Second Annual Meeting of the Society for Computation in Linguistics (SCiL 2019)

New York, New York, USA
3 - 6 January 2019

ISBN: 978-1-5108-7753-5

TABLE OF CONTENTS

Preface: SCiL 2019 Editors' Note

Gaja Jarosz, Max Nelson, Brendan O'Connor and Joe Pater
University of Massachusetts Amherst

This volume contains research presented at the second annual meeting of the Society for Computation in Linguistics (SCiL), held in New York City, January 3-6, 2019, in conjunction with the annual meeting of the Linguistic Society of America.

These proceedings include the full length paper submissions that were peer-reviewed as papers and accepted for either oral or poster presentation at SCiL 2019. The first 13 papers in the proceedings are those that were accepted as oral presentations, while the remaining 16 papers were presented as posters. Submissions to SCiL also included abstracts, which were presented as talks or posters at the conference. Further information, including the schedule and abstracts, can be found at our website: https://blogs.umass.edu/scil/scil-2019/.

In total, we received 96 submissions to the conference, 52 abstracts and 44 papers. 22 submissions were selected for oral presentation (23%) and 38 for poster presentation (40%). 51 of the submissions (53%) included a female author, and 34 (57%) of accepted submissions included a female author. 11 of the talks (50%) included a female author, and 23 of the posters (60%) included a female author[1]. We thank our reviewers for their indispensable help in selecting the research for presentation at the conference:

Adam Albright, Jacob Andreas, Michael Becker, Leon Bergen, Su Lin Blodgett, Samuel Bowman, Miriam Butt, Damir Cavar, Alexander Clark, Jennifer Culbertson, Robert Daland, Hal Daumé III, Vera Demberg, Brian Dillon, Ewan Dunbar, Chris Dyer, Jacob Eisenstein, Allyson Ettinger, Robert Frank, Matt Goldrick, Sharon Goldwater, Thomas Graf, John Hale, Jeff Heinz, Kasia Hitczenko, Tracy Holloway King, Tim Hunter, Mohit Iyer, Gerhard Jaeger, Dan Jurafsky, Roni Katzir, Greg Kobele, Andrew Lamont, Tal Linzen, Giorgio Magri, Fred Mailhot, Rob Malouf, Andrea E. Martin, Nazarré Merchant, Elliott Moreton, Emily Morgan, Aleksei Nazarov, Brendan O'Connor, Tim O'Donnell, Alexis Palmer, Martha Palmer, Lisa Pearl, Heather Pon-Barry, Christopher Potts, Brandon Prickett, Ezer Rasin, James Rogers, Asad Sayeed, Nathan Schneider, Andrea Sims, Noah Smith, Edward Stabler, Mark Steedman, Emma Strubell, Colin Wilson, Kristine Yu

Thanks also to Tom Maxfield for logistical help and Andrew Lamont for help preparing the proceedings.

SCiL 2019 also included invited tutorials by Kasia Hitczenko (on Bayesian Models) and Allyson Ettinger (on Vector Space Models), invited talks by Mark Johnson and Gaja

---

[1] The gender statistics were collected informally and may have inaccuracies. We plan to discuss better methods for collecting and reporting gender information at the business meeting. Thanks to Yiding Hao for feedback.

Proceedings of the Society for Computation in Linguistics (SCiL) 2019, pages i-ii.
New York City, New York, January 3-6, 2019

Jarosz on "Learning Hidden Linguistic Structure", and an invited panel discussion on "What Should Linguists Know About NLP/ML" by Sam Bowman, Chris Dyer, Allyson Ettinger, and Noah Smith. These invited sessions were funded by NSF conference grant BCS-1832737 to the University of Massachusetts Amherst. Further information can be found at our website: https://blogs.umass.edu/scil/scil-2019/.

Can Entropy Explain Successor Surprisal Effects in Reading?

Marten van Schijndel
Department of Cognitive Science
Johns Hopkins University
vansky@jhu.edu

Tal Linzen
Department of Cognitive Science
Johns Hopkins University
tal.linzen@jhu.edu

Abstract

Human reading behavior is sensitive to surprisal: more predictable words tend to be read faster. Unexpectedly, this applies not only to the surprisal of the word that is currently being read, but also to the surprisal of upcoming (successor) words that have not been fixated yet. This finding has been interpreted as evidence that readers can extract lexical information parafoveally. Calling this interpretation into question, Angele et al. (2015) showed that successor effects appear even in contexts in which those successor words are not yet visible. They hypothesized that successor surprisal predicts reading time because it approximates the reader's uncertainty about upcoming words. We test this hypothesis on a reading time corpus using an LSTM language model, and find that successor surprisal and entropy are independent predictors of reading time. This independence suggests that entropy alone is unlikely to be the full explanation for successor surprisal effects.

1 Introduction

One of the most robust findings in the reading literature is that more predictable words are read faster than less predictable words (Ehrlich and Rayner, 1981). Word predictability effects fit into a picture of human cognition in which humans constantly make predictions about upcoming events and test those predictions against their perceptual input (Bar, 2007).

While the effect of the predictability of the current word (w_t) on the reading time at w_t is not controversial, there is a spirited debate in the eye movement literature as to whether reading time at w_t is affected by the predictability of the *successor* word, w_{t+1} (Drieghe, 2011). Reading is characterized by a series of fixations, which bring a single word into the center of the visual field (the fovea),

where visual acuity is highest. Effects of successor predictability have been taken to indicate that readers are able to process words parafoveally, that is, even when those words are not fixated (Kliegl et al., 2006). Such an empirical finding would appear to constitute evidence against serial attention shift models such as E-Z Reader (Reichle et al., 2003), in which attention is directed at a single word at a time, and in favor of models such as SWIFT (Engbert et al., 2002), in which attention can be distributed over multiple words at the same time.

This interpretation of successor predictability effects was called into question by Angele et al. (2015), who showed that the predictability of word w_{t+1} affected reading time at w_t even when w_{t+1} was masked and was not visible until the reader fixated on it directly. A similar result was found by van Schijndel and Schuler (2017) in self-paced reading, a paradigm which similarly precludes parafoveal preview. Short of ascribing psychic abilities to readers, then, the only possible explanation for these findings is that what appears to be an effect of the predictablity of w_{t+1} is a confound driven by the relationship between the predictability of w_{t+1} and an underlying property of w_t.

Angele et al. (2015) hypothesized that the property of w_t that is confounded with the predictability of w_{t+1} is the reader's **uncertainty** about the words that could follow w_t, but they did not test this hypothesis. The present paper directly evaluates the relation between successor surprisal and uncertainty estimated from a single RNN language model (Gulordava et al., 2018). We use a self-paced reading corpus (Futrell et al., 2018), in which parafoveal preview is unavailable. To anticipate our results, we do not find evidence that the effect of successor surprisal can be reduced to uncertainty. We then explore the hypothesis that processing limitations, which lead to uncertainty

Proceedings of the Society for Computation in Linguistics (SCiL) 2019, pages 1-7.
New York City, New York, January 3-6, 2019

being calculated over a restricted number of probable words rather than over the entire vocabulary, could account for these conflicting results, with similarly negative results. We conclude that uncertainty is unlikely to be the only explanation for successor surprisal effects.

2 Surprisal and entropy

The relationship between the reading time at word w_t and the conditional probability of w_t is logarithmic (Smith and Levy, 2013); in other words, if we use *surprisal* (Hale, 2001) as our probability measure:

$$\text{surprisal}(w_t) = -\log \text{P}(w_t \mid w_{1...t-1}) \quad (1)$$

then there is a linear correlation between $\text{RT}(w_t)$ and $\text{surprisal}(w_t)$. Surprisal has been shown to be a strong predictor of reading time in linear regression models (e.g., Demberg and Keller, 2008; Roark et al., 2009).

Successor surprisal is simply the surprisal of the next observation in a sequence:

$$\text{succ. surprisal}(w_t) = -\log \text{P}(w_{t+1} \mid w_{1...t}) \quad (2)$$
$$= \text{surprisal}(w_{t+1}) \quad (3)$$

Finally, the entropy at w_t is defined as follows:

$$H(w_t) = E[\text{surprisal}(w_{t+1})] \quad (4)$$
$$= -\sum_{w_{t+1} \in V} \text{P}(w_{t+1} \mid w_{1...t}) \log \text{P}(w_{t+1} \mid w_{1...t}) \quad (5)$$

As mentioned in the introduction, Angele et al. (2015) hypothesized that the entropy at w_t is the underlying cause for successor (w_{t+1}) surprisal effects on w_t. This is a plausible hypothesis: the expected successor surprisal in a given context is the entropy at w_t (Equation 4), so in the limit, successor surprisal should be the same as the entropy over possible continuations when averaged over a corpus. In this hypothetical limit-case, we would directly observe Equation 5 in the data, as the sequence $w_{1...t+1}$ occurred exactly the expected number of times in the corpus. In practice, with a finite set of observations T which are regressed simultaneously, successor surprisal provides a Monte Carlo estimator of entropy in that

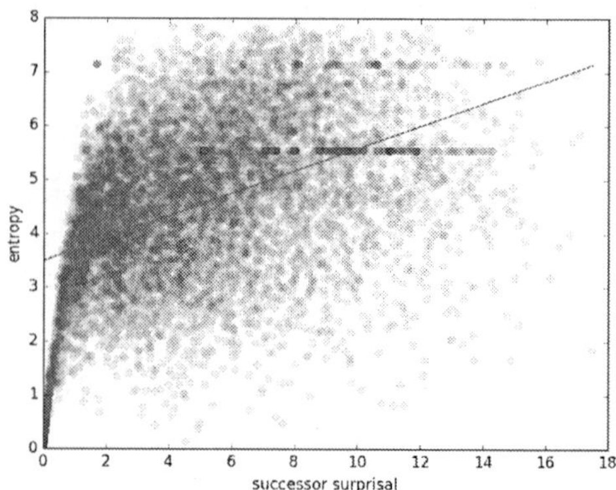

Figure 1: Successor surprisal plotted against entropy for each word in the Natural Stories Corpus. The Pearson correlation is 0.45, providing empirical validation of the theoretically strong limit-case relation between entropy and successor surprisal.

corpus:

$$\hat{H}(T) \approx -\sum_{t=1}^{|T|} \frac{1}{|T|} \log \text{P}(w_{t+1} \mid w_{1...t}) \quad (6)$$
$$= \sum_{t=1}^{|T|} \frac{1}{|T|} \text{surprisal}(w_{t+1}) \quad (7)$$

Therefore, if uncertainty over possible continuations influences reading time, then successor surprisal could be correlated with reading time simply due to its relationship with corpus-level entropy.

Importantly for the present study, if the relationship to uncertainty is the sole underlying reason that successor surprisal can predict reading time, successor surprisal should be a worse predictor of reading time than entropy when the same model distribution q is used to compute both measures. This claim follows directly from Equation 7: if entropy H_q is the true generator of the data, then it should always be a better predictor than some corpus-level approximation $\hat{H}_q$ due to noise from the Monte Carlo process.

The syntactic language models used in previous reading studies could not compute successor surprisal and entropy from the same conditional probability distribution, precluding a direct test of this hypothesis; in particular, while the Roark et al. (2009) parser can compute both surprisal and entropy, it estimates them using two different probability distributions due to its use of beam search.

3   Method

Language model: In contrast with previous work, which used grammar-based language models, we used a single recurrent neural network (RNN) language model to compute entropy and successor surprisal from the same conditional probability distribution. The language model we used was trained by Gulordava et al. (2018) on 90 million words from the English Wikipedia. The model had two LSTM layers with 650 hidden units each, 650-dimensional word embeddings, a dropout rate of 0.2 and batch size 128, and was trained for 40 epochs (with early stopping).

Unlike grammar-based language models, RNN language models do not explicitly construct syntactic dependencies, which are essential in human sentence comprehension. However, recent work has shown that RNN language models are nevertheless sensitive to the probability of syntactic structures (Linzen et al., 2016; van Schijndel and Linzen, 2018; Wilcox et al., 2018), tentatively suggesting that they are an adequate substitute for modeling human reading behavior. Importantly, they have the added benefit that all our measures of interest are easy to calculate using Equations 1, 2, and 5 on the model's softmax layer, which provides a conditional probability distribution over the upcoming word given the preceding words.

Data: The test domain in this work is the Natural Stories Corpus (Futrell et al., 2018). The corpus is a set of 10 texts (485 sentences) written to sound fluent while still containing many low-frequency and marked syntactic constructions. The sentences within each text were presented in order, and self-paced reading data were collected from 181 native English speakers. We used one third of the sentences for exploration while two thirds were set aside for statistical confirmation. We omit any words consisting of multiple tokens (e.g., *do·n't* and *boar·!·'*). In this paper, all statistical testing was done on the held-out partition.

4   Results

Successor surprisal is moderately correlated with entropy: We first tested the degree to which the Monte Carlo estimation produces a correlation between entropy and successor surprisal when each is computed with the same probability model (i.e. the LSTM language model described in Section 3) and found that the measures were mod-

erately correlated, with Pearson's $r = 0.454$ (see Figure 1). This moderate correlation between the two measures could plausibly explain the successor surprisal effects on reading time that have been observed in previous studies.

Successor surprisal predicts reading time: Before testing whether entropy can account for the effectiveness of successor surprisal in predicting reading time, we first verified that our successor surprisal measure was positively correlated with reading time as observed with the language models used in previous work (Angele et al., 2015; van Schijndel and Schuler, 2016, 2017).

Following previous studies, we used a linear mixed effects regression approach. Unlike linear regression, in which the error term is assumed to come from a single normal distribution, this approach takes into consideration clustered errors that are due to the variability across the particular participants and words in the sample ("random effects"). This makes it possible to estimate the effect of theoretically relevant "fixed effects" in a way that is more likely to generalize to new items and participants. We used the *lme4* R package (Bates et al., 2014) to perform the regression, and included fixed effects for word length, sentence position, unigram frequency, surprisal, and successor surprisal. Unigram frequencies were estimated from the Wikitext-103 training corpus (Merity et al., 2016). We included random intercepts for each word and subject, and by-subject random slopes for each fixed effect.[1] All predictors were z-transformed before fitting the models. We compared the log-likelihood of the data under that model to the log-likelihood of one without the fixed effect for successor surprisal to determine the significance of successor surprisal as a fixed effect predictor of reading time.

Successor surprisal was significant as a predictor ($\hat{\beta} = 4.3$, $\hat{\sigma} = 0.53$, $\chi^2(1) = 28$, $p < 0.001$), suggesting that the previously observed relationship between successor surprisal and reading time holds when successor surprisal is computed with our LSTM language model. We note that, in this self-paced reading setting, the regression coefficient of successor surprisal was quite large: it was over half that of the coefficient of w_t surprisal ($\hat{\beta} = 6.0$) and was larger than that of unigram fre-

---

[1] We also ran all of the analyses reported in this paper on the exploratory partition without the random word intercept and obtained qualitatively similar results.

	$\hat{\beta}$	$\hat{\sigma}$	t
(Intercept)	330.90	6.39	51.80
Sentence position	0.73	0.51	1.42
Word length	4.74	1.04	4.55
Surprisal	5.65	0.53	10.60
Unigram frequency	-1.98	1.35	-1.47
Successor surprisal	3.25	0.38	8.47
Entropy	3.12	0.58	5.34

Table 1: Fixed effect coefficients from fitting self-paced reading times. Since predictors were z-transformed, the $\hat{\beta}$ coefficients indicate the change in ms per standard deviation of each predictor.

K	Successor surprisal	Total entropy
5	0.212	0.541
50	0.335	0.820
500	0.397	0.947
5000	0.434	0.992
50000	0.454	1

Table 2: Correlations between (Center) best-K entropy and successor surprisal and (Right) best-K entropy and total entropy when best-K entropy is computed over the most probable K continuations.

quency ($\hat{\beta} = -1.7$).

Entropy and successor surprisal account for different portions of the variance: If successor surprisal is only predictive of reading time because it approximates entropy as hypothesized by Angele et al. (2015), then entropy should not only be predictive of reading time, but it should also obviate successor surprisal as a predictor since the approximation (successor surprisal) would only get credit for indirectly modeling part of the influence of entropy. To test this, we added entropy as a fixed effect and as a by-subject random slope to our linear-mixed effects model. Comparing the fit of that model to the fit of a model without each fixed effect of interest, we found that successor surprisal and entropy were both significant predictors of reading time (both $p < 0.001$; see Table 1); thus the hypothesis that the effect of entropy should subsume the effect of successor surprisal was not borne out.

5 Bounded entropy

Entropy and successor surprisal both accounted for independent portions of the variance in reading time in Section 4. Could they both provide indirect approximations of underlying reader uncertainty? So far we computed entropy over the complete distribution of possible upcoming words (*total entropy*). In this section, we explore the possibility that processing limitations cause readers to consider only the best K continuations in the psychological process that causes uncertainty effects (see bounded rationality, Simon, 1982; Jurafsky, 1996). If this is the case, then total entropy and its successor surprisal approximation could both be predictive of reading time because of their joint

correlation with the bounded entropy computed by humans.

To test this hypothesis, we computed entropy over just the best 5, 50, 500, and 5000 continuations in every context. The full vocabulary size of the model was 50000 (plus an UNK token). Successor surprisal was always computed over the full vocabulary so that every observation could be assigned a successor surprisal value.

Entropy was most correlated with successor surprisal when both measures were computed over the entire vocabulary (Table 2). This is a plausible finding given Equation 7, which indicates that successor surprisal provides a Monte Carlo approximator of the entropy of that same distribution (recall that successor surprisal was calculated over the full vocabulary). It may still be the case, however, that reading time is best predicted by one of the bounded entropy measures. For example, best-50 entropy still has a moderate correlation to successor surprisal (0.335) and a strong correlation to total entropy (0.82); it is possible that total entropy and successor surprisal both predicted reading time thanks to an underlying joint correlation with best-50 entropy.

To test whether that is the case, we used our bounded entropy variants to predict reading time, following the procedure of Section 4.[2] Bounded entropy was a consistently poorer predictor of reading time than total entropy (see Table 3). This suggests that humans may be sensitive to uncertainty over a large number of possible continuations. Moreover, successor surprisal improved as

---

[2]For these analyses, we omit by-subject random slopes for sentence position, surprisal, and unigram frequency in order to ensure that all 5 models converge. Leaving all random slopes in the models produces similar qualitative results in those models that do converge.

K	$\hat{\beta}_H$	$\hat{\sigma}_H$	$\hat{\beta}_s$	$\hat{\sigma}_s$
5	3.11	0.70	3.90	0.53
50	3.29	0.71	3.82	0.54
500	3.91	0.70	3.65	0.54
5000	4.42	0.70	3.53	0.54
50000	4.60	0.70	3.49	0.54

Table 3: Entropy (H) and successor surprisal (s) coefficients in the Section 4 RT regression model for the exploratory data partition, when H is calculated over the K most probable continuations.

a predictor of reading time as K decreased and the predictive value of bounded entropy weakened. This trade-off indicates that some of the variance in reading time is explained by both measures, which suggests that the predictivity of successor surprisal in previous studies was at least partially driven by reader uncertainty (in line with Angele et al., 2015). However, the continued predictivity of successor surprisal in the presence of entropy indicates that there are likely other factors involved as well. For example, it may be that readers make predictions of varying granularity depending on context or attention level. That is, in cases where readers make a prediction based on the best K continuations and K is similar to the bound for computing entropy, then entropy may help predict reading time. Successor surprisal could help absorb variance due to a mismatch between reader K and the model's K.

6   Related work

Previously, van Schijndel and Schuler (2017) performed a similar analysis to the reading time analysis in Section 4 in this paper using probabilistic context-free language models. They were forced to compute entropy and successor surprisal with separate models because entropy computation using a grammar-based model requires estimation of uncertainty over both words and parsing actions, and is therefore very computationally expensive. While they also found that entropy and successor surprisal independently predicted reading time, their use of multiple language models means that the independent predictivity in their study could arise from differences in their underlying models instead of from multiple independent reading time influences. In contrast, we wanted to directly compare the measures as estimated by a

single model to provide a stronger test of the original hypothesis of Angele et al. (2015).

Frank (2013) conducted a related reading time analysis which studied the relationship between entropy reduction (Hale, 2006) and surprisal as computed by neural network language models. Entropy reduction is a measure of how uncertainty about the future changes after an observation compared to before that observation. Since entropy reduction involves the difference between two levels of uncertainty, it is a distinct measure from the amount of uncertainty (entropy) over upcoming observations which we studied in this paper. That is, the fact that uncertainty is reduced after an observation says nothing about the total amount of uncertainty experienced by a reader after that lessening takes place.[3] Frank (2013) found that entropy reduction and surprisal are also distinct measures with independent reading time predictivity, similar to the findings of entropy and successor surprisal in the present paper.

Frank (2013) also tested how the relationship between entropy reduction and surprisal changed when the uncertainty used to estimate entropy reduction was computed over more than just the single next upcoming observation; he found that the predictive value of entropy reduction improves when entropy is computed over multiple future words. However, in the context of the present paper, Angele et al. (2015) observed a direct relationship between the predictability of a single word (w_{t+1}) on the reading time of the preceding word (w_t). Further, van Schijndel and Schuler (2016) previously found that successor surprisal best predicts reading time when computed over just the upcoming one or two words even when parafoveal preview is possible, so it seems unlikely that computing entropy over longer upcoming sequences like Frank (2013) could explain the remaining successor surprisal influence on self-paced reading observed in this study. Therefore, since the goal of the present paper was to test the Angele et al. (2015) hypothesis that the entropy over w_{t+1} could be the driving influence behind successor surprisal, we focused on testing the relationship between the reading time at w_t and measures of entropy over w_{t+1} and did not explore the influence of uncertainty over words beyond w_{t+1}.

---

[3]For example, $H(w_t) - 2 = H(w_{t+1})$ does not convey how large $H(w_t)$ or $H(w_{t+1})$ are. This amount of entropy reduction (2) could equally occur in a context of high uncertainty or in one of low uncertainty.

7 Discussion

This paper has used surprisal and entropy estimates from a neural network language model to test the hypothesis that successor surprisal effects in reading can be reduced to reader uncertainty. Successor surprisal and uncertainty accounted for partly non-overlapping portions of the variance in reading time. We interpret our finding of non-overlapping influences as a strong indictation that the predictivity of successor surprisal is not solely driven by uncertainty over the next word.

However, the portions of variance captured by entropy and successor surprisal are not completely disjoint: replacing entropy with bounded variants based on the best K continuations led to weaker predictive power for entropy and a stronger relationship between successor surprisal and reading time, lending support to the hypothesis that entropy is at least a contributing factor in the predictivity of successor surprisal. Finally, the finding that uncertainty was a better predictor of reading time when it was computed over the entire vocabulary rather than just the best K continuations suggests that readers may make a large number of continuation predictions simultaneously.

References

Bernhard Angele, Elizabeth R. Schotter, Timothy J. Slattery, Tara L. Tenenbaum, Klinton Bicknell, and Keith Rayner. 2015. Do successor effects in reading reflect lexical parafoveal processing? Evidence from corpus-based and experimental eye movement data. *Journal of Memory and Language*, 79–80:76–96.

Moshe Bar. 2007. The proactive brain: Using analogies and associations to generate predictions. *Trends in Cognitive Sciences*, 11(7):280–289.

Douglas Bates, Martin Maechler, Ben Bolker, and Steven Walker. 2014. *lme4: Linear mixed-effects models using Eigen and S4*. R package version 1.1-7.

Vera Demberg and Frank Keller. 2008. Data from eye-tracking corpora as evidence for theories of syntactic processing complexity. *Cognition*, 109(2):193–210.

Denis Drieghe. 2011. Parafoveal-on-foveal effects on eye movements during reading. In Simon P. Liversedge, Iain Gilchrist, and Stefan Everling, editors, *Oxford Handbook on Eye Movements*, pages 839–855. Oxford University Press.

Susan F. Ehrlich and Keith Rayner. 1981. Contextual effects on word perception and eye movements during reading. *Journal of Verbal Learning and Verbal Behavior*, 20(6):641–655.

Ralf Engbert, André Longtin, and Reinhold Kliegl. 2002. A dynamical model of saccade generation in reading based on spatially distributed lexical processing. *Vision Research*, 42(5):621–636.

Stefan Frank. 2013. Uncertainty reduction as a measure of cognitive load in sentence comprehension. *Topics in Cognitive Science*, 5:475–494.

Richard Futrell, Edward Gibson, Hal Tily, Anastasia Vishnevetsky, Steve Piantadosi, and Evelina Fedorenko. 2018. The natural stories corpus. In *Language Resources and Evaluation Conference*, pages 76–82.

Kristina Gulordava, Piotr Bojanowski, Edouard Grave, Tal Linzen, and Marco Baroni. 2018. Colorless green recurrent networks dream hierarchically. In *Proceedings of the 2018 Conference of the North American Chapter of the Association for Computational Linguistics: Human Language Technologies, Volume 1 (Long Papers)*, pages 1195–1205. Association for Computational Linguistics.

John Hale. 2001. A probabilistic Earley parser as a psycholinguistic model. In *Proceedings of the second meeting of the North American Chapter of the Association for Computational Linguistics on Language Technologies*, pages 1–8, Pittsburgh, PA. Association for Computational Linguistics.

John Hale. 2006. Uncertainty about the rest of the sentence. *Cognitive Science*, 30(4):609–642.

Daniel Jurafsky. 1996. A probabilistic model of lexical and syntactic access and disambiguation. *Cognitive Science*, 20:137–194.

Reinhold Kliegl, Antje Nuthmann, and Ralf Engbert. 2006. Tracking the mind during reading: The influence of past, present, and future words on fixation durations. *Journal of Experimental Psychology – General*, 135:12–35.

Tal Linzen, Emmanuel Dupoux, and Yoav Goldberg. 2016. Assessing the ability of LSTMs to learn syntax-sensitive dependencies. *Transactions of the Association for Computational Linguistics*, pages 521–535.

Stephen Merity, Caiming Xiong, James Bradbury, and Richard Socher. 2016. *Pointer Sentinel Mixture Models*.

Erik D. Reichle, Keith Rayner, and Alexander Pollatsek. 2003. The EZ Reader model of eye-movement control in reading: Comparisons to other models. *Behavioral and Brain Sciences*, 26(4):445–476.

Brian Roark, Asaf Bachrach, Carlos Cardenas, and Christophe Pallier. 2009. Deriving lexical and syntactic expectation-based measures for psycholinguistic modeling via incremental top-down parsing. In *Proceedings of the 2009 Conference on Empirical Methods in Natural Language Processing*, pages 324–333, Stroudsburg, PA. Association for Computational Linguistics.

Herbert A. Simon. 1982. *Models of Bounded Rationality*. MIT Press.

Nathaniel J. Smith and Roger Levy. 2013. The effect of word predictability on reading time is logarithmic. *Cognition*, 128(3):302–319.

Marten van Schijndel and Tal Linzen. 2018. Modeling garden path effects without explicit hierarchical syntax. In Charles Kalish, Martina Rau, Jerry Zhu, and Timothy T. Rogers, editors, *Proceedings of the 40th Annual Conference of the Cognitive Science Society*, pages 2600–2605. Cognitive Science Society, Austin, TX.

Marten van Schijndel and William Schuler. 2016. Addressing surprisal deficiencies in reading time models. In Dominique Brunato, Felice DellOrletta, Giulia Venturi, , Thomas Franois, and Philippe Blache, editors, *Proceedings of the Computational Linguistics for Linguistic Complexity Workshop*, pages 32–37. Association for Computational Linguistics.

Marten van Schijndel and William Schuler. 2017. Approximations of predictive entropy correlate with reading times. In Glenn Gunzelmann, Andrew Howes, Thora Tenbrink, and Eddy Davelaar, editors, *Proceedings of the 39th Annual Meeting of the Cognitive Science Society*, pages 1266–1271. Cognitive Science Society, London, United Kingdom.

Ethan Wilcox, Roger Levy, Takashi Morita, and Richard Futrell. 2018. What do RNN language models learn about filler-gap dependencies? In *Proceedings of the 2018 EMNLP Workshop BlackboxNLP: Analyzing and Interpreting Neural Networks for NLP*.

RedTyp: A Database of Reduplication with Computational Models

Hossep Dolatian and **Jeffrey Heinz**
Linguistics Department &
Institute for Advanced Computational Science
Stony Brook University
Stony Brook, NY 11790, USA
{hossep.dolatian, jeffrey.heinz}@stonybrook.edu

Abstract

Reduplication is a theoretically and typologically well-studied phenomenon, but there is no database of reduplication patterns which include explicit computational models. This paper introduces RedTyp, an SQL database which provides a computational resource that can be used by both theoretical and computational linguists who work on reduplication. It catalogs 138 reduplicative morphemes across 91 languages, which are modeled with 57 distinct finite-state machines. The finite-state machines are 2-way transducers, which provide an explicit, compact, and convenient representation for reduplication patterns, and which arguably capture the linguistic generalizations more directly than the more commonly used 1-way transducers for modeling natural language morphophonology.

1 Introduction

Reduplication is a cross-linguistically well-attested and ubiquitous morphological operation (Rubino, 2005). The World Atlas of Language Structure (WALS) database documents that 313 out of 368 languages (85%) productively use some form of reduplication to mark one or more semantic functions (Rubino, 2013).[1]

The typology of reduplication can be roughly divided into total reduplication and partial reduplication. Total reduplication copies unboundedly many segments which form some morphological constituent (e.g. a word, stem, root, etc.) as shown in (1a). Partial reduplication copies a bounded number of segments. In partial reduplication, the shape of the reduplicant is most commonly CV (2a), CVC (2b), or CVCV (2c).

---

[1]Here, the term 'reduplication' is used loosely to mean any morphosyntactic process or morpheme which systematically copies some segmental material from the stem (Hurch, 2005 ff.).

1. Indonesian (Cohn, 1989, 185)
    (a) wanita   → wanita~wanita
        'woman' → 'women'
2. Pangasinan (Rubino, 2005, 11)
    (a) too   → to~too
        'man'   → 'people'
    (b) baley   → bal~baley
        'town'   → 'towns'
    (c) manok   → mano~manok
        'chicken' → 'chickens'

There is a much more diverse typology than these relatively simple patterns. Typologists have documented various patterns of reduplication which are both common and uncommon (Moravcsik, 1978; Rubino, 2005; Inkelas and Zoll, 2005; Hurch, 2005). Interested readers are referred to Raimy (2011), Urbanczyk (2007), and Inkelas and Downing (2015) for overviews.

Reduplication is difficult to model with existing finite-state tools for two reasons. First, copying an unbounded number of segments (total reduplication) cannot be done by 1-way Finite-State Transducers (1-way FSTs) (Roark and Sproat, 2007), which are overwhelmingly used in computational linguistics (Mohri, 1997; Beesley and Karttunen, 2003). Instead, existing finite-state tools approximate total reduplication by essentially treating it as memorizing a list of existing words in the language (Hulden, 2009a; Hulden and Bischoff, 2009; Cohen-Sygal and Wintner, 2006; Roark and Sproat, 2007). If total reduplication were rare, perhaps this difficulty could be overlooked. However, total reduplication is the most common reduplicative process and it occurs in an estimated 75% of the world's languages (Rubino, 2013).

Second, while 1-way finite-state transducers can copy boundedly many segments (partial reduplication), the number of states needed can be quite large (Roark and Sproat, 2007; Hulden,

Proceedings of the Society for Computation in Linguistics (SCiL) 2019, pages 8-18.
New York City, New York, January 3-6, 2019

2009a; Chandlee and Heinz, 2012; Chandlee, 2017). This can can make them difficult to design and debug. Consequently, there are few (if any) computational resources which model reduplication in a way that is simple, small, easy to design, and linguistically motivated.

Against this background, this paper makes two contributions. First, it introduces a SQL database, which we call RedTyp, of 138 reduplicative processes from 91 languages.[2] These were gathered from various typological surveys of reduplication. We mainly used Moravcsik (1978), a classic survey on reduplication, and supplemented it with other published linguistic surveys (Rubino, 2005; Inkelas and Downing, 2015), with case studies gleaned from other smaller surveys that were narrower in scope e.g. McCarthy and Prince (1995), among others.

A copy of RedTyp exists online at our GitHub page: `github.com/jhdeov/RedTyp` and is available to the public under a Creative Commons non-commercial license (CC BY-NC 4.0).

Second, RedTyp models reduplicative processes with an understudied and under-used type of finite-state technology: 2-way deterministic finite-state transducers (2-way FSTs) (Engelfriet and Hoogeboom, 2001; Filiot and Reynier, 2016). As we explain in Subsection 2.2, and in detail in Dolatian and Heinz (2018b), 2-way FSTs can reread parts of the input string, unlike 1-way FSTs. In addition to allowing 2-way FSTs to model total reduplication exactly, this additional capacity significantly reduces the number of states needed to model partial reduplication. Consequently, 2-way FSTs for reduplication are easy to design, debug, and manage. Besides their state efficiency and practical utility, 2-way FSTs likewise capture the intensional description of reduplication. For more discussion of the role of 2-way FSTs as computational models of reduplication, see Dolatian and Heinz (2018b).

For each reduplicative process in RedTyp, we manually wrote a 2-way FST representing it. In total, we modeled 138 reduplicative processes in RedTyp with 57 2-way FSTs. The average number of states in these machines is 8.82.[3] These FSTs

are included in RedTyp, along with a Python script for using them.

The remainder of this paper is organized as follows. Although 2-way FSTs have been studied since the 1960s (Aho et al., 1969), they are a relatively unknown finite-state device in computational linguistics; outside of linguistics, there has been recently been more industrial applications for computational models equivalent to 2-way FSTs (Alur and Černý, 2011; Alur et al., 2014). In order to explain the resource RedTyp, which uses 2-way FSTs, we briefly[4] introduce and define 2-way FSTs in Section 2. Section 3 details the SQL structure of RedTyp, the software implementation of the 2-way FSTs, and the accompanying Python script. Section 4 discusses various aspects of RedTyp including a a high-level comparison of 2-way FSTs to other formal devices, a comparison of RedTyp to the only other reduplication database that exists to our knowledge (the Graz Database on Reduplication (Hurch, 2005)), the utility of RedTyp, and future research directions. Conclusions are in Section 5.

2 Reduplication with two-way finite-state transducers

Informally, both 1-way FSTs and 2-way FSTs can be thought of as machines which read their input from an input tape and write their output onto an output tape (Filiot and Reynier, 2016). In the case of 1-way FSTs, the machine only moves across the input tape from left-to-right and likewise writes the output from left-to-right. Like 1-way FSTs, 2-way FSTs also only write the output from left-to-right. However, unlike 1-way FSTs, 2-way FSTs can move back and forth along the input tape. Because of this difference, they are more expressive than 1-way FSTs. In particular, 2-way FSTs can model total reduplication exactly while 1-way FSTs cannot. In this section, we introduce them informally with an example and then provide a formalization.

2.1 Illustrating 2-way FSTs

The back and forth movement along the input tape is controlled by the transitions with a directional

---

[2]The name *RedTyp* is in homage to the "Typ" databases including the StressTyp databases (Goedemans et al., 1996; Heinz et al., 2016) and others described in Everaert et al. (2009).

[3]The largest 2-way FST in this sample, from verbal reduplication in Kinande (Downing, 2000), has 29 states. This pattern depends on the size of the root and the number and

type of suffixes and prefixes around it. In contrast, we estimate a deterministic 1-way FST would require over 1,000 states for this pattern of partial reduplication.

[4]A fuller technical illustration can be found in Dolatian and Heinz (2018b), and a more informal one in Dolatian and Heinz (In press.).

parameter d which specifies whether the machine advances left-to-right (a value of +1), stays put (a value of 0), or moves right-to-left (a value of -1). For a 1-way FST, the value of d is always +1. We further assume that input strings are flanked with the left and right boundary symbols, $\rtimes$ and $\ltimes$, respectively.

To illustrate how a 2-way FST works, consider the case of total reduplication in Indonesian. In Indonesian, plurality is marked by reduplicating the entire word or input (3). Data are from Cohn (1989, 185).

3. (a) buku $\to$ buku$\sim$buku
    'book' $\to$ 'books'

  (b) wanita $\to$ wanita$\sim$wanita
    'woman' $\to$ 'women'

  (c) maʃarakat $\to$ maʃarakat$\sim$maʃarakat
    'society' $\to$ 'societies'

  (d) kəkuraŋan $\to$ kəkuraŋan$\sim$kəkuraŋan
    'lack' $\to$ 'lacks'

This total reduplicative process cannot be modeled with a 1-way FST (Roark and Sproat, 2007), but can be easily modeled with a deterministic 2-way FST as in Figure 1. In Figure 1, transitions between states are labeled (i, o, d) where i is the input symbol, o is the output string, and d is the directional parameter. Σ represents any segment in the input which is not the left-edge or right-edge boundary. The empty string is represented by λ. The boundary symbol $\sim$ in the output plays no crucial function; it visualizes the boundary between the two copies.

To illustrate, Table 1 shows the derivation of /buku/$\to$[buku$\sim$buku] using the 2-way FST in Figure 1. Each row in the table consists of four parts: *input string, output string, current state, transition*. In the *input string*, we underline the input symbol which the 2-way FST will read next. The *output string* is what the 2-way FST has outputted up to that point. The symbol λ marks the empty string. The *current state* is what state the 2-way FST is currently in. The *transition* represents the used transition arc from input to output along with a direction value. In the first tuple, there is no transition arc used (N/A). But for other tuples, the form of the arc is:

$$\textit{input state} \xrightarrow[\text{direction}]{\text{input symbol:output string}} \textit{output state}$$

.

2.2 Defining 2-way FSTs

Here, we give a formal definition of deterministic 2-way FSTs, synthesizing definitions from Filiot and Reynier (2016) and Shallit (2008). Inputs to a 2-way FST are flanked with the start ($\rtimes$) and end boundaries ($\ltimes$). This larger alphabet is denoted by $\Sigma_\ltimes$.

4. **Definition**: A 2-way, deterministic FST is a six-tuple $(Q, \Sigma_\ltimes, \Gamma, q_0, F, \delta)$ such that:
   - Q is a finite set of states,
   - $\Sigma_\ltimes = \Sigma \cup \{\rtimes, \ltimes\}$ is the input alphabet,
   - Γ is the output alphabet,
   - $q_0 \in Q$ is the initial state,
   - $F \subseteq Q$ is the set of final states,
   - $\delta : Q \times \Sigma \to Q \times \Gamma^* \times D$ is the transition function where the direction $D = \{-1, 0, +1\}$.

A *configuration* of a 2-way FST T is an element of $\Sigma_\ltimes^* Q \Sigma_\ltimes^* \times \Gamma^*$. The meaning of the configuration (wqx, u) is that the input to T is wx and the machine is currently in state q with the read head on the first symbol of x (or has fallen off the right edge of the input tape if $x = \lambda$) and that u is currently written on the output tape.

If the current configuration is $(wqax, u)$ and $\delta(q, a) = (r, v, 0)$ then the next configuration is $(wrax, uv)$, in which case we write $(wqax, u) \to (wrax, uv)$. If the current configuration is $(wqax, u)$ and $\delta(q, a) = (r, v, +1)$ then the next configuration is $(warx, uv)$. In this case, we write $(wqax, u) \to (warx, uv)$. If the current configuration is $(waqx, u)$ and $\delta(q, a) = (r, v, -1)$ then the next configuration is $(wrax, uv)$. We write $(waqx, u) \to (wrax, uv)$.

The transitive closure of $\to$ is denoted with $\to^+$. So if $c \to^+ c'$ then there exists a finite sequence of configurations $c_1, c_2 \ldots c_n$ with $n > 1$ such that $c = c_1 \to c_2 \to \ldots \to c_n = c'$.

Next we define the string-to-string function that a 2-way FST $T = (Q, \Sigma_\ltimes, \Gamma, q_0, F, \delta)$ computes. For each string $w \in \Sigma^*$, $f_T(w) = u \in \Gamma^*$ provided there exists $q_f \in F$ such that $(q_0 \rtimes w\ltimes, \lambda) \to^+ (\rtimes w \ltimes q_f, u)$. Note that since T is deterministic it follows that if $f_T(w)$ is defined then u is unique.

There are situations where a 2-way FST T crashes on some input w and hence $f_T(w)$ is undefined. If the configuration is (qax, u) and $\delta(q, a) = (r, -1, v)$ then the derivation crashes and the transduction $f_T(ax)$ is undefined. Likewise, if the the configuration is (wq, u) and $q \notin F$

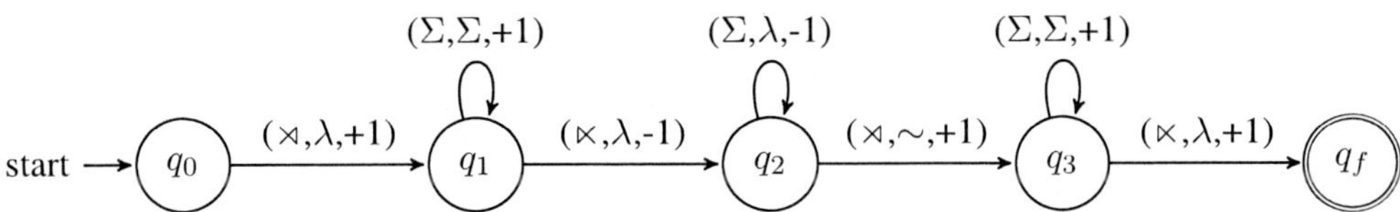

Figure 1: 2-way FST for total reduplication in Indonesian.

Outputting the first copy	Going back to the start of the tape
1. $(\underline{⋊}buku⋉,\ \lambda,\ q_0,\ \text{N/A})$	7. $(⋊buk\underline{u}⋉,\ buku,\ q_2,\ q_1 \xrightarrow[-1]{⋉:\lambda} q_2)$
2. $(⋊\underline{b}uku⋉,\ \lambda,\ q_1,\ q_0 \xrightarrow[+1]{⋊:\lambda} q_1)$	8. $(⋊bu\underline{k}u⋉,\ buku,\ q_2,\ q_2 \xrightarrow[-1]{u:\lambda} q_2)$
3. $(⋊b\underline{u}ku⋉,\ b,\ q_1,\ q_1 \xrightarrow[+1]{b:b} q_1)$	9. $(⋊b\underline{u}ku⋉,\ buku,\ q_2,\ q_2 \xrightarrow[-1]{k:\lambda} q_2)$
4. $(⋊bu\underline{k}u⋉,\ bu,\ q_1,\ q_1 \xrightarrow[+1]{u:u} q_1)$	10. $(⋊\underline{b}uku⋉,\ buku,\ q_2,\ q_2 \xrightarrow[-1]{u:\lambda} q_2)$
5. $(⋊buk\underline{u}⋉,\ buk,\ q_1,\ q_1 \xrightarrow[+1]{k:k} q_1)$	11. $(\underline{⋊}buku⋉,\ buku,\ q_2,\ q_2 \xrightarrow[-1]{b:\lambda} q_2)$
6. $(⋊buku\underline{⋉},\ buku,\ q_1,\ q_1 \xrightarrow[+1]{u:u} q_1)$	
Outputting the second copy	
12. $(⋊\underline{b}uku⋉,\ buku\sim,\ q_3,\ q_2 \xrightarrow[+1]{⋊:\sim} q_3)$	15. $(⋊buk\underline{u}⋉,\ buku\sim buk,\ q_3,\ q_3 \xrightarrow[+1]{k:k} q_3)$
13. $(⋊b\underline{u}ku⋉,\ buku\sim b,\ q_3,\ q_3 \xrightarrow[+1]{b:b} q_3)$	16. $(⋊buku\underline{⋉},\ buku\sim buku,\ q_3,\ q_3 \xrightarrow[+1]{u:u} q_3)$
14. $(⋊bu\underline{k}u⋉,\ buku\sim bu,\ q_3,\ q_3 \xrightarrow[+1]{u:u} q_3)$	17. $(⋊buku⋉,\ buku\sim buku,\ q_f,\ q_3 \xrightarrow[+1]{⋉:\lambda} q_f)$

Table 1: Derivation of /buku/→[buku∼buku].

then the transducer crashes and the transduction f_T is undefined on input w.

There is one more way in which f_T may be undefined for some input. The input may cause the transducer to go into an infinite loop.[5] This occurs for input $wx \in \Sigma_⋉^*$ whenever there exist $q \in Q$ and $u, v \in \Gamma^*$ such that $(q_0 wx, \lambda) \rightarrow^+ (wqx, u) \rightarrow^+ (wqx, uv)$.

Further information on the computational properties of 2-way FSTs can be found in Filiot and Reynier (2016). Compared to 1-way FSTs, there's relatively little work on complexity metrics for 2-way FSTs, but see Baschenis et al. (2016). See Dolatian and Heinz (2018a,b) for complexity results when using 2-way FSTs for reduplication.

3 The RedTyp Database and Python implementation of 2-way FSTs

This section details the features and organization of the RedTyp database. We likewise discuss our Python implementation of 2-way FSTs which acts as a supplement to the database.

The GitHub page for RedTyp includes the SQL file for the database, a single Python file that can read and implement the 2-way FSTs in the database, and a README textfile for instructions.

Figure 2 shows a simple Entity-Relation diagram (Elmasri and Navathe, 2010) for RedTyp. It consists of two entities: *2-way FST* for representing 2-way FSTs, and *Morpheme* for representing individual reduplicative processes in a language. They engage in a many-to-one *Match* relationship such that every *morpheme* is modeled by one *2-way FST* but a single *2-way FST* can model many reduplicative *morphemes* or reduplicative processes found within and across languages.

For example in Sundanese (Moravcsik, 1978), total reduplication expresses the meaning "not even one X" (ibid., p.301) in addition to intensity (ibid., p.321) as shown in (5)[6] and (6). Thus, in Sundanese there are two distinct morphemes, both of which are modeled with a single 2-way FST for total reduplication.

5. kali   → sakali∼kali
   'time'   → 'not even once'

---

[5]In RedTyp, all 2-way FSTs were checked to make sure they do not cause infinite loops.

[6]Moravcsik (1978, 301) calls the string 'sa' a prefix. It is not reduplicated.

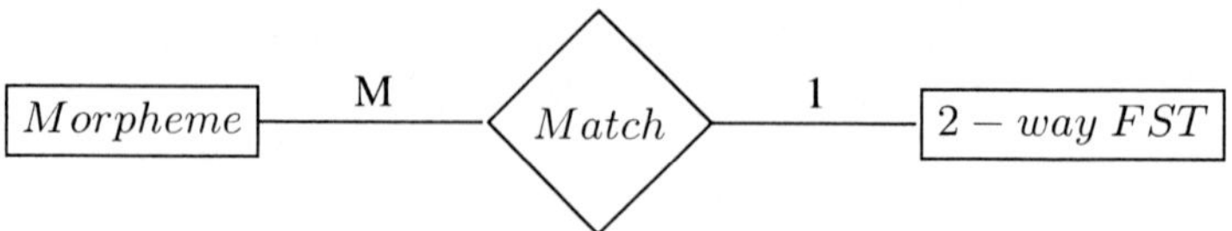

Figure 2: The Entity-Relation diagram for RedTyp.

6. hayaŋ   → hayaŋ~hayaŋ
'want'   → 'want very much'

We list and describe the attributes of each table in RedTyp below.

The 2-way FST table:

- **ID:** *string or varchar 200*
  A small descriptive name for the type of function modeled by the 2-way FST. This acts as the primary key for a **2-way FST** entry.
- **Example data:** *string or text*
  A table with example inputs and outputs, written in Markdown.
- **Description:** *string or text*
  Description of 2-way FST in terms of prose. This is written in Markdown.
- **FST diagram:** *text*
  LaTeX code for the 2-way FST diagram. It uses the following LaTeX packages/settings.

```
\usepackage{tipa}
\usepackage{tikz}
\usetikzlibrary{arrows,automata,
shapes,positioning}
```

- **FST Recipe:** *text*
  A text file that describes the alphabet and transitions for the FST in a shorthand that is human-readable and that can be read by our Python implementation.
- **FST Code:** *text*
  A text file that lists the transitions for the 2-way FST based on the shorthand description in the FST recipe. This code was created with our Python implementation of 2-way FSTs.
- **Language specific:** *Boolean*
  This field specifies if the 2-way FST entry models a reduplicative process that is unique to a specific morpheme in one language (1) or if it is general enough to model many morphemes in possibly different languages (0).

The Morpheme table:

- **Morpheme ID:** *string or varchar 200*
  The general format for a morpheme ID is ISO-FUNC-FORM where ISO is the ISO code for the morpheme's language (or the full language name if no ISO exists), FUNC is the semantic function of the morpheme based on the Leipzig glossing system[7] (otherwise the full name if the glossing abbreviation cannot be found), and the general form of the reduplicative process that is part of this morpheme. This is the primary key for the **Morpheme** entry.
- **Language:** *string or varchar 200*
  Name of the language that has this morpheme.
- **Function:** *string or varchar 200*
  The semantic function of the reduplicative morpheme.
- **Default form name:** *string or varchar 200*
  Assuming that the reduplicative morpheme has a default shape, this has the general label for it, e.g. total reduplication, initial CV, etc.
- **Sources** *text*
  Bibliographic sources used.
- **Description**: *text*
  Prosaic description of the data, patterns, and surface shapes of the morpheme, written in Markdown.
- **Data:** *text*
  A table with example inputs and outputs, written in Markdown.
- **Ambiguity:** *text*
  Description of any ambiguities present in the description of this morpheme in the bibliographic references which we used.
- **Shows allomorphy:** *Boolean*
  Specifies if the morpheme has multiple, diverse surface patterns or shapes (1) or if it has one basic shape (0).[8]
- **Has segmentalism:** *Boolean*
  Specifies if the morpheme includes any segmentalism or fixed segments (1), including

---

[7]The glossing rules can be found on: www.eva.mpg.de/lingua/resources/glossing-rules.php.

[8]It is difficult to give a consistent treatment for how to give a definite value to this attribute in some cases.

both phonological fixed segments (epenthetic vowels) or morphological fixed segments (affixes like *shm-*), or none at all (0).

- **Deeply searched:** *Boolean*
  There are some patterns that we only analyzed with secondary sources such as surveys (not deeply, thus 0); while others we analyzed using primary sources such as in-depth theoretical treatments or descriptive grammars (deeply analyzed, thus 1).
- **Possible vowel modifications:** *string or varchar 200*
  Some reduplicative process have the reduplicant vowel undergo various modifications: lengthening, shortening, diphthong reduction. This lists any vowel changes seen.
- **Morpho-phonological subconstituent involved:** *string or varchar 200*
  Some reduplicative process may target specific morphological/prosodic subconstituents, usually roots. This lists any such subconstituents involved, if any.
- **Involves affixes?:** *Boolean*
  Some reduplicative processes are either caused by or accompanied by affixes (1), while some do not involve any affixes (0).
- **Affix incorporation?:** *Boolean*
  Sometimes an affix not only triggers reduplication but it also undergoes it with the stem it attached to (1); otherwise (0).
- **Involves phonological processes?:** *Boolean*
  Sometimes a reduplicative process will involve a phonological process or opacity (1); some cases do not involve any interactions with phonology (0).
- **Data too ambiguous?:** *Boolean*
  Sometimes the source was too vague to specify the reduplicative process so no 2-way FST is provided (1). Fortunately, most cases were sufficiently described (0).
- **Miscellaneous:** *string or varchar 200*
  Miscellaneous information about this reduplicative process.

The Match table:

- **2-way FST ID:** *string or varchar 200*
  Foreign key that references the 2-way FST ID.
- **Morpheme ID:** *string or varchar 200*
  Foreign key that references the morpheme ID.

In addition to the database itself, we provide a Python script implementing 2-way FSTs. The Python program takes as input an ***FST recipe*** (that can be retrieved from the database) and a user-made text file ***input_strings*** that contains a list of strings for the 2-way FST to process. It creates two textfiles: ***output_transitions*** which contains a list of transition arcs that make up the 2-way FST, and ***output_strings*** which provides the output of every entry in the ***input strings*** using the 2-way FST.

The Python implementation can likewise take as input two textfiles: one is a list of states and transition arcs not written in shorthand (***input_transitions***), and the other is a list of input strings (***input_strings***). It will run the 2-way FST described in ***input_transitions*** and create a textfile ***output_strings*** that provides the output of each input in ***input_strings***.

Because the 2-way FSTs generally had a small number of states, we validated their correctness through manual inspection and by testing them with key examples. Our online repository contains detailed instructions and examples on how to design 2-way FSTs, extract 2-way FSTs from the database, and run them with user-made input.

Lastly, it should be noted that many of the 2-way FSTs in RedTyp define partial functions. As such, they are undefined for some logically possible inputs. For example, a 2-way FST for an initial-C reduplication is only defined for C-initial inputs. As such, it returns an error when the input is V-initial such as 'apa'.

4 Discussion

4.1 Comparison with other computational tools

Within computational morphology, many formal devices have been proposed to handle reduplication. Some of the computational models motivated by reduplication include Multiple Context-Free Grammars (MCFGs) (Seki et al., 1991, 1993; Albro, 2005) and pushdown acceptors augmented with queues (Savitch, 1989). Our reasons for using 2-way FSTs instead of MCFGs and pushdown acceptors are as follows.[9]

---

[9]The only other existing alternative to 2-way FSTs to our knowledge are pushdown transducers, which augment 1-way transducers with a stack (Allauzen and Riley, 2012). A full comparison between pushdown transducers and 2-way FSTs for modeling processes like reduplication in natural languages is an important exercise for future research.

First, unlike 2-way FSTs, MCFGs and push-down automata do not transform an input string to an output string; rather, they recognize sets of strings that may include a copying component such as the formal language $\{ww \mid w \in \Sigma^*\}$. Although Albro (2005) extended finite-state OT with MCFGs to model reduplicative processes in Malagasy, Albro's method does not provide a general machine model. We thought it judicious to provide, as resources, well-studied machine models in computer science as opposed to extending an existing formalism ourselves.

This brings us to our second reason: the class of transductions definable with 2-way FSTs are exactly the class of transductions definable with Monadic Second Order (MSO) Logic (Engelfriet and Hoogeboom, 2001). Logic, automata, and the relationship between them are foundational subjects in formal language theory (Büchi, 1960; McNaughton and Papert, 1971; Thomas, 1997), though the importance of studying string-to-string translations against this backdrop has only recently been realized (Filiot and Reynier, 2016). Our third reason is practical. As mentioned, 2-way FSTs are easy to write, debug, and implement.

4.2 Comparison with the Graz Database on Reduplication

RedTyp is not the first database for reduplication. That distinction belongs to the Graz Database on Reduplication (GDR), a SQL-database which documents and describes reduplicative processes in 82 languages (Hurch, 2005 ff.).[10]

It is the only other existing database for reduplication to our knowledge. The GDR's language sample is based on the WALS 100-language sample (Dryer and Haspelmath, 2013), but includes other languages "when these contain interesting reduplication types or when the researchers have a particular interest in any language or when there happens to be a considerable amount of information available to the researchers on the reduplication system of any language."

There are three primary distinctions between RedTyp and GDR. First, the information in the databases were collected in different ways. GDR is based on the WALS 100 language sample, and

RedTyp is based on linguistic surveys. In terms of coverage and overlap, there are 69 languages in RedTyp that are not in GDR; 60 languages in GDR that are not in RedTyp; and 22 languages common to both. They thus differ in coverage considerably. We speculate this difference is due to the goals and sources of the two databases. The GDR aims to collect examples of reduplicative processes from major and minor world languages in WALS and organize them according to form and function. There is not a specific drive to collect theoretically diverse examples of reduplication. On the other hand, the linguistic surveys and case studies used to develop RedTyp aim to document both common reduplicative processes and theoretically interesting and uncommon reduplicative processes from a morphological and phonological perspective.

Second, users can query GDR online according to pre-made and custom-made linguistically-informed searches, whereas RedTyp has no current presence online. Third, GDR does not contain any computational models of reduplication, whereas RedTyp does. Thus, RedTyp and GDR have different complementary utilities and functionalities. It is likewise an open question if RedTyp misses certain theoretically interesting patterns which are found in GDR.

4.3 Utility of RedTyp

RedTyp provides a set of 2-way FSTs representing copying processes that occur in natural language. This potentially has many uses.

For computational morphologists and phonologists working on computationally modeling or computationally implementing productive reduplicative processes in any language, RedTyp's 2-way FST examples can help them design 2-way FSTs for their own needs. To this end, RedTyp includes instructions to users on how to adapt existing 2-way FSTs by using "recipes".

For formal language theorists and theoretical linguists working on copying, the examples in RedTyp can be studied to identify additional properties, which can lead to new hypotheses about the nature of reduplicative morphology in the world's languages (cf. Heinz (2009)). For researchers interested in learning natural language patterns, RedTyp provides a computationally explicit set of learning targets. In fact, We have used RedTyp ourselves to get typological generalizations and learnability results (Dolatian and Heinz, 2018a).

---

[10]The reason why we created our own database instead of using GDR was because the GDR was offline during the time we spent collecting data for RedTyp. GDR came back online in 2017, after a hiatus of at least two years. At that time, most of the data collection for RedTyp had been completed.

Finally, our use of 2-way FSTs to model copying in natural languages opens doors on how copying, mimicry, or doubling in other domains may be modeled, including animal communication, bioinformatics and robotics.

4.4 Future Research

RedTyp also provides a focal point for different streams of future research in four general directions: improving RedTyp itself, translating linguistic theories of reduplication into 2-way FSTs, identifying subclasses of 2-way FSTs especially relevant for reduplication, and developing theory and tools to deploy 2-way FSTs in Natural Language Processing (NLP) tasks. We discuss research in both of these areas in turn.

First, although the reduplicative processes in RedTyp are fairly representative, of course more reduplicative morphemes from additional languages ought to be incorporated. We plan to grow RedTyp by exhaustively including more data from surveys such as McCarthy and Prince (1995), Inkelas and Zoll (2005), and Hurch (2005). Second, we plan to consult primary sources to verify the accuracy of the linguistic information in RedTyp. Additionally, we would like to integrate RedTyp with the Graz database (Hurch, 2005 ff.) in some fashion so that researchers interested in reduplication can take full advantage of what both databases offer, both in utility and coverage. Furthermore, an online interface should be developed.

Second, 2-way FSTs appear well-suited to capture the intuition that reduplication consists of actively copying segments from the input into multiple positions of the output. Various theoretical principles on reduplication such templatic association (Marantz, 1982), sensitivity to prominent positions in the input (Raimy, 2000), and multiple access to the same input (Steriade, 1988; Inkelas and Zoll, 2005) can be fruitfully encoded in 2-way FSTs. For results on how 2-way FSTs capture the theory behind reduplication, see Dolatian and Heinz (2018b, In press.).

Third, RedTyp contains 2-way FSTs because they were expressive enough to model both total and partial reduplication exactly and succinctly. However, reduplication does not need the full power of 2-way FSTs. Just as aspects of segmental phonology appear to be circumscribed by subclasses of 1-way FSAs/FSTs (Heinz, 2009, 2010; Chandlee, 2014; Chandlee et al., 2014,

2015; Jardine, 2016; Luo, 2017; Payne, 2017), it is likely that reduplication has stronger computational properties. We are currently investigating some promising subclasses of 2-way FSTs. One subclass in particular is the C-OSL subclass which covers the bulk of reduplicative typology and for which there are learnability results (Dolatian and Heinz, 2018a).

Finally, with respect to developing theory and tools for deploying 2-way FSTs for NLP tasks, we are optimistic. We expect that 2-way FSTs can be incorporated into existing finite-state platforms. First of all, they are straightforward extensions of 1-way FSTs, which facilitates integration. Secondly, they also have a clear logical interpretation (Engelfriet and Hoogeboom, 2001), which bolsters their status as a mathematically and computationally natural formalism. Third is the fact that computationally equivalent formalisms such as Streaming String Transducers (Alur, 2010) have industrial utility and applications (Alur and Černý, 2011; Alur et al., 2014).

Concretely, the next step for this should focus on recognition. The Python program we provided for 2-way FSTs includes code for generation, but not recognition. One route towards recognition may be non-deterministic FSTs (Alur and Deshmukh, 2011; Filiot and Reynier, 2016). Another is to see to what extent pushdown transducers (Allauzen and Riley, 2012) simulate deterministic and non-deterministic 2-way FSTs and vice versa.

To sum up, once the properties of 2-way FSTs are more more fully understood it should be possible to expand existing finite-state processing platforms for morphology, such as xfst (Beesley and Karttunen, 2003), openFST, (Allauzen et al., 2007), foma (Hulden, 2009b), and Pynini (Gorman, 2016), to include them.

5 Conclusion

RedTyp provides a publicly available record of 138 reduplicative processes and morphemes, each of which is implemented precisely with a deterministic 2-way FST. It is striking that so many reduplicative processes can be described compactly with this understudied type of finite-state machine. We hope RedTyp spurs additional research activity into computational and theoretical treatments of reduplication as well as theoretical and applied research on 2-way FSTs as models of morphophonological copying processes.

Acknowledgments

This research is supported by NIH grant #R01-HD087133 to JH. We thank audiences at CLS53, NAPhCX, ICGI, SIGMORPHON, the University of Delaware, and Stony Brook University.

References

Alfred V. Aho, John E. Hopcroft, and Jeffrey D. Ullman. 1969. A general theory of translation. *Mathematical Systems Theory*, 3(3):193–221.

Daniel M. Albro. 2005. *Studies in Computational Optimality Theory, with Special Reference to the Phonological System of Malagasy.* Ph.D. thesis, University of California, Los Angeles, Los Angeles.

Cyril Allauzen and Michael Riley. 2012. A pushdown transducer extension for the OpenFst library. In *Implementation and Application of Automata*, pages 66–77, Berlin, Heidelberg. Springer.

Cyril Allauzen, Michael Riley, Johan Schalkwyk, Wojciech Skut, and Mehryar Mohri. 2007. OpenFst: A general and efficient weighted finite-state transducer library. In *Implementation and Application of Automata*, pages 11–23, Berlin, Heidelberg. Springer.

Rajeev Alur. 2010. Expressiveness of streaming string transducers. In *Proceedings of the 30th Annual Conference on Foundations of Software Technology and Theoretical Computer Science,*, volume 8, page 112.

Rajeev Alur and Jyotirmoy V. Deshmukh. 2011. Non-deterministic streaming string transducers. In *Automata, Languages and Programming*, pages 1–20, Berlin, Heidelberg. Springer.

Rajeev Alur, Adam Freilich, and Mukund Raghothaman. 2014. Regular combinators for string transformations. In *Proceedings of the Joint Meeting of the Twenty-Third EACSL Annual Conference on Computer Science Logic (CSL) and the Twenty-Ninth Annual ACM/IEEE Symposium on Logic in Computer Science (LICS)*, CSL-LICS '14, pages 9:1–9:10, New York, NY, USA. ACM.

Rajeev Alur and Pavol Černý. 2011. Streaming transducers for algorithmic verification of single-pass list-processing programs. In *Proceedings of the 38th Annual ACM SIGPLAN-SIGACT Symposium on Principles of Programming Languages*, POPL '11, pages 599–610, New York, NY, USA. ACM.

Félix Baschenis, Olivier Gauwin, Anca Muscholl, and Gabriele Puppis. 2016. Minimizing Resources of Sweeping and Streaming String Transducers. In *43rd International Colloquium on Automata, Languages, and Programming (ICALP 2016)*, volume 55 of *Leibniz International Proceedings in Informatics (LIPIcs)*, pages 114:1–114:14, Dagstuhl, Germany. Schloss Dagstuhl–Leibniz-Zentrum fuer Informatik.

Kenneth R Beesley and Lauri Karttunen. 2003. *Finite-state morphology: Xerox tools and techniques.* CSLI Publications.

J. Richard Büchi. 1960. Weak second-order arithmetic and finite automata. *Mathematical Logic Quarterly*, 6(1-6):66–92.

Jane Chandlee. 2014. *Strictly Local Phonological Processes.* Ph.D. thesis, University of Delaware, Newark, DE.

Jane Chandlee. 2017. Computational locality in morphological maps. *Morphology*, pages 1–43.

Jane Chandlee, Rémi Eyraud, and Jeffrey Heinz. 2014. Learning strictly local subsequential functions. *Transactions of the Association for Computational Linguistics*, 2:491–503.

Jane Chandlee, Rémi Eyraud, and Jeffrey Heinz. 2015. Output strictly local functions. In *Proceedings of the 14th Meeting on the Mathematics of Language (MoL 2015)*, pages 112–125, Chicago, USA.

Jane Chandlee and Jeffrey Heinz. 2012. Bounded copying is subsequential: Implications for metathesis and reduplication. In *Proceedings of the 12th Meeting of the ACL Special Interest Group on Computational Morphology and Phonology*, SIGMORPHON '12, pages 42–51, Montreal, Canada. Association for Computational Linguistics.

Yael Cohen-Sygal and Shuly Wintner. 2006. Finite-state registered automata for non-concatenative morphology. *Computational Linguistics*, 32(1):49–82.

Abigail C Cohn. 1989. Stress in Indonesian and bracketing paradoxes. *Natural language & linguistic theory*, 7(2):167–216.

Hossep Dolatian and Jeffrey Heinz. 2018a. Learning reduplication with 2-way finite-state transducers. In *Proceedings of Machine Learning Research: International Conference on Grammatical Inference*, volume 93 of *Proceedings of Machine Learning Research*, pages 67–80, Wroclaw, Poland.

Hossep Dolatian and Jeffrey Heinz. 2018b. Modeling reduplication with 2-way finite-state transducers. In *Proceedings of the 15th SIGMORPHON Workshop on Computational Research in Phonetics, Phonology, and Morphology*, Brussells, Belgium. Association for Computational Linguistics.

Hossep Dolatian and Jeffrey Heinz. In press. Reduplication with finite-state technology. In *Proceedings of the 53rd Annual Meeting of the Chicago Linguistics Society.*

Laura J Downing. 2000. Morphological and prosodic constraints on Kinande verbal reduplication. *Phonology*, 17(01):1–38.

Matthew S. Dryer and Martin Haspelmath, editors. 2013. *WALS Online.* Max Planck Institute for Evolutionary Anthropology, Leipzig.

Ramez Elmasri and Shamkant Navathe. 2010. *Fundamentals of Database Systems*, 6th edition. Addison-Wesley Publishing Company, USA.

Joost Engelfriet and Hendrik Jan Hoogeboom. 2001. MSO definable string transductions and two-way finite-state transducers. *ACM Trans. Comput. Logic*, 2(2):216–254.

Martin Everaert, Simon Musgrave, and Alexis Dimitriadis. 2009. *The use of databases in cross-linguistic studies*, volume 41. Walter de Gruyter.

Emmanuel Filiot and Pierre-Alain Reynier. 2016. Transducers, logic and algebra for functions of finite words. *ACM SIGLOG News*, 3(3):4–19.

R.W.N. Goedemans, H.G. van der Hulst, and E.A.M. Visch. 1996. *Stress Patterns of the World Part 1: Background*. HIL Publications II. Holland Academic Graphics. The Hague.

Kyle Gorman. 2016. Pynini: A python library for weighted finite-state grammar compilation. In *Proceedings of the SIGFSM Workshop on Statistical NLP and Weighted Automata*, pages 75–80. Association for Computational Linguistics.

Jeffrey Heinz. 2009. On the role of locality in learning stress patterns. *Phonology*, 26(2):303–351.

Jeffrey Heinz. 2010. Learning long-distance phonotactics. *Linguistic Inquiry*, 41(4):623–661.

Jeffrey Heinz, Rob Goedemans, and Harry van der Hulst, editors. 2016. *Dimensions of Phonological Stress*. Cambridge University Press.

Mans Hulden. 2009a. *Finite-state machine construction methods and algorithms for phonology and morphology*. Ph.D. thesis, The University of Arizona, Tucson, AZ.

Mans Hulden. 2009b. Foma: a finite-state compiler and library. In *Proceedings of the Demonstrations Session at EACL 2009*, pages 29–32. Association for Computational Linguistics.

Mans Hulden and Shannon T Bischoff. 2009. A simple formalism for capturing reduplication in finite-state morphology. In *Proceedings of the 2009 conference on Finite-State Methods and Natural Language Processing: Post-proceedings of the 7th International Workshop FSMNLP 2008*, pages 207–214, Amsterdam. IOS Press.

Bernhard Hurch, editor. 2005. *Studies on reduplication*. 28. Walter de Gruyter, Berlin.

Bernhard Hurch. 2005 ff. Graz database on reduplication. Last accessed 10-26-2017 from `http://reduplication.uni-graz.at/redup/`.

Sharon Inkelas and Laura J Downing. 2015. What is reduplication? Typology and analysis part 1/2: The typology of reduplication. *Language and Linguistics Compass*, 9(12):502–515.

Sharon Inkelas and Cheryl Zoll. 2005. *Reduplication: Doubling in Morphology*. Cambridge University Press, Cambridge.

Adam Jardine. 2016. Computationally, tone is different. *Phonology*, 33(2):247–283.

Huan Luo. 2017. Long-distance consonant agreement and subsequentiality. *Glossa: a journal of general linguistics*, 2(1):125.

Alec Marantz. 1982. Re reduplication. *Linguistic inquiry*, 13(3):435–482.

John J McCarthy and Alan Prince. 1995. Faithfulness and reduplicative identity. In Jill N. Beckman, Laura Walsh Dickey, and Suzanne Urbanczyk, editors, *Papers in Optimality Theory*. Graduate Linguistic Student Association, University of Massachusetts, Amherst, MA.

Robert McNaughton and Seymour A Papert. 1971. *Counter-Free Automata (MIT research monograph no. 65)*. The MIT Press.

Mehryar Mohri. 1997. Finite-state transducers in language and speech processing. *Computational Linguistics*, 23(2):269–311.

Edith Moravcsik. 1978. Reduplicative constructions. In Joseph Greenberg, editor, *Universals of Human Language*, volume 1, pages 297–334. Stanford University Press, Stanford, California.

Amanda Payne. 2017. All dissimilation is computationally subsequential. *Language: Phonological Analysis*, 93(4):e353–e371.

Eric Raimy. 2000. *The Phonology and Morphology of Reduplication*. Berlin: Mouton de Gruyter.

Eric Raimy. 2011. Reduplication. In Marc van Oostendorp, Colin Ewen, Elizabeth Hume, and Keren Rice, editors, *The Blackwell companion to phonology*, volume 4, pages 2383–2413. Wiley-Blackwell, Malden, MA.

Brian Roark and Richard Sproat. 2007. *Computational Approaches to Morphology and Syntax*. Oxford University Press, Oxford.

Carl Rubino. 2005. Reduplication: Form, function and distribution. In *Studies on reduplication*, pages 11–29. Mouton de Gruyter, Berlin.

Carl Rubino. 2013. *Reduplication*. Max Planck Institute for Evolutionary Anthropology, Leipzig.

Walter J Savitch. 1989. A formal model for context-free languages augmented with reduplication. *Computational Linguistics*, 15(4):250–261.

Hiroyuki Seki, Takashi Matsumura, Mamoru Fujii, and Tadao Kasami. 1991. On multiple context-free grammars. *Theoretical Computer Science*, 88(2):191–229.

Hiroyuki Seki, Ryuichi Nakanishi, Yuichi Kaji, Sachiko Ando, and Tadao Kasami. 1993. Parallel multiple context-free grammars, finite-state translation systems, and polynomial-time recognizable subclasses of lexical-functional grammars. In *Proceedings of the 31st annual meeting on Association for Computational Linguistics*, pages 130–139. Association for Computational Linguistics.

Jeffrey Shallit. 2008. *A Second Course in Formal Languages and Automata Theory*, 1 edition. Cambridge University Press, New York, NY, USA.

Donca Steriade. 1988. Reduplication and syllable transfer in Sanskrit and elsewhere. *Phonology*, 5(1):73–155.

Wolfgang Thomas. 1997. Languages, automata, and logic. In Grzegorz Rozenberg and Arto Salomaa, editors, *Handbook of Formal Languages*, volume 3, pages 389–455. Springer-Verlag New York, Inc., New York, NY, USA.

Suzanne Urbanczyk. 2007. Themes in phonology. *The Cambridge Handbook of Phonology, edited by Paul de Lacy*, pages 473–493.

Unsupervised Learning of Cross-Lingual Symbol Embeddings Without Parallel Data

Mark Granroth-Wilding
University of Helsinki
mark.granroth-wilding@
helsinki.fi

Hannu Toivonen
University of Helsinki
hannu.toivonen@cs.helsinki.fi

Abstract

We present a new method for unsupervised learning of multilingual symbol (e.g. character) embeddings, without any parallel data or prior knowledge about correspondences between languages. It is able to exploit similarities across languages between the distributions over symbols' contexts of use within their language, even in the absence of any symbols in common to the two languages. In experiments with an artificially corrupted text corpus, we show that the method can retrieve character correspondences obscured by noise. We then present encouraging results of applying the method to real linguistic data, including for low-resourced languages. The learned representations open the possibility of fully unsupervised comparative studies of text or speech corpora in low-resourced languages with no prior knowledge regarding their symbol sets.

1   Introduction

Linguistic typology aims to map connections and similarities between different languages or dialects along multiple dimensions of comparison. A large proportion of languages spoken today have few speakers and little data annotated with linguistic analyses such as syntactic parses or part-of-speech tags. This makes mapping their typology difficult, but doing so could help in developing just such resources, for example by language transfer. There may exist digital text in these languages (e.g. forum posts or newspapers), or field recordings of speech. We attempt to learn about a language's typology purely from its surface form.

We focus on languages known to be fairly closely related (e.g. in the same language family), but where knowing more about the precise nature of the typology (e.g. regular sound correspondences in cognate words or differences in morphology) could help with resource development.

One example is the Uralic family, which contains many low-resourced languages and dialects.

To compare languages' surface forms, we must first address how to compare their basic units, characters in the case of text (List, 2014). Even closely related languages may use different writing systems, conventions, or transcription practices, as well as having systematic linguistic differences. These considerations mean that, without prior knowledge of a correspondence between two languages, it may not make sense to assume that, say, the letter a in one is directly comparable to a in the other. For example, Swedish $\mathring{a}$ typically corresponds Finnish o, and loanwords from Swedish to Finnish replace the former with the latter. Whilst such direct and well known correspondences can easily be written down by someone familiar with the language pair, capturing less clear-cut or systematic correspondences, and doing so for a large number of low-resourced language pairs, is labour intensive.

In an extreme case, two corpora may use completely distinct symbol sets, e.g. different scripts. There may be systematic linguistic differences that create a close correspondence between different symbols across languages (List, 2014), such as the phonological correspondence between Frisian f and Danish v (Fenna et al., 2014). It may also be desirable to find correspondences between sequences of symbols, e.g. Spanish $ñ$ and Portuguese nh.

We tackle this problem using unsupervised learning of vector representations (embeddings) of symbols, learning purely from unannotated, unaligned linguistic corpora. Here, we apply our method to text, learning representations of characters, but it is equally applicable to other sequences, such as phonetic sequences from speech. To be applicable to extreme cases of very little overlap between symbol vocabularies (e.g. different scripts,

Proceedings of the Society for Computation in Linguistics (SCiL) 2019, pages 19-28.
New York City, New York, January 3-6, 2019

or types of phonological transcription), it does not assume a correspondence even between common symbols. E.g., if both use *a*, it treats *a* in the two languages as distinct symbols (*1:a* and *2:a*). This means that, where such correspondences *are* found, we know that they are motivated by statistical regularities in their usages, rather than any initial bias. It may learn that *1:a* corresponds to *2:a*, or to *2:ä*, or that it has a weak correspondence to multiple characters. This makes for a challenging learning task, since it becomes impossible to exploit the idea behind typical distributional methods – that similar symbols can be recognized by similarities between their contexts of occurrences – since the contexts across languages consist of symbols from distinct sets.

We present a method that is able to discover similarities between inter-lingual symbol pairs by exploiting similarities between their respective *intra*-lingual distributions over contexts of occurrence. It must recognize that *1:a* plays a role in relation to *other symbols in language 1* that is similar to, say, *2:ä*'s role in relation to *other symbols in language 2*. It does not rely on parallel or comparable corpora, so is robust to use on whatever corpora are available for the languages of interest.

In this paper, we describe our learning method, XSYM (§3). Then we present two sets of experiments. In the first (§4), we use artificially corrupted linguistic data, allowing us to observe how well the technique recovers known mappings between character pairs obscured by the corruption. In the second (§5), we demonstrate encouraging initial results of applying the method to real linguistic data, including several low-resourced pairs, which show that it is able to build a coherent space of characters, for example placing the majority of identical characters in two related languages close to each other. This demonstrates its potential to recover correspondences between symbol pairs on the basis of distributional statistics without any other connection between the observed corpora.

Code for data preprocessing and model training, as well as trained embeddings, are available online[1].

2 Related work

Like us, Tsvetkov et al. (2016) employ a language modeling objective with neural networks to learn

multilingual embeddings for symbols (phones). They supply typological information to improve the representations. We believe that the present method is better suited to direct cross-lingual comparison of symbols and, since we aim to discover typological information, do not incorporate this in the input. Östling and Tiedemann (2016) use a character-level, multilingual language model to learn vectors to represent languages. Whilst their model shares information between languages, we focus on modeling commonalities at the level of symbol embeddings. We expect the cross-lingual information our method captures to be complementary to that in the language vectors.

A particular area where symbol alignment is required is *cognate discovery* – finding words with a common linguistic origin. List (2014) describes uses of string alignment methods, the predominant approach in the literature. He distinguishes *paradigmatic* aspects (correspondences between basic units, like phones) and *syntagmatic* aspects (comparisons in terms of sequence structure). Approaches to paradigmatic modeling include: assuming a simple set of correspondences between symbols, e.g. aligning identical symbols (Brew et al., 1996; Kondrak, 2000; Prokić et al., 2009); abstracting or normalizing symbols to comparable classes (Kondrak and Hirst, 2002; Diana Inkpen, 2005; List, 2012); and learning scoring functions or mappings to align symbols, often initializing using one of the previous assumptions (Pirkola et al., 2003; Mulloni and Pekar, 2006; Mulloni, 2007; Kondrak, 2009; Delmestri and Cristianini, 2010; Gomes and Lopes, 2011; Ciobanu and Dinu, 2014). Our approach in these terms is to learn paradigmatic correspondences from purely syntagmatic information. Some methods handle sound (e.g. phone) sequences, others text: ours, like Tsvetkov et al. (2016), can be applied to either. In contrast to alignment approaches, Hall and Klein (2010) use a Bayesian model of language change to account for differences in phonetic surface forms. McCoy and Frank (2018) use context-based character embeddings for cognate discovery and propose a method to discover cognates in a low-resourced language via a better-resourced pivot language. Our embeddings could be used with the same cognate alignment technique and evaluation scheme in future work. Our method provides an alternative, potentially more flexible, way to align with a low-resourced language.

---

[1] https://mark.granroth-wilding.co.uk/papers/unsup_symbol/

Most methods depend to some degree on linguistic resources. Many require a list of known cognate pairs (Mulloni and Pekar, 2006; Mulloni, 2007; Delmestri and Cristianini, 2010; Gomes and Lopes, 2011; Ciobanu and Dinu, 2014), or a manually aligned corpus (Navlea and Todirascu, 2011; List, 2012), others language-specific knowledge about symbols (Kondrak, 2000) or NLP tools, such as part-of-speech taggers (Brew et al., 1996; Navlea and Todirascu, 2011). Hall and Klein (2010) require a phylogeny of the input languages. We avoid reliance on any language-specific resources.

The issue of cross-lingual symbol alignment also arises in other tasks and similar approaches are used. For example, methods for computing language similarity from the surface form fall into the same categories described above for cognate identification (Batagelj et al., 1992; Kita, 1999; Petroni and Serva, 2008; Gamallo et al., 2017).

Unsupervised or semi-supervised learning of multilingual representations has been addressed at other levels of analysis (e.g. Kuhn, 2004; Snyder et al., 2009; Christodoulopoulos et al., 2012). Many could be applied to unsupervised typology, since linguistic typology concerns all levels of analysis, so are complementary to that we present. Conneau et al. (2017) present unsupervised learning of multilingual word embeddings. This could be applied to low-resourced languages and combined with our method to identify words that are related in both etymology and meaning (the *Specific Homologue Detection Problem,* List, 2014).

Conneau et al.'s learning problem is similar to ours, applied to word meaning rather than symbol correspondence. Whilst a similar technique could perhaps be applied to the present task, our method focuses specifically on similarities in local contexts of symbol use, rather than similarities in the structure of embedding spaces, which are less informative in the case of small vocabularies of characters or phonemes.

3   Method

We describe a model that assigns language model-type scores to short sequences of symbols. We train the model and use the learned embeddings and n-gram composition function. We are not ultimately interested in the predictive model, only the derived representations. The learning technique follows other representation learning algorithms

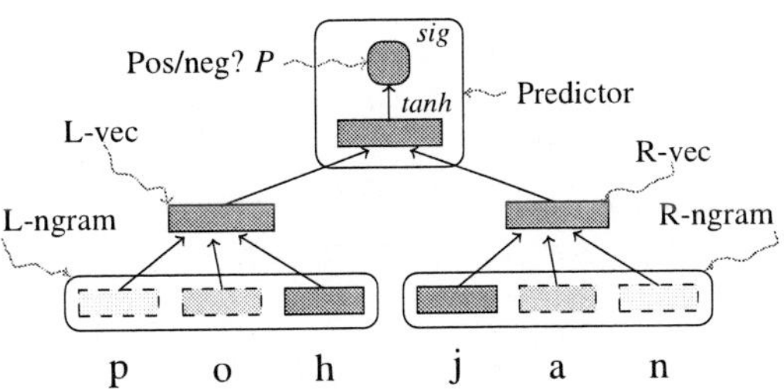

Figure 1: Structure of the neural network used to learn cross-lingual embeddings. The embeddings are used in the bottom layer. The output is a value between 0 and 1 that is used in the BPR objective function, with either positive or negative examples provided at the inputs.

(such as Mikolov et al., 2013) in using *negative sampling*. However, these methods cannot be applied directly, since the fact that the vocabularies of observed contexts are distinct for the two languages means they are unable to discover similarities between characters across languages.

In each sample seen at training time (*pohjan* in Fig. 1), all characters are from the same language, so the vectors for a Finnish character are affected only by other Finnish characters surrounding it. It is therefore possible that the resulting embeddings are grouped by language, effectively learning an independent predictor for each language. Training a high-capacity model (like an RNN) on multilingual data tends to result in this outcome. However, limiting the capacity of the network can force the model to share information between the languages at the level of embeddings. It then benefits the model to learn embeddings that exploit similarities across languages in the relationships between adjacent character sequences within a language. For example, if a is often followed by b in both languages, and there are also similarities between usage of *1:b* and *2:b*, the model can exploit this by learning similar vectors for *1:a* and *2:a*, and simultaneously *1:b* and *2:b*.

3.1   Model

Our unsupervised representation learning method, XSYM, consists of a feedforward neural network (Fig. 1) that takes as input a short sequence of characters and predicts whether or not it is a real sample from one of the languages in the training data. The character vocabularies are distinguished in the input: e.g. *fi:a* is distinct from *et:a*. The required limitation of capacity mentioned above is achieved by limiting the size of the layers and using only a small number of layers for the predictor.

The length of the input sequence is variable. Each side (L-ngram and R-ngram) may be a single symbol, represented by the symbol's embedding (which becomes L-vec/R-vec), or a bi- or tri-gram, whose embeddings are concatenated and projected by a linear transformation to get a vector for the n-gram, L-vec or R-vec. Separate transformations are learned for bi-grams and tri-grams. The same embeddings are used in each input position and the same composition function on both sides. L-vec and R-vec have the same size as the embeddings learned for individual characters.

The outputs of the two compositions are passed to a predictor function: a tanh layer and a sigmoid activation for the final output node, P. Varying the size of the two ngrams (L- and R-ngram) independently, so that a bigram is sometimes observed beside a unigram, sometimes a bigram, etc, causes the composed representations to reside in the same vector space, since they are inputs to the same predictor function.

In the experiments, we use an embedding (and composed n-gram representation) size of 30. The hidden layer in the predictor also has 30 nodes.

3.2 Learning

Positive samples are taken by passing a sliding window over the text, alternating corpora. Each positive sample is accompanied by a randomly generated negative. The positive and negative output values are used with a *Bayesian Personalized Rank* (BPR) objective function for training. BPR has been successfully used for similar representation learning tasks, where negative data is not directly available: it encourages negative samples to be ranked lower than corresponding positives (Riedel et al., 2013).

The sizes of the L- and R-ngrams are drawn independently at random. Each negative sample replaces either the L- or R-ngram of its corresponding positive (randomly, either *poh* or *jan* in Fig. 1) with characters drawn independently from the unigram distribution of the language of the sample.

All parameters, including embeddings, are initialized randomly. Dropout is applied to the embeddings and composed n-grams and a unit norm constraint is placed on the embeddings. We train using stochastic gradient descent with Adam learning rate adaptation, batch size 1000.

3.3 Validation criterion

The learned embeddings are affected by random initialization. As is typical in unsupervised learning, there is no simple way to select the best model, since we cannot evaluate the learned representations on a validation set. Conneau et al. (2017) define an *unsupervised validation criterion* to handle this problem in unsupervised alignment of word embeddings, which they use for model selection, as a proxy for word translation accuracy.

Eqn. 1 defines a validation criterion for a trained set of embeddings, *nn-sim*. To the extent that it correlates with the accuracy of correspondences found in the embeddings, it is suitable for model selection. To the extent that this holds throughout training, it can also be used for early stopping. We test these correlations in the next section. Given embeddings for languages A and B, we compute for each character in A the cosine similarity to its nearest neighbour from B, and take the mean over A's characters.

$$nn\text{-}sim = \frac{1}{|A|} \sum_{a \in A} \min_{b \in B} cos(a, b) \qquad (1)$$

Eqn. 2 defines an evaluation metric *pair-rank* that can be computed where the desired pair correspondences $(a, b) \in C$ are known. It measures how well the correspondences are retrieved by the embeddings. For each (a, b), we compute the rank, by cosine distance from a, of b among all characters in B, normalized by the size of B. We compute the same in the opposite direction and take the average of all values. A lower value reflects a better retrieval of correspondences.

$$pair\text{-}rank = \frac{1}{2|C|} \sum_{(a,b) \in C} \frac{rank_b(cos(a, B))}{|B|}$$
$$+ \frac{rank_a(cos(b, A))}{|A|} \qquad (2)$$

4 Experiments with artificial data

4.1 Motivation

For any pair of related languages, we expect to find a spectrum of correspondences between their characters, ranging from some very close pairs, through weaker correspondences, to no correspondence at all. There exists no gold-standard list of correspondences that a good model *should* find, making it difficult to evaluate representations.

Figure 2: Example sentence from the YLILAUTA corpus in its original form *(a)* and with the highest level of all three types of corruption *(b)*. The model is trained on an uncorrupted portion of the corpus as one language and a *distinct subset* to which this corruption has been applied.

We begin by testing XSYM on artificial datasets. We apply several types of corruption to real linguistic data, replacing some characters at random and combining or splitting others, then treat the corrupted data as a new language, with a distinct character set. The result is in some respects superficially similar to the relationship between related languages and presents similar challenges to the learning method. Crucially, having corrupted the data by known processes, we know which correspondences a successful method should recover.

First, we use corrupted data to measure how well the validation criterion *nn-sim* correlates with retrieval of known correspondences, measured by *pair-rank*. Then we analyze how robust the method is to the different types of corruption to get some insight into how it behaves.

4.2 Corruptions

We apply three different types of corruption. The input data has a character vocabulary V_i, the corrupted data V_o which may be different, since some corruptions add or remove characters. Corruptions are applied in the order presented. An example of the resulting text is given in Fig. 2.

Random noise: Randomly sample a given proportion p_{noise} of character tokens and, for each, sample a character at random to replace it with from the unigram distribution over V_i.

Systematic mapping: Systematically substitute a character a (randomly chosen from V_i) with b (randomly chosen from V_o). The resulting bs are indistinguishable from those that were bs in the input. a is now not in V_o, since it never occurs in the corrupted data. Characters are chosen for mapping until the expected proportion of tokens affected is $>p_{map}$. Since characters are sampled greedily to preserve randomness, the actual proportion, $\hat{p}_{map}$, may be greater than p_{map}.

Systematic splitting: Randomly choose a character a from V_o after the previous step, add new character b and randomly map half of as to b. Choose a number of characters in the same way

Metric	PCC	Slope
p_{noise}	0.35	0.22
$\hat{p}_{map}$	0.67	0.36
$\hat{p}_{split}$	-0.12	-0.06
sum	0.52	0.11

Table 1: Pearson correlation coefficient and regression slope between the level of each type of corruption and the *pair-rank* evaluation metric.

as for mapping, until the expected proportion affected is $>p_{split}$. The actual proportion is $\hat{p}_{split}$.

We train embeddings using XSYM with two corpora, as if they represented different languages. The first is a randomly chosen subset of 95k documents from the YLILAUTA corpus of Finnish forum posts[2]. The second is a distinct subset of the same size, to which the corruptions have been applied. We run the training under different levels of each type of corruption, applying all 27 combinations of $p = 0, 0.15, 0.3$ for p_{noise}, p_{map} and p_{split}.

In the first experiment, we measure the correlation between *nn-sim* and *pair-rank*. We train each model once for exactly 10 corpus iterations, outputting both metrics every 500k samples, resulting in 70 measures per model. In the second, we train all models again, using *nn-sim* as an unsupervised criterion for early stopping and model selection over 5 random intializations.

4.3 Results

Testing validation criterion *nn-sim*. We find a Pearson correlation coefficient (PCC) of $r = 0.79$ between *nn-sim* and *pair-rank* from the 1,890 measurements taken during training. The high correlation suggests that *nn-sim* is a good criterion to use for early stopping. Furthermore, measuring only at the end of training, we get $r = 0.83$, supporting the use of *nn-sim* to choose between embeddings from alternative initializations. We can expect that embeddings that maximize *nn-sim*

---

[2] http://urn.fi/urn:nbn:fi:
lb-2015031802

would also have maximized (or close) *pair-rank*, had we been able to measure it using known correspondences.

Testing effect of corruptions. Training all models with early stopping and model selection, we measured the correlation between the level of each corruption (and the sum of the three) and the *pair-rank* of the final embeddings (Table 1). We also report the slope of the regression between the corruption levels and *pair-rank*. Values of *pair-rank* range from 6%, for a low level of corruption, to 37% for a high level, with a mean of 16% over all 27 tests.

There is a high correlation for character mapping: the more characters are conflated with others in the vocabulary, the harder it is to identify the correspondences. This is unsurprising: to maintain the same level of accuracy after a mapping $a \Rightarrow b$, the method must recognize the similarity in the contexts of *2:b* in the corrupted data to those of both *1:a* and *1:b* in the uncorrupted data. The contextual distribution of *2:b*'s usage is in effect the average of those of *1:a* and *1:b*, so becomes hard to identify with either.

There is a relatively low correlation for random noise. The method is robust to this corruption, which obscures the regularities in the data, but has no systematic effect on the contextual distributions of any of the symbols.

There is no correlation for character splitting. When *1:a* is split at random so that it appears as either *2:a* or the newly added *2:b*, both *2:a* and *2:b* can be expected to have similar contextual distributions to *1:a*. The splitting reduces the amount of data from which to infer the distributions, but does not prevent the model from discovering the similarity, even under high levels of other corruptions.

These results suggest promisingly that XSYM is effective at recovering correspondences between symbols in two datasets where there are similarities in the symbols' contexts of use. It is impossible to know how these different types and levels of corruption correspond to the difficulties the method faces dealing with real data. However, this experiment confirms that the model is discovering and exploiting the sort of distributional similarities that we would hope, even where the contextual distributions are not directly comparable.

5 Experiments with linguistic corpora

We now apply XSYM to real linguistic data. To ensure that the method is not exploiting similarities between two corpora due to a shared domain (e.g., prevalence of particular cognate words peculiar to that domain), we apply it to corpora from unrelated domains, as well as in-domain pairs.

We first compare Finnish and Estonian. Whilst not low-resourced languages, it is easier to interpret results from these well-studied, closely related languages, and they are a good starting point for studying low-resourced Uralic languages. For Finnish, we use the YLILAUTA corpus again. For Estonian, we use the newspaper portion of the Estonian Reference Corpus, balanced subcorpus (Kaalep et al., 2010, henceforth EST-REF-NEWS). We use only the first 190k documents in Ylilauta, to match the size of EST-REF-NEWS ($\sim$5.8M tokens). We lower-case the text to simplify analysis and treat very rare characters ($<$ 500 occurrences) as a single out-of-vocabulary token. We also run on a single-domain corpus pair, to see how the outcome is affected by comparable versus non-comparable corpora. We train on YLILAUTA together with the forum portion of the Estonian Reference Corpus ($\sim$6.4M tokens, henceforth EST-REF-FORUM). Training parameters are identical to the previous section and *nn-sim* is used for early stopping and model selection.

We also apply the method to several combinations of low-resourced Uralic (North Finnic) languages: two dialects of Karelian (Olonets and North Karelian) and the severely endangered Ingrian language ($\sim$130 speakers). All corpora are Bible translations from the University of Helsinki Corpus Server[3], with $\sim$150k, 200k and 30k tokens respectively. We report metrics for some pairs within low-resourced languages and also for Ingrian–Finnish, since many applications will involve comparing a low-resourced language to a better-resourced one.

5.1 Results

Since this is an unsupervised learning task and there is no gold-standard set of correspondences, we cannot directly evaluate the embeddings quantitatively. Ultimately, their value will be tested by their usefulness in a downstream task, such as cognate discovery, but we leave this to future work.

---

[3]`http://urn.fi/urn:nbn:fi:lb-201403269`

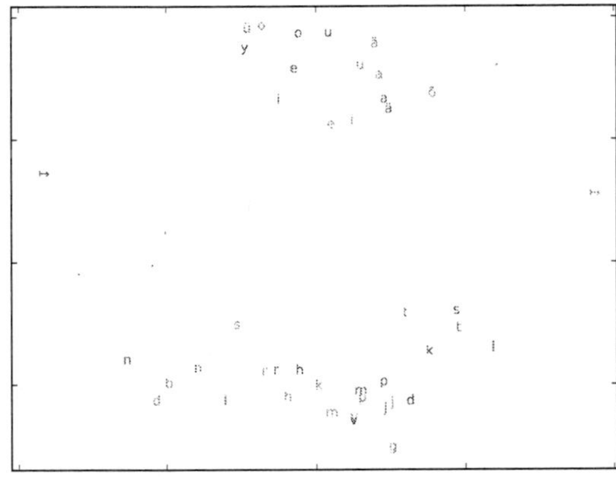

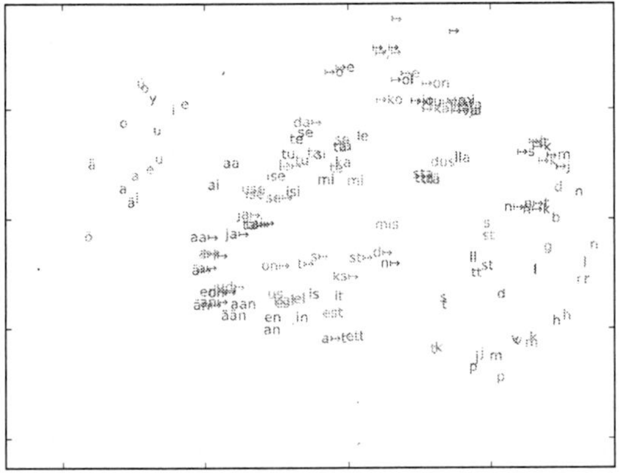

Figure 3: MDS reductions of mixed-domain embeddings for Finnish (blue) and Estonian (green). Plot of individual characters (top) and most frequent character bigrams and trigrams (bottom). '↦' represents space.

Fig. 3 shows reductions to 2D using multidimensional scaling (MDS) of the embeddings trained on Finnish and Estonian with mixed domains. We show a plot of the embeddings for all individual characters and another including the most frequent character bigrams and trigrams in each language. Fig. 4 shows single-character embeddings for single-domain corpora.

The plots give a broad notion of the layout of the space, but poorly reflect proximity between individual pairs. We also present statistics about the proximity of common characters with frequency $\geq 0.5\%$ in both corpora (e.g. *fi:t–et:t*) in Table 2. We measure where *et:t* appears in a ranking of all Estonian characters by proximity to *fi:t*, and average over all pairs, in both directions. We also report the percentage of cases where the identical character is the nearest (R@1) and within the nearest 3 characters (R@3) in the other language.

Importantly, this is *not an evaluation metric*, but

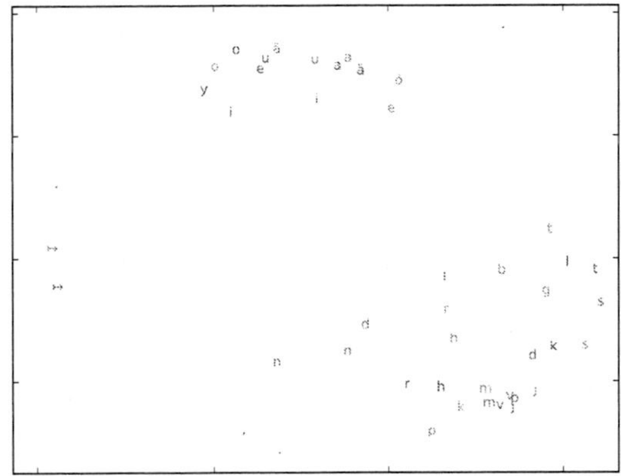

Figure 4: MDS reduction of single-domain, forum post embeddings for Finnish (b) and Estonian (g).

rather a sanity check: a lower value does not necessarily reflect better embeddings, since there may be good reasons to map non-identical characters close to each other. (Indeed, this is one of the motivations for our approach.) However, the fact that the ranking is typically low is an encouraging sign that the method is succeeding in discovering meaningful correspondences between the languages. Moreover, we see no clear difference in this respect between cross-domain and in-domain learning. The results for Uralic languages demonstrate the applicability of the method to small datasets for low-resourced languages.

To give further insight into what is being captured, in Table 3 we present, for two language pairs, nearest neighbours across languages for all cases where the nearest was not the identical character. Of particular interest here are the discovered close correspondences *š–s* and *y–ii* between North Karelian and Olonets. Table 4 shows, for one pair in one direction, other near neighbours where the nearest *is* the same character.

6   Future work

We plan to perform extrinsic evaluation of learned embeddings, like Tsvetkov et al. (2016), testing the embeddings on downstream tasks. One example is cognate discovery, where the learned similarities may bring advantages over the assumed or initial correspondences used in related work, for example where distinct symbol sets are used. Learned similarities can be incorporated into many existing cognate discovery methods (e.g. Kondrak, 2009), with McCoy and Frank (2018)

Corpus 1	Corpus 2	Chars 1	Chars 2	Common	MPR	R@1	R@3
YLILAUTA	EST-REF-NEWS	23	26	22	2.32	55%	82%
YLILAUTA	EST-REF-FORUM	23	25	25	2.11	57%	84%
NORTH KARELIAN	OLONETS KARELIAN	24	26	22	1.20	89%	95%
INGRIAN	OLONETS KARELIAN	22	26	21	1.74	64%	90%
INGRIAN	YLILAUTA	22	23	22	1.73	80%	89%

Table 2: Correspondence between common characters for cross-domain and in-domain models, as a sanity check. **Chars 1** and **2** are the number of characters in each language's vocabulary after the frequency filter. **Mean pair rank (MPR)**: mean rank of a character by cosine similarity to its identical character in the other language. **R@1** is the proportion that are nearest neighbours, **R@3** the proportion that are within the three closest.

Ing	Fi
h	v h
r	h v m r
,	n ,
.	n , s i ä .

Fi	Ing
d	k j v ...
t	k t
.	, o s .

NK	Olonets
š	k s p ...
s	l z g s
y	ü ä e ...
,	. ,

Olonets	NK
d	j t l ...
ä	e ä
g	l j s ...
s	š k p s
z	l j r ...
ü	y ä e ...
,	. ,

Table 3: Nearest neighbours across Finnish (Ylilauta)–Ingrian and North Karelian–Olonets, where the closest is not the same. **Bold** are not in the other language.

NK	Olonets
a	a o u ü e
v	v j p m r k t
ä	ä ö e ü a
e	e ä o a ü
i	i ü
h	h n
k	k s p m v j t
j	j v m p d k r z
m	m v r p j
l	l z g n r
o	o a u e
n	n h l
p	p v m r j k
r	r v m p h j
u	u o a
t	t j d k
ö	ö ä

Table 4: Nearest Olonets neighbours to North Karelian, where the nearest is identical, down to a cosine similarity of 0.5.

providing perhaps a particularly suitable way to use them. It remains an open question how n-gram similarities can be used here. Another possible application is spelling translation, for example applying the method of Pirkola et al. (2003) without requiring translation dictionaries.

A potential benefit of this method is its ability to capture correspondences between different lengths of n-grams, not just individual symbols. In our analysis (Fig. 3) we have used this by including a language's most common n-grams in projections, but other ways to select pertinent correspondences are possible, for example taking into account similarities or the structure of the vector space as well as frequency.

XSYM is similar to Polyglot language models (Tsvetkov et al., 2016). We have suggested, but not demonstrated here, that it is better suited to direct comparison of symbols. Investigation of the properties of representations learned by the two methods is required and we will test XSYM on the tasks reported by Tsvetkov et al. (2016).

We plan to apply XSYM to other symbol sequences, in particular, to sequences of phonetic symbols from speech (like List, 2014). It may be possible to use automatic transcriptions that do not require language-specific transcribers, since the symbols need not correspond to linguistically motivated systems, such as IPA. Although designed for learning about linguistic sequences, XSYM could potentially also be applied also to non-linguistic data to discover links between sequences that use distinct vocabularies. We will investigate what characteristics of sequences are essential in finding useful abstractions (e.g. vocabulary size).

7 Conclusion

We have presented an unsupervised method that uses a neural network to learn vector representations of symbols and short n-grams on the basis of their contexts observed in sequences. It is able to learn comparable representations of symbols from multiple languages that use distinct symbol sets, learning to exploit similarities in the context distributions of the symbols across languages, even though the symbols in the contexts are also drawn from distinct vocabularies.

We have demonstrated the method's ability to recover mappings between vocabularies, even when they are obscured by ambiguity in the mappings and noise, provided that the noise does not obscure the distributions over the symbols' contexts too much. We then showed some results of applying the method to real linguistic data, focusing here on characters in text and several Uralic language pairs. We found that it was able to recognize many characters that are common to the corpus pairs as being closely related by their contexts of use. An even closer correspondence was found between closely related, low-resourced dialects, despite a much smaller training set.

The learned similarities between symbols provide a way to bootstrap discovery of other linguistic similarities, such as morphology or cognate words. We leave testing on these applications to future work and have presented here some analysis of the learned representations, which appear highly promising. We suggest that the results have great potential as a first step in fully unsupervised linguistic typology. Discovered correspondences may also be able to tell us about typology in themselves. For example, some measures of orthographic difference and sound correspondences correlate with geographic factors in language development (Heeringa et al., 2013; Prokić and Cysouw, 2013). Discovered strong symbol correspondences (especially if the method is applied to phonetic sequences) could also be of typological interest in themselves.

The method presented is a generic representation learning technique for symbol sequences. As well as text, it could also be applied to other linguistic sequences, such a phonetic transcriptions, and potentially even to non-linguistic sequences. On the basis of the encouraging initial results presented here, we suggest that it warrants further investigation, including linguistic applications, such as unsupervised cognate discovery, and other aspects of linguistic typology.

8 Acknowledgements

This work was funded by the Academy of Finland *Digital Language Typology* project (no. 12933481).

References

Vladimir Batagelj, Tomaž Pisanski, and Damijana Keržič. 1992. Automatic clustering of languages. *Computational Linguistics*, 18(3):339–352.

Chris Brew, David McKelvie, et al. 1996. Word-pair extraction for lexicography. In *Proceedings of the 2nd International Conference on New Methods in Language Processing*, pages 45–55.

Christos Christodoulopoulos, Sharon Goldwater, and Mark Steedman. 2012. Turning the pipeline into a loop: Iterated unsupervised dependency parsing and PoS induction. In *Proceedings of the NAACL-HLT Workshop on the Induction of Linguistic Structure*, pages 96–99.

Alina Maria Ciobanu and Liviu P Dinu. 2014. Automatic detection of cognates using orthographic alignment. In *Proceedings of the 52nd Annual Meeting of the ACL*, volume 2, pages 99–105.

Alexis Conneau, Guillaume Lample, Marc'Aurelio Ranzato, Ludovic Denoyer, and Hervé Jégou. 2017. Word translation without parallel data. *CoRR*, abs/1710.04087.

Antonella Delmestri and Nello Cristianini. 2010. String similarity measures and PAM-like matrices for cognate identification. *Bucharest Working Papers in Linguistics*.

Grzegorz Kondrak Diana Inkpen, Oana Frunza. 2005. Automatic identification of cognates and false friends in French and English. In *Proceedings of the International Conference Recent Advances in Natural Language Processing*, pages 251–257.

Bergsma Fenna, Swarte Femke, and Gooskens Charlotte. 2014. Does instruction about phonological correspondences contribute to the intelligibility of a related language? *Dutch Journal of Applied Linguistics*, 3(1):45–61.

Pablo Gamallo, José Ramom Pichel, and Iñaki Alegria. 2017. From language identification to language distance. *Physica A: Statistical Mechanics and its Applications*, 484:152–162.

Luís Gomes and José Gabriel Pereira Lopes. 2011. Measuring spelling similarity for cognate identification. In *Proceedings of the Portuguese Conference on Artificial Intelligence*, pages 624–633.

David Hall and Dan Klein. 2010. Finding cognate groups using phylogenies. In *Proceedings of the 48th Annual Meeting of the ACL*, pages 1030–1039.

Wilbert Heeringa, Jelena Golubovic, Charlotte Gooskens, Anja Schüppert, Femke Swarte, and Stefanie Voigt. 2013. Lexical and orthographic distances between Germanic, Romance and Slavic languages and their relationship to geographic distance. *Phonetics in Europe: Perception and Production*, pages 99–137.

Heiki-Jaan Kaalep, Kadri Muischnek, Kristel Uiboaed, and Kaarel Veskis. 2010. The Estonian Reference Corpus: Its composition and morphology-aware user interface. In *Proceedings of the 4th International Conference Baltic HLT*, pages 143–146.

Kenji Kita. 1999. Automatic clustering of languages based on probabilistic models. *Journal of Quantitative Linguistics*, 6(2):167–171.

Grzegorz Kondrak. 2000. A new algorithm for the alignment of phonetic sequences. In *Proceedings of the 1st NAACL*, pages 288–295.

Grzegorz Kondrak. 2009. Identification of cognates and recurrent sound correspondences in word lists. *TAL*, 50:201–235.

Grzegorz Kondrak and Graeme Hirst. 2002. *Algorithms for language reconstruction*. Ph.D. thesis, University of Toronto.

Jonas Kuhn. 2004. Experiments in parallel-text based grammar induction. In *Proceedings of the 42nd Annual Meeting of the ACL*.

Johann-Mattis List. 2012. Lexstat: Automatic detection of cognates in multilingual wordlists. In *Proceedings of the EACL 2012 Joint Workshop of LINGVIS & UNCLH*, pages 117–125.

Johann-Mattis List. 2014. *Sequence comparison in historical linguistics*. Ph.D. thesis, Heinrich-Heine-Universität Düsseldorf. Dissertations in Language and Cognition, 1.

Richard T. McCoy and Robert Frank. 2018. Phonologically informed edit distance algorithms for word alignment with low-resource languages. In *Proceedings of the Society for Computation in Linguistics (SCiL) 2018*, pages 102–112.

Tomas Mikolov, Kai Chen, Greg Corrado, and Jeffrey Dean. 2013. Efficient estimation of word representations in vector space. *CoRR*, abs/1301.3781.

Andrea Mulloni. 2007. Automatic prediction of cognate orthography using support vector machines. In *Proceedings of the 45th Annual Meeting of the ACL: Student Research Workshop*, pages 25–30.

Andrea Mulloni and Viktor Pekar. 2006. Automatic detection of orthographic cues for cognate recognition. *Proceedings of LREC'06*.

Mirabela Navlea and Amalia Todirascu. 2011. Using cognates in a French-Romanian lexical alignment system: A comparative study. In *Proceedings of the International Conference Recent Advances in Natural Language Processing*, pages 247–253.

Robert Östling and Jörg Tiedemann. 2016. Continuous multilinguality with language vectors. *CoRR*, abs/1612.07486.

Filippo Petroni and Maurizio Serva. 2008. Language distance and tree reconstruction. *Journal of Statistical Mechanics: Theory and Experiment*, 2008(08):P08012.

Ari Pirkola, Jarmo Toivonen, Heikki Keskustalo, Kari Visala, and Kalervo Järvelin. 2003. Fuzzy translation of cross-lingual spelling variants. In *Proceedings of the 26th Annual International ACM SIGIR Conference*, pages 345–352.

Jelena Prokić and Michael Cysouw. 2013. Combining regular sound correspondences and geographic spread. *Language Dynamics and Change*, 3(2):147–168.

Jelena Prokić, Martijn Wieling, and John Nerbonne. 2009. Multiple sequence alignments in linguistics. In *Proceedings of the EACL 2009 Workshop on Language Technology and Resources for Cultural Heritage, Social Sciences, Humanities, and Education*, LaTeCH-SHELT&R '09, pages 18–25.

Sebastian Riedel, Limin Yao, Andrew McCallum, and Benjamin M Marlin. 2013. Relation extraction with matrix factorization and universal schemas. In *Proceedings of NAACL HLT 2013*, pages 74–84.

Benjamin Snyder, Tahira Naseem, and Regina Barzilay. 2009. Unsupervised multilingual grammar induction. In *Proceedings of the Joint Conference of the 47th Annual Meeting of the ACL and the 4th International Joint Conference on Natural Language Processing of the AFNLP*, pages 73–81.

Yulia Tsvetkov, Sunayana Sitaram, Manaal Faruqui, Guillaume Lample, Patrick Littell, David R. Mortensen, Alan W. Black, Lori S. Levin, and Chris Dyer. 2016. Polyglot neural language models: A case study in cross-lingual phonetic representation learning. *CoRR*, abs/1605.03832.

Q-Theory Representations are logically equivalent to Autosegmental Representations

Nick Danis
Program in Linguistics
Princeton University
ndanis@princeton.edu

Adam Jardine
Department of Linguistics
Rutgers University
adam.jardine@rutgers.edu

Abstract

We use model theory and logical interpretations to systematically compare two competing representational theories in phonology, Q-Theory (Shih and Inkelas, 2014, forthcoming) and Autosegmental Phonology (Goldsmith, 1976). We find that, under reasonable assumptions for capturing tone patterns, Q-Theory Representations are equivalent to Autosegmental Representations, in that any constraint that can be written in one theory can be written in another. This contradicts the assertions of Shih and Inkelas, who claim that Q-Theory Representations are different from, and superior to, Autosegmental Representations.

1 Introduction

Model theory and mathematical logic can be used to rigorously define phonological representations and constraints (Bird, 1995; Potts and Pullum, 2002). The logical notion of *interpretation* (Enderton, 1972; Courcelle, 1994; Hodges, 1997) between logics of different kinds of models then allows us to compare and contrast differing representational theories, and rigorously examine whether or not they are truly distinct or if they are simply notational variants of one another (Strother-Garcia and Heinz, 2017).

This paper uses these techniques to critically examine the Q-Theory Representations (QRs) of Shih and Inkelas (forthcoming, henceforth SI; see also Shih and Inkelas (2014)). SI argue for QRs as a superior alternative to Autosegmental Representations (ARs; Goldsmith (1976)), specifically with respect to phonological tone patterns. We find that, to the contrary, the differences are notational. We show that for any constraint that can be written in the first-order logic of QRs, there is an equivalent constraint in ARs, and vice versa.

The fundamental idea behind QRs is that every segment, or Q, is divided into three subsegments, or qs. Agreement and disagreement is based on *correspondence* (Hansson, 2001; Rose and Walker, 2004; Bennett, 2015), a relation that holds between qs and between Qs. To give an example, SI give the following QR in (1a) for the Basaá word [hólôl] 'ripen' (Dimmendaal, 1988; Hyman, 2003), in which the first vowel is a level high tone and the second vowel is a falling tone. Each [o] vowel Q is split into three qs, which each carry a tone. Indices on the qs represent correspondence. (Consonant qs have been abbreviated.)

a. h(ó₁ ó₁,₂ ó₂,₃)l(ó₃ ò₄ ò₄)l b. (1)

In (1a), the first q of the second vowel is high-toned while the rest are low-toned; this thus represents the falling contour of the second vowel. Furthermore, the last q of the first vowel and the first q in the second are in correspondence (and both high-toned). This indicates that the falling contour on the second vowel is the result of partial agreement with the high-toned first vowel.

In contrast, ARs would depict [hólôl] using separate strings of *autosegments* associated to one another. An AR for [hólôl], given in (1b), represents a high (H) tone associated to both the first vowel (V) and the second vowel.

SI make several claims about QRs in favor of ARs. First, they claim that representations like in (1) capture tone patterns without "the special representational machinery of autosegments and association lines" (SI, pp. 18-9). They give a number of analyses which they argue shows that QRs are "better at capturing key tone behaviors" (p. 2).

By precisely studying the nature of these representations, however, we show that QRs are logically equivalent to ARs. First, we give model-

Proceedings of the Society for Computation in Linguistics (SCiL) 2019, pages 29-38.
New York City, New York, January 3-6, 2019

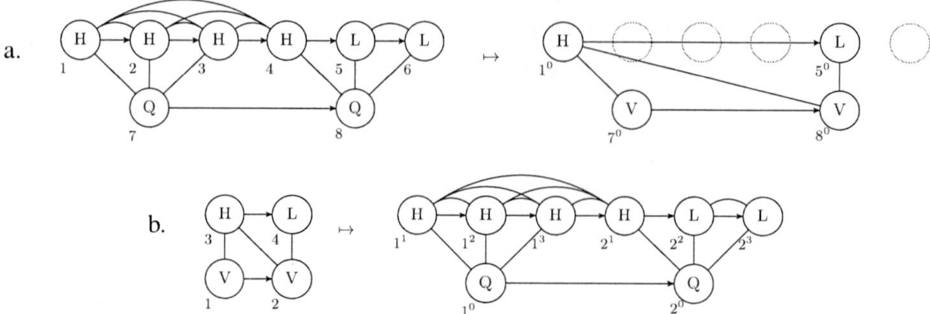

Figure 1: Overview of the transductions (a) from QRs to ARs and (b) from ARs to QRs.

theoretic definitions of both QRs and ARs. This shows that, contra to SI's claims, QRs *do* require an 'association' relation between qs and Qs. Second, based on the logical transductions of Courcelle (1994), we give a *first-order (FO) transduction* from QRs to ARs, and from ARs to QRs. This guarantees that, given any FO statement φ written over QRs, there is an equivalent FO statement φ' in ARs such that any QR model satisfies φ if and only if its equivalent AR model satisfies φ'. In phonological terms, this means that for any constraint that we can write in FO logic of QRs, there is an equivalent constraint in the FO logic of ARs (and vice versa). These models and transductions reveal an equivalence between chains of qs connected by correspondence in QRs and tonal autosegments in ARs.

This paper is not meant to be a complete rebuttal of SI, but instead to lay the formal groundwork for establishing the similarity of QRs and ARs. Throughout, we assume that FO logic as the upper bound for the expressivity necessary to capture constraints in natural language phonology (Bird, 1995; Rogers et al., 2013).

This paper is structured as follows. §2 summarizes the equivalence between structures in informal terms. §3 gives the preliminaries of model theory and logic; §4 defines ARs and QRs in terms of model theory; and §5 defines the transductions between them. §6 summarizes and discusses the results, and §7 concludes.

2 Overview

Before going into the formal details, we first give a brief overview of how transductions between the two representations proceed. These are illustrated with examples in Fig. 1 showing transductions between models for the representations in (1).

As shown in the left-hand side of Fig. 1a, defining QRs precisely reveals that there must be a relation pairing tone-bearing qs (depicted with Hs and Ls) with vowel Qs. Moving from a QR to an AR, then, is a matter of identifying the first member of a chain of corresponding qs (indicated by curved lines) and as assigning it to a tone in the output AR. All other qs in that chain are 'merged' into that autosegment—thus, for example, as both vowel Qs are associated to correspondents of 1 in the QR in Fig. 1a, both equivalent Vs in the AR are associated to its output tone 1^0.

In the other direction, illustrated in Fig. 1b, we create three additional copies of each V in the AR, representing the output qs. For example, vowel 1 in the left-hand side of Fig. 1b has copies 1^1, 1^2, and 1^3 in the right-hand side. These copies are labeled and related through correspondence according to the associations in the AR. For a series of vowels associated to the same tone in the AR, their output Qs are associated to a chain of corresponding qs of the same tone value. For example, both vowels 1 and 2 in the left-hand side of Fig. 1b are associated to the same H tone, so their output Qs are associated to a chain of corresponding H-toned qs in the output. This thus implements the equivalence of tonal autosegments to q-correspondence chains in the transduction from ARs to QRs.

3 Preliminaries

3.1 Models

The following is based on standard concepts of finite relational structures (Enderton, 1972; Libkin, 2004). A *signature* S is a fixed set $\{R_1, R_2, ..., R_n\}$ of n named relations. A *model* M over a signature is a tuple $\langle D; R_1, R_2, ..., R_n \rangle$ with a domain D of elements and a set of n relations where each $R_i \subseteq D^k$ for some k. Here, k is equal to either 1 or 2; that is, we consider only unary and binary relations.

For example, the signature $\{<, P_a, P_b\}$ can describe the set of strings over the alphabet a and b. A model in this signature is given in Fig. 2.

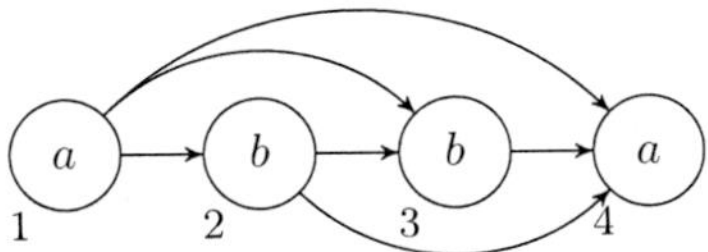

Figure 2: A model of the string $abba$. $D = \{1, 2, 3, 4\}$, P_a and P_b are indicated by labels on the nodes, and $<$ by arrows.

3.2 Logic

A fixed signature induces a first-order (FO) logical language $L_\mathcal{S}$ as follows. For every $R_i \in \mathcal{S}$, $R_i(x_1, ..., x_k)$ is an atomic formula in $L_\mathcal{S}$, which is interpreted as true in a model M when $x_1, ..., x_k$ are evaluated to $d_1, ..., d_k \in D$ and $(d_1, ..., d_k) \in R_i$ in M. We also assume an equality predicate $x \approx y$ that is true when x and y are both evaluated to some $i \in D$. We then define the FO logic of $L_\mathcal{S}$ and its semantics in the usual way; for details, see, e.g., Enderton (1972). For a FO formula $\varphi(x_1, ..., x_k)$ we write $M \models \varphi(d_1, ..., d_k)$ when $\varphi(x_1, ..., x_k)$ is true in M when $x_1, ..., x_k$ are evaluated to $d_1, ..., d_k$ in D. A *sentence* is a formula with no free variables; for a sentence φ we write $M \models \varphi$ when φ is true in M.

3.3 Transductions and interpretations

To directly compare structures in distinct signatures we use logical *transductions* (Courcelle, 1994), in which the relations in an output structure are defined using the logic of an input structure. Given an input signature $\mathcal{S}$ and an output signature $\mathcal{T} = \{R_1, ..., R_n\}$, we define each R_i in $L_\mathcal{S}$. Such a transduction thus induces an *interpretation* of $\mathcal{T}$ in $\mathcal{S}$; that is, for any formula we can write in $L_\mathcal{T}$, there exists a translation into $L_\mathcal{S}$ (Enderton, 1972; Hodges, 1997). If there then also exists a transduction back from $\mathcal{T}$ to $\mathcal{S}$, there then exists an interpretation of $\mathcal{S}$ in $\mathcal{T}$. If interpretations in both directions exist, we say that $\mathcal{S}$ and $\mathcal{T}$ are *bi-interpretable*.

A FO transduction is defined as follows. Fix a *copy set* $C = \{1, ..., k\}$, an input signature $\mathcal{S}$, and an output signature $\mathcal{T} = \{R_1, ..., R_n\}$. A FO transduction τ from $\mathcal{S}$ to $\mathcal{T}$ is thus a set of formulae $\varphi_i^{c_1, ..., c_m}(x_1, ..., x_m)$ for each $R_i \in \mathcal{T}$ and each $c_1, ..., c_m \in C^m$, where m is the arity of R_i.

The output of such a transduction is calculated as follows.[1] For a stucture M over the input signature $\mathcal{S}$, and whose domain is D, $\tau(M)$ is a structure $N = \langle D', R_1, ..., R_n \rangle$ defined as follows:

1. For every $d \in D$, there is a copy $d^c \in D'$ iff there is exactly one unary predicate $R_i^c(x)$ in τ such that $M \models \varphi_i(d)$.

2. For any R_i of arity m, $(d_1^{c_1}, ..., d_m^{c_m}) \in R_i$ if and only if there is a $d_1, ..., d_m \in D^m$ and a $\varphi_i^{c_1, ..., c_m}(x_1, ..., x_m)$ in τ such that $M \models \varphi_i^{c_1, ..., c_m}(d_1, ..., d_m)$, and each $d_i^{c_i} \in D'$ as per the requirement in (1).

Intuitively, given a structure M over $\mathcal{S}$, the output structure in $\mathcal{T}$ can have up to $|C|$ copies of elements in the domain of D, and the relations in $\mathcal{T}$ are defined relative to these copies.

For example, given the string signature $\mathcal{S}$ defined above we can define a transduction into a pseudo-autosegmental signature $\mathcal{T} = \{\lhd', A', P_c', P_b'\}$ as follows. Set the copy set to $C = \{1, 2\}$. Then define a transduction τ as

$$x \lhd'^{1,1} y \overset{\text{def}}{=} x < y \wedge \neg(\exists z)[x < z \wedge z < y],$$
$$x \lhd'^{2,2} y \overset{\text{def}}{=} x < y \wedge \neg(\exists z)[x < z \wedge z < y],$$
$$x A'^{1,2} y \overset{\text{def}}{=} x \approx y,$$
$$P_b'^2(x) \overset{\text{def}}{=} P_b(x),$$
$$P_c'^1(x) \overset{\text{def}}{=} P_b(x) \vee P_a(x),$$

and for all other $i, j \in C$, $x \lhd'^{i,j} y \overset{\text{def}}{=} x A'^{i,j} y \overset{\text{def}}{=}$ False, and $P_b'^1 \overset{\text{def}}{=} P_c'^2 \overset{\text{def}}{=}$ False.

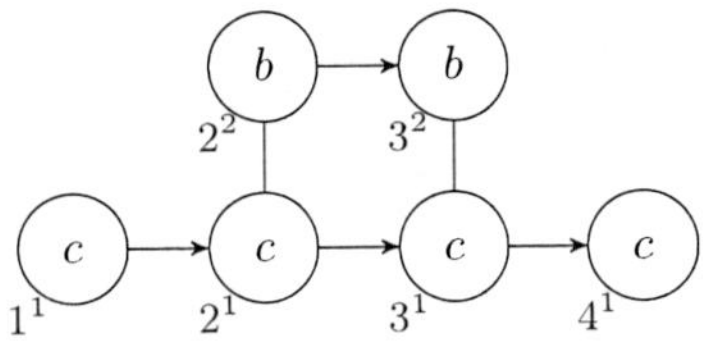

Figure 3: Output structure in $\mathcal{T}$ obtained by applying τ to the string model in Fig. 2. Arrows denote $\lhd'$ and lines without arrows denote A'. Indices of the nodes are of the form d^c, where d is a node from Fig. 2 and $c \in C$.

---

[1] We use an abbreviated construction used for those in strings, based on (Engelfriet and Hoogeboom, 2001). For the full construction see (Courcelle et al., 2012).

We interpret τ as follows; an example is given in Fig. 3. As $P_c'^1(x) \stackrel{\text{def}}{=} P_b(x) \vee P_a(x)$, every node d in the input string is given a copy d^1 in the output labeled c. Similarly, as $P_b'^2(x) \stackrel{\text{def}}{=} P_b(x)$ means that for any d labeled b in the input, there is a second copy d^2 labeled b in the output. As $P_b'^1(x) = P_c'^2(x) = \texttt{False}$, no other copies are produced. Thus, the b nodes in Fig. 2 have both a corresponding c node and b node in Fig. 3, but the a nodes only have a corresponding c node.

The definitions for $x \lhd'^{1,1} y$ and $x \lhd'^{2,2} y$ then establish a *successor* relation between the first and second copies of nodes, respectively. Thus, for two nodes d_1 and d_2 in the input structure, d_2^1 is the successor of d_1^1 if and only if $i < j$ in in the input structure and no node intervenes between them; likewise for d_1^2 and d_2^2. As $x \lhd'^{i,j} y$ is `False` for all other $i, j \in C$, the first and second copies are not ordered with respect to each other. Instead, $x A'^{1,2} y \stackrel{\text{def}}{=} x \approx y$ establishes that for any d, d^1 in the output is associated to its own second copy d^2 in the output (assuming that it survives according to (1) above). This can be seen for the copies of the b nodes 2 and 3 from Fig. 2 in Fig. 3.

As such a transduction is defined in terms of the atomic predicates of the output signature, it also induces an interpretation from the logic of the output signature to the logic of the input signature.

Lemma 1 (Courcelle et al. (2012)) *A FO transduction τ from S to T induces a translation f from the FO language L_S of S to the FO language L_T of T such that for every sentence φ in L_S there is a sentence $f(\varphi)$ in L_T such that for any structure M over S, $M \models \varphi$ if and only if $\tau(M) \models f(\varphi)$.*

In terms of phonology, if there is a FO transduction from one representational theory S to another T, Lemma 1 means that for any FO constraint C over S there is a FO constraint C' over T such that a representation in S satisfies C if and only if its equivalent representation in T satisfies C'.

4 Phonological representations as models

We now apply this technique to studying the relationship between ARs and QRs. First, we define the representations in model-theoretic terms.

4.1 Autosegmental representations

We assume a basic theory of autosegmental representations (ARs), which also follows SI's characterization of ARs (p. 2). The crucial assumptions are that there exists a tier of timing units (in our case, vowels), and featural elements are associated to elements on this tier. Each type of featural element (for our purposes, Hs and Ls) are also on their own tier, ordered together. For the patterns discussed in SI, a single tonal tier is sufficient. The signature for ARs is thus as below.

$$\mathcal{A} = \{\lhd_{\mathcal{A}}, A_{\mathcal{A}}, V_{\mathcal{A}}, H_{\mathcal{A}}, L_{\mathcal{A}}\} \tag{2}$$

$V_{\mathcal{A}}$, $H_{\mathcal{A}}$, and $L_{\mathcal{A}}$ are unary relations that label elements as vowels, H tones, and L tones, respectively. The association relation is $A_{\mathcal{A}}$; to simplify definitions we treat $A_{\mathcal{A}}$ as antisymmetric and directed from vowels to tones; that is, $x A_{\mathcal{A}} y$ holds only if $V_{\mathcal{A}}(x)$ is true and either $H_{\mathcal{A}}(y)$ or $L_{\mathcal{A}}(y)$.

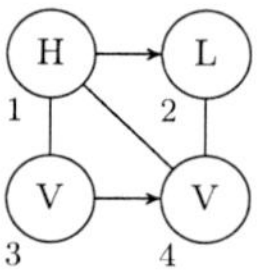

Figure 4: An example AR of the sequence V́V̂.

Each tier is ordered by the $\lhd_{\mathcal{A}}$ successor relation. Thus, the set of elements labeled $V_{\mathcal{A}}$ are ordered, as are the set of elements labeled $H_{\mathcal{A}}$ or $L_{\mathcal{A}}$. A vowel can be associated to more than one tone (a contour) or a tone can be associated to more than one vowel (spreading). This is shown in Figure 4. For further simplicity, we also assume full specification: there are no toneless vowels and no floating tones. This last assumption is somewhat generous, as by SI's own admission, QRs cannot capture floating tones (see SI §6.1).

Next, we assume two axioms that specially require the use of precedence ($<$). The first is No Gapping (NG), which prohibits autosegments from being linked to non-contiguous elements on the timing tier (Ní Chiośain and Padgett, 2001).

$$\text{NG} \stackrel{\text{def}}{=} (\forall x, y, z, w)\big[\; (x < y < z \wedge A_{\mathcal{A}}(x, w) \\ \wedge A_{\mathcal{A}}(z, w)) \to A_{\mathcal{A}}(y, w)\big]$$

We also adopt the No-Crossing Constraint (NCC), which states that association must respect precedence on each tier (Goldsmith, 1976).

$$\text{NCC} \stackrel{\text{def}}{=} (\forall x, y, v, w)\big[\; (x A_{\mathcal{A}} v \wedge y A_{\mathcal{A}} w \\ \wedge x < y) \to v < w\big]$$

Thus, models in $\mathcal{A}$ satisfy NG $\wedge$ NCC.

Finally, we assume that vowels can only associate to at most three tones—this maintains equivalence between ARs and QRs. While this has not traditionally been explicitly stated as an axiom of ARs, recent proposals do state such constraints (Yli-Jyrä, 2013; Jardine and Heinz, 2015).

4.2 Q-Theory representations

Q-Theory Representations (QRs) consist of two sets of ordered elements: one of Qs, and one of qs. Each Q consists of exactly 3 qs, and every q is part of exactly one Q. According to SI, qs are subsegments; the featural information of the segment is carried on the q. For our purposes, the relevant features are the tone features H and L. Thus, because constraints in SI refer to the featural information of some Q, it must be able to "see" what qs are relevant; a Q and its qs must be in some relation. We denote this relation A_Q.

We thus consider the following signature for QRs. Fig. 5 gives an example model in this signature of the QR for [hólôl] from (1).

$$\mathcal{Q} = \{\triangleleft_\mathcal{Q}, R_\mathcal{Q}, A_\mathcal{Q}, Q_\mathcal{Q}, H_\mathcal{Q}, L_\mathcal{Q}\} \qquad (3)$$

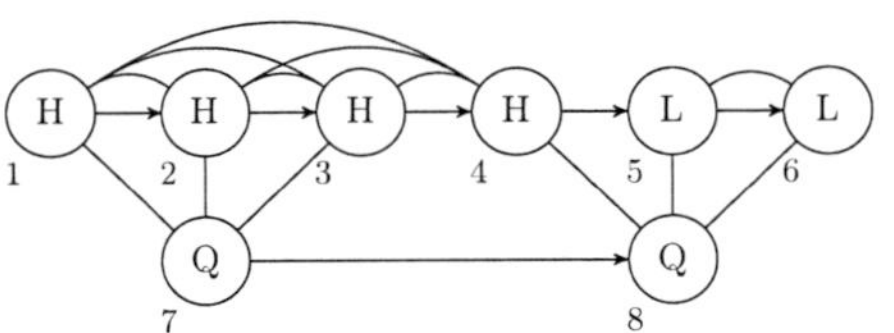

Figure 5: An example QR of the sequence V́V̂.

This signature includes a sucessor relation $\triangleleft_\mathcal{Q}$, a correspondence relation $R_\mathcal{Q}$ (the curved lines in Fig. 5), the relation $A_\mathcal{Q}$ associating Qs to qs, and three unary relations $Q_\mathcal{Q}$, $H_\mathcal{Q}$, and $L_\mathcal{Q}$, labeling Qs, H-toned qs, and L-toned qs, respectively.

The axioms that govern $R_\mathcal{Q}$ are not straightforward and so we discuss them here. We base our axioms for $R_\mathcal{Q}$ on both the explicit and implicit discussion in SI.

First, we assume that $R_\mathcal{Q}$ is transitive. While SI claim their correspondence to be non-transitive, their constraints crucially refer to *correspondence chains*, or unbroken chains of corresponding elements. They state: "[A] sequence of three identical consecutive segments S in a grammar requiring that identical segments correspond would satisfy that constraint as follows: $S_1 S_{1,2} S_2$, where coindexation encodes correspondence" (SI, p. 5). In other words, the first S_1 and third S_2, although they do not directly correspond, satisfy any correspondence constraints because there is a correspondence chain connecting them (through the intermediary $S_{1,2}$). Thus, in practice, the correspondence relation of SI is transitive.

For ease of definition we further assume $R_\mathcal{Q}$ is also reflexive and symmetric and thus an equivalence relation (per Bennett (2015)).

$$\text{EQ} \stackrel{\text{def}}{=} \forall (x, y, z)[\ (xR_\mathcal{Q}y \rightarrow yR_\mathcal{Q}x) \wedge \\ (xR_\mathcal{Q}x\ ) \wedge \\ ((xR_\mathcal{Q}y \wedge yR_\mathcal{Q}z) \rightarrow xR_\mathcal{Q}z)\ ]$$

However, this choice is not crucial to our results.

Furthermore, like SI, we define $R_\mathcal{Q}$ to be local: "'Local' means consecutive; thus V-to-V correspondence is still considered local even if a consonant intervenes, as long as the closest two vowels in the string correspond" (SI: 4–5). In all of their case studies, correspondence is always between adjacent vowels. (The only candidate that includes non-local correspondence in terms of vowels is SI:(8d), which is not an optimum.) In the models here, consonants are not included, so vowels are strictly adjacent.

To restrict correspondence to a span of adjacent elements, we must adopt the following axiom.

$$\text{ADJ} \stackrel{\text{def}}{=} (\forall x, y, z)[(x < y \wedge y < z \wedge xR_\mathcal{Q}z) \\ \rightarrow (xR_\mathcal{Q}y \wedge yR_\mathcal{Q}z)]$$

ADJ states that for any x and z in correspondence, all intervening y must also be in correspondence. Note that this axiom requires specially adopting the $<$ relation, as it must hold for *all* intervening elements y. This is stricter than SI's requirement of 'consecutivity', which instead restricts correspondence to intervening elements of some type— e.g., vowels—but as they are vague about how this is determined we ignore this here, and note only that relativizing 'consecutivity' to a particular type of element is also FO-definable (Graf, 2017).

Thus, we assume $\mathcal{Q}$ models satisfy EQ $\wedge$ ADJ. (For comparison to models that do not, see §6.2.)

Finally, correspondence implies identity. As SI state: "Our operating assumption is that GEN does not even produce candidates in which elements obey CORR but violate the associated IDENT-XX constraint" (SI: 6). Thus, correspondence between two qs implies they are either both H or both L. Similarly, correspondence between Qs implies they are associated to identical strings of qs.

5 Transductions

We now show the FO-equivalence between these two representational theories by defining a transduction from $\mathcal{Q}$ to $\mathcal{A}$, and then from $\mathcal{A}$ to $\mathcal{Q}$.

5.1 From Q-Theory Representations

We begin with a transductions from QRs in $\mathcal{Q}$ to ARs in $\mathcal{A}$. Intuitively, this transduction is based on the idea that a correspondence chain of qs in a QR is equivalent to a tone in an AR.

We identify qs by the fact that they carry tones.

$$q_{\mathcal{Q}}(x) \stackrel{\text{def}}{=} H_{\mathcal{Q}}(x) \vee L_{\mathcal{Q}}(y)$$

Then, to uniquely identify each chain of corresponding qs, we define the following predicate $\text{FC}(x)$, which identifies the *first correspondent*; i.e., the first element in a correspondence chain.

$$\text{FC}(x) \stackrel{\text{def}}{=} \neg(\exists y)[xR_{\mathcal{Q}}y \wedge y \vartriangleleft_{\mathcal{Q}} x]$$

This is possible with a successor relation $\vartriangleleft_{\mathcal{Q}}$ because of the adjacency axiom ADJ. If $y \vartriangleleft_{\mathcal{Q}} x$ and $\neg yR_{\mathcal{Q}}x$ and there is no z such that $z <_{\mathcal{Q}} x$ and $zR_{\mathcal{Q}}x$, then x must be first in the chain.

The transduction is thus as given in Table 1. The copy set is $C = \{1\}$, so we omit superscripts indicating copies. An example output structure, given Fig. 5 as an input, is given in Fig. 6.

$$V_{\mathcal{A}}(x) \stackrel{\text{def}}{=} Q_{\mathcal{Q}}(x)$$
$$H_{\mathcal{A}}(x) \stackrel{\text{def}}{=} H_{\mathcal{Q}}(x) \wedge \text{FC}(x)$$
$$L_{\mathcal{A}}(x) \stackrel{\text{def}}{=} L_{\mathcal{Q}}(x) \wedge \text{FC}(x)$$
$$x \vartriangleleft_{\mathcal{A}} y \stackrel{\text{def}}{=} \big(Q_{\mathcal{Q}}(x) \wedge Q_{\mathcal{Q}}(y) \wedge x \vartriangleleft_{\mathcal{Q}} y\big) \vee$$
$$\big(q_{\mathcal{Q}}(x) \wedge q_{\mathcal{Q}}(y) \wedge \text{FC}(x) \wedge \text{FC}(y) \wedge$$
$$(\exists z)[xR_{\mathcal{Q}}z \wedge z \vartriangleleft_{\mathcal{Q}} y]\big)$$
$$xA_{\mathcal{A}}y \stackrel{\text{def}}{=} \text{FC}(x) \wedge (\exists z)[xR_{\mathcal{Q}}z \wedge zA_{\mathcal{Q}}y]$$

Table 1: Transduction from $\mathcal{Q}$ to $\mathcal{A}$.

First, the definitions of $V_{\mathcal{A}}(x)$, $H_{\mathcal{A}}(x)$, and $L_{\mathcal{A}}(x)$, are straightforward. As vowels in ARs and Qs in QRs are equivalent, we set $V_{\mathcal{A}}(x)$ equal to $Q_{\mathcal{Q}}(x)$. For $H_{\mathcal{A}}(x)$, and $L_{\mathcal{A}}(x)$, we set each to the first q of a chain that is valued either H or L, respectively. Thus, for example in Fig. 6, only nodes 1 and 5 are copied over from Fig. 5.

The definition of $x \vartriangleleft_{\mathcal{A}} y$, then, is relativized to elements for which these predicate are true. The

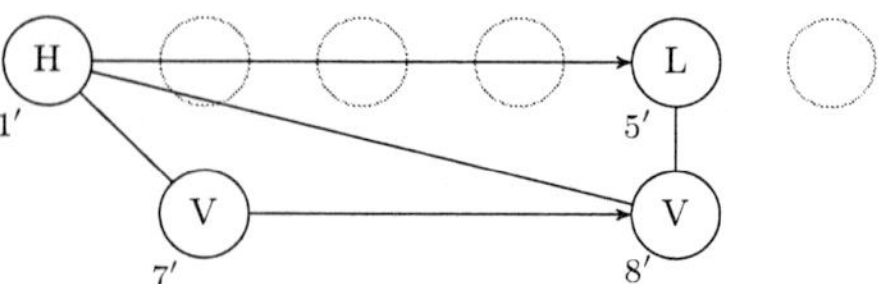

Figure 6: Output of the transduction in Table 1 given Fig. 5 as input; i' indicates a surviving copy of node i from Fig. 5.

disjunct $\big(Q_{\mathcal{Q}}(x) \wedge Q_{\mathcal{Q}}(y) \wedge x \vartriangleleft_{\mathcal{Q}} y\big)$ means that the successor relation between vowels in the AR is identical to the successor relation between Qs in the QR. The other disjunct defines the successor relation between tones. This has two parts: $q_{\mathcal{Q}}(x) \wedge q_{\mathcal{Q}}(y) \wedge \text{FC}(x) \wedge \text{FC}(y)$ ensures that the successor relation only holds between first elements in correspondence chains, and $(\exists z)[xR_{\mathcal{Q}}z \wedge z \vartriangleleft_{\mathcal{Q}} y]$ identifies for some x the element y that starts the next correspondence chain; that is, it succeeds the element z that is the last element in x's correspondence chain. This can be seen in Fig. 6 between $1'$ and $5'$. In Fig. 5, in both 1 and 5 are first in their chains and 5 is the successor of 4, which corresponds with 1; thus $5'$ succeeds $1'$ in Fig. 6.

In a similar fashion, the definition for $xA_{\mathcal{A}}y$ holds true when x is the first member of a chain and y that is associated to some z that corresponds with x. Thus, for example, since 4 is associated to 8 in Fig. 5 and 4 is a member of 1's correspondence chain, $1'$ and $8'$ are associated in Fig. 6. Thus, $\mathcal{A}$ is definable from $\mathcal{Q}$.

Lemma 2 $\mathcal{A}$ *is FO-definable from* $\mathcal{Q}$.

Proof: Witnessed by transduction defined in Table 1. Note that these ARs will satisfy NG and NCC. Briefly, this is because $A_{\mathcal{A}}$ and $\vartriangleleft_{\mathcal{A}}$ are defined through $R_{\mathcal{Q}}$, which satisfies ADJ as outlined in Sec. 4.2. ADJ essentially orders correspondence chains, and thus the tones and association relations defined via $R_{\mathcal{Q}}$. $\square$

5.2 From Autosegmental Representations

For this transformation, the copy set is $\mathcal{C} = \{0, 1, 2, 3\}$. For each vowel, we need both the vowel itself (for the Q; let this be copy 0) and three copies (for each q; let these be copies 1, 2, and 3).

The tones themselves in the AR are not copied. Instead, the values of the qs will be determined by the string of tones associated to the vowel in the

AR, as (partially) summarized in Table 2.[2]

Tones	qs	Tones	qs
H	$\to H_1 H_{1,2} H_2$	L	$\to L_1 L_{1,2} L_2$
HL	$\to H_1 L_2 L_2$	LH	$\to L_1 H_2 H_2$
HLH	$\to H_1 L_2 H_3$	LHL	$\to L_1 H_2 L_3$

Table 2: Mapping from strings of tones associated to a vowel (AR) to strings of qs associated to a Q (QR).

a. $\texttt{first}(x,y) \overset{\text{def}}{=} \neg(\exists z)[x A_A z \wedge z \triangleleft_A y]$

b. $\texttt{last}(x,y) \overset{\text{def}}{=} \neg(\exists z)[x A_A z \wedge y \triangleleft_A z]$

c. $\texttt{second}(x,y) \overset{\text{def}}{=} (\exists z)[x A_A z \wedge z \triangleleft_A y \\ \wedge \texttt{first}(x,z)]$

d. $\texttt{only}(x,y) \overset{\text{def}}{=} \texttt{first}(x,y) \wedge \texttt{last}(x,y)$

Table 3: Predicates used in the AR to QR transduction

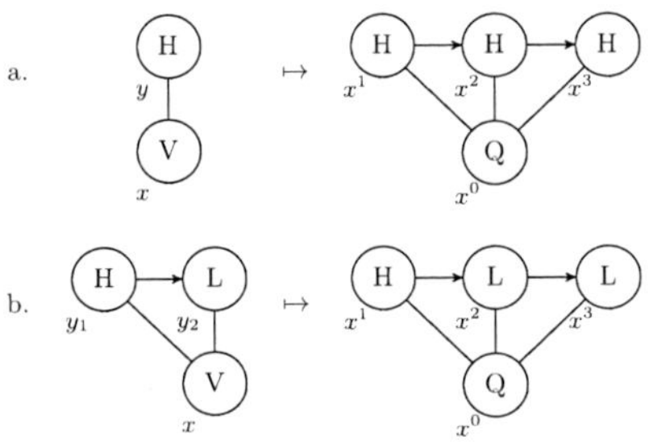

Figure 7: Deriving strings of qs from strings of tones. On the right, x^i indicates the ith copy of x.

These correspondences are FO-definable. First, we define a series of predicates $\texttt{first}(x,y)$, $\texttt{second}(x,y)$, $\texttt{last}(x,y)$, and $\texttt{only}(x,y)$ that indicate when y is the first, second, last, or only tone associated to x, respectively. These definitions are given in Table 3. (These do not explicitly associate y to x; this will be invoked in later definitions.)

From these predicates we can determine, for each vowel in the AR, how to label its q copies in the QR. This is given in Table 4b. For example, $H_Q^1(x)$ is true when there is a H tone y that is the first tone associated to x. This means that copy 1 of x will be a q valued H. Similarly, $H_Q^2(x)$ is true when there is some H tone associated to x that is either the second tone or the *only* tone associated to x. This last disjunct is necessary in case x has a

single H associated to it in the AR, for its equivalent QR all three qs will be H (see Fig. 7a).

Table 4a specifies when Qs are built: the 0th copy of each vowel x is labeled Q. Table 4c then specifies that the 0th copy of x is associated to each of its own copies 1, 2, and 3 (i.e., the qs). The specification that $x \approx y$ ensures that the Q for each vowel is associated to each of its q copies. Likewise, Table 4d specifies that the successor relation $\triangleleft_A$ between vowels is preserved between Qs (i.e., the 0 copies of vowels) and, that for the 1st through 3rd copies of vowel x, its ith copy is succeeded by its own $i + 1$th copy. The reader can confirm this via the examples in Fig. 7.

Finally, we define R_Q. First, as described in §4.2, correspondence between Qs is dependent on identity between Qs, which again depends on their associated qs. Thus, $x R_Q^{0,0} y$ should be true when the output Qs of x and y are associated to identical strings of qs. The values of q copies of are determined by the tones associated to x and y, respectively. Thus, Table 4e defines $x R_Q^{0,0} y$ with the predicate $\texttt{ident}(x,y)$, which is true if and only if the first, second, and last tones of x and y have the same value. (Let $\texttt{same}(x,y) \overset{\text{def}}{=} (H_A(x) \wedge H_A(y)) \vee (L_A(x) \wedge L_A(y))$.) For example, this is true of the vowels in Fig. 8a, but not in 8b.

Between qs, we define correspondence based on shared associations. Table 4f thus defines $x R_Q^{i,j} y$ for $1 \leq i, j \leq 3$ to be true when there is some z for which both x and y are associated. However, which qs of x and y correspond depend on z's position relative to other tones associated to x and y. Thus, z must also satisfy requirements $\varphi_i(x,z)$ and $\varphi_j(y,z)$ based on the value of i and j.

For example, when $i = 1$ and $j = 1$—that is, when defining correspondence between the 1st q of x and the 1st q of y—z must satisfy both $\texttt{first}(x,z)$ and $\texttt{first}(y,z)$. Intuitively, the first q of x and the first q of y correspond only if x and y share an association to z and z is the *first* tone associated to both x and y. This can be seen in Fig. 8; for example, in Fig. 8b, both x and y share an initial tone z, and so x^1 and y^1 correspond.

Thus, Table 4 is a transduction from $\mathcal{A}$ to $\mathcal{Q}$.

Lemma 3 $\mathcal{Q}$ *is FO-definable from* $\mathcal{A}$.

Proof: Witnessed by the transduction defined in Table 4. In particular, we sketch why R_Q is guaranteed to be an equivalence relation over the copy set. First, $x R_Q^{i,i} y$ holds when $x \approx y$ and thus R_Q is

---

[2]It is also the case that, e.g., a vowel associated to a string of three H tones (i.e., HHH) will be output as a Q associated to a string of three, non-corresponding H qs ($H_1 H_2 H_3$).

a. $Q_Q^i(x) \overset{\text{def}}{=} V_A(x)$ for $i = 0$; False otherwise

b. For $T \in \{H, L\}$, $T_Q^0(x) \overset{\text{def}}{=}$ False

$$T_Q^1(x) \overset{\text{def}}{=} (\exists y)[xA_Ay \wedge T_A(y) \wedge \texttt{first}(x,y)]$$
$$T_Q^2(x) \overset{\text{def}}{=} (\exists y)[xA_Ay \wedge T_A(y) \wedge (\texttt{only}(x,y) \vee \texttt{second}(x,y))]$$
$$T_Q^3(x) \overset{\text{def}}{=} (\exists y)[xA_Ay \wedge T_A(y) \wedge \texttt{last}(x,y)]$$

c. $xA_Q^{i,j}y \overset{\text{def}}{=} x \approx y$ for $i = 0$ and $1 \leq i \leq 3$; False otherwise.

d. $x \triangleleft_Q^{i,j} y \overset{\text{def}}{=} x \triangleleft y$ for $i, j = 0$ or $i = 3, j = 1$; $x \approx y$ for $1 \leq i, j \leq 3, j = i + 1$; False otherwise.

e. $xR_Q^{0,0}y \overset{\text{def}}{=} \texttt{ident}(x,y) \wedge (x \triangleleft_Q y \vee y \triangleleft_Q x)$, where

$$\texttt{ident}(x,y) \overset{\text{def}}{=} (\forall v, w)\big[((xA_Av \wedge yA_Aw) \wedge ((\texttt{first}(x,v) \wedge \texttt{first}(y,w))\vee$$
$$((\texttt{only}(x,v) \vee \texttt{second}(x,v) \wedge (\texttt{only}(y,w) \vee \texttt{second}(y,w))\vee$$
$$(\texttt{last}(x,v) \wedge \texttt{last}(y,w)))) \to \texttt{same}(v,w)\big];$$

$xR_Q^{i,0}y \overset{\text{def}}{=} xR_Q^{0,j}y \overset{\text{def}}{=}$ False for any $1 \leq i, j \leq 3$

f. $xR_Q^{i,j}y \overset{\text{def}}{=} (\exists z)[xA_Az \wedge yA_Az \wedge \varphi_i(x,z) \wedge \varphi_j(y,z)]$,

where $\varphi_n(v,w) \overset{\text{def}}{=} \texttt{first}(v,w)$ if $n = 1$,
$(\texttt{only}(v,w) \vee \texttt{second}(v,w))$ if $n = 2$, and
$\texttt{last}(v,w)$ if $n = 3$, for $1 \leq i, j \leq 3$.

Table 4: Transduction from $\mathcal{A}$ to $\mathcal{Q}$

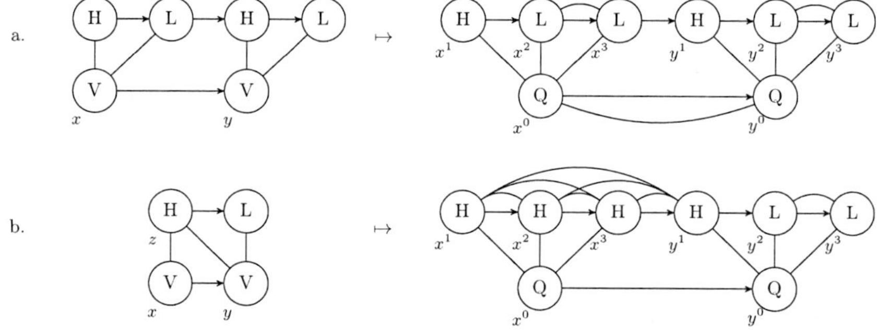

Figure 8: Deriving R_Q from tonal associations.

reflexive and symmetric. Finally, the fact that R_Q is transitive derives from the fact that the relation defined by $(\forall z)[xA_Az \wedge yA_Az]$ is transitive.

Also, because any input AR satisfies NG, x and y in an AR only share associations if they are adjacent, and thus R_Q will satisfy ADJ. $\square$

6   Summary and discussion

6.1   Equivalence of the models

We have now shown that $\mathcal{A}$ is definable from $\mathcal{Q}$ and $\mathcal{Q}$ is definable from $\mathcal{A}$.

Theorem 1 $\mathcal{A}$ and $\mathcal{Q}$ are FO bi-interpretable.

Proof: From Lemmas 2 and 3. $\square$

As stated in the introduction, this means that for any FO constraint written for QRs, there is an equivalent FO constraint on ARs, and vice-versa. Thus, while QRs may be based on a particular set of axioms and constraints, an equivalent set of axioms and constraints can be written in ARs, without changing the complexity of the constraints.

Furthermore, while SI argue that QRs are a fundamental reimagining of phonological structure, our model-theoretic analysis shows that they are remarkably similar to ARs in which each vowel is associated to three autosegments. To illustrate this point, one reported benefit of QRs is that the fixed number of 3 subsegments predicts contrasts between HHL and HLL-toned vowels, for instance (SI, p. 14). While not commonly proposed for ARs, this contrast is possible for ARs as well if the OCP is relaxed (as argued by Odden 1986).

6.2 Relation to other correspondence models

As noted in Sec. 4.2, we follow SI in restricting the correspondence relation to adjacent elements. This is more restrictive than other theories of correspondence; the formulation of Bennett (2013), for example, obeys EQ but not ADJ. How do ARs compare to QRs given a less restrictive correspondence relation? We conjecture that $\mathcal{A}$ and $\mathcal{Q}$ are incomparable to such a signature.

To see why, consider a signature identical to $\mathcal{Q}$ with the exception that models in $\mathcal{Q}'$ only satisfy EQ, thus allowing unbounded correspondence. Defining $R_\mathcal{Q}$ from R' would require defining a binary predicate in the FO logic of $\mathcal{Q}'$ that satisfies ADJ. However, it is likely that no such predicate exists, because the definition of ADJ crucially requires $<$, and it is well-known that $<$ cannot be defined from $\lhd$. (See, e.g., Libkin (2004).)

Going the other way, $\mathcal{Q}'$ essentially allows for quantification over a single abstract binary predicate whose only restriction is that it is an equivalence relation. For example, the FO language of $\mathcal{Q}'$ includes sentences such as

$$(\forall x, y)\big[\ (\texttt{first}(x) \wedge \texttt{last}(y) \to xR'y)\wedge$$
$$(\forall z, w)[w \lhd'_\mathcal{Q} x \wedge y \lhd'_\mathcal{Q} z \to wR'z]\ \big],$$

where $\texttt{first}(x) = (\forall y)[\neg y \lhd_\mathcal{Q} x]$ and $\texttt{last}(x) = (\forall y)[\neg x \lhd_\mathcal{Q} y]$. This enforces 'center embedding' correspondence where in a string of elements $a_0 a_1 a_2 ... a_{\ell-2} a_{\ell-1} a_\ell$, each a_i and $a_{\ell-i}$ (for $i \leq \ell/2$) are in correspondence.

Such a relation is almost certainly more expressive than anything definable in $\mathcal{Q}$ and $\mathcal{A}$. First, $\mathcal{A}$ is FO-definable from strings with $<$ (Jardine, 2017). FO-transductions are closed under composition (Courcelle et al., 2012). If $\mathcal{Q}'$ were to be FO-definable from $\mathcal{A}$, it would then have to be FO-definable from strings. As 'center embedding'-type relations are well-known to not be FO-definable, this is very likely not to be true.

6.3 Future work

An even stronger result would be that $\mathcal{A}$ and $\mathcal{Q}$ are equivalent under quantifier-free (QF) transductions (Chandlee and Lindell, forthcoming;

Strother-Garcia, 2017). However, QF transductions of Chandlee and Lindell and Strother-Garcia crucially use models with functions instead of pure relational models. Here, in order to hew to the standard definitions of association and correspondence as relations, we leave the interesting question of QF transductions for future work.

The result here is based on the machinery necessary to capture the case studies from SI, which all involve local tone interactions. As they also suggest extending their theory to segmental phonology, the obvious next direction is long-distance segmental phenomena. This involves more features, or unary predicates on qs, in addition to relaxing the ADJ axiom.

7 Conclusion

Model theory and logic provide for a powerful way to compare representational theories in phonology. Here, we have shown that ARs and QRs are not as different as they appear. This paper also serves as a case study for how logical transformations can be used to precisely evaluate theories of representation in phonology.

References

William Bennett. 2013. *Dissimilation, Consonant Harmony, and Surface Correspondence*. Ph.D. thesis, Rutgers, the State University of New Jersey.

William G. Bennett. 2015. *The phonology of consonants: Harmony, dissimilation, and correspondence*. Cambridge, UK: Cambridge University Press.

Steven Bird. 1995. *Computational phonology: A constraint-based approach*. Studies in Natural Language Processing. Cambridge University Press.

Jane Chandlee and Steven Lindell. forthcoming. A logical characterization of strictly local functions. In Jeffrey Heinz, editor, *Doing Computational Phonology*. OUP.

Bruno Courcelle. 1994. Monadic second-order definable graph transductions: a survey. *Theoretical Computer Science*, 126:53–75.

Bruno Courcelle, Joost Engelfriet, and Maurice Nivat. 2012. *Graph structure and monadic second-order logic: A language-theoretic approach*. Cambridge University Press.

Gerrit Dimmendaal. 1988. Aspects du basaa. In *Bibliographie de la SELAF 96*. Paris, France: Peeters/SELAF. Trans. Luc Bouquiaux.

Herbert Enderton. 1972. *A mathematical introduction to logic*. Academic Press.

Joost Engelfriet and Hendrik Jan Hoogeboom. 2001. MSO definable string transductions and two-way finite-state transducers. *ACM Transations on Computational Logic*, 2:216–254.

John Goldsmith. 1976. *Autosegmental Phonology.* Ph.D. thesis, Massachussets Institute of Technology.

Thomas Graf. 2017. The power of locality domains in phonology. *Phonology*, 34:385–405.

Gunnar Ólafur Hansson. 2001. *Theoretical and Typological Issues in Consonant Harmony*. Ph.D. thesis, University of California, Berkeley.

Wilfred Hodges. 1997. *A Shorter Model Theory*. Cambridge: Cambridge University Press.

Larry Hyman. 2003. Basaa a.43. In Derek Nurse and Gérard Philippson, editors, *The Bantu Languages*, pages 257–282. London, UK: Routledge.

Adam Jardine. 2017. On the logical complexity of autosegmental representations. In *Proceedings of the 15th Meeting on the Mathematics of Language*, pages 22–35, London, UK. Association for Computational Linguistics.

Adam Jardine and Jeffrey Heinz. 2015. A concatenation operation to derive autosegmental graphs. In *Proceedings of the 14th Meeting on the Mathematics of Language (MoL 2015)*, pages 139–151, Chicago, USA. Association for Computational Linguistics.

Leonid Libkin. 2004. *Elements of Finite Model Theory*. Berlin: Springer-Verlag.

Maire Ní Chiośain and Jaye Padgett. 2001. Markedness, segment realization, and locality in spreading. In Linda Lombardi, editor, *Segmental phonology in Optimality Theory*, pages 118–156. Cambridge University Press.

David Odden. 1986. On the role of the Obligatory Contour Principle in phonological theory. *Language*, 62(2):353–383.

Christopher Potts and Geoffrey K. Pullum. 2002. Model theory and the content of OT constraints. *Phonology*, 19:361–393.

James Rogers, Jeffrey Heinz, Margaret Fero, Jeremy Hurst, Dakotah Lambert, and Sean Wibel. 2013. Cognitive and sub-regular complexity. In *Formal Grammar*, volume 8036 of *Lecture Notes in Computer Science*, pages 90–108. Springer.

Sharon Rose and Rachel Walker. 2004. A typology of consonant agreement as correspondence. *Language*, 80:475–531.

Stephanie Shih and Sharon Inkelas. 2014. A subsegmental correspondence approach to contour tone (dis)harmony patterns. In *Proceedings of the 2013 Meeting on Phonology (UMass Amherst)*, Proceedings of the Annual Meetings on Phonology. LSA.

Stephanie Shih and Sharon Inkelas. forthcoming. Autosegmental aims in surface optimizing phonology. Ms. available at lingbuzz/002520.

Kristina Strother-Garcia. 2017. Imdlawn Tashlhiyt Berber syllabification is quantifier-free. In *Proceedings of the first annual meeting of the Society for Computation in Linguistics*, volume 1, pages 145–153.

Kristina Strother-Garcia and Jeffrey Heinz. 2017. Logical foundations of syllable representations. Poster presented at the 5th Annual Meeting on Phonology, New York University, New York City.

Anssi Yli-Jyrä. 2013. On finite-state tonology with autosegmental representations. In *Proceedings of the 11th International Conference on Finite State Methods and Natural Language Processing*, pages 90–98. Association for Computational Linguistics.

Modeling Clausal Complementation for a Grammar Engineering Resource

Olga Zamaraeva
University of Washington
olzama@uw.edu

Kristen Howell
University of Washington
kphowell@uw.edu

Emily M. Bender
University of Washington
ebender@uw.edu

Abstract

We present a grammar engineering library for modeling objectival declarative clausal complementation patterns attested cross-linguistically. Our primary contribution is positing a set of syntactico-semantic analyses couched within a variant of the HPSG syntactic formalism and integrating them with a variety of phenomena already implemented in a grammar engineering toolkit. We evaluate the addition to the system on testsuites from genetically diverse languages that were not considered during development.

1 Introduction

Grammar engineering is the modeling of language rules in a machine-readable fashion, such that the resulting system (the *grammar*) can parse grammatical strings while not *overgenerating* (licensing incorrect or spurious analyses). Linguistic grammar engineering prioritizes *precision* (how many parses are syntactically and semantically correct with respect to the linguistic formalism) over *recall* (how many input strings get parsed).

A *precision grammar* documents and models linguistic phenomena on the one hand, and is a program that parses and generates, on the other. This makes precision grammars a resource for rigorous linguistic hypothesis testing as well as for NLP tasks. While precision grammars are expensive—broad-coverage grammars like Flickinger 2000, 2011 or Siegel et al. 2016 take years to build—there are efforts to automate this process. We present a contribution to one such initiative, adding a clausal complements library to a grammar engineering starter toolkit.

Clausal complements are a kind of subordinate clause. Modeling subordinate clauses in general and clausal complements in particular is important not only because of their corpus frequency, but also because of their interaction with other phenomena. A grammar that cannot support subordinate clauses will fail to provide analyses for a big portion of a typical corpus and will not support the grammar engineer in exploring how well the analyses used for modeling simple clauses generalize.

To fill this gap, we incorporate a cross-linguistic account of clausal complements into a grammar engineering questionnaire and customization system. The questionnaire elicits typological information about hypothetically any language and the customization system outputs a starter precision grammar to specifications. In this way, the toolkit supports the rapid development of precision grammars, giving both novice and experienced grammar developers a means to create a grammar fragment customized to their language of interest and ready for extension to broader coverage.

In the meta-grammar engineering context, an *analysis* is a set of theoretically-grounded elements which comply with the requirements of the specific implementation framework and are used by the grammar engineering system so as to produce functioning grammars. In our case, the analysis is couched within Head-Driven Phrase Structure Grammar (HPSG; Pollard and Sag, 1994) and Minimal Recursion Semantics (MRS; Copestake et al., 2005) and is implemented as an extension to the LinGO Grammar Matrix (Bender et al., 2002, 2010). Our main challenges lie in accounting for a large space of typological possibilities while at the same time integrating our analysis of clausal complements into a complex system which outputs streamlined grammars. We start by motivating the choice of the grammar engineering system and briefly summarizing the formal underpinnings associated with this choice (§2). We then present a concise summary of the typological literature on clausal complementation (§3), and describe our analysis and implementation in §4. The evaluation

Proceedings of the Society for Computation in Linguistics (SCiL) 2019, pages 39-49.
New York City, New York, January 3-6, 2019

results featuring held-out languages from different families are given in §5. All of the resources mentioned in the paper are freely available.[1]

2 Background

2.1 The Grammar Matrix

We develop a cross-linguistic analysis of clausal complements as part of the LinGO Grammar Matrix[2] (Bender et al., 2002, 2010). Other examples of multilingual grammar engineering projects include ParGram (Butt and King, 2002) and CoreGram (Müller, 2015). What is unique about the Grammar Matrix, however, is that it allows the user to obtain a starter grammar customized from typological choices, making it possible to easily test the analysis on multiple languages, including systematic testing of each part of the analysis using artificially constructed languages (see §4.3).

The Grammar Matrix consists of a web-based questionnaire and a back-end customization system. The input to the system is user answers to the typological questions (elicited in the questionnaire and serialized as a *choices file*) and the output is an implemented starter precision grammar. There are currently multiple libraries, including word order (Bender and Flickinger, 2005; Fokkens, 2014); person, number, gender, and case systems (Drellishak, 2009); tense, aspect, and mood (Poulson, 2011); argument optionality (Saleem and Bender, 2010); matrix yes/no questions, lexicon, (Bender and Flickinger, 2005); morphotactics (O'Hara, 2008; Goodman and Bender, 2010); nominalized clauses (Howell et al., 2018), and clausal modifiers (Howell and Zamaraeva, 2018).[3] The contribution of this paper is the clausal complements library. In the context of the Grammar Matrix, our analysis consists of a new web questionnaire page with a set of choices describing clausal complements crosslinguistically, a set of new types available for the back-end customization logic, and revisions to the types already existing in the system.

Building on the existing resource of the Grammar Matrix to develop our library has dual benefits: On the one hand, we can reuse existing implementations of phenomena that occur in embedded clauses and focus our attention primarily on clause embedding itself. On the other hand, we are able to explore the interaction of our analyses with the existing analyses of other phenomena in order to validate both the existing and new libraries. Finally, because we contribute our library to the Grammar Matrix code base, it can in turn serve as part of the background infrastructure for future library development.

2.2 DELPH-IN Joint Reference Formalism, HPSG and MRS

The Grammar Matrix uses the DELPH-IN Joint Reference Formalism (Copestake, 2000), a version of the HPSG syntactic formalism (Pollard and Sag, 1994), developed to balance expressive power with computational efficiency. Every part of the grammar (lexical items, lexical rules, and phrase structure rules) is encoded with typed feature structures.[4] Phrase structure rules can have any fixed number of daughters in a fixed order,[5] but are typically either binary branching or unary constructions. Lexical rules are always unary projections and are furthermore restricted to the lower parts of the tree, i.e. below any phrase structure rules.

A customized grammar consists of a type hierarchy where typed feature structures (*types*) inherit constraints from other types and add their own constraints. The typed feature structures defined by the grammar are combined using the operation of unification in order to build analyses of sentences. If no analysis can be found for a string using a grammar, then the string is deemed ungrammatical by that grammar. Because the feature structures encode both syntactic and semantic constraints, any derivation tree produced by the grammar also includes an MRS semantic representation (Copestake et al., 2005). When evaluating a grammar created via the Grammar Matrix customization system, the correctness of both syntactic and semantic representations of strings is taken into account.

2.3 Clausal Complements in HPSG

To our knowledge, there is no previous cross-linguistic account of clausal complements in HPSG. Language-specific analyses include Ginzburg and Sag 2000 for English and Crysmann 2013 for German, among others. We could not di-

---

[1] `svn://lemur.ling.washington.edu/shared/matrix/trunk`, revision 42067 (code and testsuites).

[2] `http://matrix.delph-in.net/customize/matrix.cgi`

[3] The nonexhaustive list of cited libraries includes the ones with which we tested the interaction of our library.

[4] These are exemplified in §4.2 in (4)-(10).

[5] This contrasts with other versions of HPSG formalisms which separate immediate dominance from linear precedence (e.g. Engelkamp et al., 1992) as well as those that allow variable-arity rules, like Sag et al. 2003.

rectly incorporate them for two reasons. First, most of the existing theoretical analyses are not within the DELPH-IN JRF. Second, the literature mostly concerns itself with the level of clause complexity which is beyond the Grammar Matrix's current scope. The analyses which informed us the most are actual grammar implementations within the DELPH-IN JRF and include Siegel et al. 2016 for Japanese and Flickinger 2000, 2011 for English.

3   The Typology of Clausal Complements

Clausal arguments are clauses which serve as core arguments to verbs (Noonan, 2007). They can be subjects or complements (objects) and typically occur with verbs of thought, perception, knowledge, etc. An example of an objectival clausal argument is given in (1).

(1)   Kim thinks [that Sandy left]. [eng]

Clausal complements can be finite clauses that can occur on their own (1) or they can be *reduced*. Reduced clauses can share the subject with the matrix clause, have the verb in a dependent form or have case marking on the arguments that differs from what is normal for finite clauses in the language (*ibid.*). Complementation strategies include parataxis (several clauses joined without subordination); complementizer + finite complement; nominalization; infinitival and participial complements.

Here we focus on the complementation phenomena which involve embedded clauses that are declarative, objectival and clearly marked as subordinate, and that contain a full proposition. Embedded clauses that are subjects, interrogative clauses, subject sharing, paratactic, infinitival or participial complements are not covered at this point. Our library supports clausal complements marked by special morphology on the verb, special word order, and/or a complementizer attaching to one of the edges of the embedded clause. Special morphology on the embedded verb is illustrated in (2), a Turkish example with nominalization. Special word order in the matrix clause[6] is illustrated by (3): Uzbek is a SOV language, but clausal complements can be extraposed to the end of the sentence. Note that the order of the complementizer and the embedded clause here also does not follow the same rule as, for example, a transitive verb and

its nominal object. Complementizers can be seen in both (3) and (1).

(2)   [senin   sinema-ya   gel-me-n-i]
      [2SG.GEN cinema-DAT come-NMZ-2SG-ACC]
      isti-yor-um
      want-PROG-1SG
      'I want you to come to the movies.' [tur] (adapted
      from Kornfilt 2013, p. 48)

(3)   Men bilamen   [ki   bu ɔdam ǰoǰa-ni
      I   know-1SG [COMP this man   chicken-OBJ
      oğirladi]
      stole-3SG]
      'I know that the man stole the chicken.' [uzb] (Noonan, 2007)

4   Developing the Library

Development starts with mapping typological descriptions of the phenomenon to a set of choices to be presented to the user via the web questionnaire (§4.1). This characterizes our analysis in the broad sense. In particular, upon reviewing the typological literature and restricting the scope of the library as outlined in §3, we provide an analysis for languages that mark clausal complements in a set of certain ways, e.g. with complementizers, nominalization, aspect or other marking on the embedded verb.[7] We posit HPSG analyses for all combinations of the choices we target, without claiming to have identified or modeled all dimensions of variation. We start with basic analyses for complementizers and clause-embedding verbs (§4.2) and implement a holistic analysis in a test-driven fashion (§4.3).

4.1   Web Questionnaire

As summarized in §3, clausal complements can be marked with a complementizer, special morphology on the embedded verb, or word order changes in either the matrix or the embedded clause. Combinations of these phenomena are also possible. There may be several distinct strategies in a language and clausal complement-taking verbs may select for specific ones. We add a web page to the questionnaire which elicits all the relevant choices from the user.

A language may have multiple complementizers which belong to distinct complementation strategies (i.e. with different word order consequences, different selecting verbs, or different morphological requirements on the embedded verb). To ac-

---

[6]See §4.2.4 regarding the word order in subordinate clauses in German.

[7]While our analysis draws on a comprehensive review of typological literature, we do not make any typological claims as part of this work.

count for this, we generalize the FORM feature, previously available for verbs to distinguish different syntactically relevant inflected forms, to complementizers, and reflect this in the questionnaire.

To handle complementation strategies that require specific morphology on the embedded verb, we leverage several existing libraries: The morphotactics library (Goodman, 2013) provides a means of associating morphological features with inflected forms of verbs; the tense/aspect/mood library (Poulson, 2011) allows users to define morphology associated with those features (as well as additional arbitrary features on the 'Other Features' page) and the nominalization library (Howell et al., 2018) accounts for nominalized clauses. In all cases, the lexical rules defined by these libraries include morphosyntactic or morphosemantic features which allow an embedding verb or complementizer to select for a clausal complement headed by a verb with appropriate morphology. This lexically introduced information is available at the clause level thanks to constraints in the shared core grammar that pass the information up the tree.

We also provide an analysis of clause-bounded extraposition of clausal complements. One of the salient syntactic characteristics of clausal complements is that they tend to be dispreferred in sentence-medial position, as seen in (3). We allow the user to choose this type of extraposition and indicate whether it is obligatory or optional.[8]

Finally, the user must add lexical types for clause-embedding verbs, at least one per complementation strategy, as we operate within a lexicalist view of syntax and the lexical type of the clause-embedding verb is therefore responsible for choosing which type of clausal complement to take. Here, we extended an already existing part of the questionnaire (the Lexicon) so that verb types can select for a complementation strategy.

4.2 Syntactic Analysis

As discussed in §2.3, there appears to be little in the theoretical HPSG literature focused on a cross-linguistic account of basic complementation that can be directly incorporated into our library. However, we can leverage the existing Grammar Matrix analyses of various phenomena as well as those from other implemented grammars and extend or adapt them to cover clausal complementation; the Grammar Matrix provides us with a theoretical as well as an engineering basis. As is consistent with the Grammar Matrix's overarching goal, the main goal of our analysis is to provide the user-linguist with a range of typologically motivated possibilities rather than to focus on specific predictions of what is possible vs. what is not possible in the world's languages. In this section, we describe the building blocks of our analysis.

4.2.1 Lexical Types

Complementizers can be treated as semantically empty elements that take a proposition as a complement (e.g. Siegel et al. 2016). The Grammar Matrix already had a complementizer type which did not contribute its own predication but raised its complement's semantic identifier via the HOOK identity, as shown in (4).[9]

$$(4)\quad \begin{bmatrix} \textit{comp-lex-item} \\[4pt] \text{HEAD} & \begin{bmatrix} \textit{comp} \\ \text{MOD} & \langle\,\rangle \end{bmatrix} \\[8pt] \text{SUBJ} & \langle\,\rangle \\[4pt] \text{COMPS} & \langle\;\boxed{1}\begin{bmatrix} \text{HEAD} & \textit{verb} \\ \text{SUBJ} & \langle\,\rangle \\ \text{COMPS} & \langle\,\rangle \\ \text{HOOK} & \boxed{2} \end{bmatrix}\;\rangle \\[8pt] \text{ARG-ST} & \langle\;\boxed{1}\;\rangle \\ \text{RELS} & \langle!\ !\rangle \\ \text{HOOK} & \boxed{2} \end{bmatrix}$$

While posited originally for question particles in the yes/no questions library (Bender and Flickinger, 2005), it was intended to generalize to clausal complementizers. In order to have clausal complementizers inherit from this supertype we move the MC ('main clause') value from the supertype (4) where it was posited originally to the clausal complementizer subtypes (5). This way question particles (not shown) can take main clauses as their complements but clausal complementizers cannot. Another change implemented to support our analysis is that complementizers now have the FORM feature (with user-specified array of values). This is used to license certain complementizers only in combination with certain verb types.[10]

---

[8]Displacement to sentence-initial position is less mentioned in the typological literature, though it appears to be possible. We leave it to future work.

[9]Empty semantic relations (RELS) lists and HOOK identities as in (4) are characteristic of semantically empty elements.

[10]AVMs are abbreviated to focus on the primary points of interest. Note also that all such feature structures are arranged into a type hierarchy, such that more specific types, like (5), inherit all of the constraints of their supertypes, like (4).

(5)
$$\begin{bmatrix} \textit{ccomp-lex-item} \\ \text{HEAD} \quad \begin{bmatrix} \text{FORM} & \textit{form} \end{bmatrix} \\ \text{COMPS} \quad \langle \begin{bmatrix} \text{MC} & - \end{bmatrix} \rangle \end{bmatrix}$$

To model clausal complement-taking verbs,[11] we introduce new lexical types. Lexical types in the Grammar Matrix typically specify both syntactic and semantic requirements on their dependents. Because cross-linguistically clausal complement-taking verbs can take both verbal and nominalized complements, our supertype in this space (6) leaves both underspecified. Otherwise, it is similar to *transitive-verb-lex*, which also specifies two arguments.[12]

(6)
$$\begin{bmatrix} \textit{cl-verb-lex} \\ \text{SUBJ} \quad \langle \boxed{1} \rangle \\ \text{COMPS} \quad \langle \boxed{2} \begin{bmatrix} \text{SUBJ} & \langle \rangle \\ \text{COMPS} & \langle \rangle \end{bmatrix} \rangle \\ \text{ARG-ST} \quad \langle \boxed{1} \begin{bmatrix} \text{HEAD} & \textit{noun} \end{bmatrix}, \boxed{2} \rangle \end{bmatrix}$$

Further subtypes inheriting from *cl-verb-lex* are based on the specific choices made by the user and make use of one of two already existing types: either *transitive-lex-item*, for nominalized complements, or *clausal-second-arg-trans-lex-item*, for all other types of clausal complements. This allows us to model the primary semantic effect of nominalization: the introduction of an *individual*-type variable corresponding to the nominalized clause, which in turn allows for e.g. adjectival modifiers of that clause. In the semantic composition, *transitive-lex-item* takes the *individual*-type index of its complement as a semantic argument. *Clausal-second-arg-trans-lex-item*, on the other hand, expects an argument with an *event*-type index and combines with it semantically via a handle constraint to accommodate the MRS analysis of quantifier scope (Copestake et al., 2005).

For proper interaction with the case library (Drellishak, 2009), clausal complement-taking verbs require a hierarchy which is aware of various case frames. In modeling a language with case, the user must specify a case frame for each verb type. For example, a verb can have nominative-accusative argument structure, meaning the type will constrain its syntactic subject to bear nominative case and its object accusative. We added

---

[11]Often called the CTP, complement-taking predicate, in syntactic and typological literature.

[12]In future work, we will extend the lexical types available to provide for more valence patterns with clausal complements, such as *Kim told me that Sandy left.*

clausal complement strategies as argument structure choices and allowed the case frames that are available for non-clause-embedding verbs to be available for clausal complement strategies as well. The option which specifies a case constraint on the verb's object is not always available: it only makes sense for nominalized clausal objects.

4.2.2 Lexical Rules, Features, Nominalization

As noted in §4.1 above, we leverage existing libraries to account for constraints on the morphology of embedded verbs imposed by complementizers or clausal-complement verbs. The result is that users can specify, for example, that the clausal complement be nominalized, at which point the resulting clausal-complement verb type will include the constraint shown in (7). We also extended the Morphotactics library to allow nominalized verbs to bear case inflections.

(7)
$$\begin{bmatrix} \textit{cl-verb-lex} \\ \text{COMPS} \quad \langle \begin{bmatrix} \text{NMZ} & + \end{bmatrix} \rangle \end{bmatrix}$$

For a specific example of how we accommodate lexical variation in complementation, consider Turkish, which has several complementation strategies. The verb *isti* ('want') can not only take nominalized complements like in (2) but also clauses headed by verbs in the optative form, as in (8).

(8) herkes   [yarin   ben-im-le sinema-ya
     everybody [tomorrow I-GEN-WITH cinema-DAT
     gel-esin]   isti-yor
     come-2SG.OPT] want-PRES.PROG
     'Everybody wants you to come along to the movies
     with me tomorrow.' [tur] (from Kornfilt 2013, p. 48)

To model this, the user can add separate complementation strategies in the questionnaire for nominalization and for optative on the embedded verb, and a corresponding clausal complement-taking verb type to go with each strategy. The resulting grammar will include two lexical entries for *isti*, each belonging to a different type. One will only take complements with [NMZ +, FORM nonfinite] and the other [NMZ −, FORM opt].

4.2.3 Phrase Structure Rules, INIT and EXTRA

The most intricate part of this library is its interaction with the existing analysis of word order. To account for basic word order, any Grammar Matrix-generated grammar will have some basic head-subject and head-complement rules, one of each when the word order is strict (e.g. SOV) and more if the order is flexible.

When the complementizer or the main verb participates in a word order that is different from other verbs, we posit an additional head-complement rule (HCR) and, in some cases, an additional head-subject rule (HSR). Then we constrain them (as well as all lexical types that use the HCRs and HSRs) for one or both Boolean features, INIT and EXTRA. While similar features have been used before (Keller 1995; Crysmann 2013; see also Siegel et al. 2016, 59), we incorporate them into a new customization logic so that sets of correct constraints are emitted automatically based on user choices. Examples (9)–(10) illustrate the general HCR and the additional one for extraposition that are emitted for one of many possible user-defined languages: an OVS language with extraposition.

$$(9) \quad \begin{bmatrix} HCR1 \\ \text{COMPS} & \boxed{1} \\ \text{H-DTR} & \begin{bmatrix} \text{INIT} & - \\ \text{SUBJ} & \langle\,\rangle \\ \text{COMPS} & \langle\boxed{3}\rangle \oplus \boxed{1} \end{bmatrix} \\ \text{NH-DTR} & \boxed{3} \\ \text{ARGS} & \langle\,\boxed{3}\,,\boxed{2}\,\rangle \end{bmatrix} \qquad \text{Top}_{HCR1} \; \begin{array}{cc} O & V_{HSR} \\ & V \quad S \end{array}$$

$$(10) \quad \begin{bmatrix} HCR2 \\ \text{COMPS} & \boxed{1} \\ \text{H-DTR} & \begin{bmatrix} \text{INIT} & + \\ \text{SUBJ} & \langle\,\rangle \\ \text{COMPS} & \langle\boxed{3}\rangle \oplus \boxed{1} \end{bmatrix} \\ \text{NH-DTR} & \boxed{3} \\ \text{ARGS} & \langle\,\boxed{2}\,,\boxed{3}\,\rangle \end{bmatrix} \qquad \text{Top}_{HCR2} \; \begin{array}{cc} V_{HSR} & O \\ V \quad S & \end{array}$$

We use INIT (a HEAD feature) on lexical types and on the head daughters of phrase structure rules to account for word order variations associated with subordinator attachment and with extraposition of objects from OV languages. [INIT +] is associated with head-initial rules and [INIT −] with head-final rules. We need a separate feature, EXTRA (not shown), to handle extraposition in VOS and V-initial languages, because the order in these languages remains head-initial despite extraposition to the end of sentence. EXTRA is constrained on COMPS list elements of clausal-complement selecting heads and on the non-head daughter of head-initial HCRs.[13]

4.2.4 German-like V2/V-final Variation

In German, the word order is verb second (V2), but in clausal complements marked by a comple-

---

[13]For an example of how EXTRA is used, see Zamaraeva et al. 2018.

mentizer the order is verb final. Fokkens (2014) implemented this type of word order variation in the Grammar Matrix framework but did not fully integrate it into the customization system. We incorporate part of her analysis so that the user can choose this type of word order variation directly via the questionnaire.

4.3 Implementation

Encoding any particular structure is straightforward; the challenge is in emitting the right sets of structures with the right constraints given user choices, where the space of possible combinations is large. Furthermore, any additions need to be well integrated so that the constraints the new code emits should not interfere with what other libraries create. At the same time, it is not desirable to add unique structures where an existing one can be adapted, since this leads to unnecessarily large, complex and potentially overgenerating grammars. The goal is to implement an analysis that is sufficiently general to handle any typologically plausible language while at the same time emitting reasonably streamlined grammars.

4.3.1 Test-driven Development

We begin by describing the procedure we use for creating test cases, both in development and in evaluation (§5). Test-driven development in the context of the Grammar Matrix relies on two components: the testsuites and the test choices files (i.e. grammar specifications). There is a testsuite and a choices file for each language that is used in development or evaluation. While the testsuite and the choices file are created separately, both are based on the descriptive grammar for the language in question (with the exception of artificial pseudolanguages discussed below which function more like 'unit tests' for the bits of our analysis). Specifically, we first collect the sentences illustrating clausal complementation from the descriptive grammar to compile the testsuites. Then, in a separate iteration, we read the descriptive grammar to the extent necessary to fill out the Grammar Matrix questionnaire for this language.

We build testsuites and choices files for *pseudolanguages* (defined by combinations of choices) and for 5 development languages (see §5 for the details). The number of possible pseudolanguages is large: a conservative estimate which treats some bundles of choices as single dimensions is 2300, assuming one strategy per language. In testing we work with a 50 language sample which includes several languages with more than one complementation strategy. A testsuite consists of grammatical and ungrammatical sentences illustrating what is possible/impossible with respect to clausal complements in a given language.

For pseudolanguages testsuites, we construct all possible nonrecursive sentences[14] illustrating the clausal complementation strategies that this language has. For development languages, the sentences either come directly or are adapted from the sections in descriptive grammars explaining how clausal complements work in this language. Here the sentences feature interacting phenomena such as tense and case.[15] Crucially, we include corresponding impossible (ungrammatical) sentences to make sure they are not parsed. Consider a language with one strict strategy: SOV word order, obligatory complementizer attaching before the embedded clause, and obligatory extraposition of clausal complements. The testsuite will consist of 2 grammatical sentences, one for a simple SOV sentence and another that has an extraposed clausal complement with the complementizer. The ungrammatical sentences will include: a complex sentence with no complementizer, one with a complementizer attaching after the clause, one with a non-extraposed clausal complement, and a simple clause with SVO order. The more flexible the language, the more grammatical and fewer ungrammatical examples the testsuite will have.

From the choices files which are created independently from the testsuites, grammar fragments are created with the original customization system. The grammars are loaded into the LKB software(Copestake, 2002) which can parse strings. Then we edit these grammars by hand until they behave correctly with respect to the yet unsupported clausal complements choices (as reflected by the grammars' coverage and overgeneration over the corresponding testsuites). Then we generalize the solutions in the resulting grammars and incorporate them in the customization system, continually testing with the regression tests. The result of this development is frozen before evaluation on held-out languages, described in §5 below.

4.3.2 Adding Types

We update the customization system as follows. A supertype for clausal-complement verbs (described in §4.2) is now added in all cases when any clausal complement strategy is specified. A supertype for a complementizer is added whenever the user says there is a complementizer associated with any of the strategies. Appropriate subtypes are added based on the user choices, one per strategy, and constrained as described in §4.3.3.[16]

Additional phrase structure rules are added according to the user choices. An additional HSR is added for VOS orders with extraposition. An additional HCR is added whenever the complementizer or the clause-embedding verb cannot use the basic HCR. In general, this means all situations when the basic order is e.g. head-final but there is either extraposition or the complementizer can attach clause-initially (or symmetrically, if the basic order is head-initial but the complementizer can attach clause-finally). In practice, it means checking combinations of choices: 8 for the word orders;[17] 3 for complementizer (obligatory, no, optional); 3 for complementizer attachment (before the clause, after, or both); 3 for extraposition (obligatory, no, optional).

4.3.3 Adding Constraints

After adding the types, we constrain them for the grammar to generate only grammatical strings (e.g. for features FORM, NMZ, INIT, EXTRA). We need to add constraints so that they do not clash with those placed by other libraries while not positing new types unless necessary.

The information about whether FORM or NMZ (nominalization) constraints are needed on the relevant types comes directly from the choices files: the user would have specified a FORM value or a nominalization strategy associated with the complementation strategy. The treatment of INIT and EXTRA however must be inferred from a fairly large space of choices combinations.

Figure 1 shows the logic that we add to the customization system that lets it decide whether to use the INIT feature.[18] The decision depends on

---

[14]The vocabulary is minimal.

[15]In developing these testsuites, we sometimes must adapt the sentences to exclude phenomena that are not supposed to be supported by the system or to capture the full spectrum described by the grammar's author in prose but not fully illustrated by examples. This, along with the initial selection of which sentences to include in the grammar, introduces a certain amount of bias to the testsuites.

[16]A type can be instantiated by multiple lexical entries.

[17]Excluding V2 and free.

[18]Abbreviations for Figure and Tables: comp (complementizer); extrap (extraposition); fam (family); morph (morpheme); neg (ungrammatical sentences); nmz (nominalization); oblig (obligatory); opt (optional); OV (object pre-

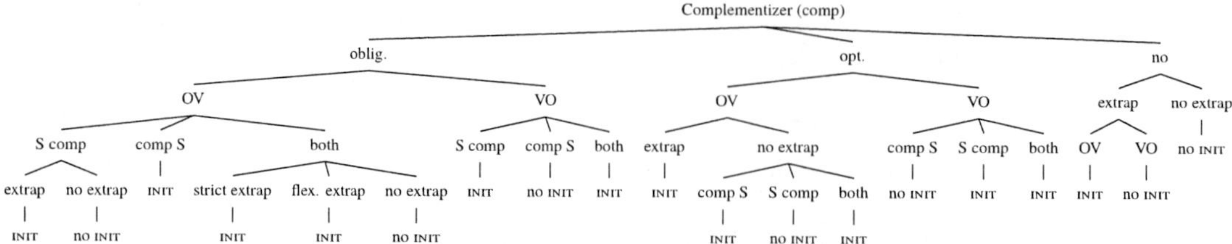

Figure 1: Decision tree illustrating the logic of using the INIT feature based on user choices

whether there is a complementizer, whether it is obligatory or optional, what is the basic word order, is there extraposition and is it strict or flexible, and how does the complementizer attach to the clause. If the INIT feature is used, then all HCR and all lexical items which can go through the HCR must be properly constrained for INIT + or −. The logic associated with the EXTRA feature is simpler: it is used only with VOS and V-initial word orders when there is extraposition.

4.3.4 Summary

This section described the process and the main techniques used to implement the Clausal Complements library for the Grammar Matrix. We operate in a large space of theoretically possible user choices combinations (over 2300) where the ultimate goal is to emit streamlined grammars which behave correctly for any valid combination of choices (and a language defined by them). The development was driven by a sample of pseudo- and illustrative (development) languages and was evaluated as described in the next section.

5 Testing, Evaluation, and Error Analysis

To test the typological legitimacy and the rigor of our analysis, we apply a three-stage process where we test grammars against testsuites. The process used in all stages is described in §4.3.1. The first two stages involving 50 pseudolanguages and 5 development languages are part of the test-driven development. We chose the development languages which exhibited the full range of in-scope complementation phenomena and for which we had both some sentences and a description sufficient for us to fill out the questionnaire. Table 1 summarizes

the phenomena covered by the development languages.[19]

As for testing the interaction with other libraries, we included all the choices that were relevant to the testsuites. For example, if the language has case and the sentences with clausal complements showed this, we filled out the Case portion of the questionnaire and added appropriate lexical rules on the Morphology page. Case, word order, morphology, and tense, aspect and mood choices came up most often.

After addressing a few issues uncovered by the pseudo- and development languages, we achieve 100% coverage and 0% overgeneration on their testsuites (Table 1). Furthermore, we checked that all parses for each sentence are warranted, i.e. there is no unwanted ambiguity. At the same time, the library was used in a course where students implemented grammar fragments for 5 more languages,[21] which helped us discover an issue in the interaction with the information structure library (Song, 2014).

Finally, we evaluate the library on 5 held-out languages from different language families than the development languages.[22] The results are presented in Table 2. Coverage and overgeneration are given in numbers of sentences in the testsuite (4/8 means 4 out of 8 were parsed).

In Jalkunan (SOV), there is a kind of clausal

---

cedes verb); pos (grammatical sentences); S comp (clause followed by complementizer); strat (strategy); VO (verb precedes object); WO (word order). Language families: AA (Afro-Asiatic); Astrn (Austronesian); Awk (Arawak); IE (Indo-European); NS (Nilo-Saharan); NC (Niger-Congo); PN (Pama-Nyungan); PP (Plateau Penutian); Tur (Turkic).

[19]German (Sapp, 2006), Tagalog (Hoenigswald et al., 1975), Lango (Noonan, 2007), Turkish (Kornfilt, 2013). The first author, a native speaker of Russian, provided the testsuite and the choices for Russian.

[20]We targeted a fragment of German with obligatory complementizers and V2/V-final word order variation.

[21]Akuntsu [aqz] (Tupian); Lhasa Tibetan [bod] (Tibeto-Burman), Dzongkha [dzo] (Tibeto-Burman), Dagaare [gur] (Niger-Congo), Yolmo [scp] (Tibeto-Burman).

[22]The number of languages is limited by time constraints. We pick held-out languages randomly from a pool of descriptive grammars and reject them if they come from a language family already used or if the grammars do not cover basic clausal complements. Grammars: Jalkunan (Heath, 2017), Paresi-Haliti (Brandão), Sahaptin (Jansen, 2010), Hebrew (Zuckermann, 2006), Wangkangurru (Hercus, 1994).

Language	iso639-3	fam	WO	comp	order	morph	extrap	# strat	pos	neg
Russian	rus	IE	free	opt	comp S	nmz,form	-	3	6	11
German	deu	IE	V2/V-fin	oblig[20]	comp S.	-	-	1	6	4
Tagalog	tgl	Astrn.	V-in	oblig	comp S	-	flexible	1	3	4
Lango	laj	NS	SVO	oblig	comp S	mood	-	3	4	4
Turkish	tur	Tur	SOV	opt	both	nmz, form	strict	4	7	9

Table 1: Phenomena covered in the development languages. Coverage is 100%, overgeneration is 0%.

Language	iso639-3	fam	WO	comp	order	morph	extrap	# strat.	Cov.	Overgen.
Jalkunan	bxl	NC	SOV	opt	comp S	-	strict	1	4/8	0/12
Paresi-Haliti	pab	Awk	SOV	-	-	nmz	strict	1	5/5	0/5
Yakima Sahaptin	yak	PP	free	-	-	nmz	-	1	10/10	0/6
Modern Hebrew	heb	AA	SVO	oblig	comp S	-	-	1	2/2	0/9
Wangkangurru	wgg	PN	free	-	-	aspect	-	1	10/10	0/3

Table 2: Coverage and overgeneration on sentences from held-out language families.

complement extraposition where a "dummy" 3SG pronoun (similar to *it* in English) stays in the sentence-medial position while the clausal complement is extraposed (Heath, 2017). We had not considered this strategy during the development since we hadn't come across it in the literature, so we could not parse those items. In addition, we discovered a bug in the interaction with the word order library which places constraints on the order of auxiliaries and their complements. Some of the Jalkunan sentences had auxiliaries, and we also could not parse them due to the bug; hence the 50% coverage. On all other languages we achieve 100% coverage and 0% overgeneration (again, with no spurious ambiguity).

The testsuites represent typologically diverse languages, and so one testsuite may emphasize word order variation, another morphology, etc. The descriptive grammars for held-out languages only included one in-scope strategy per language. In general, our held-out grammars contain relatively few examples which illustrated basic complementation.[23] Our source for Modern Hebrew, Zuckermann 2006, for example, identified a single strict complementation strategy, and so for that language we have just one grammatical sentence illustrating simple noun complementation and one grammatical sentence illustrating clausal complementation. The more strategies in a language, the more flexible they are, and the clearer the author of the grammar describes them in isolation from other phenomena, the more sentences we can include. The point of the evaluation is to approx-

imate quantitatively how well a system would do for a linguist working from a reasonably thorough description of a language we had not worked with.

6 Conclusion

We presented a clausal complements library for the LinGO Grammar Matrix. To this end, we implemented an HPSG-based analysis of a range of complementation phenomena attested in the typological literature. The library allows the grammar engineer to include basic clausal complements in their starter grammar in a streamlined system with appropriate interaction with other phenomena, thus extending the initial coverage of the grammar fragment that can be obtained automatically. Available choices define thousands of possible combinations for which the library needs to emit correct code. We make sure we have correct behavior on a sample of 50 choices combinations and 5 development languages; on testsuites from 5 held-out languages, we achieve 88% coverage and no overgeneration.

In the future, we plan to extend the system to handle such related phenomena as subject sharing, sentential subjects, embedded questions, and displacement to the beginning of the clause. In terms of interactions with other libraries, we will look at complex sentences combining clausal complements and clausal modifiers and coordinated clausal complements. Our library will also serve as a foundation for testing future additions to the Grammar Matrix for their interaction with subordinate clauses, e.g. *wh*-questions. Finally, we plan to explore how to infer answers to our additions to the questionnaire from collections of interlinear glossed text, along the lines of Bender et al. (2013) and Bender et al. (2014).

---

[23]Descriptive grammars seem to prioritize complicated examples of complex clauses. This differs from the data from development languages which were picked so as to better inform the implementation of the library.

Acknowledgements

We thank the anonymous reviewers for SCiL 2019 for helpful discussion.

This material is based upon work supported by the National Science Foundation under Grant No. BCS-1561833. Any opinions, findings, and conclusions or recommendations expressed in this material are those of the authors and do not necessarily reflect the views of the National Science Foundation.

References

Emily M. Bender, Joshua Crowgey, Michael Wayne Goodman, and Fei Xia. 2014. Learning grammar specifications from IGT: A case study of Chintang. In *Proceedings of the 2014 Workshop on the Use of Computational Methods in the Study of Endangered Languages*, pages 43–53. Association for Computational Linguistics.

Emily M Bender, Scott Drellishak, Antske Fokkens, Laurie Poulson, and Safiyyah Saleem. 2010. Grammar customization. *Research on Language & Computation*, 8(1):23–72. 10.1007/s11168-010-9070-1.

Emily M. Bender and Dan Flickinger. 2005. Rapid prototyping of scalable grammars: Towards modularity in extensions to a language-independent core. In *Proceedings of the 2nd International Joint Conference on Natural Language Processing IJCNLP-05 (Posters/Demos)*, Jeju Island, Korea.

Emily M. Bender, Dan Flickinger, and Stephan Oepen. 2002. The Grammar Matrix: An open-source starter-kit for the rapid development of cross-linguistically consistent broad-coverage precision grammars. In *Proceedings of the Workshop on Grammar Engineering and Evaluation at the 19th International Conference on Computational Linguistics*, pages 8–14, Taipei, Taiwan.

Emily M. Bender, Michael Wayne Goodman, Joshua Crowgey, and Fei Xia. 2013. Towards creating precision grammars from interlinear glossed text: Inferring large-scale typological properties. In *Proceedings of the 7th Workshop on Language Technology for Cultural Heritage, Social Sciences, and Humanities*, pages 74–83, Sofia, Bulgaria. Association for Computational Linguistics.

Ana Paula Barros Brandão. *A Reference Grammar of Paresi-Haliti (Arawak)*. Ph.D. thesis, The University of Texas at Austin.

Miriam Butt and Tracy Holloway King. 2002. Urdu and the Parallel Grammar project. In *Proceedings of the 3rd workshop on Asian language resources and international standardization-Volume 12*, pages 1–3. Association for Computational Linguistics.

Ann Copestake. 2000. Appendix: Definitions of typed feature structures. *Natural Language Engineering*, 6(01):109–112.

Ann Copestake. 2002. *Implementing typed feature structure grammars.* CSLI publications Stanford.

Ann Copestake, Dan Flickinger, Carl Pollard, and Ivan A Sag. 2005. Minimal recursion semantics: An introduction. *Research on language and computation*, 3(2-3):281–332.

Berthold Crysmann. 2013. On the locality of complement clause and relative clause extraposition. *Rightward movement in a comparative perspective*, 200:369–395.

Scott Drellishak. 2009. *Widespread but Not Universal: Improving the Typological Coverage of the Grammar Matrix*. Ph.D. thesis, University of Washington.

Judith Engelkamp, Gregor Erbach, and Hans Uszkoreit. 1992. Handling linear precedence constraints by unification. In *Proceedings of the 30th annual meeting on Association for Computational Linguistics*, pages 201–208. Association for Computational Linguistics.

Dan Flickinger. 2000. On building a more efficient grammar by exploiting types. *Natural Language Engineering*, 6(01):15–28.

Dan Flickinger. 2011. Accuracy v. robustness in grammar engineering. In Emily M. Bender and Jennifer E. Arnold, editors, *Language from a Cognitive Perspective: Grammar, Usage and Processing*, pages 31–50. CSLI Publications, Stanford, CA.

Antske Sibelle Fokkens. 2014. *Enhancing Empirical Research for Linguistically Motivated Precision Grammars*. Ph.D. thesis, Department of Computational Linguistics, Universität des Saarlandes.

Jonathan Ginzburg and Ivan Sag. 2000. *Interrogative investigations*. Stanford: CSLI publications.

Michael Wayne Goodman. 2013. Generation of machine-readable morphological rules from human-readable input. *Seattle: University of Washington Working Papers in Linguistics*, 30.

Michael Wayne Goodman and Emily M. Bender. 2010. What's in a word? Refining the morphotactic infrastructure in the LinGO Grammar Matrix customization system. In *Workshop on Morphology and Formal Grammar, Paris*.

Jeffrey Heath. 2017. *A grammar of Jalkunan (Mande, Burkina Faso)*. Language Description Heritage Library.

Luise A Hercus. 1994. *A grammar of the Arabana-Wangkangurru language: Lake Eyre Basin, South Australia*. Australian National Univ.

Henry M Hoenigswald, Paul Schachter, and Fe T Otanes. 1975. *Tagalog Reference Grammar*.

Kristen Howell and Olga Zamaraeva. 2018. Clausal modifiers in the grammar matrix. In *Proceedings of the 27th International Conference on Computational Linguistics*, pages 2939–2952.

Kristen Howell, Olga Zamaraeva, and Emily M. Bender. 2018. Nominalized clauses in the Grammar Matrix. In *Proceedings of the 25th International Conference on Head-Driven Phrase Structure Grammar*, pages 68–88.

Joana Worth Jansen. 2010. *A Grammar of Yakima Ichishkíin/Sahaptin*. Ph.D. thesis, University of Oregon.

Frank Keller. 1995. Towards an account of extraposition in HPSG. In *Proceedings of the seventh conference on European chapter of the Association for Computational Linguistics*, pages 301–306. Morgan Kaufmann Publishers Inc.

Jaklin Kornfilt. 2013. *Turkish*. Routledge, London.

Stefan Müller. 2015. The CoreGram project: Theoretical linguistics, theory development and verification. *Journal of Language Modelling*, 3(1):21–86.

Michael Noonan. 2007. Complementation. In Timothy Shopen, editor, *Language Typology and Syntactic Description*, volume 2. Cambridge University Press, Cambridge, UK.

Kelly O'Hara. 2008. *A morphotactic infrastructure for a grammar customization system*. Ph.D. thesis, University of Washington.

Carl Pollard and Ivan A. Sag. 1994. *Head-Driven Phrase Structure Grammar*. Studies in Contemporary Linguistics. The University of Chicago Press and CSLI Publications, Chicago, IL and Stanford, CA.

Laurie Poulson. 2011. Meta-modeling of tense and aspect in a cross-linguistic grammar engineering platform. *University of Washington Working Papers in Linguistics (UWWPL)*, 28.

Ivan A. Sag, Thomas Wasow, and Emily M. Bender. 2003. *Syntactic Theory: A Formal Introduction*, second edition. CSLI, Stanford, CA.

Safiyyah Saleem and Emily M Bender. 2010. Argument optionality in the LinGO Grammar Matrix. In *Proceedings of the 23rd international conference on computational linguistics: posters*, pages 1068–1076. Association for Computational Linguistics.

Christopher D Sapp. 2006. *Verb order in subordinate clauses from Early New High German to Modern German*. Indiana University.

Melanie Siegel, Emily M. Bender, and Francis Bond. 2016. *Jacy: An Implemented Grammar of Japanese*. CSLI Studies in Computational Linguistics. CSLI Publications, Stanford CA.

Sanghoun Song. 2014. *A grammar library for information structure*. Ph.D. thesis, University of Washington.

Olga Zamaraeva, Kristen Howell, and Emily M Bender. 2018. A cross-linguistic account of subordinator and subordinate clause position. Poster presented at The 25th International Conference on Head-Driven Phrase Structure Grammar, Tokyo, Japan.

Ghil'ad Zuckermann. 2006. Complement clause types in Israeli. Oxford University Press.

Do RNNs learn human-like abstract word order preferences?

Richard Futrell[1] and **Roger P. Levy**[2]

[1]Department of Language Science, UC Irvine, rfutrell@uci.edu
[2]Department of Brain and Cognitive Sciences, MIT, rplevy@mit.edu

Abstract

RNN language models have achieved state-of-the-art results on various tasks, but what exactly they are representing about syntax is as yet unclear. Here we investigate whether RNN language models learn humanlike word order preferences in syntactic alternations. We collect language model surprisal scores for controlled sentence stimuli exhibiting major syntactic alternations in English: heavy NP shift, particle shift, the dative alternation, and the genitive alternation. We show that RNN language models reproduce human preferences in these alternations based on NP length, animacy, and definiteness. We collect human acceptability ratings for our stimuli, in the first acceptability judgment experiment directly manipulating the predictors of syntactic alternations. We show that the RNNs' performance is similar to the human acceptability ratings and is not matched by an *n*-gram baseline model. Our results show that RNNs learn the abstract features of weight, animacy, and definiteness which underlie soft constraints on syntactic alternations.

The best-performing models for many natural language processing tasks in recent years have been recurrent neural networks (RNNs) (Elman, 1990; Sutskever et al., 2014; Goldberg, 2017), but the black-box nature of these models makes it hard to know exactly what generalizations they have learned about their linguistic input: Have they learned generalizations stated over hierarchical structures, or only dependencies among relatively local groups of words (Linzen et al., 2016; Gulordava et al., 2018; Futrell et al., 2018)? Do they represent structures analogous to syntactic dependency trees (Williams et al., 2018), and can they represent complex relationships such as filler–gap dependencies (Chowdhury and Zamparelli, 2018; Wilcox et al., 2018)? In order to make progress

with RNNs, it is crucial to determine what RNNs actually learn given currently standard practices; then we can design network architectures, objective functions, and training practices to build on strengths and alleviate weaknesses (Linzen, 2018).

In this work, we investigate whether RNNs trained on a language modeling objective learn certain syntactic preferences exhibited by humans, especially those involving word order. We draw on a rich literature from quantitative linguistics that has investigated these preferences in corpora and experiments (e.g., McDonald et al., 1993; Stallings et al., 1998; Bresnan et al., 2007; Rosenbach, 2008).

Word order preferences are a key aspect of human linguistic knowledge. In many cases, they can be captured using local co-occurrence statistics: for example, the preference for subject–verb–object word order in English can often be captured directly in short word strings, as in the dramatic preference for *I ate apples* over *I apples ate*. However, some word order preferences are more abstract and can only be stated in terms of higher-order linguistic units and abstract features. For example, humans exhibit a general preference for word orders in which words linked in syntactic dependencies are close to each other: such sentences are produced more frequently and comprehended more easily (Hawkins, 1994; Futrell et al., 2015; Temperley and Gildea, 2018).

We are interested in whether RNNs learn abstract word order preferences as a way of probing their syntactic knowledge. If RNNs exhibit these preferences for appropriately controlled stimuli, then on some level they have learned the abstractions required to state them.

Knowing whether RNNs show human-like word order preferences also bears on their suitability as language generation systems. White and Rajkumar (2012) have shown that language gener-

Proceedings of the Society for Computation in Linguistics (SCiL) 2019, pages 50-59.
New York City, New York, January 3-6, 2019

ation systems produce better output when human-like word order preferecences are built in; it may turn out that RNN language models reproduce such preferences such that they do not need to be built in explicitly.

As part of this work, we validate and quantify these word order preferences for humans by collecting acceptability ratings for English sentences with different word orders. To our knowledge, this is the first experimental acceptability-judgment study of these word order preferences using fully controlled stimuli; previous experimental work has used naturalistic stimuli derived from corpora, in which the predictors of word order are not directly manipulated (Rosenbach, 2003; Bresnan, 2007).

Alternations studied

We study four syntactic alternations in English: **particle shift**, in which a verbal particle can appear directly after the verb or later (e.g., *give up the habit* vs. *give the habit up*); **heavy NP shift**, in which a verb is followed by an NP and a PP with order NP–PP or PP–NP; the **dative alternation** (e.g. *give a book to Tom* vs. *give Tom a book*); and the **genitive alternation** (e.g. *the movie's title* vs. *the title of the movie*).

In all these alternations, three common factors influencing word order preferences are evident: short constituents go before long constituents; words which are definite go earlier; and words referring to animate entities go earlier. In fact these preferences are very general patterns across languages, and in some languages constitute hard constraints (Bresnan et al., 2001).

1 Methods

We investigate the learned word order preferences of RNNs by studying the total probability they assign to sentences with various word order properties. Specifically, we create sentences by hand which can appear in a number of configurations, and study how these manipulations affect the SUR-PRISAL value assigned by an RNN to a sentence. Surprisal is the negative log probability:

$$S(x_{i=1}^n) = -\log_2 p(x_{i=1}^n)$$

$$= -\sum_{i=1}^n \log_2 p(x_i|x_{j=1}^{i-1}),$$

where $x_{i=1}^n$ is a sequence of n words forming a sentence and the conditional probability $p(x_i|x_{j=1}^{i-1})$ is calculated as the RNN's normalized softmax activation for x_i given its hidden state after consuming $x_{j=1}^{i-1}$.

Surprisal has a number of interpretations that make it convenient as a dependent variable for examining language model behavior. First, surprisal is equivalent to the contribution of a sentence to a language model's cross-entropy loss: effectively, our RNN language models are trained with the sole objective of minimizing the average surprisal of training sentences, so surprisal is directly related to the model's performance. Second, word-by-word surprisal has been found to be an effective predictor of human comprehension difficulty (Hale, 2001; Levy, 2008; Smith and Levy, 2013); interpreting surprisal as metric of "difficulty" allows us to analyze RNN behavior analogously to human processing behavior (van Schijndel and Linzen, 2018; Futrell et al., 2018). Third, surprisal more generally reflects the dispreference or **markedness** of a sequence according to a language model. High surprisal for a sentence corresponds to a relative dispreference for that sentence. When the logarithm is taken to base 2, surprisal is equivalent to the bits of information required to encode a sentence under a model.

In the studies below, we test hypotheses statistically using maximal linear mixed-effects models (Baayen et al., 2008; Barr et al., 2013) fit to predict surprisals given experimental conditions.

1.1 Models tested

We study the behavior of two LSTMs trained on a language modeling objective over English text: the one presented in Jozefowicz et al. (2016) as "BIG LSTM+CNN Inputs", which we call "JRNN", which was trained on the One Billion Word Benchmark (Chelba et al., 2013) with two hidden layers of 8196 units and CNN character embeddings as input; and the one presented in Gulordava et al. (2018), which we call "GRNN", with two hidden layers of 650 units, trained on 90 million tokens of English Wikipedia.

As a control, we also study surprisals assigned by an *n*-gram model trained on the One Billion Word Benchmark (a 5-gram model with modified Kneser-Ney interpolation, fit by KenLM with default parameters) (Heafield et al., 2013). The *n*-gram surprisals tell us to what extent the patterns under study can be learned purely from co-occurrence statistics with a small context window without any generalization over words. To the extent that LSTMs yield more humanlike performance than the *n*-gram model, this indicates one of two things. Either they have learned generalizations that are formulated in terms of more abstract linguistic features, or they have learned generalizations that can span larger distances than the *n*-gram window.

1.2 Human acceptability ratings

We also compare RNN surprisals against human preferences on our experimental items. We collected acceptability judgments on a scale of 1 (least acceptable) to 5 (most acceptable) over Amazon Mechanical Turk.[1] For the studies of heavy NP shift, the dative alternation, and the genitive alternation, we collected data from 64 participants, filtering out participants who were not native English speakers or who could not correctly answer 80% of simple comprehension questions about the experimental items. After filtering, we had data from 55 participants. For the study of particle shift, we used data from a previous (unpublished) acceptability rating experiment with 196 subjects, and the same filtering criteria. After filtering, we had data from 156 participants.

2 Heavy NP Shift

HEAVY NP SHIFT describes a scenario where constituent weight preferences become so strong that an order which would otherwise be unacceptable becomes more acceptable, as shown in Example (1).

(1)   a.   The publisher announced a book on Thursday.

        b.   *The publisher announced on Thursday a book.

        c.   The publisher announced a new book from a famous author who always produced bestsellers on Thursday.

        d.   The publisher announced on Thursday a new book from a famous author who always produced bestsellers.

In these examples, the verb *announced* is followed by a noun phrase (*a (new) book...*) and a temporal PP adjunct (*on Thursday*). The usual order for these elements is to put the NP before the PP, but when the NP becomes very heavy, the PP might

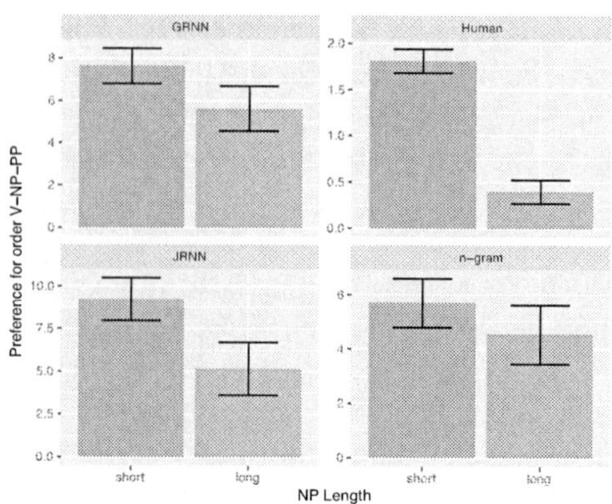

Figure 1: Mean preference for standard word order by NP length. In this and other figures, for computational models, preference is measured as total sentence surprisal for Verb–NP–PP order minus total sentence surprisal for Verb–PP–NP order; error bars represent 95% confidence intervals of the contrasts between conditions, computed by subtracting out the by-item means before calculating the intervals (Masson and Loftus, 2003). For the human data, preference is measured as the difference in mean acceptability for Verb–PP–NP minus Verb–NP–PP, and error bars represent 95% confidence intervals of the contrasts between conditions after subtracting out by-item and by-subject means.

be placed closer to the verb, which case the word order is called SHIFTED. Heavy NP shift is the primary example of locality effects in word order preferences, in that it creates shorter dependencies from the verb to the NP and the PP.

We tested whether RNNs show length-based preferences similar to Example (1).[2] We adapted 40 items from Stallings et al. (1998) which consist of a verb followed by an NP and a temporal PP adjunct, where the order of the NP and the PP and the length of the NP are manipulated. If the networks show human-like word ordering preferences, there should be a penalty for PP–NP order when the NP is short, but this penalty should be smaller or nonexistent when the NP is long.

Figure 1 shows the models' preference for the standard word order (Verb–NP–PP) over the shifted word order (Verb–PP–NP), calculated as the surprisal of sentences in shifted word order minus their surprisal in standard word order. Also included are the human acceptability ratings, where the preference for the order Verb–NP–PP is calculated as the average acceptability difference between Verb–NP–PP and Verb–PP–NP

---

[1]Preregistered at https://aspredicted.org/sh9zf.pdf.

[2]The preregistration for this experiment can be viewed at https://aspredicted.org/ea6m8.pdf.

across items. In all cases, we see that the shifted order becomes more preferred when the NP is long, although it never becomes the most preferred order.

Our experimental design allows us to control for the effect of sentence length on RNN surprisals. The sentences with long NPs are naturally expected to have higher RNN surprisal than the ones with short noun phrases, since they have more words and thus higher information content. However, the Verb–NP–PP preference is quantified as the *difference* between surprisal of order Verb–PP–NP and surprisal of the order Verb–NP–PP, for both the long and short NP conditions. The long NP conditions may have higher surprisal overall, but this will be cancelled out in the difference. The crucial question is then whether this preference is larger in the long NP case than in the short NP case—whether the red and blue values in Figure 1 are significantly different across items. The crucial statistic for each item i is given by the interaction I_i:

$$I_i = \left(S_i(\text{short}, \text{Verb–NP–PP}) - S_i(\text{short}, \text{Verb–PP–NP})\right)$$
$$- \left(S_i(\text{long}, \text{Verb–NP–PP}) - S_i(\text{long}, \text{Verb–PP–NP})\right),$$

where S_i is the surprisal for the ith item in the given condition. If I_i is significantly positive across items, then we have evidence that NP length causes a preference for Verb–PP–NP order even when controlling for the intrinsic effects of length and of the particular words in each item. The same logic is applied to the analysis of the acceptability ratings data. All studies in this paper apply this same design and analysis. Similar designs are common in psycholinguistics, and are applied to RNN surprisal data in Futrell et al. (2018) and Wilcox et al. (2018).

To test the significance of the interaction, we use mixed-effects modeling with random intercepts and slopes by item. We find that the interaction is statistically significant in JRNN (interaction size 4.0 bits, $p < 0.001$) and GRNN (2.0 bits, $p = 0.02$), but not in the n-gram baseline (1.2 bits, $p = 0.13$). The interaction in JRNN is significantly stronger than in the n-gram baseline ($p = 0.03$), but the interaction in GRNN is not significantly stronger than the n-gram baseline ($p = 0.48$). None of the models show the effect as strongly as the human acceptability judgments.

Thus we find that both JRNN and GRNN exhibit human-like word order biases for Heavy NP shift, but do not find evidence for such a bias in the n-gram baseline. The result suggests that the LSTM models have learned a higher-order generalization that is not trivially present in n-gram statistics.

3 Phrasal verbs and particle shift

Another domain of word order variation similar to Heavy NP shift is phrasal verbs, which consist of a verb and a particle, such as *give up*. The object NP of a transitive phrasal verb can appear in two positions: it can be SHIFTED (after the particle) or UNSHIFTED (before the particle). As in Heavy NP shift, the shifted order is generally preferred when the NP is long:

(2) a. Kim gave up the habit. [shifted]
    b. Kim gave the habit up. [unshifted]
    c. Kim gave up the habit that was preventing success in the workplace. [shifted]
    d. Kim gave the habit that was preventing success in the workplace up. [unshifted]

The fact that both word orders are possible is called PARTICLE SHIFT. Particle shift provides another arena to test whether RNNs have learned the basic short-before-long constituent ordering preference in English. Furthermore, particle shift is also affected by the animacy of the object NP, in that the unshifted order is preferred when the object NP is animate (Gries, 2003), so we can use this construction to test order preferences involving both length and animacy.

We designed 32 experimental items consisting of sentences with phrasal verbs as in Example (2), where each item could occur with either a long or a short object NP. Long NPs were created by adding adjectives and postmodifiers to short NPs. Half of the items had inanimate objects; half had animate objects. All NPs were definite. We tested the effects of NP length, NP animacy, and word order on language model surprisal.[3]

Figure 2 shows the average preference for shifted word order according to each model, calculated as the surprisal of the shifted order minus the surprisal of the unshifted order. In general, we see that when the object NP is long, the shifted order is relatively preferred; the effect is

---

[3]The preregistration for this experiment can be viewed at `https://aspredicted.org/uu7am.pdf`.

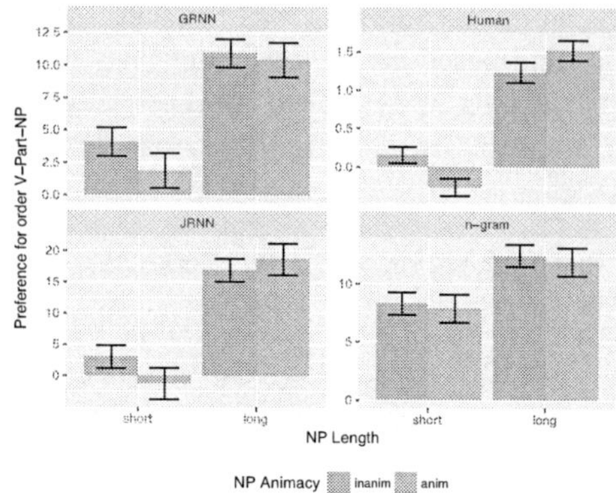

Figure 2: Preference for shifted word order (total sentence surprisal for Verb–Particle–NP order minus Verb–NP–Particle order) by NP length, NP animacy, and model.

strongest in JRNN. In regressions, we found that the interaction of NP length and word order is significant in JRNN (16.9 bits, $p < 0.001$), GRNN (7.8 bits, $p < 0.001$), and the n-gram baseline (4.1 bits, $p < 0.001$). However, the interaction in the n-gram baseline is significantly smaller than in JRNN ($p < 0.001$) and GRNN ($p < 0.01$).

The effects of animacy are unexpectedly intricate. Numerically, GRNN and the n-gram baseline show the expected effect: an animate NP favors unshifted order. However, in the human ratings we find that the expected animacy effect for short NPs actually reverses for long NPs, and this is reflected numerically in JRNN. No effects of animacy are significant in any model. In the human data, animacy has a significant interaction favoring the unshifted word order for short NPs ($p < 0.001$) with an interaction that reverses the effect for long NPs ($p < 0.001$). This reversal is surprising given what was previously known about word order in phrasal verbs.

Our investigation of particle shift has shown that LSTM models learn short-before-long length preferences in regard to word order in phrasal verb constructions; n-gram models show these preferences as well, though weaker. We do not find evidence that the models learned human word order preferences based on NP animacy in this case, but the experimental results suggest that the effects of animacy on this alternation might be more complex than previously believed.

4   Dative alternation

The DATIVE ALTERNATION refers to the fact that in many cases the following forms are substitutable:

(3)   a.   The man gave the woman the book. [Double-object (DO) construction]

        b.   The man gave the book to the woman. [Prepositional-object (PO) construction]

The dative alternation is one of the most studied topics in syntax. The two constructions have been argued to convey subtly different meanings, with the DO construction indicating caused possession and the PO construction indicating caused motion (Green, 1974; Oehrle, 1976; Gropen et al., 1989; Levin, 1993). However, the semantic preference of each construction appears to be only one factor among many when it comes to determining which form will be used in any given instance. Other factors include the animacy, definiteness, and length of the THEME (*the book* in Example (3)) and the RECIPIENT (*the woman*) (Bresnan et al., 2007).

The human preferences in the dative alternation work out such that the NP which is more animate, definite, and short goes earlier. An extreme case is exemplified in (4): the sentences marked with ? are relatively dispreferred by native English speakers.

(4)   a.   The man gave the woman a very old book that was about historical topics.

        b.   ?The man gave a very old book that was about historical topics to the woman.

        c.   The man gave the book to a woman who was waiting patiently in the hallway.

        d.   ?The man gave a woman who was waiting patiently in the hallway a book.

In order to examine whether LSTMs show human-like preferences in the dative alternation, we designed 16 items on the pattern of (3), with 8 verbs of caused possession (such as *give*) and 8 verbs of caused motion (such as *throw*).[4] In all items, the theme was inanimate and the recipient was animate. We manipulated the definiteness of the

---

[4]The preregistration for this experiment can be viewed at `https://aspredicted.org/ky9ne.pdf`.

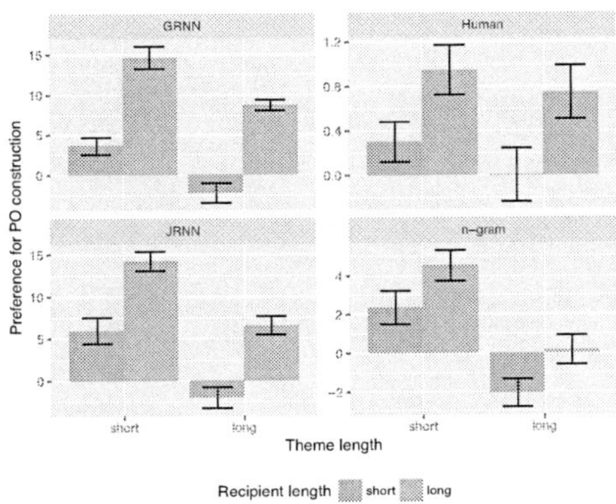

Figure 3: Average PO preference by length of theme and recipient.

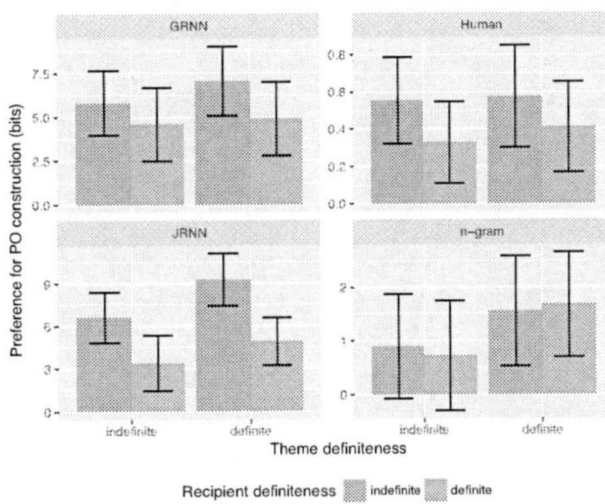

Figure 4: Average PO preference by definiteness of theme and recipient.

theme and the recipient using the articles *the* and *a*, and the length of the theme and the recipient by adding relative clauses to either or both.

Figure 3 shows the strength of the models' preference for the PO construction as a function of the length of the theme and recipient. The LSTMs have an overall preference for the PO form, which is mirrored in the human data. In addition, we see that a long recipient is strongly associated with a stronger preference for the PO form, and a long theme is strongly associated with a relative preference for the DO form, in line with human preferences. The *n*-gram baseline shows these effects but with a smaller magnitude, and without the overall PO preference shown by humans.

All interactions of length and word order are significant at $p < .001$ in all models, with the exception of the effect of recipient length in the *n*-gram model, where $p = 0.01$. The effects of recipient and theme length are significantly weaker in the *n*-gram baseline than in JRNN ($p < 0.01$); for GRNN, the effect of recipient definiteness is significantly stronger than the *n*-gram baseline ($p = 0.02$) but the effect of theme definiteness is not significantly stronger than in the *n*-gram baseline. In human data, the interaction of recipient length and word order is significant at $p < .001$ and the interaction of theme length and word order is significant at $p = .01$.

Now we turn to word order preferences based on NP definiteness. Figure 4 shows the PO preference by the definiteness of the theme and recipient. In line with the linguistic literature, the PO preference is numerically smaller for definite recipients in both LSTM models and in human data,

but not in the *n*-gram model. The interaction of recipient definiteness and word order is significant in the expected direction in JRNN at $p < 0.001$ and GRNN at $p = 0.01$. Theme definiteness has a small positive interaction with word order (at $p < 0.01$) for JRNN, favoring the PO construction. These results are broadly in line with the linguistic literature, but they are not reflected in the human data for these experimental items: in the human ratings data, there are no significant interactions of definiteness and word order.

Overall, we find evidence for humanlike ordering preferences in the dative alternation with respect to length and definiteness of theme and recipient. The strongest effects which are most in line with the linguistic literature come from JRNN.

5   Genitive alternation

Similarly to the dative alternation, the GENITIVE ALTERNATION involves two constructions with opposite word orders expressing similar meanings:

(5)   a.   The woman's house [*s*-genitive, definite possessor]
  b.   The house of the woman [*of*-genitive, definite possessor]
  c.   A woman's house [*s*-genitive, indefinite possessor]
  d.   The house of a woman [*of*-genitive, indefinite possessor]

As in the dative alternation, whatever semantic difference exists between the two constructions is only one factor conditioning which form is used

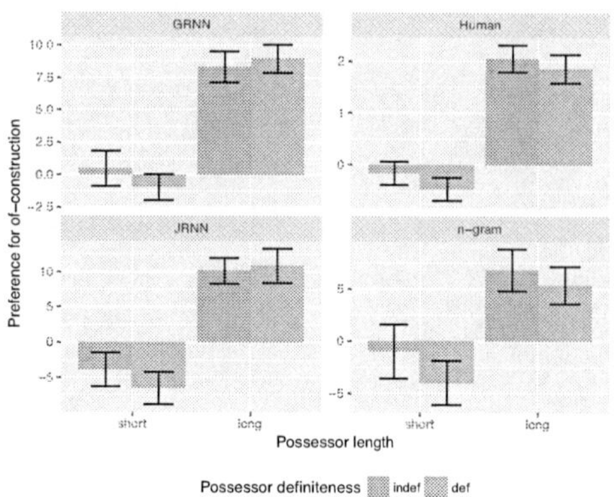
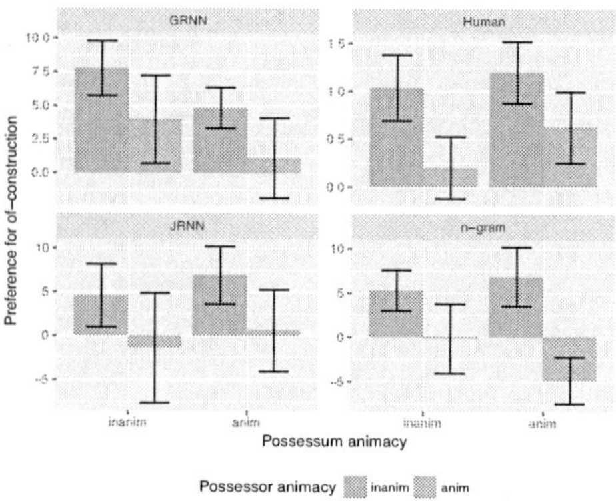

Figure 5: Average *of*-genitive preference by length and definiteness of possessor.

Figure 6: Average *of*-genitive preference by animacy of possessor and possessum.

in each particular case. The other factors are the usual suspects: animacy, definiteness, and length of the POSSESSOR (*the woman* in (5)) and POSSESSUM (*the house* in (5)) (Kreyer, 2003; Rosenbach, 2003, 2008; Shih et al., 2015).

In order to study the genitive alternation in RNNs, we designed 16 items on the pattern of (5). We varied the definiteness and length of the possessor as in the dative alternation.[5] We also varied the animacy of the possessor and possessum, between items.[6]

Figure 5 shows the RNNs' preferences for the *of*-genitive form based on the definiteness and length of the possessor. In all models and in human data, we see that the *of*-genitive is preferred generally when the possessor is long, and the *s*-genitive when it is short. The interaction of possessor length with word order is significant in models and human data ($p < 0.001$ in all cases). Turning to possessor definiteness, we see that it relatively favors the *s*-genitive in human data and in the *n*-gram baseline, in line with the linguistic literature, but no such effect is found in the RNN models. However, the interaction of definiteness with word order is not significant in our data ($p = .09$ in human data and higher for the language models).

Now we turn to effects of animacy. Figure 6 shows the *of*-genitive preference by the animacy of the possessor and possessum. In all models, in line with human preferences, we see that possessor animacy favors the *s*-genitive. The interaction

of possessor animacy and word order is significant in JRNN ($p = 0.03$) and GRNN ($p < 0.001$) but not in the *n*-gram baseline ($p = 0.09$); the effect is significantly stronger in JRNN than in the *n*-gram baseline ($p = 0.02$) but not significantly stronger in GRNN. The effect of possessum animacy is more complex: it seems to favor the *s*-genitive in GRNN, but the *of*-genitive in the other models and in human preferences; in any case, the effect is small, and the interaction is not significant in any of the data collected here.

Overall, it appears that the LSTMs tested show humanlike order preferences in the genitive alternation when it comes to possessor length and animacy; they show more evidence for effects of possessor animacy than an *n*-gram baseline. They do not appear to pick up on definiteness preferences, but based on human experimental data these preferences might be weak in the first place.

6 Discussion

We have explored RNN language models' ability to represent soft word order preferences whose formulation requires abstract features such as animacy, definiteness, and length. We found that RNN language models generally do so, and outperform an *n*-gram baseline, indicating that they learn generalizations which are not trivially present in local co-occurrence statistics of words. The extent to which RNNs learn such preferences varies: effects of length are strongly and consistently represented, with weaker evidence for effects of animacy and definiteness.

Much recent work has focused on whether RNNs can learn to represent discrete syntactic

---

[5] For both constructions to be legitimate syntactic options, the possesssum must be definite and unmodified by relative clauses.

[6] The preregistration for this experiment can be viewed at https://aspredicted.org/f2sk8.pdf.

structures such as long-distance number agreement (Linzen et al., 2016), wh-dependencies (McCoy et al., 2018; Chowdhury and Zamparelli, 2018; Wilcox et al., 2018), anaphora, negative polarity item licensing, and garden path sentences (van Schijndel and Linzen, 2018; Marvin and Linzen, 2018; Futrell et al., 2018). The current work focuses on soft preferences which have been studied in quantitative syntax, and the abstract features that have been discovered to underly these preferences, finding that RNNs are able to represent many of the required features. The same features underlying these soft preferences in English often play a role in hard constraints in other languages (Bresnan et al., 2001): thus our findings indicate that RNNs can learn crosslinguistically useful abstractions.

Our results also demonstrate that some of the key features underlying syntactic alternations can be learned from text data alone, without any particular innate bias toward such features. Qualifying this point, note that the language models we studied here were exposed to many more tokens of linguistic input than a typical child learner.

In addition to the results about RNNs, our work provides human data from directly controlled experimental manipulations of animacy, definiteness, and length in particle shift, genitive, and dative alternations. Our human acceptability ratings experiments have revealed some unexpected patterns, such as the sign reversal in the effect of animacy for long NPs in particle shift (Section 3), which should be investigated in more detail in future work.

An interesting question which has been studied in the functional linguistic literature is *why* these particular word order preferences exist across languages. The preferences are often explained in terms of cognitive pressures on language comprehension and production. The short-before-long preference is most likely a manifestation of the pressure for short dependencies (Wasow, 2002), which is motivated by working memory limitations in sentence processing (Gibson, 1998); this word order preference is reversed in predominantly head-final languages such as Japanese, where there is a general preference for long constituents to come before short ones (Yamashita and Chang, 2001). The biases for animate and definite nouns to come early are usually linked to biases in the human language production process whereby words and constituents which are easier to produce come earlier (Bock, 1982).

It is possible that these same cognitively motivated biases might also be present in RNNs. For example, Futrell and Levy (2017) have argued that there should be a preference for short dependencies in any system that predicts words incrementally given lossy representations of the preceding context: since RNNs represent context using fixed-length vectors, their context representations must be lossy in this way. Furthermore, Chang (2009) has shown that the preference to place animate words earlier can arise in simple recurrent networks without this bias being present in training data, suggesting that RNNs may be subject to similar pressures to produce certain kinds of words earlier.

More generally, we have treated RNN language models essentially as human subjects delivering acceptability judgments, observing their behavior on carefully controlled linguistic stimuli rather than examining their internals. By using controlled experimental designs, we are able to control for factors such as sentence length and the particular lexical items in each sentence (cf. Lau et al., 2017). We believe this approach will allow us to derive initial insight into the limits of what RNNs can do, and will guide work that explains the behavior we document here in terms of network internals.

Acknowledgments

This work was supported in part by a gift from the NVIDIA corporation. RPL gratefully acknowledges support from the MIT-IBM AI Research Laboratory. All code and data is available at `https://github.com/langprocgroup/rnn_soft_constraints`.

References

R. Harald Baayen, D.J. Davidson, and Douglas M. Bates. 2008. Mixed-effects modeling with crossed random effects for subjects and items. *Journal of Memory and Language*, 59(4):390–412.

Dale J. Barr, Roger Levy, Christoph Scheepers, and Harry J Tily. 2013. Random effects structure for confirmatory hypothesis testing: Keep it maximal. *Journal of Memory and Language*, 68(3):255–278.

J. Kathryn Bock. 1982. Toward a cognitive psychology of syntax: Information processing contributions to sentence formulation. *Psychological Review*, 89:1–47.

Joan Bresnan. 2007. Is syntactic knowledge probabilistic? Experiments with the English dative alternation. In *Roots: Linguistics in Search of its Evidential Base*, pages 77–96. Mouton de Gruyter, Berlin.

Joan Bresnan, Anna Cueni, Tatiana Nikitina, and Harald Baayen. 2007. Predicting the dative alternation. In *Cognitive Foundations of Interpration*, pages 69–94. Royal Netherlands Academy of Science, Amsterdam.

Joan Bresnan, Shipra Dingare, and Christopher D. Manning. 2001. Soft constraints mirror hard constraints: Voice and person in English and Lummi. In *Proceedings of the LFG 01 Conference*, pages 13–32. CSLI Publications.

Franklin Chang. 2009. Learning to order words: A connectionist model of Heavy NP Shift and accessibility effects in Japanese and English. *Journal of Memory and Language*, 61:374–397.

Ciprian Chelba, Tomas Mikolov, Mike Schuster, Qi Ge, Thorsten Brants, Phillipp Koehn, and Tony Robinson. 2013. One billion word benchmark for measuring progress in statistical language modeling. *arXiv preprint arXiv:1312.3005*.

Shammur Absar Chowdhury and Roberto Zamparelli. 2018. RNN simulations of grammaticality judgments on long-distance dependencies. In *Proceedings of the 27th International Conference on Computational Linguistics*, Sante Fe, NM.

Jeffrey L. Elman. 1990. Finding structure in time. *Cognitive Science*, 14(2):179–211.

Richard Futrell and Roger Levy. 2017. Noisy-context surprisal as a human sentence processing cost model. In *Proceedings of the 15th Conference of the European Chapter of the Association for Computational Linguistics: Volume 1, Long Papers*, pages 688–698, Valencia, Spain.

Richard Futrell, Kyle Mahowald, and Edward Gibson. 2015. Large-scale evidence of dependency length minimization in 37 languages. *Proceedings of the National Academy of Sciences*, 112(33):10336–10341.

Richard Futrell, Ethan Wilcox, Takashi Morita, and Roger Levy. 2018. RNNs as psycholinguistic subjects: Syntactic state and grammatical dependency. *arXiv*, 1809.01329.

Edward Gibson. 1998. Linguistic complexity: Locality of syntactic dependencies. *Cognition*, 68(1):1–76.

Yoav Goldberg. 2017. Neural network methods for natural language processing. *Synthesis Lectures on Human Language Technologies*, 10(1):1–309.

Georgia M. Green. 1974. *Semantics and syntactic regularity*. Indiana Univ Pr.

Stefan Thomas Gries. 2003. *Multifactorial analysis in corpus linguistics: A study of particle placement*. A&C Black.

Jess Gropen, Steven Pinker, Michelle Hollander, Richard Goldberg, and Ronald Wilson. 1989. The learnability and acquisition of the dative alternation in English. *Language*, pages 203–257.

Kristina Gulordava, Piotr Bojanowski, Edouard Grave, Tal Linzen, and Marco Baroni. 2018. Colorless green recurrent networks dream hierarchically. In *Proceedings of NAACL*.

John T. Hale. 2001. A probabilistic Earley parser as a psycholinguistic model. In *Proceedings of the Second Meeting of the North American Chapter of the Association for Computational Linguistics and Language Technologies*, pages 1–8.

John A. Hawkins. 1994. *A performance theory of order and constituency*. Cambridge University Press, Cambridge.

Kenneth Heafield, Ivan Pouzyrevsky, Jonathan H. Clark, and Philipp Koehn. 2013. Scalable modified Kneser-Ney language model estimation. In *Proceedings of the 51st Annual Meeting of the Association for Computational Linguistics*, Sofia, Bulgaria.

Rafal Jozefowicz, Oriol Vinyals, Mike Schuster, Noam Shazeer, and Yonghui Wu. 2016. Exploring the limits of language modeling. *arXiv*, 1602.02410.

Rolf Kreyer. 2003. Genitive and of-construction in modern written English: Processability and human involvement. *International Journal of Corpus Linguistics*, 8(2):169–207.

Jey Han Lau, Alexander Clark, and Shalom Lappin. 2017. Grammaticality, acceptability, and probability: A probabilistic view of linguistic knowledge. *Cognitive Science*, 41(5):1202–1241.

Beth Levin. 1993. *English verb classes and alternations: A preliminary investigation*. University of Chicago press.

Roger Levy. 2008. Expectation-based syntactic comprehension. *Cognition*, 106(3):1126–1177.

Tal Linzen. 2018. What can linguistics and deep learning contribute to each other? *Language*.

Tal Linzen, Emmanuel Dupoux, and Yoav Goldberg. 2016. Assessing the ability of LSTMs to learn syntax-sensitive dependencies. *Transactions of the Association for Computational Linguistics*, 4:521–535.

Rebecca Marvin and Tal Linzen. 2018. Targeted syntactic evaluation of language models. In *Proceedings of EMNLP*, Brussels.

Michael E. J. Masson and Geoffrey R. Loftus. 2003. Using confidence intervals for graphically based data interpretation. *Canadian Journal of Experimental Psychology/Revue canadienne de psychologie expérimentale*, 57(3):203.

R. Thomas McCoy, Robert Frank, and Tal Linzen. 2018. Revisiting the poverty of the stimulus: hierarchical generalization without a hierarchical bias in recurrent neural networks. *arXiv preprint arXiv:1802.09091*.

Janet L. McDonald, J. Kathryn Bock, and Michael H. Kelly. 1993. Word and world order: Semantic, phonological, and metrical determinants of serial position. *Cognitive Psychology*, 25:188–230.

Richard Thomas Oehrle. 1976. *The grammatical status of the English dative alternation*. Ph.D. thesis, Massachusetts Institute of Technology.

Anette Rosenbach. 2003. Aspects of iconicity and economy in the choice between the s-genitive and the of-genitive in english. *Determinants of grammatical variation in English*, 379412.

Anette Rosenbach. 2008. Animacy and grammatical variation: Findings from English genitive variation. *Lingua*, 118(2):151–171.

Marten van Schijndel and Tal Linzen. 2018. Modeling garden path effects without explicit hierarchical syntax. In *Proceedings of the 40th Annual Meeting of the Cognitive Science Society*.

Stephanie Shih, Jason Grafmiller, Richard Futrell, and Joan Bresnan. 2015. Rythm's role in the genitive construction choice in spoken english. In Ralf Vogel and Reuben van de Vijver, editors, *Rhythm in phonetics, grammar, and cognition*, pages 208–234. De Gruyter Mouton, Berlin, Germany.

Nathaniel J. Smith and Roger Levy. 2013. The effect of word predictability on reading time is logarithmic. *Cognition*, 128(3):302–319.

Lynne M. Stallings, Maryellen C. MacDonald, and Padraig G. O'Seaghdha. 1998. Phrasal ordering constraints in sentence production: Phrase length and verb disposition in heavy-NP shift. *Journal of Memory and Language*, 39(3):392–417.

Ilya Sutskever, Oriol Vinyals, and Quoc V. Le. 2014. Sequence to sequence learning with neural networks. In *Advances in Neural Information Processing Systems*, pages 3104–3112.

David Temperley and Dan Gildea. 2018. Minimizing syntactic dependency lengths: Typological/cognitive universal? *Annual Review of Linguistics*, 4:1–15.

Thomas Wasow. 2002. *Postverbal Behavior*. CSLI Publications, Stanford, CA.

Michael White and Rajakrishnan Rajkumar. 2012. Minimal dependency length in realization ranking. In *Proceedings of the 2012 Joint Conference on Empirical Methods in Natural Language Processing and Computational Natural Language Learning*, pages 244–255. Association for Computational Linguistics.

Ethan Wilcox, Roger Levy, Takashi Morita, and Richard Futrell. 2018. What do RNN language models learn about filler–gap dependencies? In *Proceedings of BlackboxNLP*, Brussels.

Adina Williams, Andrew Drozdov, and Samuel R Bowman. 2018. Do latent tree learning models identify meaningful structure in sentences? *Transactions of the Association for Computational Linguistics*, 6:253–267.

Hiroko Yamashita and Franklin Chang. 2001. "Long before short" preference in the production of a head-final language. *Cognition*, 81(2):B45–B55.

Segmentation and UR Acquisition with UR Constraints[*]

Max Nelson
University of Massachusetts Amherst
manelson@umass.edu

Abstract

This paper presents a model that treats segmentation and underlying representation acquisition as parallel, interacting processes. A probability distribution over mappings from underlying to surface representations is defined using a Maximum Entropy grammar which weights a set of underlying representation constraints (URCs) (Apoussidou, 2007; Pater et al., 2012). URCs are induced from observed surface strings and used to generate candidates. Structural ambiguity arising from the comparison of segmented outputs to unsegmented surface strings is handled with Expectation Maximization (Dempster et al., 1977; Jarosz, 2013). The model successfully learns a simple voicing assimilation rule and segmentation via correspondences between surface phones and input meanings. The trained grammar is also able to segment novel forms affixed with familiar morphemes.

1 Introduction

Segmentation is the task by which continuous speech is broken up into discrete words. This task is complicated by the fact that there are no universal cues to word boundary location. Language-specific morphological, phonotactic, and prosodic cues to word boundaries do exist, but these cues are unavailable in early acquisition because their cooccurrence with word boundaries has not yet been observed (Perruchet and Vinter, 1998).

The lexicon and accompanying phonological knowledge provide a rich source of potential information about boundary location. If any substring from an utterance can be mapped onto a lexical item, then boundaries can be inferred by identifying the correspondences between the phones in the surface string and those in the underlying form. However, using this knowledge requires that some of the lexicon is known to the learner and that segmentation has already been used successfully to identify surface forms.

The fact that segmentation is a prerequisite to build the lexicon only precludes lexical information from being used in segmentation if the two processes take place in serial, with learners developing the ability to segment speech before storing any lexical information. Previous models of segmentation either ignore the acquisition of the lexicon (Saffran et al., 1996a; Saffran et al., 1996b; Perruchet and Vinter, 1998) or do not fully utilize the richness of lexical knowledge (Johnson et al., 2015; Goldwater et al., 2009). This paper presents a model of segmentation in which the lexicon, represented by phonological underlying forms which correspond to meanings, is being acquired in parallel with segmentation, and the two processes are mutually informing. This type of joint inference has been explored elsewhere, particularly with regards to the interaction of segmentation with phonetic categorization and lexical acquisition (Elsner et al., 2013; Elsner et al., 2016), but little work has been done on the interaction of other processes with the acquisition of phonological alternations.

---

[*]Thank you to Katherine Blake, Gaja Jarosz, Andrew Lamont, Joe Pater, Brandon Prickett, UMass Phonology Reading Group, and three anonymous reviewers for comments. Remaining errors are my own.

Proceedings of the Society for Computation in Linguistics (SCiL) 2019, pages 60-68.
New York City, New York, January 3-6, 2019

2 Background

2.1 Segmentation

Early work on segmentation excluded the use of
phonological knowledge by design. Saffran et al.
(1996a; 1996b) conducted a series of experiments
in which both infants and adults were tasked with
segmenting continuous speech that had no prosodic
cues to word boundaries, finding in all cases that participants were able to segment the data into the composite words. This led to the hypothesis that learners
are able to identify word boundaries solely by tracking transitional probability minima in the input.

However, the storage and update of transitional
probabilities is computationally costly and statistical models have been shown to be successful without relying on their direct computation. One such
model is Perruchet and Vinter's PARSER (1998).
The PARSER model takes advantage of the fact that
any randomly selected set of syllables is more likely
to reoccur if the syllables are a word than if they
are not, storing a set of weights on encountered substrings rather than explicitly storing and computing
transitional probabilities.

Both of these approaches model segmentation
in isolation. Johnson and Jusczyk (2001) suggested that when phonological cues to word boundaries are available, they supercede statistics in word
boundary identification. Infants in their study were
more likely to learn word boundaries cued by
prosodic/phonological information than competing
boundaries cued by statistical information. Furthermore, segmentation is a necessary step toward the
identification of phonological surface forms, which
are the necessary precursor to the learning of phonotactics, phonological grammars and underlying representations. Phonological acquisition both feeds
and is fed by segmentation; therefore a model of
segmentation that does not incorporate phonological
processes and underlying forms is incomplete.

Similarly, a model of segmentation should not
only model acquisition, but should also model adult-
like behavior. A simple Wug task (Berko Gleason, 1958) involves the use of lexical and phonological knowledge to identify correspondences between phonological content in the surface form and
known morphemes. This results in a segmentation
of the novel word, but this kind of segmentation task
is largely absent from the literature. The use of lexical knowledge to predict segmentations requires that
the learner entertain multiple possible lexical entries
for a given meaning. The model presented below
uses underlying representation constraints (URCs)
within a standard constraint-based grammar (Prince
and Smolensky, 19932004; Pater et al., 2012; Smith,
2015) to allow the learner to entertain multiple possible URs. The likelihood of a segmentation is affected by the likelihood of the corresponding URs
and phonological alternations.

2.2 Underlying Representation Constraints

Underlying representation constraints (URCs),
also referred to as lexical constraints, specify the
underlying form for a meaning and are violated
when an alternative underlying form is chosen
(Apoussidou, 2007; Kager, 2008; Eisenstat, 2009).
URCs allow the selection of underlying forms to
happen in parallel with phonological optimization, allowing the grammar to choose between
multiple URs with an eye to the phonological
consequences of the decision (Pater et al., 2012).
A sample UR constraint is defined below, using
language from Smith (2015). This constraint specifies the underlying form /ə/ for the indefinite article.

> {IND}=/ə/ : Assign one violation for
> every input set of morphosyntactic fea-
> tures corresponding to IND (indefinite
> determiner) that is not realized by /ə/

URCs represent non-discrete lexical entries. The
phonological representation of a lexical item is distributed over the set of relevant URCs. When there
are multiple candidate URs and corresponding surface allomorphs, the choice between URs is made
in the phonology in parallel with other phonological
operations (Pater et al., 2012; Smith, 2015) . Inputs to the phonology are sets of meanings without
any inherent phonological material; following Smith
(2015), these are formalized as sets of morphosyntactic features. Candidates evaluated by the grammar are mappings from underlying to surface forms.

To illustrate how UR constraints interact with the
rest of the phonology, consider the a~an alternation
in English. Simplifying slightly by ignoring vowel
reduction, the indefinite determiner surfaces as [ə]

before a consonant and [ən] before a vowel.

If the UR of the indefinite determiner were always /ə/, describing this process would require /n/ insertion and the analyst would be tasked with accounting for the fact that [n]-epenthesis occurs in only this specific environment. Likewise, if the UR were assumed to be /ən/, this process would require preconsonantal /n/-deletion and the analyst would have to account for the lack of /n/-deletion elsewhere. With UR constraints however there is a third possibility: UR selection. The tableaux in (1) and (2) illustrate how UR selection can result in a non-default form surfacing due to pressure from the standard markedness constraint HIATUS, which penalizes adjacent vowels.

{IND} + DOG	HIATUS	IND=ə	IND=ən
☞ a. ə+dɔg → ədɔg			*
b. ən+dɔg → əndɔg		*W	L

Tableau 1: The default UR, /ə/, is chosen when there is no interaction with markedness constraints

In Tableau (1) there is no possible HIATUS violation so /ə/, the default UR, is chosen. The default status of /ə/ is captured by the ranking IND=ə≫IND=ən. Tableau (2) illustrates how a potential HIATUS violation can result in the selection of a non-default form, creating a surface alternation. When a markedness constraint outranks the constraint specifying the default UR then a non-default UR can be chosen to repair the markedness violation.

{IND} + ANT	HIATUS	IND=ə	IND=ən
a. ə+ænt → əænt	*W	L	*W
☞ b. ən+ænt → ənænt		*	

Tableau 2: The non-default UR, /ən/ is rendered optimal by a high ranked markedness constraint

The tableaux in (1) and (2) do not consider candidates in which the UR→SR mapping is unfaithful. In the URC model, faithfulness constraints evaluate faithfulness between the selected UR and corresponding surface form. To illustrate the role of faithfulness in UR selection Tableaux (1) and (2) are repeated in Tableaux (3) and (4) with MAX and DEP added to the constraint set and the relevant unfaithful candidates considered.

{IND} + DOG	DEP	MAX	HIATUS	IND=ə	IND=ən
☞ a. ə+dɔg → ədɔg					*
b. ən+dɔg → əndɔg				*W	L
c. ə+dɔg → əndɔg	*W				*
d. ən+dɔg → ədɔg		*W		*W	L

Tableau 3: The default UR is chosen and sufaces faithfully when there are no interacting markedness constraints

Candidate (d) in (3) illustrates why an /n/-deletion account if the a∼an alternation does not work, it is harmonically bounded by (b) due to the lack of a markedness constraint motivating deletion and (a) due to the lack of a markedness constraint motivating non-default UR selection.

{IND} + ANT	DEP	MAX	HIATUS	IND=ə	IND=ən
a. ə+ænt → əænt			*W	L	*W
☞ b. ən+ænt → ənænt				*	
c. ə+ænt → ənænt	*W			L	*W
d. ən+ænt → əænt		*W	*W	*	

Tableau 4: High ranked faithfulness prevent an unfaithful mapping from the default UR from being optimal

Candidate (c) in (4) illustrates why an /n/-epenthesis analysis of the a∼an alternation does not work, it is ruled out by high ranked DEP which is necessary to account for the with the lack of /n/-epenthesis elsewhere in English in response to HIATUS violations.

UR selection is a viable alternative to faithfulness-violating phonological alternations when the alternation is either unmotivated or highly restricted. However, UR selection as described thus far remains a possibility even in cases in which a standard phonological explanation is preferred. The URC model provides no convincing reason that UR selection should not be used in, for example, the English plural alternation. Smith (2015) holds that the use of UR selection is limited by the fact that not all inputs have multiple UR constraints. UR selection is limited to suppletive forms because only those forms have multiple URCs. This claim creates problems for the learnability of URCs. A learner cannot restrict the creation of URCs to suppletive forms without first knowing that those forms are suppletive. The model presented below shows that this stipulation is unnecessary. Removing these restrictions makes the URC induction task tractable and does not result in rampant use of UR selection when a simple phonological solution is available.

3   Model

3.1   The grammar and learning algorithm

The present model uses URCs along with standard phonological constraints in a Maximum Entropy (MaxEnt) grammer (Goldwater and Johnson, 2003) to learn a probability distribution over segmented phonological surface forms for any input set of morphosyntactic objects. The training data consists of mappings from morphosyntactic objects to surface forms, which have no surface-apparent segmentation. At no point are segmentations provided to the learner: segmentations of inputs emerge as a result of the acquisition of URs, through the induction and weighting of URCs, and the acquisition of phonological alternations.

In a MaxEnt grammar, constraints are weighted and candidates' violations of constraints are represented by negative integers. The weighted sum of constraint violations is referred to as the *harmony* of a candidate. The closer to 0 the harmony is, the more likely that candidate is to surface. The probability distribution over the set of candidates is calculated by applying the softmax function to the set of harmonies. In this case a single candidate x is a mapping from underlying to surface form and an input M is a set of morphosyntactic features. This is shown explicitly in the formula in (1), where c_i represents the number of violations the mapping of M to x incurs on constraint i, w_i represents the current weight of i, and Ω_M represents the set of all candidates in the tableau for input M.

$$p(x \mid M) = \frac{e^{-(\sum_i w_i c_i(M,x))}}{\sum_{x' \in \Omega_M} e^{-(\sum_i w_i c_i(M,x'))}} \quad (1)$$

The learner's goal is to find the set of weights that maximize the likelihood of the training data T or, in other words, minimize the negative log likelihood:

$$\mathcal{L} = -\sum_{x \in T} \log p(x) \quad (2)$$

This is used as the current model's objective function with no regularization. Learning is error-driven and trained via stochastic gradient descent. In standard MaxEnt the calculation of the gradient is relatively simple. For a single training datum y, which in this case is a mapping from a set of morphosyntactic features to a surface string, the gradient of the loss function with respect to a given weight can be calculated as follows:

$$\frac{\partial \mathcal{L}}{\partial w_i} = c_i(M, y) - \sum_{x \in \Omega_M} c_i(M, x) p(x) \quad (3)$$

The update to a constraint's weight given a training datum is the learning rate times the difference between the observed number of violations of that constraint, $c_i(M, y)$, and the expected number of violations based on the current state of the model, $\sum_{x \in \Omega_M} c_i(M, x) p(x)$.

In this model, however, things are complicated by the fact that there can be multiple possible segmented outputs that, when segmentation is removed, produce the observed surface string. As framed here, the segmentation problem is therefore a problem of learning structural ambiguity - a topic of much recent work in the phonological learning literature (see Jarosz (2019) for a recent review). This creates two challenges for standard stochastic gradient descent in MaxEnt.

First, the definition of an error must be revised. In standard error-driven learning it is straighforward to compare the predicted output and the observed form. However, in this case the predicted output has more structure than the observed. Tesar and Smolensky's (1998) Robust Interpretive Parsing algorithm overcomes this issue by using the current grammar to assign structure to the observed form before making a prediction, allowing for the observed and predicted forms to both be fully structured. Jarosz's hidden structure learning algorithm, Expected Interpretive Parsing (2013), is the basis for the algorithm used here, and the definition of 'error' adopted follows her account: an error occurs when the predicted form, stripped of structure, does not match the observed form. The learner is therefore agnostic about segmentation with regard to errors. Both ðə₁#dɔg₂ and ðəd₁#ɔg₂ are acceptable segmented outputs for the input {DEF}₁+{DOG}₂, where # represents a word boundary.

Second, in the update rule above, $c_i(M, y)$ refers to the number of violations of a constraint incurred by the observed form. However, because the observed form has no structure, the corresponding structured candidate in the tableau is unknown and the violations cannot be counted. A solution to this problem relies on the use of expectation maximization (Dempster et al., 1977; Jarosz, 2013; Jarosz, 2015). An estimate of the observed violations of a constraint can be made given the grammar's current belief about the likelihood of the different segmentations of the unsegmented input. Given a training datum y, an estimate of the observed violations for a constraint i can be calculated as in (4), where Z_y is the set of all outputs that are possible segmentations of the observed string.

$$\hat{c}_i(M, y) = \sum_{z \in Z_y} c_i(M, z) \frac{p(z)}{\sum_{z \in Z_y} p(z)} \qquad (4)$$

This is equivalent to defining a probability distribution over the set of segmented candidates that overtly produce the unsegmented observed form, and then assigning a probabilistic segmentation to the observed form that is the average of all possible segmentations weighted by their probabilities.

3.2 URC induction

The training data take the form of observed surface strings and their underlying sets of morphosyntactic objects. Upon encountering a novel datum, the learner first constructs the complete set of UR constraints for all present morphosyntactic objects given that datum and adds them to the current grammar. These constraints are then immediately used in the generation of the candidate set and evaluation of the grammar.

Given a string and a set of n corresponding morphosyntactic objects, URC induction begins by computing every possible partition of the string into n non-empty substrings. A URC is then added to the grammar specifying that every substring is the UR for every morphosyntactic object in the input. This process is illustrated below for a sample training datum: the observed surface form [abc] for the morphosyntactic objects {M1}+{M2}.

Segmentation	New UR constraints	
a#bc	{M1}=a,	{M1}=bc,
	{M2}=a,	{M2}=bc
ab#c	{M1}=ab,	{M1}=c,
	{M2}=ab,	{M2}=c

Table 1: UR constraints generated from the two possible segmentations of [abc] into two non-vacuous substrings

This method of constraint induction implicitly assumes that all morphosyntactic objects will have some phonological exponent. It also provides no mechanism for URCs to specify strings that do not occur at any point in the training data. In other words, every underlying form must surface faithfully at least once in order to be considered a possible UR. This assumption is shared by other models of UR acquisition, such as Albright (2002), and of segmentation and UR acquisition (Johnson et al., 2015).

3.3 Candidate generation

For each tableau, candidates are generated from the input and constraint set. Each URC that makes reference to a morphosyntactic object in the input defines a possible UR for that object. Candidates are generated by combining every possible UR for each morphosyntactic object in the input. Tableau (5) illustrates the set of candidates that would be generated for the {M1}+{M2} input given the constraints that had been induced from the [abc] surface form in Table (5). For the sake of brevity the M1 preceding M2 order is assumed, cutting the number of constraints and candidates in half by eliminating all candidates that place the exponents of {M2} before that of {M1}. The actual model assumes no knowledge of the relative orderings of morphosyntactic objects, and the candidates with opposite correspondence relations would also be generated. Candidates shown in bold are consistent with the observed surface form [abc] and would not produce an error in training.

$\{M1\}_1+\{M2\}_2$	$\{M1\}$=a	$\{M1\}$=ab	$\{M2\}$=bc	$\{M2\}$=c
a. $\mathbf{a_1\#bc_2}$		-1		-1
b. $\mathbf{ab_1\#c_2}$	-1		-1	
c. $a_1\#c_2$		-1	-1	
d. $ab_1\#bc_2$	-1			-1

Tableau 5: Candidates and violations generated from the constraints in (5) - the ordering {M1} precedes {M2} is imposed for brevity

4 Test case: English plural

Voicing assimiliation of the English plural morpheme, by which the plural morpheme surfaces as [s] after a voiceless consonant and [z] after a voiced consonant or vowel, was used as a test case for the model. The model was tasked with segmenting utterences that contained either the definite or indef-

English Phrase	Input String	Input Morphemes
a dog	ədɔg	IND, DOG
a cat	əkæt	IND, CAT
the dog	ðədɔg	DEF, DOG
the cat	ðəkæt	DEF, CAT
the dogs	ðədɔgz	DEF, DOG, PLURAL
the cats	ðəkæts	DEF, CAT, PLURAL

Table 2: Training strings and corresponding sets of morphosyntactic objects for the English plural alternation

inite determiner (DEF/IND) and a singular or plural noun that ended with either a voiced or voiceless consonant. The complete set of inputs to the learner is listed in Table (2); sets of morphemes are unordered. The task of the learner then, is to learn the segmentation of the input strings and underlying representations for the definite and indefinite determiners, the roots DOG and CAT, and the plural. To make possible the learning of voicing assimilation, the constraints AGREE(VOICE), which assigns violations to adjacent consonants that do not share the same voicing specification, and IDENT(VOICE), which assigns violations to corresponding consonants in the UR and surface form that have different voicing specifications, are added to the constraint set. The candidate generation algorithm is expanded to have the ability to generate all IDENT(VOICE) violating candidates.

It is worth addressing the small size of this test language, especially in comparison to the corpora often used to train and test models of segmentation alone. While small for a model of segmentation, toy languages of similar size are often used to test models of phonological alternations (Tesar, 2006; Pater et al., 2012; Jarosz, 2016) and are justified by the complexity of the task. The constraint set increases linearly with the number of unique utterances in the language, but the number of candidates for any input increases exponentially with the size of the constraint set. The small test case was chosen to minimize the computational cost of evaluating an exponentially increasing number of candidates in each tableau and to ensure an interpretable output.

In all simulations the learner was able segment with near perfect accuracy. Table (3) shows the total probability assigned to correct segmentations for all six inputs after 1000 epochs with a learning rate of 0.1 and an initialization of 1.0 for all weights.

A segmentation was considered correct if a mor-

pheme's phonological exponent was correctly identified as corresponding with that morpheme, even if the resulting phonological surface form was incorrect. For example, the probability that the grammar maps the input $\{\sqrt{DOG}\}_1 + \{PLURAL\}_2$ to the phonological mapping $/dɔg_1 + s_2/ \rightarrow [dɔg_1 \# s_2]$ would be included in the total probability for a correct parse of *dogs* even though the phonological surface form is incorrect. However, the probabilities assigned to correct segmentations with incorrect surface forms were very small in all simulations and should make minimal difference to the total probability of correct segmentations.

Input String	Segmentation	Probability
ədɔg	ə#dɔg	0.962
əkæt	ə#kæt	0.959
ðədɔg	ðə#dɔg	0.947
ðəkæt	ðə#kæt	0.948
ðədɔgz	ðə#dɔg#z	0.954
ðəkæts	ðə#kæt#s	0.933

Table 3: Probability assigned to the correct segmentation of all phrases after training

The UR learning problem as given to the model has three solutions. There are two standard solutions in which there is a fixed underlying representation for the plural, either /s/ or /z/, and it either voices or devoices, violating IDENT, in order to satisfy AGREE. Given the data in Table (2) there is no reason to believe that /s/ or /z/ is a more likely UR for the plural, so the learner should reach these two solutions with equal likelihood. The third solution is UR selection, which is specific to the use of URCs, and involves choosing between the URs /s/ and /z/ to satisfy AGREE without violating IDENT. The data in (2) do not suggest that any one solution is preferable over another, so any solution is considered correct as long as it results in the desired outputs and segmentations.

In 100 simulations with all weights initialized at 1.0, the learner converged on a single voicing assimilation solution to the critical data points, *the cats* and *the dogs*, 51 times. A dominant solution is defined here as a solution in which there is a single candidate in both relevant tableau with a probability greater than 0.70. In 24 of these 51 solutions the plural was underlyingly voiceless and mapped unfaith-

{DOG}+{PLURAL}	4.00 {PLURAL}=/z/	3.75 AGREE	3.70 {PLURAL}=/s/	0.00 IDENT	$\mathcal{H}$	p
/dɔg+z/→[dɔg#z]	0	0	-1	0	-3.70	0.57
/dɔg+s/→[dɔg#z]	-1	0	0	-1	-4.00	0.42
/dɔg+s/→[dɔg#s]	-1	-1	0	0	-7.75	0.01

Tableau 6: A final grammar with free variation between voicing assimilation and UR selection

fully to [+VOICE] after /dɔg/, in the remaining 27 the plural was underlyingly [+VOICE] and mapped unfaithully to [-VOICE] after /kæt/.

In the other 49 runs, UR selection was used to an extent, but there was no clear dominant solution. In these cases there was free variation between UR selection and voicing assimilation candidates which yielded the same phonological surface form. Because an error is defined as a mismatch between an observed surface form and a structureless version of the predicted surface form, the learner has no reason to select between two candidates with equivalent surface forms. An example of this type of solution is shown in Tableau (6). The data as presented in Table (2) do not favor voicing assimilation or UR selection, so it is expected that the learner converge on these kinds of ambiguous solutions frequently.

The effect of a data point that forced one specific solution to be preferred was tested by adding the vowel final word *eye* to the training data in the singular and plural. The plural form, *eyes*, surfaces as [aiz], taking a [+VOICE] plural morpheme with no possible AGREE violation. To the analyst this suggests that /-z/ is the underlying form of the plural morpheme and that voicing assimilation is responsible for the [s] that surfaces after voiceless consonants. In 100 more simulations identical to those described above but with the *eye(s)* data points added to the language, the learner now converged on voicing assimilation with a [+VOICE] UR 96 times. The remaining four final grammars represented ambiguous solutions similar to that shown in Tableau (6) and segmentation accuracy remained near ceiling.

Finally, to test the ability of the model to perform adult like parsing of novel words the trained grammar from one of the previous 100 simulations was used to make predictions about the segmentations of the previously unencountered surface forms [wuks] and [wugz] from the morphosyntactic elements {WUK} and {WUG} plus {PLURAL}.

The probabilities of key candidate segmentations are shown in Table (4). Generated candidates which are not possible segmentations of the input string, such as [wug$_1$#ugz$_2$] are not included in (4), but are all assigned near zero probabilities.

Input	Segmentation	Probability
{WUG}$_1$, {PLURAL}$_2$	w$_1$#ugz$_2$	0.024
	wu$_1$#gz$_2$	0.009
	wug$_1$#z$_2$	0.967
{WUK}$_1$, {PLURAL}$_2$	w$_1$#uks$_2$	0.061
	wu$_1$#ks$_2$	0.061
	wuk$_1$#s$_2$	0.878

Table 4: Probability of key segmentations of novel words suffixed with the plural morpheme

In these cases the model was able to correctly segment the novel words based solely on a high ranked constraint that the underlying form for the plural morpheme is /z/. In the [wuks] case, the probability of the correct segmentation is slightly hurt by the lack of a surface [z] but [s] here is a possible and likely phonological exponent of underlying /z/, making the correct segmentation drastically more likely than its competitors.

5 Discussion

When the *eye(s)* data points were included the training data were no longer agnostic towards the solution and the learner converged on the expected assimilation solution nearly all of the time. Recall that Smith (2015) stipulates that only suppletive forms can have multiple URCs in order to prevent the rampant use of UR selection rather than unfaithful phonological mappings. In this case, there were a large number of URCs for every word in the lexicon but the UR selection solution was reached only 4 out of 100 times. Consequently the restriction placed on URCs by Smith seems unnecessary. While there exists a solution to the dataset in which UR selection is responsible for every alternation, that solution appears strongly disfavored by the learner.

Assimilation represents a large portion of the space of possible weights compared to UR selection, making it easier for the learner to find. Setting aside extraneous UR constraints, the Hasse diagram in Figure (1) shows the necessary rankings for assimilation and UR selection. A direct line between two constraints means that the weight of the higher constraint must be greater than that of the lower one.

Assimilation: **UR selection:**

AGREE   {PL}=/z/   AGREE   IDENT

IDENT   {PL}=/s/   {PL}=/z/

                                      {PL}=/s/

Figure 1: Ranking arguments for assimilation and UR selection

Randomly sampling one million sets of weights from the uniform distribution between 0 and 5, the range of the final weights of most simulations run above, the ranking arguments for assimilation are satisfied 14.68% of the time, and for UR selection only 3.86%. Assimilation occupies roughly 80% of the solution space. The model implemented here used no regularization term, but regularization will further decrease the likelihood of UR selection as the assimilation solution requires that two constraints have weights greater than 0 (AGREE and IDENT) where the UR selection solution requires three (AGREE, IDENT, and {PL}=/z/).

6   Conclusions

The acquisition of segmentation, underlying representations, and phonological alternations are treated here as parallel and interacting processes. The result is a model that succeeds in learning phonological alternations while also learning segmentation with near perfect accuracy, albeit on a very simple test case.

This model succeeds at segmentation for the same reason that the transitional probability and PARSER models work. A UR constraint that refers to a correct UR, such as {√DOG}=/dɔg/, will be reinforced by every observed output, regardless of the word's context. A UR constraint that refers to an 'incorrect' UR, such as {√DOG}=/dɔgz/, will be reinforced only by surface forms that result from one particular concatenation of morphemes. Because of transitional probability minima, the correct UR constraints will end up highly ranked. Like PARSER, this approach effectively tracks statistical trends in the data without the need to explicitly store them. Unlike PARSER, this model does so using a pre-existing phonological framework which allows for the incorporation of segmentation into a larger model of phonological learning.

This model relies on the strong assumption that the meaning of the utterance is known to the learner as a set of morphosyntactic objects. Consequently, this model cannot account for Saffran et al.'s (1996) result, in which participants were able to segment a language consisting only of nonce words. However, the Saffran et al. tasks are far removed from naturalistic language acquisition. Segmentation is not learned in isolation before the rest of acquisition. Information regarding segmentation, phonological processes, and underlying representations are made available to the learner simultaneously.

The assumption that the set of meanings are known to the learner greatly reduces the complexity of the segmentation task by providing the learner with the number of boundaries to be drawn, however this does not necessarily reduce the validity of the model. A slightly relaxed assumption, that infants have at least partial knowledge about the meaning of an utterance and are actively trying to identify correspondences between the phonological material and this partial meaning, does not seem empirically unsound. It is likely that infants are making use of contextual cues to make hypotheses about the semantic content of sentences from an early stage of learning, as evidenced by research showing that lexical representations are present as early as 6 months (Bergelson and Aslin, 2017). There is no reason that the infant needs to directly discover how many boundaries are in an utterance, they need only look for as many substrings as there are hypothesized meanings.

Beyond acquisition, this model captures the ability of adult speakers to segment novel words after a single exposure. Statistical models assume the minimum amount of linguistic knowledge of the learner, often relying only on representations of phonemes or syllables. This may be a sound assumption to make about infants in the earliest stages of acquisition, but it fails to allow a mechanism for higher level linguistic information to be incorporated as it is acquired. The end state of the presented model represents a speaker that is able to make simultaneous use of lexical and phonological knowledge to segment novel forms.

References

Adam Albright. 2002. *The identification of bases in morphological paradigms*. Ph.D. thesis, University of California, Los Angeles.

Diana Apoussidou. 2007. *The learnability of metrical phonology*. Ph.D. thesis, University of Amsterdam.

Elika Bergelson and Richard N. Aslin. 2017. Nature and origins of the lexicon in 6-mo-olds. *Proceedings of the National Academy of Sciences*, 114(49).

Jean Berko Gleason. 1958. The child's learning of English morphology. *Word*, 14, 08.

Arthur Dempster, Natalie Laird, and Donald B. Rubin. 1977. Maximum likelihood from incomplete data via the EM algorithm. *Journal of the Royal Statistical Society Series B*, 39:1–38.

Sarah Eisenstat. 2009. Learning underlying forms with MaxEnt. Master's thesis, Brown University.

Micha Elsner, Sharon Goldwater, Naomi H. Feldman, and Frank Wood. 2013. A joint learning model of word segmentation, lexical acquisition and phonetic variability. In *Proceedings of the 2013 Conference on Empirical Methods in Natural Language Processing*, pages 42–54.

Micha Elsner, Stephanie Antetomaso, and Naomi H. Feldman. 2016. Joint word segmentation and phonetic category induction. In *Proceedings of the 54th Annual Meeting of the Association for Computational Linguistics*, pages 59–65.

Sharon Goldwater and Mark Johnson. 2003. Learning OT constraint rankings using a maximum entropy model. *Proceedings of the Stockholm Workshop on Variation in Optimality Theory*, pages 111–120.

Sharon Goldwater, Thomas L. Griffiths, and Mark Johnson. 2009. A bayesian framework for word segmentation: Exploring the effects of context. *Cognition*, 112:21–54.

Gaja Jarosz. 2013. Learning with hidden structure in optimality theory and Harmonic Grammar: beyond robust interpretive parsing. *Phonology*, 30(1):27–71.

Gaja Jarosz. 2015. Expectation driven learning of phonology. *Unpublished Manuscript*.

Gaja Jarosz. 2016. Learning opaque and transparent interactions in Harmonic Serialism. In *Proceedings of the 2015 Annual Meetings and Phonology, Vancouver BC*.

Gaja Jarosz. 2019. Computational modeling of phonological learning. *Annual Review of Linguistics*, 5:To appear.

Elizabeth K. Johnson and Peter W. Jusczyk. 2001. Word segmentation by 8-month-olds: When speech cues count more than statistics. *Journal of Memory and Language*, 44:548–567.

Mark Johnson, Joe Pater, Robert Staubs, and Emmanuel Dupoux. 2015. Sign constraints on feature weights improve a joint model of word segmentation and phonology. In *Proceedings of the 2015 Conference of the North American Chapter of the Association for Computational Linguistics: Human Language Technologies*, pages 303–313. Association for Computational Linguistics.

René Kager. 2008. Lexical irregularity and the typology of contrast. In Kristin Hanson and Sharon Inkelas, editors, *The Nature of the Word: Studies in Honor of Paul Kiparsky*, pages 397–432. MIT Press.

Joe Pater, Robert Staubs, Karen Jesney, and Brian Smith. 2012. Learning probabilities over underlying representations. In *Proceedings of the Twelfth Meeting of the Special Interest Group on Computational Morphology and Phonology*.

Pierre Perruchet and Annie Vinter. 1998. PARSER: A model for word segmentation. *Journal of Memory and Language*, 39:246–263.

Alan Prince and Paul Smolensky. 1993/2004. *Optimality Theory: Constraint Interaction in Generative Grammar*. Blackwell Publishing, Malden, MA.

Jenny R. Saffran, Richard N. Aslin, and Elissa L. Newport. 1996a. Statistical learning by 8-month-old infants. *Science*, 274.

Jenny R. Saffran, Elissa L. Newport, and Richard N. Aslin. 1996b. Word segmentation: The role of distributional cues. *Journal of Memory and Language*, 35:606–621.

Brian Smith. 2015. *Phonologically conditioned allomorphy and UR constraints*. Ph.D. thesis, University of Massachusetts Amherst.

Bruce Tesar and Paul Smolensky. 1998. Learnability in Optimality Theory. *Linguistic Inquiry*, 29:229–268.

Bruce Tesar. 2006. Faithful contrastive features in learning. *Cognitive Science*, 30:863–903.

Constraint breeding during on-line incremental learning[*]

Elliott Moreton
University of North Carolina, Chapel Hill
moreton@unc.edu

Abstract

An evolutionary algorithm for simultaneously inducing and weighting phonological constraints (Winnow-MaxEnt-Subtree Breeder) is described, analyzed, and illustrated. Implementing weights as sub-population sizes, reproduction with selection executes a new variant of Winnow (Littlestone, 1988), which is shown to converge. A flexible constraint schema, based on the same prosodic and autosegmental trees used in representations, is described, together with algorithms for mutation and recombination (mating). The algorithm is applied to explaining abrupt learning curves, and predicts an empirical connection between abruptness and language-particularity.

1 Introduction

This paper aims to unite, within the framework of Harmonic Grammar (Legendre et al., 1990), two facts about phonological learning. One is that not all constraints can be innate; some are parochial and must be induced from language data (e.g., Prince and Smolensky 1993, 101), raising the question of

how new constraints are induced. The other is that phonological learning can be abrupt, in the sense that a flat learning curve can later accelerate, both in nature (Smith, 1973; Macken and Barton, 1978; Vihman and Velleman, 1989; Barlow and Dinnsen, 1998; Levelt and van Oostendorp, 2007; Gerlach, 2010; Becker and Tessier, 2011; Guy, 2014) and in the lab (Moreton and Pertsova, 2016), raising the question of what is going on during the period of apparent stagnation .

The proposed answer to both is that constraint induction and constraint reweighting happen simultaneously via a single mechanism. Constraint weights are represented as sub-population sizes, i.e., the number of copies of a given constraint ("micro-constraints" in a "macro-constraint"). Error-driven reweighting of the macro-constraints happens when micro-constraints reproduce with fitness dependent on their contribution to error reduction. This process is shown to implement a modestly new incremental HG learning algorithm, Winnow-MaxEnt ($\S2$), which is then analyzed ($\S\S3, 4, 5$). A flexible prosodic and Feature-Geometric constraint schema, the Subtree Schema($\S6$), is used to add mutation and recombination ($\S7$), so that fitter constraint variants can evolve and rapidly supersede their predecessors, leading to abrupt changes in performance ($\S8$). The paper ends with discussion ($\S9$).

2 Weights as population sizes

The first step towards constraint breeding is to replace constraint weights with population sizes so that differential reproductive success implements up- or down-weighting. Without changing the har-

[*]The author is indebted to Brian Hsu, Katya Pertsova, and Jen Smith, Chris Wiesen of the Odum Institute at UNC-CH, and three anonymous SCiL reviewers for comments on previous drafts. The paper benefited from audience comments on portions of Sections 6 and 7 at the Workshop on Computational Modelling of Sound Pattern Acquisition (University of Alberta, February 14, 2010), at an MIT departmental colloquium (April 9, 2010), and at the Workshop on Grammar Induction (Cornell University, May 14, 2010). The research was supported in part by NSF BCS 1651105, "Inside phonological learning", to E. Moreton and K. Pertsova.

Proceedings of the Society for Computation in Linguistics (SCiL) 2019, pages 69-80.[*]
New York City, New York, January 3-6, 2019

mony of any candidate, we can replace any constraint of weight w with k "micro-constraints", i.e., clones of that constraint, each with weight w/k. Across an entire grammar, we can fix a parameter ζ to be the quantum of harmony, and replace every ("macro-") constraint of weight w with a population of w/ζ microconstraints of fixed weight ζ.

Changes in weight of a macro-constraint result from changes in population size of a micro-constraint. When an error occurs, each micro-constraint produces an offspring with probability $(1 + \epsilon)^d$, where d is the difference between the winner's and loser's score on that constraint and ϵ is the learning-rate parameter. If $(1+\epsilon)^d > k$ for some integer $k \geq 1$, the constraint produces k offspring with certainty, and another with probability $(1 + \epsilon)^d - k$. The new generation replaces the current generation.

The weight update at the macro level is therefore not described by a Perceptron-like algorithm, in which weights change by a fixed absolute increment, implementing gradient ascent on log-likelihood (Rosenblatt, 1958; Sutton and Barto, 1981; Jäger, 2007; Boersma and Pater, 2016), but rather by one in which the increment is proportional to the weight, i.e., by a variant of Winnow-2 (Littlestone, 1988). This algorithm is analyzed in Sections 3–5 below.

The weights grow exponentially in the number of mistakes (Propositions 1 and 2, below), so a population explosion may threaten to overwhelm the learner's limited computational substrate. That problem can be addressed using weight decay: On each update (or on each trial), the learner can delete each micro-constraint with a fixed probability, causing the macro-constraint weights to decay by an amount proportional to their magnitude and slowing population growth. Alternatively, the decay rate can be adjusted dynamically, randomly deleting or duplicating micro-constraints to maintain a fixed total micro-constraint population size.

3 The Winnow-MaxEnt algorithm

Winnow-MaxEnt, the learning algorithm induced by the constraint-breeding algorithm, is similar to Winnow-2 (Littlestone, 1988), but with the following differences. Winnow-MaxEnt (1) models k-alternative forced choices rather than yes-no clas-

sification, (2) responds probabilistically rather than deterministically, and (3) supports non-binary constraint scores. The original Winnow-2 was first suggested as a possible HG learner by Magri (2013). This section describes the two-alternative Winnow-MaxEnt. Generalization to $k > 2$ and to negative constraints is discussed in Section 5 below.

Each of n constraints (macro-constraints) gives a non-negative score to any candidate. The algorithm sees only the score vectors, and so is equally applicable to pure phonotactic learning (where each candidate is a surface form and there are no faithfulness constraints) and to alternation learning (where each candidate is an input-output pair and there are faithfulness constraints). We write x_i for the score given by C_i to Candidate x. Each constraint C_i has weight $w_i > 0$, so that the state of the learner is described by the weight vector $\mathbf{w} = (w_1, \ldots, w_n)$.

Given the experimenter's intended winner x^+ and intended loser x^-, the learner chooses x^+ with a probability that depends on the harmonies of the candidates. The version of the model discussed here uses the Luce choice rule applied to the exponentiated harmonies:

$$\Pr(x^+ \mid x^+, x^-) = \frac{\exp(\sum_{i=1}^{n} x_i^+ w_i)}{\exp(\sum_{i=1}^{n} x_i^+ w_i) + \exp(\sum_{i=1}^{n} x_i^- w_i)} \tag{1}$$

This rule (Luce, 1959, 23) is an independently-justified model of human choice behavior across a wide range of domains (Bradley and Terry, 1952; Luce, 1977; Strauss, 1992; Macmillan and Creelman, 2004). Its use with exponentiated harmonies yields a conditional Maximum Entropy (MaxEnt) model (Goldwater and Johnson, 2003; Jäger, 2007; Hayes and Wilson, 2008). The losers ("negative evidence") may be presented to the learner explicitly in the form of a 2AFC experimental trial, or implicitly in the form of an internally-generated candidate set.

If x^+ is chosen, nothing changes. If x^- is chosen, the weights of winner-preferring constraints grow, and those of loser-preferring constraints shrink, according to the update rule

$$w_i' = w_i \alpha^{d_i} \tag{2}$$

where $\alpha = 1 + \epsilon$ for some fixed learning-rate parameter $\epsilon > 0$, and $d_i = x_i^+ - x_i^-$.

4 Convergence of Winnow-MaxEnt

Winnow-MaxEnt is different enough from Winnow-2 that convergence cannot be assumed on the basis of Littlestone (1988)'s proof for Winnow-2, though ideas from that proof are useful here. In fact, since the probability of an error cannot be zero, Winnow-MaxEnt does not converge at all, in the sense of ceasing to make mistakes. However, we will see that the error rate can be made arbitrarily small.

4.1 Consequences of the update rule

The Propositions presented in this subsection are derived from the update rule (Equation 2) and do not depend on the response rule, the candidate-set size, or the sign of the marks awarded.

We proceed as usual (Novikoff, 1963) by first assuming that the target concept is representable in the learner, and then finding lower and upper bounds on a function of the weights in terms of the number of mistakes. Let D be the (multi-)set of candidate pairs used in the experiment. Each pair consists of an intended winner x^+ and an intended loser x^-. The same pair may occur multiple times, and not all possible pairs need occur. A candidate that is the positive member of one pair may be the negative member of another. Suppose that there exist nonnegative weights $\mu = (\mu_1, \ldots, \mu_n)$ and a δ_μ such that for every candidate pair $(x^+, x^-) \in D$,

$$\sum_{i=1}^{n} \mu_i(x_i^+ - x_i^-) > \delta_\mu > 0 \tag{3}$$

Proposition 1 (analogous to Littlestone (1988)'s Lemma 9). *Let* $W = \sum_{i=1}^{n} w_i$, *and let a target concept satisfying Inequality 3 be given. Let* $A_\mu = \delta_\mu / \sum_{i=1}^{n} \mu_i$. *Then after the t-th update,*

$$\log W(t) > \min_i(\log w_i(0)) + t \cdot A_\mu \log(1+\epsilon) \tag{4}$$

Proof. Taking the logarithm of Equation 2 yields $\log w_i' = \log w_i + (x_i^+ - x_i^-)\log\alpha$. Hence

$$\sum_{i=1}^{n} \mu_i \log w_i' = \sum_{i=1}^{n} \mu_i \log w_i + (\log\alpha)\sum_{i=1}^{n} \mu_i(x_i^+ - x_i^-) \tag{5}$$

Substituting from Equation 3 we have

$$\sum_{i=1}^{n} \mu_i \log w_i' > \sum_{i=1}^{n} \mu_i \log w_i + (\log\alpha)\cdot\delta_\mu \tag{6}$$

and so after t updates,

$$\sum_{i=1}^{n} \mu_i \log w_i(t) > \sum_{i=1}^{n} \mu_i \log w_i(0) + (\log\alpha)\cdot\delta_\mu \cdot t \tag{7}$$

Since all the μ_i's are nonnegative, the sum on the left doesn't get smaller if we replace all the weights with the largest weight, and the sum on the right doesn't get larger if we replace all the weights with the smallest weight. Let $i^* = \arg\max_i w_i(t)$ and $\hat{i} = \arg\min_i w_i(0)$; then

$$\log w_{i^*}(t)\sum_{k=1}^{n}\mu_k > \log w_{\hat{i}}(0)\sum_{k=1}^{n}\mu_k + (\log\alpha)\cdot\delta_\mu\cdot t \tag{8}$$

Since the μ_i's are all nonnegative, we can divide through by their sum to conclude that

$$\log w_{i^*}(t) > \log w_{\hat{i}}(0) + t \cdot A_\mu \cdot \log\alpha \tag{9}$$

Since $\log W(t) = \log \sum_{i=0}^{n} w_i(t) > \log w_{i^*}(t)$, the claim is proven. $\qquad\square$

Proposition 2. *Let a target concept satisfying Inequality 3 be given. Let* $\Sigma^+ = \sum_{i=1}^{n} x_i^+ w_i$ *and* $\Sigma^- = \sum_{i=1}^{n} x_i^- w_i$ *for a given winner-loser pair* (x^+, x^-). *Then for any* $\epsilon \leq 1/(d_{max} - 1)$,

$$\log W(t) \leq \log W(0) + \epsilon \cdot \sum_{\tau=0}^{t-1} \frac{\Sigma^+(\tau) - \Sigma^-(\tau)}{W(\tau)}$$
$$+ t \cdot \frac{d_{max}^2 \epsilon^2}{1 - (d_{max} - 1)\epsilon} \tag{10}$$

Proof. From the update rule in Equation 2 plus the binomial theorem,

$$W' = W + \sum_{i=1}^{n}(\alpha^{d_i} - 1)w_i$$
$$= W + \sum_{i=1}^{n}(d_i\epsilon + O(\epsilon^2))w_i \tag{11}$$
$$= W + \epsilon(\Sigma^+ - \Sigma^-) + O(\epsilon^2)W$$

To bound the $O(\epsilon^2)$ term explicitly, we rewrite Equation 11 as

$$W' = W + \sum_{i|d_i>0}(\alpha^{d_i} - 1)w_i + \sum_{i|d_i<0}(\alpha^{d_i} - 1)w_i \tag{12}$$

Since $\epsilon(\Sigma^+ - \Sigma^-) = \sum_{i=1}^{n} \epsilon d_i w_i$, we can rewrite that again as

$$W' = W + \epsilon(\Sigma^+ - \Sigma^-)$$
$$+ \underbrace{\sum_{i|d_i>0}(\alpha^{d_i} - 1 - \epsilon d_i)w_i}_{Y} + \underbrace{\sum_{i|d_i<0}(\alpha^{d_i} - 1 - \epsilon d_i)w_i}_{Z} \tag{13}$$

By Theorem 2 of Mitrinović (1970, p. 34),

$$(1+x)^n - 1 \le \frac{nx}{1 - (n-1)x} \tag{14}$$

for $n > 1$ and $-1 \le x \le 1/(n-1)$. This clearly also holds for $n = 0$ and $n = 1$ as long as $x \ge 0$. Hence for $d_i \ge 0$ and $\epsilon \le 1/(d_{\max} - 1)$,

$$\alpha^{d_i} - 1 \le \frac{d_i\epsilon}{1 - (d_i - 1)\epsilon} \tag{15}$$

with strict equality if $d_i = 0$ or $d_i = 1$. Therefore,

$$Y \le \sum_{i|d_i>0} d_i\epsilon\left(\frac{1}{1 - (d_i - 1)\epsilon} - 1\right)w_i \tag{16}$$
$$\le \sum_{i|d_i>0} d_i\epsilon\left(\frac{(d_i - 1)\epsilon}{1 - (d_i - 1)\epsilon}\right)w_i$$

Likewise,

$$Z = \sum_{i|d_i<0}(\alpha^{-|d_i|} - 1 + \epsilon|d_i|)w_i \tag{17}$$

If $n, x \ge 0$, then by the binomial theorem, $(1 + x)^n \ge 1 + nx$, so

$$(1+x)^{-n}-1 = \frac{1}{(1+x)^n}-1 \le \frac{1}{1+nx}-1 = \frac{-nx}{1+nx} \tag{18}$$

Hence,

$$Z \le \sum_{i|d_i<0}\left(\frac{-|d_i|\epsilon}{1 + |d_i|\epsilon} + |d_i|\epsilon\right)w_i \le \sum_{i|d_i<0}\frac{(|d_i|\epsilon)^2}{1 + |d_i|\epsilon}w_i \tag{19}$$

The sum $Y + Z$ is therefore bounded by

$$Y + Z \le \sum_{i=0}^{n}\max\left\{\begin{array}{c}\frac{|d_i|(|d_i|-1)\epsilon^2}{1-(|d_i|-1)\epsilon} \\ \frac{|d_i|^2\epsilon^2}{1+|d_i|\epsilon}\end{array}\right\}w_i \tag{20}$$

Combining the larger numerator and smaller denominator to get a fraction that is larger than either, we have

$$Y + Z \le \sum_{i=1}^{n}\frac{d_i^2\epsilon^2}{1 - (|d_i| - 1)\epsilon}w_i \tag{21}$$
$$\le \frac{d_{\max}^2\epsilon^2}{1 - (d_{\max} - 1)\epsilon}W$$

Combining Inequalities 13 and 21 yields

$$W' \le W\left(1 + \epsilon\frac{\Sigma^+ - \Sigma^-}{W} + \frac{d_{\max}^2\epsilon^2}{1 - (d_{\max} - 1)\epsilon}\right) \tag{22}$$

Since $\log(1 + x) \le x$, we have

$$\log W' \le \log W + \epsilon\frac{\Sigma^+ - \Sigma^-}{W} + \frac{d_{\max}^2\epsilon^2}{1 - (d_{\max} - 1)\epsilon} \tag{23}$$

from which the proposition follows by summation from $\tau = 0$ to $\tau = t - 1$. $\square$

Proposition 3. *Let a target concept satisfying Inequality 3 be given, and let A_{max} be the least upper bound on A_{μ} over all μ. Let $V = \log W(0) - \min_i(\log w_i(0))$, and let $a = (\Sigma^+ - \Sigma^-)/W$ for a given winner-loser pair (x^+, x^-). Then for any $\theta > 0$, there exist ϵ_θ and t_θ such that when Winnow-MaxEnt is run with $\epsilon = \epsilon_\theta$,*

$$\frac{1}{t}\cdot\sum_{\tau=0}^{t-1}a(\tau) \ge A_{max} - \theta \tag{24}$$

for all $t \ge t_\theta$.

Proof. Propositions 1 and 2 together imply that for all $t \ge 0$ and $\epsilon \le 1/(d_{\max} - 1)$,

$$\epsilon\sum_{\tau=0}^{t-1}a(\tau) \ge -V + tA\log(1 + \epsilon) - \frac{td_{\max}^2\epsilon^2}{1 - (d_{\max} - 1)\epsilon} \tag{25}$$

Since $\log 1 + x \ge x - x^2/2$,

$$\frac{1}{t}\cdot\sum_{\tau=0}^{t-1}a(\tau) \ge A - \frac{1}{2}A\epsilon - \frac{d_{\max}^2\epsilon}{1 - (d_{\max} - 1)\epsilon} - \frac{V}{\epsilon t} \tag{26}$$

Sufficiently small ϵ and large t make the right-hand side as close to A as desired. $\square$

To bound t_θ, we note that the remainder in Inequality 26 is bounded above by

$$f(\epsilon, t) = \frac{1}{2}A\epsilon + \frac{d_{\max}^2\epsilon}{1 - (d_{\max} - 1)\epsilon} + \frac{V}{\epsilon t} \tag{27}$$
$$< \frac{1}{2}A\epsilon + \frac{d_{\max}^2\epsilon}{1 - d_{\max}\epsilon} + \frac{V}{\epsilon t}$$

so that $f(\epsilon, t) < g(d_{\max}\epsilon, 1/t)$,

$$g(x, y) = Fx + d_{\max}\frac{x}{1 - x} + \frac{Gy}{x} \tag{28}$$

where $F = A/2d_{\max}$ and $G = Vd_{\max}$. Any pair (ϵ, t) that satisfies $g(d_{\max}\epsilon, 1/t) = \theta$ also satisfies

$f(\epsilon, t) < \theta$. Setting $g(x, y) = \theta$ and solving for y yields

$$y = h(x) = \frac{1}{G}\left(\theta x - Fx^2 - d_{\max}\frac{x^2}{1-x}\right) \quad (29)$$

for $x \in (0, 1)$. We want to choose $x(= d_{\max}\epsilon)$ so as to maximize $y(= 1/t)$. The function $h(x)$ is hard to maximize analytically, so instead we maximize a more tractable minorant $i(x)$ to bound the maximum of $h(x)$ below. Using the fact that $1/(1-x) \leq 1 + 2x$, $x \in [0, 1/2]$, we have

$$i(x) = \frac{1}{G}\left(\theta x - Fx^2 - d_{\max}(x^2 + 2x^3)\right) \quad (30)$$

Then $h(x) \geq i(x)$ for all $x \in (0, 1/2]$. Differentiation shows that $i(x)$ attains a maximum at

$$x_\theta = \frac{\sqrt{(d_{\max} + F)^2 + 6d_{\max}\theta} - (d_{\max} + F)}{6d_{\max}} \quad (31)$$

Whatever the global maximum of $h(x)$ might be, it is at least as big as $i(x_\theta)$, i.e. $\max_{x \in (0,\infty)} h(x) \geq \max_{x \in (0,1/2]} h(x) \geq h(x_\theta) \geq i(x_\theta)$, which is

$$i(x_\theta) = \frac{(T + U^2)\left(\sqrt{T + U^2} - U\right) - \frac{1}{2}TU}{54V} \quad (32)$$

where $T = 6\theta/d_{\max}$ and $U = 1 + A/2d_{\max}^2$. Therefore, there exist an $\epsilon_\theta = x_\theta/d_{\max}$ and a $t_\theta = 1/i(x_\theta)$ such that $f(\epsilon_\theta, t_\theta) \leq g(x_\theta, i(x_\theta)) = \theta$. Thus, $t_\theta = O(\theta^{-3/2})$. The smallest possible V occurs when all the initial weights are equal, in which case $V = \log n$ and $t_\theta = O(\log n)$; i.e., the time bound is not very sensitive to the number of constraints.

4.2 2AFC performance

This subsection addresses the question of how the bound on the relative harmony gap (Proposition 3) translates into a bound on 2AFC error probability. From Equation 1, the log-odds of choosing the correct candidate is

$$\log \text{odds}(x^+ \mid x^+, x^-, \mathbf{w}) = \Sigma^+ - \Sigma^- = aW \quad (33)$$

where a is defined as in Proposition 3. The cumulative average log-odds of a correct response across all trials where an error actually occurred is therefore

$$L(t) = \frac{1}{t}\sum_{\tau=0}^{t-1} a(\tau)W(\tau) \quad (34)$$

where τ indexes errors as in Propositions 2 and 3. Let θ be given and let ϵ_θ and t_θ be as in Proposition 3, and $t \geq t_\theta$. From Proposition 1, for any $\tau \geq 0$,

$$W(\tau) \geq \exp(\min_i(\log w_i(0)) + A_{\max}(\log \alpha_\theta)\tau)$$
$$\geq \min_i(w_i(0))\exp(A_{\max}\log(\alpha_\theta)\tau)$$
$$\geq \min_i(w_i(0))\exp(A_{\max}\epsilon_\theta\tau)$$
$$(35)$$

since $1 + x \geq \log x$. This lower bound on $W(\tau)$ is a strictly increasing function of τ. The same is not necessarily true of $a(\tau)$, but we can see that for a fixed value of $A(t) = (1/t)\sum_{\tau=0}^{t-1} a(\tau)$, the lower bound on $L(t)$ is minimized when $a(0), a(1), \ldots, a(\tau^*)$ are as big as possible — i.e., equal to $d_{\max}$ — and the rest of the $a(\tau)$ are zero. Thus $\tau^* = t \cdot A(t)/d_{\max}$. To skirt complications when τ^* is not an integer, we switch to a continuous approximation, using the fact that $\sum_{k=0}^{n} e^k \geq \int_0^n e^x dx$:

$$L(t) \geq \frac{1}{t}\int_0^{\tau^*} d_{\max}W(\tau)d\tau$$
$$\geq \frac{d_{\max}}{t}\int_0^{\tau^*} \mu_0\exp(A_{\max}\epsilon_\theta\tau)d\tau$$
$$\geq \frac{\mu_0 d_{\max}}{A_{\max}\epsilon_\theta}\frac{1}{t}\left(\exp\left(\frac{A_{\max}\epsilon_\theta}{d_{\max}}tA(t)\right) - 1\right)$$
$$(36)$$

where $\mu_0 = \min_i(w_i(0))$. From Proposition 3, we know that $A(t) \geq A_{\max} - \theta$, so

$$L(t) \geq \frac{\mu_0 d_{\max}}{A_{\max}\epsilon_\theta}\frac{1}{t}\left(\exp\left(\frac{A_{\max}\epsilon_\theta(A_{\max} - \theta)}{d_{\max}}t\right) - 1\right)$$
$$(37)$$

Thus, the cumulative mean log-odds of a correct response on error trials (i.e., the log-odds of a correct response immediately before each error was committed) is bounded below by a function that is only slightly less than exponential in the number of mistakes. (This of course causes the mistakes themselves to become less and less frequent, so the log-odds grows slower in terms of the number of trials.)

This is a worst-case bound that does not depend on how the training sequence is constructed. Since error trials oversample error-prone 2AFC pairs, the cumulative mean log-odds of a correct response on all trials is expected to be greater than that on the error trials.

4.3 Simulation results

The analysis was checked by a simulation whose parameters were chosen to roughly approximate a typical Harmonic Grammar phonological analysis. For each replication of the simulation, n was sampled uniformly from $\{2, \ldots, 20\}$, and $d_{\max}$ from $\{1, 2, 3, 4\}$. Numbers m and r were uniformly sampled from 4 to 64 and from 8 to 256, respectively. A weight vector μ of length n was made by uniformly sampling each entry from the interval $(0, 1)$. The cells of an $m \times n$ tableau (candidates $\times$ constraints) were filled by uniformly sampling each from $\{-d_{\max}, \ldots, 0\}$, and one was randomly (uniformly) chosen to be the most-harmonic positive stimulus, so long as it was not the most- or least-harmonic of all. The other candidates' harmonies thus determined their positive/negative status. The least upper bound $A_{\max}$ was approximated by maximizing A_μ over all μ consistent with the concept using the quasi-Newton method of Byrd et al. (1995) as implemented in the `optim` function of Version 3.2.2 of the `stats` package in R (R Core Team, 2015). A number r of winner-loser pairs was made by randomly sampling (uniformly, with replacement) from the positive and negative candidates, provided that some intended winners had less-than-perfect scores. A θ was sampled uniformly from $[1/32, 1/8]$, ϵ_θ was chosen as in Equation 31, and t_θ was chosen as in Equation 32. Initial weights were all set to 1. Winnow-MaxEnt was trained until the learner's cumulative average relative harmony gap (the left-hand side of Inequality 26) reached or exceeded $A_{\max} - \theta/2$, or until $5t_\theta$ errors had occurred. (If that criterion was already met before any training, the simulation was discarded and replaced.)

In 10,000 replications, the bound of Inequality 26 always underestimated the cumulative average harmony gap at every time point (error) in every replication by a margin of at least 0.0823 (median, 0.9732). The bound of Inequality 32 always overestimated the actual number of errors required to reach $A_{\max} - \theta$ by a factor of at least 3.93, and usually by very much more (the median was a factor of 52.60). The bound in Inequality 37 always underestimated the actual log-odds at $t = t_\theta$ by at least a margin of 1.084 (median, 280.3). Average-case performance in actual applications may therefore be much better.

5 Beyond 2AFC with positive constraints

Because the Luce choice rule describes how to choose one item out of a set of alternatives on the basis of nonnegative harmony values, k-AFC for $k > 2$ requires no amendment for positive constraints. For negative constraints, we let the alternatives be, not individual candidates $x_i \in X$, competing to be the winning individual on the basis of their harmonies $h_{\mathbf{w}}(x_i)$, but rather sets of $k - 1$ candidates $X_i = X - \{x_i\}$, competing to be the losing set on the basis of their harmonies $H_{\mathbf{w}}(X_j) = \sum_{x \in X_j} h_{\mathbf{w}}(x) = \left(\sum_{x \in X} h_{\mathbf{w}}(x) \right) - h_{\mathbf{w}}(x_j)$. Then

$$
\begin{aligned}
\Pr(x_i \mid X, \mathbf{w}) &= \frac{\exp\left(\sum_{x \in X} h_{\mathbf{w}}(x) \right) / \exp(h_{\mathbf{w}}(x_j))}{\sum_{j=1}^{k} \exp\left(\sum_{x \in X} h_{\mathbf{w}}(x) \right) / \exp(h_{\mathbf{w}}(x_j))} \\
&= \frac{\exp(-h_{\mathbf{w}}(x_i))}{\sum_{j=1}^{k} \exp(-h_{\mathbf{w}}(x_j))}
\end{aligned}
\tag{38}
$$

In other words, negative (penalizing) constraints can be implemented by simply inverting the sign of the marks awarded.

6 Constraints as representation subtrees

The next step is a constraint schema that enables breeding and mutation. We can define markedness constraints as subtrees of autosegmental representations, such that every representation is itself a constraint (Burzio, 1999). The representational system in the implemented model is a hierarchical prosodic and featural tree structure simplified from Gussenhoven and Jacobs (2005, Ch. 5) by omitting feet and moras. Figure 6 shows an example.

A markedness constraint is a representation, rooted at a PrWd, which awards a mark to a candidate for each time it matches part of that candidate. Examples of familiar markedness constraints expressed in this schema are shown in Figure 2. The symbols L and R mark left and right constituent boundaries.

The Subtree Schema (Moreton, 2010b,a,c) differs from previous explicitly described constraint schemas used in implemented inductive learning models (Hayes and Wilson, 2008; Adriaans and Kager, 2010; Pizzo, 2013; Rasin and Katzir, 2016) in that it imposes no extra limits on constraint structure beyond those inherited from representational structure; it integrates autosegmental tier structure

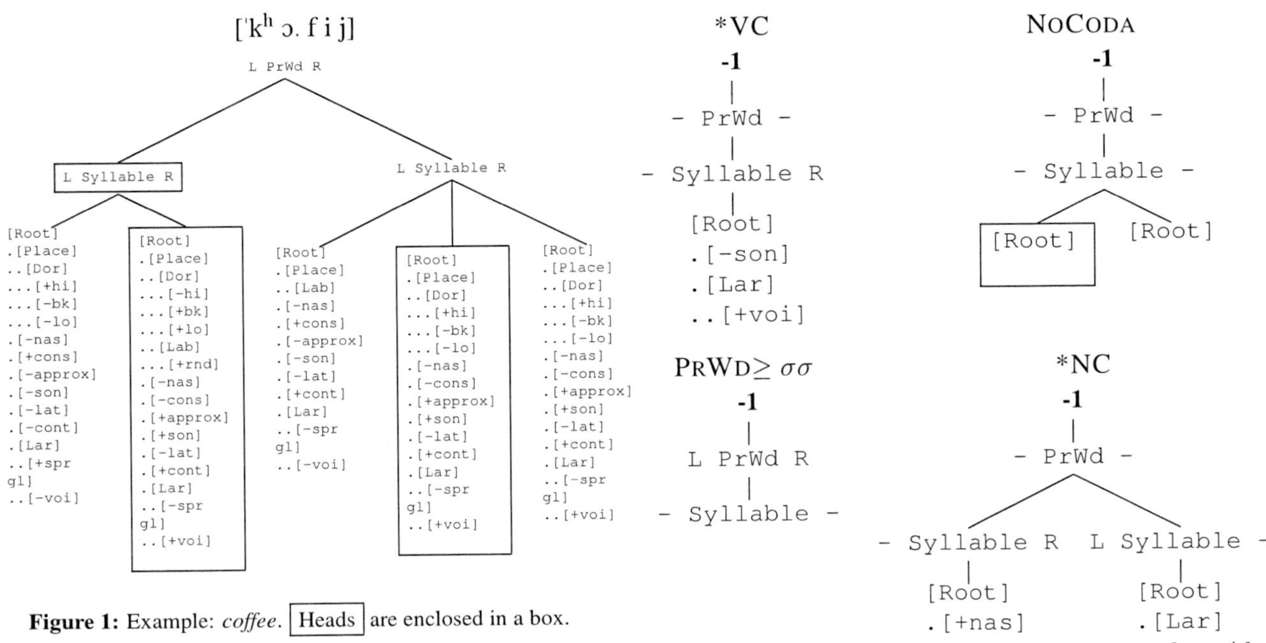

Figure 1: Example: *coffee*. Heads are enclosed in a box.

Figure 2: Some familiar markedness constraints in the Subtree Schema: *VC, final-obstruent devoicing (Ito and Mester, 2003); NoCoda (Prince and Smolensky, 1993); a constraint enforcing a disyllabic minimal prosodic word; *NC (Pater, 2004).

with prosodic constituent structure, thus supporting positional constraints; it accommodates non-adjacent dependencies; it allows variables (not discussed here) for (e.g.) AGREE, OCP, and reduplication; and it provides continuity between constraints and representations (Golston, 1996; Burzio, 1999). The tree structure also lends itself to a recursive breeding algorithm, as described in the next section.

7   Mutation, recombination, and selection

We now let the micro-constraints reproduce with variation, so that the Winnow-MaxEnt rule acts as a selective force in an evolutionary algorithm. Evolutionary algorithms have long been applied to problems closely related to the ones addressed here, including evolving receptive fields for inputs to the single-layer perceptron (Nakano et al., 1995) and evolving tree structures (Cramer, 1985; Koza, 1989). Replication of mental representations with variation, recombination, and selection is a leading theory of human creativity in other domains (Simonton, 1999, 2004; Dietrich and Haider, 2015).

Each constraint which is chosen to breed is randomly paired with another chosen breeder of equal or greater fitness (reproductive probability). The two constraints are mated recursively. The offspring of two prosodic-category nodes randomly copies node-level properties (left and right anchors) from the par-

ents. Immediate dependents of each parent node are randomly paired, preserving left-to-right order, and leaving some dependents unpaired if one parent node has more than the other. Each pair of dependents then breeds to make one node in the offspring. An unpaired dependent is either inherited intact or deleted, with probability 1/2. The offspring of paired compatible unary-feature nodes (e.g., [+Cor] bred with [+Cor]) is computed analogously: Subfeature nodes common to both parents are paired and bred recursively; unpaired nodes are either copied intact or deleted, with probability 1/2. The offspring of paired compatible binary-feature nodes (e.g., [+voice] bred with [−voice]) is identical to each of the parents with probability 1/2. An example is shown in Figure 3.

The offspring then undergoes undirected mutation. Mutation is recursive (when a node is exposed to the hazard, so are its dependents). Mutations include gaining, losing, or duplicating a dependent node; designating, undesignating, or redesignating a constituent as a prosodic head; setting or unsetting the left and right prosodic anchors; and invert-

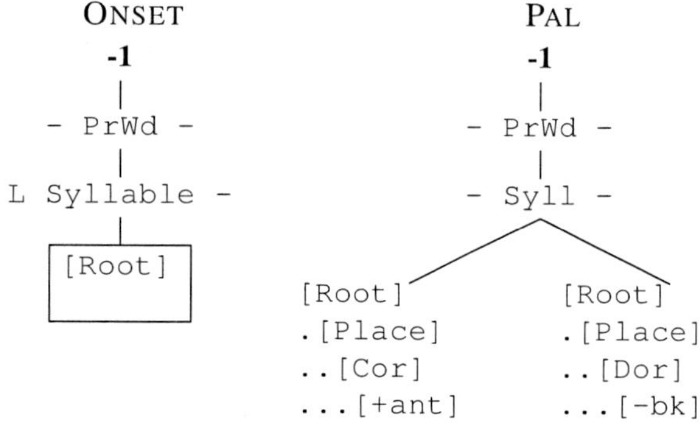

One offspring, before mutation:

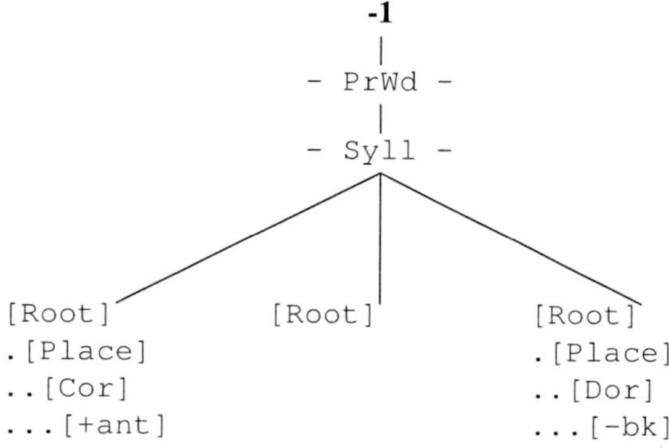

Same offspring, mutated:

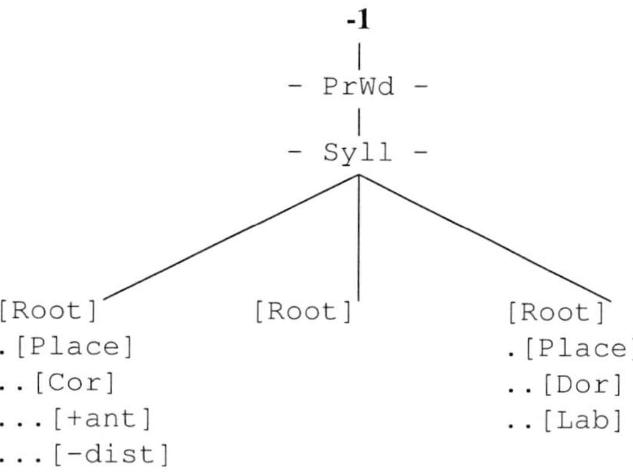

Figure 3: Breeding and mutation, illustrated with parents ONSET (à la Smith 2003, 2012) and PAL (McCarthy, 1999).

ing the coefficient on a binary feature. The probability of each is controlled by a separate parameter. A macro-constraint thus becomes an equivalence class of formally diverse micro-constraints which assign the same marks to all of the candidates.

8 Constraint breeding in practice

The combination of Winnow-MaxEnt with the Subtree Schema is illustrated using an artificial phono-

tactic pattern. Candidates were the initial syllables from the stimuli of Saffran and Thiessen (2003, 494). The positive stimuli (winners) had the form $\{p, t, k\}V\{b, d, g\}$ and the negative stimuli (losers) $\{b, d, g\}V\{p, t, k\}$. The population size was fixed at $n = 1000$ (micro-)constraints, which initially were identical clones that gave -1 mark to every PrWd. On each trial, a random candidate pair was presented for 2AFC judgement. When a mistake happened, the quantity $r_i = \alpha^{x_i^+ - x_i^-}$ was calculated for each constraint C_i. If $r_i \geq 1$, the constraint made one offspring with certainty, then another with probability $1 - r_i$. If $r_i < 1$, the constraint made one offspring with probability r_i. If the offspring violated a "hard" restriction on representations (e.g., a ban on [+high +low]), or scored all candidates alike, breeding was retried up to 100 times before giving up and accepting the undesirable offspring. The new generation then completely replaced the old.

For one set of 50 simulations, the harmony quantum ζ was set to 0.01, the learning rate ϵ to 0.25, the mutation probability to 0.25, and the probabilities of each individual mutation type to 0.1. In 17 of them, performance on the 1000th trial was above 0.90 correct. Two examples are shown in Figure 4 to illustrate the variety of simulation behavior.

In the top panel, performance is initially at chance on all pairs. As the constraint population diversifies, so do the error probabilities of the individual pairs, but average performance stays at chance. That changes after two near-simultaneous innovations, the fell-swoop constraint $C_9 = *[-\text{voice}]]_\sigma$ (Trial 378) and a parochial version $C_{11} = *V : [-\text{voice}]]_\sigma$ (Trial 384) that applies only when the vowel is long (tense). Both macro-constraints prosper, but greater generality of C_9 gives it a reproductive advantage (it breeds whenever C_{11} does, but not vice versa). By Trial 999, C_9 is represented 591 times in the population (equivalent to a weight of $591 \cdot \zeta = 5.91$). The slight bifurcation at the end, visible as a thickening of the gray line, is due to 48 instances of C_{11} that cause slightly better accuracy for long vowels.

In the bottom panel, the fell-swoop constraint $*[-\text{voice}]]_\sigma$ does not arise until Trial 732, by which time two parochial constraints, one for long- and one for short-vowelled syllables, have already established themselves and slowed the learning rate. The

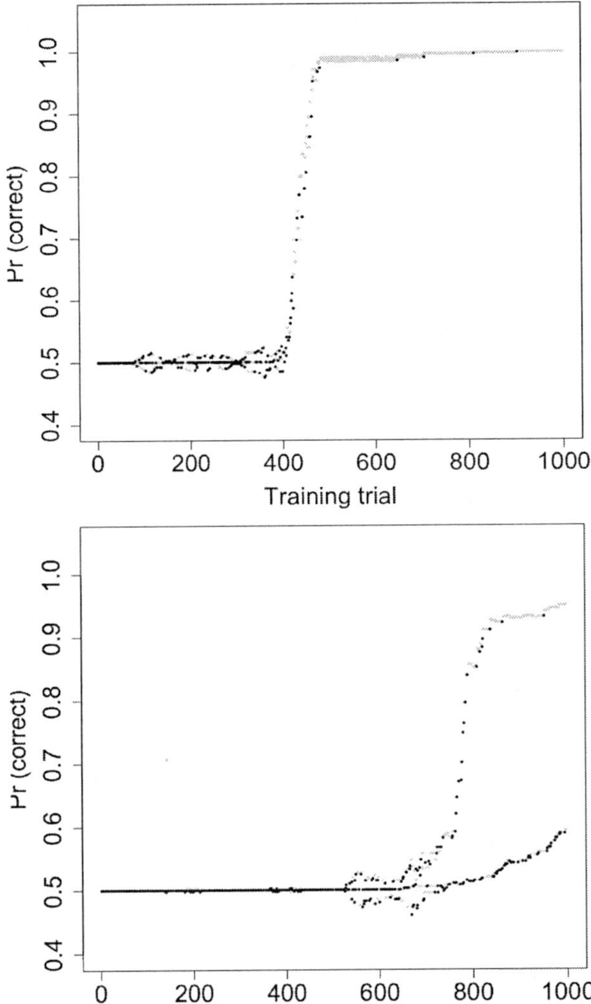

Figure 4: Probability of correct response to the specific winner-loser pair presented on each trial, for one run of the simulation. Black points show errors.

two have prospered unequally (284× vs. 28× on Trial 999), so that the learning curves for the two syllable types diverge. The fell-swoop constraint is still feeble (7×) because the learner nearly stopped making errors on long-vowel syllables before it was discovered, so its weight now grows in tandem with that of the short-vowel constraint. When the simulation ends the learner is near-perfect when the vowel is long, but only a bit above chance when it is short. The early discovery of a solution for a subset of the data has inhibited a more general solution.

9 Discussion

Sigmoidal abruptness in an observed learning curve has often been taken as distinguishing "rule-based" learning by serial hypothesis testing from "cue-based" associative learning by gradual weight changes (Ashby et al., 1998; Love, 2002; Maddox and Ashby, 2004; Smith et al., 2012; Kurtz et al., 2013). The theory is that while the curve is flat, the learner is serially testing and discarding incorrect rule hypotheses, and the jump occurs when the correct rule is found. The Winnow-MaxEnt-Subtree Breeder model shows that the same observation is consistent with an incremental constraint-based learner. While the curve is flat, this learner is exploring the space of possible constraints, and the jump occurs when a useful mutant arises and prospers.

This behavior leads to a hypothesis. Becker and Tessier (2011) have proposed a correlation between abruptness and innateness (or at least pre-existingness), viz., that a U-shaped kink in an L1 learning curve means that the learner has innovated a constraint and added it at the top of the hierarchy, causing a transient drop in adult-like performance. Analogously, the behavior of Winnow-MaxEnt-Subtree Breeder implies that patterns which depend only on preexisting constraints (supplied by Universal Grammar, or transferred from a previously-acquired language) should be acquired less abruptly than patterns which depend on constraints that are specific to the particular natural or artificial language.

Another consequence is an emergent bias in favor of more-general constraints. In Winnow-MaxEnt-Subtree Breeder, general constraints automatically outcompete parochial ones because they are more fit (see discussion of Figure 4, above; Pater and Moreton 2012; Moreton et al. 2017, §4.1). In that respect, the model is akin to the Minimum Description Length learner of Rasin and Katzir (2016), which adds, removes, and changes constraints without trying to anticipate their effects, rather than learners in which a drive towards generalization is hard-wired into the constraint-generation component (Hayes and Wilson 2008, §4.2.2, Adriaans and Kager 2010, 317f.).

References

Adriaans, F. and R. Kager (2010). Adding generalization to statistical learning: the induction of phonotactics from continuous speech. *Journal of Memory and Language 62*(3), 311–331.

Ashby, F. G., L. A. Alfonso-Reese, A. U. Turken, and E. M. Waldron (1998). A neuropsychological theory of multiple systems in category learning. *Psychological Review 105*(3), 442–481.

Barlow, J. A. and D. A. Dinnsen (1998). Asymmetrical cluster development in a disordered system. *Language Acquisition 7*(1), 1–49.

Becker, M. and A. Tessier (2011). Trajectories of faithfulness in child-specific phonology. *Phonology 28*, 163–196.

Boersma, P. and J. Pater (2016). Convergence properties of a gradual learning algorithm for Harmonic Grammar. In J. J. McCarthy and J. Pater (Eds.), *Harmonic Grammar and Harmonic Serialism*, pp. 389–434. Sheffield, England: Equinox.

Bradley, R. A. and M. E. Terry (1952). Rank analysis of incomplete block designs: I. the method of paired comparisons. *Biometrika 39*(3/4), 324–345.

Burzio, L. (1999). Surface-to-surface morphology: when your representations turn into constraints. MS, Department of Cognitive Science, Johns Hopkins University. ROA-341.

Byrd, R. H., P. Lu, J. Nocedal, and C. Zhu (1995). A limited memory algorithm for bound constrained optimization. *SIAM Journal of Scientific Computing 16*, 1190–1208.

Cramer, N. L. (1985). A representation for the adaptive generation of simple sequential programs. In J. Grefenstette (Ed.), *Proceedings of the First International Conference on Genetic Algorithms*, pp. 183–187.

Dietrich, A. and H. Haider (2015). Human creativity, evolutionary algorithms, and predictive representations: the mechanics of thought trials. *Psychonomic Bulletin and Review 22*, 897–915.

Gerlach, S. R. (2010). *The acquisition of consonant feature sequences: harmony, metathesis, and deletion patterns in phonological development*. Ph. D. thesis, University of Minnesota.

Goldwater, S. J. and M. Johnson (2003). Learning OT constraint rankings using a maximum entropy model. In J. Spenader, A. Erkisson, and O. Dahl (Eds.), *Proceedings of the Stockholm Workshop on Variation within Optimality Theory*, pp. 111–120.

Golston, C. (1996). Direct Optimality Theory: Representation as pure markedness. *Language 72*(4), 713–748.

Gussenhoven, C. and H. Jacobs (2005). *Understanding phonology* (2nd ed.). Understanding Language Series. London: Hodder Arnold.

Guy, G. R. (2014). Linking usage and grammar: generative phonology, exemplar theory, and variable rules. *Lingua 142*, 57–65.

Hayes, B. and C. Wilson (2008). A Maximum Entropy model of phonotactics and phonotactic learning. *Linguistic Inquiry 39*(3), 379–440.

Ito, J. and R. A. Mester (2003). On the sources of opacity in OT: coda processes in German. In C. Féry and R. van de Vijver (Eds.), *The syllable in Optimality Theory*, pp. 271–303. Cambridge, England: Cambridge University Press.

Jäger, G. (2007). Maximum Entropy models and Stochastic Optimality Theory. In J. Grimshaw, J. Maling, C. Manning, J. Simpson, and A. Zaenen (Eds.), *Architectures, rules, and preferences: a festschrift for Joan Bresnan*, pp. 467–479. Stanford, California: CSLI Publications.

Koza, J. R. (1989). Hierarchical genetic algorithms operating on populations of computer programs. In *Proceedings of the 11th International Joint Conference on Artificial Intelligence*, Volume 1, San Mateo, California, pp. 768–774. Morgan Kaufmann.

Kurtz, K. J., K. R. Levering, R. D. Stanton, J. Romero, and S. N. Morris (2013). Human learning of elemental category structures: revising the classic result of Shepard, Hovland, and Jenkins (1961). *Journal of Experimental Psychology: Learning, Memory, and Cognition 39*(2), 552–572.

Legendre, G., Y. Miyata, and P. Smolensky (1990). Can connectionism contribute to syntax? Harmonic Grammar, with an application. In M. Ziolkowski, M. Noske, and K. Deaton (Eds.), *Proceedings of the 26th Regional Meeting of the Chicago Linguistic Society*, Chicago, pp. 237–252. Chicago Linguistic Society.

Levelt, C. and M. van Oostendorp (2007). Feature

co-occurrence constraints in L1 acquisition. *Linguistics in the Netherlands 24*(1), 162–172.

Littlestone, N. (1988). Learning quickly when irrelevant attributes abound: a new linear-threshold algorithm. *Machine Learning 2*, 285–318.

Love, B. C. (2002). Comparing supervised and unsupervised category learning. *Psychonomic Bulletin and Review 9*(4), 829–835.

Luce, R. D. (1977). The Choice Axiom after twenty years. *Journal of Mathematical Psychology 15*, 215–233.

Luce, R. D. (2005 [1959]). *Individual choice behavior: a theoretical analysis*. New York: Dover.

Macken, M. A. and D. Barton (1978, March). The acquisition of the voicing contrast in English: a study of voice-onset time in word-initial stop consonants. Report from the Stanford Child Phonology Project.

Macmillan, N. A. and C. D. Creelman (2004). *Detection Theory: A User's Guide*. Cambridge, England: Lawrence Erlbaum.

Maddox, W. T. and F. G. Ashby (2004). Dissociating explicit and procedural-learning based systems of perceptual category learning. *Behavioural Processes 66*, 309–332.

Magri, G. (2013). HG has no computational advantages over OT: toward a new toolkit for computational OT. *Linguistic Inquiry 44*(4), 569–609.

McCarthy, J. J. (1999). Introductory OT on CD-ROM. Graduate Linguistic Students' Association, University of Massachusetts, Amherst.

Mitrinović, D. S. (1970). *Analytic inequalities*. New York: Springer-Verlag.

Moreton, E. (2010a, April). Connecting paradigmatic and syntagmatic simplicity bias in phonotactic learning. Department colloquium, Department of Linguistics, MIT.

Moreton, E. (2010b, February). Constraint induction and simplicity bias. Talk given at the Workshop on Computational Modelling of Sound Pattern Acquisition, University of Alberta.

Moreton, E. (2010c, May). Constraint induction and simplicity bias in phonotactic learning. Handout from a talk at the Workshop on Grammar Induction, Cornell University.

Moreton, E. (2018). Conditions on abruptness in a gradient-ascent Maximum Entropy learner. In G. Jarosz and J. Pater (Eds.), *Proceedings of the Society for Computation in Linguistics*, Volume 1, pp. Article 13.

Moreton, E., J. Pater, and K. Pertsova (2017). Phonological concept learning. *Cognitive Science 41*(1), 4–69.

Moreton, E. and K. Pertsova (2016). Implicit and explicit processes in phonotactic learning. In TBA (Ed.), *Proceedings of the 40th Boston University Conference on Language Development*, Somerville, Mass., pp. TBA. Cascadilla.

Nakano, K., H. Hiraki, and S. Ikeda (1995). A learning machine that evolves. In *Proceedings of ICEC–95*, pp. 808–813.

Novikoff, A. B. (1963). On convergence proofs for perceptrons. Technical report, Stanford Research Institute.

Pater, J. (2004). Austronesian nasal substitution and other $*NC$ effects. In J. J. McCarthy (Ed.), *Optimality Theory in phonology: a reader*, Chapter 14, pp. 271–289. Malden, Mass.: Blackwell.

Pater, J. and E. Moreton (2012). Structurally biased phonology: complexity in learning and typology. *Journal of the English and Foreign Languages University, Hyderabad 3*(2), 1–44.

Pizzo, P. (2013, January 19). Learning phonological alternations with online constraint induction. Slides from a presentation at the 10th Old World Conference on Phonology (OCP 10).

Prince, A. and P. Smolensky (1993). *Optimality Theory: constraint interaction in generative grammar*. Department of Linguistics, Rutgers University.

R Core Team (2015). *R: A Language and Environment for Statistical Computing*. Vienna, Austria: R Foundation for Statistical Computing.

Rasin, E. and R. Katzir (2016). On evaluation metrics in optimality theory. *Linguistic Inquiry 47*(2), 235–282.

Rosenblatt, F. (1958). The perceptron: a probabilistic model for information storage and organization in the brain. *Psychological Review 65*(6), 386–408.

Saffran, J. R. and E. D. Thiessen (2003). Pattern induction by infant language learners. *Developmental Psychology 39*(3), 484–494.

Simonton, D. K. (1999). Creativity as blind variation and selective retention: is the creative process Darwinian? *Psychological Inquiry 10*(4), 309–

328.

Simonton, D. K. (2004). *Creativity in science: chance, logic, genius, and Zeitgeist*. Cambridge University Press.

Smith, J. D., M. E. Berg, R. G. Cook, M. S. Murphy, M. J. Crossley, J. Boomer, B. Spiering, M. J. Beran, B. A. Church, F. G. Ashby, and R. C. Grace (2012). Implicit and explicit categorization: a tale of four species. *Neuroscience and Biobehavioral Reviews 36*(10), 2355–2369.

Smith, J. L. (2003). Onset sonority constraints and subsyllabic structure. MS, Department of Linguistics, University of North Carolina, Chapel Hill. ROA-602.

Smith, J. L. (2012). The formal definition of the ONSET constraint and implications for Korean syllable structure. In T. Borowsky, S. Kawahara, T. Shinya, and M. Sugahara (Eds.), *Prosody matters: essays in honor of Elisabeth Selkirk*, pp. 73–108. Equinox.

Smith, N. V. (1973). *The acquisition of phonology: a case study*. Cambridge, England: Cambridge University Press.

Strauss, D. (1992). The many faces of logistic regression. *American Statistician 46*(4), 321–327.

Sutton, R. S. and A. G. Barto (1981). Toward a modern theory of adaptive networks: expectation and prediction. *Psychological Review 88*(2), 135–170.

Vihman, M. M. and S. Velleman (1989). Phonological reorganization: a case study. *Language and Speech 32*, 149–170.

An Incremental Iterated Response Model of Pragmatics

Reuben Cohn-Gordon
Stanford

Noah D. Goodman
Stanford

Christopher Potts
Stanford

{reubencg, ngoodman, cgpotts}@stanford.edu

Abstract

Recent *Iterated Response* (IR) models of pragmatics conceptualize language use as a recursive process in which agents reason about each other to increase communicative efficiency. These models are generally defined over complete utterances. However, there is substantial evidence that pragmatic reasoning takes place incrementally during production and comprehension. We address this with an incremental IR model. We compare the incremental and global versions using computational simulations, and we assess the incremental model against existing experimental data and in the TUNA corpus for referring expression generation, showing that the model can capture phenomena out of reach of global versions.

1 Introduction

A number of recent Bayesian models of pragmatics conceptualize language use as a recursive process in which abstract speaker and listener agents reason about each other to increase communicative efficiency and enrich the meanings of the utterances they hear in context-dependent ways (Jäger 2007, 2012; Franke 2009; Frank and Goodman 2012; for overviews, see Franke and Jäger 2014; Goodman and Frank 2016). For example, in these models, pragmatic listeners reason, not about the literal semantics of the utterances they hear, but rather about pragmatic speakers reasoning about simpler listeners that are defined directly in terms of the literal semantics. In this back-and-forth, many phenomena characterized by Grice (1975) as *conversational implicatures* emerge naturally as probabilistic inferences.

In general, these *iterated response* (IR) models separate pragmatic reasoning from incremental processing, in that the calculations are done in terms of complete utterances. However, there is substantial evidence that pragmatic processing is incremental: listeners venture pragmatic inferences over the time-course of the utterances they hear, which influences the choices that speakers make. To address this, we develop an IR model that is incremental in the sense that pragmatic reasoning takes place word-by-word (though the process could be defined in terms of different linguistic units, like morphemes or phrases).

A variant of this model was applied successfully to *pragmatic image captioning* by Cohn-Gordon et al. (2018); here we concentrate on its qualitative behavior and linguistic predictions. We present computational experiments which demonstrate that incremental and global pragmatics make different predictions, and we show that a speaker that incrementally makes pragmatically informative choices arrives at an utterance which is globally informative. We then argue that an incremental model can account for two empirical observations out of reach of a global model: (i) the asymmetry between adjective–noun and noun–adjective languages in over-informative referential behavior (Rubio-Fernández, 2016), and (ii) the anticipatory implicatures arising from contrastive modifiers (Sedivy, 2007). The first of these observations requires a model of language production, while the second requires a model of language interpretation, and as such these case studies serve to demonstrate both aspects of incremental pragmatics. Finally, we apply the model to the TUNA corpus for referring expression generation (Gatt et al., 2009), showing that it makes more realistic predictions about attributive modifiers than does its global counterpart.

2 Iterated Response Models

We construct our model within the *Rational Speech Acts* (RSA) paradigm (Frank and Goodman, 2012; Goodman and Stuhlmüller, 2013).

Proceedings of the Society for Computation in Linguistics (SCiL) 2019, pages 81-90.
New York City, New York, January 3-6, 2019

RSA and its extensions have been applied to a wide range of pragmatic phenomena, including scalar implicatures (Frank et al., 2016; Potts et al., 2016), manner implicatures (Bergen et al., 2016), hyperbole (Kao et al., 2014), metaphor, and politeness (Yoon et al., 2016). In addition, RSA can be cast as a machine learning model, thereby allowing us to study pragmatic reasoning in large corpora and complex environments (Vogel et al., 2013; Monroe and Potts, 2015; Monroe et al., 2017; Andreas and Klein, 2016).

Standard RSA models are global in the sense that the pragmatic reasoning is defined over complete utterances. Speakers are conditional distributions of the form $P(u|w)$, while listeners are of the form $P(w|u)$, for an utterance u and state w. We first present this global formulation (section 2.1), and then we show how to reformulate it so that utterances are sequences of linguistic units $u = [u_1, \ldots, u_n]$ and the core RSA reasoning is applied to each step u_i given $[u_1, \ldots u_{i-1}]$.

Figure 1 presents a running illustrative example. We imagine there are three referents, a red dress (R1), a blue dress (R2), and a red hat (R3). We have a simple language composed of three utterances, *dress*, *red dress*, and *red object*, each with its expected semantics. For the RSA calculation, we make the background assumption that the speaker and listener are playing a coordination game: they succeed to the extent that the listener can use the speaker's utterance to identify the speaker's intended referent.

2.1 Global Pragmatics

We define our global RSA agents as follows:

$$L_0^{\text{UTT}}(w|u) \propto [\![u]\!](w) \tag{1}$$

$$S_1^{\text{UTT-GP}}(u|w) \propto e^{\log(L_0^{\text{UTT}}(w|u)) - cost(u)} \tag{2}$$

$$L_1^{\text{UTT}}(w|u) \propto S_1^{\text{UTT-GP}}(u|w) \tag{3}$$

Here, $[\![\cdot]\!]$ is an interpretation function mapping utterances to functions from referents to $\{0, 1\}$. Thus, the literal listener L_0^{UTT} is simply a probabilistic version of the truth conditions established by $[\![\cdot]\!]$; given an utterance u, L_0^{UTT} evenly distributes probability mass to the worlds compatible with u according to $[\![\cdot]\!]$.

The pragmatic speaker $S_1^{\text{UTT-GP}}$ is more sophisticated than a literal agent, in that $S_1^{\text{UTT-GP}}$ reasons about L_0^{UTT}, taking message costs into account. We take *cost* to be a language model, which could either be estimated from data (higher probability

to attested utterances), derived from a grammar (higher probability to grammatical utterances), or simply assign longer utterances more cost. Intuitively, $S_1^{\text{UTT-GP}}$ prefers utterances which are not only true but best convey to L_0^{UTT} which world the speaker is in. This is illustrated in figure 1b: whereas all three messages are true of R1, $S_1^{\text{UTT-GP}}$ prefers *red dress* because it is the most specific. In this sense, $S_1^{\text{UTT-GP}}$ is a model of a Gricean informative speaker.

The pragmatic listener L_1^{UTT} in turn reasons about what world state $S_1^{\text{UTT-GP}}$ must be in such that the observed utterance was chosen, and thus draws more refined inferences than L_0^{UTT}. We see this in figure 1b as well, with respect to *dress* and *red object*. Whereas L_0^{UTT} regards these messages as completely ambiguous, L_1^{UTT} (softly) disambiguates them: *dress* is heavily biased toward R2, and *red object* is heavily biased toward R3. This inference formalizes the intuitive reasoning that if the speaker of *red object* had been referring to R1, they would have used the more specific, informative *red dress*; their avoidance of this means they must be referring to R3.

2.2 Incremental Pragmatics

In natural language, speakers and listeners produce and comprehend utterances segment by segment. For present purposes, we define this process at the word level, but we emphasize that the proposed approach extends both to sub-word segments (Cohn-Gordon et al., 2018) and to larger syntactic units.

To approximate this incremental process, we represent utterances as sequences of words and allow RSA-style reasoning to happen at the point of production or comprehension of each word, in the order they are uttered. We represent the end of an utterance as a STOP token, so that the choice of STOP as the next "word" represents the decision that the utterance is complete.

Roughly speaking, we want to define listener models $P(w|word, c)$ and speaker models $P(word|w, c)$, where c is a sequence of words constituting the utterance so far. In order to do this, we first must define an incremental semantics. This incremental semantics is defined in terms of a global semantics and the set of available complete utterances. For any partial sequence c and set of referents W, $[\![c]\!](w) \in [0, 1]$ is the number of full-utterance extensions of c true in w divided

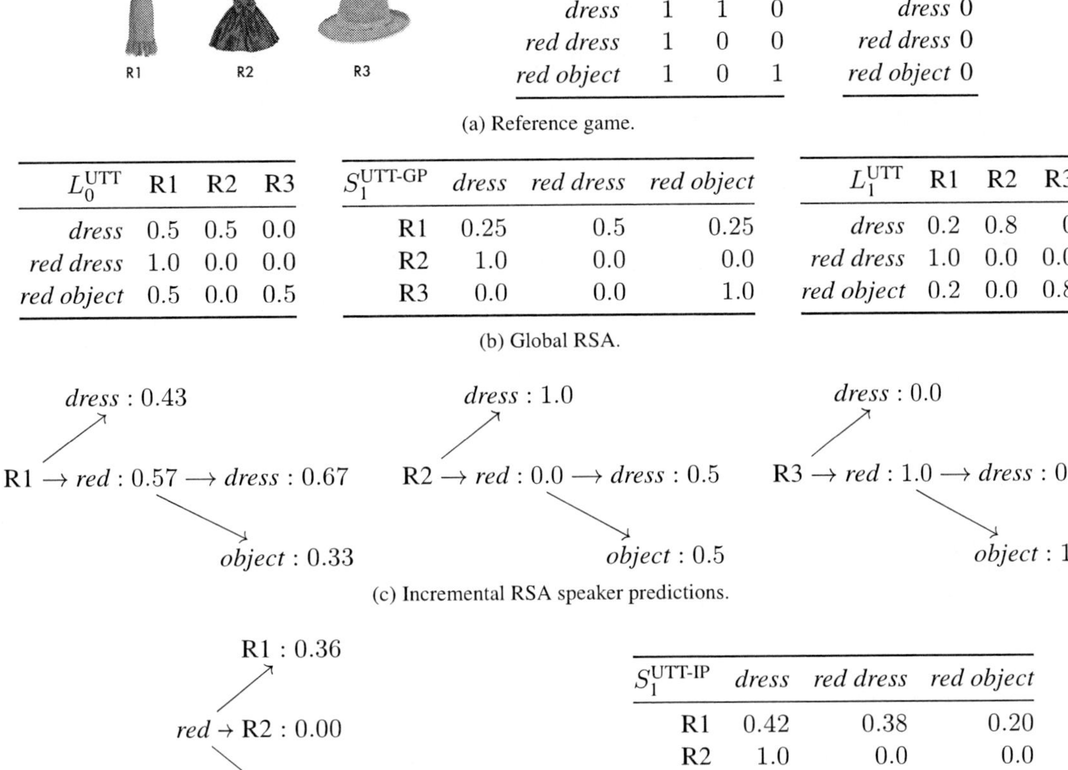

	$[\![\cdot]\!]$	R1	R2	R3		cost	
	dress	1	1	0		*dress*	0
	red dress	1	0	0		*red dress*	0
	red object	1	0	1		*red object*	0

(a) Reference game.

L_0^{UTT}	R1	R2	R3
dress	0.5	0.5	0.0
red dress	1.0	0.0	0.0
red object	0.5	0.0	0.5

$S_1^{\text{UTT-GP}}$	*dress*	*red dress*	*red object*
R1	0.25	0.5	0.25
R2	1.0	0.0	0.0
R3	0.0	0.0	1.0

L_1^{UTT}	R1	R2	R3
dress	0.2	0.8	0
red dress	1.0	0.0	0.0
red object	0.2	0.0	0.8

(b) Global RSA.

$dress : 0.43$

$R1 \rightarrow red : 0.57 \longrightarrow dress : 0.67$

$object : 0.33$

$dress : 1.0$

$R2 \rightarrow red : 0.0 \longrightarrow dress : 0.5$

$object : 0.5$

$dress : 0.0$

$R3 \rightarrow red : 1.0 \longrightarrow dress : 0.0$

$object : 1.0$

(c) Incremental RSA speaker predictions.

$R1 : 0.36$

$red \rightarrow R2 : 0.00$

$R3 : 0.64$

(d) Incremental RSA listener predictions upon hearing *red*.

$S_1^{\text{UTT-IP}}$	*dress*	*red dress*	*red object*
R1	0.42	0.38	0.20
R2	1.0	0.0	0.0
R3	0.0	0.0	1.0

(e) Incremental utterance-level predictions from $S_1^{\text{UTT-IP}}$.

Figure 1: Illustrative example comparing global and incremental RSA. For ease of comparison to the global model, we do not depict the STOP token for the incremental model.

by the number of possible extensions of c into full utterances that are true of any world in W. Where c is a full utterance, $[\![c]\!](w) \in \{0, 1\}$ is as in the global model; where c is a partial utterances, $[\![c]\!]$ represents the biases created by c.

This is not the only possible way to define an incremental semantics. One alternative is to define a probabilistic S_0 or L_0 directly (as in Cohn-Gordon et al. 2018). We choose the method defined above since it is as close as possible to a standard truth-conditional semantics and thus permits direct comparison. Furthermore, since our incremental semantics can be generated from an utterance-level semantics, only the latter needs to be stipulated.

Just as the standard RSA model presented in section 2.1 uses as global semantics to define successive speakers and listeners, we can now define an incremental literal listener L_0^{WORD} and incre-

mental pragmatic speaker and listener S_1^{WORD} and L_1^{WORD}:

$$L_0^{\text{WORD}}(w|c, word) \propto [\![c + word]\!](w) \quad (4)$$

$$S_1^{\text{WORD}}(word|c, w) \propto \quad (5)$$
$$e^{\log(L_0^{\text{WORD}}(w|c,word)) - cost(word)}$$

$$L_1^{\text{WORD}}(w|c, word) \propto S_1^{\text{WORD}}(word|c, w) \quad (6)$$

Figure 1c summarizes the reasoning of the incremental pragmatic speaker S_1^{WORD}, assuming 0 cost on all words for simplicity. This agent prefers *red* as a first word when conveying R1: $S_1^{\text{WORD}}(red|c = [], w = \text{R1}) = 0.57$. However, if R3 is the intended referent, the agent *must* begin its utterance with *red* (since *hat* is not an available word in this simple example). As shown in figure 1d, this fact allows the pragmatic listener to infer from hearing *red* that the referent is most likely R3: $L_1^{\text{WORD}}(\text{R3}|c = [], red) = 0.64$.

There may be cases in which there is no possible true continuation of a sequence of words into a true utterance. For instance, no continuation of *red* constitutes a truthful description of R2. In such situations, we say that probability is evenly distributed over all choices of word, so that $S_1^{\text{WORD}}(dress|c = [red], w = R2) = S_1^{\text{WORD}}(object|c = [red], w = R2) = 0.5$.

2.3 An Utterance-level Incremental Speaker

From the word level agent S_1^{WORD}, we can use the chain rule to obtain $S_1^{\text{UTT-IP}}$, an *utterance-level speaker* whose values are the result of incremental pragmatic inferences:[1]

$$S_1^{\text{UTT-IP}}(u|w) = \prod_{i=1}^{n} S_1^{\text{WORD}}(u_i|c = [u_1 \ldots u_{i-1}], w)$$

(7)

Whereas $S_1^{\text{UTT-GP}}$ in (2) makes pragmatic calculations on the basis of whole utterances, $S_1^{\text{UTT-IP}}$ makes incremental pragmatic decisions about each choice of word, which together also give rise to a distribution over utterances.

This allows for an efficient strategy, namely *greedy unrolling*, to generate an utterance from a referent r. We choose the first word $word_1$ of the utterance to be $\arg\max_{word} S_1^{\text{WORD}}(word|w = r, c = [])$, and this decision then becomes part of the context for choosing the second word: $word_2$ is $\arg\max_{word} S_1^{\text{WORD}}(word|w = r, c = [word_1])$. And so on through the entire utterance.

2.4 Relating the Global and Incremental Models

Figure 2 depicts the core relationships between the global and local models, focusing on the pragmatic speaker. The agents along the solid green path define the global model of section 2.1, while those along the dashed red path define the incremental model of section 2.2 as defined by $S_1^{\text{UTT-IP}}$. Importantly, while $S_1^{\text{UTT-GP}}$ and $S_1^{\text{UTT-IP}}$ are of the same *type*, in the sense of being conditional probability distributions over full utterances, they are not the same distribution.

For instance, the predictions of $S_1^{\text{UTT-IP}}$ for our illustrative example are given in figure 1e. Comparing them with the global pragmatic speaker predictions in figure 1b, we see that the two make

[1]We use $u[n]$ for the nth element of a list u, and $u[: n]$ for the sublist of u up to but not including $u[n]$.

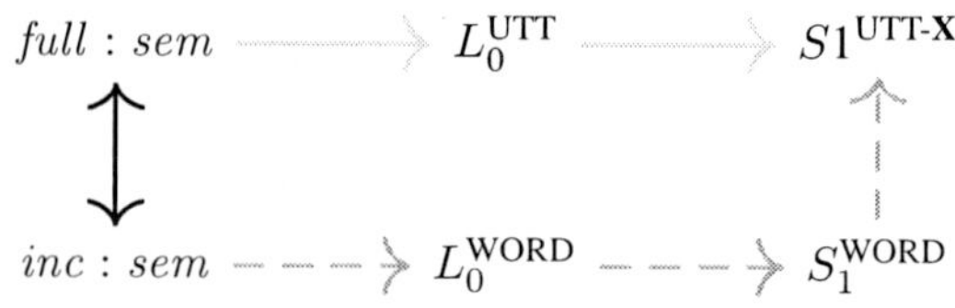

Figure 2: Two ways of constructing an utterance-level pragmatic speaker from a semantics. The solid green path is to obtain a literal listener over full utterances and then perform pragmatics, which gives rise to $S_1^{\text{UTT-GP}}$ while the dashed red path is to obtain an incremental literal listener, use it to construct a word-level pragmatic speaker from L_0^{WORD} and then use this to define an utterance-level pragmatic speaker, $S_1^{\text{UTT-IP}}$.

substantively different predictions. In the global model, the speaker who wishes to refer to R1 prefers *red dress*. In contrast, in the incremental model, the speaker referring to R1 prefers *dress*. The reason for $S_1^{\text{UTT-IP}}$ having these values is that saying *dress* ensures the termination of the utterance (given the set of utterances that are available in this example), which therefore has probability 1.0 at the next time step, while saying *red* leaves two options, *dress* and *object*. Thus, $S_1^{\text{UTT-GP}}$ and $S_1^{\text{UTT-IP}}$ are not only quantitatively different, but even differ in their predictions about which utterances are optimal.

Figure 3 provides an abstract example which further reinforces this difference. Moving from left to right, the numbers in green depict the S_1^{WORD} probabilities at each of the two steps in the generation of a complete utterance, when the target reference is W1 instead of distractor W2. The probability of the full utterance at $S_1^{\text{UTT-IP}}$ is the product of the two S_1^{WORD} steps.

An example of the difference to $S_1^{\text{UTT-GP}}$ is shown in green. When referring to W1, $S_1^{\text{UTT-GP}}$ gives equal weight to *AA*, *BA* and *BB*. $S_1^{\text{UTT-IP}}$, however, first chooses between *A* and *B*: in this decision, *B* is preferred, since one of the two continuations of *A*, namely *AB*, is not compatible with W1. However, if *A* is chosen, the subsequent choice is fully determined to be *B* ($p(A|[A], \text{W1} = 1.0$). This results in a preference for *AA*.

While we focus largely on the differences between incremental and global pragmatics, it is worth highlighting a regard in which the former behaves like the latter.

Given a referent r, call an utterance u *weakly*

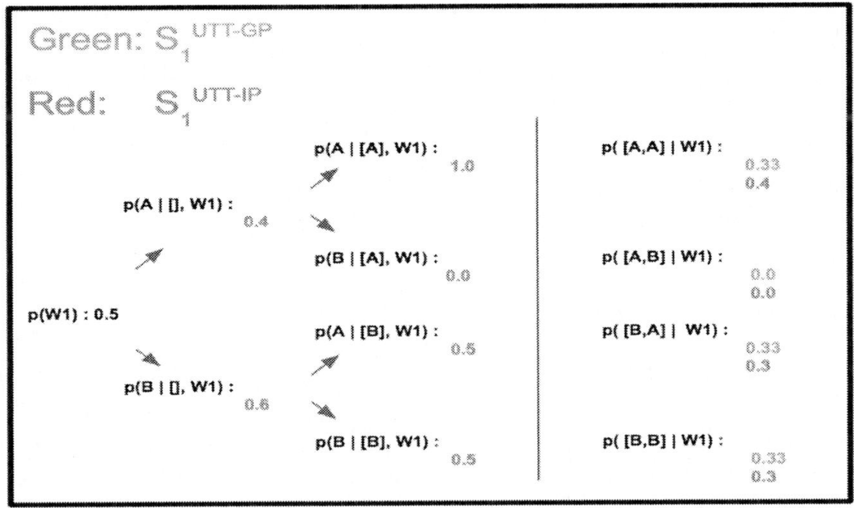

Figure 3: A depiction of the probabilities of the $S_1^{\text{UTT-IP}}$ in red and $S_1^{\text{UTT-GP}}$ in green, for a simple abstract example. The four utterances are *AA*, *AB*, *BA* and *BB*, while the two worlds are W1 and W2. The semantics assigns $u = \text{W1}$ and $w = AB$ to 0 but all other utterance–world pairs to 1. Given a world w, the incremental speaker first chooses the first letter to be *A* or *B*, and then chooses the second letter conditioned jointly on w and the first letter, to obtain a full utterance. The resulting full utterance probabilities are compared with the predictions of the global $S_1^{\text{UTT-GP}}$. As can be seen, the incremental and global speakers assign different probabilities to each utterance and are consequently distinct from each other.

informative if $L_0^{\text{UTT}}(r|u) \geq \frac{1}{|W|}$, where W is the set of possible referents. In other words, given u, the literal listener L_0^{UTT} will guess the correct referent with probability at least at chance (when costs are 0). We note that the utterance $u*_r$ obtained by greedy unrolling at each step of generation, as described in section 2.3, is weakly informative. To see this, observe that the nth word of $u*_r$ is $\arg\max_{word} S_1^{\text{WORD}}(word|w = r, c = u *_r [:n])$. Since at each step S_1^{WORD} produces a word which, at worst, does not rule out any referents for L_0^{WORD}, the resulting sentence $u*$ at worst gives $L_0^{\text{UTT}}(r|u*_r) \geq \frac{1}{|W|}$. In other words, greedily unrolling the incremental speaker will produce an utterance which is true and has the literal listener infer the probability of the intended referent as being at least at chance.

This result suggests that the strategy of choosing the most informative word (or syntactic unit) at each point in the generation of an utterance can be used as a substitute for choosing, from all utterances, the one which is most informative. Exploring the gap in this informativity bound is an important future direction.

One potential advantage of $S_1^{\text{UTT-IP}}$ as a plausible model of referring expression generation (over a small, discrete set of referents) is computational

tractability in real-world settings where the set of possible utterances U is large or unbounded. In such settings, $S_1^{\text{UTT-GP}}$ becomes intractable, owing to the normalizing term required over U.

However, it is important to note that in the setup presented here, $S_1^{\text{UTT-IP}}$ is not more tractable than $S_1^{\text{UTT-GP}}$. The reason for this is that the calculation of the incremental semantics depends on factoring the global semantics: this involves an intractable normalization akin to that present in the $S_1^{\text{UTT-GP}}$. Thus, $S_1^{\text{UTT-IP}}$ is only computationally tractable if the incremental semantics in terms of which it is defined is tractable. In the present work, we define an incremental semantics in terms of a global one, in order to allow for a maximally clear comparison between the global and incremental models of pragmatics that ensue. However, an incremental semantics (or literal speaker model) can be defined or learned independently, as in Vedantam et al. 2017 and Cohn-Gordon et al. 2018.

3 Application to Prior Experiments

We now briefly consider two cases where incremental pragmatics provides an explanation of a phenomenon where global pragmatics does not seem to suffice.

3.1 Over-informative Referring Expressions

It has been observed that, when generating referring expressions (REs), humans often provide more information than necessary to refer unambiguously (Engelhardt et al., 2006; Herrmann and Deutsch, 1976). For instance, Rubio-Fernández (2016) shows that English speakers often use redundant color terms (e.g., *the red dress*) in a scene with only a single dress, where the shorter utterance *dress* would suffice. However, Rubio-Fernández also notes that Spanish speakers are less likely to over-describe with the analogous referring expression, *el vestido rojo*, in the same situation. This difference is a challenge for non-incremental pragmatic accounts, since, *ceteris paribus*, we would expect semantically equivalent Spanish and English REs to have the same production probability.

Using incremental pragmatics, we model the English case as follows: let the referents be a red dress (R1) and a blue hat (R2), and the possible utterances be *dress*, *red dress*, *hat*, and *blue hat*, with the obvious semantics.

We make the following assumption regarding the *cost* term: assume a cost of 1.0 for all words but a cost of 0.0 for the STOP token. Further assume that an utterance's cost is the sum of the cost of its words. The effect of this cost term is to penalize longer utterances, all else being equal.

On these assumptions, the globally pragmatic speaker $S_1^{\text{UTT-GP}}$ prefers *dress* to *red dress*, since both are fully informative but the latter is costlier: $S_1^{\text{UTT-GP}}(dress|\text{R1}) = 0.73 > S_1^{\text{UTT-GP}}(red\ dress|\text{R1}) = 0.27$. Meanwhile the incremental pragmatic speaker $S_1^{\text{UTT-IP}}$ is undecided: $S_1^{\text{UTT-IP}}(dress|\text{R1}) = S_1^{\text{UTT-IP}}(red\ dress|\text{R1}) = 0.5$. The increase in mass on the over-informative RE *red dress* in $S_1^{\text{UTT-IP}}$ as compared to $S_1^{\text{UTT-GP}}$ is the result of incremental processing: the decision between *red* and *dress* is made on the basis of informativity, and both words are equally informative. However, if *red* is chosen, the subsequent, now over-informative word *dress* has to follow, since *red* on its own is not an utterance.

We explore the generality of this dynamic – that incremental pragmatics may lead to the language model being compelled to produce longer utterances – in section (4), where we apply the model to real-world data, in the form of the TUNA corpus.

However, this effect does not obtain in Spanish, where adjectives are post-nominal. In the Spanish case, let our utterances be *vestido*, *vestido rojo*, *sombrero*, and *sombrero azul*, with the same referents and costs as before. Then there is no difference between the global and incremental models:

$$S_1^{\text{UTT-GP}}(vestido|\text{R1}) = 0.73 >$$
$$S_1^{\text{UTT-GP}}(vestido\ rojo|\text{R1}) = 0.27$$
$$S_1^{\text{UTT-IP}}(vestido|\text{R1}) = 0.73 >$$
$$S_1^{\text{UTT-IP}}(vestido\ rojo|\text{R1}) = 0.27$$

When choosing the word to follow *vestido*, the incremental pragmatic speaker has no need to say *rojo* rather than STOP, since the goal of communicating the referent has already been completed by *vestido*. As a result, the speaker chooses the less costly option, STOP. The relevant difference here from the English case is that it is grammatical to stop after the first word (since the first word is a noun, not an adjective as in English).

A qualitative property which this example illustrates is a dislike in $S_1^{\text{UTT-IP}}$ for utterances which begin with a sequence of words which would mislead the incremental literal listener L_0^{WORD}. This is the basis on which anticipatory implicatures are formed, as discussed in section 3.2. This is not a hard constraint: utterances which would initially mislead an incremental listener are not categorically ruled out. However, the question of whether this behavior is empirically justified is a worthwhile topic for future investigation.

3.2 Anticipatory Implicatures

We now turn to a phenomenon concerning language interpretation, which we will model with an RSA listener, L_1^{WORD}.

Sedivy (2007) provides compelling empirical evidence that humans draw pragmatic inferences partway through utterances. For instance, when shown a scene with a tall cup, a tall pitcher, a short cup, and a key, a listener who hears "Give me the tall–" will fixate on the tall cup before the utterance is complete.

We take this as evidence for an incremental pragmatic listener L_1^{WORD} which can calculate an implicature by reasoning that, had the speaker intended to refer to the pitcher, they would not have had any motivation to say "tall". By contrast, on the assumption that the speaker's referent is the tall cup, the contrastive modifier serves to distinguish the intended referent from the short cup.

To model this implicature formally, we make the simplifying assumption that the possible utterances are *tall cup*, *short cup*, *tall pitcher*, *cup*, *pitcher*, and *key*. For consistency with the previous example, we assume the additive *cost* function from section 3.1.

On hearing *tall* as the first word of an utterance, L_1^{WORD}, the incremental pragmatic listener, can draw the following inference: the intended referent is likely to have been the tall cup, since had it been the tall pitcher, there would have been no need to use the contrastive modifier *tall*: $L_1^{\text{WORD}}(\text{the pitcher}|c = [\,], tall) = 0.4$ while $L_1^{\text{WORD}}(\text{the tall glass}|c = [\,], tall) = 0.6$.

This implicature is cancelable, and indeed, were the next word to be *pitcher*, we would exclude all referents but the pitcher. In this respect, the model represents the confusion created by uttering "tall pitcher", where after the first word of the utterance, the majority of probability mass is on a referent (*the tall cup*) which, after the second word, has no probability mass.

4 Experimental Validation with TUNA

In order to observe the behavior of our incremental pragmatic model on real data, we make use of the TUNA corpus (van Deemter et al., 2006). TUNA is built around a referring expression task grounded in images. The images are coded using a fixed set of attributes, and the human-produced utterances are coded using the same attributes. Thus, TUNA lets us study the core content of naturally produced referring expressions without forcing us to confront the full complexity of natural language.

Our goal is to show that, when a cost is imposed which prefers shorter utterances, the incremental model $S_1^{\text{UTT-IP}}$ is less affected, and on average produces more two-word utterances than $S_1^{\text{UTT-GP}}$.

We hypothesize this on the basis of the preference of $S_1^{\text{UTT-IP}}$ for utterances where the choice of each word is made with high certainty. This means that informative one-word utterances which have reasonable probability of being extended with a second word will score lower than two-word utterances where the choice of the first word all but fixes the choice of the second. Since most one-word utterances admit the possibility of an extension to a second word, this dynamic would result in a preference for the longer, two-word utterances. This would provide further evidence that

Figure 4: An example target entity from the *furniture* domain, along with its coding as a dictionary, and the human generated referring expression for it in a context of other images.

the dynamic described in section 3.1 generalizes from an idealized example to real language.

4.1 Data

The TUNA corpus defines a reference game in the sense of figure 1a. Each *trial* contains a set of images (entities), of which one or several are the target, and a human-generated referring expression for the target in the context of all the images. We refer to the full set of target and non-target entities as the *context set*.

Both images and utterances are coded as sets of attributes (figure 4). This coding defines a semantics. For instance, in figure 4, the utterance "the grey desk" is true of the entity, since `type:desk` and `colour:grey` are included in its attributes. For the *furniture* domain, attributes such as color, object type, and size are coded. The *people* domain is more complex, coding for more attributes, including age, clothing, hair color, glasses, and orientation. Both domains also code for the position of the image relative to the other images in the context set.

4.2 Methods

For simplicity, we restrict our model to the *furniture* and *people* domains where only a single referent is provided, and consider only utterances of two words or fewer. These constitute 32% of the total utterances in the single referent corpora, and to our knowledge are not distinct in other ways than their length.

For each trial, the possible utterances are those from the set of all two-word utterances across the entire corpus (either of furniture or people) which are compatible with at least one of the entities in the trial. We predict the set of optimal utterances (since there may be more than one utterance with maximum probability) for both $S_1^{\text{UTT-GP}}$ and $S_1^{\text{UTT-IP}}$. For our cost function, we assume all words have a cost of 1.0 except the STOP token, which has cost 0.0. Utterances cost the sum of their words. This has the effect of penalizing longer utterances.

For each trial, we have a set of entities as referents, with the designated target identified among these entities. In addition, we can define the set of all possible true utterances for a given trial. Thus, it is possible to make predictions according to both $S_1^{\text{UTT-GP}}$ and $S_1^{\text{UTT-IP}}$ for each trial without having to enrich the TUNA dataset in any way.

4.3 Results

As expected, we find a preference for longer utterances; out of the 114 *people* trials, $S_1^{\text{UTT-GP}}$ identifies 120 two-word utterances as optimal, compared to 287 for $S_1^{\text{UTT-IP}}$. In the 83 trials of the *furniture* domain, $S_1^{\text{UTT-GP}}$ marks 88 two word utterances as optimal, compared to 149 for $S_1^{\text{UTT-IP}}$. (More than one utterance may be optimal for a given trial, in the event that multiple utterances have the same, maximal probability of being chosen.)

An example of a representative case is the trial where the entity in figure 4 is the target, and no other distractors are grey, although others are desks. In this case, both "grey" and "a grey desk" are fully informative, in the sense of only being compatible with the target. With the cost term having the effect of penalizing longer utterances, $S_1^{\text{UTT-GP}}$ chooses "grey" as optimal. For $S_1^{\text{UTT-IP}}$, however, neither of these utterances are optimal, because probability is divided between stopping after "grey" and continuing with "desk". Instead, the optimal utterance, "right middle", describes the position of the target among the images of the context set. "Right" is not an available full utterance (as it is not attested in the data) and so no probability mass is lost by being divided between stopping and continuing with "middle".

While this result offers a possible motivation for over-informative behavior, the nature of the relation is clearly nuanced – two-word utterances are not always more informative than one-word utterances – and merits further work. In particular, it

would be desirable to use a more direct proxy for over-informativity than preference for longer utterances.

5   Conclusion

In summary, we have defined a formal notion of incremental pragmatics, with respect to both production and comprehension, and shown that it differs in meaningful ways from global pragmatic behavior, at least within the RSA paradigm. The core differences are the sensitivity to word order, which varies cross-linguistically in a way which core pragmatic reasoning does not, and the ability of an incremental model to calculate implicatures partway through an utterance. We compared these models using simulations, and we assessed them using existing psycholinguistic data and using a new experiment with the TUNA corpus.

Exploration of RSA as a machine learning model is now underway, and this is helping to show the value of pragmatic reasoning in important NLP tasks. Such work forces us to confront the fact that the idealized RSA speaker agent must reason about all possible utterances – the normalization constant in (3) demands this. Prior work has sought to get around this by simplifying the space of possible utterances (Monroe and Potts, 2015) or by sampling a small set of utterances to approximate this normalization (Andreas and Klein, 2016; Monroe et al., 2017). Neither solution is ideal. The incremental approach offers a scalable alternative, as long as the incremental semantics is learned, as in Cohn-Gordon et al. 2018 and Vedantam et al. 2017.

There is also much to be done in assessing the incremental model in the context of on-line sentence processing. We have begun to identify the key properties of the model, but the degree to which these properties accord with empirical data on production and comprehension remains a largely open question.

6   Acknowledgments

Many thanks to the insightful comments of the reviewers, regarding both the presentation of the material and the substantive technical comments regarding the model itself.

This material is based in part upon work supported by the Stanford Data Science Initiative and by the NSF under Grant No. BCS-1456077.

References

Jacob Andreas and Dan Klein. 2016. Reasoning about pragmatics with neural listeners and speakers. In *Proceedings of the 2016 Conference on Empirical Methods in Natural Language Processing*, pages 1173–1182. Association for Computational Linguistics.

Leon Bergen, Roger Levy, and Noah D. Goodman. 2016. Pragmatic reasoning through semantic inference. *Semantics and Pragmatics*, 9(20).

Reuben Cohn-Gordon, Noah Goodman, and Christopher Potts. 2018. Pragmatically informative image captioning with character-level inference. In *Proceedings of the 2018 Conference of the North American Chapter of the Association for Computational Linguistics: Human Language Technologies, Volume 2 (Short Papers)*, pages 439–443. Association for Computational Linguistics.

Kees van Deemter, Ielka van der Sluis, and Albert Gatt. 2006. Building a semantically transparent corpus for the generation of referring expressions. In *Proceedings of the Fourth International Natural Language Generation Conference*, pages 130–132. Association for Computational Linguistics.

Paul E Engelhardt, Karl GD Bailey, and Fernanda Ferreira. 2006. Do speakers and listeners observe the gricean maxim of quantity? *Journal of Memory and Language*, 54(4):554–573.

Michael C. Frank, Andrés Gómez Emilsson, Benjamin Peloquin, Noah D. Goodman, and Christopher Potts. 2016. Rational speech act models of pragmatic reasoning in reference games. Ms., Stanford University.

Michael C. Frank and Noah D. Goodman. 2012. Predicting pragmatic reasoning in language games. *Science*, 336(6084):998.

Michael Franke. 2009. *Signal to Act: Game Theory in Pragmatics*. ILLC Dissertation Series. Institute for Logic, Language and Computation, University of Amsterdam.

Michael Franke and Gerhard Jäger. 2014. Pragmatic back-and-forth reasoning. In Salvatore Pistoia Reda, editor, *Pragmatics, Semantics and the Case of Scalar Implicatures*, pages 170–200. Palgrave Macmillan UK, London.

Albert Gatt, Anja Belz, and Eric Kow. 2009. The TUNA-REG Challenge 2009: Overview and evaluation results. In *Proceedings of the 12th European Workshop on Natural Language Generation (ENLG 2009)*, pages 174–182, Athens, Greece. Association for Computational Linguistics.

Noah D Goodman and Michael C Frank. 2016. Pragmatic language interpretation as probabilistic inference. *Trends in Cognitive Sciences*, 20(11):818–829.

Noah D. Goodman and Andreas Stuhlmüller. 2013. Knowledge and implicature: Modeling language understanding as social cognition. *Topics in Cognitive Science*, 5(1):173–184.

H. Paul Grice. 1975. Logic and conversation. In Peter Cole and Jerry Morgan, editors, *Syntax and Semantics*, volume 3: Speech Acts, pages 43–58. Academic Press, New York.

Theo Herrmann and Werner Deutsch. 1976. *Psychologie der objektbenennung*. Huber.

Gerhard Jäger. 2007. Game dynamics connects semantics and pragmatics. In Ahti-Veikko Pietarinen, editor, *Game Theory and Linguistic Meaning*, pages 89–102. Elsevier, Amsterdam.

Gerhard Jäger. 2012. Game theory in semantics and pragmatics. In Claudia Maienborn, Klaus von Heusinger, and Paul Portner, editors, *Semantics: An International Handbook of Natural Language Meaning*, volume 3, pages 2487–2425. Mouton de Gruyter, Berlin.

Justine T. Kao, Jean Y. Wu, Leon Bergen, and Noah D. Goodman. 2014. Nonliteral understanding of number words. *Proceedings of the National Academy of Sciences*, 111(33):12002–12007.

Will Monroe, Robert X. D. Hawkins, Noah D. Goodman, and Christopher Potts. 2017. Colors in context: A pragmatic neural model for grounded language understanding. *Transactions of the Association for Computational Linguistics*, 5:325–338.

Will Monroe and Christopher Potts. 2015. Learning in the Rational Speech Acts model. In *Proceedings of 20th Amsterdam Colloquium*, Amsterdam. ILLC.

Christopher Potts, Daniel Lassiter, Roger Levy, and Michael C. Frank. 2016. Embedded implicatures as pragmatic inferences under compositional lexical uncertainty. *Journal of Semantics*, 33(4):755–802.

Paula Rubio-Fernández. 2016. How redundant are redundant color adjectives? an efficiency-based analysis of color overspecification. *Frontiers in psychology*, 7:153.

Julie C Sedivy. 2007. Implicature during real time conversation: A view from language processing research. *Philosophy compass*, 2(3):475–496.

Ramakrishna Vedantam, Samy Bengio, Kevin Murphy, Devi Parikh, and Gal Chechik. 2017. Context-aware captions from context-agnostic supervision. In *Computer Vision and Pattern Recognition (CVPR)*, volume 3.

Adam Vogel, Max Bodoia, Christopher Potts, and Dan Jurafsky. 2013. Emergence of Gricean maxims from multi-agent decision theory. In *Human Language Technologies: The 2013 Annual Conference of the North American Chapter of the Association for Computational Linguistics*, pages 1072–1081, Stroudsburg, PA. Association for Computational Linguistics.

Erica J. Yoon, Michael Henry Tessler, Noah D. Goodman, and Michael C. Frank. 2016. Talking with tact: Polite language as a balance between kindness and informativity. In *Proceedings of the 38th Annual Conference of the Cognitive Science Society*, pages 2771–2776. Cognitive Science Society.

Learning exceptionality and variation with lexically scaled MaxEnt[*]

Coral Hughto, Andrew Lamont, Brandon Prickett, and **Gaja Jarosz**
University of Massachusetts Amherst
{coralwilliam, alamont, bprickett, jarosz}@linguist.umass.edu

Abstract

A growing body of research in phonology addresses the representation and learning of variable processes and exceptional, lexically conditioned processes. Linzen et al. (2013) present a MaxEnt model with additive lexical scales to account for data exhibiting both variation and exceptionality. In this paper, we implement a learning model for lexically scaled MaxEnt grammars which we show to be successful across a range of data containing patterns of variation and exceptionality. We also explore how the model's parameters and the rate of exceptionality in the data influence its performance and predictions for novel forms.

1   Introduction

While phonological research often focuses on categorical generalizations, a growing body of research addresses the representation and learning of variable processes and exceptional processes, where application is lexically conditioned (see Coetzee and Pater (2011) and Pater (2010) for overviews). A few recent studies have modeled processes that exhibit both variation *and* exceptionality (Hayes and Londe, 2006; Pater et al., 2012; Linzen et al., 2013; Nazarov, 2018; Shih, 2018; Zymet, 2018).

Linzen et al. (2013) model co-existing exceptionality and variation in Russian using a Maximum En-

tropy (MaxEnt) grammar (Goldwater and Johnson, 2003) with additive, lexically specified scales. Russian contains a vowel alternation process that exhibits both variation and idiosyncratic lexical conditioning (exceptionality). Linzen et al. show that speakers apply this process variably and that its variation differs across lexical items. In their lexical scaling framework, each lexical item is associated with a vector of scales that are added to the general weights of the grammar's constraints. These summed weights are used to calculate the probability of the input's surface realization. This allows the likelihood of a phonological process to differ across morphemes, since the scales can modulate how constraints are weighted for different lexemes. While Linzen et al. (2013) show that a lexically scaled MaxEnt grammar can successfully represent Russian speakers' knowledge of a pattern that is both variable and exceptional, they do not show how such a grammar would be learned.

In this paper, we introduce a model for learning lexically scaled MaxEnt grammars from data exhibiting both variation and exceptionality.[1] The primary challenge for formalizing learning in this framework is generalizing appropriately beyond the learning data and limiting the learner's reliance on lexical scales. Since every morpheme can potentially scale the weight of every constraint, there is potential for massively over-fitting the learning data

---

[*]We wish to thank the SCiL 2019 anonymous reviewers, the UMass Linguistics Sound Workshop, Brendan O'Connor, and Joe Pater for valuable comments.

[1]Our code is publicly available at https://github.com/chughto/Lexically-Scaled-MaxEnt

Proceedings of the Society for Computation in Linguistics (SCiL) 2019, pages 91-101.
New York City, New York, January 3-6, 2019

and failing to generalize. We approach this challenge as a problem of feature selection and seek a learner that utilizes scales (i.e., assigning them non-zero weights) only when needed to account for lexical conditioning. We propose an objective function relying on an L1 (linear) prior (§2), rather than the more commonly used L2 (quadratic) prior (§4.1), to formalize these criteria.

Our approach differs in a number of ways from previous models for learning exceptionality and variation. We assume the learner must induce a weighting for general phonological constraints and make lexical conditioning choices without prior knowledge of which lexical items behave exceptionally (Allen and Becker, 2015; Becker and Gouskova, 2016). Rather than splitting the learning of general phonological patterns and the learning of exceptions/classes into distinct learning phases (Nazarov, 2018; Shih, 2018), or treating the learning of lexical conditioning as emergent from repeated exposure to the lexicon (Zuraw, 2000; Zuraw, 2010), we seek to formally characterize the criteria that favor the desired balance of lexical sensitivity and generalization in a model that optimizes general weights and lexical conditioning in parallel. Our approach is most similar to Moore-Cantwell and Pater (2016); however, we argue for an L1 prior rather than an L2 prior (§4.1). We demonstrate the capacity of our model to learn variation and exceptionality using a variety of toy languages based on the Russian process mentioned above (§3).

We also explore the model's predictions for novel data, examining how the learner decides which patterns to treat as exceptional and which to generalize (§4). Previous behavioral investigations of speakers' productive knowledge of lexically conditioned (morpho-)phonological alternations have found that speakers extend statistical tendencies in the lexicon to novel forms (Zuraw, 2000; Ernestus and Baayen, 2003; Hayes and Londe, 2006; Hayes et al., 2009; Linzen et al., 2013; Becker and Gouskova, 2016). In some cases, the absolute rates of application of a process in nonce forms closely follow rates observed in the lexicon, yielding so-called "frequency-matching" behavior (Hayes and Londe, 2006; Hayes et al., 2009; Zymet, 2018). In other cases, however, rates of application of exceptional processes are systematically skewed lower as compared to the lexical rates (Zuraw, 2000; Albright and Hayes, 2003; Ernestus and Baayen, 2003). Under a variety of learning assumptions, frequency-matching behavior is not automatic. To better understand some of the factors that may play a role in these divergent findings, we examine the properties of the data distribution and parameters of the model that affect frequency-matching behavior on nonce forms.

2 Lexically scaled MaxEnt

Linzen et al.'s (2013) scaled weights framework uses weighted constraints to represent probabilistic phonological patterns, and adds scales on those weights to represent lexicalized behavior for individual morphemes. In MaxEnt (Goldwater and Johnson, 2003), the probability of some surface representation (SR), given a grammar and an underlying representation (UR), is calculated as in (1):

$$p(i) = \frac{e^{\mathcal{H}_i}}{\sum_{k \in K_i} e^{\mathcal{H}_k}} \qquad (1)$$

Here $\mathcal{H}_i$ is the harmony of a given (UR, SR) pair i, and K_i is the set of candidates that share the same UR as i (including i itself). Typically, harmony is the weighted sum of a candidate's constraint violations (Goldwater and Johnson, 2003), however in Linzen et al.'s (2013) framework, harmony is a function of a candidate's violations, the general weights, and the relevant scales, as shown formally in (2):

$$\mathcal{H}_i = \sum_{\gamma \in \Gamma} (w_\gamma + \sum_{m \in \mu_i} s_{\gamma m})(v_{\gamma i}) \qquad (2)$$

Here Γ is the set of constraints, w_γ is the general weight of constraint γ, μ_i is the set of morphemes in the (UR, SR) pair i, $s_{\gamma m}$ is the scale that morpheme m has for constraint γ, and $v_{\gamma i}$ is the number of violations assigned to candidate i by constraint γ. The parameters of the model are the general constraint weights and the additive lexical scales. For succinctness, we refer to these simply as "weights" and "scales", respectively. Every morpheme is associated with a scale for every constraint that is added to that constraint's weight. This model is closely related to other approaches relying on additive scales (Boersma and Hayes, 2001; Coetzee and Kawahara, 2013; Hsu and Jesney, 2016) and multiplicative scales (Kimper, 2011). However, in Linzen et al.'s framework, scaling is not restricted to faithfulness constraints or systematic factors (e.g., register, frequency): all constraints are available for lexical scaling by all morphemes. Using both weights and scales enables the model to represent lexicalized exceptions by employing the scales to modulate the effect of some constraints. We leave exploring the relationship between this approach and indexed constraints (Kraska-Szlenk, 1995; Pater, 1996), a closely related framework, to future work.

We formalized learning as minimizing the objective function in (3), the sum of the negative log likelihood and an L1 prior on weights and scales.

$$-\sum_i \log p(i) + C \sum_{\gamma \in \Gamma} |w_\gamma| + C \sum_{\gamma \in \Gamma} \sum_{m \in M} |s_{\gamma m}| \quad (3)$$

Here, M is the set of morphemes in the language, and C is a parameter that controls the overall strength of the prior. Our goal was to determine whether learning of phonological generalizations could occur without formally distinguishing between weights and scales. Accordingly, this prior penalizes both weights and scales with a single strength parameter C. In simulations reported here, both weights and scales are restricted to nonnegative values, but this is not a inherent restriction of the model. For optimization, we used a form of gradient descent adapted for L1 priors – the "L1 (Clipping)" method described by Tsuruoka et al. (2009).

3 Learning variation and exceptionality

To explore the capacity of this model to learn a range of variable and exceptional patterns, it was trained on four toy languages based on the Russian vowel alternation described by Linzen et al. (2013).

In Russian, underlyingly CV prepositions surface as C before words beginning with vowels or single consonants; we follow Linzen et al. (2013, §5.1) in treating this alternation as deletion. Before words beginning with consonant clusters, vowel deletion is variable and lexically conditioned. For example, the vowel in /sa/ "from, with" variably surfaces with certain cluster-initial words (4a), categorically deletes with certain others (4b), and categorically surfaces with others (4c) (Linzen et al., 2013, 455).

(4) a. [s ∼ sa] mnóʐəstvəm "with a large
          amount, (mathematical) set"

b. [s ∼ *sə] prikázəm "with the order"

c. [*s ∼ sə] stərikóm "with the old man"

The factors influencing vowel deletion in Russian span multiple phonological dimensions such as stress and sonority profile. For the purposes of testing our learning model, we focused on whether words began with one or two consonants. The four toy languages consisted of 3 prefixes /ape-/, /ate-/, and /ake-/ concatenated with 420 stems, giving 1260 forms in total. Stems were all consonant-initial, beginning either with a single consonant ("C-stems"), or a biconsonantal cluster ("CC-stems"). Six consonants were used {v, r, l, n, s, t}, giving 6 unique C-stem types, and 36 CC-stem types. Each stem type was replicated 10 times, yielding 420 stems in total.

In all four languages, prefix vowels categorically deleted with C-stems, e.g., /ape-naba/ → [apnaba]. Vowel deletion was conditioned with CC-stems, either categorically failing to apply (§3.1) or with its application subject to free variation (§3.2), lexical specification (§3.3), or both (§3.4).

We used three categorically evaluated constraints (see Linzen et al. (2013, 489-490)): ALIGN, MAX, and *CCC. ALIGN prefers vowel deletion, and is violated by candidates containing the final prefix vowel. MAX disprefers vowel deletion, and is violated by candidates lacking the final prefix vowel. *CCC is violated by candidates with triconsonantal clusters, and so disprefers deletion with CC-stems.

After training, the model was tested by evaluating its performance on the learning data and its predictions on a set of nonce forms comprising 3 novel prefixes concatenated with 42 novel stems. Following previous work, we assume that predictions for novel forms are generated using only the general weights.

Learning was evaluated according to quantitative and qualitative criteria. Quantitatively, learning was considered successful if the KL-Divergence (Kullback and Leibler, 1951) between the likelihood assigned by the model and the observed probability in the training data was close to zero, indicating that the model succeeded in accounting for the learning data.[2] Qualitatively, learning was considered successful only if the model appropriately divided weight between the general constraints and

---

[2] MaxEnt grammars cannot exactly represent categorical behavior, but probabilities can get arbitrarily close to 0 or 1.

/ape-taba/	*CCC	MAX	ALIGN	O	E
a. apetaba	0	0	-1	0.00	0.00
b. aptaba	0	-1	0	1.00	1.00
/ape-tnaba/	11.5	0.0	4.5	O	E
a. apetnaba	0	0	-1	1.00	1.00
b. aptnaba	-1	-1	0	0.00	0.00

Tableau 1: Categorical language

the scales, only using scales when presented with lexically conditioned data. Finally, we required that the model generalizes the observed pattern to nonce forms, deleting (nearly) categorically for novel C-stems while predicting variation for CC-stems in languages with variation and/or lexical conditioning.

For all experiments in this section, the model was run with weights and scales initialized at 0.0, for 20,000 epochs, with a learning rate of .001, and prior term C set to 1.0, unless otherwise noted.

Overall, the model performed well, successfully learning the four toy languages and using the scales appropriately. In all runs, ALIGN received non-zero weight, reflecting (near) categorical vowel deletion with C-stems. In languages with variable or exceptional deletion, *CCC was weighted closer to ALIGN, predicting variation in nonce forms.

3.1 Categorical language

In the Categorical language, prefix vowels always delete with C-stems and never with CC-stems. The solution learned by the model captures this pattern using the general weights only, putting no weight on the scales, as summarized in Table (1). The weight on *CCC is much higher than the weight on ALIGN so that tri-consonantal clusters block vowel deletion, and the weight of ALIGN is above that of MAX, so that prefix vowels always delete with C-stems.

	*CCC	MAX	ALIGN
General Weights	11.5	0.0	4.5
Morpheme Scales	0.0	0.0	0.0

Table 1: Categorical weights and mean scales

The model's performance on forms in the training data is illustrated in Tableau (1) with a C-stem, /taba/, and a CC-stem, /tnaba/. Candidate probabil-

ities observed in the training data are given in column O. Column E gives the expected candidate probabilities generated by the model, rounded to two decimal places. The model fits the training data extremely well (KL divergence ≈ 0.002) and, because only the general weights are used, the model predicts that the trained pattern should generalize, yielding the same predicted probabilities for nonce forms.

3.2 Variable language

In the Variable language, prefix vowels always delete with C-stems and variably delete 33% of the time with CC-stems. As desired, the model captures this pattern using the general weights only, putting no weight on the scales, as shown in Table (2).

	*CCC	MAX	ALIGN
General Weights	5.2	0.0	4.5
Morpheme Scales	0.0	0.0	0.0

Table 2: Variable weights and mean scales

The model's performance on trained forms is illustrated in Tableau (2) below with a C-stem and a CC-stem. The weight of *CCC is above that of ALIGN, but by a smaller margin than in the Categorical language, yielding variable rather than categorical deletion with CC-stems. MAX is weighted below ALIGN, so that deletion occurs (nearly) categorically for C-stems. The probabilities generated by the model (E) fit the training data (O) extremely well (KL divergence ≈ 0.002) and, because only the general constraints are used, the model predicts that the trained pattern should generalize, yielding the same predicted probabilities for nonce forms.

/ape-taba/	*CCC	MAX	ALIGN	O	E
a. apetaba	0	0	-1	0.00	0.01
b. aptaba	0	-1	0	1.00	0.99
/ape-tnaba/	5.2	0.0	4.5	O	E
a. apetnaba	0	0	-1	0.67	0.67
b. aptnaba	-1	-1	0	0.33	0.33

Tableau 2: Variable language

3.3 Lexical language

The Lexical language is identical to the Categorical language, except that one prefix, /ape-/, is exceptional: its vowel always deletes with CC-stems. Averaged across the lexicon, the rate of deletion with CC-stems is therefore 33%, but this pattern cannot be captured using the general weights alone. The scales must be used to distinguish the behavior of the exceptionally deleting prefix from the other two prefixes. As Table (3) shows, the model's solution weights the general constraints in the same order as in the Categorical language: *CCC > ALIGN > MAX. The model additionally scales up the weight of ALIGN for the deleting prefix /ape-/, yielding (near) categorical deletion for it, and scales up the weight of *CCC for each of the non-deleting prefixes, preventing deletion for those prefixes.

	*CCC	MAX	ALIGN
General Weights	4.6	0.0	4.1
Deleting Prefix	0.0	0.0	6.4
Non-Deleting Prefixes	5.3	0.0	0.0
Stems	0.0	0.0	0.0

Table 3: Lexical weights and mean scales

The model's performance on forms in the training data is illustrated in Tableau (3) with a CC-stem /tnaba/ paired with a non-deleting prefix /ake-/, and the deleting prefix /ape-/. The weights shown for each input are the sums of the general weights and scales associated with the input morphemes for each constraint. The model's solution fits the training data well (KL divergence $\approx$ 0.004), predicting deletion for the deleting prefix and no deletion for each non-deleting prefix. These weights additionally yield deletion of all prefix vowels before C-stems (not shown) in the learning data, as expected. Since this is captured by general constraint weights, the same prediction is made for novel C-stems.

Because the general weight of ALIGN is somewhat lower but still close to the general weight of *CCC, variable deletion (37%) is predicted for novel prefixes attached to novel CC-stems. Tableau (4) illustrates with the nonce prefix /aʔe-/ and the nonce stem /pmaba/. Because this form was not present in the training data, only the expected probabilities are reported. As discussed above, predicting variable deletion is desirable given experimental find-

/ake-tnaba/	*CCC	MAX	ALIGN	O	E
a. aketnaba	0	0	-1	1.00	1.00
b. aktnaba	-1	-1	0	0.00	0.00
/ape-tnaba/	4.6	0.0	10.5	O	E
a. apetnaba	0	0	-1	0.00	0.00
b. aptnaba	-1	-1	0	1.00	1.00

Tableau 3: Lexical language – known prefixes and stems; /ape-/ exceptionally undergoes vowel deletion with CC-stems

ings that speakers extend lexical trends to nonce forms (Hayes et al., 2009). Deletion is the dispreferred outcome in both the training data and the predictions for novel forms, but the predicted rate of deletion for novel forms (37%) is a little higher than that observed in the training data (33%).

Interestingly, by using scales for each prefix, the model did not single out any prefix as qualitatively exceptional, despite the fact that such a solution is available. Removing the weight from the scales of the non-deleting prefixes and dividing it between the weight of general *CCC and the deleting prefix's scale of ALIGN produces a solution that is identical in terms of fit to the training data and the total sum of weights across all constraints and scales. That solution identifies only the deleting prefix as exceptional, and produces different predictions for nonce forms. The proposed objective function does not always differentiate among distinct ways of encoding exceptionality. The solution selected by the model in this experiment is arbitrarily influenced by starting the weights at zero. In experiments with weights initialized to random values between 0 and 10, the solutions selected by the model all have equivalent fit to the training data and total weight but vary somewhat in terms of how exceptionality is encoded and the deletion rate predicted for nonce forms. The availability of such varied solutions depends on the rate

/aʔe-pmaba/	*CCC	MAX	ALIGN	E
a. aʔepmaba	0	0	-1	0.63
b. aʔpmaba	-1	-1	0	0.37

Tableau 4: Lexical language – nonce prefix and stem

of exceptionality in the training data and the prior. These factors are further explored in §4.

3.4 Variable-Lexical language

The Variable-Lexical language is largely identical to the Variable language, except that 20% of CC-stems are exceptional triggers of categorical vowel deletion. The model's solution is summarized in Table (4). Tableau (5) illustrates the learned weights with a triggering stem /vraba/ and a non-triggering stem /tnaba/. The model learned a set of general weights which closely, but not exactly, reproduces the trained general pattern of variable deletion, and weights the scale of ALIGN higher for triggering CC-stems, though not enough to yield (near) categorical deletion. Again, ALIGN is weighted sufficiently above MAX to motivate (near) categorical deletion with C-stems. The model's fit to the training data for the Variable-Lexical language, while worse than the other languages, is still good (KL divergence $\approx$ 0.08). Examining the general weights, the model generalizes appropriately, predicting (near) categorical deletion for novel C-stems, and variable deletion for novel CC-stems.

	*CCC	MAX	ALIGN
General Weights	4.8	0.0	4.5
Prefixes	0.0	0.0	0.0
Exceptional Stems	0.0	0.0	1.0
Regular Stems	0.0	0.0	0.0

Table 4: Variable-Lexical weights and mean scales

	*CCC	MAX	ALIGN		
/ape-vraba/	4.8	0.0	5.5	O	E
a. apevraba	0	0	-1	0.00	0.33
b. apvraba	-1	-1	0	1.00	0.67
/ape-tnaba/	4.8	0.0	4.5	O	E
a. apetnaba	0	0	-1	0.67	0.58
b. aptnaba	-1	-1	0	0.33	0.42

Tableau 5: Variable-Lexical language – known prefixes and stems; /vraba/ exceptionally triggers prefix vowel deletion

Fit with the training data is not as close as with the other languages due to pervasive exceptionality: 20% of the stems (84 morphemes) must utilize

scales to capture their behavior, which conflicts with the prior's pressure to keep the total weights and scales low. The effect of the prior is explored systematically in the next section, but it is worth noting here that a closer fit with the training data for this language is straightforwardly achieved with a weaker prior; for example, setting $C = 0.1$ yields a deletion rate of 97% for /ape-vraba/.

4 Generalizing from exceptional data

This section examines the model's predictions for nonce data, focusing on how the choice of the prior and the rate of exceptionality in the training data affect generalization.

4.1 Effect of the prior

Recall that the previous section reported on experiments with the prior term C set to 1.0. Here, we vary C and examine its effects on the model's predictions, using the Lexical language as a test case.

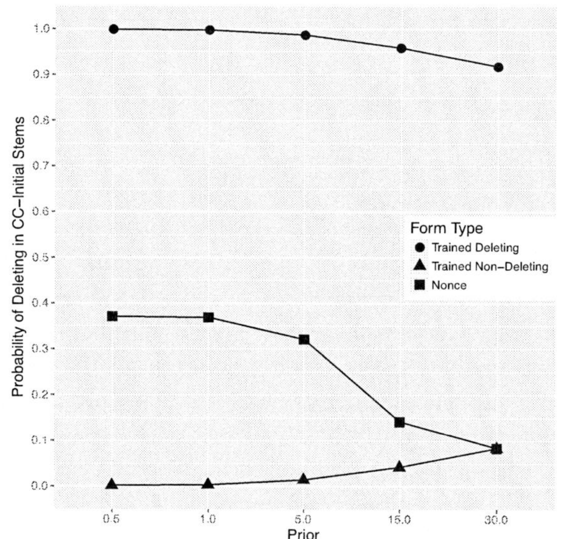

Figure 1: Probability of deletion with CC-stems by C values

Unsurprisingly, the model's fit to the training data decreases as the strength of the prior increases, as there is more pressure to keep all weights and scales close to zero. The model's predictions for novel forms also vary with C, as shown in Figure (1), which plots the probability of deletion for CC-stems by values of C. As C increases, there is a poorer fit to the training data: known forms which should undergo vowel deletion are slightly less likely to, and known forms which should not undergo vowel deletion are slightly more likely to.

The most striking trend is the convergence of nonce form behavior with the behavior of non-deleting forms. In the Lexical language, two prefixes, and thus two-thirds of the data, categorically do not undergo deletion with CC-stems. As discussed in §3.3, these proportions make multiple ways of encoding exceptionality available to the model. When the prior is weak, the model encodes exceptionality in a distributed way, and its predicted deletion rate for novel forms is intermediate between the deleting and non-deleting forms in the training data. When the prior is strong, however, the learner is forced to set more weights to zero, and the non-deleting forms in the learning data are more easily accommodated by the general constraint weights. This leads the learner to designate one of the prefixes as exceptional and to generalize to novel forms on the basis of the non-deleting prefixes. Thus, with a stronger prior, there is more pressure on the learner to over-extend the more general pattern in the data.

This pattern is clear when we examine the learned weights. Table (5) reports the weights learned with C set to 0.5 and 30. With C set low, the learner assigns weight to the exceptionally deleting prefix as well as the non-deleting prefixes. With C set high, the learner only assigns weight to the exceptional prefix, picking it out as exceptional.

	$C = 0.5$			$C = 30$		
	*CCC	MAX	ALIGN	*CCC	MAX	ALIGN
General Wts	5.3	0.0	4.8	2.4	0.0	0.01
Except. Prefix	0.0	0.0	7.1	0.0	0.0	4.8
Reg. Prefixes	6.0	0.0	0.0	0.0	0.0	0.0
Stems	0.0	0.0	0.0	0.0	0.0	0.0

Table 5: Lexical weights and mean scales, $C = 0.5$ and 30

4.2 Effect of exceptionality

Following Moore-Cantwell and Pater (2016), this section reports the effect of varying the proportion of exceptional forms in the training data on nonce form predictions. To test this, we started with the Categorical language, in which prefix vowels always delete with C-stems but never delete with CC-stems, and then created data sets which increased the per-

centage of CC-stems that trigger deletion of the prefix vowel by 10% increments, forming a total of 11 data sets (with deletion rates of 0%, 10%, ..., 90%, 100%). In these simulations, epochs were increased up to 80000 (we found this to be necessary to guarantee convergence for languages with pervasive exceptionality and weaker priors).

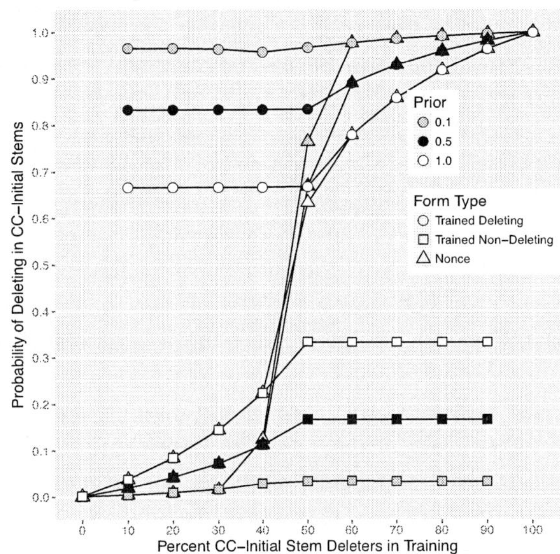

Figure 2: Probability of deletion with CC-stems by percentage of deletion-triggering CC-stems in the training data

Figure (2) plots the probability of deletion as a function of the percentage of triggering CC-stems in the training data. To show how the strength of the prior interacts with the rate of exceptionality in the data, we show curves for three settings of the prior parameter ($C = 0.1, 0.5, 1.0$). The patterns are qualitatively similar for all three settings, with closer fit to the data for weaker priors. As the percentage of triggering CC-stems in the training data increases, the probability of deleting the prefix vowel before any CC-stem increases. For trained stems, the probability of deleting with a non-triggering stem is always much lower than the probability of deleting with a triggering stem, with rates closer to categorical for lower C values. The rate of exceptionality affects learning of both the majority and minority patterns: the more extreme the imbalance, the more poorly the minority pattern is learned and the more categorically the majority pattern is learned.

The behavior of nonce forms mirrors the behavior of non-triggering stems when they form a majority of the training data (0%-30%), and mirrors the behavior of triggering stems when they form a majority in the training data (60%-100%), with the probability of deleting in nonce forms rising sharply across those data sets where there is not a clear majority (40%-50%). This indicates that, when there is a clear majority pattern, the model more strongly trends towards using the general weights to capture the majority pattern and the scales to capture the behavior of exceptional forms. When there is no clear majority pattern, the model will trend towards learning general weights which more closely reflect the lexical statistics in the training data, using scales to account for the idiosyncratic behavior of each stem.

Also noteworthy are the non-linear shape and the displacement of the nonce form curves. As Moore-Cantwell and Pater (2016) found for indexed constraints, we show here that the lexically scaled model also predicts nonce form rates that exaggerate the proportions in the training data. For example, when 70% of the stems trigger deletion in the training data, the model with $C = 1.0$ exaggerates this to over 85% in novel forms, and when 30% of stems trigger deletion in training, the model predicts fewer than 15% deletion in novel forms. Our results demonstrate two further influences. First, the exaggeration effect is greater for weaker priors since the curves are overall steeper. Second, the curve is shifted leftward: when 50% of the CC-stems are triggers, the predicted rate of deletion for nonce forms is above 50%, regardless of C. The predicted deletion rate is generally higher than might be expected on the basis of the trained deletion rate in CC-stems alone. The presence of categorically deleting C-stems in the data exerts an independent pressure to weight ALIGN more heavily than MAX, favoring deletion overall. When the $C = 1.0$ model is trained without C-stems (not shown), no skew is predicted: 50% deletion is predicted for nonce forms in the 50% training condition. These results indicate that predictions for nonce forms in one context can be influenced by other processes in the language.

5 Discussion

5.1 Why not L2 regularization?

Existing MaxEnt models of phonology overwhelmingly utilize L2 priors rather than L1 priors (Goldwater and Johnson, 2003; Wilson, 2006; Pater et al., 2012). For our purposes, however, we found that the choice of an L1 prior was crucial. While both L1 and L2 priors penalize higher weights, L1 priors are more effective for learning sparse vectors of weights, with as many zeroes as possible (Yan, 2016). The primary challenge for learning in the lexically scaled MaxEnt framework is to use scales sparingly. This requires a strong pressure to set weights exactly to zero, which an L1 prior provides. L2 priors favor solutions with small weights distributed across many parameters; setting weights to zero is not generally the optimal solution.

$$-\sum_i \log p(i) + \frac{1}{2\sigma^2}\left(\sum_{\gamma \in \Gamma} w_\gamma^2 + \sum_{\gamma \in \Gamma}\sum_{m \in M} s_{\gamma m}^2\right) \quad (5)$$

In experiments with an L2 prior, we found there was no weighting of the prior that simultaneously eliminated weights from the scales in languages without exceptionality while satisfactorily accounting for the training data. An example of the weights learned for the Variable language with a weak L2 prior is shown in Table (6). These weights were learned using the standard L-BFGS-B optimizer (Byrd et al., 1995) and the objective function in (5).

	*CCC	MAX	ALIGN
General Weights	3.00	0.00	2.50
Prefix Scales	1.00	0.00	0.80
C-Stem Scales	0.00	0.00	0.08
CC-Stem Scales	0.01	0.01	0.00

Table 6: Variable weights and mean scales, L2 prior, $\sigma^2 = 1$

While predicted probabilities for trained C-stems and CC-stems fit the training data well (Tableau 6), the model makes wide-spread use of scales: all morphemes use scales to some degree even though the Variable language does not require them. Consequently, the weight of ALIGN is not high enough to predict (near) categorical deletion for C-stems. The wide-spread use of scales also prevents the model from generalizing the rate of deletion to novel forms: deletion is predicted to apply more frequently to novel forms. Using a stronger prior (lowering σ), all weights and scales decrease, but weight remains on the scales and the fit with the training data deteriorates. Thus, the L2 prior fails to predict frequency-matching behavior for free variation, predicting skews not only for lexically-conditioned variation (as predicted by the L1 prior) but also for patterns without lexical conditioning.

As discussed earlier, we characterized successful learning in terms of feature selection, using scales only when needed to capture lexical conditioning, and we have shown that the L2 prior does not succeed on this criterion, affecting generalization of categorical, lexicalized, and freely variable processes. However, the extent to which language users encode predictable properties of lexical items is not known, and further behavioral research is needed to understand whether and how generalization of variable and exceptional processes is skewed.

	*CCC	MAX	ALIGN		
/ape-taba/	4.00	0.00	3.38	O	E
a. apetaba	0	0	-1	0.00	0.03
b. aptaba	0	-1	0	1.00	0.97
/ape-tnaba/	4.01	0.01	3.30	O	E
a. apetnaba	0	0	-1	0.67	0.66
b. aptnaba	-1	-1	0	0.33	0.34

Tableau 6: Variable language tableau – L2 prior, $\sigma^2 = 1$

5.2 No extra penalty for scales

We found that a general L1 prior was sufficient for keeping the model from overusing scales and generalizing beyond the data. The objective function penalizes weights and scales equally, but scales are more costly when many morphemes require the same scaling. Thus, the pressure against scales follows automatically from their limited utility in the grammar. This contrasts with other approaches to MaxEnt learning of exceptionality, which require either additional priors on some constraints to ensure that the model generalizes (Pater et al., 2012) or distinct phases of learning for general and lexical generalizations (Nazarov, 2018; Shih, 2018).

5.3 Multiple correct solutions

We also found that, when lexical exceptionality is present, there are multiple correct solutions for a given problem with different predictions about generalization. Any model that is tasked with learning both general and exceptional patterns must decide which items in the lexicon are the exceptions and which represent the generalizable pattern. We found that the objective function for our model favors overextending clear majority patterns, but is more ambivalent about what to treat as exceptional given balanced data (§3.3). This ambivalence was modulated by the strength of the prior (§4.1) and the presence of related processes in the data (§4.2).

5.4 Future work

A number of avenues for future work remain. As mentioned in §2, the differences between this approach and lexically indexed constraints (Pater, 2010) remain to be explored, as do differences from alternative models for learning variability and exceptionality (Nazarov, 2018; Shih, 2018). Another natural continuation of this research is to apply the learning paradigm described here to more realistic datasets. Following Pater (2007), Linzen et al. (2013, 489) limit scales to only penalizing exponents of the morphemes they are associated with. This locality condition will be important to incorporate before exploring more complex datasets.

Further investigations of the effect of the prior on generalization are needed. While we investigated the consequences of varying C, our focus was limited to the Lexical language. We found that the data distribution, the strength of the prior, and the existence of related processes in the language already introduce strong pressures on the learner's encoding of exceptionality. In some cases, however, we found the proposed prior did not uniquely favor a single solution. Ultimately, these and other modeling decisions require an understanding of how humans perform under similar learning conditions. Connections with experimental work on how humans generalize variable and exceptional patterns is crucial to defining desirable behavior for any learning model.

6 Conclusion

This paper introduces and tests a method for learning lexically scaled MaxEnt grammars. We show that an L1 prior places strong constraints on the encoding of exceptionality and identify a number of factors that affect the model's performance on training data and generalizations to nonce forms, which can be tested against human behavior.

References

Adam Albright and Bruce Hayes. 2003. Rules vs. analogy in English past tenses: A computational/experimental study. *Cognition*, 90(2):119–161.

Blake Allen and Michael Becker. 2015. Learning alternations from surface forms with sublexical phonology. Unpublished manuscript, University of British Columbia and Stony Brook University. Available as lingbuzz/002503.

Michael Becker and Maria Gouskova. 2016. Source-oriented generalizations as grammar inference in Russian vowel deletion. *Linguistic Inquiry*, 47(3):391–425.

Paul Boersma and Bruce Hayes. 2001. Empirical tests of the Gradual Learning Algorithm. *Linguistic Inquiry*, 32(1):45–86.

Richard H. Byrd, Peihuang Lu, Jorge Nocedal, and Ciyou Zhu. 1995. A limited memory algorithm for bound constrained optimization. *SIAM Journal on Scientific Computing*, 16(5):1190–1208.

Andries W. Coetzee and Shigeto Kawahara. 2013. Frequency biases in phonological variation. *Natural Language and Linguistic Theory*, 31(1):47–89.

Andries W. Coetzee and Joe Pater. 2011. The place of variation in phonological theory. In John A. Goldsmith, Jason Riggle, and Alan C. L. Yu, editors, *The Handbook of Phonological Theory*, pages 401–434. Wiley, 2nd edition.

Mirjam Ernestus and R. Harald Baayen. 2003. Predicting the unpredictable: Interpreting neutralized segments in Dutch. *Language*, pages 5–38.

Sharon Goldwater and Mark Johnson. 2003. Learning OT constraint rankings using a Maximum Entropy model. In *Proceedings of the Stockholm Workshop on Variation within Optimality Theory*, pages 111–120.

Bruce Hayes and Zsuzsa Cziráky Londe. 2006. Stochastic phonological knowledge: The case of Hungarian vowel harmony. *Phonology*, 23(1):59–104.

Bruce Hayes, Péter Siptár, Kie Zuraw, and Zsuzsa Londe. 2009. Natural and unnatural constraints in Hungarian vowel harmony. *Language*, 85(4):822–863.

Brian Hsu and Karen Jesney. 2016. Scalar positional markedness and faithfulness in Harmonic Grammar. In *Proceedings of the Annual Meeting of the Chicago Linguistic Society*, volume 51, pages 241–255.

Wendell Kimper. 2011. *Competing Triggers: Transparency and Opacity in Vowel Harmony*. Ph.D. thesis, University of Massachusetts Amherst.

Iwona Kraska-Szlenk. 1995. *The phonology of stress in Polish*. Ph.D. thesis, University of Illinois at Urbana-Champaign.

Solomon Kullback and Richard A. Leibler. 1951. On information and sufficiency. *The Annals of Mathematical Statistics*, 22(1):79–86, 03.

Tal Linzen, Sofya Kasyanenko, and Maria Gouskova. 2013. Lexical and phonological variation in Russian prepositions. *Phonology*, 30(3):453–515.

Claire Moore-Cantwell and Joe Pater. 2016. Gradient exceptionality in Maximum Entropy grammar with lexically specific constraints. *Catalan Journal of Linguistics*, 15:53–66.

Aleksei Nazarov. 2018. Learning within- and between-word variation in probabilistic OT grammars. In Gillian Gallagher, Maria Gouskova, and Sora Yin, editors, *Supplemental Proceedings of the 2017 Annual Meeting on Phonology*, Washington, DC. Linguistic Society of America.

Joe Pater, Karen Jesney, Robert Staubs, and Brian Smith. 2012. Learning probabilities over underlying representations. In *Proceedings of the Twelfth Meeting of the Special Interest Group on Computational Morphology and Phonology*, pages 62–71. Association for Computational Linguistics.

Joe Pater. 1996. *Consequences of Constraint Ranking*. Ph.D. thesis, McGill University.

Joe Pater. 2007. The locus of exceptionality: Morpheme-specific phonology as constraint indexation. In Leah Bateman, Michael O'Keefe, Ehren Reilly, and Adam Werle, editors, *University of Massachusetts Occasional Papers in Linguistics 32: Papers in Optimality Theory III*, pages 259–296. GLSA, Amherst, MA.

Joe Pater. 2010. Morpheme-specific phonology: Constraint indexation and inconsistency resolution. In Steve Parker, editor, *Phonological argumentation: Essays on evidence and motivation*, pages 123–154. Equinox, London.

Stephanie S. Shih. 2018. Learning lexical classes from variable phonology. In Yuki Seo and Haruya Ogawa, editors, *Selected Papers from Asian Junior Linguists Conference 2*, pages 1–15. ICUWPL.

Yoshimasa Tsuruoka, Jun'ichi Tsujii, and Sophia Ananiadou. 2009. Stochastic gradient descent training for L1-regularized log-linear models with cumulative penalty. In *Proceedings of the Joint Conference of the 47th Annual Meeting of the ACL and the 4th International Joint Conference on Natural Language Processing of the AFNLP: Volume 1*, pages 477–485. Association for Computational Linguistics.

Colin Wilson. 2006. Learning phonology with substantive bias: An experimental and computational study of velar palatalization. *Cognitive Science*, 30:945–982.

Shi Yan. 2016. L1 norm regularization and sparsity explained for dummies. https://medium.com/mlreview/l1-norm-regularization-

and-sparsity-explained-for-dummies-5b0e4be3938a.

Kie Zuraw. 2000. *Patterned Exceptions in Phonology*. Ph.D. thesis, University of California, Los Angeles.

Kie Zuraw. 2010. A model of lexical variation and the grammar with application to Tagalog nasal substitution. *Natural Language & Linguistic Theory*, 28(2):417–472.

Jesse Zymet. 2018. *Lexical propensities in phonology: corpus and experimental evidence, grammar, and learning*. Ph.D. thesis, University of California, Los Angeles.

Learning complex inflectional paradigms through blended gradient inputs

Eric Rosen
Johns Hopkins University
errosen@mail.ubc.ca

Abstract

Through Gradient Symbolic Computation (Smolensky and Goldrick, 2016), in which input forms can consist of gradient blends of more than one phonological realization, we propose a way of deriving surface forms in complex inflectional paradigms that dispenses with direct references to inflectional classes and relies solely on relatively simple blends of input expressions.

In languages whose inflectional systems have a highly complex paradigmatic structure, it becomes a challenge to explain how a speaker can produce a correct inflectional form when the number of possible forms is exceedingly large. As Ackerman and Malouf (2013, p. 429) (henceforth A&M) comment: "That speakers are able to do this is a truly puzzling accomplishment given the extraordinary variation and complexity attested in the morphological systems of the world." When it becomes extremely difficult for a speaker to memorize every possible inflectional form for every lexeme in their language, it becomes attractive to posit some means by which they can produce a correct unmemorized form.

Three interacting types of paradigmatic complexity that put a burden on learning are addressed here: (a) differences in inflectional material across lexemes, which, descriptively, result in division of lexemes into inflectional classes; (b) syncretism, where the same inflectional material occurs in different paradigm cells; (c) independent subsystems of inflectional class behaviour, evident in Mazatec (see §3.) These complexities are all ways in which inflectional patterns depart from *canonicity* as defined in detail by Corbett (2009); Baerman and Corbett (2010); Stump (2016).

Through Gradient Symbolic Computation (Smolensky and Goldrick, 2016), a type of Harmonic Grammar, and with examples from Russian and Mazatec[1], we propose a system that enables a speaker to produce correct forms of complex paradigms through learnable input representations without indexing to inflectional classes.

The paper is organized as follows. §1 introduces GSC and how it can be applied to learning exponents of inflectional paradigms. §2 shows how Russian noun inflection can be acquired through this framework. §2.1 shows how GSC limits the kinds of inflectional patterning that are possible. §3 analyses complex paradigms in Mazatec, where inflectional classes vary in three cross-cutting dimensions. §4 discusses testing and comparison with other models. §5 summarizes how this framework can both explain departures from canonicity in inflectional paradigms and also constrain the degree of departure from the canonical.

1 Gradient Symbolic Computation

We adopt here Gradient Symbolic Computation (henceforth GSC), in which gradient inputs are given numerical activation levels, which we shall show to be learnable, and are evaluated with weighted constraints that calculate the Harmony of input candidates, where the candidate with the greatest Harmony surfaces. This formalism is part of a larger research program in which computation derives outputs from gradient representations in phonology, syntax and semantics (Cho et al., 2017; Faust and Smolensky, 2017; Faust, 2017; Goldrick et al., 2016; Hsu, 2018; Müller, 2017; Rosen, 2016, 2018; Smolensky et al., 2014; Smolensky and Goldrick, 2016; Van Hell et al.,

---

[1] In response to a reviewer's question about the effects and degree of simplification of the paradigms of these two languages, we contend that (a) any linguistic analysis will have some degree of simplification, (b) the paradigms are no more simplified than those analysed by A&M and in fact include *more* paradigm positions than are represented in their table A6 (p. 457), and (c) nothing in the analysis was excluded because the model couldn't handle it.

Proceedings of the Society for Computation in Linguistics (SCiL) 2019, pages 102-112.
New York City, New York, January 3-6, 2019

2016; Zimmermann, 2017b,a, forthcoming).[2]

In the examples in §2 from Russian noun inflection, the surface exponents that can represent genitive singular among the descriptive inflectional classes, form a blend of input segments, which we shall call 'inflectional input': $\{a, i\}$. A lexeme (basic element of the lexicon) in descriptive class 1 whose genitive sg. is *vina*, 'wine' contributes an input we shall call 'base input' that consists of what is traditionally thought of as a stem plus a blend of word-final segments $\{a, u, o\}$ that mirrors segments that can occur in surface-final position. We propose that it derives as follows, with numerical details shown later in table 4.

	Lexical base	Inflectional affix
Input:	root vin $\{a, u, o\}$	GEN.SG. = $\{a, i\}$
Output:	vin a root exponent affixal exponent	

Table 1: Gen.sg. of lexeme, descriptive class 1

In this framework, a discrete output form is chosen from possible candidates by the action of Faithfulness constraints that are familiar from Optimality Theory (Prince and Smolensky, 1993), but which, in GSC, have weighted values and evaluate gradient input activations. We assume a highly-weighted *quantization* constraint quantified by an equation in Cho et al. (2017) that disfavours blended outputs and gives a higher Harmony to discrete non-blended forms. The tableaux below thus ignore blended output candidates.[3]

Surface material that some models view as deriving solely from an affix input is derived here from two distinct input sources, thus blending two competing analyses: a constructivist approach that builds whole words out of morphemes and a word-based approach that seeks relationships between whole word forms. The input representation of a lexeme that includes affixal material as an intrinsic part of the word is based upon a whole-word model; an affix as a fully independent input follows a morpheme-based model. A simi-

CLASS	1	2	3	4
		SINGULAR		
NOM	-o	-∅	-a	-∅
ACC	-o	-∅	-u	-∅
GEN	-a	-a	-i	-i
DAT	-u	-u	-e	-i
LOC	-e	-e	-e	-i
INST	-om	-om	-oj	-ju
		PLURAL		
NOM	-a	-i	-i	-i
ACC	-a	-i	-i	-i
GEN	-∅	-ov	-∅	-ej
DAT	-am	-am	-am	-am
LOC	-ax	-ax	-ax	-ax
INST	-am'i	-am'i	-am'i	-am'i

Table 2: Russian noun paradigm

lar approach is taken by Smolensky and Goldrick (2016), treating French liaison as derived from both the end of a preceding word and the beginning of a following word, thus combining two competing approaches to liaison in the literature.

Any matching phonological material from the two sources will combine through coalescence. When there are multiple descriptive inflectional classes, the exponent for a given inflectional combination varies, depending not only on the lexeme, but on the stem when there is stem allomorphy (Stump, 2016). The current proposal for blended word-final input segments that mirror affixes, directly encodes the fact that lexeme/stem choice will affect affix-choice. Non-concatenative and suppletive alternations can thus be represented as well, as blends of different stem alternants occurring underlyingly.

2 Learning Russian noun inflection

For ease of exposition, we first examine the relatively simple paradigms of case/number noun suffixes in Russian, with data from A&M p. 460 given in table 2. For presentation purposes, we ignore here the paradigm defectiveness of some Russian nouns (Corbett, 2007).

The exponent that surfaces for a given stem and person/number combination is the one with the highest aggregate activation that surpasses a threshold determined by MAX and DEP constraints to be defined below. When two instances of the same exponent occur in both base and inflectional input, they can coalesce together in the output, with an aggregate input activa-

---

[2] A reviewer asks what advantages this model has over a "genuine connectionist model" such as Goldsmith and O'Brien (2006); Kann and Schütze (2016); Malouf (2018). In this model, the knowledge it contains is completely transparent, whereas in the last two models cited by the reviewer, it is not clear what kind of knowledge is contained in those networks. (See §4 for further discussion.)

[3] But see Zimmermann (2017b,a, 2018) for analyses of other phenomena in which outputs are also gradient.

Source	☞ a	u	o	i
Base input	0.1	0.02	0.16	
GEN-SG	0.3			0.26
Total	**0.4**	0.02	0.16	0.26

Table 3: Summed activations for class 1 GEN-SG

$vin(0.1 \cdot a, 0.02 \cdot u, 0.16 \cdot o)$ 'wine' $+$ GEN-SG$(0.3 \cdot a, 0.26 \cdot i)$			
	MAX 5	DEP -2	Harmony
☞ **vin-a**	2.0	-1.2	**0.8**
vin-u	0.1	-1.96	-1.86
vin-o	0.8	-1.68	-0.88
vin-i	1.3	-1.48	-0.18
vin-e		-2.0	-2.0
vin			0.0

Table 4: Tableau for class 1 GEN-SG

$vin(0.1 \cdot a, 0.02 \cdot u, 0.16 \cdot o)$ 'wine' $+$ GEN-PL$(0.28 \cdot ov, 0.22 \cdot ej)$			
	MAX 5	DEP -2	Harmony
vin-a	0.5	-1.8	-1.3
vin-u	0.1	-1.96	-1.86
vin-o	0.8	-1.68	-0.88
vin-ov	1.4	-1.44	-0.04
vin-ej	1.1	-1.56	-0.46
vin-e		-2.0	-2.0
☞ **vin**			**0.0**

Table 5: Tableau for class 1 GEN-PL

tion that is the sum of the two source activations. Consider again the same genitive singular form *vina* given above in table 1. Suppose that the base input has a blend of three affix-mirroring segments with the following activity levels: vin + (0.1·a, 0.02·u, 0.16·o) and affixal GEN-SING is a blend of segments (0.3·a, 0.26·i). There are then four possible candidate segments that have a non-zero input activation: /-a/, /-u/, /-o/ and /-i/, whose input activations will be the sums of any pair of co-occurring segments that can coalesce in the output as shown in table 3.

The segment *a* surpasses the relevant threshold and surfaces, having the highest aggregate input activation. Table 4 shows a harmonic tableau for this form. In GSC, a MAX constraint (here weighted 5.0) contributes positive Harmony proportionate to the surfacing of underlying activation. A DEP constraint (here weighted at -2.0) contributes negative Harmony for the deficit between input and output activations. We assume that quantization will only allow surface activations of 0 or 1 so the tableau only considers candidates with those values. The positive contribution to Harmony from MAX for the winning candidate is is 5 times the sum of its input activations for /a/ which are 0.1 from the base input plus 0.3 from gen.sg. inflection input. The winning candidate has the highest Harmony.

An affixless candidate incurs no MAX reward or DEP penalty and will be optimal when all other candidates have negative Harmony (table 5.)

The following simple algorithm[4] learned blended base and inflectional input values such that the optimal output candidate is the correct target of learning for all 48 forms. Following Faust and Smolensky (2017, page 2), not just an individual segment but also other structures can have an activity level.

- Initialize all activations at zero.
- Calculate the Harmony for each descriptive stem-class/number/case combination.
- If the wrong affix is predicted, decrease its two input activations if nonzero and increase the activations of the desired affix. Stepsize 0.02.
- Repeat until all 48 paradigm positions are correctly predicted.

Tables 6 and 7 show the learned input values after 72 iterations.

Nonzero inputs for an inflectional combination indicate its set of possible exponents. A co-occurring nonzero base input narrows down the choice of those exponents. For example, the locative singular affix is *-e* for all descriptive classes except class 4, where *-i* surfaces. The activation of 0.12 for *-i* for a class 4 base input allows it to surpass other competitors where it surfaces.

In summary, representing both base and inflectional inputs with a blend of partially activated exponents allows a speaker to encode all the information in a multi-class inflectional paradigm directly on the relevant input forms.

---

[4]A reviewer suggests that the contribution of this model is theoretical rather than computational and that the learning algorithm is 'fairly trivial.' We see no advantage in a model of human learning that is intentionally complex; the focus of this proposal is to contribute to computationally-based theories of human language rather than to test new computational techniques.

Class	1	2	3	4
a	0.1		0.04	
e			0.12	
u	0.02		0.06	
om		0.04		
ov		0.02		
ax				
am				
am'i				
i			0.1	0.12
oj			0.06	
ju				0.06
o	0.16			
ej				0.08

Table 6: Learned nonzero input values

Cell	NSg	ASg	GSg	DSg	LSg	ISg
a	0.28		0.3			
e				0.26	0.3	
u		0.28		0.3		
om						0.3
ov						
ax						
am						
am'i						
i			0.26	0.22	0.24	
oj						0.26
ju						0.26
o	0.24	0.22				
ej						
Cell	NPl	APl	GPl	DPl	LPl	IPl
a	0.24	0.24				
e						
u						
om						
ov			0.4			
ax					0.3	
am				0.3		
am'i						0.3
i	0.3	0.3				
oj						
ju						
o						
ej			0.22			

Table 7: Learned inflectional input values

2.1 Restricting possible paradigms

The Russian noun paradigm exhibits both syncretism within descriptive inflectional classes and variance of exponents for a given position across inflectional classes. Our model predicts that there are limits to such departures from canonicity. In the dative singular, the affix is e in class 3 and i in class 4. In the genitive singular, it is i for both classes, making i syncretic across those two feature combinations for class 4. Our model predicts the impossibility of the pattern in the right-hand half of table 8.

	Real		Impossible	
	Class 3	Class 4	Class 3	Class 4
Gen. Sg.	i	i	i	e
Dat. Sg.	e	i	e	i

Table 8: Crossing diagonals

In the impossible paradigm, lines connecting the two instances of i (coloured blue) and connecting the two instances of e (coloured red) would cross. Such diagonal crossing can be shown to mathematically imply activation hierarchies that lead to a contradiction (table 9) , where ι represents the activation of i and ϵ of e for a given (subscripted) feature value or descriptive inflectional class.

$$\iota_{g.sg.} + \iota_3 > \epsilon_{g.sg.} + \epsilon_3 \tag{1}$$

$$\epsilon_{g.sg.} + \epsilon_4 > \iota_{g.sg.} + \iota_4 \tag{2}$$

$$\iota_{dat.sg.} + \iota_4 > \epsilon_{dat.sg.} + \epsilon_4 \tag{3}$$

$$\epsilon_{dat.sg.} + \epsilon_3 > \iota_{dat.sg.} + \iota_3 \tag{4}$$

$$(1) + (2) : \iota_3 + \epsilon_4 > \epsilon_3 + \iota_4 \tag{5}$$

$$(3) + (4) : \iota_4 + \epsilon_3 > \epsilon_4 + \iota_3 \tag{6}$$

$$(6) \text{ contradicts } (5)$$

Table 9: Contradictory inequalities

Thus, in spite of a common misconception that "you can do anything with numbers", the proposed GSC model predicts that many conceivable paradigms are impossible.

3 Learning inputs in Mazatec

We now consider verb paradigms in Chiquihuitlán Mazatec, a language with a high degree of paradigmatic complexity. Jamieson (1982) shows that its verbal inflectional morphology has three separate dimensions in the affirmative forms of the neutral and incompletive aspects: (a) a stem formative (table 12), with 35 possible exponents, (b) a final vowel (table 19), with 11 possible exponents, and (c) a tone pattern (table 15), with 15 possible exponents. For example, in the neutral 1st person singular form in table 10, ba^{3}sæ^1, the stem is merely the segment s. The stem formative is ba, the final vowel is $æ$ and the tone pattern is 3-1. Yet these $35 \times 11 \times 15 = 5775$ hypothetically

NEUTRAL   INCOMPLETIVE

	SG	PL	SG	PL
1INCL		$ča^2sē^2$		$ča^2sē^{42}$
1	$ba^3sæ^1$	$ča^2sĩ^{24}$	$k^wa^3sæ^1$	$ča^4sĩ^{24}$
2	$ča^2se^2$	$ča^2sū^2$	$ča^4se^2$	$ča^4sū^2$
3		ba^3se^2		$k^wa^4se^2$

Table 10: Paradigm for 'remember'

possible combinations are actually reduced to 20 in Jamieson's list of paradigms. Table 10 gives the paradigm for ba^3se^2 'remember' from A&M:450, taken from Jamieson (1982, p. 167). This lexeme is in stem formative descriptive class 11, tone pattern class B 3-1 and final vowel class 2.

Combinations of morphosyntactic features are represented by combinations of multiple exponents, but there is no apparent correspondence between individual feature values and individual exponents. The surface form for a verb expresses feature values for aspect, person and number, with a stem formative, a tone pattern and a suffix vowel.

Stems in many cases consist merely of a single segment. As A&M:447 observe, a stem is much more easily identified by "its membership in an inflectional class in each of three distinct cross-cutting dimensions: tone pattern, final vowel, and stem formative." In the proposed blended representations, a lexeme's base input carries much of the information that predicts what exponents it occurs with, in this way identifying what can descriptively be called its stem. It also directly encodes what is descriptively its inflectional class in a way that is not possible in a model in which paradigm information and stem information are separate. Table 11 shows, with activation values omitted for now, an example basic input-output structure, which contains gradient blends of consonants in the input.

Tone and final vowel omitted here		
	Lexical base	Stem formative
Input:	{b, k^w, č} a $\overset{\frown}{}$ s (root)	3rd.p.def.incomp. { $\widehat{sk}$, k^{wh}, s, k^w }
Output:	k^wa $\underbrace{}$ s $\underbrace{}$	
	stem formative root exponent	

Table 11: Input-output for 'remember' 3rd.p.def.inc.

Some further complexities in Jamieson's data are omitted here for simplicity of exposition but

Class	Stem formatives				Representations	
	3def or 1s		Oth.prsns			
	Neu.	Incomp.	Neu.	Incomp.	blend	vowel
1	be	k^we	be	k^we	b,**k^w**	e
2	ba	k^wa	ba	k^wa	b, **k^w**	a
3	bo	$\widehat{sk}o$	čo	čo	b, **$\widehat{sk}$**, č	o
4	bu	$\widehat{sk}u$	ču	ču	b, **$\widehat{sk}$**, č	u
5	hu	$\widehat{sk}u$	$č^hu$	$č^hu$	h, **$\widehat{sk}$**, $č^h$	u
6	hi	$\widehat{sk}i$	$č^hi$	$č^hi$	h, **$\widehat{sk}$**, $č^h$	i
7	^hba	$k^{wh}a$	^hba	$k^{wh}a$	^hb, **k^{wh}**	a
8	¢i	¢i	nĩ	nĩ	**¢**, n	i
9	su	su	nũ	nũ	**s**, n	u
10	bu	ku	bu	ku	b,**k**	u
11	ba	k^wa	ča	ča	b, k^w, č	a
12	ka	$\widehat{sk}a$	ča	ča	k, **$\widehat{sk}$**, č	a
13	^hba	$k^{wh}a$	nã	nã	^hb, **k^{wh}**, n	a
14	ba	k^wa	nã	nã	b,**k^w**, n	a
15	bi	k^wi	bi	k^wi	b,**k^w**	i
16	bu	$\widehat{sk}u$	^ntu	^ntu	b, **$\widehat{sk}$**, ^nt	u
17	hi	si	či	ši	h, s, č, š	i
18	^hba	$k^{wh}a$	$č^ha$	$č^ha$	^hb, **k^{wh}**, $č^h$	a

Table 12: Representations of stem formatives

can be explained by our analysis. These include suffixing of verbs, verb compounding, verbs with no stem formative[5] and stem suppletion.[6]

Among the 35 possible stem formatives, 11 possible final vowels and 15 possible tone patterns, a given lexeme's input form only needs a blend of a small subset of each of these exponents.

3.1 Learning inputs for stem formatives

Consider first the stem formatives, shown in table 12 (Data from Jamieson (1982).)[7]

The proposed representation for each base input is simply a blend of all its possible initial consonants. The vowels stay the same across a class. Which consonant surfaces depends on how this blend interacts through coalescence of identical consonants with an inflectional input blend of consonant features.

Tables 13 and 14 show the results of the same kind of algorithm discussed on page 3 for learning input activations of inflectional person-number combinations and base inputs respectively.

It took 22 iterations to learn activations that derive the correct stem formative consonants for each of 4 person-number groups in 18 classes.

Abstracting away for now from tone and final

---

[5]If a stem formative is absent from the base input, an anchoring constraint will prevent an inflection-based stem-formative input from surfacing.

[6]Stem suppletion can be accounted for by an input that includes a blend of different stem allomorphs each linked to different inflectional features.

[7]Following Golston and Kehrein (1998), we take what Jamieson transcribes as complex onsets and nuclei to be simplex segments with secondary articulations.

3def,1sg,neu		3def,1sg,incomp	
b	0.27	sk	0.21
k	0.06	k^{wh}	0.21
h	0.12	s	0.12
^{h}b	0.12	k^w	0.12
Other Neu.		Other Incomp	
b	0.21	č	0.15
č	0.21	k^{wh}	0.12
n	0.21	n	0.21
^{n}t	0.12	š	0.15

Table 13: Input activations for person/number

vowels, for $k^w a^4 se^2$ 'remember' (class 11), 3rd p. def. incompl., the activations for the input given above in table 11 are as follows.

Base input: $(0.1 \cdot b, 0.3 \cdot k^w, 0.3 \cdot č)$as

Inflectional input:
$(0.21 \cdot \widehat{sk}, 0.21 \cdot k^{wh}, 0.12 \cdot s, 0.12 \cdot k^w)$

For each candidate, an inflectional input can coalesce with a base input. The segment with the highest combined activation surfaces, namely k^w, with an underlying activation of $0.3 + 0.12 = 0.42$. We assume the stem consonant and the vowel of the stem formative to both have full 1.0 underlying activations; thus no Harmony is gained by having a gradient inflectional stem formative consonant incorrectly coalesce with the stem consonant nor for a gradient inflectional final vowel to incorrectly coalesce with the stem formative vowel.

3.2 Learning inputs for tone patterns

Tone patterns, which fall into 11 descriptive classes, were also learned by an algorithm that separately learned patterns for the first and second syllables.

Table 15 shows tone patterns listed by class and person-number-aspect combination. (Data from Jamieson (1982).)

There is some phonological predictability for the tones of the second syllable, where 1 is the highest tone and 4 the lowest:

- The initial tone on the second syllable can be no lower than the final tone of the first syllable.
- If the initial tone of the second syllable is 3 or 4 and the same as the final tone of the first, there is a further rise of two tone levels:

  – e.g. 4 can be followed by 42 but not simple 4;
  – 3 can be followed by 31 but not 3.
  – 2 can only be followed by 2 or 24.

Class	stem formative	input activation
1	b	0.2
	k^w	0.3
2	b	0.1
	k^w	0.3
3	b	0.1
	$\widehat{sk}$	0.2
	č	0.2
4	b	0.1
	$\widehat{sk}$	0.2
	č	0.3
5	$\widehat{sk}$	0.2
	h	0.2
	č	0.3
6	$\widehat{sk}$	0.2
	h	0.2
	č	0.3
7	^{h}b	0.3
	k^{wh}	0.2
8	¢	0.4
	n	0.2
9	n	0.2
	s	0.3
10	b	0.2
	k	0.3
Class	stem formative	input activation
11	b	0.1
	k^w	0.3
	č	0.3
12	$\widehat{sk}$	0.2
	k	0.3
	č	0.3
13	^{h}b	0.2
	k^{wh}	0.2
	n	0.2
14	b	0.1
	k^{wh}	0.2
	n	0.3
15	b	0.2
	k^w	0.2
16	b	0.1
	$\widehat{sk}$	0.2
	^{n}t	0.3
17	s	0.2
	h	0.2
	š	0.3
	č	0.1
18	^{h}b	0.2
	k^{wh}	0.1
	č	0.3

Table 14: Input activations for stem formatives

– 1 can only be followed by 1.

- We can take the level 4 tone that occurs last in

Neutral aspect						
Class	3def	1s	1in	2s	1ex	2p
A	3-1	3-1	3-31	3-1	3-14	3-1
B1-1	2-2	1-1	2-2	2-2	2-24	2-2
B3-1	3-2	3-1	2-2	2-2	2-24	2-2
C	3-24	14-3	14-42	14-3	14-34	14-3
D1-1	1-1	1-1	3-2	3-2	3-24	3-2
D3-1	3-2	3-1	3-2	3-2	3-24	3-2
Incompletive aspect						
A(1-7)	4-2	3-1	3-31	3-1	3-14	3-1
A(8-18)	4-2	3-1	4-31	4-1	4-14	4-1
B1-1 (1-7)	4-2	1-1	2-2	2-2	2-24	2-2
B1-1 (8-13)	4-2	1-1	4-42	4-2	4-24	4-2
B1-1 (14-18)	4-1	1-1	4-42	4-3	4-34	4-3
B3-1 (1-7)	4-2	3-1	2-2	2-2	2-24	2-2
B3-1 (8-13)	4-2	3-1	4-42	4-2	4-24	4-2
B3-1 (14-18)	4-1	3-1	4-42	4-3	4-34	4-3
C	3-24	14-3	14-42	14-3	14-34	14-3
D1-1 (8-13)	4-2	1-1	4-42	4-2	4-24	4-2

Table 15: Tone patterns

the 1st exclusive to be a separate tonal input for 1st-exclusive.

Tables 16 and 17 show the results of learning algorithms for first and second syllable tones. Ten iterations were required for syllable 1 and 22 iterations for syllable 2, with a stepsize of 0.05 for syllable 1 and 0.1 for syllable 2. Activations were initialized at 0.2 for each base-input and tonal person-number input for each tone pattern that actually occurs. We assume there exists a Harmonic Grammar analysis of the above constraints, in which they have higher weight than Faithfulness, which will otherwise derive the pattern with the highest aggregate activation.

A two-syllable base input has a tone linked to the mora of each syllable. The inflectional input has a linearly ordered sequence of two tones on the tonal tier.[8] A strongly-weighted anchoring constraint will require the tones on the inflectional input to line up with the tones on the base input when they coalesce.

Consider the second person singular incompletive of 'remember', $\check{c}a^4se^2$. This is tonal class B-3-1 (8-13) with inputs shown in table 18. When the two input sources coalesce on each syllable, tone level 4 has the highest activation for syllable 1 of $0.25 + 0.1 = 0.35$ and tone level 2 on syllable 2 of $0.4 + 0.0 = 0.4.$, both the correct tones.

3.3 Learning inputs for final vowels

Table 19, with data from Jamieson (1982) shows the 10 descriptive classes of final vowels.

---

[8]In the 1st person exclusive, a level 4 tone will occur further to the right of other tones.

First syllable tones					
Tone class	1	2	3	4	14
A1-7			0.25	0.15	
A8-18			0.2	0.25	
B1-1-1-7	0.15	0.25		0.05	
B1-1-18-13	0.2	0.25		0.2	
B1-1-14-18	0.15	0.25		0.2	
B3-1-1-7		0.3	0.2	0.1	
B3-1-8-13		0.25	0.15	0.25	
B3-1-14-18		0.25	0.1	0.25	
C			0.2		0.35
D1-1	0.2		0.15	0.25	
D3-1	0.15		0.2	0.25	
Person/number	1	2	3	4	14
3def Neu.		0.05	0.25		
1s Neu.	0.15		0.15		0.1
1in Neu.		0.2	0.15		0.05
2s Neu.		0.15	0.15		0.05
1ex Neu.		0.2	0.15		0.05
2p Neu.		0.1	0.1		
3def Inc.			0.15	0.35	
1s Inc.	0.25		0.15		0.1
1in Inc.		0.05	0.05	0.1	0.05
2s Inc.		0.05	0.1	0.1	
1ex Inc.		0.05	0.05	0.1	
2p Inc.		0.05	0.05	0.1	

Table 16: Input activations for σ_1 tones

Second syllable tones					
Tone class	1	2	3	4	24
A1-7	0.2	0.2	-0.1		
A8-18	0.5		0.2	0.2	
B1-1-1-7	0.2	0.2			
B1-1-18-13		0.4		0.2	
B1-1-14-18	0.1		0.6	0.4	
B3-1-1-7	0.2	0.2			
B3-1-8-13		0.4		0.2	
B3-1-14-18	0.5		0.4	0.2	
C			0.3	0.3	0.2
D1-1		0.5		0.2	
D3-1	0.1	0.5		0.2	
Person/number	1	2	3	4	24
3def Neu.	0.2	0.4			0.2
1s Neu.	0.5		0.2		
1in Neu.		0.1	0.5	0.8	
2s Neu.	0.2	0.1	0.2		
1ex Neu.	0.2	0.1	0.2		
2p Neu.	0.2	0.1	0.2		
3def Inc.	0.2	0.3	0.1		0.2
1s Inc.	0.5		0.3		
1in Inc.			0.3	0.7	
2s Inc.	0.1		0.3		
1ex Inc.	0.1		0.2		
2p Inc.	0.1		0.2		

Table 17: Input activations for σ_2 tones

The algorithm learns input values, shown in table 20, for $\pm hi$, $\pm lo$, $\pm bk$ and *nas* features, with coalescence of values from the two input sources. A negative value in the table represents a positive value for the negative binary feature: e.g. -0.1

	Syllable 1			
Tone →	1	2	3	4
Tonal class B-31 (8-13)		0.25	0.15	0.25
2nd sg. incomp.		0.05	0.1	0.1
Total		0.3	0.25	**0.35**
	Syllable 2			
Tone →	1	2	3	4
Tonal class B-31 (8-13)		0.4		0.2
2nd sg. incomp.	0.1		0.3	
Total	0.1	**0.4**	0.3	0.2

Table 18: Aggregate activations

Class	3def (basic)	1s	1in	2s	1ex	2p
1	i	æ	ẽ	i	ĩ	ũ
2	e	æ	ẽ	e	ĩ	ũ
3	æ	æ	ẽ	e	ĩ	ũ
4	u	u	ũ	i	ĩ	ũ
5	o	o	õ	e	ĩ	ũ
6	a	a	ã	e	ĩ	ũ
7	ĩ	ẽ	ẽ	ĩ	ĩ	ũ
8	ẽ	ẽ	ẽ	ĩ	ĩ	ũ
9	ũ	ũ	ũ	ĩ	ĩ	ũ
10	ã	ã	ã	ĩ	ĩ	ũ

Table 19: Classes of final vowels

hi means 0.1 $-hi$. We assume that $\forall i$ both $+f_i$ and $-f_i$ do not occur in the same source. Table 21 shows input vowel features for $\check{c}a^4se^2$ 'remember', final-vowel class 2 in the 2nd sg. incomp. (W_v denotes base input.)

	hi	lo	bk	nas
3def	-0.1			
1s	-0.2	0.2		
1in	-0.2			0.2
2s	0.1	-0.3	-0.2	
1ex	0.4	-0.2	-0.2	0.2
2p	0.4	-0.2	0.3	0.2
	hi	lo	bk	nas
Class 1	0.2		-0.1	
Class 2	-0.2	-0.1	-0.1	
Class 3	-0.2	0.2	-0.1	
Class 4	0.4	-0.2	0.1	
Class 5	-0.2	-0.3	0.1	
Class 6	-0.2	0.1	0.1	
Class 7	0.2	-0.1	-0.2	0.2
Class 8			-0.1	0.2
Class 9	0.4	-0.2	0.1	0.1
Class 10			0.1	0.1

Table 20: Input activations for vowel features

We adopt a second, strongly-weighted quantiza-

tion constraint from Cho et al. (2017) that requires the sum of activations from a binary feature group such as $\{+hi, -hi\}$ to be 1. Thus $-hi$ competes with $+hi$ and $-hi$ surfaces because its higher aggregate activation results in greater Harmony.

Feature	2nd-sg.	W_v	Winner
hi	0.1	-0.2	$-hi$
lo	-0.3	-0.1	$-lo$
bk	-0.2	-0.1	$-bk$
nas			$0\ nas$

Table 21: Values for final-vowel class 2, 2nd-sg.

$[-hi, -lo, -bk, 0\ nas] = e$, the correct final vowel, is the output after quantization.

4 Testing and comparison with other models

To test how a learner could predict an unseen inflectional form for a given stem, we ran cross-vaidation on Mazatec stem formatives, tone patterns and final vowels, with training set items (70% of the total stemclass×inflection combinations) picked randomly from a Zipf-Mandelbrot distribution. On ten runs for each, the average test accuracy was 83% for stem formatives, 87% on tone 1, 92% on tone 2 and 89% on the final vowel. As a baseline, we simultaneously tested prediction of unseen forms based on frequency of occurring stem formatives, for which the accuracy was 9.5%. The relative success of the model in cross-validation is due to the syncretism that occurs both within paradigms and across classes. The following tableau shows how the correct stem formative k^{wh} is predicted for a never-encountered 3rd-definite-incomplete form of a class 7 stem 'weave' $a\mathit{?}y^9$ in the holdout set, using activation values that were learned for encountered forms.[10]

The strength of this model is that it directly encodes knowledge of the tendency of an exponent to occur for a given stem and for a given morphosyntactic combination. For example, a Mazatec class 1 stem with a stem-formative blend (0.2·b, 0.3·k^w) encodes the relative tendencies of these two exponents to occur with this stem, with zero-valued exponents having no inclination to occur. In Kann and Schütze (2016) and Malouf

[9] Since the vowel a of the stem formative does not vary, for convenience we can take it here to be part of the stem.

[10] Because the activation values were learned just for a random training set, they will be different from those given in tables 13 and 14 above.

3RD-DEF-INC$(0.1{\cdot}a, 0.15{\cdot}\widehat{sk}, 0.09{\cdot}k^{wh}, 0.12{\cdot}s, 0.12{\cdot}k^{w})$ $+(0.20{\cdot}{}^{h}b, 0.20{\cdot}k^{wh})$ *aʔy-* 'weave'			
	MAX 5	DEP −1	Harmony
$\widehat{sk}$-aʔy-	0.75	−0.85	−0.10
☞ k^{wh}-aʔy-	1.45	−0.71	0.74
s-aʔy-	0.6	−0.88	−0.28
k^{w}-aʔy-	0.6	−0.88	−0.28
^{h}b-aʔy-	1.0	−0.80	−0.20

Table 22: Tableau for 'weave' class 7 3rd-def-inc.

(2018), there is no indication of what kind of knowledge is represented by a given node or connection. Goldsmith and O'Brien (2006)[11] is more similar to the present model but it is not clear how weights from input to hidden-layer nodes translate into feature-values on a symbolic level. And its winner-take-all mechanism with no threshold to surpass means than zero exponents in a paradigm must be represented as such, rather than resulting from any exponent failing to surpass a threshold. This results in awkward representations when a form is expressed by multiple zero affixes. The advantage of the GSC model, (see Smolensky et al. (2014, p. 1103)) is that it combines a subsymbolic neural level with a symbolic level, i.e. 'microlevel representations and algorithms' with symbolic grammatical theory, with an interface between the two. The subsymbolic level provides a platform for optimization and allows gradient activations. When output activations are quantized to discrete values they percolate to the symbolic level which contains symbolic descriptions that are familiar from symbol-based linguistic theory.

5 Summary

Inflectional patterns in Russian and Mazatec depart from canonicity in a number of ways, as was outlined on page 1. If these systems were completely canonical, each morphosyntactic combination of feature values would have a unique, lexeme-invariant exponent. In our model, in Russian, the variance of an exponent across inflectional classes is expressed directly by a *blend* of segments in an underlying form, e.g. (*a, i*) for genitive singular. Syncretism across inflectional feature combinations, such as multiple instances of *-i* in several classes is expressed by its occurrence as

a base input, so that it can coalesce with a matching inflectional input[12] for several feature combinations. If a different exponent occurred in each cell and there were no inflectional class divisions, the URs could simply be a single non-blended exponent for each inflectional input, with no inflectional formatives on base inputs. So the representations proposed here directly encode and capture the kinds of departures from canonicity that occur.

In Mazatec, blended inputs capture not just deviation from paradigm canonicity but patterns of predicability within its paradigm structure. Out of 12^{35} possible stem-formative combinations that could occur in 12 paradigm positions, Jamieson only lists 18 classes. Blended input representations, in which no more than four phonemes occur for a base input or inflectional input, limit how many stem formatives occur for a given lexeme and along with the occurrence of the same blended inflectional inputs in multiple person-number combinations, derive the syncretism that occurs across those paradigm positions.

This approach can also derive subtractive morphology, suppletion, umlaut and moraic augmentation. For example, if an inflectional form is subtractive relative to a base, the subtractable part can have partial or negative-valued underlying activation in the UR and express morphosyntactic features that affect its surfacing. Umlaut (Trommer, 2017) can be derived from a blend of different vowel features where alternation occurs.

Given the vast number of ways that languages can deviate from canonical inflection (Corbett, 2009, 2007; Baerman and Corbett, 2010; Stump, 2016), we hope with future research to explore in the GSC framework how it is possible to learn complex paradigmatic patterns in other languages.

6 Acknowledgements

Thanks to Paul Smolensky, Matt Goldrick, Farrell Ackerman, three anonymous reviewers and members of the Johns Hopkins Neurosymbolic Computation Group and the Surrey Morphology Group for valuable discussion and suggestions. Research was generously funded by NSF INSPIRE grant BCS-1344269. All errors are my own.

---

[11]See also Goldsmith and Rosen (2017), which has similarities with the present model but differs in crucial ways.

[12]In terms of correspondence, this model employs the converse of what Pulleyblank (2008) proposes for his account of reduplication in which a single input has mutiple outputs. Here, pairs of identical input features or segments can each coalesce on a single output feature or segment.

References

Ackerman, Farrell, and Robert Malouf. 2013. Morphological Organization: the Low Conditional Entropy Conjecture. *Language* 89:429–464.

Baerman, Matthew, and Greville Corbett. 2010. A typology of inflectional class interaction. In *14th International Morphology Meeting*. Budapest, Hungary.

Cho, Pyeong Whan, Matthew Goldrick, and Paul Smolensky. 2017. Incremental parsing in a continuous dynamical system: sentence processing in Gradient Symbolic Computation: Supplementary Materials 3: processing. *Linguistics Vanguard* 3.

Corbett, Greville. 2007. Canonical typology, suppletion and possible words. *Language* 83:8–42.

Corbett, Greville. 2009. Canonical inflectional classes. In *Selected Proceedings of the 6th Décembrettes: Morphology in Bordeaux*, 1–11.

Faust, Noam. 2017. How much for that vowel? Talk, Strength in Grammar Workshop, University of Leipzig.

Faust, Noam, and Paul Smolensky. 2017. Activity as an alternative to autosegmental association. In *Manchester Phonology Meeting*. Manchester, United Kingdom.

Goldrick, Matthew, Michael Putnam, and Lara Schwarz. 2016. Coactivation in bilingual grammars: A computational account of code mixing. *Bilingualism: Language and Cognition* 19:857–876. ROA 1441.

Goldsmith, John, and Jeremy O'Brien. 2006. Learning inflectional classes. *Language Learning and Development* 2:219–250.

Goldsmith, John, and Eric Rosen. 2017. Geometrical morphology. *CoRR* abs/1703.04481. URL http://arxiv.org/abs/1703.04481.

Golston, Chris, and Wolfgang Kehrein. 1998. Mazatec Onsets and Nuclei. *International Journal of American Linguistics* 64:311–337.

van Hell, Janet G., Clara Cohen, and Sarah Grey. 2016. Testing tolerance for lexically-specific factors in gradient symbolic computation. *Bilingualism: Language and Cognition* 19:897–899.

Hsu, Brian. 2018. Scalar constraints and gradient symbolic representations generate exceptional prosodification effects without exceptional prosody. Handout, West Coast Conference on Formal Linguistics 36.

Jamieson, Carol. 1982. Conflated subsystems marking person and aspect in Chiquihuitlán Mazatec verbs. *Language* 48:139–167.

Kann, Katharina, and Hinrich Schütze. 2016. Single-Model Encoder-Decoder with Explicit Morphological Representation for Reinflection. In *Proceedings of the 54th Annual Meeting of the Association for Computational Linguistics (Volume 2: Short Papers)*, 555–560. Association for Computational Linguistics.

Malouf, Robert. 2018. Generating morphological paradigms with a recurrent neural network. *San Diego Linguistic Papers* 6.

Müller, Gereon. 2017. Gradient symbolic representations in syntax. Handout, IGRA 02: Syntax II.

Prince, Alan, and Paul Smolensky. 1993. Optimality Theory: Constraint Interaction in Generative Grammar. Technical report, Rutgers University Center for Cognitive Science and Computer Science Department, University of Colorado at Boulder.

Pulleyblank, Douglas. 2008. *The nature of the word: Studies in honor of paul kiparsky*, chapter Patterns of Reduplication in Yoruba. MIT Press.

Rosen, Eric. 2016. Predicting the unpredictable: Capturing the apparent semi-regularity of rendaku voicing in japanese through gradient symbolic computation. In *Proceedings of the Berkeley Linguistics Society*, volume 42. ROA 1299.

Rosen, Eric. 2018. Predicting semi-regular patterns in morphologically complex words. *Linguistics Vanguard* 4. ROA 1339.

Smolensky, Paul, and Matt Goldrick. 2016. Gradient Symbolic Representations in Grammar: The case of French Liaison. Rutgers Optimality Archive 1552, Rutgers University.

Smolensky, Paul, Matthew Goldrick, and Donald Mathis. 2014. Optimization and Quantization in Gradient Symbol Systems: A Framework for Integrating the Continuous and the Discrete in Cognition. *Cognitive Science* 38:1102–1138.

Stump, Gregory. 2016. *Inflectional paradigms: Content and from at the syntax-morphology interface*, volume 149 of *Cambridge Studies in Linguistics*. Cambridge, UK: Cambridge University Press.

Trommer, Jochen. 2017. Scalar Cumulativity in German Umlaut. Talk, Strength in Grammar Workshop, University of Leipzig.

Zimmermann, Eva. 2017a. Being (slightly) stronger: Lexical stress in Moses Columbian Salish. Handout, Strength in Grammar Workshop, University of Leipzig.

Zimmermann, Eva. 2017b. Gradient symbols and gradient markedness: A case study from Mixtec tones. Handout: Manchester Phonology Meeting.

Zimmermann, Eva. 2018. Gradient symbolic representations and the typology of ghost segments: An argument from gradient markedness. Handout and slides, Annual Meeting on Phonology, UC San Diego.

Zimmermann, Eva. forthcoming. Gradient Symbolic Representations in the output: A case study from Moses Columbian Salishan stress. In *Proceedings of NELS*, volume 48.

Jabberwocky Parsing: Dependency Parsing with Lexical Noise

Jungo Kasai *
University of Washington
jkasai@cs.washington.edu

Robert Frank
Yale University
robert.frank@yale.edu

Abstract

Parsing models have long benefited from the use of lexical information, and indeed current state-of-the art neural network models for dependency parsing achieve substantial improvements by benefiting from distributed representations of lexical information. At the same time, humans can easily parse sentences with unknown or even novel words, as in Lewis Carroll's poem *Jabberwocky*. In this paper, we carry out *jabberwocky* parsing experiments, exploring how robust a state-of-the-art neural network parser is to the absence of lexical information. We find that current parsing models, at least under usual training regimens, are in fact overly dependent on lexical information, and perform badly in the jabberwocky context. We also demonstrate that the technique of word dropout drastically improves parsing robustness in this setting, and also leads to significant improvements in out-of-domain parsing.

1 Introduction

Since the earliest days of statistical parsing, lexical information has played a major role (Collins, 1996, 1999; Charniak, 2000). While some of the performance gains that had been derived from lexicalization can be gotten in other ways (Klein and Manning, 2003), thereby avoiding increases in model complexity and problems in data sparsity (Fong and Berwick, 2008), recent neural network models of parsing across a range of formalisms continue to use lexical information to guide parsing decisions (constituent parsing Dyer et al. (2016)); dependency parsing: Chen and Manning (2014); Kiperwasser and Goldberg (2016); Dozat and Manning (2017); CCG parsing: Ambati et al. (2016); TAG parsing: Kasai et al. (2018); Shi and

Lee (2018)). These models exploit lexical information in a way that avoids some of the data sparsity issues, by making use of distributed representations (i.e., word embeddings) that support generalization across different words.

While humans certainly make use of lexical information in sentence processing (MacDonald et al., 1994; Trueswell and Tanenhaus, 1994), it is also clear that we are able to analyze sentences in the absence of known words. This can be seen most readily by our ability to understand Lewis Carroll's poem, *Jabberwocky* (Carroll, 1883), in which open class items are replaced by non-words.

> Twas brillig, and the slithy toves
> Did gyre and gimble in the wabe;
> All mimsy were the borogoves,
> And the mome raths outgrabe

Work in neurolinguistics and psycholinguistics has demonstrated the human capacity for unlexicalized parsing experimentally, showing that humans can analyze syntactic structure even in presence of pseudo-words (Stromswold et al., 1996; Friederici et al., 2000; Kharkwal, 2014).

The word embeddings used by current lexicalized parsers are of no help in sentences with nonce words. Yet, it is at present unknown the degree to which these parsers are dependent on the information contained in these embeddings. Parsing evaluation on such nonce sentences is, therefore, critical to bridge the gap between cognitive models and data-driven machine learning models in sentence processing. Moreover, understanding the degree to which parsers are dependent upon lexical information is also of practical importance. It is advantageous for a syntactic parser to generalize well across different domains. Yet, heavy reliance upon lexical information could have detrimental effects on out-of-domain parsing because

---

*Work done at Yale University.

Proceedings of the Society for Computation in Linguistics (SCiL) 2019, pages 113-123.
New York City, New York, January 3-6, 2019

lexical input will carry genre-specific information (Gildea, 2001).

In this paper, we investigate the contribution of lexical information (via distributed lexical representations) by focusing on a state-of-the-art graph-based dependency parsing model (Dozat and Manning, 2017) in a series of controlled experiments. Concretely, we simulate jabberwocky parsing by adding noise to the representation of words in the input and observe how parsing performance varies. We test two types of noise: one in which words are replaced with an out-of-vocabulary word without a lexical representation, and a second in which words are replaced with others (with associated lexical representations) that match in their Penn TreeBank (PTB)-style fine-grained part of speech. The second approach is similar to the method that Gulordava et al. (2018) propose to assess syntactic generalization in LSTM language models.

In both cases, we find that the performance of the state-of-the-art graph parser dramatically suffers from the noise. In fact, we show that the performance of a lexicalized graph-based parser is substantialy worse than an unlexicalized graph-based parser in the presence of lexical noise, even when the lexical content of frequent or function words is preserved. This dependence on lexical information presents a severe challenge when applying the parser to a different domain or heterogeneous data, and we will demonstrate that indeed parsers trained on the PTB WSJ corpus achieve much lower performance on the Brown corpus.

On the positive side, we find that word dropout (Iyyer et al., 2015), applied more aggressively than is commonly done (Kiperwasser and Goldberg, 2016; de Lhoneux et al., 2017; Nguyen et al., 2017; Ji et al., 2017; Dozat and Manning, 2017; Bhat et al., 2017; Peng et al., 2017, 2018), remedies the susceptibility to lexical noise. Furthermore, our results show that models trained on the PTB WSJ corpus with word dropout significantly outperform those trained without word dropout in parsing the out-of-domain Brown corpus, confirming the practical significance of jabberwocky parsing experiments.

2 Parsing Models

Here we focus ourselves on a graph-based parser with deep biaffine attention (Dozat and Manning, 2017), a state-of-the-art graph-based parsing

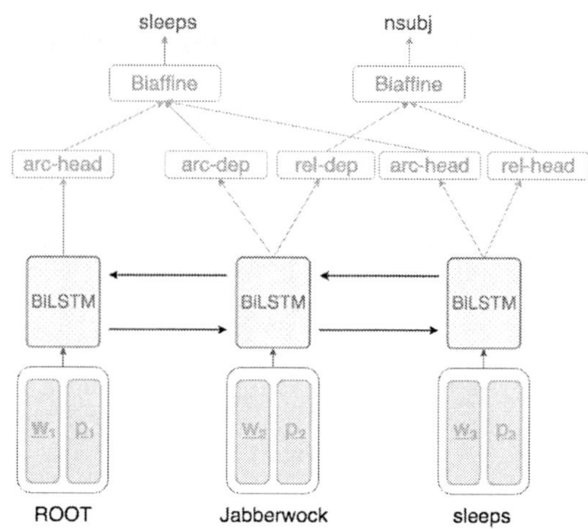

Figure 1: Biaffine parsing architecture. W and p denote the word and POS embeddings.

model, and assess its ability to generalize over lexical noise.

Input Representations The input for each word is the concatenation of a 100-dimensional embedding of the word and a 25-dimensional embedding of the PTB part of speech (POS). We initialize all word embeddings to be a zero vector and the out-of-vocabulary word is also mapped to a zero vector in testing. The POS embeddings are randomly initialized. We do not use any pretrained word embeddings throughout our experiments in order to encourage the model to find abstractions over the POS embeddings. Importantly, PTB POS categories also encode morphological features that should be accessible in jabberwocky situations. We also conducted experiments by taking as input words, universal POS tags, and character CNNs (Ma and Hovy, 2016). We observed similar patterns throughout the experiments. While those approaches can more easily scale to other languages, one concern is that the character CNNs can encode the identity of short words along side their morphological properties, and therefore would not achieve a pure jabberwocky situation. For this reason, we only present results using fine-grained POS.

Biaffine Parser Figure 1 shows our biaffine parsing architecture. Following Dozat and Manning (2017) and Kiperwasser and Goldberg (2016), we use BiLSTMs to obtain features for each word in a sentence. We first perform unlabeled arc-factored scoring using the final output vectors from the BiLSTMs, and then label the resulting arcs. Specifically, suppose that we score edges coming into the ith word in a sentence i.e. assigning scores to the potential parents of the ith word. Denote the final output vector from the BiLSTM for the kth word by h_k and suppose that h_k is d-dimensional. Then, we produce two vectors from two separate multilayer perceptrons (MLPs) with the ReLU activation:

$$h_k^{\text{arc-dep}} = \text{MLP}^{(\text{arc-dep})}(h_k)$$
$$h_k^{\text{arc-head}} = \text{MLP}^{(\text{arc-head})}(h_k)$$

where $h_k^{\text{arc-dep}}$ and $h_k^{\text{arc-head}}$ are d_{arc}-dimensional vectors that represent the kth word as a dependent and a head respectively. Now, suppose the kth row of matrix $H^{(\text{arc-head})}$ is $h_k^{\text{arc-head}}$. Then, the probability distribution s_i over the potential heads of the ith word is computed by

$$s_i = \text{softmax}(H^{(\text{arc-head})}W^{(\text{arc})}h_i^{\text{arc-dep}}$$
$$+H^{(\text{arc-head})}b^{(\text{arc})}) \quad (1)$$

where $W^{(\text{arc})} \in \mathbb{R}^{d_{arc} \times d_{arc}}$ and $b^{(arc)} \in \mathbb{R}^{d_{arc}}$. In training, we simply take the greedy maximum probability to predict the parent of each word. In the testing phase, we use the heuristics formulated by Dozat and Manning (2017) to ensure that the resulting parse is single-rooted and acyclic.

Given the head prediction of each word in the sentence, we assign labeling scores using vectors obtained from two additional MLP with ReLU. For the kth word, we obtain:

$$h_k^{\text{rel-dep}} = \text{MLP}^{(\text{rel-dep})}(h_k)$$
$$h_k^{\text{rel-head}} = \text{MLP}^{(\text{rel-head})}(h_k)$$

where $h_k^{\text{rel-dep}}, h_k^{\text{rel-head}} \in \mathbb{R}^{d_{rel}}$. Let p_i be the index of the predicted head of the ith word, and r be the number of dependency relations in the dataset. Then, the probability distribution ℓ_i over the possible dependency relations of the arc pointing from the p_ith word to the ith word is calculated by:

$$\ell_i = \text{softmax}(h_{p_i}^{T(\text{rel-head})}U^{(\text{rel})}h_i^{(\text{rel-dep})}$$
$$+W^{(\text{rel})}(h_i^{(\text{rel-head})} + h_{p_i}^{(\text{rel-head})}) + b^{(\text{rel})}) \quad (2)$$

where $U^{(\text{rel})} \in \mathbb{R}^{d_{rel} \times d_{rel} \times r}$, $W^{(\text{rel})} \in \mathbb{R}^{r \times d_{rel}}$, and $b^{(\text{rel})} \in \mathbb{R}^r$.

We generally follow the hyperparameters chosen in Dozat and Manning (2017). Specifically, we use BiLSTMs layers with 400 units each. Input, layer-to-layer, and recurrent dropout rates are all 0.33. The depth of all MLPs is 1, and the MLPs for unlabeled attachment and those for labeling contain 500 (d_{arc}) and 100 (d_{rel}) units respectively. We train this model with the Adam algorithm to minimize the sum of the cross-entropy losses from head predictions (s_i from Eq. 1) and label predictions (ℓ_i from Eq. 2) with $\ell = 0.001$ and batch size 100 (Kingma and Ba, 2015). After each training epoch, we test the parser on the dev set. When labeled attachment score (LAS) does not improve on five consecutive epochs, training ends.

3   Dropout as Regularization

Dropout regularizes neural networks by randomly setting units to zero with some probability during training (Srivastava et al., 2014). In addition to usual dropout, we consider applying word dropout, a variant of dropout that targets entire words and therefore entire rows in the lexical embedding matrix (Iyyer et al., 2015). The intuition we follow here is that a trained network will be less dependent on lexical information, and more successful in a jabberwocky context, if lexical information is less reliably present during training. We consider a number of ways of word dropout.

Uniform Word Dropout Iyyer et al. (2015) introduced the regularization technique of word dropout in which lexical items are replaced by the "unknown" word with some fixed probability p and demonstrated that it improves performance for the task of text classification. Replacing words with the out-of-vocabulary word exposes the networks to out-of-vocabulary words that only occur in testing. In our experiments, we will use word dropout rates of 0.2, 0.4, 0.6, and 0.8.

Frequency-based Word Dropout Dropping words with the same probability across the vocabulary might not behave as an ideal regularizer. The network's dependence on frequent words or function words is less likely to lead to overfitting on the training data or corpus-specific properties, as the distribution of such words is less variable across different corpora. To avoid penalizing the networks for utilizing lexical information (in the form of word embeddings) for frequent words, Kiperwasser and Goldberg (2016) propose that word dropout should be applied to a word with a probability inversely proportional to the word's frequency. Specifically, they drop out each word w that appears $\#(w)$ times in the training data with probability:

$$p_w = \frac{\alpha}{\#(w) + \alpha} \tag{3}$$

Kiperwasser and Goldberg (2016) set $\alpha = 0.25$, which leads to relatively little word dropout. In our WSJ training data, $\alpha = 0.25$ yields an expected word dropout rate of 0.009 in training, an order of magnitude less than commonly used rates in uniform word dropout. We experimented with $\alpha = 0.25, 1, 40, 352, 2536$ where the last three values yield expected word dropout rates of 0.2, 0.4, and 0.6 (the uniform dropout rates we consider). In fact, we will confirm that α needs to be much larger to significantly improve robustness to lexical noise.

Open Class Word Dropout The frequency-based word dropout scheme punishes the model less for relying upon frequent words in the training data. However, some words may occur frequently in the training data because of corpus-specific properties of the data. For instance, in the PTB WSJ training data, the word "company" is the 40th most frequent word. If our aim is to construct a parser that can perform well in different domains or across heterogeneous data, the networks should not depend upon such corpus-specific word senses. Hence, we propose to apply word dropout only on open class (non-function) words with a certain probability. We experimented with open class word dropout rates of 0.38 and 0.75 (where open class words are zeroed out 38% or 75% of the time), corresponding to the expected overall dropout rates of 0.2 and 0.4 respectively. To identify open class words in the data we used the following criteria. We consider a word as an open class word if and only if: 1) the gold UPOS is "NOUN", "PROPN", "NUM", "ADJ", or "ADV", or 2) the gold UPOS is "VERB" and the the gold XPOS (PTB POS) is not "MD" and the lemma is not "'be", "have", or "do".

4 Experiments

We test trained parsers on input that contains two types of lexical noise, designed to assess their ability to abstract away from idiosyncratic/collocational properties of lexical items: 1) *colorless green* noise and 2) *jabberwocky* noise. The former randomly exchanges words with PTB

POS preserved, and the latter zeroes outs the embeddings for words (i.e. replacing words with an out-of-vocabulary word). In either case, we keep POS input to the parsers intact.

Colorless Green Experiments Gulordava et al. (2018) propose a framework to evaluate the generalization ability of LSTM language models that abstracts away from idiosyncratic properties of words or collocational information. In particular, they generate nonce sentences by randomly replacing words in the original sentences while preserving part-of-speech and morphological features. This can be thought of as a computational approach to producing sentences that are "grammatical" yet meaningless, exemplified by the famous example "colorless green ideas sleep furiously" (Chomsky, 1957). Concretely, for each PTB POS category, we pick the 50 most frequent words of that category in the training set and replace each word w in the test set by a word uniformly drawn from the 50 most frequent words for w's POS category. We consider three situations: 1) full *colorless green* experiments where all words are replaced by random words, 2) top 100 *colorless green* experiments where all words but the 100 most frequent words are replaced by random words, and 3) open class *colorless green* experiments where the input word is replaced by a random word if and only if the word is an open class word.[1]

Jabberwocky Experiments One potential shortcoming with the approach above is that it produces sentences which might violate constraints that are imposed by specific lexical items, but which are not represented by the POS category. For instance, this approach could generate a sentence like "it stays the shuttle" in which the intransitive verb "stay" takes an object (Gulordava et al., 2018).[2] Such a violation of argument structure constraints could mislead parsers (as well as language models studied in Gulordava et al. (2018)) and we will show that is indeed the

---

[1] We use the same criteria for open class words as in the open class word dropout.

[2] This shortcoming might be overcome by using lexical resources like PropBank (Palmer et al., 2005) or NomBank (Meyers et al., 2004) to guide word substitutions. In this paper, we do not do this, follow Gulordava et al.'s approach for the creation of colorless green sentences. We instead use the jabberwocky manipulation to avoid creating sentences that violate selectional constraints.

case.[3] To address this issue, we also experiment with *jabberwocky* noise, in which input word vectors are zeroed out. This noise is equivalent to replacing words with an out-of-vocabulary word by construction. Because fine-grained POS information is retained in the input to the parser, the parser is still able to benefit from the kind of morphological information present in Carroll's poem. We again consider three situations 1) full jabberwocky experiments where all word embeddings are zeroed out, 2) top 100 jabberwocky experiments where word embeddings for all but the most frequent 100 words are zeroed out, and 3) open class jabberwocky experiments where the input word vector is zeroed out if and only if the word is an open class word. Open class jabberwocky experiments are the closest to the situation when humans read Lewis Carroll's *Jabberwocky*.[4]

Out-of-domain experiments We also explore a practical aspect of our experiments with lexical noise. We apply our parsers that are trained on the WSJ corpus to the Brown corpus and observe how parsers with various configurations perform.[5] Prior work showed that parsers trained on WSJ yield degraded performance on the Brown corpus (Gildea, 2001) despite the fact that the average sentence length is shorter in the Brown corpus (23.85 tokens for WSJ; 20.56 for Brown). We show that robustness to lexical noise improves out-of-domain parsing.

Baseline Parsers Lexical information is clearly useful for certain parsing decisions, such as PP-attachment. As a result, a lexicalized parser clearly should make use of such information when it is available, and may well perform less well when it is not. In fact, in *jabberwocky* and *colorless green* settings, the absence of lexical information may lead to an underdetermination of the parse by the POS or word sequence, so that there is no non-arbitrary "gold standard" parse. As a result, simply observing a performance drop of a parser in the face of lexical noise does not help to establish an appropriate baseline with respect to how well a parser can be expected to perform in a lexically noisy setting. We propose three baseline parsers: 1) an unlexicalized parser where the network input is only POS tags, 2) a "top 100" parser where the network input is only POS tags and lexical information for the 100 most frequent words and 3) a "function word" parser where the network input is only POS tags and lexical information for function words. Each baseline parser can be thought of as specialized to the corresponding *colorless green* and *jabberwocky* experiments. For example, the unlexicalized parser gives us an upper bound for full *colorless green* and *jabberwocky* experiments because the parser is ideally adapted to the unlexicalized situation, as it has no dependence on lexical information.

Experimental Setup We use Universal Dependency representations obtained from converting the Penn Treebank (Marcus et al., 1993) using Stanford CoreNLP (ver. 3.8.0) (Manning et al., 2014). We follow the standard data split: sections 2-21, 22, and 23 for training, dev, and test sets respectively. For the out-of-domain experiments, we converted the Brown corpus in PTB again using Stanford CoreNLP into Universal Dependency representations.[6]

We only use gold POS tags in training for simplicity,[7] but we conduct experiments with both gold and predicted POS tags. Experiments with gold POS tags allow us to isolate the effect of lexical noise from POS tagging errors, while those with predicted POS tags simulate more practical situations where POS input is not fully reliable. Somewhat surprisingly, however, we find that relative performance patterns do not change even when using predicted POS tags. All pre-

---

[3] Prior work in psycholinguistics argued that verbs can in fact be used in novel argument structure constructions, and assigned coherent interpretations on the fly (Johnson and Goldberg, 2013). Our colorless green parsing experiments can be interpreted as a simulation for such situations.

[4] An anonymous reviewer notes that because of its greater complexity, human performance on a jabberwocky version of the WSJ corpus may not be at the level we find when reading the sentences of Lewis Carroll's poem or in the psycholinguistic work that has explored human ability to process jabberwocky-like sentences. We leave it for future work to explore whether human performance in such complex cases is indeed qualitatively different, and also whether the pattern of results changes if we restrict our focus to a syntactically simpler corpus, given a suitable notion of simplicity.

[5] We initially intended to apply our trained parsers to the Universal Dependency corpus (Nivre et al., 2015) as well for out-of-domain experiments, but we found annotation inconsistency and the problem of conversion from phrase structures to universal dependencies. We leave this problem for future.

[6] We exclude the domains of CL and CP in the Brown corpus because the Stanford CoreNLP converter encountered an error.

[7] One could achieve better results by training a parser on predicted POS tags obtained from jackknife training, but improving normal parsing performance is not the focus of our work.

dicted POS tags are obtained from a BiLSTM POS tagger with character CNNs, trained on the same training data (sections 2-21) with hyperparameters from Ma and Hovy (2016) and word embeddings initialized with GloVe vectors (Pennington et al., 2014). We train 5 parsing models for each training configuration with 5 different random initializations and report the mean and standard deviation.[8] We use the CoNLL 2017 official script for evaluation (Zeman et al., 2017).

5 Results and Discussions

Normal Parsing Results Table 1 shows normal parsing results on the dev set. In both gold and predicted POS experiments, we see a significant discrepancy between the performance in rows 2-4 and the rest, suggesting that lexicalization of a dependency parser greatly contributes to parsing performance; having access to the most frequent 100 words (row 3) or the function words (row 4) recovers part of the performance drop from unlexicalization (row 2), but the LAS differences from complete lexicalization (row 1, row 5 and below) are still significant. For each of the three word dropout schemes in gold POS experiments, we see a common pattern: performance improves up to a certain degree of word dropout (Uniform 0.2, Frquency-based 1-40, Open Class 0.38), and it drops after as word dropout becomes more aggressive. This suggests that word dropout also involves the bias-variance trade-off. Although performance generally degrades with predicted POS tags, the patterns of relative performance still hold. Again, for each of the three dropout schemes, there is a certain point in the spectrum of word dropout intensity that achieves the best performance, and such points are almost the same both in the models trained with gold and predicted POS tags. This is a little surprising because a higher word dropout rate encourages the model to rely more on POS input, and noisy POS information from the POS tagger can work against the model. Indeed, we observed this parallelism between experiments with gold and predicted POS tags consistently throughout the *colorless green* and *jabberwocky* experiments, and therefore we only report results with gold POS tags for the rest of the *colorless green* and *jabberwocky* experiments for simplicity.

---

[8]Our code is available at https://github.com/jungokasai/graph_parser for easy replication.

Model	Gold		Predicted	
	UAS	LAS	UAS	LAS
No Dropout	$93.6_{0.2}$	$92.3_{0.2}$	$92.7_{0.1}$	$90.6_{0.1}$
Unlexicalized	$88.0_{0.1}$	$85.4_{0.1}$	$87.1_{0.1}$	$83.8_{0.1}$
Top 100	$92.5_{0.1}$	$90.8_{0.1}$	$91.7_{0.1}$	$89.2_{0.1}$
Function	$90.7_{0.4}$	$88.1_{0.6}$	$90.0_{0.3}$	$86.8_{0.5}$
Uniform 0.2	$93.9_{0.1}$	$92.6_{0.1}$	$93.0_{0.1}$	$90.9_{0.2}$
Uniform 0.4	$94.0_{0.1}$	$92.5_{0.1}$	$93.0_{0.1}$	$90.8_{0.1}$
Uniform 0.6	$93.7_{0.1}$	$92.2_{0.1}$	$92.7_{0.1}$	$90.5_{0.1}$
Uniform 0.8	$93.0_{0.1}$	$91.4_{0.1}$	$92.1_{0.1}$	$89.7_{0.2}$
Freq 0.25	$93.7_{0.1}$	$92.4_{0.1}$	$92.9_{0.1}$	$90.8_{0.1}$
Freq 1	$93.9_{0.1}$	$92.6_{0.1}$	$93.0_{0.1}$	$91.0_{0.1}$
Freq 40	$94.0_{0.2}$	$92.6_{0.2}$	$93.0_{0.2}$	$90.9_{0.2}$
Freq 352	$93.6_{0.1}$	$92.2_{0.1}$	$92.7_{0.1}$	$90.5_{0.1}$
Freq 2536	$92.9_{0.1}$	$91.4_{0.1}$	$92.0_{0.1}$	$89.7_{0.1}$
Open Cl 0.38	$93.9_{0.1}$	$92.5_{0.2}$	$93.0_{0.1}$	$90.9_{0.2}$
Open Cl 0.75	$93.5_{0.1}$	$92.1_{0.1}$	$92.7_{0.1}$	$90.5_{0.1}$

Table 1: Normal Parsing Results on the Dev Set. The subscripts indicate the standard deviations.

Full Experiments Table 2 shows results for full *colorless green* and *jabberwocky* experiments. The models without word dropout yield extremely poor performance both in *colorless* and *jabberwocky* settings, suggesting that a graph-based parsing model learns to rely heavily on word information if word dropout is not performed. Here, unlike the normal parsing results, we see monotone increasing performance as word dropout is more aggressively applied, and the performance rises more dramatically. In particular, with uniform word dropout rate 0.2, full *jabberwocky* performance increases by more than 40 LAS points, suggesting the importance of the parser's exposure to unknown words to abstract away from lexical information. Frequency-based word dropout needs to be performed more aggressively ($\alpha \geq 40$) than has previously been done for dependency parsing (Kiperwasser and Goldberg, 2016; Dozat and Manning, 2017) in order to achieve robustness to full lexical noise similar to that obtained with uniform word dropout with $p > 0.2$. Open class word dropout does not bring any benefit to parsers in the full *jabberwocky* and *colorless green* settings. This is probably because parsers trained with open class word dropout has consistent access to function words, and omitting the lexical representations of the function words is very harmful to such parsers. Interestingly, in some of the cases, *colorless green* outperforms *jabberwocky* performance, perhaps because noisy word information, even with argument constraint violations, is better than no word information.

Model	Colorless		Jabberwocky	
	UAS	LAS	UAS	LAS
No Dropout	$62.6_{0.2}$	$56.3_{0.1}$	$51.9_{2.3}$	$39.1_{1.9}$
Unlexicalized	$88.0_{0.1}$	$85.4_{0.1}$	$88.0_{0.1}$	$85.4_{0.2}$
Top 100	$71.7_{0.4}$	$67.1_{0.3}$	$72.7_{0.3}$	$68.2_{0.5}$
Function	$69.2_{0.9}$	$62.1_{0.7}$	$58.8_{3.0}$	$39.8_{3.4}$
Uniform 0.2	$74.0_{0.2}$	$69.1_{0.2}$	$85.7_{0.3}$	$82.7_{0.3}$
Uniform 0.4	$76.9_{0.3}$	$72.3_{0.2}$	$87.1_{0.1}$	$84.3_{0.1}$
Uniform 0.6	$79.2_{0.2}$	$75.0_{0.2}$	$87.7_{0.1}$	$85.0_{0.1}$
Uniform 0.8	$82.0_{0.3}$	$78.5_{0.3}$	$88.0_{0.1}$	$85.4_{0.1}$
Freq 0.25	$62.9_{0.2}$	$56.4_{0.1}$	$55.0_{1.4}$	$43.4_{2.5}$
Freq 1	$63.6_{0.4}$	$57.1_{0.1}$	$60.1_{1.7}$	$48.8_{3.6}$
Freq 40	$67.5_{0.7}$	$61.6_{0.6}$	$76.4_{1.0}$	$72.0_{1.2}$
Freq 352	$74.5_{0.5}$	$69.7_{0.5}$	$82.9_{0.4}$	$79.5_{0.6}$
Freq 2536	$82.6_{0.2}$	$78.8_{0.3}$	$86.5_{0.4}$	$85.4_{0.2}$
Open Cl 0.38	$65.0_{0.5}$	$58.8_{0.4}$	$53.7_{2.6}$	$36.8_{3.6}$
Open Cl 0.75	$66.7_{0.2}$	$60.5_{0.3}$	$53.8_{1.0}$	$34.0_{1.3}$

Table 2: Full Colorless Green and Jabberwocky Experiments on the Dev Set.

Model	Colorless		Jabberwocky	
	UAS	LAS	UAS	LAS
No Dropout	$85.5_{0.1}$	$82.7_{0.1}$	$86.4_{0.8}$	$83.4_{0.9}$
Unlexicalized	$88.0_{0.1}$	$85.4_{0.1}$	$88.0_{0.1}$	$85.4_{0.2}$
Top 100	$92.5_{0.1}$	$90.8_{0.1}$	$92.5_{0.1}$	$90.8_{0.1}$
Function	$88.7_{0.4}$	$85.4_{0.7}$	$90.8_{0.3}$	$88.0_{0.6}$
Uniform 0.2	$87.5_{0.2}$	$84.9_{0.2}$	$90.2_{0.6}$	$88.2_{0.6}$
Uniform 0.4	$88.5_{0.2}$	$86.0_{0.2}$	$90.8_{0.4}$	$88.9_{0.4}$
Uniform 0.6	$89.2_{0.2}$	$86.8_{0.1}$	$91.0_{0.3}$	$89.1_{0.2}$
Uniform 0.8	$89.7_{0.1}$	$87.4_{0.2}$	$90.6_{0.2}$	$88.6_{0.2}$
Freq 0.25	$85.8_{0.2}$	$83.0_{0.2}$	$87.8_{0.6}$	$85.0_{0.6}$
Freq 1	$86.1_{0.1}$	$83.3_{0.1}$	$88.9_{0.4}$	$86.3_{0.4}$
Freq 40	$88.1_{0.2}$	$85.5_{0.1}$	$90.9_{0.2}$	$88.7_{0.4}$
Freq 352	$89.7_{0.1}$	$87.4_{0.1}$	$91.9_{0.2}$	$90.0_{0.2}$
Freq 2536	$90.7_{0.2}$	$88.6_{0.3}$	$91.3_{0.2}$	$89.3_{0.3}$
Open Cl 0.38	$88.6_{0.3}$	$86.2_{0.3}$	$90.6_{0.2}$	$88.3_{0.2}$
Open Cl 0.75	$89.6_{0.1}$	$87.4_{0.2}$	$90.8_{0.3}$	$88.0_{0.6}$

Table 3: Top 100 Colorless Green and Jabberwocky Experiments on the Dev Set.

Model	Colorless		Jabberwocky	
	UAS	LAS	UAS	LAS
No Dropout	$84.1_{0.3}$	$81.3_{0.2}$	$84.9_{0.6}$	$82.1_{0.6}$
Unlexicalized	$88.0_{0.1}$	$85.4_{0.1}$	$88.0_{0.1}$	$85.4_{0.2}$
Top 100	$90.5_{0.2}$	$88.4_{0.2}$	$91.8_{0.1}$	$89.9_{0.1}$
Function	$90.7_{0.4}$	$88.1_{0.6}$	$90.7_{0.4}$	$88.1_{0.6}$
Uniform 0.2	$87.4_{0.2}$	$84.8_{0.2}$	$89.7_{0.7}$	$87.8_{0.7}$
Uniform 0.4	$88.3_{0.2}$	$85.9_{0.3}$	$90.6_{0.4}$	$88.7_{0.4}$
Uniform 0.6	$89.2_{0.2}$	$86.8_{0.2}$	$90.9_{0.3}$	$89.0_{0.3}$
Uniform 0.8	$89.9_{0.2}$	$87.7_{0.1}$	$90.5_{0.3}$	$88.6_{0.2}$
Freq 0.25	$84.7_{0.2}$	$82.0_{0.2}$	$86.7_{0.5}$	$84.3_{0.6}$
Freq 1	$85.2_{0.4}$	$82.4_{0.4}$	$88.1_{0.6}$	$85.9_{0.6}$
Freq 40	$87.7_{0.2}$	$85.2_{0.2}$	$91.2_{0.3}$	$89.2_{0.3}$
Freq 352	$89.5_{0.2}$	$87.3_{0.1}$	$92.0_{0.1}$	$90.2_{0.1}$
Freq 2536	$90.7_{0.2}$	$88.7_{0.2}$	$91.7_{0.2}$	$89.9_{0.1}$
Open Cl 0.38	$89.0_{0.2}$	$86.7_{0.3}$	$92.1_{0.2}$	$90.3_{0.2}$
Open Cl 0.75	$90.7_{0.1}$	$88.4_{0.2}$	$92.4_{0.1}$	$90.7_{0.1}$

Table 4: Open Class Colorless Green and Jabberwocky Experiments on the Dev Set.

Model	Gold		Predicted	
	UAS	LAS	UAS	LAS
No Dropout	$89.7_{0.1}$	$87.5_{0.1}$	$88.8_{0.1}$	$85.7_{0.1}$
Unlexicalized	$83.0_{0.1}$	$79.3_{0.2}$	$81.3_{0.1}$	$76.7_{0.1}$
Top 100	$89.4_{0.1}$	$86.8_{0.1}$	$88.5_{0.1}$	$84.9_{0.1}$
Function	$88.3_{0.3}$	$84.8_{0.7}$	$87.4_{0.3}$	$83.1_{0.7}$
Uniform 0.2	$90.0_{0.1}$	$87.8_{0.2}$	$89.1_{0.1}$	$86.0_{0.2}$
Uniform 0.4	$90.1_{0.1}$	$87.9_{0.1}$	$89.3_{0.1}$	$86.1_{0.1}$
Uniform 0.6	$90.1_{0.1}$	$87.7_{0.1}$	$89.1_{0.1}$	$85.8_{0.1}$
Uniform 0.8	$89.4_{0.1}$	$86.8_{0.1}$	$88.5_{0.1}$	$85.0_{0.1}$
Freq 0.25	$89.9_{0.2}$	$87.7_{0.2}$	$89.1_{0.2}$	$86.0_{0.2}$
Freq 1	$90.2_{0.2}$	$88.1_{0.2}$	$89.3_{0.1}$	$86.3_{0.1}$
Freq 40	$90.7_{0.2}$	$\mathbf{88.5_{0.3}}$	$89.8_{0.2}$	$\mathbf{86.7_{0.2}}$
Freq 352	$90.3_{0.1}$	$88.0_{0.1}$	$89.3_{0.1}$	$86.1_{0.1}$
Freq 2536	$89.3_{0.2}$	$86.8_{0.2}$	$88.4_{0.1}$	$85.0_{0.2}$
Open Cl 0.38	$90.3_{0.2}$	$88.1_{0.2}$	$89.4_{0.1}$	$86.2_{0.2}$
Open Cl 0.75	$90.3_{0.1}$	$88.0_{0.1}$	$87.4_{0.3}$	$86.1_{0.1}$

Table 5: Brown CF Results.

Top 100 Experiments Table 3 shows the results of top 100 *colorless green* and *jabberwocky* experiments. Performance by parsers trained without word dropout is substantially better than what is found in the full *colorless green* or *jabberwocky* settings. However, the performance is still much lower than the unlexicalized parsers (2.7 LAS points for *colorless green* and 2.0 LAS points for *jabberwocky*), meaning that the parser without word dropout has significant dependence on less frequent words. On the other hand, parsers trained with a high enough word dropout rate outperform the unlexicalized parser (e.g., uniform 0.4, frequency-based $\alpha = 40$, and open class 0.38). Frequency-based word dropout is very effective. Recall that $\alpha = 352, 2536$ correspond to the expected word dropout rates of 0.4 and 0.6. The two configurations yield better results than uniform 0.4 and 0.6.

Open Class Experiments Table 4 gives the results of open class *colorless green* and *jabberwocky* experiments. We see similar patterns to the top 100 *jabberwocky* experiments except that open class word dropout performs better and frequency-based word dropout performs worse, which naturally follows from the way we train the parsers.

Out-of-domain Parsing Table 5 reports parsing performance on the CF domain in the Brown corpus.[9] POS tagging accuracy was 96.4%, relatively low as compared to in-domain performance in WSJ. Gildea (2001) demonstrated that removing lexical information from lexicalized PCFG does not deteriorate out-of-domain parsing perfor-

---

[9]We found similar patterns in relative performance when applied to the other domains of the Brown corpus.

	Colorless			Jabberwocky		
relation	Pre	Rec	F1	Prec	Rec	F1
nsubj	87.8	86.2	87.0	91.0	90.0	90.5
dobj	79.2	81.4	80.3	83.0	90.7	86.7
iobj	29.4	27.8	28.6	71.4	55.6	62.5
csubj	30.4	46.7	36.8	33.3	60.0	42.9
ccomp	75.3	75.3	75.3	77.2	78.2	77.7
xcomp	69.0	69.2	69.1	78.7	64.3	70.8
others	83.6	83.6	83.6	86.7	86.6	86.6

Table 6: Performance Breakdown by Dependency Relation.

mance in the Brown corpus. In contrast, our results show that lexicalization of the neural network dependency parsers via distributed representations facilitates parsing performance. Most of the gains from lexicalization stem from the 100 most frequent words (row 3) and function words (row 4), but we get a significant improvement by performing relatively aggressive word dropout ($\alpha = 40$). This confirms the practical significance of *jabberwocky* parsing experiments.

6 Analysis of Results

Colorless Green vs. Jabberwocky Earlier we hypothesized that *colorless green* lexical noise could mislead the parser by violating argument structure constraints. And in fact, we saw in the previous section that *jabberwocky* parsing results are generally better than *colorless green* parsing results. In order to further test our hypothesis, we provide a breakdown of parsing performance broken down by dependency type (Nivre et al., 2015). Table 6 provides the open class performance breakdown for a parser trained with uniform word dropout rate 0.2. We observe that in the *colorless green* situation, the parser particularly suffers in "iobj" and "dobj", consistent with what we would expect for parsing sentences with argument structure violations. For example, the *colorless green* scheme does not prevent us from replacing a ditransitive verb with a non-ditransitive verb. This result validates our hypothesis, and the *colorless green* scheme is limited as a framework to purely assess parser's generalization ability.

Trained Word Embeddings The logic of our *jabberwocky* experiments and the role of word dropout involves the assumption that the parser will succeed in the absence of lexical information if it depends more heavily on the grammatical category information present in the POS embeddings. However, this fails to allow for the possibility that

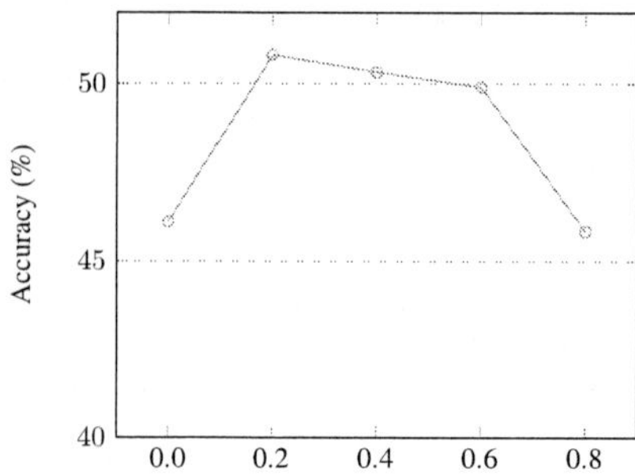

Figure 2: POS Prediction Results from the Word Embedding Induced in Varying Uniform Dropout Rates.

the word embeddings themselves might also represent POS information. It might instead be the case that what word dropout does is merely discouraging the model from constructing grammatical abstractions in the word embeddings, depending instead on the information present in the POS embeddings.

To test this possibility, we attempt to use a simple softmax regression on top of the induced word embeddings to detect the presence of grammatical category information. Concretely, we find the set of words that occur 100 times or more in the training data whose unigram probability for the most frequent POS tag is greater than 0.5. In this way, we obtain a set of pairs of a word and its most frequent POS tag, and we then randomly split the set to run 5-fold cross validation. Figure 2 shows POS prediction accuracy over varying uniform word dropout rates. These results do not support the idea that word dropout reduces the representation of grammatical category information in word embedding. On the contrary, word dropout rates of 0.2 through 0.6 leads to word embeddings that *better* represent POS.

Parser Weight Sizes What then is the effect of word dropout on the network? Figure 3 shows L2 norms of the trained POS embeddings (46 by 25) and the input/output gate weights for POS input in the first BiLSTM layer (400 by 25) across varying uniform word dropout rates. We can observe that L2 norm for each becomes larger as the word dropout rate increases. This suggests that what word dropout does is to encourage the model to make greater use of POS information.

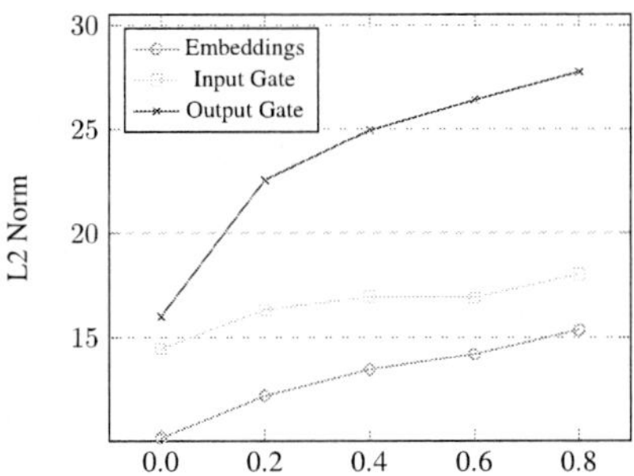

Figure 3: POS Embeddings and Weight Sizes over Uniform Word Dropout Rates.

7   Conclusion and Future Work

We conducted extensive analysis on the robustness of a state-of-the-art graph-based dependency parser against lexical noise. Our experiments showed that parsers trained under usual regimens performed poorly in the face of lexical noise. However, we demonstrated that the technique of word dropout, when applied aggressively, remedies this problem without sacrificing parsing performance. Word dropout is commonly used in literature, but our results provide further guidance about how it should be used in the future. In future work, we would like to compare our results with different parsing architectures such as transition-based parsers.

References

Bharat Ram Ambati, Tejaswini Deoskar, and Mark Steedman. 2016. Shift-reduce ccg parsing using neural network models. In *NAACL*.

Riyaz Ahmad Bhat, Irshad Ahmad Bhat, and Dipti Misra Sharma. 2017. Leveraging newswire treebanks for parsing conversational data with argument scrambling. In *IWPT*.

Lewis Carroll. 1883. *Through the Looking-Glass*. Macmillan and Co., New York.

Eugene Charniak. 2000. A maximum-entropy-inspired parser. In *ANLP*.

Danqi Chen and Christopher Manning. 2014. A fast and accurate dependency parser using neural networks. In *EMNLP*, pages 740–750, Doha, Qatar. Association for Computational Linguistics.

Noam Chomsky. 1957. *Syntactic Structures*. Mouton & Co., Berlin, Germany.

Michael Collins. 1996. A new statistical parser based on bigram lexical dependencies. In *ACL*.

Michael Collins. 1999. . *Head-Driven Statistical Models for Natural Language Parsing*. Ph.D. thesis, University of Pennsylvania.

Timothy Dozat and Christopher Manning. 2017. Deep biaffine attention for neural dependency parsing. In *ICLR*.

Chris Dyer, Adhiguna Kuncoro, Miguel Ballesteros, and Noah A. Smith. 2016. Recurrent neural network grammars. In *NAACL*.

Sandiway Fong and Robert C. Berwick. 2008. Treebank parsing and knowledge of language : A cognitive perspective. In *CogSci*.

Angela D. Friederici, Mia Viktoria Meyer, and D. Yves von Cramon. 2000. Auditory language comprehension: an event-related fmri study on the processing of syntactic and lexical information. *Brain and language*, 75 3:289–300.

Daniel Gildea. 2001. Corpus variation and parser performance. In *EMNLP*.

Kristina Gulordava, Piotr Bojanowski, Edouard Grave, Tal Linzen, and Marco Baroni. 2018. Colorless green recurrent networks dream hierarchically. In *NAACL*. Association for Computational Linguistics.

Mohit Iyyer, Varun Manjunatha, Jordan L. Boyd-Graber, and Hal Daumé. 2015. Deep unordered composition rivals syntactic methods for text classification. In *ACL*.

Tao Ji, Yuanbin Wu, and Man Lan. 2017. A fast and lightweight system for multilingual dependency parsing. In *CoNLL Shared Task*.

Matt A. Johnson and Adele E. Goldberg. 2013. Evidence for automatic accessing of constructional meaning: Jabberwocky sentences prime associated verbs. *Language and Cognitive Processes*, 28(10):14391452.

Jungo Kasai, Robert Frank, Pauli Xu, William Merrill, and Owen Rambow. 2018. End-to-end graph-based TAG parsing with neural networks. In *NAACL*. Association for Computational Linguistics.

Gaurav Kharkwal. 2014. *Taming the Jabberwocky: Examining Sentence Processing with Novel Words*. Ph.D. thesis, Rutgers University.

Diederik P. Kingma and Jimmy Lei Ba. 2015. ADAM: A Method for Stochastic Optimization. In *ICLR*.

Eliyahu Kiperwasser and Yoav Goldberg. 2016. Simple and accurate dependency parsing using bidirectional LSTM feature representations. *TACL*, 4:313–327.

Dan Klein and Christopher D. Manning. 2003. Accurate unlexicalized parsing. In *ACL*.

Miryam de Lhoneux, Yan Shao, Ali Basirat, Eliyahu Kiperwasser, Sara Stymne, Yoav Goldberg, and Joakim Nivre. 2017. From raw text to universal dependencies - look, no tags! In *CoNLL Shared Task*.

Xuezhe Ma and Eduard Hovy. 2016. End-to-end sequence labeling via bi-directional LSTM-CNNs-CRF. In *ACL*, pages 1064–1074, Berlin, Germany. Association for Computational Linguistics.

Maryellen C. MacDonald, Neal J. Pearlmutter, and Mark S. Seidenberg. 1994. Lexical nature of syntactic ambiguity resolution. *Psychological Review*, 101:676–703.

Christopher D. Manning, Mihai Surdeanu, John Bauer, Jenny Finkel, Steven J. Bethard, and David Mc-Closky. 2014. The Stanford CoreNLP natural language processing toolkit. In *Association for Computational Linguistics (ACL) System Demonstrations*.

Mitchell Marcus, Beatrice Santorini, and Mary Ann Marcinkiewicz. 1993. Building a large annotated corpus of english: The Penn Treebank. *Computational Linguistics*, 19(2):313–330.

Adam Meyers, Ruth Reeves, Catherine Macleod, Rachel Szekely, Veronika Zielinska, Brian Young, and Ralph Grishman. 2004. The NomBank project: An interim report. In *Proceedings of the Workshop on Frontiers in Corpus Annotation at HLT-NAACL*.

Dat Quoc Nguyen, Mark Dras, and Mark Johnson. 2017. A novel neural network model for joint pos tagging and graph-based dependency parsing. In *CoNLL Shared Task*.

Joakim Nivre, Željko Agić, Maria Jesus Aranzabe, Masayuki Asahara, Aitziber Atutxa, Miguel Ballesteros, John Bauer, Kepa Bengoetxea, Riyaz Ahmad Bhat, Cristina Bosco, Sam Bowman, Giuseppe G. A. Celano, Miriam Connor, Marie-Catherine de Marneffe, Arantza Diaz de Ilarraza, Kaja Dobrovoljc, Timothy Dozat, Tomaž Erjavec, Richárd Farkas, Jennifer Foster, Daniel Galbraith, Filip Ginter, Iakes Goenaga, Koldo Gojenola, Yoav Goldberg, Berta Gonzales, Bruno Guillaume, Jan Hajič, Dag Haug, Radu Ion, Elena Irimia, Anders Johannsen, Hiroshi Kanayama, Jenna Kanerva, Simon Krek, Veronika Laippala, Alessandro Lenci, Nikola Ljubešić, Teresa Lynn, Christopher Manning, Cătălina Mărănduc, David Mareček, Héctor Martínez Alonso, Jan Mašek, Yuji Matsumoto, Ryan McDonald, Anna Missilä, Verginica Mititelu, Yusuke Miyao, Simonetta Montemagni, Shunsuke Mori, Hanna Nurmi, Petya Osenova, Lilja Øvrelid, Elena Pascual, Marco Passarotti, Cenel-Augusto Perez, Slav Petrov, Jussi Piitulainen, Barbara Plank, Martin Popel, Prokopis Prokopidis, Sampo Pyysalo, Loganathan Ramasamy, Rudolf Rosa, Shadi Saleh, Sebastian Schuster, Wolfgang Seeker, Mojgan Seraji, Natalia Silveira, Maria Simi, Radu Simionescu, Katalin Simkó, Kiril Simov, Aaron Smith, Jan Štěpánek, Alane Suhr, Zsolt Szántó, Takaaki Tanaka, Reut Tsarfaty, Sumire Uematsu, Larraitz Uria, Viktor Varga, Veronika Vincze, Zdeněk Žabokrtský, Daniel Zeman, and Hanzhi Zhu. 2015. Universal dependencies 1.2. LINDAT/CLARIN digital library at the Institute of Formal and Applied Linguistics, Charles University.

Martha Palmer, Dan Gildea, and Paul Kingsbury. 2005. The proposition bank: A corpus annotated with semantic roles. *Computational Linguistics*, 31(1).

Hao Peng, Sam Thomson, and Noah A. Smith. 2017. Deep multitask learning for semantic dependency parsing. In *ACL*.

Hao Peng, Sam Thomson, Swabha Swayamdipta, and Noah A. Smith. 2018. Learning joint semantic parsers from disjoint data. In *NAACL*.

Jeffrey Pennington, Richard Socher, and Christopher D. Manning. 2014. Glove: Global vectors for word representation. In *EMNLP*.

Tianze Shi and Lillian Lee. 2018. Valency-augmented dependency parsing. In *EMNLP*. Association for Computational Linguistics.

Nitish Srivastava, Geoffrey Hinton, Alex Krizhevsky, Ilya Sutskever, and Ruslan Salakhutdinov. 2014. Dropout: A simple way to prevent neural networks from overfitting. *Journal of Machine Learning Research*, 15:1929–1958.

Karen Stromswold, David O. Caplan, Nathaniel M. Alpert, and Scott L. Rauch. 1996. Localization of syntactic comprehension by positron emission tomography. *Brain and language*, 52 3:452–73.

John C. Trueswell and Michael K. Tanenhaus. 1994. Toward a lexicalist framework for constraint-based syntactic ambiguity resolution. In Charles Clifton, Jr., Lyn Frazier, and Keith Rayner, editors, *Perspectives on Sentence Processing*, pages 155–179. Lawrence Erlbaum Associates, Hillsdale, NJ.

Daniel Zeman, Martin Popel, Milan Straka, Jan Hajic, Joakim Nivre, Filip Ginter, Juhani Luotolahti, Sampo Pyysalo, Slav Petrov, Martin Potthast, Francis Tyers, Elena Badmaeva, Memduh Gokirmak, Anna Nedoluzhko, Silvie Cinkova, Jan Hajic jr., Jaroslava Hlavacova, Václava Kettnerová, Zdenka Uresova, Jenna Kanerva, Stina Ojala, Anna Missilä, Christopher D. Manning, Sebastian Schuster, Siva Reddy, Dima Taji, Nizar Habash, Herman Leung, Marie-Catherine de Marneffe, Manuela Sanguinetti, Maria Simi, Hiroshi Kanayama, Valeria dePaiva, Kira Droganova, Héctor Martínez Alonso, Çağr Çöltekin, Umut Sulubacak, Hans Uszkoreit, Vivien Macketanz, Aljoscha Burchardt, Kim Harris, Katrin Marheinecke, Georg Rehm, Tolga Kayadelen, Mohammed Attia, Ali Elkahky, Zhuoran Yu, Emily Pitler, Saran Lertpradit, Michael Mandl, Jesse Kirchner, Hector Fernandez Alcalde, Jana Strnadová, Esha Banerjee, Ruli Manurung, Antonio Stella, Atsuko Shimada, Sookyoung Kwak, Gustavo

Mendonca, Tatiana Lando, Rattima Nitisaroj, and Josie Li. 2017. CoNLL 2017 shared task: Multilingual parsing from raw text to universal dependencies. In *Proceedings of the CoNLL 2017 Shared Task: Multilingual Parsing from Raw Text to Universal Dependencies*, pages 1–19, Vancouver, Canada. Association for Computational Linguistics.

Learnability and Overgeneration in Computational Syntax

Yiding Hao
Department of Linguistics
Department of Computer Science
Yale University
`yiding.hao@yale.edu`

Abstract

This paper addresses the hypothesis that unnatural patterns generated by grammar formalisms can be eliminated on the grounds that they are unlearnable. I consider three examples of formal languages thought to represent dependencies unattested in natural language syntax, and show that all three can be learned by grammar induction algorithms following the Distributional Learning paradigm of Clark and Eyraud (2007). While learnable language classes are restrictive by necessity (Gold, 1967), these facts suggest that learnability alone may be insufficient for addressing concerns of overgeneration in syntax.

1 Introduction

A longstanding debate in linguistics concerns the division of labor in language acquisition between innate universal assumptions about natural language and the learner's ability to recognize patterns in data. The *rationalist* position, famously championed by the Principles and Parameters framework, follows the Poverty of the Stimulus argument (POS, Chomsky, 1965, 1968, 1971, 1980) in assuming a rich Universal Grammar (UG) that allows individual languages to vary along a narrow range of dimensions. On the other hand, the Distributional Learning paradigm of grammatical inference (Clark and Eyraud, 2007) has shown that it is possible to create *empiricist* representations of grammar optimized for extracting generalizations from data with theoretical guarantees of convergence.

Recent advances in mathematical linguistics have suggested that the rationalist–empiricist debate may be of interest to the program of formally characterizing the typology of syntax. Shieber's (1985) argument that Swiss German is not context-free shows that substantial expressive power is needed in order to adequately describe syntactic phenomena. At the same time, the class of context-free languages and its extensions include pathological dependencies unattested in natural language. Kobele (2011), for instance, shows that the context-free Merge operation allows Minimalist Grammars (MGs) to define languages that require every syntactically well-formed sentence to have at least one semantic type conflict. In light of this overgeneration problem, learnability has been proposed as a possible way to refine existing language classes so as to better align with empirical facts. Under such an approach, UG specifies the formalism in which grammars are represented, while language acquisition is modelled by a grammar induction algorithm that correctly converges on a subset of the possible grammars. Since no strict superclass of the finite languages admits a general learning procedure (Gold, 1967), there necessarily exist languages that are permitted by UG but that cannot be learned by the language acquisition algorithm.

This paper takes some preliminary steps toward evaluating the potential of learnability to produce restricted language classes that exclude unnatural patterns. Recent work in Distributional Learning has produced a hierarchy of context-free and multiple context-free language classes defined by learning algorithms. I examine three examples of unnatural patterns—structure-independent constraints on sentence length, free word order with unbounded crossing dependencies, and unlimited copying of deep context-free structure—and show that these patterns appear in small classes of the learnable hierarchy. This suggests that current approaches to grammar induction for syntax may fail to yield learnability-based accounts for the absence of these patterns in syntactic typology.

After basic definitions and notation are presented in Section 2, Section 3 introduces the learnable language classes considered in this paper.

Proceedings of the Society for Computation in Linguistics (SCiL) 2019, pages 124-134.
New York City, New York, January 3-6, 2019

The three unnatural patterns, drawn from Graf's (2013) discussion of overgeneration in MGs, are defined in Section 4. There, it will be shown that the three patterns exist within the language classes from Section 3. Section 5 concludes with a discussion of these facts and their relationship with the rationalist–empiricist debate.

2   Preliminaries

As usual, $\mathbb{N}$ denotes the set of nonnegative integers, and for any set A, $\mathcal{P}(A)$ denotes the power set of A. Unless otherwise specified, the letter Σ denotes a finite alphabet. The length of a string x is denoted by $|x|$, and ε denotes the empty string. For each $a \in \Sigma$, $|x|_a$ denotes the number of occurrences of a in x. Alphabet symbols are identified with strings of length 1. For strings a and b, ab denotes the concatenation of a and b. As usual, this notation is extended elementwise to sets of strings. For $k \in \mathbb{N}$, α^k denotes α concatenated with itself k-many times; $\alpha^{\leq k}$ denotes $\bigcup_{i=0}^{k} \alpha^i$; α^* denotes $\bigcup_{i=0}^{\infty} \alpha^i$; and α^+ denotes $\alpha^* \backslash \{\varepsilon\}$. This notation does not apply to $(\Sigma^*)^k$, which denotes the cartesian product $\prod_{i=1}^{k} \Sigma^*$. The *length of a tuple* $\mathbf{x} = \langle x_1, x_2, \ldots, x_k \rangle$ is defined as $|\mathbf{x}| := \sum_{i=1}^{k} |x_i|$. For $a \in \Sigma$, $|\mathbf{x}|_a$ denotes $|x_1 x_2 \ldots x_k|_a$.

For $k \in \mathbb{N}$, a *k-context over* Σ is a $(k+1)$-tuple of strings $\langle c_0, c_1, \ldots, c_k \rangle \in (\Sigma^*)^k$, denoted $c_0 \square c_1 \square \ldots \square c_k$. For sets $L_1, L_2, \ldots, L_k \subseteq \Sigma^*$, $L_0 \square L_1 \square \ldots \square L_k$ denotes the cartesian product $\prod_{i=0}^{k} L_i$. The *wrapping operation* $\odot$ between k-contexts and k-tuples of strings is defined by

$$c_0 \square c_1 \square \ldots \square c_k \odot \langle x_1, x_2, \ldots, x_k \rangle$$
$$:= c_0 x_1 c_1 x_2 c_2 \ldots x_k c_k$$

and extended elementwise to sets of contexts and sets of strings. For $\alpha \in (\Sigma^*)^k \cup \mathcal{P}\big((\Sigma^*)^k\big)$ and $L \subseteq \Sigma^*$, the *contexts of α with respect to L* are defined to be the set

$$\alpha^{|L\rangle} := \Big\{ \mathbf{c} \in (\Sigma^*)^{k+1} \Big| \mathbf{c} \odot \alpha \subseteq L \Big\},$$

with the "$\subseteq$" above replaced by "$\in$" when $\alpha \in (\Sigma^*)^k$. For $\gamma \in (\Sigma^*)^{k+1} \cup \mathcal{P}\big((\Sigma^*)^{k+1}\big)$, we define the set

$$\gamma^{\langle L|} := \Big\{ \mathbf{x} \in (\Sigma^*)^k \Big| \gamma \odot \mathbf{x} \subseteq L \Big\},$$

with the "$\subseteq$" above replaced by "$\in$" when $\gamma \in (\Sigma^*)^{k+1}$. When the identity of the language L is clear from context, we may denote $\alpha^{|L\rangle}$ by $\alpha^{\triangleright}$ and $\gamma^{\langle L|}$ by $\gamma^{\triangleleft}$.

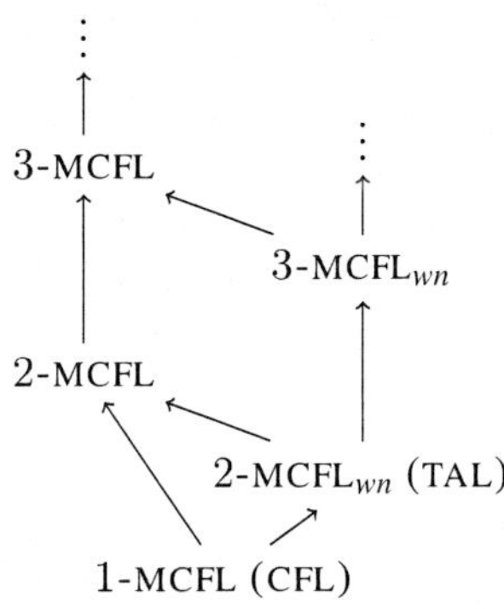

Figure 1: The MCFL hierarchy.

2.1   Multiple Context-Free Grammars

This paper considers *multiple context-free grammars* (MCFGs, Seki et al., 1991), a mildly context-sensitive (MCS) formalism equivalent to MGs (Harkema, 2001; Michaelis, 2001). MCFGs are a generalization of context-free grammars (CFGs) in which nonterminals derive tuples of strings. Whereas CFG rules concatenate strings derived from nonterminals on their right-hand sides, MCFGs interleave nonterminal-derived tuples. Let us consider an example to illustrate how MCFGs generate strings.

Example 1. The following four rules define an MCFG generating the copy language $L = \{ww \mid w \in \{a, b\}^*\}$. The start symbol is S.

$$S(xy) \leftarrow T(x, y) \tag{2a}$$
$$T(ax, ay) \leftarrow T(x, y) \tag{2b}$$
$$T(bx, by) \leftarrow T(x, y) \tag{2c}$$
$$T(\varepsilon, \varepsilon) \leftarrow \tag{2d}$$

A rule of the form

$$A(\mathbf{y}) \leftarrow B_1(\mathbf{x_1}) B_2(\mathbf{x_2}) \ldots B_n(\mathbf{x_n})$$

is interpreted as an axiom stating that if each nonterminal B_i on the right-hand side generates the tuple $\mathbf{x}_i$, then the nonterminal A on the left-hand side generates the tuple $\mathbf{y}$. In rule (2d), the right-hand side is empty; this means that we assume T to generate the tuple $\langle \varepsilon, \varepsilon \rangle$.

The string $abab \in L$ is derived as follows. By rule (2d), T generates $\langle \varepsilon, \varepsilon \rangle$. By (2c), T generates $\langle b, b \rangle$. By (2b), T generates $\langle ab, ab \rangle$. By (2a), the start symbol S generates $abab$.

An MCFG rule may be thought of as a function that describes how tuples generated by nonterminals on the right-hand side may be combined with one another. These functions must satisfy a condition known as *linearity*, which asserts that MCFG rules cannot copy their inputs.[1]

Definition 3. Fix $k \in \mathbb{N}$. Consider a function $f : \prod_{i=1}^{k}(\Sigma^*)^{d_i} \to (\Sigma^*)^{d_0}$. For each i, write $\mathbf{x}_i = \langle x_{i,1}, x_{i,2}, \ldots, x_{i,d_i} \rangle$. We say that f is a *linear function* if it is of the form

$$f(\mathbf{x}_1, \mathbf{x}_2, \ldots, \mathbf{x}_k) = \langle \alpha_1, \alpha_2, \ldots, \alpha_{d_0} \rangle,$$

where the concatenated string $\alpha = \alpha_1 \alpha_2 \ldots \alpha_{d_0}$ satisfies the following criteria:

- α contains exactly one occurrence of each variable $x_{i,j}$; and

- for each i and j, $x_{i,j}$ occurs to the left of $x_{i,j+1}$ in α.[2]

Furthermore, we say that f is *well-nested* if there are no indices i, j, i', j', and j'', with $i \neq i'$ and $j' \neq j''$, such that the variable $x_{i',j'}$ occurs between $x_{i,j}$ and $x_{i,j+1}$ in α, but $x_{i',j''}$ does not.

Definition 4. A *multiple context-free grammar* (MCFG) is an ordered quadruple $G = \langle N, \Sigma, R, I \rangle$, where

- N is a finite set of *nonterminals*;

- Σ is a finite set of *terminals*;

- $I \subseteq N$ is the set of *start symbols*; and

- letting $\mathcal{F}$ be the set of all linear functions, $R \subseteq N \times \mathcal{F} \times N^*$ is a finite set of *rules*.

We always assume that N and Σ are disjoint. Each nonterminal $A \in N$ is associated with a number $\dim(A)$ known as its *dimension*. All start symbols must have dimension 1. We denote each rule $r = \langle A, f, B_1 B_2 \ldots B_k \rangle$ by

$$A(\mathbf{y}) \leftarrow B_1(\mathbf{x}_1) B_2(\mathbf{x}_2) \ldots B_k(\mathbf{x}_k),$$

where each $\mathbf{x}_i$ is a $\dim(B_i)$-tuple of variables and $\mathbf{y} = f(\mathbf{x}_1, \mathbf{x}_2, \ldots, \mathbf{x}_k)$. We say that r is *well-nested* if f is well-nested.

---

[1]While individual MCFG rules cannot copy, Example 1 shows that MCFGs can perform copying by combining several different rules.

[2]Technically, the definition of linear functions only requires that α contain at least one occurrence of each $x_{i,j}$. Seki et al. (1991) and Kracht (2003) show that the other assumptions can be made without changing the generative capacity of MCFGs.

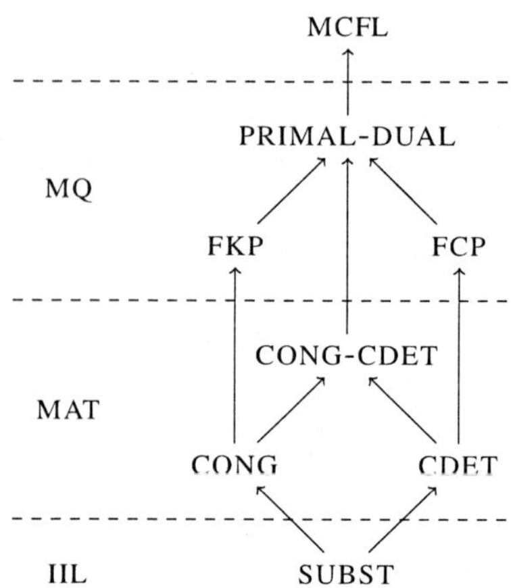

Figure 2: The hierarchy of Distributionally Learnable MCFLs (see Clark and Yoshinaka 2016).

We say that G is a *k-multiple context free grammar* (*k*-MCFG) if every nonterminal has dimension at most k. We say that G is *well-nested* if every rule in R is well-nested. For each nonterminal A, we define $\mathcal{L}(G, A) \subseteq (\Sigma^*)^{\dim(A)}$ as follows. For each rule $A(\mathbf{y}) \leftarrow B_1(\mathbf{x}_1) B_2(\mathbf{x}_2) \ldots B_k(\mathbf{x}_k)$ with $\mathbf{y} = f(\mathbf{x}_1, \mathbf{x}_2, \ldots, \mathbf{x}_k)$, if $\mathbf{z}_i \in \mathcal{L}(G, B_i)$ for each i, then $f(\mathbf{z}_1, \mathbf{z}_2, \ldots, \mathbf{z}_k) \in \mathcal{L}(G, A)$. Identifying 1-tuples with strings, the *language generated by G* is the language $\mathcal{L}(G) := \bigcup_{S \in I} \mathcal{L}(G, S)$. We say that a language $L \subseteq \Sigma^*$ is a *k-multiple context-free language* (*k*-MCFL) if it is generated by a *k*-MCFG. We say that L is *well-nested* if G is well-nested.

MCFLs naturally subsume other common language classes: the class of context-free languages (CFLs) is the same as the class of 1-MCFLs, while the class of tree-adjoining languages (TALs) is the same as the class of well-nested 2-MCFLs (Kanazawa, 2009b). Seki et al. (1991) and Rambow and Satta (1999) prove a separation result showing that k-MCFLs are strictly contained within the class of $(k + 1)$-MCFLs. This MCFL hierarchy, along with its well-nested counterpart (Kanazawa, 2009a), is shown in Figure 1.

3   Learnable Classes of Languages

The theory of learnability considered here is based on the *Identification in the Limit* (IIL) model of Gold (1967). Under this paradigm, the learner receives an infinite data stream containing all possible strings drawn from a target language L, arranged in an unspecified order. After observing each string, the learner must guess a grammar for L. We consider a class of languages $\mathcal{C} \subseteq \mathcal{P}(\Sigma^*)$ to be learnable if there is a learner whose guesses converge to a correct grammar for L for any target $L \in \mathcal{C}$ and any presentation of the strings of L.

IIL-learning of formal languages was pioneered by Angluin (1982), who gave an algorithm that learns the class of regular languages satisfying a criterion known as *reversibility*. While the full class of regular languages is not learnable under the IIL paradigm, Angluin (1987) showed that learner can learn all regular languages if it is equipped with a *minimally adequate teacher* (MAT): a black-box oracle that answers certain questions about the target language. These algorithms were extended to CFLs by Clark and Eyraud (2007) and Clark (2010), respectively, and to MCFLs by Yoshinaka (2011a) and Yoshinaka and Clark (2012), respectively. Since the MAT-learning algorithm fails to learn the full classes of CFLs and MCFLs, further results by Yoshinaka (2011b), Yoshinaka (2012), and Clark and Yoshinaka (2012) expand the MAT-learnable classes via algorithms using *membership queries* (MQs). These learnable language classes are visually summarized in Figure 2.

The remainder of this section formally defines several classes of MCFLs. Subsection 3.1 defines the IIL-learnable *substitutable* MCFLs ("SUBST" in Figure 2), the MCFL analogue of Angluin's reversible regular languages. Subsection 3.2 defines the MAT-learnable *congruential* MCFLs ("CONG" in Figure 2). Subsection 3.3 defines two MQ-learnable classes of MCFLs: those generated by MCFGs with the *finite kernel property* ("FKP" in Figure 2) and those generated by MCFGs with the *finite context property* ("FCP" in Figure 2).

3.1 Substitutable Languages

The IIL algorithms of Clark and Eyraud (2007) and Yoshinaka (2011a) rely upon the strong assumption that whenever two k-tuples $\mathbf{x}$ and $\mathbf{y}$ appear in the same context—i.e., $\mathbf{x}^{\triangleright} \cap \mathbf{y}^{\triangleright} \neq \varnothing$— they must be generated by the same k-dimensional nonterminal. This property is known as *substitutability*.

Definition 5. For $k \in \mathbb{N}$, a language $L \subseteq \Sigma^*$ is *k-substitutable* if for all k-tuples $\mathbf{x}, \mathbf{y} \in (\Sigma^*)^k$, either $\mathbf{x}^{|L\rangle} = \mathbf{y}^{|L\rangle}$ or $\mathbf{x}^{|L\rangle} \cap \mathbf{y}^{|L\rangle} = \varnothing$.

For each k, a language L induces an equivalence relation $\equiv_L^k$ on $(\Sigma^*)^k$ in which $\mathbf{x} \equiv_L^k \mathbf{y}$ if and only if $\mathbf{x}^{\triangleright} = \mathbf{y}^{\triangleright}$. The grammar G constructed by the algorithm identifies each nonterminal A with an equivalence class $[a]$ of $\equiv_L^{\dim(A)}$, so that $a \in \mathcal{L}(G, A) \subseteq [a]$. It turns out that linear functions map tuples of subsets of equivalence classes to subsets of equivalence classes, allowing nonterminals to combine with one another via MCFG rules.

When L is a k-substitutable k-MCFL, the learner determines whether or not $\mathbf{x}$ and $\mathbf{y}$ are equivalent based on whether or not a common context in $\mathbf{x}^{\triangleright} \cap \mathbf{y}^{\triangleright}$ has been observed so far, with the understanding that such a context must appear in the data eventually. At each time step, the learner finds all equivalence classes seen so far, and constructs all rules such that a representative from the equivalence class on the left-hand side has been observed in the data. The learner converges when the data contain enough equivalence classes to construct a correct grammar for L.

3.2 Congruential Languages

In Clark (2010) and Yoshinaka and Clark (2012), the learner again identifies each nonterminal A with an equivalence class of $\equiv_L^{\dim(A)}$ and seeks to find all equivalence classes needed to construct the grammar. Without the assumption of substitutability, the learner relies on the minimally adequate teacher to determine which tuples are equivalent. To do this, the learner asks the teacher two types of questions: *membership queries* (Is $x \in L$?) and *equivalence queries* (What is an example of a string in $L \backslash \mathcal{L}(G)$?). At each time step, an equivalence query is used to identify an equivalence class not covered by an existing nonterminal, and membership queries are used to construct all possible rules involving the new nonterminal. Note that training data are not needed, since the learner asks the teacher for data through equivalence queries. MCFGs constructed through this procedure are known as *congruential* MCFGs.

Definition 6. A k-MCFG G is *congruential* if for every nonterminal A, $\mathcal{L}(G, A)$ is completely contained within an equivalence class of $\equiv_{\mathcal{L}(G)}^{\dim(A)}$. A k-MCFL is *congruential* if it is generated by a congruential k-MCFG.

3.3 The FKP and the FCP

The learning algorithms for the substitutable and congruential CFLs and MCFLs attempt to find equivalence classes of $\equiv_L^k$. Yoshinaka (2011b) and

Clark and Yoshinaka (2012) generalize beyond this approach by dropping the requirement that nonterminals correspond to equivalence classes. Instead, each nonterminal A is identified with a finite set of strings or contexts with the same distribution as A.

Definition 7. Fix $k \in \mathbb{N}$. An MCFG G has the *k-finite kernel property* (k-FKP) if for every nonterminal A of G, there exists $K_A \subseteq (\Sigma^*)^{\dim A}$ such that $|K_A| \leq k$ and $\mathcal{L}(G, A)^{\triangleright} = K_A^{\triangleright}$. G has the *k-finite context property* (k-FCP) if for every nonterminal A, there exists $C_A \subseteq (\Sigma^*)^{\dim(A)+1}$ such that $|C_A| \leq k$ and $\mathcal{L}(G, A)^{\triangleright \triangleleft} = C_A^{\triangleleft}$.[3]

At each time step, the learner constructs nonterminals by considering all possible size-k sets of tuples or contexts. The learner constructs rules $r = A(\mathbf{y}) \leftarrow B_1(\mathbf{x}_1) B_2(\mathbf{x}_2) \ldots B_n(\mathbf{x}_n)$ by determining whether or not the right-hand side and the left-hand side have the same distribution. This is done heuristically by asking membership queries for strings of the form $\mathbf{c} \odot f(\mathbf{b}_1, \mathbf{b}_2, \ldots, \mathbf{b}_n)$, where f is the linear function associated with r. When L is assumed to have the k-FKP, $\mathbf{c}$ is drawn from the contexts in $K_A^{\triangleright}$ observed so far, and for each i, $\mathbf{b}_i \in K_{B_i}$. When L is assumed to have the k-FCP, $\mathbf{c} \in C_A$, while each $\mathbf{b}_i$ is drawn from the substrings in $C_{B_i}^{\triangleleft}$ observed so far.

4 Overgeneration

The formal problem of overgeneration has a long history in linguistics, starting from Peters and Ritchie's (1973) proof that Transformational Grammars can generate all recursively enumerable languages. Recent interest in the overgeneration problem arises from the model-theoretic approach pioneered by Rogers (1994, 1998) for the formalization of syntactic theories. Relying upon the equivalence of monadic second-order (MSO) logic over trees with tree automata (Thatcher and Wright, 1968), Rogers constructs a context-free implementation of Rizzi's (1990) constraint-based Relativized Minimality theory by stating the constraints in MSO logic. Morawietz (2008) extends the model-theoretic approach to MCS formalisms by combining MSO constraints on derivation trees with MSO-definable transductions from derivation trees to derived structures. Considering the case of MGs, Kobele (2011) and Graf (2011) show

that MG derivation trees are closed under intersection with arbitrary MSO constraints, and Graf (2012) shows that complex movement operations can be added to MGs by enhancing the transduction from derivation trees to derived trees. These closure properties allow Graf (2013) to develop a full MG-based treatment of Minimalist syntax within Morawietz's framework, showing that Minimalist constraints on derivation trees and derived trees, as well as transderivational constraints, can be implemented using Merge by carefully choosing categories and selection features for lexical items.

These findings have highlighted the relevance of overgeneration to mainstream Minimalist syntax. As discussed in Graf (2017), existing constraints on movement can be circumvented by using Merge to create non-local dependencies. On the other hand, any pathological pattern is a logically possible MG as long as it is MSO-definable. Illustrating the latter point, Graf (2013, pp. 117–118) identifies three kinds of unnatural dependencies that can be generated by MGs:

(8)   a. patterns sensitive to "non-linguistic" information, such as the number of words in a sentence;

        b. languages with completely free word order, subject to no restrictions; and

        c. creating arbitrarily many copies of context-free structure.

In Subsections 4.1 and 4.2, I show that the patterns described in (8a) and (8b), respectively, can be represented as substitutable MCFLs. In Subsection 4.3, we will see that the arbitrary copying of (8c) is not congruential, but it can be generated by an MCFG with both the 2-FKP and the 1-FCP.

4.1 Structure-Independent Patterns

One of the earliest motivations for the rationalist position is the observation that syntactic dependencies are universally sensitive to constituency structure. Chomsky (1968) argues:

> … grammatical transformations are invariably *structure-dependent* in the sense that they apply to a string of words by virtue of the organization of these words into phrases. It is easy to imagine *structure-independent* operations that apply to a string of elements quite independently of its ab-

---

[3]The definition presented here is for the *weak* versions of the FKP and the FCP. Other versions of these properties are discussed in Kanazawa and Yoshinaka (2017).

stract structure as a system of phrases. ... Yet no human language contains structure-independent operations .... The language-learner knows that [such operations] need not be considered as tentative hypotheses.

Examples of "structure-independent" patterns typically consist of operations whose targets are based on arithmetic criteria. One such example appears in the passage quoted above, where Chomsky imagines an auxiliary-fronting operation targeting the first auxiliary in a sentence. This produces the ungrammatical question (9b) from the corresponding declarative (9a).

(9) a. The subjects who will act as controls will be paid.

b. * Will the subjects who t act as controls will be paid?

c. Will the subjects who will act as controls t be paid?

Along these lines, Graf imagines a requirement that the length of a sentence or phrase be a multiple of some fixed number n.

Definition 10. For each $n > 0$, let us define

$$\mathrm{MOD}_n := \{x \mid |x| \equiv 0 \mod n\}.$$

Despite its structure-independence, MOD_n is easily shown to be substitutable.

Proposition 11. MOD_n *is k-substitutable for every $k \in \mathbb{N}$ and $n > 0$.*

Proof. For any k-tuple $\mathbf{x}$ and k-context $\mathbf{c}$, $\mathbf{c} \odot \mathbf{x} \in \mathrm{MOD}_n$ if and only if $|\mathbf{c}| + |\mathbf{x}|$ is a multiple of n. Therefore,

$$\mathbf{x}^\triangleright = \{\mathbf{c} \mid |\mathbf{c}| \equiv -|\mathbf{x}| \mod n\}.$$

It is clear that for any $\mathbf{x}, \mathbf{y} \in (\Sigma^*)^k$, $\mathbf{x}^\triangleright$ and $\mathbf{y}^\triangleright$ are either equal or disjoint, so MOD_n is k-substitutable for every k. $\square$

4.2 Free Word Order

Following Shieber's (1985) argument that Swiss German is not context-free, Joshi (1985) proposed the MCS languages as a characterization of the possible natural languages. This class is defined by grammar formalisms that admit a polynomial-time parsing algorithm, exhibit constant growth, and express limited cross-serial dependencies. The notion of "limited cross-serial dependencies" was left vague, but Joshi et al. (1990, 1991) provide some elaboration:

[MCS grammars] capture only certain kinds of dependencies, e.g., nested dependencies and certain limited kinds of crossing dependencies (e.g., in the subordinate clause constructions in Dutch or some variations of them, but perhaps not in the so-called MIX (or Bach) language ... [).]

The language MIX mentioned above is the focus of this subsection.

Definition 12. The language MIX is defined as

$$\mathrm{MIX} := \{x \in \{a, b, c\}^* \mid |x|_a = |x|_b = |x|_c\}.$$

According to Joshi (1985), MIX "represents the extreme case of the degree of free word order permitted in a language," and is therefore "linguistically not relevant." The fact that MIX is a 2-MCFL but not a TAL (Salvati, 2011, 2015; Kanazawa and Salvati, 2012) has been used to argue that the TALs are a more suitable formalization of the MCS languages than the MCFLs. This kind of reasoning may be seen as a rationalist position asserting that MIX is not a possible natural language because UG requires natural languages to be TALs. An empiricist account for the absence of MIX-like natural languages might claim that the learners fail to converge on MIX even though MIX is allowed by UG. However, it turns out that MIX is substitutable, so such an account would not be supported by Distributional Learning as a model of language acquisition.

Proposition 13 (Clark and Yoshinaka, 2016). MIX *is k-substitutable for every $k \in \mathbb{N}$.*

Proof. Suppose $\mathbf{c} \odot \mathbf{x}, \mathbf{c} \odot \mathbf{y}, \mathbf{d} \odot \mathbf{x} \in \mathrm{MIX}$. We want to show that $\mathbf{d} \odot \mathbf{y} \in \mathrm{MIX}$. To that end, observe that for any context γ and symbol $i \in \{a, b, c\}$,

$$|\gamma \odot \mathbf{y}|_i = |\gamma \odot \mathbf{x}|_i - |\mathbf{x}|_i + |\mathbf{y}|_i. \tag{14}$$

Taking $\gamma = \mathbf{c}$, we obtain

$$-|\mathbf{x}|_i + |\mathbf{y}|_i = |\mathbf{c} \odot \mathbf{y}|_i - |\mathbf{c} \odot \mathbf{x}|_i.$$

Next, we take $\gamma = \mathbf{d}$ and substitute the above into (14), giving us

$$|\mathbf{d} \odot \mathbf{y}|_i = |\mathbf{d} \odot \mathbf{x}|_i + |\mathbf{c} \odot \mathbf{y}|_i - |\mathbf{c} \odot \mathbf{x}|_i.$$

Since the terms on the right-hand side have the same value for all i, so must the left-hand side. This means that $\mathbf{d} \odot \mathbf{y} \in \mathrm{MIX}$, as desired. $\square$

4.3 Copying

The third unnatural dependency that Graf considers is represented by the *double-copying language* $\mathrm{COPY}_3(D_1)$.

Definition 15. For $L \subseteq \Sigma^*$ and $n \in \mathbb{N}$, define

$$\mathrm{COPY}_n(L) := \{(x\#)^n \mid x \in L\},$$

where $\# \notin \Sigma$.[4]

Definition 16. The language D_1 is the language generated by the following 1-MCFG.

$$S(xy) \leftarrow S(x)S(y)$$
$$S([\,x\,]) \leftarrow S(x)$$
$$S(\varepsilon) \leftarrow$$

Copy languages have two interpretations in mathematical linguistics. On the one hand, $\mathrm{COPY}_2(\{a,b\}^*)$ represents the cross-serial dependencies found in Swiss German, since it is a homomorphic image of the embedded-clause verb–argument sequences that Shieber shows is not context-free. On the other hand, the idea of copying structure often appears explicitly in syntactic analyses. Kobele (2006), for instance, argues that Yoruba has a relative clause construction that involves copying VPs. Apart from overtly attested instances of copying, Merchant (1999, 2001) develops a theory of sluicing in which CPs are copied and their TP complements are deleted. It turns out that Distributional Learning can distinguish between these two interpretations of copying.

Proposition 17. $\mathrm{COPY}_n(L)$ *is a congruential n-MCFL if and only if L is regular.*[5]

If we consider non-regular Ls to represent copying of structure, then only the former interpretation is captured by the congruential n-MCFLs.

Lemma 18. *Let $\mathbf{x} = \langle x_1, x_2, \ldots, x_m \rangle$, with $m \leq n$. If $|\mathbf{x}|_\# < n$, then either $|x_i|_\# \geq 2$ for some i, $\mathbf{x}^{|\,\mathrm{COPY}_n(L))} = \varnothing$, or $\mathbf{x}$ belongs to a finite equivalence class of $\equiv^m_{\mathrm{COPY}_n(L)}$.*

Proof. Suppose $\mathbf{x}^\triangleright \neq \varnothing$, $|x_i|_\# \leq 1$ for all i, and $|\mathbf{x}|_\# \leq n - 2$. Then, $\mathbf{x}$ has a context $\mathbf{c} = c_0 \square c_1 \square \ldots \square c_n$ such that $|c_i|_\# \geq 2$ for some i. Writing $c_i = l\#w\#r$, observe that every $\mathbf{y} \in \mathbf{c}^\triangleleft$ satisfies $\mathbf{c} \odot \mathbf{y} = (w\#)^n$. There are only finitely

---

[4]The language considered in Graf (2013) does not have a final $\#$. However, adding the final $\#$ allows $\mathrm{COPY}_n(L)$ to be congruential when L is regular (Proposition 17).

[5]However, it is easy to show that $\mathrm{COPY}_n(\{a^i b^i \mid i \geq 0\})$ is a congruential $(n+1)$-MCFL.

many such **y**s, so only finitely many strings may share the context $\mathbf{c}$ with $\mathbf{x}$.

Next, suppose that $\mathbf{x}^\triangleright \neq \varnothing$, $|x_i|_\# \leq 1$ for all i, and $|\mathbf{x}|_\# = n - 1$. Then, we have $|x_p|_\# = 0$ for some p, and for $i \neq p$ we can write $x_i = y_i\#z_i$ with $|y_i|_\# = |z_i|_\# = 0$. Let y be the longest y_i and z be the longest z_i, and let $y_{m+1} = z_0 := \varepsilon$. Observe that $\mathbf{c} \in x^\triangleright$ if and only if $\mathbf{c} \odot \mathbf{x} = (w\#)^n$ for some $w \in z\Sigma^*y \cap z_{p-1}\Sigma^*x_p\Sigma^*y_{p+1}$. Thus, if $\mathbf{x}'^\triangleright = \mathbf{x}^\triangleright$, then $\mathbf{x}' = \langle x_1', x_2', \ldots, x_m' \rangle$, where $x_q' = x_p$ for some q, $x_i' = y_i'\#z_i'$ for $i \neq q$, y is the longest y_i', z is the longest z_i', $y_{q+1}' = y_{q+1}$, and $z_{q-1}' = z_{p-1}$. There are only finitely many such $\mathbf{x}'$, so the lemma follows. $\square$

Proof of Proposition 17. First, suppose L is regular. Let M be the minimal right-to-left deterministic finite-state automaton recognizing L. We can construct an MCFG G for $\mathrm{COPY}_n(L)$ as follows. The nonterminals of G are the states of M. If A is the start state of M, then G has the rule $A(\#,\#,\ldots,\#) \leftarrow$. If M transitions from state B to state A after reading a, then G has a rule $A(ax_1, ax_2, \ldots, ax_n) \leftarrow B(x_1, x_2, \ldots, x_n)$. Finally, for each accept state S of M, G has a start symbol I_S and a rule $I_S(x_1 x_2 \ldots x_n) \leftarrow S(x_1, x_2, \ldots, x_n)$. It is clear that for each $x \in \mathcal{L}(G, I_S)$, $x^\triangleright = \{\square\}$. Observe that for each nonterminal A of G, $\mathcal{L}(G, A)$ is the set of strings $(w\#)^n$ such that M is in state A after reading w. Thus, elements of $\mathcal{L}(G, A)$ are of the form $(w\#)^n$. For each such $(w\#)^n$, we have

$$((w\#)^n)^\triangleright = \{c\square c\square \ldots \square c \mid cw \in L\}.$$

Since M is minimal, if $(u\#)^n, (v\#)^n \in \mathcal{L}(G, A)$, then by the Myhill–Nerode Theorem we must have

$$\{c \mid cu \in L\} = \{c \mid cv \in L\},$$

thus

$$((u\#)^n)^\triangleright = \{c\square c\square \ldots \square c \mid cu \in L\}$$
$$= \{c\square c\square \ldots \square c \mid cv \in L\}$$
$$= ((v\#)^n)^\triangleright.$$

This means that G is congruential.

Now, suppose $\mathrm{COPY}_n(L)$ is generated by a congruential n-MCFG G. By Lemma 18, without loss of generality each copy of $w \in L$ in $(w\#)^n \in \mathrm{COPY}_n(L)$ is generated exclusively using rules of the form

$$A(l_1 x_1 r_1, l_2 x_2 r_2, \ldots, l_n x_n r_n)$$

$$\leftarrow B(x_1, x_2, \ldots, x_n),$$

where $l_i, r_i \in \Sigma^*$ for each i and $\mathcal{L}(G, B) \subseteq (\Sigma^* \# \Sigma^*)^n$. Since x_1 must already contain a $\#$, such rules can only append a constant string to the left of the first copy of w, so the set of possible ws must be regular. $\qquad\square$

Graf argues that $\mathrm{COPY}_3(D_1)$ is unnatural because "embeddings of unbounded depth are copied and fully realized in three distinct positions in the utterance." According to Proposition 17, the property of unbounded depth disqualifies $\mathrm{COPY}_3(D_1)$ from congruentiality, but the existence of more than two copies does not, as long as $\mathrm{COPY}_3(D_1)$ is generated by a 3-MCFG. $\mathrm{COPY}_3(D_1)$ is still learnable, however, because it belongs to the class of 3-MCFLs defined by the FKP and the FCP.

Proposition 19. $\mathrm{COPY}_3(D_1)$ *is generated by a 3-MCFG G with the 2-FKP and the 1-FCP.*

Proof. G is defined as follows.

$$S(x \# y \# z \#) \leftarrow T(x, y, z)$$
$$T(x_1 x_2, y_1 y_2, z_1 z_2) \leftarrow T(x_1, y_1, z_1)$$
$$T(x_2, y_2, z_2)$$
$$T([x], [y], [z]) \leftarrow T(x, y, z)$$
$$T(\varepsilon, \varepsilon, \varepsilon) \leftarrow$$

We have

$$\mathcal{L}(G, S)^{\triangleright} = \mathrm{COPY}_3(D_1)^{\triangleright} = \{\square\} = \{\#\#\#\}^{\triangleright}$$
$$\mathcal{L}(G, T)^{\triangleright} = \{\langle w, w, w \rangle \mid w \in D_1\}^{\triangleright}$$
$$= \left\{ l\square r \# l\square r \# l\square r \# \,\middle|\, l\square r \in D_1^{\langle D_1|} \right\}$$
$$= \{\langle [\,[\,]\,], [\,[\,]\,], [\,[\,]\,] \rangle,$$
$$\langle [\,]\,[\,], [\,]\,[\,], [\,]\,[\,] \rangle\}^{\triangleright},$$

so G has the 2-FKP.[6] We also have

$$\mathcal{L}(G, S)^{\triangleright\triangleleft} = \{\square\}^{\triangleleft}$$
$$\mathcal{L}(G, T)^{\triangleright\triangleleft} = \{\square \# \square \# \square \#\}^{\triangleleft},$$

so G has the 1-FCP. $\qquad\square$

5 Conclusion

We have seen that MOD_n and MIX are k-substitutable for every k, while $\mathrm{COPY}_3(D_1)$ is generated by a 3-MCFG with the 2-FKP and the

1-FCP. If the Distributional Learning hierarchy of Figure 2 is taken to be a measure of complexity, then we may conclude from these facts that MOD_n and MIX are very simple from the perspective of learnability. Proposition 17 gives us the interesting result that in general, the complexity of $\mathrm{COPY}_n(L)$ with respect to learnability is related to the language-theoretic complexity of L, so that $\mathrm{COPY}_3(D_1)$ is slightly more complex than the congruential languages. Since natural language grammars are not congruential,[7] any class in the learnable hierarchy that might plausibly include natural language syntax would also likely include MOD_n, MIX, and $\mathrm{COPY}_3(D_1)$.

The discussions in Subsections 4.2 and 4.3 should be contrasted with language-theoretic analyses of MIX and $\mathrm{COPY}_3(D_1)$, respectively. As mentioned previously, MIX falls outside the TALs, which is identical to the well-nested 2-MCFLs. Similarly, Kanazawa and Salvati (2010) show that $\mathrm{COPY}_3(D_1)$ is not a well-nested n-MCFL for any n. The criterion of well-nestedness, then, provides an elegant rationalist explanation for the absence of MIX- or $\mathrm{COPY}_3(D_1)$-like natural languages. Such a criterion could also be justified on functionalist grounds, since well-nested MCFGs admit a more efficient parsing algorithm than MCFGs in general (Gómez-Rodríguez et al., 2010). While the well-nestedness requirement does not eliminate MOD_n, an anonymous reviewer observes that intersecting the language of a CFG with MOD_n increases the size of that CFG by a factor of n^2. Thus, when n is large, languages with MOD_n-like dependencies may be eliminated by functionalist considerations regarding grammar size.

The case of MOD_n shows that the regular languages capture many patterns that do not resemble natural language dependencies. Although the inclusion of the regular languages in natural language has traditionally been taken for granted,[8] recent work on the *subregular hierarchy* has shown that markedness constraints in phonotactics and morphotactics typically belong to restricted, IIL-learnable subclasses of the regular languages (Heinz et al., 2011; Aksënova et al.,

---

[6]G does not have the 1-FKP because for any $\langle x, x, x \rangle \in \mathcal{L}(G, T)^{\triangleright\triangleleft}$, $x\square \# \square x \# x \square \# \in \langle x, x, x \rangle^{\triangleright} \backslash \mathcal{L}(G, T)^{\triangleright}$.

[7]For example, congruentiality would preclude the possibility of a single word such as *effect* or *affect* having the distribution of both a noun and a verb if nonterminals are identified with syntactic categories.

[8]Additionally, Joshi et al. (1990, 1991) mention strict inclusion of the CFLs as a fourth defining property of the MCS languages.

2016) that formalize notions of locality. It may be the case that a refinement of the regular languages is needed for syntax as well. While the study of the equivalence relation $\equiv_L^k$ may be seen as an algebraic treatment of the notion of structure (Clark, 2015), the learnability of MOD_n may reveal a point of divergence between the algebraic approach and the intuitive notion of syntactic constituencies.

In conclusion, this paper has shown that the restricted language classes in the Distributional Learning hierarchy are rich enough to raise the very questions of overgeneration that they were hypothesized to solve. While Distributional Learning does not provide a learnability-based account for the typological absence of patterns modelled by MOD_n, MIX, or $\mathrm{COPY}_3(D_1)$, all three patterns can plausibly be eliminated on rationalist or functionalist grounds. These findings suggest that learnability may play a smaller role in determining natural language typology than once expected.

References

Alëna Aksënova, Thomas Graf, and Sedigheh Moradi. 2016. Morphotactics as Tier-Based Strictly Local Dependencies. In *Proceedings of the 14th SIG-MORPHON Workshop on Computational Research in Phonetics, Phonology, and Morphology*, pages 121–130, Berlin, Germany. Association for Computational Linguistics.

Dana Angluin. 1982. Inference of Reversible Languages. *Journal of the Association for Computing Machinery*, 29(3):741–765.

Dana Angluin. 1987. Learning Regular Sets from Queries and Counterexamples. *Information and Computation*, 75(2):87–106.

Noam Chomsky. 1965. *Aspects of the Theory of Syntax*, 1 edition. MIT Press, Cambridge, MA.

Noam Chomsky. 1968. *Language and Mind*, 1 edition. Harcourt, Brace & World, New York, NY.

Noam Chomsky. 1971. *Problems of Knowledge and Freedom: The Russell Lectures*, 1 edition. Pantheon Books, New York, NY.

Noam Chomsky. 1980. On Cognitive Structures and their Development: A Reply to Piaget. In Piatelli M. Palmerini, editor, *Language and Learning: The Debate Between Jean Piaget and Noam Chomsky*, pages 35–54. Routledge & Kegan Paul, London, United Kingdom.

Alexander Clark. 2010. Distributional Learning of Some Context-Free Languages with a Minimally Adequate Teacher. In *Grammatical Inference: Theoretical Results and Applications*, pages 24–37, Valencia, Spain. Springer Berlin Heidelberg.

Alexander Clark. 2015. The syntactic concept lattice: Another algebraic theory of the context-free languages? *Journal of Logic and Computation*, 25(5):1203–1229.

Alexander Clark and Rémi Eyraud. 2007. Polynomial Identification in the Limit of Substitutable Context-free Languages. *Journal of Machine Learning Research*, 8(Aug):1725–1745.

Alexander Clark and Ryo Yoshinaka. 2012. Beyond Semilinearity: Distributional Learning of Parallel Multiple Context-free Grammars. In *Proceedings of the Eleventh International Conference on Grammatical Inference, PMLR 21:1-3, 2012*, volume 21 of *Proceedings of Machine Learning Research*, pages 84–96, College Park, MD. PMLR.

Alexander Clark and Ryo Yoshinaka. 2016. Distributional Learning of Context-Free and Multiple Context-Free Grammars. In Jeffrey Heinz and José M. Sempere, editors, *Topics in Grammatical Inference*, pages 143–172. Springer Berlin Heidelberg, Berlin, Germany.

E Mark Gold. 1967. Language identification in the limit. *Information and Control*, 10(5):447–474.

Carlos Gómez-Rodríguez, Marco Kuhlmann, and Giorgio Satta. 2010. Efficient Parsing of Well-Nested Linear Context-Free Rewriting Systems. In *Human Language Technologies: The 2010 Annual Conference of the North American Chapter of the Association for Computational Linguistics*, pages 276–284, Los Angeles, CA. Association for Computational Linguistics.

Thomas Graf. 2011. Closure Properties of Minimalist Derivation Tree Languages. In *Logical Aspects of Computational Linguistics: 6th International Conference, LACL 2011, Montpellier, France, June 29 – July 1, 2011. Proceedings*, pages 96–111, Berlin, Germany. Springer Berlin Heidelberg.

Thomas Graf. 2012. Movement-Generalized Minimalist Grammars. In *7th International Conference, LACL 2012, Nantes, France, July 2-4, 2012. Proceedings*, volume 7351 of *Lecture Notes in Computer Science*, pages 58–73, Berlin, Germany. Springer Berlin Heidelberg.

Thomas Graf. 2013. *Local and Transderivational Constraints in Syntax and Semantics*. PhD Dissertation, University of California, Los Angeles, Los Angeles, CA.

Thomas Graf. 2017. A computational guide to the dichotomy of features and constraints. *Glossa: a journal of general linguistics*, 2(1):18.1–36.

Henk Harkema. 2001. A Characterization of Minimalist Languages. In *Logical Aspects of Computational Linguistics: 4th International Conference, LACL 2001 Le Croisic, France, June 27–29, 2001 Proceedings*, pages 193–211, Berlin, Germany. Springer Berlin Heidelberg.

Jeffrey Heinz, Chetan Rawal, and Herbert G. Tanner. 2011. Tier-based Strictly Local Constraints for Phonology. In *Proceedings of the 49th Annual Meeting of the Association for Computational Linguistics: Human Language Technologies*, pages 58–64, Portland, OR. Association for Computational Linguistics.

Aravind K. Joshi. 1985. Tree adjoining grammars: How much context-sensitivity is required to provide reasonable structural descriptions? In Arnold M. Zwicky, David R. Dowty, and Lauri Karttunen, editors, *Natural Language Parsing: Psychological, Computational, and Theoretical Perspectives*, Studies in Natural Language Processing, pages 206–250. Cambridge University Press, Cambridge, United Kingdom.

Aravind K. Joshi, K. Vijay Shanker, and David Weir. 1990. The Convergence of Mildly Context-Sensitive Grammar Formalisms. Technical Report MS-CIS-90-01, University of Pennsylvania Department of Computer and Information Science, Philadelphia, PA.

Aravind K. Joshi, K. Vijay Shanker, and David Weir. 1991. The Convergence of Mildly Context-Sensitive Grammar Formalisms. In Stuart M. Shieber, Peter Sells, and Thomas Wasow, editors, *Foundational Issues in Natural Language Processing*, System Development Foundation Benchmark Series, pages 31–81. MIT Press, Cambridge, MA.

Makoto Kanazawa. 2009a. The Convergence of Well-Nested Mildly Context-Sensitive Grammar Formalisms.

Makoto Kanazawa. 2009b. The Pumping Lemma for Well-Nested Multiple Context-Free Languages. In *Developments in Language Theory: 13th International Conference, DLT 2009, Stuttgart, Germany, June 30-July 3, 2009. Proceedings*, volume 5583 of *Lecture Notes in Computer Science*, pages 312–325, Berlin, Germany. Springer Berlin Heidelberg.

Makoto Kanazawa and Sylvain Salvati. 2010. The Copying Power of Well-Nested Multiple Context-Free Grammars. In *Language and Automata Theory and Applications: 4th International Conference, LATA 2010, Trier, Germany, May 24-28, 2010. Proceedings*, volume 6031 of *Lecture Notes in Computer Science*, pages 344–355, Berlin, Germany. Springer Berlin Heidelberg.

Makoto Kanazawa and Sylvain Salvati. 2012. MIX Is Not a Tree-Adjoining Language. In *Proceedings of the 50th Annual Meeting of the Association for Computational Linguistics*, volume 1, pages 666–674, Jeju, South Korea. Association for Computational Linguistics.

Makoto Kanazawa and Ryo Yoshinaka. 2017. The Strong, Weak, and Very Weak Finite Context and Kernel Properties. In *Language and Automata Theory and Applications: 11th International Conference, LATA 2017, Umeå, Sweden, March 6-9, 2017, Proceedings*, pages 77–88, Cham, Switzerland. Springer International Publishing.

Gregory M. Kobele. 2006. *Generating Copies: An Investigation into Structural Identity in Language and Grammar*. PhD Dissertation, University of California, Los Angeles, Los Angeles, CA.

Gregory M. Kobele. 2011. Minimalist Tree Languages Are Closed Under Intersection with Recognizable Tree Languages. In *Logical Aspects of Computational Linguistics: 6th International Conference, LACL 2011, Montpellier, France, June 29 – July 1, 2011. Proceedings*, pages 129–144, Berlin, Germany. Springer Berlin Heidelberg.

Marcus Kracht. 2003. *The Mathematics of Language*. Number 63 in Studies in Generative Grammar. De Gruyter Mouton, Berlin, Germany.

Jason Merchant. 1999. *The Syntax of Silence: Sluicing, Islands, and Identity in Ellipsis*. PhD Dissertation, University of California, Santa Cruz, Santa Cruz, CA.

Jason Merchant. 2001. *The Syntax of Silence: Sluicing, Islands, and the Theory of Ellipsis*, 1 edition. Oxford Studies in Theoretical Linguistics. Oxford University Press, Oxford, United Kingdom.

Jens Michaelis. 2001. Derivational Minimalism Is Mildly Context–Sensitive. In *Logical Aspects of Computational Linguistics: Third International Conference, LACL'98 Grenoble, France, December 14–16, 1998 Selected Papers*, pages 179–198, Berlin, Germany. Springer Berlin Heidelberg.

Frank Morawietz. 2008. *Two-Step Approaches to Natural Language Formalism*, 1 edition. Number 64 in Studies in Generative Grammar. De Gruyter Mouton, Berlin, Germany.

P. Stanley Peters and R. W. Ritchie. 1973. On the generative power of transformational grammars. *Information Sciences*, 6(Supplement C):49–83.

Owen Rambow and Giorgio Satta. 1999. Independent parallelism in finite copying parallel rewriting systems. *Theoretical Computer Science*, 223(1):87–120.

Luigi Rizzi. 1990. *Relativized Minimality*. Number 16 in Linguistic Inquiry Monographs. MIT Press, Cambridge, MA.

James Rogers. 1994. *Studies in the Logic of Trees with Applications to Grammar Formalisms*. PhD Dissertation, University of Delaware, Newark, DE.

James Rogers. 1998. *A Descriptive Approach to Language-Theoretic Complexity*. Studies in Logic, Language, and Information. CSLI Publications, Stanford, CA.

Sylvain Salvati. 2011. MIX is a 2-MCFL and the word problem in $\mathbb{Z}^2$ is solved by a third-order collapsible pushdown automaton.

Sylvain Salvati. 2015. MIX is a 2-MCFL and the word problem in Z2 is captured by the IO and the OI hierarchies. *Journal of Computer and System Sciences*, 81(7):1252–1277.

Hiroyuki Seki, Takashi Matsumura, Mamoru Fujii, and Tadao Kasami. 1991. On multiple context-free grammars. *Theoretical Computer Science*, 88(2):191–229.

Stuart M. Shieber. 1985. Evidence against the context-freeness of natural language. *Linguistics and Philosophy*, 8(3):333–343.

J. W. Thatcher and J. B. Wright. 1968. Generalized Finite Automata Theory with an Application to a Decision Problem of Second-Order Logic. *Mathematical systems theory*, 2(1):57–81.

Ryo Yoshinaka. 2011a. Efficient learning of multiple context-free languages with multidimensional substitutability from positive data. *Theoretical Computer Science*, 412(19):1821–1831.

Ryo Yoshinaka. 2011b. Towards Dual Approaches for Learning Context-Free Grammars Based on Syntactic Concept Lattices. In *Developments in Language Theory: 15th International Conference, DLT 2011, Milan, Italy, July 19-22, 2011. Proceedings*, pages 429–440, Berlin, Germany. Springer Berlin Heidelberg.

Ryo Yoshinaka. 2012. Integration of the Dual Approaches in the Distributional Learning of Context-Free Grammars. In *6th International Conference, LATA 2012, A Coruña, Spain, March 5-9, 2012. Proceedings*, volume 7183 of *Lecture Notes in Computer Science*, pages 538–550, Berlin, Germany. Springer Berlin Heidelberg.

Ryo Yoshinaka and Alexander Clark. 2012. Polynomial Time Learning of Some Multiple Context-Free Languages with a Minimally Adequate Teacher. In *Formal Grammar: 15th and 16th International Conferences, FG 2010, Copenhagen, Denmark, August 2010, FG 2011, Ljubljana, Slovenia, August 2011, Revised Selected Papers*, Lecture Notes in Computer Science, pages 192–207, Berlin, Germany. Springer Berlin Heidelberg.

A Conceptual Spaces Model of Socially Motivated Language Change

Heather Burnett and **Olivier Bonami**
Laboratoire de Linguistique Formelle
Université Paris Diderot & CNRS

Abstract

This paper outlines a formal model of socially motivated language change which unites insights from identity-oriented theories of language change with formal theories of language use and understanding. We use (Gärdenfors, 2000)'s *Conceptual Spaces* framework to formalize socially motivated ideological change and use signaling games with an *iterated best response* solution concept (Franke, 2009; Frank and Goodman, 2012) to formalize the link between ideology, linguistic meaning and language use. We then show how this new framework can be used to shed light on the mechanisms underlying socially-motivated change in French grammatical gender.

1   Introduction

Since the mid 1990s, the development of mathematical and computational models of language variation and change, such as (Clark and Roberts, 1993; Niyogi and Berwick, 1997; Yang, 2000; Yang, 2002; Kauhanen and Walkden, 2018) among others, has yielded enormous advances in our understanding of the cognitive processes that underly these phenomena. However, although it has been observed since at least (Labov, 1963) that many (if not most) linguistic changes are socially conditioned, formal models have been almost exclusively focused on the grammatical and/or psychological aspects of change, neglecting its social aspects. On the other hand, many non-mathematically oriented approaches in sociolinguistics and linguistic anthropology (see (Bucholtz and Hall, 2005; Bucholtz and

Hall, 2008) for an overview) have stressed the role that social meaning, ideologies and identity construction play in language use, and they have developed articulated theories of how meaning and ideological structure mediate the relation between social change and language change. The goal of this paper is to outline a model which brings together insights from identity-oriented theories of language change and unites them with formal theories of language use and understanding. More specifically, we use (Gärdenfors, 2000; Gärdenfors, 2014)'s *Conceptual Spaces* framework to formalize speaker/listener ideological change and use epistemic game theory, particularly signaling games with an *iterated best response* solution concept, such as the *Rational Speech Act* model (RSA) (Franke, 2009; Frank and Goodman, 2012; Burnett, 2017) to formalize the link between ideology, linguistic meaning and language use. We then show how this new framework can be used to shed light on the mechanisms underlying socially-motivated change in French grammatical gender.

2   Variation and change in French g-gender

French is a g(rammatical) gender language, which means that its grammar sorts all nouns into two classes, masculine and feminine, that determine patterns of agreement in sentences (Hockett, 1958; Corbett, 1991). Although with inanimate nouns, there is no relation between noun meaning and g-gender, there is a non-arbitrary relation between social and grammatical gender with most human nouns. This paper focuses on change in the use of nouns denoting social functions. When referring to a woman,

Proceedings of the Society for Computation in Linguistics (SCiL) 2019, pages 135-145.
New York City, New York, January 3-6, 2019

either the feminine or the masculine can be used with these nouns; whereas, only the masculine can be used to refer to a man (1)-(2).

(1) a. **Le** président   *'the (fe)male president'*
   b. **La** présiden**te**   *'the female president'*

(2) a. **Le** ministre   *'the (fe)male minister'*
   b. **La** ministre   *'the female minister'*

(Burnett and Bonami, 2018) present a study of variation and change in g-gender of terms of address for women (*Madame **le/la** N*[1]) in the transcripts of the debates of the *Assemblée Nationale* (French House of Representatives) from 1983-2005. This corpus features a high degree of intra-speaker variation in g-gender, an example of which is shown in (3) for *Madame **le/la** ministre* 'Madam Minister'.

(3) a. **M. Jean-Marc Ayrault.** Madame **le** ministre de l'environnement, plus de 6 000 personnes ont défilé, samedi dernier, dans les rues de Nantes...   (29/01/1997)
   b. **M. Jean-Marc Ayrault**. Monsieur le président, madame **la** ministre, mes chers collègues,...   (19/12/1997)

The use of grammatical gender in expressions referring to women has been the subject of enormous amounts of prescription and language planning, see (Houdebine, 1998; Burr, 2003; Viennot, 2014) among others, and these actions can be naturally divided into two main waves of activism at the end of the 20th century. The first wave centered around on March 11th 1986, when the Socialist Prime Minister Laurent Fabius legislated the use feminine grammatical gender (eg. *la ministre*, *la présidente*) in the Assemblée Nationale and in official documents. Figure 1 shows the proportion of the use of feminine vs masculine grammatical gender in female terms of address (*Madame le/la N*) in the Assemblée Nationale from 1983 to 2005. This figure shows that use of the feminine form is extremely limited throughout the 1980s, and that Fabius' language policy in 1986 had little to no effect on the speech of the politicians.

However, twelve years later, on March 6th 1998,

the Socialist Prime Minister Lionel Jospin issued a statement (a *circulaire*) acknowledging that Fabius' policy was never obeyed/enforced and recalling to the government that they are supposed to be using feminine g-gender. Figure 1 shows that the second wave of activism has very different results, with use of the feminine form rising dramatically in 1997-98, around the time of Jospin's statement.

(Burnett and Bonami, 2018) argue that the striking contrast between the mid 1980s and the mid 1990s, and the reason Jospin's reiteration of Fabius' language policy was successful when the original policy failed, was due to a change in the **social context** in which the policies were enacted. Whereas, in the 1980s, social and political attention to issues of gender equality was limited, the mid-1990s saw an explosion of public reflection on the properties of female politicians and the place of women in government within the context of the *parité* political movement (Gaspard et al., 1992), which aimed to ensure equal representation of men and women across electoral lists.

(Burnett and Bonami, 2018) show that the spread of the use of feminine g-gender mirrors the spread of the support for parité, with left wing politicians, who supported *parité* early, using significantly more feminine (61% F 1356/2133) than right wing politicians (28% F 793/2023), who only supported the movement after mid 1998 (Bereni, 2007). Furthermore, right wing politicians who actively support *parité*, such as Roselyne Bachelot (81% F 105/129), behave like left wing politicians. Following (Ramsay, 2003; Achin et al., 2007; Julliard, 2012; Montini, 2017) among others, (Burnett and Bonami, 2018) argue that the parité movement was accompanied by enormous discussion in news and literary media, and many of the discourses emerging from these discussions constructed female politicians as having stereotypically feminine properties, such as being *sensitive, pragmatic* and *honest*. Thus, the authors propose that the parité movement and the public discussion surrounding it served to introduce new social types (or **personae**) for female politicians into the ideologies of French speakers in the late 1990s. (Burnett and Bonami, 2018) show that politicians in their corpus, such as Bachelot and Ségolène Royal, who personally construct a new feminine persona, use significantly more feminine than their female

---

[1] The authors focused on terms of address because the title (*Madame*) allowed for the automatic identification of female referents from the transcripts.

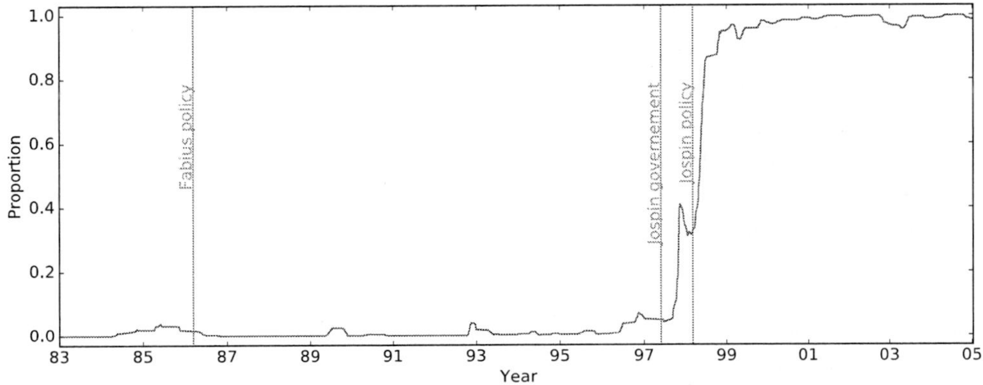

Figure 1: Prop. of *Madame la N* vs *Madame le N* (1983-2005).

party colleagues who have a more masculine gender construction, such as Michèle Alliot-Marie and Martine Aubry. Furthermore, women constructing a feminine persona, such as Royal, are referred to significantly more often in the feminine than women constructing less a feminine persona, like Aubry.

Social meaning of French g-gender

To account for these patterns, following (McConnell-Ginet, 2013), (Burnett and Bonami, 2018) propose that French feminine g-gender marking has **social meaning**; in particular, the authors propose that feminine g-gender marking (F) is associated with, or *indexes* (Ochs, 1992), sets of properties called their *indexical fields* (Eckert, 2008), notated [F], which contain properties stereotypically associated with women at the time, such as those referenced in the discourses on female politicians mentioned above (4-a). Correspondingly, masculine g-gender marking indexes properties stereotypically associated with men at the time (4-b).

(4) a. [F] = {sensitive, pragmatic, non-dominant, honest...}

b. [M] = {tough, abstract, dominant, dishonest...}

Since the new feminine personae have stereotypically feminine properties, speakers are predicted to use the feminine when attempting to construct such a persona and/or when describing someone who instantiates one. Conversely, they are predicted to use the masculine when constructing a more stereo-

typically masculine persona or when referring to women with a more stereotypically masculine gender presentation. In the 1980s, all personae for female politicians had masculine properties; therefore, the masculine form dominated. As speaker ideologies change to incorporate the new feminine personae in the mid 1990s and speakers started viewing themselves and others in these terms, and the feminine became more useful and eventually replaced the masculine in the Assemblée Nationale with the help of Jospin's *circulaire*.

(Burnett and Bonami, 2018) provide an intuitive explanation of the change and why Jospin's reiteration of Fabius' policy was successful; however, they do not make completely explicit how the development of the new personae translates into the change from masculine g-gender to feminine g-gender, and why Fabius' and Jospin's language policies had different statuses. Therefore, in the rest of this paper, we flesh out the relation between ideological change, language change and language policy in terms of the *Conceptual Spaces* and signaling games.

3   Ideological change in Conceptual Spaces

To formalize ideological change, we will make use of formal tools from the *Conceptual Spaces* framework for lexical semantics (Gärdenfors, 2000; Gärdenfors, 2014). In this approach speaker and listener conceptual and ideological structures are represented as a tuple $\langle D, \text{sim}, \text{PERS} \rangle$, where $\langle D, \text{sim} \rangle$ is an $|D|$-dimensional vector space with a relation sim measuring distance between points, and PERS is a distinguished set of points. Socially meaningful expressions are interpreted into these vector spaces whose dimensions are found in their indexical fields. In synchronic research, the dimensions and personae in the spaces can be constructed based on experimental data, as in (Douven, 2016), and the indexical fields associated with sociolinguistic variants can likewise be determined by experimentation (see, for instance, (Campbell-Kibler, 2007; Levon, 2014; Podesva et al., 2015)). The study that we are modeling in this paper is a historical one, and it's possible that g-gender's indexical fields have changed in the past twenty years. Therefore, we will use simulations to illustrate how our formal model works.

In the analysis of the social meaning of French g-gender, we will take the dimensions from public discourses about French politicians in the 1990s described in (Burnett and Bonami, 2018), shown in (5). This being said, for ease of visualisation, we will limit our illustration to a three dimensional space consisting of *Institutional dominance*, *Abstraction* and *Toughness*.

(5)   **4 dimensions of ideological space**

    a. Institutional dominance
       (dominant ↔ non-dominant)
    b. Abstraction (abstract ↔ pragmatic)
    c. Toughness (tough ↔ sensitive)
    d. Honesty (dishonest ↔ honest)

We propose that personae are represented as distinguished points within this space (i.e. PERS) according to their properties,[2] and changes in speakers and listeners' ideological structure will be modeled as changes in how personae are distributed across the ideological space. For example, suppose we consider most politicians' ideological structures in 1986, i.e. when Fabius formulated the first language policy. (Burnett and Bonami, 2018) argue that there was a very tight correlation in the minds of politicians between institutional dominance, abstraction and toughness at this time, and we can represent this as a correlation between values on the different dimensions. Of course we do not know exactly how many personae a speaker represents and how exactly they are arranged in the ideological space, so as a demonstration of how the framework works, we generated 20 points in the conceptual space such that

---

[2]Our personae play the role of Gärdenfors' *prototypes*.

10 occupy the higher two thirds of the space on the dominance, abstraction, and toughness scales, while 10 occupy the lower two thirds of the space, using the *rand* function in Octave (Eaton et al., 2015). Thus, we propose that most politicians in the AN have an ideological structure similar to that found in Figure 2 in 1986.

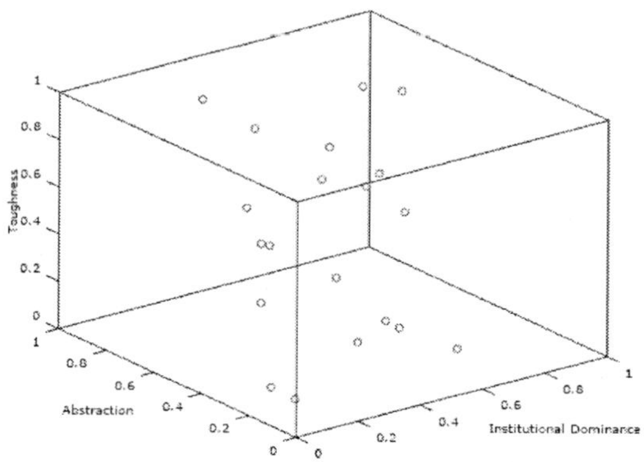

Figure 2: Ideological structure in the late 1980s (PERS$_{86}$)

Observe that there are some significant empty spaces in the cube shown in Figure 2. Most importantly, no personae are highly dominant, very pragmatic and also very sensitive in this model.

Both the truth conditional and social meanings of linguistic expressions pick out regions of the ideological space, and speakers use their language to communicate information about the location of the individual that they are talking about. By analogy with Gärdenfors's work on prototypes in lexical semantics, we assume that the arrangement of personae in the space imposes constraints on which regions noun phrases like *le ministre* and *la ministre* can identify. Given an n-dimensional conceptual space and a distinguished set of points, there is a natural way of partitioning this space into discrete regions: **voronoi polygons**. The voronoi polygon associated with a persona p_i, $v(p_i)$, is the set of points that lie closer to p_i than to any other persona in the domain (6-a). The **Voronoi tesselation** generated by a set of personae PERS, V(PERS), is the collection of voronoi polygons associated with every persona in PERS (6-b).

(6)   Let $p_i \in$ PERS be a persona.

    a. $v(p_i) := \{x | \forall j (\text{sim}(x, p_i) \leq \text{sim}(x, p_j))\}$

b. $V(\textsc{pers}) := \{v(p_i)|p_i \in \textsc{pers}\}$

Thus, the voronoi tessalation of the personae in the 1986 model are shown (in two dimensions for readability) in Figures 3 and 4.[3]

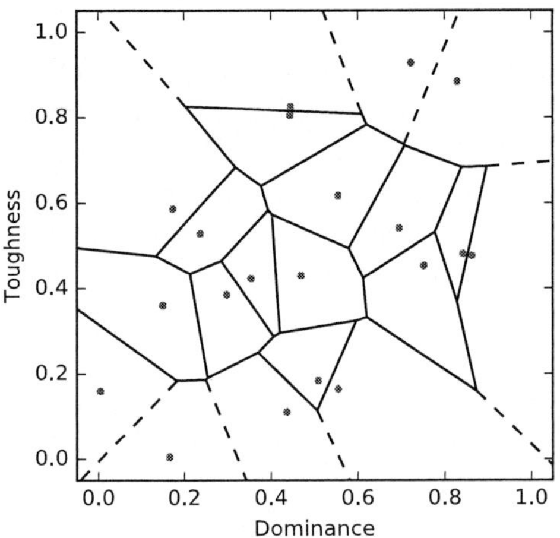

Figure 3: 1986 ideological space: Dominance vs Toughness

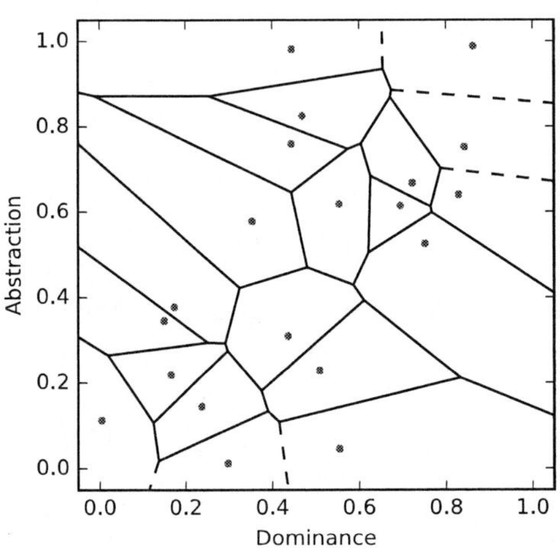

Figure 4: 1986 ideological space: Dominance vs Abstraction

Crucially, in this model, individuals that are both highly institutionally dominant and very sensitive fall within the ideological region of a less dominant persona (Figure 3). Likewise, highly dominant and very pragmatic individuals are obligatorily grouped

---

[3]All the tesselations in this paper were calculated using Octave.

into the region defined by the less dominant persona (Figure 4).

Function nouns and indexical fields

The nouns that alternate in the Assemblée Nationale corpus all refer to very powerful government positions (*ministre, garde des sceaux, président(e)* etc.). Therefore, it seems reasonable to assume that, in virtue of occupying one of these positions, individuals in the denotation of a word like *ministre* (written ⟦ministre⟧) acquire a high level of institutional dominance. For convenience, we will assume that the level of institutional dominance of ministers is greater than or equal to 0.7, as shown in (7). This is materialized by the red line in Figures 5 and 6: all ministers are by virtue of their function to the right of that line.

(7) ⟦ministre⟧ is a subset of the set of individuals that lie in the voronoi polygons associated with personae whose institutional dominance exceeds 0.7.

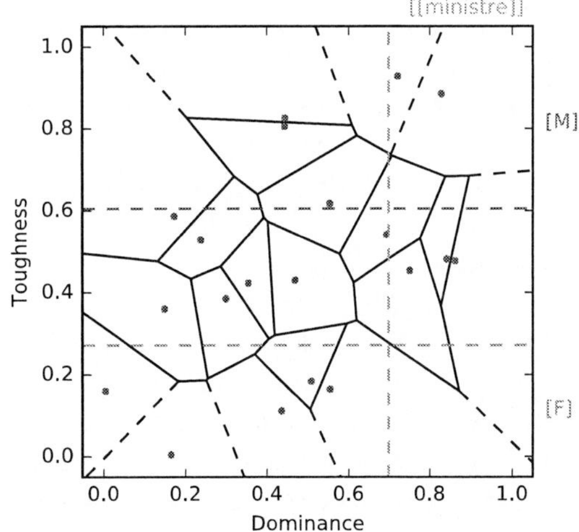

Figure 5: Dominance vs. toughness in 1986: No minister is sensitive enough to be within the feminine indexical field

We propose that grammatical gender marking (M/F) also picks out regions: the space associated with all the personae that have a high level of **at least one** of the properties in the indexical field (Burnett, 2017). So the social meaning of masculine g-gender is the concave region within the cube containing all the personae that are above the third quartile on

139

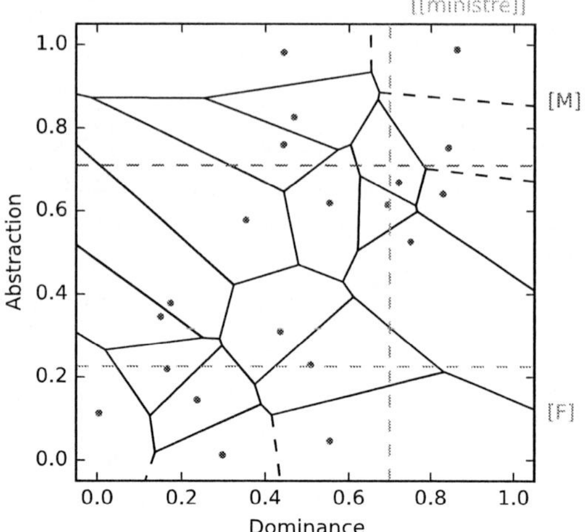

Figure 6: Dominance vs. abstraction in 1986: No minister is pragmatic enough to be within the feminine indexical field

the institutional dominance, abstraction or toughness scales. In the two-dimensional projections of Figures 5 and 6, this is materialized by the horizontal blue lines: all and only individuals above those lines are in the masculine indexical field. In 1986, it happens that there is a strong correlation between the three dimensions. As a result, 1986 personae compatible with masculine cluster in the upper right corners of the two squares in Figures 5 and 6.

Following the analysis in (4), the social meaning of feminine g-gender corresponds to the concave region associated with all the personae that are lower than the first quartile on the dimensions in the indexical field. In the two-dimensional projections of Figures 5 and 6, this is materialized by the horizontal green lines: all and only individuals below those lines are in the feminine indexical field. Again, in 1986, having a low value in one dimension predicts having a low value in other dimensions, so that personae compatible with the feminine cluster in the lower left corners of the two squares in Figures 5 and 6.

The ideological structure in 1986 is such that the space picked out by the indexical field of the feminine is disjoint from ⟦ministre⟧: in both Figure 5 and Figure 6, the rectangle to the right of the red line and below the blue line is empty. So, in this model, the expression *la ministre* does not pick out a populated chunk of ideological space; this makes reference to

a woman minister in the feminine very unlikely.

In contrast, in 1998, speakers' ideological structures are very different: the lower righthand corner of the ideological space contains personae who are both sensitive and pragmatic, but also highly dominant. These are the *feminine political personae* described above, who are instantiated by individuals like Bachelot and Royal. A model of such an ideological space is shown in Figure 7: although the relationship between other dimensions has not changed (i.e. there is still a correlation between abstraction and toughness), there has been a weakening of the relationship between institutional dominance and the other dimensions.

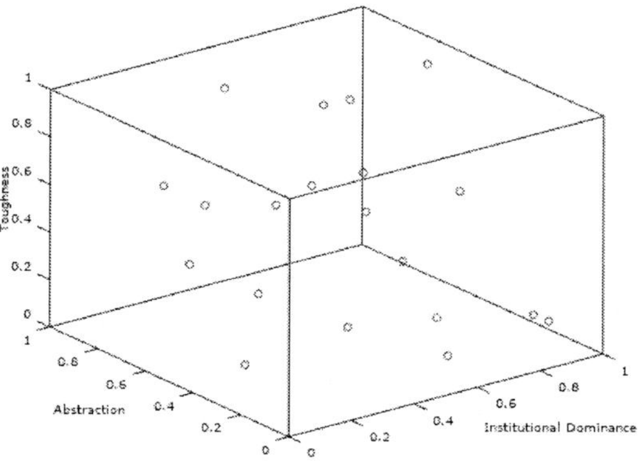

Figure 7: Ideological structure in the late 1990s (PERS$_{98}$)

Keeping the same definitions as in the 1986 model, we see that these new personae change the denotation of *ministre* and the indexical fields of M and F. Firstly, ⟦ministre⟧ now has more polygons of personae in its denotation. This is materialized in the two-dimensional projections in Figures 8 and 9 by having more points to the right of the red line.

Secondly, some of these ministers stand within the indexical field of the feminine, because they are very sensitive or pragmatic (Figure 8). Thus, we observe the following facts comparing the models:

(8) a. $⟦\text{ministre}⟧_{86} \cap [F]_{86} = \varnothing$.
     b. $⟦\text{ministre}⟧_{98} \cap [F]_{98} \neq \varnothing$.

We propose that this difference is what explains that use of the feminine to refer to a female minister was just unavailable in 1986 but was possible in 1998.

Also noticeable is the fact that the relevant ministers, by virtue of being dominant, also stand within

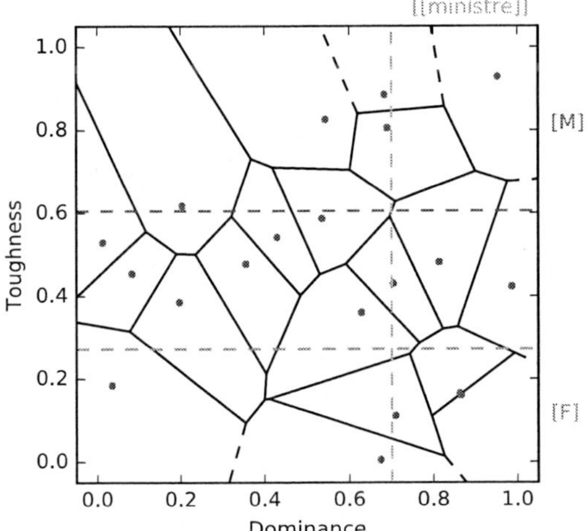

Figure 8: Dominance vs. toughness in 1998: Some ministers are sensitive enough to be within the feminine indexical field

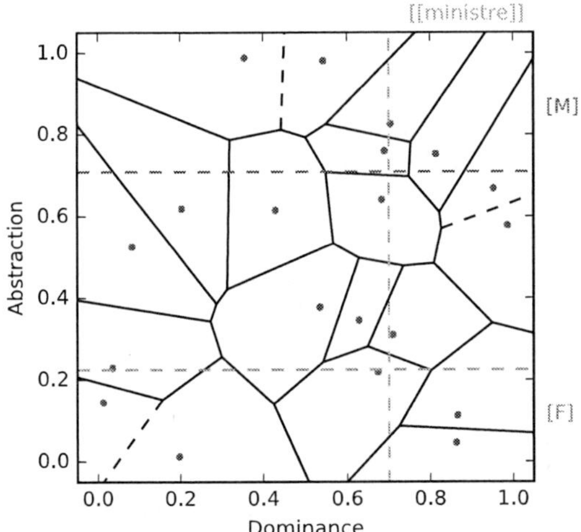

Figure 9: Dominance vs. abstraction in 1998: Some ministers are pragmatic enough to be within the feminine indexical field

the masculine indexical field (the third quartile of dominance, not materialized in the Figures, is at 0.76, just to the to the right of the red line).

(9) $[\![\text{ministre}]\!]_{98} \cap [F]_{98} \cap [M]_{98} \neq \emptyset.$

This explains why there can be variation in 1998: both the use of the feminine and the use of the masculine to refer to a female minister convey a relevant social message.

4 Linking ideology and language use

When it comes to capturing the relationship between conceptual spaces and communication, the majority of the work has focused on how multi-dimensional spaces with prototypes constrain meanings in the context of **signaling games** (Jäger, 2007; Jäger and Van Rooij, 2007; Warglien and Gärdenfors, 2013; Gärdenfors, 2014). In this paper, we will also use signaling game architecture combined with an iterated best response solution concept of the kind used by (Franke, 2009; Frank and Goodman, 2012; Burnett, 2017) and many others. The basic structure of the game is as follows: the speaker (S) knows the location of a (female) minister in ideological space and wishes to communicate that location to the listener. In order to do this, they choose how they gender mark *ministre* using the determiner *le* or *la*. The listener (L) hears *le/la ministre* and updates their beliefs with respect to the location of the referent in their conceptual space. More formally, we represent each time period as a game as follows:

(10)   **Model for 1986**
$G_{86} = \langle S, L, \langle D, \text{sim}, \text{PERS}_{86} \rangle, M, [\cdot], C, P \rangle$:

a. S, L are the players.

b. $\langle D, \text{sim}, \text{PERS}_{86} \rangle$ is the ideological space in Figure 2.

c. M = {*le, la*} is a set of messages.

d. $[\cdot]$ is an indexation relation mapping each message to its indexical field.
$[le] = [M]_{86}$
$[la] = [F]_{86}$

e. C is a **cost function** assigning a natural number to each message.

f. P_{86} is a probability distribution over $\{v(p) : p \in \text{PERS}_{86} \cap [\![\text{ministre}]\!]_{86}\}$, encoding L's **prior beliefs** concerning in which voronoi polygon the referent is located.

(11)   **Model for 1998**
$G_{98} = \langle S, L, \langle D, \text{sim}, \text{PERS}_{98} \rangle, M, [\cdot], C, P \rangle$:

a. S, L are the players.

b. $\langle D, \text{sim}, \text{PERS}_{98} \rangle$ is the ideological space in Figure 7.

c. M = {*le, la*} is a set of messages.

d. $[\cdot]$ is an indexation relation mapping each message to its indexical field.
$[le] = [M]_{98}$

$[la] = [F]_{98}$

   e. C is a cost function assigning a natural number to each message.

   f. P_{98} is a probability distribution over $\{v(p) : p \in \text{PERS}_{98} \cap [\![\text{ministre}]\!]_{98}\}$.

For convenience, we assume that both P_{86} and P_{98} are uniform distributions over $\{v(p) : p \in \text{PERS}_{86} \cap [\![\text{ministre}]\!]_{86}\}$ and $\{v(p) : p \in \text{PERS}_{98} \cap [\![\text{ministre}]\!]_{98}\}$,[4] as shown in Tables 1 and 2.

Dominance	Abstraction	Toughness	P
0.83	0.64	0.88	0.2
0.75	0.53	0.45	0.2
0.84	0.75	0.48	0.2
0.72	0.67	0.93	0.2
0.86	0.99	0.48	0.2

Table 1: L's prior belief distribution over voronoi polygons associated with personas in the 1986 model

Dominance	Abstraction	Toughness	P
0.70	0.83	0.43	0.143
0.81	0.75	0.48	0.143
0.95	0.67	0.93	0.143
0.71	0.31	0.11	0.143
0.99	0.58	0.42	0.143
0.87	**0.11**	**0.16**	0.143
0.86	**0.05**	**0.16**	0.143

Table 2: L's prior belief distribution over voronoi polygons associated with personas in the 1998 model

Following (Frank and Goodman, 2012), we assume that S and L's actions are calculated based on a number of steps. When L hears a message, the first thing they do is condition their prior beliefs on the meaning of the message, as shown in (12) (for the 1986 model).

(12) $P_{86}(v(p)|m) = \frac{P_{86}(v(p) \cap [m])}{P_{86}([m])}$

As shown in Table 3, since there are no ministers who are located within the indexical field of la, $P_{86}(v(p)|la) = 0$, for all $p \in [\![\text{ministre}]\!]_{86}$. However, since there are two personae in [F] in $[\![\text{ministre}]\!]_{98}$, P_{86} conditioned under la for these two personae is 0.5.

---

[4]This assumption does not affect our formal results.

Dominance	Abstraction	Toughness	le	la
0.83	0.64	0.88	0.2	0
0.75	0.53	0.45	0.2	0
0.84	0.75	0.48	0.2	0
0.72	0.67	0.93	0.2	0
0.86	0.99	0.48	0.2	0

Table 3: L's belief distribution over polygons conditioned on the indexical field associated with a message, in the 1986 model

Dominance	Abstraction	Toughness	le	la
0.70	0.83	0.43	0.143	0
0.81	0.75	0.48	0.143	0
0.95	0.67	0.93	0.143	0
0.71	0.31	0.11	0.143	0
0.99	0.58	0.42	0.143	0
0.67	**0.11**	**0.16**	0.143	0.5
0.86	**0.05**	**0.16**	0.143	0.5

Table 4: L's belief distribution over polygons conditioned on the indexical field associated with a message, in the 1998 model

Again following (Frank and Goodman, 2012), we assume that speaker utility is calculated based on message **informativity**, which is calculated based on the *negative surprisal* (positive natural log probability (Shannon, 1948)) of the prior conditioned on the the the message, minus whatever costs are assigned to m by C, as shown in (13) (for the 1986 model).

(13) $U_S(v(p), m) = log(P_{98}(v(p)|m)) - C(m)$

We will use the cost functions to model the effects of the language policies.[5] Both in 1986 and 1998, we have two situations: **before** the policy, where there no message costs: $C(le) = C(la) = 0$, and **after** the policy, where there is a cost for using the masculine: $C(la) = 0, C(le) \neq 0$.

To account for variability in action selection, we assume that the speaker chooses a message based on the *soft-max choice rule* (Luce, 1959; Sutton and Barto, 1998) (14), where λ is a parameter governing how (non)deterministic the choice is.

(14) $S(m|v(p)) \propto exp(\lambda * U_S(v(p), m))$

---

[5]This seems reasonable, given that disobeying the policy has monetary costs. For example, in 2014, Julien Aubert (UMP) was required to pay 1378 euros for saying *Madame le président*.

Results

Our model makes predictions concerning the probability that the speaker will use *le* or *la* to describe some female minister. Firstly, as shown in Theorem 1, in the 1986 model, where there are no costs put on the messages (i.e. before Fabius' policy), we predict that speakers categorically use the masculine in the 1986 model. This is due to the fact in (8-a): the regions picked out by the feminine's indexical field are disjoint from where the ministers lie.

Theorem 1 *Before Fabius' policy (1986).* *Let* $C(le) = C(la) = 0$. *For all (non-∞) values for* λ, *all* $v(p) \in \text{PERS}_{86} \cap [\![ministre]\!]_{86}$, $S(la|v(p)) = 0$ *and* $S(le|v(p)) = 1$.[6]

Furthermore, we show that, with the 1986 ideological structure, adding costs to the masculine does not predict an increase in use of the feminine, as shown in Theorem 2. This is because the calculation of speaker utility (13) in the RSA model prioritizes informativity over message costs.

Theorem 2 *After Fabius' policy (1986).* *Let* $C(la) = 0$. *For all values* $n \in \mathbb{N}$ *such that* $C(le) = n$, *and for all (non-∞) values for* λ, *all* $v(p) \in \text{PERS}_{86} \cap [\![ministre]\!]_{86}$, $S(la|v(p)) = 0$ *and* $S(le|v(p)) = 1$.[7]

On the other hand, in both models for 1998, the feminine is predicted to be used, particularly to communicate that the referent lies close to the new feminine personae. For example, if we set $\lambda = 2$, for illustration, we see that use of *la* to communicate the polygons in the bottom right corner of the ideological space is predicted to be 0.925 in 1998, as shown in Table 5.

Dominance	Abstraction	Toughness	*le*	*la*
0.87	0.11	0.16	0.075	0.925
0.86	0.05	0.16	0.075	0.925

Table 5: Probability of S choosing a message conditioned on the polygon in which S locates the referent, before policy

---

[6]PROOF. Suppose $\lambda = n \neq \infty$ and let $p \in \text{PERS}_{86} \cap [\![ministre]\!]_{86}$. By Table 3, $P_{86}(v(p)|la) = 0$, so by (13), $U_S(v(p), la) = -\infty$. Therefore, by (14), $S(la|v(p)) = 0$ and $S(le|v(p)) = 1$. ∎

[7]PROOF. Let $C(le) = n$, $\lambda = m$ and $p \in \text{PERS}_{86} \cap [\![ministre]\!]_{86}$. Since $P_{86}(v(p)|la) = 0$ (see proof of Theorem 1, $U_S(v(p), la) = -\infty + 1 = -\infty$. So, by (14), $S(la|v(p)) = 0$ and $S(le|v(p)) = 1$. ∎

Likewise, if we add a cost to using the masculine (say $C(le) = 1$), the probability of using *la* increases to 0.971, as shown in Table 6.

Dominance	Abstraction	Toughness	*le*	*la*
0.87	0.11	0.16	0.029	0.971
0.86	0.05	0.16	0.029	0.971

Table 6: Probability of S choosing a message conditioned on the polygon in which S locates the referent, after policy

Thus, the model correctly predicts 1) increase of the feminine from 1986 to 1998, and 2) effectiveness of language policy in 1998 but not in 1986.

5 Conclusion

We presented a formal model of socially driven linguistic change that is centered around the relationship between ideological structure and linguistic meaning. In our approach, which follows (Foucault, 1976; Butler, 1993; Butler, 1997; Livia and Hall, 1997) among others, social changes and discourse about them construct and change speaker/listener ideologies. These ideologies then constrain what meanings can be assigned to linguistic expressions in the way proposed by (Gärdenfors, 2000; Gärdenfors, 2014). Expressions' meanings then determine how they can be used in communication, as in the *Rational Speech Act* model.

We used our model to explicitly characterize both the ideological change in late 1990s and the consequences that this change had on the use of *le ministre* vs *la ministre*. We therefore conclude that frameworks such as *Conceptual Spaces* and the *RSA* are promising for capturing the link between ideologies and linguistic production, and that tools from formal semantics and pragmatics have a role to play in the study of sociolinguistic phenomena.

Acknowledgments

We thank Paul Égré, Gerhard Jäger, Denis Paperno, three anonymous reviewers, and audiences at ENS Paris, ZAS Berlin, Stanford University and the Ohio State University for helpful comments. This work was supported by a grant overseen by the French National Research Agency (ANR) as part of the "Investissements d'Avenir" program (reference: ANR-10-LABX-0083).

References

Catherine Achin, Lucie Bargel, Delphine Dulong, Eric Fassin, Christine Guillonnet, Stéphanie Guyon, Clémence Labrouche, Stphane Latté, Pierre Leroux, Sandrine Lévêque, Frdrique Matonti, Marion Paoletti, Christiane Restier-Melleray, Philippe Teillet, and Aurlia Troupel. 2007. *Sexes, genre et politique*. Economica, Paris.

Laure Bereni. 2007. *De la cause à la loi. Les mobilisations pour la parité politique en France (1992-2000)*. Ph.D. thesis, Université Panthéon-Sorbonne-Paris I.

Mary Bucholtz and Kira Hall. 2005. Identity and interaction: A sociocultural linguistic approach. *Discourse studies*, 7(4-5):585–614.

Mary Bucholtz and Kira Hall. 2008. All of the above: New coalitions in sociocultural linguistics. *Journal of Sociolinguistics*, 12(4):401–431.

Heather Burnett and Olivier Bonami. 2018. Linguistic prescription, ideological structure and the actuation of linguistic changes: Grammatical gender in French parliamentary debates. *in revision for Language in Society*.

Heather Burnett. 2017. Sociolinguistic interaction and identity construction: The view from game-theoretic pragmatics. *Journal of Sociolinguistics*, 21(2):238–271.

Elisabeth Burr. 2003. Gender and language politics in France. *Gender across languages*, 3:119–139.

Judith Butler. 1993. *Bodies that matter: On the discursive limits of sex*. Taylor & Francis.

Judith Butler. 1997. *Excitable speech: A politics of the performative*. Psychology Press.

Kathryn Campbell-Kibler. 2007. Accent,(ing), and the social logic of listener perceptions. *American speech*, 82(1):32–64.

Robin Clark and Ian Roberts. 1993. A computational model of language learnability and language change. *Linguistic Inquiry*, 24(2):299–345.

Corbett. 1991. *Gender (Cambridge textbooks in linguistics)*. Cambridge University Press.

Igor Douven. 2016. Vagueness, graded membership, and conceptual spaces. *Cognition*, 151:80–95.

John W. Eaton, David Bateman, Sören Hauberg, and Rik Wehbring. 2015. *GNU Octave version 4.0.0 manual: a high-level interactive language for numerical computations*.

Penelope Eckert. 2008. Variation and the indexical field. *Journal of sociolinguistics*, 12(4):453–476.

Michel Foucault. 1976. *Histoire de la sexualité (Tome 1)-La volonté de savoir*. Editions Gallimard.

Michael C Frank and Noah D Goodman. 2012. Predicting pragmatic reasoning in language games. *Science*, 336(6084):998–998.

Michael Franke. 2009. *Signal to act: Game theory in pragmatics*. Ph.D. thesis, Institute for Logic, Language and Computation, Amsterdam.

Peter Gärdenfors. 2000. *Conceptual spaces: The geometry of thought*. MIT press.

Peter Gärdenfors. 2014. *The geometry of meaning: Semantics based on conceptual spaces*. MIT Press.

Françoise Gaspard, Claude Servan-Schreiber, and Anne Le Gall. 1992. *Au pouvoir citoyennes!: Liberté, égalité, parité*. Seuil.

Charles F. Hockett. 1958. *A course in modern linguistics*. New York: Macmillan.

Anne-Marie Houdebine. 1998. La féminisation des noms de métiers. *Paris: Harmattan*.

Gerhard Jäger and Robert Van Rooij. 2007. Language structure: psychological and social constraints. *Synthese*, 159(1):99–130.

Gerhard Jäger. 2007. The evolution of convex categories. *Linguistics and Philosophy*, 30(5):551–564.

Virginie Julliard. 2012. *De la presse à Internet: la parité en questions*. Hermès science publications.

Henri Kauhanen and George Walkden. 2018. Deriving the constant rate effect. *Natural Language & Linguistic Theory*, 36(2):483–521.

William Labov. 1963. The social motivation of a sound change. *Word*, 19(3):273–309.

Erez Levon. 2014. Categories, stereotypes, and the linguistic perception of sexuality. *Language in Society*, 43(05):539–566.

Anna Livia and Kira Hall. 1997. It's a girl!: Bringing performativity back to linguistics. *Queerly phrased: Language, gender, and sexuality*, pages 3–18.

R Duncan Luce. 1959. On the possible psychophysical laws. *Psychological review*, 66(2):81.

Sally McConnell-Ginet. 2013. Gender and its relation to sex: the myth of ''natural'' gender. *The Expression of Gender*, pages 3–38.

Frédérique Montini. 2017. *Le genre présidentiel*. Editions la découverte.

Partha Niyogi and Robert C Berwick. 1997. A dynamical systems model for language change. *Complex Systems*, 11(3):161–204.

Elinor Ochs. 1992. Indexing gender. *Rethinking context: Language as an interactive phenomenon*, 11:335.

Robert J Podesva, Jermay Reynolds, Patrick Callier, and Jessica Baptiste. 2015. Constraints on the social meaning of released /t/: A production and perception study of us politicians. *Language Variation and Change*, 27(01):59–87.

Raylene L Ramsay. 2003. *French women in politics: writing power, paternal legitimization, and maternal legacies*. Berghahn Books.

Claude Shannon. 1948. A mathematical theory of communication. *Bell System Technical Journal*, 27:379–423.

Richard S Sutton and Andrew G Barto. 1998. *Reinforcement learning: An introduction*. MIT press.

Éliane Viennot. 2014. Non, le masculin ne lemporte pas sur le féminin. *Petite histoire des résistances de la langue française*.

Massimo Warglien and Peter Gärdenfors. 2013. Semantics, conceptual spaces, and the meeting of minds. *Synthese*, pages 1–29.

Charles D Yang. 2000. Internal and external forces in language change. *Language variation and change*, 12(3):231–250.

Charles D Yang. 2002. *Knowledge and learning in natural language*. Oxford University Press.

Identifying Participation of Individual Verbs or VerbNet Classes in the Causative Alternation

Esther Seyffarth

Heinrich Heine University Düsseldorf

Düsseldorf, Germany

`esther.seyffarth@hhu.de`

Abstract

Verbs that participate in diathesis alternations have different semantics in their different syntactic environments, which need to be distinguished in order to process these verbs and their contexts correctly. We design and implement 8 approaches to the automatic identification of the causative alternation in English (3 based on VerbNet classes, 5 based on individual verbs). For verbs in this alternation, the semantic roles that contribute to the meaning of the verb can be associated with different syntactic slots. Our most successful approaches use distributional vectors and achieve an F1 score of up to 79% on a balanced test set. We also apply our approaches to the distinction between the causative alternation and the unexpressed object alternation. Our best system for this is based on syntactic information, with an F1 score of 75% on a balanced test set.

1 Introduction

English verbs impose syntactic and semantic restrictions on their arguments, but some verbs are more flexible than others. A number of verbs in English have different syntactic frames (subcategorization frames, SCFs) that are associated with different semantics. This behavior of a subset of the verbs in a language is known as *diathesis alternations*, or verb alternations (Levin, 1993).

Verbs that participate in one or more alternations are potentially problematic in the context of natural language processing tasks. In order to be able to process an instance of an alternating verb in a text, it is necessary to distinguish between the different possible uses, so that the correct meaning can be assigned to the given instance.

The causative alternation is one of the regular verb alternations in English. Verbs in this alternation can be used intransitively, with an inchoative meaning, or transitively, leading to a causative meaning. The choice of a transitive or intransitive syntactic frame has an impact on the semantic roles that are part of the meaning of the verb. Consider sentences (1) and (2).

(1)   The number of students has decreased.

(2)   We have decreased the number of students.

Both sentences make a statement about the number of students having changed. In (1), the only semantic role that is explicitly encoded is the THEME (the thing that has decreased). In addition to this role, sentence (2) also specifies an AGENT that has causative control over the event.

The automatic identification of verbs that participate in the causative alternation is not trivial, because the semantic roles involved in the events described by the different uses of these verbs are encoded in the syntactic frames in different ways. In the sentences above, the THEME is located in the syntactic subject position in (1), but in the syntactic direct object position in (2).

It is insufficient to use the presence or absence of syntactic arguments, such as the direct object, as indicators for or against a verb's participation in the alternation, since verbs can occur with different sets of arguments for other reasons. Many verbs in English have optional direct objects; in the terminology of Levin (1993), they participate in the *unexpressed object alternation*. Distinguishing between different alternations is essential for tasks that rely on correct semantic analyses of a verb and its arguments. Examples for applications where this is important are question answering, information extraction, or summarization.

This paper describes, compares and evaluates a total of 8 approaches to the automatic identification of verbs in the causative alternation. Of particular interest to us is the comparison of different evaluation conditions and different test sets, which give

Proceedings of the Society for Computation in Linguistics (SCiL) 2019, pages 146-155.

New York City, New York, January 3-6, 2019

a wide range of accuracy scores depending on the setup.

Our results show that some of our setups are more robust than others against different evaluation conditions. The different evaluation conditions are useful because they can expose problems of individual setups, such as a tendency to assign false positive labels.

We also evaluate the performance of our systems on the distinction between verbs in the causative alternation and verbs in the unexpressed-object alternation. Although these alternations resemble each other in the SCFs they allow, our results show that some systems perform well on both classification tasks.

While English alternating verbs can be identified by looking them up in one of the resources that exist for such purposes, we find it desirable to create dynamic systems for the identification of alternating verbs, for two main reasons. First, the phenomenon may be productive to a certain degree, which means that resources can become outdated; and second, there are other languages with similar phenomena for which no (large) resources like this exist. A system that does well on English alternation identification can be helpful in building this type of resource for other languages.

2   Related Work

While diathesis alternations have been a topic of linguistic discussion for some time, the idea of identifying these alternations automatically has mostly been discussed after the publication of Levin (1993). Her lists of verb alternations and of verb classes made it possible to design systems that cluster verbs automatically and to evaluate the outputs of those systems against Levin's data.

The creation of resources like WordNet (Miller, 1998) and VerbNet (Kipper et al., 2000) made this even easier. For instance, approaches like the one by McCarthy (2000, 2001) use the WordNet hierarchy to predict whether a verb participates in the causative or conative alternation. Using a sub-categorization lexicon derived from the BNC, she calculates the similarity of the role fillers for each position in the verb's syntactic frame to identify cases where different slots have a systematic overlap in their semantic preferences, which is seen as an indicator for the alternation. McCarthy (2000) hand-picks a set of 46 positive and 53 negative verbs that are being classified. Human annotators

decide whether each verb participates in the alternation. The author describes several different setups; the highest accuracy on her test set for the causative alternation is 73%.

Merlo and Stevenson (2001) distinguish three types of optionally intransitive verbs using a number of features. Their distinction is between unergative, unaccusative, and object-drop verbs. Their features include semantic features like animacy or causativity, as well as syntactic features like passive voice or presence of a VBN tag. The combination of all features leads to a classification accuracy of 69.8% on a test set of 20 unergative verbs, 19 unaccusative verbs, and 20 object-drop verbs. From their experiments with human annotators, they derive an "expert-based upper bound" accuracy around 86.5% for the task.

Sun et al. (2013) present an unsupervised approach to the semantic classification of verbs that uses approximations of diathesis alternations as features. While they evaluate their system on verb class induction tasks, their method for approximating diathesis alternations is also of interest in isolation from the clustering results. The approximation takes into account the subcategorization frames that are observed for each verb in a corpus and the likelihood of individual verbs and individual SCFs. As each diathesis alternation gives rise to several SCFs, the joint probability can be used to predict whether the SCFs of a verb are observed by chance or due to the verb's participation in an alternation.

An area of research that is related to, but distinct from the task we discuss here is the clustering of verbs into Levin classes, VerbNet classes, or other semantic classes. Examples for this are presented in Lapata and Brew (1999); Schulte Im Walde (2000); Joanis (2002); Joanis and Stevenson (2003); Stevenson and Joanis (2003); Schulte Im Walde (2006); Joanis et al. (2008); Sun et al. (2008); Korhonen (2009). While verb classes are associated with diathesis alternations, there is no one-to-one relation between a verb class and an alternation. Thus, strategies that are useful for verb class prediction cannot always be used in the same way for the prediction of verb alternations. In this paper, we develop systems for the identification of diathesis alternations because we are specifically interested in properties of verbs at the syntax-semantics interface.

One of the contributions of our work that has not been discussed in depth in the literature is the comparison of the performance of different classification methods on the lists by Levin (1993) and on VerbNet classes, and on different subsets of verbs from those lists. We show that the scores of each method sometimes vary by a large margin, which makes it difficult to compare the performance of previous approaches when the evaluation technique is not described in detail.

3 Methods

We develop three class-based systems and five verb-based systems for the classification of English verbs regarding their participation in the causative alternation. Class-based systems classify verbs that belong to the same VerbNet class together. Verb-based systems classify each verb lemma individually.

3.1 Data

Syntactic patterns and frequency counts are derived from a dependency-parsed version of the BNC corpus (Burnard, 2007)[1]. The approaches that classify individual verbs refer to the dependency annotations in the corpus and in some cases to distributional word vectors, but do not make use of any external, manually-created resources.

For the class-based approaches, we collect information about individual verbs from verb class definitions in VerbNet 3.3 (Kipper et al., 2000). The information we gather from the resource is limited to determining which verbs form a class together; nothing else is being read from VerbNet.

We evaluate our systems on two different test sets[2], each including examples of alternating verbs as well as examples of non-alternating verbs. One of the test sets is the list given by Levin (1993, pp. 27–32), where Levin lists 365 examples of verbs that participate in the alternation and 238 examples of verbs that do not participate. The other test set is extracted from VerbNet; the set of alternating verbs consists of all members of all VerbNet classes that are marked as having causative and inchoative uses. As negative examples for this test set, we use verbs that are marked in VerbNet as having transitive and intransitive uses (i.e., they are syntactically flexible), but not as having causative and inchoative uses. This leads to 469 positive examples and 454 negative examples.

Our strategy for collecting verbs outside the causative alternation creates a negative set that is not too large and contains only verbs that exhibit behavior similar to alternating verbs. Effectively, we select verbs that participate in the unexpressed-object alternation (see also Section 6).

One difficulty in evaluating our classification systems is that verbs are not distinguished by verb sense. For instance, Levin lists *advance* as an alternating verb in its (CAUSED-)CHANGE-OF-STATE sense, but also as a non-alternating verb in its FUTURE-HAVING sense. We plan to examine these issues and their implications for the task more closely in future work. For now, in order to achieve a clear separation of alternating and non-alternating verbs, we decide to drop verbs with multiple class membership from the test sets for our experiments, leading to a set of 358 positive and 236 negative examples[3].

While the positive examples from both sources share a specific syntactic and semantic behavior, the negative examples are less homogeneous, and it is not necessarily useful to treat the negative examples as a closed set. Theoretically, all verbs that are not listed as positive examples should be usable as negative examples, provided the list of positive examples is complete and covers all verbs in the language that participate in the alternation.

However, using all unlisted verbs as negative examples would make the classification much more difficult to evaluate, due to the overwhelming majority of negative items. Instead, we use the sets described above and propose three test conditions to base our evaluations on. The test conditions are described in Section 4.

3.2 Class-Based Methods

We define three class-based approaches to the task. The information these approaches rely on is extracted from VerbNet 3.3. The measures used to calculate the likelihood of each verb to alternate are inspired by Bonial et al. (2011). There, the authors define scores that are used as indicators for how likely the members of each VerbNet class are to occur in the CAUSED-MOTION construction. In a similar way, we define scores that indicate the likelihood of participation in the causative alternation for the members of each VerbNet class.

---

[1] 112,298,424 tokens in 6,026,307 sentences. Parsed with the Stanford CoreNLP Library (Manning et al., 2014).

[2] The full test sets are available from the author upon request.

[3] Levin also lists some verbs more than once, such as *bleed*. We group words with the same surface forms together without performing word sense disambiguation.

The motivation for the approaches in this section is that the causative alternation is closely related to the question whether a verb can be used transitively and intransitively. Although transitive and intransitive uses can also be an indicator of optional complements or of the unexpressed object alternation, we implement three setups based on the transitivity behavior of verbs to determine how indicative the use of transitive and intransitive SCFs is for the causative alternation.

3.2.1 VNType

Our first classifier, VNTYPE, assigns the alternating label to all members of the VerbNet class if all members occur in both SCFs at least once in the corpus, following the rule in Equation 1.

$$a_1(v \in C) = 1 \text{ iff } \forall v' \in C : c(v'_{trans}) > 0 \atop \wedge\, c(v'_{intrans}) > 0 \quad (1)$$

The alternatability score 1 (verb participates in the alternation) is given to the verb v iff all verbs in the same VerbNet class C occur at least once in a transitive SCF and at least once in an intransitive SCF.

In all other cases, including the case that one or more verbs in the class are not found in the corpus at all, the classifier assigns the non-alternating label to all members of the VerbNet class. This approach is type-based: Frequencies of transitive and intransitive uses are not taken into account.

3.2.2 VNRank

Our second approach, VNRANK, derives the alternatability score from the percentage of verb types in a VerbNet class that were observed at least once transitively and at least once intransitively, following Equation 2.

$$a_2(v \in C) = \frac{|\{v' \in C : c(v'_{trans}) > 0 \wedge c(v'_{intrans}) > 0\}|}{|C|} \quad (2)$$

a_2 assigns each verb v an alternatability score between 0 and 1 that reflects the percentage of verbs in the same VerbNet class C that occur at least once in a transitive SCF and at least once in an intransitive SCF.

If a class C contains one or more verbs v' that are not observed in the corpus, the likelihood for that class and its member v to be labeled as alternating becomes lower.

3.2.3 VNToken

Our third approach, VNTOKEN, is a token-based variation of VNRANK, assigning a score following Equation 3.

$$a_3(v \in C) = \frac{\sum\limits_{v' \in C} \min(c(v'_{trans}), c(v'_{intrans}))}{\sum\limits_{v' \in C} c(v')} \quad (3)$$

a_3 assigns each verb v an alternatability score that is based on the frequency of transitive or intransitive uses (whichever is lower) of verbs in the same VerbNet class C.

Since we use the lower of the two numbers as indicator for how strong the verb's ability to alternate is, the highest possible score that verbs in a VerbNet class C can achieve according to a_3 is 0.5, meaning that the overall number of transitive occurrences of members of C in the corpus was exactly as high as the overall number of intransitive occurrences of verbs in C. The lowest score is 0, which is the case when all members of C occur exclusively transitively or exclusively intransitively in the corpus.

Verbs that do not occur in the corpus do not impact the score calculated by a_3, since they do not add anything to either the numerator or the denominator in the equation.

3.3 Verb-Based Methods

The following methods classify or rank verbs individually, without taking their VerbNet classes into account.

3.3.1 SCFFlag

Our first verb-based approach, SCFFLAG, is a variation of VNTYPE that classifies verbs individually, not based on their VerbNet classes. Equation 4 shows how the score is calculated.

$$a_4(v) = 1 \text{ iff } c(v_{trans}) > 0 \wedge c(v_{intrans}) > 0 \quad (4)$$

The alternatability score 1 (verb participates in the alternation) is given to a verb v iff v is observed at least once with a transitive SCF and at least once with an intransitive SCF.

Since this approach is purely syntactic, it is prone to misclassifying verbs that have optional direct objects as verbs that participate in the causative alternation. We include it here in order to compare other systems against it. Unattested verbs are labeled as non-alternating, as they do not fulfill the criteria defined here for alternating verbs.

3.3.2 SCFRatio

Our second verb-based approach, SCFRATIO, is a variation on SCFFLAG that takes the frequency of each syntactic frame into account, as shown in Equation 5.

$$a_5(v) = \frac{c(v_{trans})}{c(v_{intrans})} \qquad (5)$$

The result of a_5 is a continuous value that reflects the relation between the number of transitive and intransitive occurrences of v. In the special case that the denominator is zero, a value of 0 is assigned.

While SCFFLAG only checks whether both transitive and intransitive frames are possible, this approach looks at their relative frequency, as observed in the corpus. If a verb is mostly used transitively and is only intransitive in one instance, it does not necessarily participate in the causative alternation; the one intransitive instance might be due to an error or a coerced usage of the verb. If it occurs transitively and intransitively with similar frequencies, it is more likely for that verb to participate in the causative alternation.

Verbs that are not found in the corpus are treated like syntactically inflexible verbs, that is, they are unlikely to alternate. Like SCFFLAG, we expect this setup to be prone to misclassifying verbs with optional objects as participating in the causative alternation.

The method is similar to that of Sun et al. (2013), but unlike that system, it does not take the overall frequency of each SCF over all verbs in the corpus into account. In SCFFLAG and SCF-RATIO, the SCFs are simplified and distinguished by (in)transitivity; the presence or absence of other dependents and the order of the items in the SCF are disregarded. The main reason for this simplification is that it minimizes sparsity problems by generalizing over different SCFs that share the property of being (in)transitive.

The following approaches explore the idea that verbs in the alternation will impose the same selectional preferences on their direct objects as on their intransitive subjects, as illustrated by examples (1) and (2). Therefore, the set of possible direct objects should be more similar to the set of possible intransitive subjects if a verb alternates than it is for verbs that do not alternate. We implement two vector-based approaches to test this.

3.3.3 CentroidDistance

Our third verb-based approach, CENTROIDDIS-TANCE, makes use of distributional information about the arguments observed for each verb in the BNC corpus. Our source for distributional information is a set of pre-trained word vectors derived from a 100-billion word portion of the Google News dataset[4]. The vector set covers 3 million words and phrases and represents each item with a 300-dimensional vector created with word2vec (Mikolov et al., 2013). The formula that calculates the alternatability score is given in Equation 6.

$$a_6(v) = \cos(\overrightarrow{objects}, \overrightarrow{intr\text{-}subjects}) \qquad (6)$$

a_6 derives a verb's alternatability score from the difference between the centroid of the verb's direct objects in the corpus, and the centroid of its intransitive subjects. The difference is represented by the cosine similarity between the centroids. The method is an unsupervised approximation of the WordNet-based approach by McCarthy (2001).

Verbs that are unattested in the corpus or occur with only one SCF are treated as unlikely to alternate. Some verb argument slot fillers, particularly proper names, are not covered by the Google News vectors. These arguments are disregarded.

3.3.4 CentroidSubjVsObj

Our fourth verb-based approach, CENTROIDSUBJ-VSOBJ, extends the CENTROIDDISTANCE approach by another criterion. Verbs can impose similar selectional preferences on different argument slots, e.g. when they require animate subjects as well as animate direct objects. CENTROIDDIS-TANCE may not be successful in classifying such verbs. This approach takes that fact into account by comparing the centroid distance calculated in a_6 above to the distance between the centroids for transitive and intransitive subjects of the given verb, as shown in Equation 7.

$$a_7(v) = a_6(v) - \cos(\overrightarrow{tr\text{-}subjects}, \overrightarrow{intr\text{-}subjects}) \qquad (7)$$

The assumption is that verbs whose subjects tend to be more similar to each other than their intransitive subjects are to their objects are likely to participate in the object-drop alternation, not the causative alternation. Unattested verbs and arguments that cannot be associated with a vector are handled as in the CENTROIDDISTANCE approach.

---

[4]Available from `https://code.google.com/archive/p/word2vec/`.

3.3.5 RNN-LM

Our fifth verb-based approach, RNN-LM, determines the alternatability score of a verb based on automatically-generated acceptability scores for the verb's uses in transitive and intransitive environments. We extract ordered, lemma-based argument sequences from the corpus and use a script to turn transitive sentences into intransitive sentences by deleting the direct object, and to turn intransitive sentences into transitive sentences by adding dummy arguments in the form of personal pronouns. Thus, the sentence "Pat invites Kim" becomes the (transitive) argument sequence "invite-Pat-Kim" and is turned into the (intransitive) sequence "invite-Pat". The sentence "Sandy slept" becomes "sleep-Sandy", and is turned into the sequence "sleep-Sandy-her".

Having extended the input data with these alternated sentences, the system now compares the average acceptability of all transitive and intransitive uses of each verb, as shown in Equation 8.

$$a_8(v) = \frac{1}{|avg\_acc(v_{trans}) - avg\_acc(v_{intrans})|} \tag{8}$$

Acceptability is approximated by a modified version of the Recurrent Neural Network from Lau et al. (2015). That work is concerned with the prediction of acceptability judgments that are normalized for factors like sentence length or word frequency. This makes the measure more useful for our task than the mere probability of an input sequence (because changing the transitivity in a sentence always changes the length of the sentence, and thus, its probability). For details on the algorithm, see the original paper (Lau et al., 2015). By using argument sequences instead of sentences, we reduce noise. Unattested verbs are treated as unlikely to alternate.

We expect that the artificially-alternated sentences will receive lower acceptability scores for non-alternating verbs, while verbs that participate in the alternation are more acceptable in their generated alternate uses. Thus, the difference in acceptability scores should be lower for alternating verbs.

4   Results

We report the scores of our systems evaluated in three different conditions, to show the impact of the size and contents of the test set on the score.

The first test condition, ALL, evaluates the accuracy of each setup on the full verb sets. It uses all positive and negative examples from Levin, and all positive examples and syntactically-flexible negative examples from VerbNet.

The second test condition, FREQ, evaluates the accuracy of each setup on the 300 most frequent verbs from the full Levin and VerbNet sets. The selection is based on the number of occurrences of each verb in the BNC corpus. For the Levin set, the frequency cut-off leads to a slight majority of alternating verbs in the test set (177 alternating, 123 non-alternating). For the VerbNet set, it leads to a slight majority of non-alternating verbs (138 alternating, 162 non-alternating).

The third test condition, BALANCED, evaluates the accuracy of each setup on the 150 most frequent verbs from each class for each source, so that we force a balance of 150 positive and 150 negative examples per source, where each verb occurs with high frequency in the corpus.

Since the ALL condition has the largest majority of alternating verbs, the setups that perform better in this condition are the ones that are more likely to assign the alternating label. We find that the BALANCED condition gives the best indicator of the accuracy of a setup.

Table 1 shows the F1 scores of our setups. For comparison, we also include the results of a random baseline. Bold font indicates the highest scores achieved in each condition.

For the systems that employ a ranking to classify the verbs, we report the scores achieved by splitting the ranked lists at a pre-defined index. The results reported here correspond to the split index that leads to the same number of alternating and non-alternating verbs as in the test sets.

Initially, we had split the ranked lists at the index leading to the optimal score. This introduced a strong bias in favor of the ranking approaches. In another setup, we used the mean ranking score to separate the classes, which sometimes also achieved better results than the fixed-index split. We decided to report the score as described above because we find that it best reflects the ability of each approach to predict the data in the test sets.

5   Discussion

For those of our systems that use corpus data for the classification, the frequency of individual verbs has an impact on the likelihood of the system to

	Levin			VerbNet		
	ALL	**FREQ**	**BALANCED**	**ALL**	**FREQ**	**BALANCED**
RANDOM BASELINE	0.51	0.54	0.52	0.53	0.47	0.56
VNTYPE	0.20	0.31	0.32	0.10	0.18	0.17
VNRANK	0.67	0.63	0.52	0.60	0.42	0.52
VNTOKEN	0.61	0.59	0.50	**0.83**	0.68	0.71
SCFFLAG	**0.71**	**0.74**	**0.67**	0.59	0.63	0.67
SCFRATIO	**0.71**	0.72	0.65	0.68	0.57	0.60
CENTROIDDISTANCE	0.62	0.60	0.62	0.64	0.78	**0.79**
CENTROIDSUBJVSOBJ	0.63	0.63	0.57	0.64	**0.79**	**0.79**
RNN-LM	0.66	0.69	0.59	0.66	0.78	**0.79**

Table 1: F1 scores of all setups

assign the correct label. Verbs that are listed in the Levin or VerbNet sets as participating in the alternation cannot be classified correctly with these approaches if they are unattested in the corpus.

All setups except VNTYPE outperform the random baseline. While this approach had a precision of roughly 50% in each of the setups, the recall was extremely low, leading to the low F1 scores shown in the table. VNTYPE is generally prone to mislabeling alternating verbs as non-alternating. The reason for the prevalence of such errors is the lack of tolerance in assigning the alternating label. Recall that a verb is only labeled as alternating by this setup if it is a member of a VerbNet class in which *all* members are observed in transitive and intransitive SCFs in the corpus. Data sparsity may lead to individual VerbNet class members not being attested at all, or being attested only in one syntactic configuration, even when the other one is possible. Thus, the criterion that *all* members of the class need to be observed in both types of SCFs is apparently too strict for successful classification.

Relaxing this condition leads to the approach VNRANK, where a high percentage of syntactically flexible members in a VerbNet class leads to all members of that class being classified as alternating verbs, but it is not necessary for all verbs in the class to be observed with both types of SCFs. Table 1 shows that relaxing the conditions for syntactic flexibility leads to high performance gains. Compared to VNTYPE, this approach assigns a lower number of false negatives.

VNTOKEN performs slightly worse than VNRANK on the Levin test sets, but is among the best setups on the VerbNet test sets. A closer look at its false positives and false negatives shows that they consist mainly of verbs that are unattested or infrequent in the BNC.

The approaches SCFFLAG and SCFRATIO perform surprisingly well on the task, particularly on the Levin test sets. These approaches derive a verb's alternatability score from a comparison of the numbers of transitive and intransitive occurrences of the verb in the corpus. The fact that SCFFLAG is one of the best-scoring approaches on the Levin test sets, while its accuracy is less impressive for the VerbNet test sets, indicates one of the main differences in the two test sets. The approach simply checks whether the verb was used at least once in each SCF type. That it performs well on the Levin set mainly tells us that the syntactic flexibility of the negative examples used in that test set is lower than that of the positive examples.

SCFFLAG and SCFRATIO are also discussed below, in Section 6.

On the VerbNet test set, the systems that rely on word vectors achieved good scores, together with the RNN-LM setup. In some other evaluation setups, the RNN method slightly outperformed the vector-based ones.

The RNN-LM approach generally preferred transitive verb uses over intransitive ones. This was even the case when lexically-intransitive verbs were involved. For instance, "John-sleep" received a lower acceptability score than "John-sleep-it", even though the verb *to sleep* rarely takes a direct object in English. This shows that the way the RNN-LM scores were calculated is not necessarily a good approximation of acceptability.

Thus, even though the RNN setup was among the best-scoring ones on the balanced VerbNet test set, we find the vector-based approaches preferable. For the Levin test sets, the SCFFLAG setup achieves the highest scores throughout the test conditions.

A common source of errors for many of our approaches were mistakes in the parse trees in the corpus. They influenced our results in two ways. First, some tokens were erroneously annotated as arguments of a verb. These cases added noise to the modeling of the verb's behavior and argument preferences. They may also be responsible for the preference of the RNN-LM approach for transitive sentences; possibly, the preference is simply a result of the dependency parser having the same preference. Second, some verbs in our test sets were systematically not annotated as being verbs, including verbs that have noun homographs, such as *circle* or *drip*, and verbs that have adjective homographs, such as *yellow* or *awake*. Since our approaches rely on the dependency trees observed in the corpus in order to model the behavior of each verb, the absence of correctly-parsed sentences for these verbs had a negative impact on our overall performance. These issues may be resolved by adding a word-sense disambiguation step to the process. We will explore this in future work.

Our vector-based systems perform much better on VerbNet than on the Levin test set. This is probably because the VerbNet classes are organized semantically, which means that even when one verb is not attested frequently enough to draw conclusions about it based on its arguments, the availability of vectors for other verbs in the same VerbNet class improves the score by a large margin.

We expected our class-based approaches that rely on VerbNet class groupings (VNTYPE, VNRANK, VNTOKEN) to generally perform better when evaluated against VerbNet than when evaluated against the Levin test set. This is the case for VNTOKEN, but the other approaches in the set achieve better scores on the Levin set. Particularly surprising is the better performance on the Levin set of the VNTYPE method. However, since this approach achieved scores well below the random baseline, we do not explore it further.

Our strategy for assembling the negative test set for the VerbNet setup by collecting verbs from classes that are annotated as having both transitive and intransitive uses, but not as having both causative and inchoative uses, has an influence on the results reported in Table 1. In particular, the approaches that use the presence or absence of transitive and intransitive SCFs (SCFFLAG, SCFRATIO, VNTYPE, VNRANK, VNTOKEN) have a high risk of false positives on this test set. This is not ideal, since the ability to distinguish between the causative alternation and the unexpressed-object alternation is one of the motivations for the alternation identification task. If the identification of one of these alternations relies on features that both classes of verbs share, that distinction may not be feasible.

The following section shows how our approaches perform when they do not assign alternating and non-alternating labels, but instead separate verbs in the causative alternation from verbs in the unexpressed-object alternation.

6 Distinguishing Causative and Unexpressed-Object Alternation

The way we collected the VerbNet test set already filters the verbs in such a way that optionally-transitive verbs that do not participate in the causative alternation make up the negative set. This criterion has the result that we effectively separate causatively-alternating verbs from verbs in the unexpressed-object alternation.

Table 2 shows the performance of our systems on the task of distinguishing the causative alternation from the unexpressed-object alternation on verbs from Levin. The verbs that participate in the unexpressed-object alternation were taken from Levin (1993, pp. 33–40). The full set contained 343 verbs, which we reduced for the FREQ and BALANCED conditions as in the previous task.

The performance of our systems on this task differs only slightly from the scores reported above. Against our expectations, the vector-based approaches CENTROIDDISTANCE and CENTROIDSUBJ-VSOBJ perform slightly worse when applied to the distinction between the two alternations. These approaches are designed to take each verb's semantic preferences for its argument slots into account. Since CENTROIDSUBJVSOBJ performs better than CENTROIDDISTANCE, the poor performance of the latter is probably due to overlapping semantic preferences for the different slots.

To assess the merit of our approaches, we compare them to the work of Merlo and Stevenson (2001). They achieve an accuracy of 69% on the three-way distinction of unaccusative, unergative, and unexpressed-object verbs (our distinction combines the first two of these). Our verb-based approach SCFRATIO outperforms that of Merlo and Stevenson by 6%. Our setup is simpler than that of Merlo and Stevenson, requiring only a dependency-

	all	freq	balanced
RANDOM BASELINE	0.48	0.50	0.49
VNTYPE	0.19	0.30	0.30
VNRANK	**0.79**	0.67	0.68
VNTOKEN	0.61	0.51	0.51
SCFFLAG	0.64	0.66	0.67
SCFRATIO	0.68	**0.73**	**0.75**
CENTROIDDISTANCE	0.53	0.55	0.55
CENTROIDSUBJVSOBJ	0.59	0.61	0.61
RNN-LM	0.58	0.63	0.63

Table 2: F1 scores of all setups when applied to the causative-versus-unexpressed-object task, on verbs from Levin (1993)

parsed corpus from which to derive SCF statistics, whereas their system makes use of features like animacy or causativity, which pose problems when a verb is attested infrequently.

Our best-performing setup SCFRATIO assigned the causative-alternation label for verbs that occur in transitive or intransitive SCFs with very dissimilar frequencies (that is, where one of the SCFs was dominant in the corpus), while verbs whose frequencies with transitive and intransitive SCFs were closer to each other were more likely to participate in the unexpressed-object alternation.

7 Conclusion

Our results are difficult to compare to those reported in previous work. Early work, such as McCarthy (2000); Schulte Im Walde (2000); McCarthy (2001); Merlo and Stevenson (2001), tends to evaluate on small test sets. Some of our approaches exceed the performance of the systems for the identification of the causative alternation presented in these publications. Note that our test conditions achieve varying scores even with minimal changes in the test sets; previous work in this area often did not specify the exact conditions of the evaluation.

More recent work in this area has focused less on the identification of diathesis alternations, and more on the induction of Levin-like verb classes, with a stronger focus on semantics. In contrast to this, our work focuses on the classification of verbs based on properties at the syntax-semantics interface. The good results of the SCFRATIO approach on the distinction between verbs in the causative alternation and verbs in the unexpressed-object alternation shows that this system learns something about the verbs that are being classified.

The experiments in this paper were performed on English verbs because gold data for the task was readily available for the two alternations in English. However, since many of our approaches do not rely on manually-compiled resources, they can be applied to other languages with little effort, as long as dependency parsers and corpora to use as a source for distributional information are available. However, the quality of available dependency parsers for the language will always influence the performance of our methods.

The methods presented here may be applied to any role-switching alternation (McCarthy, 2001) in any language for which the necessary preprocessing tools are available. Comparing the performance of our approaches to the performance they achieve on other languages will be informative from a typological perspective. We plan to conduct similar experiments on at least one language from another language family in the future.

Due to the interest in transferring our findings to similar phenomena in other languages, we find that verb-based methods are preferable for this task. As Table 1 shows, they perform reasonably well in comparison with our other systems, and the cases where class-based methods perform better (VNTOKEN on the VerbNet test sets) are likely the result of overfitting on the structure of VerbNet.

Acknowledgments

The work presented in this paper was financed by the Deutsche Forschungsgemeinschaft (DFG) within the CRC 991 "The Structure of Representations in Language, Cognition, and Science". The author wishes to thank Laura Kallmeyer, Kilian Evang, Jakub Waszczuk, and three anonymous reviewers for their valuable feedback and helpful comments.

References

Claire Bonial, Susan Windisch Brown, Jena D Hwang, Christopher Parisien, Martha Palmer, and Suzanne Stevenson. 2011. Incorporating Coercive Constructions into a Verb Lexicon. In *Proceedings of the ACL 2011 Workshop on Relational Models of Semantics*, pages 72–80. Association for Computational Linguistics.

Lou Burnard. 2007. Reference Guide for the British National Corpus (XML Edition) .

Eric Joanis. 2002. Automatic Verb Classification Using a General Feature Space. *Master's thesis, Department of Computer Science, University of Toronto*.

Eric Joanis and Suzanne Stevenson. 2003. A General Feature Space for Automatic Verb Classification. In *10th Conference of the European Chapter of the Association for Computational Linguistics*.

Eric Joanis, Suzanne Stevenson, and David James. 2008. A general feature space for automatic verb classification. *Natural Language Engineering*, 14(3):337–367.

Karin Kipper, Hoa Trang Dang, and Martha Palmer. 2000. Class-Based Construction of a Verb Lexicon. In *Proceedings of the Seventeenth National Conference on Artificial Intelligence*, pages 691–696.

Anna Korhonen. 2009. Automatic Lexical Classification - Balancing between Machine Learning and Linguistics. In *Proceedings of the 23rd Pacific Asia Conference on Language, Information and Computation, Volume 1*.

Maria Lapata and Chris Brew. 1999. Using Subcategorization to Resolve Verb Class Ambiguity. In *1999 Joint SIGDAT Conference on Empirical Methods in Natural Language Processing and Very Large Corpora*, pages 266–274.

Jey Han Lau, Alexander Clark, and Shalom Lappin. 2015. Unsupervised Prediction of Acceptability Judgements. In *Proceedings of the 53rd Annual Meeting of the Association for Computational Linguistics and the 7th International Joint Conference on Natural Language Processing (Volume 1: Long Papers)*, pages 1618–1628. Association for Computational Linguistics.

Beth Levin. 1993. *English Verb Classes and Alternations: A Preliminary Investigation*. University of Chicago press.

Christopher D. Manning, Mihai Surdeanu, John Bauer, Jenny Finkel, Steven Bethard, and David McClosky. 2014. The Stanford CoreNLP Natural Language Processing Toolkit. In *Proceedings of 52nd Annual Meeting of the Association for Computational Linguistics: System Demonstrations*, pages 55–60. Association for Computational Linguistics.

Diana McCarthy. 2000. Using Semantic Preferences to Identify Verbal Participation in Role Switching Alternations. In *1st Meeting of the North American Chapter of the Association for Computational Linguistics*, pages 256–263. Association for Computational Linguistics.

Diana McCarthy. 2001. *Lexical Acquisition at the Syntax-Semantics Interface: Diathesis Alternations, Subcategorization Frames and Selectional Preferences*. Ph.D. thesis, University of Sussex.

Paola Merlo and Suzanne Stevenson. 2001. Automatic Verb Classification Based on Statistical Distributions of Argument Structure. *Computational Linguistics*, 27(3):373–408.

Tomas Mikolov, Ilya Sutskever, Kai Chen, Greg S Corrado, and Jeff Dean. 2013. Distributed Representations of Words and Phrases and their Compositionality. In *Advances in Neural Information Processing Systems*, pages 3111–3119. Curran Associates, Inc.

George Miller. 1998. *WordNet: An electronic lexical database*. MIT press.

Sabine Schulte Im Walde. 2000. Clustering Verbs Semantically According to their Alternation Behaviour. In *COLING 2000 Volume 2: The 18th International Conference on Computational Linguistics*, pages 747–753. Association for Computational Linguistics.

Sabine Schulte Im Walde. 2006. Experiments on the Automatic Induction of German Semantic Verb Classes. *Computational Linguistics*, 32(2):159–194.

Suzanne Stevenson and Eric Joanis. 2003. Semi-supervised Verb Class Discovery Using Noisy Features. In *Proceedings of the Seventh Conference on Natural Language Learning at HLT-NAACL 2003*, pages 71–78. Association for Computational Linguistics.

Lin Sun, Anna Korhonen, and Yuval Krymolowski. 2008. Verb Class Discovery from Rich Syntactic Data. In *International Conference on Intelligent Text Processing and Computational Linguistics*, pages 16–27. Springer.

Lin Sun, Diana McCarthy, and Anna Korhonen. 2013. Diathesis alternation approximation for verb clustering. In *Proceedings of the 51st Annual Meeting of the Association for Computational Linguistics (Volume 2: Short Papers)*, pages 736–741. Association for Computational Linguistics.

Using Sentiment Induction to Understand Variation
in Gendered Online Communities

Li Lucy
Symbolic Systems Program
Department of Computer Science
Stanford University
lucy3@stanford.edu

Julia Mendelsohn
Department of Linguistics
Department of Computer Science
Stanford University
jmendels@stanford.edu

Abstract

We analyze gendered communities defined in three different ways: text, users, and sentiment. Differences across these representations reveal facets of communities' distinctive identities, such as social group, topic, and attitudes. Two communities may have high text similarity but not user similarity or vice versa, and word usage also does not vary according to a clearcut, binary perspective of gender. Community-specific sentiment lexicons demonstrate that sentiment can be a useful indicator of words' social meaning and community values, especially in the context of discussion content and user demographics. Our results show that social platforms such as Reddit are active settings for different constructions of gender.

1 Introduction

Social groups can be described by many factors, such as the demographics of its participants or its physical location. To detect sociolinguistically significant groups, linguists have built upon the concept of *communities of practice*, which are characterized by their participants' shared actions, beliefs, values, and language styles (Eckert and McConnell-Ginet, 1992; Eckert, 2006). This concept initially emerged to understand the complex interplay between language and gender, and has been applied to study social identities in numerous communities (e.g. Eckert, 1989; Mendoza-Denton, 1996; Hall, 2009). While previous variationist work has primarily studied traditional physical communities, we focus instead on online ones.

Online communities have been shown to form collective linguistic norms, which give rise to a rich amount of language variation across communities, even on the same website (Danescu-Niculescu-Mizil et al., 2013; Yang and Eisenstein, 2015). One of the largest content aggre-gator and discussion platforms, Reddit, contains thousands of unique communities, known as *subreddits*. These subreddits vary in topic, such as r/sport and r/history, content type, such as r/pics and r/videos, and format, such as the Q&A style of r/IamA and the narratives on r/confession. Online communities such as subreddits are often characterized by language use and user membership (Hamilton et al., 2016; Datta et al., 2017; Bamman et al., 2014; Martin, 2017).

Sociolinguists have primarily analyzed phonological and syntactic variables (Eckert, 2012), though some have studied lexical variables (e.g. Wong, 2005). Previous computational work also focuses on lexical variation (Bamman et al., 2014). We approach variation from a new direction, where we examine the salient semantic dimension of sentiment to understand *how* users use the same words to convey different meanings. We also create representations for subreddits that encode text and user membership to situate insights gained from sentiment-based representations and to understand the intersection of speaker identity (user), content (text), and affect (sentiment). This paper focuses on explicitly gendered subreddits, which cater towards masculine- or feminine-identifying groups.

We provide two main contributions:

1) Salient aspects of social group identities, such as gender, can produce low user overlap in communities sharing similar topics.

2) Sentiment-based representations of communities can reveal a type of variation across social groups that word-choice alone cannot. An in-depth study of words' sentiments in gendered subreddits reveals patterns of how linguistic resources construct a wide array of gendered identities in the online sphere.

Proceedings of the Society for Computation in Linguistics (SCiL) 2019, pages 156-166.
New York City, New York, January 3-6, 2019

2 Previous Work

The study of online communities is highly interdisciplinary, spanning machine learning, natural language processing, social network analysis, communications, and sociolinguistics. Twitter, online news, and other websites have been a rich source of data for computational social scientists, and Reddit in particular has been of interest to much previous work (Althoff et al., 2014; Kumar et al., 2018; Newell et al., 2016; Jaech et al., 2015; Hamilton et al., 2017). Research in this area expands beyond quantitative measures, by comparing results with social science theories and employing qualitative thinking to highlight trends of individual words and communities (Bamman et al., 2014; Danescu-Niculescu-Mizil et al., 2013; Zhang et al., 2017; Althoff et al., 2014).

In particular, the characterization and identification of gender is a common use case for online data. Language is often used to infer demographics of users, especially in classification tasks that tend to find clear distinctions between men and women (e.g. Burger et al., 2011; Argamon et al., 2007; Schler, 2006; Rao et al., 2010). Previous work have found strong patterns of gender differences in language (Newman et al., 2008; Mulac et al., 2001). For example, Volkova et al. (2013) showed that the sentiment of words, hashtags, and emoticons vary between men and women on Twitter and used gender-dependent features to improve sentiment classification of tweets. Our work aims to look beyond a straightforward divide between men and women, particularly because gender is not a fixed biological variable, but rather a dynamic, social one that is actively created and reinforced through repeated behaviors (Butler, 1988; Nguyen et al., 2014; Herring and Paolillo, 2006).

Language is used to simultaneously co-construct multiple identities, so the plethora of gendered identities that emerge from communities of practice may substantially differ from mainstream stereotypes of "femininity" and "masculinity" (Eckert, 1989; Mendoza-Denton, 1996; Hall, 2009). On Twitter, Bamman et al. (2014) investigated cross-community lexical variation and the varied ways of constructing gender identities. They clustered users based on bag-of-words representations of their posts, and the resulting clusters corresponded not only to topical interest but also gender. Some clusters had language patterns that were orthogonal to expected language differences between men and women, demonstrating diversity in gendered language styles.

We compare text, user, and sentiment representations of communities by their predictions of similarity and identify cases where these predictions agree or disagree. Pavalanathan et al. (2017) suggested that subreddits with similar topics can have dissimilar user groups due to differences in preferred interactional styles. Datta et al. (2017) introduced a method for finding misalignments of inferred user-based and text-based networks on Reddit. They found that pairs with high text but low user similarity tend to be communities that conflict (such as political subreddits) as well as communities with hierarchical relationships (such as a niche subreddit with a more generic one). High user but low text similarity suggested a single overarching community scattered across multiple subreddits. We assessed Datta et al. (2017)'s z^2-score method in section 5.1, but found that its results hid important misalignments.

We use domain-specific lexicon induction techniques for creating sentiment-based subreddit representations. Previous work has built or adapted word embeddings or scores to flexibly encode semantic dimensions or specific domains, and some have applied their techniques to social media communities (Rothe et al., 2016; Yang and Eisenstein, 2015; Hamilton et al., 2016). Rothe et al. (2016)'s DENSIFIER model involves dense word embeddings created by mapping generic word embeddings into meaningful subspaces. These learned embeddings may even contain a single dimension, which can act as labels for an induced lexicon, and are best applied to corpora with several billion tokens, which is far greater than any subreddit that we study.

While Rothe et al. (2016) learned lexicons for generic domains such as news and Twitter, Hamilton et al. (2016)'s SENTPROP method solves a similar task across fine-grained domains, including Reddit communities. They applied a label propagation method to 250 Reddit communities, and found a wide range of sentiment variation. For example, *insane* is negative in r/twoxchromosomes but positive in r/sports, while *soft* shows the opposite pattern. SENTPROP was the most suitable approach for our purposes due to its ability to operate on smaller datasets. We extend this work by examining how vector representations created from subreddit-specific sen-

Subreddit	Description
r/actuallesbians	"A place for cis and trans lesbians, bisexual girls, chicks who like chicks..."
r/askgaybros	"Where you can ask the manly men for their opinions on various topics."
r/mensrights	"For those who wish to discuss men's rights and the ways said rights are infringed upon."
r/askmen	"A semi-serious place to ask men casual questions about life, career, and more."
r/askwomen	"Dedicated to asking women questions about their thoughts, lives, and experiences."
r/xxfitness	"For women and gender non-binary redditors who are fit, want to be fit..."
r/femalefashionadvice	"A subreddit dedicated to learning about and discussing women's fashion."
r/malefashionadvice	"Making clothing less intimidating and helping you develop your own style."
r/trollxchromosomes	"A subreddit for rage comics and other memes with a girly slant."

Table 1: Gendered communities with descriptions from their sidebars or subreddit search listings.

timent lexicons compare to text-based and user-based representations, with gendered communities as a case study.

3 Data

In order to gain a broad perspective of how gendered subreddits relate to each other and other communities within the larger Reddit context, we consider data from subreddits with 50,000+ subscribers, as provided in a user-curated list[1]. These subreddits span topics ranging from plants to cryptocurrency, and provide a glimpse into Reddit's long tail of diverse niche communities, which is a primary draw to the platform (Newell et al., 2016). The most popular subreddits tend to be part of a set of "default" subreddits to which users have historically been auto-subscribed (Newell et al., 2016; Datta et al., 2017). To focus on more niche and non-artificially inflated communities, we filtered out about 50 default subreddits based on lists in r/defaults created during May 07 2014, May 26 2016, and March 26 2017.

We took the top 400 remaining subreddits and used their comments created between May 2016 and April 2017. The vast majority of these subreddits contain between 10^7 and 10^8 tokens, with r/politics (the largest) containing over 764 million tokens to r/accidentalwesanderson (the smallest) containing over 7 million. From these subreddits we manually selected nine subreddits with clearly gender-oriented names (Table 1).

4 Approach

4.1 Text & User Representations

To provide a basis of comparison for our sentiment-based representations, we created term frequency-inverse document frequency (tf-idf) vectors for each subreddit using user and unigram

Positive	love, loved, loves, awesome, nice, amazing, best, fantastic, correct, happy
Negative	hate, hated, hates, terrible, nasty, awful, worst, horrible, wrong, sad

Table 2: Positive and negative Twitter seed words from Hamilton et al. (2016)

frequencies. Here, we define subreddit user frequencies as the number of times a user comments to a specific subreddit. For unigram or user t in subreddit d, its tf-idf weighted frequency is

$$w_{t,d} = (1 + \log tf_{t,d}) \log(N/df_t),$$

where $tf_{t,d}$ is the frequency of t in d, df_t is the number of subreddits in which t appears, and N is the total number of subreddits.

We filtered out rare users and bots, with $1 < df_t \leq 380$ for users, and filtered out rare words and stop words, with $5 < df_t \leq 380$ for unigrams. We used truncated singular value decomposition (SVD) to reduce these vectors to 100 dimensions and normalized them to each have a unit norm (Pedregosa et al., 2011; Halko et al., 2011).

4.2 Sentiment Representations

We induced community-specific sentiment lexicons using the SENTPROP method introduced by Hamilton et al. (2016). This framework was demonstrated to perform well on moderately sized domains of 10^7 tokens, which matches the majority of our subreddits.

SENTPROP begins by creating community-specific word embeddings. All comments from a given subreddit were first concatenated into a single document, separated by 5 dummy tokens so adjacent comments did not influence the linguistic contexts of the first and last words. Following Hamilton et al. (2016), word co-occurrence matrices for each subreddit were created with a symmetric context window of 4 words and

---

[1]Available here.

reweighted using positive pointwise mutual information (PPMI) with context distribution smoothing $c = 0.75$ (Levy et al., 2015). The dimensionality of each word embedding was then reduced to 100 using SVD.

After obtaining subreddit-specific word embeddings, we introduce a small set of seed words with positive and negative polarity. We used the same seed words as Hamilton et al. (2016) did for Twitter, another social media platform (Table 2). SENTPROP runs a series of random walks from both the positive and negative seed words, and the resulting sentiment value for each word is based on the probabilities that the word was hit by the positive random walk versus the negative one. We used SENTPROP's default parameters for the Reddit lexicon induction portion of their paper, setting $\beta = 0.9$ and $K = 25$, where K is the number of nearest neighbors in the semantic space to which edges are drawn in graph construction. A higher β favors similar labels for neighbors and a lower β favors correct labels on seed words. We induced sentiment for the top 5000 words by frequency in each subreddit.

Adjusting the parameters β and K did not change our main conclusions or observations. Lowering β from 0.9 to as far as 0.5 shrinks the overall range of sentiment values from -3 to 3 to about -2 to 2. Words with neutral sentiment tend to be slightly more positive or negative with lower values of β, but words with the highest polarities are consistent. Sentiment scores also remain steady when varying K. With $\beta = 0.9$, the Pearson correlation of sentiment scores between $K = 25$ and $K = 15$ is 0.9183 ($p < 0.001$) and 0.9668 between $K = 25$ and $K = 35$ ($p < 0.001$) for r/xxfitness.

We standardized values for each word to have zero mean and unit variance. The resulting sentiment vectors were then an array of negative and positive values corresponding to sentiment, averaged over 50 bootstrap-sampled runs. Each index in these vectors maps to a word in the vocabulary, which is the union of all subreddits' vocabularies. If a word's sentiment was not induced in a certain subreddit, its sentiment value is set to a neutral zero.

4.3 Metrics

We performed agglomerative clustering on all 400 subreddits' user- and text-based representations to see where gendered subreddits' users and content are situated within Reddit. We fixed the number of clusters to 20 and compared cluster sets provided by different representations by calculating their adjusted mutual information (AMI), where the possible range of values is 0 for random cluster and 1 for identical ones (Vinh et al., 2010). To further compare the different representations, we calculated the Spearman correlation between subreddits' pairwise similarities. We identify misalignments as subreddit pairs that have high similarity for one representation but low similarity for another.

We also implemented the misalignment identification method proposed by Datta et al. (2017). This method subtracts two pairwise similarity rank matrices created by two different representation types, such as text and user, and z-score normalizes the difference matrix's columns and rows. Values in the final misalignment matrix are called z^2-scores. Pairs of subreddits with a high positive z^2-score have a higher similarity than expected with the first representation compared to the second, while a large negative z^2-score signifies the opposite.

5 Analysis

5.1 Text & Users

The clusterings of user- and text-based representations are similar, with an AMI of 0.5610, and the text-based clusterings are more topically coherent. For example, r/femalefashionadvice and r/malefashionadvice are in the same text-based cluster but different user-based clusters, since both are about fashion but cater towards different genders. Subsets of the clusters in which gendered subreddits appear can be found in Table 3. The feminine subreddits are all in the same user-based cluster, while the masculine ones are more scattered. Female Reddit users may find themselves pushed into this cluster because of an overall predominant masculine culture throughout the platform which can be hostile to women (Massanari, 2017). A majority of the gendered subreddits occur in the text-based cluster containing those related to personal topics, such as families and relationships. These clusters situate our gendered communities based on *what* they talk about and *who* is talking, and changing the representation type alters the perceived geography of Reddit.

The Spearman correlation between text and

User-based Clusters	Text-based Clusters
femalefashionadvice askwomen xxfitness trollxchromosomes actuallesbians weddingplanning makeupaddiction justnomil skincareaddiction raisedbynarcissists dogs childfree vegan parenting running teachers unresolvedmysteries	**askwomen actuallesbians askmen askgaybros trollxchromosomes** suicidewatch justnomil deadbedrooms babybumps seduction raisedbynarcissists dogs childfree casualiama legaladvice parenting foreveralone dating_advice teachers polyamory
mensrights sandersforpresident changemyview neutralpolitics forwardsfromgrandma the_donald anarchism economics atheism subredditdrama	**mensrights** thathappened teenagers forwardsfromgrandma niceguys blackpeopletwitter roastme trashy facepalm photoshopbattles outoftheloop 4chan cringe
askgaybros askmen suicidewatch teenagers sex bodybuilding depression seduction offmychest ama advice foreveralone dating_advice tinder polyamory	**xxfitness** fatlogic loseit keto cooking vegan running bodybuilding
malefashionadvice houston cooking churning entrepreneur seattle financialindependence investing travel homeimprovement jobs photography homebrewing bicycling personalfinance	**femalefashionadvice malefashionadvice** weddingplanning makeupaddiction skincareaddiction sneakers streetwear asianbeauty fashionreps

Table 3: The gendered subreddits and a subset of the subreddits that occur in the same clusters as them.

user vectors' pairwise similarities is 0.549 ($p <$ 0.0001), plotted in Figure 1. The vast majority of the pairs with high user and low text similarity are those pertaining to European countries, where comments are in different languages. The pairs with high text and low user similarity include subreddits pertaining to cities, as well as those divided by gender, sexual orientation, or personal topics. Thus, user demographics are important motivators for community formation on Reddit. User-based similarities for gendered subreddits tend to vary based on whether they cater towards the same gender, though some subreddits act as bridges between them: r/askmen and r/askwomen have a user similarity of 0.417, which is above the average among gendered subreddits (0.2880). The structure of these communities facilitates this by encouraging questions posted by users of any gender, and follow-up dialogue across groups accompanies the targeted gender's answers in the comments.

The misalignments identified by raw similarities are more intuitive than those identified by z^2-scores. Pairs in the top 20 with high text and low user similarity based on z^2-scores included understandable ones such as r/casualconversation-r/tinder, but also many pairs on very different topics such as r/bodybuilding-r/learningprogramming and r/makeupaddiction-r/legaladvice. Pairs in the top 20 with low text and high user similarity were easier to interpret and included r/truegaming-r/askmen and r/vegan-r/askscience. The z^2 score method normalizes any subreddit's skewed distribution of similarities. For example, country subreddits in general have lower text similarity to other subreddits since Reddit is mostly in English,

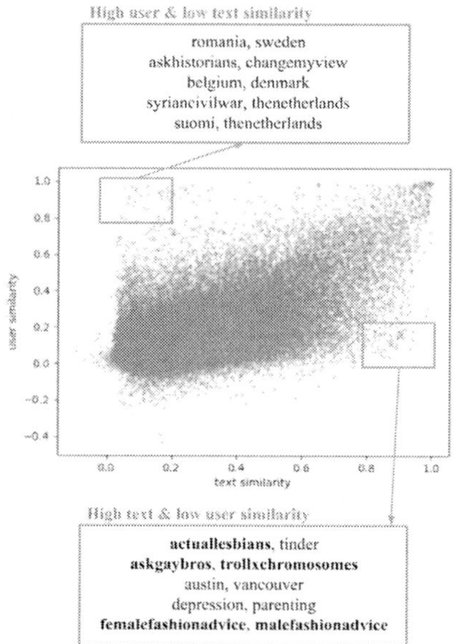

Figure 1: Subreddit similarities, with text similarities on the horizontal axis and user similarities on the vertical axis. Each point represents a pair of subreddits. The listed subreddit pairs are examples of outliers, where one type of similarity is very small (< 0.2) and another is large (> 0.8).

and normalization causes inter-country similarities to match their expected similarity differences. Thus, normalization steps may reduce meaningful variation in how some subreddit similarities deviate from the norm of Reddit as a whole.

5.2 Sentiment

We calculated the pairwise cosine similarities between each of the nine explicitly gendered sub-

Highest	Similarity	Lowest	Similarity
askmen, askwomen	0.6702	femalefashionadvice, mensrights	0.1802
askgaybros, askmen	0.6144	askwomen, malefashionadvice	0.1876
askwomen, trollxchromosomes	0.6003	malefashionadvice, trollxchromosomes	0.2162
actuallesbians, trollxchromosomes	0.5462	malefashionadvice, mensrights	0.2170
askgaybros, askwomen	0.5310	mensrights, xxfitness	0.2181

Table 4: Highest and lowest sentiment similarities between gendered subreddits, with a mean of 0.3701.

	Spearman ρ	p
text, user	0.4268	< 0.01
text, sentiment	0.6371	< 0.0001
user, sentiment	0.4219	$= 0.01$

Table 5: Correlations of text, user, and sentiment representations using pairwise cosine similarity between nine gendered subreddits. Though sentiment and text are related, they provide different information.

reddits using text, user, and sentiment community representations. Table 5 shows the resulting Spearman correlation between these representations. Sentiment representations correlate more strongly with those of text, which could be explained by how they are both linguistically motivated. However, this correlation is far from 1, suggesting that sentiment representations capture some aspects of communities that weighted word counts do not.

The pairs of subreddits with highest and lowest sentiment similarity can be found in Table 4. Some of the highest similarities are between subreddits oriented towards the same gender, and while some of the lowest are between those of different genders, but there are several exceptions. Therefore, sentiment does not divide itself evenly based on gender. The high sentiment similarity between r/askmen and r/askwomen misaligns with their low text similarity (0.2874) and near average user similarity (0.4168). Another outlier across text, user, and sentiment similarities is r/actuallesbians and r/trollxchromosomes, which have high user similarity (0.8856), above average sentiment similarity (0.5462), and high text similarity (0.9415).

The most positive and negative non-seed words in each subreddit are consistent with the concepts we expect to be relevant to them (some examples[2] in Table 6.). Many negative words

in r/trollxchromosomes and r/femalefashionadvice revolve around pain and health, while those in r/mensrights refer to gender bias (within the top fifteen most negative words are *misandrist* and *manhating*). The most positive words in r/xxfitness are similar to those in other subreddits since many are adjectives such as *great* and *fun*, but its most negative words almost entirely focus on physical ailments, such as *flu, infection* and *headache*. The words *brothers* and *brother* have highest sentiment in r/mensrights compared to other gendered subreddits, suggesting that this community values masculine solidarity. Likewise, even though the words *troll* and *trolls* are predominantly negative, they have high positive sentiment in r/trollxchromosomes, as users in this community have re-appropriated these terms to refer positively to themselves.[3]

Subreddits with high text similarity such as r/malefashionadvice and r/femalefashionadvice still contain distinct cultures. The highly positive words in r/femalefashionadvice reflect their custom of referencing daily outfits using days of the week, while users on r/malefashionadvice do not follow this format. The expressive elongation in r/femalefashionadvice's highly positive *loooove* has previously been shown to be a female marker (Bamman et al., 2014; Rao et al., 2010). Sentiment is a helpful but sometimes superficial metric for determining community values, and its interpretation is best understood in context with topic and users. For example, *men* is most negative in r/mensrights compared to other gendered subreddits, but that does not mean these users dislike men, since the opposite is actually the case. The strong negativity here is instead associated with how their discussions center on injustices towards men.

Table 7 shows the words with the highest variance in sentiment with the subreddits in which they have the most positive and negative polarity. Much of the cross-community variation in

---

[2] The token *lt3* is a punctuation-stripped HTML heart. Similarly, *d* is often a happy emoji *:D*.

[3] The full lexicons can be found in our Github repo here.

TrollXChromosomes		FemaleFashionAdvice		MaleFashionAdvice		MensRights	
Positive	Negative	Positive	Negative	Positive	Negative	Positive	Negative
lovely	infections	gorgeous	gross	sweet	gross	wonderful	vile
gorgeous	yeast	adore	marks	beautiful	annoying	favorite	evil
beautiful	pain	lovely	blood	cool	dirty	excellent	disgusting
wonderful	dealing	stunning	rough	those	stupid	watch	horribly
congratulations	mess	thursdays	painful	vouch	armpits	enjoyed	cruel
fabulous	horrific	mondays	worse	plus	shitty	honey	hating
congrats	painful	tuesdays	messed	dig	crap	clip	misogynistic
yay	minor	killer	causing	perfect	garbage	enjoying	hateful
d	uti	loooove	horribly	makes	crappy	fan	sexist
lt3	infection	fabulous	poor	interesting	sweaty	episode	bigots

Table 6: Most positive and negative non-seed words for a selected set of subreddits.

Word	Variance	Positive Subreddits	Negative Subreddits
sounds	2.775	femalefashionadvice, actuallesbians	askgaybros, askmen
smells	2.652	actuallesbians, malefashionadvice	askgaybros, askmen
hilarious	2.547	askwomen, actuallesbians	askgaybros, malefashionadvice
absolutely	2.231	femalefashionadvice, malefashionadvice	askwomen, askmen
obsessed	2.094	askwomen, femalefashionadvice	mensrights, askmen
sharp	2.087	actuallesbians, femalefashionadvice	xxfitness, trollxchromosomes

Table 7: Words with greatest variance in sentiment across all gendered subreddits, along with the subreddits in which they are the most positive and most negative.

sentiment is likely due to polysemy, where different senses of a given word are predominant in different communities. For example, when calculating the sentiment of *sick* (13th highest variance) in each subreddit's semantic space, SENT-PROP encounters neighbors such as *nauseous* (r/xxfitness), *disgusting* (r/mensrights), or *dope* (r/malefashionadvice).

> *i never thought id see sitting on a tricycle look so badass looks **sick** love it*[4] (r/malefashionadvice)

> *...what kind of **sick** twisted person could do that to another human being truly disgusting what some people are willing to do to others* (r/mensrights)

Furthermore, words may adopt the sentiment polarities that reflect the overall discourse style. In r/femalefashionadvice, seemingly negative words such as *jealous* (10th highest variance) take on a positive meaning as they are used to compliment the original poster:

> *that is amazing congratulations i am so **jealous*** (r/femalefashionadvice)

This relationship with overall discourse style may be even more pronounced for judgment-related words such as *sounds*, whose polarity reflects whether communities tend to use it to evaluate other users or entities positively or negatively.

> *...that **sounds** like a really polite and productive way to deal with the gift issues* (r/femalefashionadvice)

> ***sounds** like you just have shitty friends* (r/askgaybros)

Finally, many affective differences emerge depending on whether a subreddit's users talk about their own feelings, beliefs, and passions (personal) or make claims about other people's mental states (impersonal). In particular, sentiment of words such as *jealous* or *obsessed* varies depending on whether one uses it to describe themselves or somebody else (Figure 2).

> *...recently became **obsessed** with this podcast this is super cool* (r/trollxchromosomes)

> *so sad that so many female teachers are feminist **obsessed**...* (r/mensrights)

Volkova et al. (2013) studied sentiment variation using Twitter data, but treated gender as a binary variable of male versus female. They listed examples with large gender differences: *weakness* is used positively by women and negatively by men, while *overdressed* is used positively by men and negatively by women. Their most polarized words, with hashtags removed, do not split according to a binary in our subreddits. We observe diverse language styles: *weakness* is strongly negative in r/xxfitness (-2.0634 $\pm$ 0.5577) but positive in r/actuallesbians (0.9112 $\pm$ 0.2100), and the sentiment score of *overdressed* is similar in r/malefashionadvice (-0.6016 $\pm$ 0.5273) and r/femalefashionadvice (-0.6696 $\pm$ 0.8512). This implies that though gender can be a helpful variable for improving sentiment analysis, its expression is not fixed across multiple contexts.

The word *omg* seems to be used in far broader

---

[4]Examples transcribed as they appear after preprocessing.

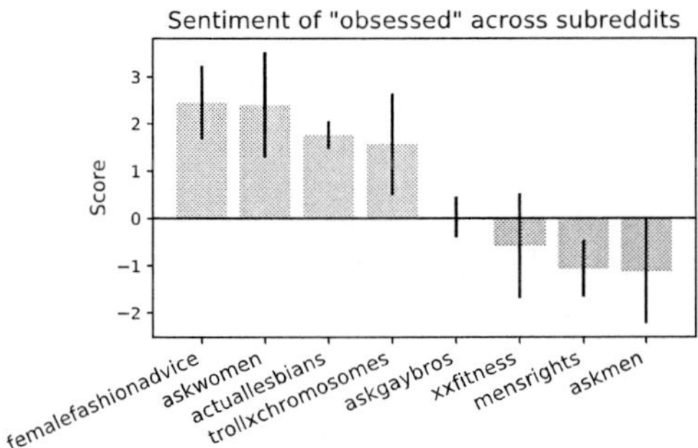

Figure 2: Words with high variance across communities such as *obsessed* can be strongly positive or negative.

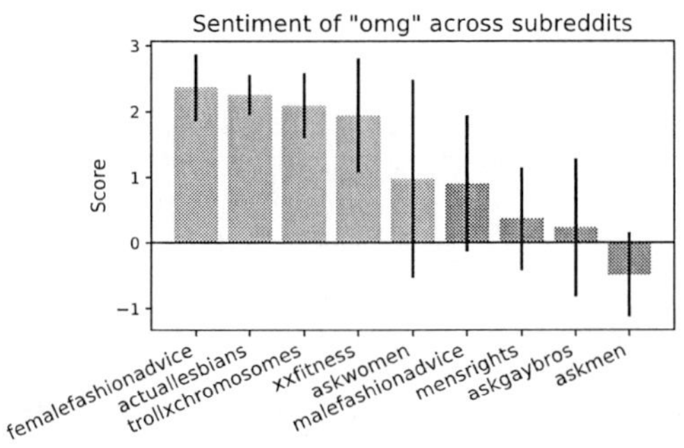

Figure 3: Average sentiment scores and standard deviations of "omg" in explicitly-gendered subreddits, sorted in decreasing order, based on 50 SENTPROP runs. Women-oriented subreddits are marked in red, and men-oriented are in blue.

contexts and have a substantially different meaning than its origin phrase, *oh my god*. In Figure 3, the sentiment of *omg* is highest among the five women-oriented subreddits, and lower in the men-oriented subreddits. This finding is consistent with prior results that show that forms predominant in computer-mediated communication are more commonly used by and highly associated with women (Bamman et al., 2014; Carpenter et al., 2017). However, these results have implications beyond just associating forms such as *omg* with women. In particular, *omg* is not a filler word devoid of meaning in women-oriented communities. Rather, it conveys highly positive affect and may also indicate cooperativeness and engagement in a conversation. It seems to not play the same role in men-oriented communities, where *omg* is used frequently in indirect quotes of others' speech.

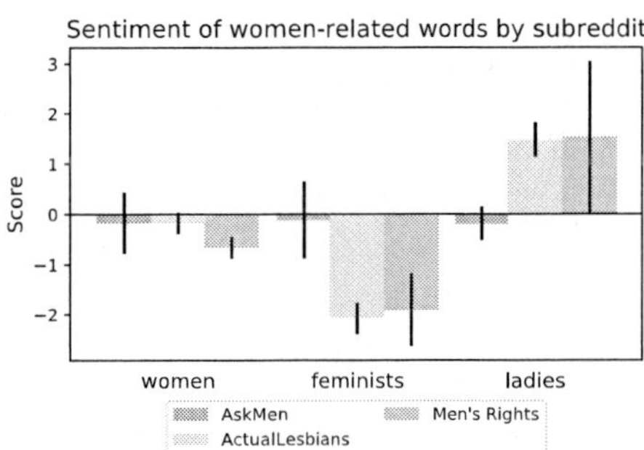

Figure 4: Sentiment scores of the words "women", "feminists", and "ladies" across three subreddits, with error bars showing the standard deviation of 50 bootstrap-sampled SENTPROP runs.

> ***omg*** *love her did you see that shoeprinted dress she had on this weeks episode* (r/femalefashionadvice)

> *...if anything it was usually **omg** you two would have the most beautiful babies...* (r/askmen)

Sentiment-based representations can also detect words that may be denotationally similar but have different social meanings due to repeated associations with certain beliefs and stereotypes. Figure 4 demonstrates community variation in the affective meaning of the denotationally similar terms *women* and *ladies* and the related but semantically distinct *feminists* across three subreddits. This variation demonstrates the potential for denotationally similar terms to acquire community-dependent connotational and affective meanings.

Unsurprisingly, *feminists* is highly negative in r/mensrights. However, it is similarly negative in r/actuallesbians, while neutral in r/askmen. Members of r/actuallesbians tend to not disapprove of feminists in general; instead, much of the discourse that includes this word focuses on the perceived exclusivity of many feminist movements towards LGBTQ individuals.

> *...didnt realize that transphobia was such an organized and politically influential problem especially from some **feminists** and not just old white guys...* (r/actuallesbians)

The words *women* and *ladies* are associated with many distinct social meanings. For example, *women* is seen as both a neutral and cold label, while *ladies* can be seen as traditional, patronizing, and sexual (Cralley and Ruscher, 2005; Friedman, 2013). More recently, *ladies* has also been reclaimed as an age-agnostic label popular with modern feminists (Friedman, 2013).

Both *women* and *ladies* are used in r/actuallesbians to name the target group of romantic and sexual attraction. However, the much more positive sentiment of *ladies* may be due to its additional meaning as an in-group label.

> *its a pretty slow reddit but **ladies** do say hello and interact* (r/actuallesbians)

Even though *ladies* also has positive sentiment in r/mensrights, the word is used very differently there. Instead of being used to sexualize women, *ladies* was far more commonly written in a patronizing manner.

> *...**ladies** this is what equality looks like time to give up some of your numerous privileges* (r/mensrights)

This reveals one limitation of a sentiment-only approach to analyzing sociolinguistic variation. The patronizing and sometimes sarcastic usage of *ladies* is a complex phenomenon that cannot be easily captured by methods based on vector space models. SENTPROP mistakenly arrives at a positive polarity for *ladies* in r/mensrights, although its high standard deviation hints at some underlying source of inconsistency.

6 Conclusion

Sentiment representations are useful for understanding variation both on a broad scale as well as among specific lexemes, particularly when combined with in-depth qualitative analyses. We focused on only explicitly gendered subreddits, but other subreddits can also be implicitly gendered. From the user-based clusters, we may be able to infer that subreddits like r/weddingplanning and r/makeupaddiction have mostly feminine users. In the future, we would like to situate our sentiment analysis of gendered subreddits in the larger context of Reddit. For example, comparing r/xxfitness with its fitness-related neighbors may allow a understanding of how explicitly targeting some demographic changes words' sentiment.

Sentiment is a salient semantic dimension, but it may also be illuminating to define subreddits along some other dimension, such as arousal, concreteness, or various emotions (Brysbaert et al., 2014; Warriner et al., 2013; Mohammad and Turney, 2010). Rarely are subreddit communities redundant. Though two subreddits may align with high similarities with some type of representation, they should differ in some other one. Still, a comparison of sentiment and emotion could result in strong alignment; negativity underlies anger and sadness, while positivity is fundamental to happiness and surprise.

7 Acknowledgements

We would like to thank Chris Potts, Will Hamilton, and Bill MacCartney for their helpful ideas and comments. Additional thanks to Will for Reddit data.

References

Tim Althoff, Cristian Danescu-Niculescu-Mizil, and Dan Jurafsky. 2014. How to ask for a favor: A case study on the success of altruistic requests. In *Proceedings of International Conference on Web and Social Media*.

Shlomo Argamon, Moshe Koppel, James W Pennebaker, and Jonathan Schler. 2007. Mining the blogosphere: Age, gender and the varieties of self-expression. *First Monday*, 12(9).

David Bamman, Jacob Eisenstein, and Tyler Schnoebelen. 2014. Gender identity and lexical variation in social media. *Journal of Sociolinguistics*, 18(2):135–160.

Marc Brysbaert, Amy Beth Warriner, and Victor Kuperman. 2014. Concreteness ratings for 40 thousand generally known english word lemmas. *Behavior research methods*, 46(3):904–911.

John D Burger, John Henderson, George Kim, and Guido Zarrella. 2011. Discriminating gender on twitter. In *Proceedings of the conference on empirical methods in natural language processing*, pages 1301–1309. Association for Computational Linguistics.

Judith Butler. 1988. Performative acts and gender constitution: An essay in phenomenology and feminist theory. *Theatre journal*, 40(4):519–531.

Jordan Carpenter, Daniel Preotiuc-Pietro, Lucie Flekova, Salvatore Giorgi, Courtney Hagan, Margaret L Kern, Anneke EK Buffone, Lyle Ungar, and Martin EP Seligman. 2017. Real men dont say cute using automatic language analysis to isolate inaccurate aspects of stereotypes. *Social Psychological and Personality Science*, 8(3):310–322.

Elizabeth L Cralley and Janet B Ruscher. 2005. Lady, girl, female, or woman: Sexism and cognitive busyness predict use of gender-biased nouns. *Journal of Language and Social Psychology*, 24(3):300–314.

Cristian Danescu-Niculescu-Mizil, Robert West, Dan Jurafsky, Jure Leskovec, and Christopher Potts. 2013. No country for old members: User lifecycle and linguistic change in online communities. In *Proceedings of the 22nd international conference on World Wide Web*, pages 307–318. ACM.

Srayan Datta, Chanda Phelan, and Eytan Adar. 2017. Identifying misaligned inter-group links and communities. *Proc. ACM Hum.-Comput. Interact.*, 1(CSCW):37:1–37:23.

Penelope Eckert. 1989. *Jocks and burnouts: Social categories and identity in the high school.* Teachers College Press.

Penelope Eckert. 2006. Communities of practice. *Encyclopedia of language and linguistics*, 2(2006):683–685.

Penelope Eckert. 2012. Three waves of variation study: The emergence of meaning in the study of sociolinguistic variation. *Annual review of Anthropology*, 41:87–100.

Penelope Eckert and Sally McConnell-Ginet. 1992. Think practically and look locally: Language and gender as community-based practice. *Annual review of anthropology*, 21(1):461–488.

Ann Friedman. 2013. Hey "ladies": The unlikely revival of a fusty old label. *The New Republic.*

Nathan Halko, Per-Gunnar Martinsson, and Joel A Tropp. 2011. Finding structure with randomness: Probabilistic algorithms for constructing approximate matrix decompositions. *SIAM review*, 53(2):217–288.

Kira Hall. 2009. Boys talk: Hindi, moustaches and masculinity in new delhi. In *Gender and spoken interaction*, pages 139–162. Springer.

William L Hamilton, Kevin Clark, Jure Leskovec, and Dan Jurafsky. 2016. Inducing domain-specific sentiment lexicons from unlabeled corpora. In *Proceedings of the 2016 Conference on Empirical Methods in Natural Language Processing*, pages 595–605.

William L Hamilton, Justine Zhang, Cristian Danescu-Niculescu-Mizil, Dan Jurafsky, and Jure Leskovec. 2017. Loyalty in online communities. In *Proceedings of the International AAAI Conference on Weblogs and Social Media*, volume 2017, page 540. NIH Public Access.

Susan C Herring and John C Paolillo. 2006. Gender and genre variation in weblogs. *Journal of Sociolinguistics*, 10(4):439–459.

Aaron Jaech, Victoria Zayats, Hao Fang, Mari Ostendorf, and Hannaneh Hajishirzi. 2015. Talking to the crowd: What do people react to in online discussions? In *Proceedings of the 2015 Conference on Empirical Methods in Natural Language Processing*, pages 2026–2031.

Srijan Kumar, William L Hamilton, Jure Leskovec, and Dan Jurafsky. 2018. Community interaction and conflict on the web. In *Proceedings of the 2018 World Wide Web Conference on World Wide Web*, pages 933–943. International World Wide Web Conferences Steering Committee.

Omer Levy, Yoav Goldberg, and Ido Dagan. 2015. Improving distributional similarity with lessons learned from word embeddings. *Transactions of the Association for Computational Linguistics*, 3:211–225.

Trevor Martin. 2017. community2vec: Vector representations of online communities encode semantic relationships. In *Proceedings of the Second Workshop on NLP and Computational Social Science*, pages 27–31.

Adrienne Massanari. 2017. # gamergate and the fappening: How reddits algorithm, governance, and culture support toxic technocultures. *New Media & Society*, 19(3):329–346.

Norma Mendoza-Denton. 1996. muy macha: Gender and ideology in gang-girls discourse about makeup. *Ethnos*, 61(1-2):47–63.

Saif M Mohammad and Peter D Turney. 2010. Emotions evoked by common words and phrases: Using mechanical turk to create an emotion lexicon. In *Proceedings of the NAACL HLT 2010 workshop on computational approaches to analysis and generation of emotion in text*, pages 26–34. Association for Computational Linguistics.

Anthony Mulac, James J Bradac, and Pamela Gibbons. 2001. Empirical support for the gender-as-culture hypothesis: An intercultural analysis of male/female language differences. *Human Communication Research*, 27(1):121–152.

Edward Newell, David Jurgens, Haji Mohammad Saleem, Hardik Vala, Jad Sassine, Caitrin Armstrong, and Derek Ruths. 2016. User migration in online social networks: A case study on reddit during a period of community unrest. In *Tenth International AAAI Conference on Web and Social Media*.

Matthew L Newman, Carla J Groom, Lori D Handelman, and James W Pennebaker. 2008. Gender differences in language use: An analysis of 14,000 text samples. *Discourse Processes*, 45(3):211–236.

Dong Nguyen, Dolf Trieschnigg, A Seza Doğruöz, Rilana Gravel, Mariët Theune, Theo Meder, and Franciska De Jong. 2014. Why gender and age prediction from tweets is hard: Lessons from a crowdsourcing experiment. In *Proceedings of COLING 2014, the 25th International Conference on Computational Linguistics: Technical Papers*, pages 1950–1961.

Umashanthi Pavalanathan, Jim Fitzpatrick, Scott Kiesling, and Jacob Eisenstein. 2017. A multidimensional lexicon for interpersonal stancetaking. In *Proceedings of the 55th Annual Meeting of the Association for Computational Linguistics (Volume 1: Long Papers)*, volume 1, pages 884–895.

F. Pedregosa, G. Varoquaux, A. Gramfort, V. Michel, B. Thirion, O. Grisel, M. Blondel, P. Prettenhofer, R. Weiss, V. Dubourg, J. Vanderplas, A. Passos, D. Cournapeau, M. Brucher, M. Perrot, and

E. Duchesnay. 2011. Scikit-learn: Machine learning in Python. *Journal of Machine Learning Research*, 12:2825–2830.

Delip Rao, David Yarowsky, Abhishek Shreevats, and Manaswi Gupta. 2010. Classifying latent user attributes in twitter. In *Proceedings of the 2nd international workshop on Search and mining user-generated contents*, pages 37–44. ACM.

Sascha Rothe, Sebastian Ebert, and Hinrich Schütze. 2016. Ultradense word embeddings by orthogonal transformation. In *Proceedings of the 2016 Conference of the North American Chapter of the Association for Computational Linguistics: Human Language Technologies*, pages 767–777.

Jonathan Schler. 2006. Effects of age and gender on blogging. In *Proceedings of AAAI Symposium on Computational Approaches for Analyzing Weblogs, 2006*, pages 199–205.

Nguyen Xuan Vinh, Julien Epps, and James Bailey. 2010. Information theoretic measures for clusterings comparison: Variants, properties, normalization and correction for chance. *Journal of Machine Learning Research*, 11(Oct):2837–2854.

Svitlana Volkova, Theresa Wilson, and David Yarowsky. 2013. Exploring demographic language variations to improve multilingual sentiment analysis in social media. In *Proceedings of the 2013 Conference on Empirical Methods in Natural Language Processing*, pages 1815–1827.

Amy Beth Warriner, Victor Kuperman, and Marc Brysbaert. 2013. Norms of valence, arousal, and dominance for 13,915 english lemmas. *Behavior research methods*, 45(4):1191–1207.

Andrew D Wong. 2005. The reappropriation of tongzhi. *Language in society*, 34(5):763–793.

Yi Yang and Jacob Eisenstein. 2015. Putting things in context: Community-specific embedding projections for sentiment analysis. *Arxiv-Social Media Intelligence*.

Justine Zhang, William L Hamilton, Cristian Danescu-Niculescu-Mizil, Dan Jurafsky, and Jure Leskovec. 2017. Community identity and user engagement in a multi-community landscape. In *Proceedings of the... International AAAI Conference on Weblogs and Social Media. International AAAI Conference on Weblogs and Social Media*, volume 2017, page 377. NIH Public Access.

On the difficulty of a distributional semantics of spoken language

Grzegorz Chrupała
Tilburg University
`g.chrupala@uvt.nl`

Lieke Gelderloos
Tilburg University
`l.j.gelderloos@uvt.nl`

Ákos Kádár
Tilburg University
`a.kadar@uvt.nl`

Afra Alishahi
Tilburg University
`a.alishahi@uvt.nl`

Abstract

In the domain of unsupervised learning most work on speech has focused on discovering low-level constructs such as phoneme inventories or word-like units. In contrast, for written language, where there is a large body of work on unsupervised induction of semantic representations of words, whole sentences and longer texts. In this study we examine the challenges of adapting these approaches from written to spoken language. We conjecture that unsupervised learning of the semantics of spoken language becomes feasible if we abstract from the surface variability. We simulate this setting with a dataset of utterances spoken by a realistic but uniform synthetic voice. We evaluate two simple unsupervised models which, to varying degrees of success, learn semantic representations of speech fragments. Finally we present inconclusive results on human speech, and discuss the challenges inherent in learning distributional semantic representations on unrestricted natural spoken language.

1 Introduction

In the realm of NLP for written language, unsupervised approaches to inducing semantic representations of words have a long pedigree and a history of substantial success (Landauer et al., 1998; Blei et al., 2003; Mikolov et al., 2013b). The core idea behind these models is to build word representations that can predict their surrounding context. In search for similarly generic and versatile representations of whole sentences, various composition operators have been applied on word representations (e.g. Socher et al., 2013; Kalchbrenner et al., 2014; Kim, 2014; Zhao et al., 2015). Alternatively, sentence representations are induced via

the objective to predict the surrounding sentences (e.g. Le and Mikolov, 2014; Kiros et al., 2015; Arora et al., 2016; Jernite et al., 2017; Logeswaran and Lee, 2018). Such representations capture aspects of the meaning of the encoded sentences, which can be used in a variety of tasks such as semantic entailment or text understanding.

In the case of spoken language, unsupervised methods usually focus on discovering relatively low-level constructs such as phoneme inventories or word-like units. This is mainly due to the fact that the key insight from distributional semantics that "you shall know the word by the company it keeps" (Firth, 1957) is hopelessly confounded in the case of spoken language. In text two words are considered semantically similar if they co-occur with similar neighbors. However, speech segments which occur in the same utterance or situation often have many other features in addition to similar meaning, such as being uttered by the same speaker or accompanied by similar ambient noise.

In this study we show that if we can abstract away from speaker and background noise, we can effectively capture semantic characteristics of spoken utterances in an unsupervised way. We present SegMatch, a model trained to match segments of the same utterance. SegMatch utterance encodings are compared to those in Audio2Vec, which is trained to decode the context that surrounds an utterance. To investigate whether our representations capture semantics, we evaluate on speech and vision datasets where photographic images are paired with spoken descriptions. Our experiments show that for a single synthetic voice, a simple model trained only on image captions can capture pairwise similarities that correlate with those in the visual space.

Proceedings of the Society for Computation in Linguistics (SCiL) 2019, pages 167-173.
New York City, New York, January 3-6, 2019

Furthermore we discuss the factors preventing effective learning in datasets with multiple human speakers: these include confounds between semantic and situational factors as well as artifacts in the datasets.

2   Related work

Studies of unsupervised learning from speech typically aim to discover the phonemic or lexical building blocks of the language signal. Park and Glass (2008) show that words and phrase units in continuous speech can be discovered using algorithms based on dynamic time warping. van den Oord et al. (2017) introduce a Vector Quantised-Variational AutoEncoder model, in which a convolutional encoder trained on raw audio data gives discrete encodings that are closely related to phonemes. Recently several unsupervised speech recognition methods were proposed that segment speech and cluster the resulting word-like segments (Kamper et al., 2017a) or encode them into segment embeddings containing phonetic information (Wang et al., 2018). Scharenborg et al. (2018) show that word and phrase units arise as a by-product in end-to-end tasks such as speech-to-speech translation. In the current work, the aim is to directly extract semantic, rather than word form information from speech.

Semantic information encoded in speech is used in studies that ground speech to the visual context. Datasets of images paired with spoken captions can be used to train multimodal models that extract visually salient semantic information from speech, without access to textual information (Harwath and Glass, 2015; Harwath et al., 2016; Kamper et al., 2017b; Chrupała et al., 2017; Alishahi et al., 2017; Harwath and Glass, 2017). This form of semantic supervision, through contextual information from another modality, has its limits: it can only help to learn to understand speech describing the here and now.

On the other hand, the success of word embeddings derived by distributional semantic principles has shown how rich the semantic information within the structure of language itself is. Semantic representations of words obtained through Latent Semantic Analysis have proven to closely resemble human semantic knowledge (Blei et al., 2003; Landauer et al., 1998). Word2vec models produce semantically rich word embeddings by learning to predict the surrounding words in text (Mikolov

et al., 2013a,b) and this principle is extended to sentences in the Skip-thought model (Kiros et al., 2015) and several subsequent works (Arora et al., 2016; Jernite et al., 2017; Logeswaran and Lee, 2018).

In the realm of spoken language, in Chung and Glass (2017) the sequence-to-sequence Audio2vec model learns semantic embeddings for audio segments corresponding to words, by predicting the audio segments around it. Chung and Glass (2018) further experiment with this model and rename it to Speech2vec. Chen et al. (2018) train semantic word embeddings from word-segmented speech as part of their method of training an ASR system from non-aligned speech and text. These works are closely related to our current study, but crucially, unlike them we do *not* assume that speech is already segmented into discrete words.

3   Models

3.1   Encoder

All the models in this section use the same encoder architecture. The encoder is loosely based on the architecture of Chrupała et al. (2017), i.e. it consists of a 1-dimensional convolutional layer which subsamples the input, followed by a stack of recurrent layers, followed by a self-attention operator. Unlike Chrupała et al. (2017) we use GRU layers (Chung et al., 2014) instead of RHN layers (Zilly et al., 2017), and do not implement residual connections. These modifications are made in order to exploit the fast native CUDNN implementation of a GRU stack and thus speed up experimentation in this exploratory stage of our research. The encoder Enc is defined as follows:

$$\mathrm{Enc}(\mathbf{x}) = \mathrm{unit}(\mathrm{Attn}(\mathrm{GRU}_\ell(\mathrm{Conv}_{\mathrm{s,d,z}}(\mathbf{x}))))$$

$$(1)$$

where Conv is a convolutional layer with length s, d channels, and stride z, GRU_ℓ is a stack of ℓ GRU layers, Attn is self-attention and unit is L2-normalization. The self-attention operator computes a weighted sum of the RNN activations at all timesteps:

$$\mathrm{Attn}(\mathbf{x}) = \sum_t \alpha_t \mathbf{x}_t \qquad (2)$$

where the weights α_t are determined by an MLP with learned parameters $\mathbf{U}$ and $\mathbf{W}$, and passed through the timewise softmax function:

$$\alpha_t = \frac{\exp(\mathbf{U} \tanh(\mathbf{W}\mathbf{x}_t))}{\sum_{t'} \exp(\mathbf{U} \tanh(\mathbf{W}\mathbf{x}_{t'}))} \tag{3}$$

3.2 Audio2vec

Firstly we define a model inspired by Chung and Glass (2017) which uses the multilayer GRU encoder described above, and a single-layer GRU decoder, conditioned on the output of the encoder.

The model of Chung and Glass (2017) works on word-segmented speech: the encoder encodes the middle word of a five word sequence, and the decoder decodes each of the surrounding words. Similarly, the Skip-thought model of (Kiros et al., 2015) works with a sequence of three sentences, encoding the middle one and decoding the previous and next one. In our fully unsupervised setup we do not have access to word segmentation, and thus our Audio2vec models work with arbitrary speech segments. We split each utterance into three equal sized chunks: the model encodes the middle one, and decodes the first and third one.

The decoder predicts the MFCC features at time $t + 1$ based on the state of the hidden layer at time t. From reading Chung and Glass (2017) it is not clear whether in addition to the hidden state their decoder also receives the MFCC frame at t as input. We thus implemented two versions, one with and one without this input.

Audio2vec-C The decoder receives the output of the encoder as the initial state of the hidden layer, and the frame at t as input as it predicts the next frame at $t + 1$.

$$\hat{\mathbf{x}}_{t+1}^{\text{first}} = \mathbf{F}\mathbf{h}_t \tag{4}$$

$$\mathbf{h}_t = \text{gru}(\mathbf{h}_{t-1}, \mathbf{x}_t^{\text{first}}) \tag{5}$$

$$\mathbf{h}_0 = \text{Enc}\left(\mathbf{x}^{\text{middle}}\right) \tag{6}$$

where $\mathbf{x}_t^{\text{first}}$ are the MFCC features of the previous chunk at time t, $\hat{\mathbf{x}}_{t+1}^{\text{first}}$ are the predicted features at the next time step, $\mathbf{F}$ is a learned projection matrix, $\text{gru}(\cdot, \cdot)$ is a single step of the GRU recurrence, and $\mathbf{x}^{\text{middle}}$ is the sequence of the MFCC features of the input. The decoder for the third chunk $\mathbf{x}^{\text{third}}$ is defined in the same way.

Audio2vec-U The decoder receives the output of the encoder as the input at each time step, but does not have access to the frame at t.

$$\hat{\mathbf{x}}_{t+1}^{\text{first}} = \mathbf{F}\mathbf{h}_t \tag{7}$$

$$\mathbf{h}_t = \text{gru}(\mathbf{h}_{t-1}, \text{Enc}(\mathbf{x}^{\text{middle}})) \tag{8}$$

In this version $\mathbf{h}_0$ is a learned parameter. There are two separate decoders: i.e. the weights of the decoder for the first chunk and for the third chunk are *not* shared.

For both versions of **Audio2vec** the loss function is the Mean Squared Error.

3.3 SegMatch

This model works with segments of utterances also: we split each utterance approximately in half, while erasing a short portion in the center in order to prevent the model from finding trivial solutions based on matching local patterns at the edges of the segments. The encoder is as described above. After encoding the segments, we project the initial and final segments via separate learned projection matrices:

$$\mathbf{b} = \mathbf{B}\text{Enc}(\mathbf{x}_{0:m}) \tag{9}$$

$$\mathbf{e} = \mathbf{E}\text{Enc}(\mathbf{x}_{m+k:n}) \tag{10}$$

where $\mathbf{x}_{0:n}$ is the sequence of MFCC frames for an utterance, k is the size of the erased segment, $\text{Enc}(\cdot)$ is the encoder and $\mathbf{B}$ and $\mathbf{E}$ are the projection matrices for the beginning and end segment respectively. That is, there is a single shared encoder for both types of speech segments (beginning and end), but the projections are separate. There is no decoding, but rather the model learns to match encoded segments from the same utterance and distinguish them from encoded segments from different utterances within the same mini-batch. The loss function is similar to the one for matching spoken utterances to images in Chrupała et al. (2017), with the difference that here we are matching utterance segments to each other:

$$\mathcal{L} = \sum_{\mathbf{b},\mathbf{e}} \left(\sum_{\mathbf{b}'} \max[0, \alpha + d(\mathbf{b}, \mathbf{e}) - d(\mathbf{b}', \mathbf{e})] \right.$$
$$\left. + \sum_{\mathbf{e}'} \max[0, \alpha + d(\mathbf{b}, \mathbf{e}) - d(\mathbf{b}, \mathbf{e}')] \right) \tag{11}$$

where $(\mathbf{b}, \mathbf{e})$ are beginning and end segments from the same utterance, and $(\mathbf{b}', \mathbf{e})$ and $(\mathbf{b}, \mathbf{e}')$ are beginning and end segments from two different utterances within a batch, while $d(\cdot, \cdot)$ is the cosine distance between encoded segments. The loss function thus attempts to make the cosine distance between encodings of matching segments less than the distance between encodings of mismatching segment pairs, by a margin.

Note that the specific way we segment speech is not a crucial component of either of the models: it is mostly driven by the fact that we run our experiments on speech and vision datasets, where speech consists of isolated utterances. For data consisting of longer narratives, or dialogs, we could use different segmentation schemes.

4 Experimental setup

4.1 Datasets

In order to facilitate evaluation of the semantic aspect of the learned representations, we work with speech and vision datasets, which couple photographic images with their spoken descriptions. Thanks to the structure of these data we can use the evaluation metrics detailed in section 4.2.

Synthetically spoken COCO This dataset was created by Chrupała et al. (2017), based on the original COCO dataset (Lin et al., 2014), using the Google TTS API. The captions are spoken by a single synthetic voice, which is realistic but simpler than human speakers, lacking variability and ambient noise. There are 300,000 images, each with five captions. Five thousand images each are held out for validation and test.

Flickr8k Audio Caption Corpus This dataset (Harwath and Glass, 2015) contains the captions in the original Flickr8K corpus (Hodosh et al., 2013) read aloud by crowdworkers. There are 8,000 images, each image with five descriptions. One thousand images are held out for validation, and another one thousand for the test set.

Places Audio Caption Corpus This dataset was collected by (Harwath et al., 2016) using crowdworkers. Here each image is described by a single spontaneously spoken caption. There are 214,585 training images, and 1000 validation images (there are no separate test data).

4.2 Evaluation metrics

We evaluate the quality of the learned semantic speech representations according to the following criteria.

Paraphrase retrieval For the Synthetically Spoken COCO dataset as well as for the Flickr8k Audio Caption Corpus each image is described via five independent spoken captions. Thus captions describing the same image are effectively paraphrases of each other. This structure of the data allows us to use a paraphrasing retrieval task as a measure of the semantic quality of the learned speech embeddings. We encode each of the spoken utterances in the validation data, and rank the others according to the cosine similarity. We then measure: (a) Median rank of the top-ranked paraphrase; and (b) recall@K: the proportion of paraphrases among K top-ranked utterances, for $K \in \{1, 5, 10\}$.

Representational similarity to image space Representational similarity analysis (RSA) is a way of evaluating how pairwise similarities between objects are correlated in two object representation spaces (Kriegeskorte et al., 2008). Here we compare cosine similarities among encoded utterances versus cosine similarities among vector representations of images. Specifically, we create two pairwise $N \times N$ similarity matrices: (a) among encoded utterances from the validation data, and (b) among images corresponding to each utterance in (a). Note that since there are five descriptions per image, each image is replicated five times in matrix (b). We then take the upper triangulars of these matrices (excluding the diagonal) and compute Pearson's correlation coefficient between them. The image features for this evaluation are obtained from the final fully connected layer of VGG-16 (Simonyan and Zisserman, 2014) pre-trained on Imagenet (Russakovsky et al., 2014) and consist of 4096 dimensions.

4.3 Settings

We preprocess the audio by extracting 12-dimensional mel-frequency cepstral coefficients (MFCC) plus log of the total energy. We use 25 milisecond windows, sampled every 10 miliseconds. Audio2vec and SegMatch models are trained for a maximum of 15 epochs with Adam, with learning rate 0.0002, and gradient clipping at 2.0. SegMatch uses margin $\alpha = 0.2$. The encoder GRU has 5 layers of 512 units. The convolutional layer has 64 channels, size of 6 and stride 3. The hidden layer of the attention MLP is 512. The GRU of the Audio2vec decoder has 512 hidden units; the size of the output of the projections $\mathbf{B}$ and $\mathbf{E}$ in SegMatch is also 512 units. For SegMatch the size of the erased center portion of the utterance is 30 frames. We apply early stopping and report all the results of each model after the epoch for which it scored best on recall@10. When applying SegMatch on human data, each mini-batch includes utterances spoken only by one speaker: this is in order to discourage the model from encoding speaker-specific features.

5 Results

5.1 Synthetic speech

Table 1 shows the evaluation results on synthetic speech. Representations learned by Audio2vec and SegMatch are compared to the performance of random vectors, mean MFCC vectors, as well as visually supervised representations (VGS, model from Chrupała et al. (2017)). Audio2vec works better than chance and mean MFCC on paraphrase retrieval, but does not correlate with the visual space. SegMatch works much better than Audio2vec according to both criteria. It does not come close to VGS on paraphrase retrieval, but it does correlate with the visual modality even better.

5.2 Human speech

Places This dataset only features a single caption per image and thus we only evaluate according to RSA: with both SegMatch and Audio2vec we found the correlations to be zero.

Flickr8K Initial experiments with Flickr8K were similarly unsuccessful. Analysis of the learned SegMatch representations revealed that in spite of partitioning the data by speaker for training, speaker identity can be decoded from them.

Enforcing speaker invariance We thus implemented a version of SegMatch where an auxiliary speaker classifier is connected to the encoder via a gradient reversal operator (Ganin and Lempitsky, 2015). This architecture optimizes the main loss, while at the same time pushing the encoder to remove information about speaker identity from the representation it outputs. In preliminary experiments we saw that this addition was able to prevent speaker identity from being encoded in the representations during the first few epochs of training. Evaluating this speaker-invariant representation gave contradictory results, shown in Table 2: very good scores on paraphrase retrieval, but zero correlation with visual space.

Further analysis showed that there seems to be an artifact in the Flickr8K data where spoken captions belonging to consecutively numbered images share some characteristics, even though the images do not. As a side effect, this causes captions belonging to the same image to also share

some features, independent of their semantic content, leading to high paraphrasing scores. The artifact may be due to changes in data collection procedure which affected some aspect of the captions in ways which correlate with their sequential ordering in the dataset.

If we treat the image ID number as a regression target, and the first two principal components of the SegMatch representation of one of its captions as the predictors, we can account for about 12% of the holdout variance in IDs using a non-linear model (using either K-Nearest Neighbors or Random Forest). This effect disappears if we arbitrarily relabel images.

6 Conclusion

For synthetic speech the SegMatch approach to inducing utterance embeddings shows very promising performance. Likewise, previous work has shown some success with word-segmented speech. There remain challenges in carrying over these results to natural, unsegmented speech. Word segmentation is a highly non-trivial research problem in itself and the variability of spoken language is a serious and intractable confounding factor.

Even when controlling for speaker identity there are still superficial features of the speech signal which make it easy for the model to ignore the semantic content. Some of these may be due to artifacts in datasets and thus care is needed when evaluating unsupervised models of spoken language: for example use of multiple evaluation criteria may help spot spurious results. In spite of these challenges, in future we want to further explore the effectiveness of enforcing desired invariances via auxiliary classifiers with gradient reversal.

References

Afra Alishahi, Marie Barking, and Grzegorz Chrupała. 2017. Encoding of phonology in a recurrent neural model of grounded speech. In *Proceedings of the 21st Conference on Computational Natural Language Learning (CoNLL 2017)*, pages 368–378. Association for Computational Linguistics.

Sanjeev Arora, Yingyu Liang, and Tengyu Ma. 2016. A simple but tough-to-beat baseline for sentence embeddings. In *ICLR*.

David M Blei, Andrew Y Ng, and Michael I Jordan. 2003. Latent dirichlet allocation. *Journal of machine Learning research*, 3(Jan):993–1022.

	Recall@10 (%)	Median rank	RSA$_{image}$
VGS	27	6	0.4
SegMatch	**10**	**37**	**0.5**
Audio2vec-U	5	105	0.0
Audio2vec-C	2	647	0.0
Mean MFCC	1	1,414	0.0
Chance	0	3,955	0.0

Table 1: Results on Synthetically Spoken COCO. The row labeled VGS is the visually supervised model from Chrupała et al. (2017).

	Recall@10 (%)	Median rank	RSA$_{image}$
VGS	15	17	0.2
SegMatch	12	17	0.0
Mean MFCC	0	711	0.0

Table 2: Results on Flickr8K. The row labeled VGS is the visually supervised model from Chrupała et al. (2017).

Yi-Chen Chen, Chia-Hao Shen, Sung-Feng Huang, and Hung-yi Lee. 2018. Towards unsupervised automatic speech recognition trained by unaligned speech and text only. *arXiv preprint arXiv:1803.10952*.

Grzegorz Chrupała, Lieke Gelderloos, and Afra Alishahi. 2017. Representations of language in a model of visually grounded speech signal. In *Proceedings of the 55th Annual Meeting of the Association for Computational Linguistics*.

Junyoung Chung, Caglar Gulcehre, KyungHyun Cho, and Yoshua Bengio. 2014. Empirical evaluation of gated recurrent neural networks on sequence modeling. In *NIPS 2014 Deep Learning and Representation Learning Workshop*.

Yu-An Chung and James Glass. 2017. Learning word embeddings from speech. In *NIPS ML4Audio Workshop*.

Yu-An Chung and James Glass. 2018. Speech2vec: A sequence-to-sequence framework for learning word embeddings from speech. *arXiv preprint arXiv:1803.08976*.

John Rupert Firth. 1957. A synopsis of linguistic theory 1930-1955, volume 1952-59. The Philological Society.

Yaroslav Ganin and Victor Lempitsky. 2015. Unsupervised domain adaptation by backpropagation. In *Proceedings of the 32nd International Conference on Machine Learning*, volume 37 of *Proceedings of Machine Learning Research*, pages 1180–1189, Lille, France. PMLR.

David Harwath and James Glass. 2015. Deep multimodal semantic embeddings for speech and images. In *IEEE Automatic Speech Recognition and Understanding Workshop*.

David Harwath and James R Glass. 2017. Learning word-like units from joint audio-visual analysis. *arXiv preprint arXiv:1701.07481*.

David Harwath, Antonio Torralba, and James Glass. 2016. Unsupervised learning of spoken language with visual context. In *Advances in Neural Information Processing Systems*, pages 1858–1866.

Micah Hodosh, Peter Young, and Julia Hockenmaier. 2013. Framing image description as a ranking task: Data, models and evaluation metrics. *Journal of Artificial Intelligence Research*, 47:853–899.

Yacine Jernite, Samuel R Bowman, and David Sontag. 2017. Discourse-based objectives for fast unsupervised sentence representation learning. *arXiv preprint arXiv:1705.00557*.

Nal Kalchbrenner, Edward Grefenstette, and Phil Blunsom. 2014. A convolutional neural network for modelling sentences. *arXiv preprint arXiv:1404.2188*.

Herman Kamper, Aren Jansen, and Sharon Goldwater. 2017a. A segmental framework for fully-unsupervised large-vocabulary speech recognition. *Computer Speech & Language*, 46:154–174.

Herman Kamper, Shane Settle, Gregory Shakhnarovich, and Karen Livescu. 2017b. Visually grounded learning of keyword prediction from untranscribed speech. In *Proc. Interspeech 2017*, pages 3677–3681.

Yoon Kim. 2014. Convolutional neural networks for sentence classification. *arXiv preprint arXiv:1408.5882*.

Ryan Kiros, Yukun Zhu, Ruslan R Salakhutdinov, Richard Zemel, Raquel Urtasun, Antonio Torralba, and Sanja Fidler. 2015. Skip-thought vectors. In *Advances in Neural Information Processing Systems*, pages 3276–3284.

Nikolaus Kriegeskorte, Marieke Mur, and Peter A Bandettini. 2008. Representational similarity analysis-connecting the branches of systems neuroscience. *Frontiers in systems neuroscience*, 2:4.

Thomas K Landauer, Peter W Foltz, and Darrell Laham. 1998. An introduction to latent semantic analysis. *Discourse processes*, 25(2-3):259–284.

Quoc Le and Tomas Mikolov. 2014. Distributed representations of sentences and documents. In *International Conference on Machine Learning*, pages 1188–1196.

Tsung-Yi Lin, Michael Maire, Serge Belongie, James Hays, Pietro Perona, Deva Ramanan, Piotr Dollár, and C Lawrence Zitnick. 2014. Microsoft COCO: Common objects in context. In *Computer Vision–ECCV 2014*, pages 740–755. Springer.

Lajanugen Logeswaran and Honglak Lee. 2018. An efficient framework for learning sentence representations. *arXiv preprint arXiv:1803.02893*.

Tomas Mikolov, Kai Chen, Greg Corrado, and Jeffrey Dean. 2013a. Efficient estimation of word representations in vector space. *arXiv preprint arXiv:1301.3781*.

Tomas Mikolov, Ilya Sutskever, Kai Chen, Greg S Corrado, and Jeff Dean. 2013b. Distributed representations of words and phrases and their compositionality. In *Advances in Neural Information Processing Systems*, pages 3111–3119.

Aäron van den Oord, Oriol Vinyals, and Koray Kavukcuoglu. 2017. Neural discrete representation learning. *CoRR*, abs/1711.00937.

Alex S Park and James R Glass. 2008. Unsupervised pattern discovery in speech. *IEEE Transactions on Audio, Speech, and Language Processing*, 16(1):186–197.

Olga Russakovsky, Jia Deng, Hao Su, Jonathan Krause, Sanjeev Satheesh, Sean Ma, Zhiheng Huang, Andrej Karpathy, Aditya Khosla, Michael Bernstein, Alexander C. Berg, and Li Fei-Fei. 2014. ImageNet large scale visual recognition challenge.

Odette Scharenborg, Laurent Besacier, Alan Black, Mark Hasegawa-Johnson, Florian Metze, Graham Neubig, Sebastian Stüker, Pierre Godard, Markus Müller, Lucas Ondel, et al. 2018. Linguistic unit discovery from multi-modal inputs in unwritten languages: Summary of the Speaking Rosetta JSALT 2017 workshop. *arXiv preprint arXiv:1802.05092*.

Karen Simonyan and Andrew Zisserman. 2014. Very deep convolutional networks for large-scale image recognition. *CoRR*, abs/1409.1556.

Richard Socher, Alex Perelygin, Jean Wu, Jason Chuang, Christopher D Manning, Andrew Ng, and Christopher Potts. 2013. Recursive deep models for semantic compositionality over a sentiment treebank. In *Proceedings of the 2013 conference on empirical methods in natural language processing*, pages 1631–1642.

Yu-Hsuan Wang, Hung-yi Lee, and Lin-shan Lee. 2018. Segmental audio word2vec: Representing utterances as sequences of vectors with applications in spoken term detection. In *2018 IEEE International Conference on Acoustics, Speech, and Signal Processing. Proceedings.*

Han Zhao, Zhengdong Lu, and Pascal Poupart. 2015. Self-adaptive hierarchical sentence model. In *IJCAI*, pages 4069–4076.

Julian Georg Zilly, Rupesh Kumar Srivastava, Jan Koutník, and Jürgen Schmidhuber. 2017. Recurrent highway networks. In *Proceedings of the 34th International Conference on Machine Learning*, volume 70 of *Proceedings of Machine Learning Research*, pages 4189–4198, International Convention Centre, Sydney, Australia. PMLR.

Distributional Effects of Gender Contrasts Across Categories

Timothee Mickus
Université Paris Diderot,
Laboratoire de
linguistique formelle

Olivier Bonami[*]
Université Paris Diderot,
Laboratoire de
linguistique formelle

Denis Paperno[*]
Loria (UMR7503)
CNRS
Université de Lorraine

Abstract

This paper proposes a methodology for comparing grammatical contrasts across categories with the tools of distributional semantics. After outlining why such a comparison is relevant to current theoretical work on gender and other morphosyntactic features, we present intrinsic and extrinsic predictability as instruments for analyzing semantic contrasts between pairs of words. We then apply our method to a dataset of gender pairs of French nouns and adjectives. We find that, while the distributional effect of gender is overall less predictable for nouns than for adjectives, it is heavily influenced by semantic properties of the adjectives.

1 Introduction

Grammatical gender (henceforth **g-gender**) is the phenomenon by which some languages group nouns in classes that exhibit different behavior in agreement, as in French une_F $petite_F$ *table* 'a small table' vs. un_M $petit_M$ *bureau* 'a small desk' (Hockett, 1958). In languages that have such a system, g-gender entertains a complex relationship with the social gender of referents (henceforth **s-gender**). On the one hand, the assignment of g-gender to nouns is often arbitrary. This is massively the case in languages like French, which have only two genders, and need to assign all inanimate nouns to either masculine or feminine. On the other hand, as Corbett (1991) highlights, all g-gender assignment systems have a semantic core, which usually entails lexicalizing different nouns for male and female referents, and assigning them to a matching g-gender (une_F $petite_F$ *fille* 'a small girl' vs. un_M $petit_M$ *garçon* 'a small boy') to masculine g-gender (Corbett, 2013). While this not a categorical rule (some nouns refer to either men or women

MAS	FEM	translation
candidat	*candidate*	'candidate'
marchand	*marchande*	'merchant'
infirmier	*infirmière*	'nurse'

Table 1: Sample pairs of human nouns

MAS	FEM	translation
délicat	*délicate*	'delicate'
grand	*grande*	'tall'
plénier	*plénière*	'plenary'

Table 2: Sample pairs of adjectives

while having a single gender, e.g. *personne* 'person' is always feminine), it is a very strong tendency.

In this paper we focus on pairs of morphologically-related nouns such as *candidat, candidate* where g-gender signals s-gender[1]; Table 1 exhibits a few relevant examples. The nature of the relationship between such nouns is an understudied but pressing issue for morphological theory. One position holds that *candidat* and *candidate* are two separate lexical items or *lexemes* (Matthews, 1974), related by derivational morphology (Zwanenburg, 1988). Under such a view, the relationship between the two nouns is similar to that between *danser* 'to dance' and *danseur* 'dancer'. The opposite view holds that *candidat* and *candidate* are forms of the same lexeme, related by inflectional morphology (Bonami and Boyé, in press). Under such a view, the relation between the a masculine and a feminine

---

[1]More precisely, Burnett and Bonami (in press(a); in press(b)) argue that g-gender carries social meaning rather than denotational meaning: using a feminine signals the speaker's perception of gender-stereotypical properties of the referent, leading to a situation where g-gender and s-gender will mostly match but differ in principled ways in some situations.

Olivier Bonami and Denis Paperno share senior authorship and are listed in alphabetic order.

Proceedings of the Society for Computation in Linguistics (SCiL) 2019, pages 174-184.
New York City, New York, January 3-6, 2019

noun (*candidat* vs. *candidate*) is similar to that between a singular and a plural noun (*candidat* vs. *candidats*) or a masculine and feminine forms of an adjective (*petit* and *petite*).

While these two views make different theoretical predictions on the nature of g-gender systems, they are remarkably difficult to tease apart empirically, given the elusiveness of the empirical divide between inflection and derivation (see e.g. Dressler 1989; Corbett 2010; Spencer 2013). In this paper we build on the well-known observation that inflection is semantically more regular than derivation (Robins, 1959; Matthews, 1974; Wurzel, 1989; Stump, 1998). While the meaning of the English 3SG verb form *dines* can readily be predicted from the meaning of its base form *dine*, the range of meanings of *diner* (including a particular kind of restaurant) is unpredictable. Bonami and Paperno (forthcoming) operationalize this idea by quantifying the diversity of semantic contrasts between pairs of morphologically-related words, and found, consistently with the theoretical literature, that pairs of words in derivational relations contrast in more diverse ways than pairs of word forms related by inflection.

It is not immediately obvious how diverse the semantic contrasts between pairs of gender-contrasting human nouns are. On the one hand, these are systematic enough that dictionaries do not list separate entries for masculine and feminine nouns. On the other hand, the existence of gender biases does lead to some interesting unpredictable differences. For instance, until very recently, masculine nouns referring to a stereotypically male occupation (e.g. *ambassadeur* 'ambassador') were often paired with a feminine noun (e.g. *ambassadrice*) referring to the wife of a man with that occupation, rather than to a woman with that occupation. While social change towards gender equality led to a change in usage in this particular case, the pervasiveness of gender biases leads one to expect differences in meaning or in usage between masculine vs. feminine nouns which have comparable meanings otherwise; cf. Bolukbasi et al. (2016), who highlighted the omnipresence of gender stereotypes in the distribution of English nouns.

This paper compares of the semantic import of g-gender contrasts in human nouns, as illustrated in Table 1, as opposed to g-gender contrasts in adjectives (Table 2). We ask two kinds of questions:

1. Are the semantic contrasts between human nouns **more diverse** than the contrasts between adjectives?

2. Are the semantic contrasts between human nouns **similar** to the semantic contrasts between adjectives?

Different views on the nature of g-gender lead to contradictory predictions as to the answers to questions 1 and 2. Under a naive view of g-gender assignment as completely arbitrary, we would expect to find semantic contrasts among neither nouns nor adjectives, leading to a negative answer to the first question and a positive answer to the second.[2] On the other hand, if g-gender on human nouns does signal s-gender of the referent, then the different takes on the relationship between paired nouns will lead to distinct expectation. If the relation is inflectional, we expect little or no difference between nouns and adjectives, and hence a negative answer to question 1. If it is derivational, following Bonami and Paperno (forthcoming), we expect more irregularity among nouns, and hence a positive answer to question 1. As to question 2, if g-gender signals s-gender, we expect similar contrasts for human nouns and adjectives that modify a nominal expression with human reference. However, we have no such expectation of similarity for those adjective instances that modify an inanimate nominal expression; hence the answer to question 2 should be different for different subsets of adjective usages.

The structure of the paper is as follows. Section 2 presents our new methodology to study morphological contrasts. In Section 3, we test the validity of our methodology by applying it to the study of grammatical gender contrasts in French human nouns (**HN**s) and adjectives and report what differences are observed between these categories. In Section 4, we probe the variability of contrast among adjectives, and in Section 5 we specifically investigate the differences between usages of adjectives to qualify human nouns (**HQA**s) vs. usages of adjectives to qualify non-human nouns (**NHQA**s). Our findings are summarized in Section 6.

---

[2]In a distributional operationalization, we expect small, erratic differences that cancel each other on average.

175

2 Methodology

2.1 Framework

In distributional semantics (Lenci, 2018), the meaning of a word is represented in the mathematical form of a vector computed on the basis of the word's contexts of occurrence in a large text corpus. Distributional vectors have a number of applications, ranging from predicting semantic relatedness judgments (Agirre et al., 2009) to initializing neural machine translation systems (Artetxe et al., 2017; Lample et al., 2017). Among the wide range of theoretical and practical applications, distributional semantic modeling has been used in two domains of direct relevance to the present study. First, on the basis of German data, Dye et al. study the relation of distributional similarity and g-gender assigment. Second, distributional methods have been used to characterize natural language morphology, including the issue of semantic transparency in derivation (Marelli and Baroni, 2015), analysis of morphological variation (Varvara, 2017), as well as the nature of the inflectional and derivational relations (Bonami and Paperno, forthcoming).

Our method is closely related to the latter work, and is based on two assumptions. First, following Mikolov et al.'s (2013b) model for solving proportional semantic analogy, we assume that a semantic contrast between two words is represented by the shift between the corresponding word vectors, so that words in identical relations are expected to have similar shifts[3]. The second assumption is that the semantics of a morphological relation can be approached by averaging vector differences for multiple word pairs in the relation. This has the double benefit of cancelling out some of the noise inherent in distributional vectors and evening out variation in the contrast between pairs of words entering the same relation.

Other authors have stressed that some relations were not accurately represented using vector shifts. For instance, Gladkova et al. (2016) have highlighted that "derivational and lexicographic relations remain a major challenge"; Levy and Goldberg (2014) and Linzen (2016) both stress that simple additive models do not suffice to model

relations. However, we do expect that even if a linear shift is an imperfect approximation of the relation in a distributional vector space, the regularity of such an approximation still corresponds to the semantic regularity of a specific relation. Therefore we do not make any strong claim regarding the correct representation of a relation in a DSM, but we do assume that the more regular a relation is, the more akin to a linear function – *ie.* a vector offset – its representation will be. More generally, the aim of this work is not to discuss how to accurately capture lexical relations between words, but rather to assess the relative regularity of different relations.

Therefore, although we use an evaluation setup similar to Mikolov et al.'s, our goal here is not to solve the propositional analogy task, but to analyze and assess the predictability of different relations. Hence, we emphasize that we mention intrinsic and extrinsic 'predictions' of word vector values only for the sake of convenience, which is also the reason why we do not employ various improvements on the vector shift method proposed in the literature such as the multiplicative method of Levy and Goldberg (2014), and stick to the simplest, most transparent option suitable for our purposes. Likewise, as we are not attempting to solve the analogy task but merely measuring the relative regularity of different relations, we do not report predictive strength.

2.2 Experimental Procedure

The framework and assumptions we adopt naturally dictate how one can predict the vector of a word from information about a related word. The prediction is based on the computation of the mean shift vector for a morphological relation, as illustrated in Figures 1 and 2. First, we compute the difference between the vectors representing each pair of related words, e.g. $\vec{candidate} - \vec{candidat}$; these **shift vectors** are shown in red for adjectives and in blue for nouns in Figure 1. A shift vector can be seen as a functional representation of the semantic contrast that holds between two words. Second, for each morphological relation, we compute the average of all shift vectors. This gives rise to the mean shift vectors $\vec{ms}_A$ for adjective pairs and $\vec{ms}_N$ for noun pairs in Figure 2. The mean shift vectors thus represent the average semantic contrast between pairs of words in the relation.

The next step is to use these mean shift vectors

---

[3]The utility of vector shifts as inputs to word relation classification –Jameel et al. (2018) showed that difference vectors achieve a performance just slightly lower than specialized representations learned for this task– further confirms that, to some extent, they can be used to represent lexical relations.

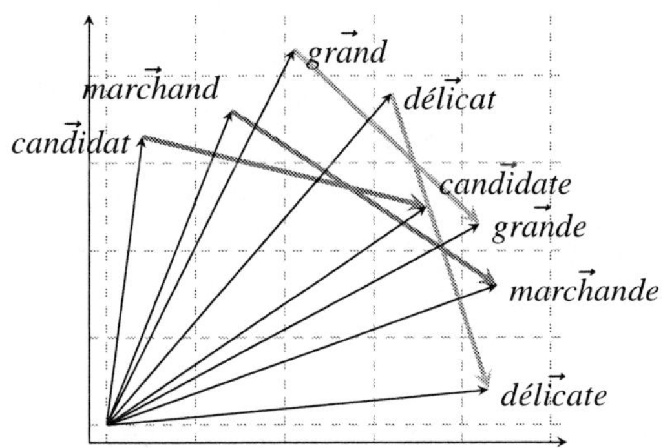

Figure 1: G-gender alternations

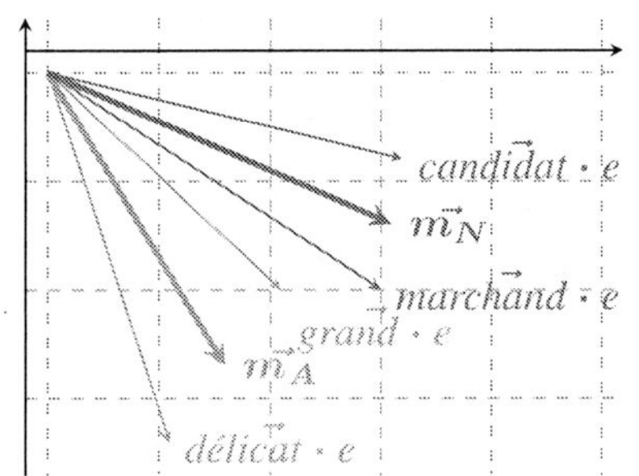

Figure 2: Mean shifts for the two processes

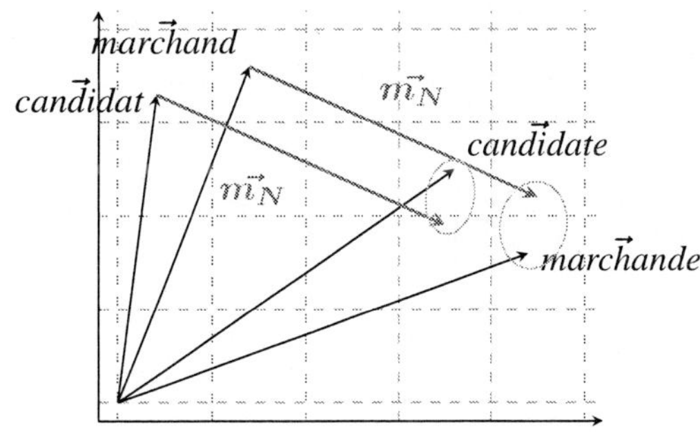

Figure 3: Intrinsic predictions for HNs

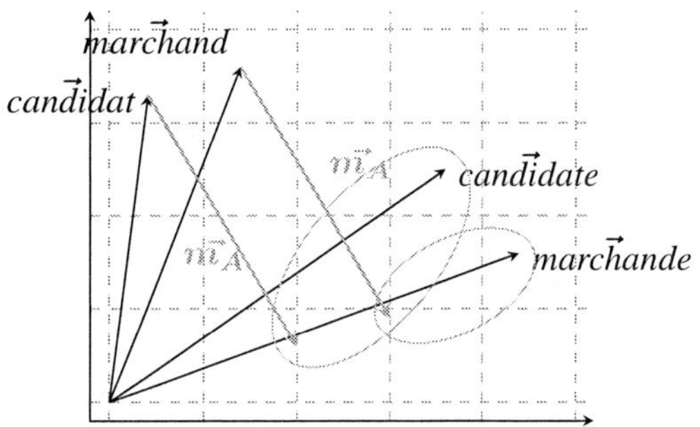

Figure 4: Extrinsic predictions for HNs

as prediction functions. The basic scenario, which we label **intrinsic prediction** (illustrated in Figure 3), can be used to address question 1 above. Given a word w_1 (e.g. the masculine noun *marchand*) participating in some morphological relation R, we add to the vector representation $\vec{w}_1$ of w_1 the mean shift vector for R (here $\vec{m}_N$). This gives us the predicted vector for the morphological alternant w_2 (in this example, the feminine noun *marchande*). We may now assess how far the predicted vector $\vec{w}_1 + \vec{m}_N$ falls from the actual observed vector $\vec{w}_2$ of the morphological alternant. Various measures can be used to quantify predictability in this case. In this paper we use two: the Euclidean distance between the predicted and observed vectors for the alternant, and the log rank of the actual vector in terms of distance from the predicted vector within the vector space.

The more diverse the shifts within a relation, the less accurate this intrinsic prediction will be on average. To address question 1, we will therefore compare the quality of intrinsic prediction for pairs of nouns and pairs of adjectives: the answer to it will be positive if prediction is less accurate for nouns than for adjectives.

A different procedure, which we call **extrinsic**

prediction, allows us to address question 2 above, and is illustrated in Figure 4. Informally, we test to what extent two relations have the same distributional footprint. Given a word w_1 (e.g. the masculine noun *marchand*) participating in morphological relation R, we add to the vector representation of that word the mean shift vector for the *other* relation R' (here $\vec{m}_A$). If relations R and R' are semantically equivalent (i.e., g-gender alternation has the same effects for nouns and adjectives), then extrinsic prediction should be just as accurate as intrinsic prediction. If, on the other hand, the two relations are not equivalent, we expect extrinsic prediction to be less accurate.

3 Experiment 1: Overall comparison of HNs and adjectives

We start by addressing questions 1 and 2 in broad terms, and will proceed with a more fine-grained analysis of adjectives in subsequent sections.

3.1 Stability of contrast

Research Question The first question addressed in our paper concerns the relative degrees of semantic regularity of gender alternation in human nouns vs. adjectives. We compare the quality of

Measure	t-statistic	p-value
Distance	2.8824	0.0047
Log rank	1.1095	0.2694

Table 3: T-test results for intrinsic predictions of HNs and adjectives in the $\mathcal{M}_1$ model

Measure	t-statistic	p-value
Distance	-5.772	$< 10^{-7}$
Log rank	-6.245	$< 10^{-8}$

Table 4: T-test results for HNs, intrinsic vs. extrinsic prediction in the $\mathcal{M}_1$ model

Measure	t-statistic	p-value
Distance	-39.328	$< 10^{-15}$
Log rank	-33.169	$< 10^{-15}$

Table 5: T-test results for adjectives, intrinsic vs. extrinsic prediction in the $\mathcal{M}_1$ model

intrinsic predictions for the two processes.

Materials The corpus used in our experiments is the concatenation of FRWAC (Baroni et al., 2009), FRCOW (Schäfer, 2015) and a dump of French Wikipedia, a total of 14 bln tokens, annotated with Coavoux's (2017) parser. FRWAC was cleaned to remove sentences containing characters not belonging to standard French and duplicate sentences. This corpus was used to compute a word2vec (Mikolov et al., 2013a) model (parameters: CBOW, negative sampling, window of 5), referred to as $\mathcal{M}_1$, where feminine and masculine homographs as well as noun and adjective homographs were disambiguated. HNs were selected from the GLAWI database (Hathout et al., 2014), enriched with information from the Lexeur lexicon (Fabre et al., 2004). To obtain a sample of homogeneous frequency, we only selected word forms occurring between 100 and 1000 times in our corpus. These constraints resulted in 120 HN pairs and 4874 adjective pairs.

Statistical Results We compute the discrepancy between predicted vector and observed vector using both log-normalized rank and euclidean distance[4]. The predictions were compared using a Welch t-test, cf. Table 3. We find that, in terms of distance, adjective predictions are closer to their respective targets than HN predictions.

Discussion The observed difference between adjectives and HNs provides evidence that the semantic relationships between masculine and feminine nouns are less predictable than those between masculine and feminine adjectives. This is coherent with the hypothesis that masculine and feminine nouns are related by derivation, and hence entertain a less regular relation than inflectionally related masculine and feminine adjectives.

3.2 Similarity of Semantic Effects

Research Question Turning to question 2, we test whether gender alternations in nouns and adjectives have the same semantic effect. We do so by comparing the intrinsic and the extrinsic predictions for adjectives, and the intrinsic and the extrinsic predictions for HNs.

Statistical Results Using the same materials as previously, we test whether the two processes yield similar outputs for the same input. Table 4 presents the Welch t-test results for HNs, and Table 5 reports those for adjectives. All tests highlight a significant statistical difference between the intrinsic and the extrinsic predictions: intrinsic predictions always yield lower measurements.

Discussion Comparing predictability measures allows us to test the similarity of the semantic effects of g-gender alternation in HNs and in adjectives. The morphological and syntactic similarity of these processes does not logically imply a semantic identity; the measurements described above provide evidence for the opposite.

Perhaps this decline in predictability indicates a difference between the meaning of g-gender for nouns and adjectives. However, it might also be due to an imbalance in the data: we compared human nouns, where g-gender plausibly signals s-gender, with all adjectives, despite the fact that many adjective tokens describe inanimate entities and hence cannot receive any interpretation in terms of s-gender. To assess this, we need to examine how the human reference of entities described by adjectives influences their distributional properties.

---

[4]We preferred testing both rank and distance measurements over the more widespread cosine similarity measure so as to take into account neighborhood structure (Linzen, 2016).

Predictor	Estimate	t-statistic	p-value
Intercept	0.2288	34.35	$< 10^{-15}$
Log freq.	0.0578	42.65	$< 10^{-15}$
Ratio	0.1657	10.20	$< 10^{-15}$
10.20	$< 10^{-15}$		
Shift size	-0.0140	-40.38	$< 10^{-15}$

Table 6: Fixed effects for model of homogeneity of gender contrast in adjectives

4 Experiment 2: Differences among adjectives

Research Question Adjectives describing primarily humans might be more similar to HNs than other adjectives: they should mostly share the same context and convey similar s-gender information. If so, the more an adjective is used to qualify HNs rather than other nouns, the more similar its gender shift will be to the mean shift of HNs. Adjective shifts can then be expected to express a continuous trend from adjectives primarily used to describe humans (e.g. *talentueux, talentueuse,* 'talented') to those not necessarily describing humans (e.g. *grand, grande,* 'tall'), and to those (almost) never describing human referents (e.g. *plénier, plénière,* 'plenary').

Materials We compute the mean HN gender shift and compare it to the shift vector for each pair of adjectives. The same set of HNs extracted from GLAWI and Lexeur was used as in the previous experiment. We only considered HNs occurring at least 50 times to compute this mean shift. Adjectives were extracted from the GLAWI database; for each adjective we also computed its number of occurrences (in either gender) as the modifier of a HN on the basis of the dependency annotation by Coavoux's (2017) parser. When divided by the total number of occurrences of the adjective, this defines a ratio of usage as qualifying a HN. As with HNs, we only considered adjective forms occurring more than 50 times in our corpus for this experiment, resulting in a total of 15624 adjective pairs.

Statistical Results The hypothesis was tested using a mixed-effects model. Linear effects include log-frequency and shift size (factors of statistical noise), as well as the human qualification ratio. The lexical identity of the adjective was used as a random effect. To obtain a normal distribution, the dependent variable was transformed to $-\log(\log(\frac{1}{\cos(\vec{A^i_f} - \vec{A^i_m}, \vec{m_N})}))$ with $\vec{A^i_f} - \vec{A^i_m}$ the shift for a given adjective and $\vec{m_N}$ the mean noun shift, then rescaled between 0 and 1 for interpretabilty purposes. Note that the dependent variable is monotonic with respect to cosine similarity.

The model was run using the R-Studio LME4 library (Bates et al., 2015), and converged to the results described in 6. All predictors were deemed significant. An analysis of residuals showed that the model is sound and accurate. The quantitatively most important effect is associated with the ratio, which contributes to higher cosine values.

Discussion The model highlights the importance of the type of nouns that the adjective qualifies to the semantic effect of the g-gender alternation. It stresses that regularity of gender alternation does not hold in an absolute fashion, and that the semantic contrasts between two related words is modulated by their common lexical semantics.

The precise nature of the sub-regularity indicates that adjective g-gender alternation in some cases resembles that of nouns. This provides an objective basis to disambiguate adjectives according to their usage. We can now use this information to tease apart adjectives which are semantically comparable to human nouns from those that are not.

5 Experiment 3: Comparing HNs to two classes of adjectives

The next experiment aims at studying g-gender alternation within three groups: human noun qualifying adjectives (HQAs), non-human noun qualifying adjectives (NHQAs), and HNs.

5.1 Stability of contrast

Research Question We first compare intrinsic predictions pairwise to assess the relative regularity of our three classes. Since NHQAs modify inanimate or abstract nouns, which do not possess an s-gender, we expect a different degree of regularity within NHQAs than within HQAs.

Materials We extract from the GLAWI database nouns which can only refer to humans, as well as nouns which never refer to humans. We define NHQAs as the adjectives which only qualify nouns that never refer to humans, and HQAs as the adjectives which only qualify nouns that always refer to humans.

Predictors		diff.	Adj. p-val.
HNs	vs. HQAs	-0.00783	0.79589
HNs	vs. NHQAs	0.04846	0.00741
NHQAs	vs. HQAs	-0.05629	0.00005

Table 7: Tukey HSD test results for distance measurements of intrinsic predictions in model $\mathcal{M}_2$

Predictors		Diff.	Adj. p-val.
HNs	vs. HQAs	-0.62057	0.04685
HNs	vs. NHQAs	0.85721	0.03510
NHQAs	vs. HQAs	-1.47778	$< 10^{-15}$

Table 8: Tukey HSD test results for log rank measurements of intrinsic predictions in model $\mathcal{M}_2$

A new model, dubbed $\mathcal{M}_2$, is computed so as to provide a distinct representation for HNs, HQAs and NHQAs. We once again use a word2vec model (CBOW, 5 negative samples, window of 5). In this $\mathcal{M}_2$ model, we disambiguate feminine vs. masculine, adjectives vs. nouns, and HQAs vs. NHQAs vs. ambiguous usages of adjectives.

Consistently with our first experiment, we only consider items occurring between 100 and 1000 times. However, this constraint resulted in sets of very different sizes: 118 noun pairs, 481 HQA pairs and 5074 NHQA pairs. Our NHQA sample is an order of magnitude bigger than the other classes and, more importantly, constitutes less of a natural class semantically. Such a disbalance might impact the results, therefore it was necessary to select the most cohesive group of NHQAs. This was done by retrieving the bottom-most cluster containing enough samples from UPGMA hierarchical clustering[5] and resulted in a set of 101 NHQA pairs.

Statistical Results We compare three morphological processes simultaneously, conducting an analysis of variance (ANOVA) to see if a given measure could discriminate the different processes; if it does, we apply Tukey's Honest Significant Difference (HSD) test to provide estimated factor and adjusted probabilities for each pair of processes. In all the case studies shown here, ANOVAs give strong evidence for differences with the processes ($p < 10^{-4}$, both for Euclidian distance and log rank). We report only HSD test results in the interest of space.

The adjusted p-values for distance of the Tukey HSD test in Table 7 underscore no significant difference between nouns and HQAs, but NHQAs are shown to yield lower measurements than HQAs and HNs; both p-values are under 0.05. This sug-

gests that in terms of distance NHQAs are more regular than nouns and HQAs, and that nouns and HQAs cannot be really distinguished from one another in terms of regularity.

Rank measurements, cf. Table 8, accordingly highlight the same difference between NHQAs on the one hand and nouns and HQAs on the other. Moreover, adjusted p-values indicate that there is a significant difference in measurements not only when comparing nouns and HQAs to NHQAs, but also when comparing nouns to HQAs. This suggests that NHQAs embody the most regular process, followed by HNs, and that HQAs correspond to the least regular process.

Discussion The hypotheses that this experiment tested were that HQA g-gender alternation was more similar to HN g-gender alternation than NHQA due to similarity in lexical meaning, and that NHQA pairs exhibited more regular shifts than HQA pairs.

A significant difference between the two processes was found: NHQAs yield lower rank and distance measurements than HQAs. It is however noteworthy that the difference between the measurements for the two processes is very small, so the distinction it introduces is subtle.

Another point of interest is that HN pairs exhibit more regularity than HQAs, but less than NHQAs. This suggests that, when compared to semantically comparable adjectives, human nouns fall within the scope of semantic regularity expected for inflectional alternations. This more careful experiment hence disproves the tentative conclusions reached after experiment 1: if anything, distributional evidence points to an inflectional status for g-gender alternations in human nouns.

5.2 Similarity of Semantic Effects

Research Question We now turn to the comparison of extrinsic and intrinsic predictions. The expectation is that g-gender alternation of HNs is more similar to that of HQAs than to the alterna-

---

[5] We tested using a Tukey HSD test whether class influenced pairwise distances measures within groups of distinct gender and class. NHQAs initially introduced a difference of ten times what we observed for other classes. With clustering, we observed a variation of means of 0.016 ± 0.008. Applying the same constraint to HQAs as well made HQAs overly cohesive but did not substantially affect the results.

Predictors	Diff.	Adj. p-val.
nouns vs. HQAS	-0.10139	$< 10^{-6}$
nouns vs. NHQAS	-0.11102	$< 10^{-15}$
NHQAS vs. HQAS	0.00963	0.86564

(a) Tukey HSD test results for distance measurements

Predictors	Diff.	Adj. p-val.
nouns vs. HQAS	-2.00157	$< 10^{-6}$
nouns vs. NHQAS	-3.19196	$< 10^{-15}$
NHQAS vs. HQAS	1.19039	0.00427

(b) Tukey HSD test results for log rank measurements

Table 9: Tukey HSD tests results for HNs, intrinsic vs. extrinsic prediction in model $\mathcal{M}_2$

Predictors	Diff.	Adj. p-val.
HQAS vs. nouns	-0.07383	$< 10^{-15}$
HQAS vs. NHQAS	-0.08725	$< 10^{-15}$
nouns vs. NHQAS	-0.01342	0.22433

(a) Tukey HSD test results for distance measurements

Predictors	Diff.	Adj. p-val.
HQAS vs. nouns	-0.99466	$< 10^{-15}$
HQAS vs. NHQAS	-2.75437	$< 10^{-15}$
nouns vs. NHQAS	-1.75971	$< 10^{-15}$

(b) Tukey HSD test results for log rank measurements

Table 10: Tukey HSD tests results for HQAS, intrinsic vs. extrinsic prediction in model $\mathcal{M}_2$

tion of NHQAS, due to their greater semantic relatedness; moreover, if g-gender alternation in nouns is indeed derivational, we expect nouns to diverge significantly from adjectives.

Statistical Results We start with examining predictions for HNs. An ANOVA shows that both distance and log-scaled rank measurements highlight a variation among the different prediction setups. We thus perform Tukey HSD tests, summarized in Table 9, to study more precisely what these differences in distance and log rank entail. From distance measurements (cf. 9a), we see that using information from either HQA g-gender alternation or NHQA g-gender alternation clearly deteriorates the measurements for HNs. Moreover, no significant statistical effect is attested when comparing the two extrinsic predictions.

When studying log rank measurements (cf. 9b), the same deterioration can be observed. However, log rank measurements also reveal a significant difference when comparing the two extrinsic predictions: NHQAS yield even higher measurements than HQAS, suggesting that the semantics of HQA alternation are more similar to that of HNs than the gender alternation of NHQAS.

The second group of extrinsic predictions concerns HQAS. Tukey HSD tests in Table 10 display the same results as with nouns, both in terms of distance (cf. 10a) and in terms of log-rank (cf. 10b) which clearly indicate that noun-based extrinsic predictions are a better fit than NHQA-based extrinsic predictions. This might entail that there is a gradation of semantic effects' similarity: HNs would be more similar to HQAS than NHQAS.

The last group of extrinsic predictions are those

Predictors	Diff.	Adj. p-val.
NHQAS vs. nouns	-0.34385	$< 10^{-15}$
NHQAS vs. HQAS	-0.41443	$< 10^{-15}$
nouns vs. HQAS	-0.07061	$< 10^{-06}$

(a) Tukey HSD test results for distance measurements

Predictors	Diff.	Adj. p-val.
NHQAS vs. nouns	-5.49577	$< 10^{-15}$
NHQAS vs. HQAS	-7.24153	$< 10^{-15}$
nouns vs. HQAS	-1.74575	$< 10^{-6}$

(b) Tukey HSD test results for log rank measurements

Table 11: Tukey HSD tests results for NHQAS, intrinsic vs. extrinsic prediction in model $\mathcal{M}_2$

for NHQAS. As previously, after an ANOVA, a Tukey HSD test is conducted for each pair of measurements; the results are summarized in Table 11. When studying either distance (cf. 11a) or log-rank (cf. 11b) variation, we observe both that intrinsic prediction performs better than extrinsic predictions, and that the extrinsic prediction based on HNs yields better measurements than the one based on HQAS. This implies that the semantic effects of NHQAS are more similar to those of HNs than to those of HQAS.

Discussion Intrinsic prediction is systematically better than any of the extrinsic predictions, highlighting that all three groups embody different semantic processes. We, however, observe a gradient: gender alternations for HQAS and HNs are more similar to each other than to NHQAS, and HNs are somewhere in between the two classes of adjectives. HNs and HQAS form a more cohesive group from which NHQAS differ systematically.

Although the cohesiveness of HNs and HQAS might be explained by the mechanics of distributional semantics, this in and of itself does not suffice to explain the gradient effect we observe. One could tentatively conclude from these facts that s-gender plays a greater role for HQAS compared to HNs. The concreteness of HNs may entail that all speakers agree on their semantics: a woman manning a checkout desk shall necessarily be *une caissière*; on the other hand, whether to use a specific adjective, such as *délicat*, to qualify a human referent, depends on the speaker's judgment which can be sensitive to s-gender. In other words, the person at the cash register is objectively a cashier regardless of their s-gender, but the standards of being *delicate* can be different for men and women, which in turn might explain the relatively idiosyncratic character of g-gender alternation in HQAS.

6 General Discussion

In this paper, we have detailed a data-driven methodology which enables a comparison of the distributional effects of a grammatical feature across categories. This methodology has allowed us to make several observations on g-gender alternation in HNs and adjectives.

In the first set of experiments, we compared the grammatical gender feature of French HNs to its counterpart in adjectives. We observed a greater semantic regularity in adjectives, which we tentatively attributed to the status of the gender distinction in nouns vs. adjectives: pairs of nouns are related by derivation, but pairs of adjectives are related by inflection. In addition, the comparison of intrinsic and extrinsic predictions highlighted a clear semantic difference between g-gender contrasts in nouns and adjectives.

Experiment 2 showed that another factor comes into play: the shift for an average adjective pair is more likely to resemble that of nouns, when the adjective pair itself is used to qualify HNs. This lead us to compare HNs with HQAS and NHQAS in the following section.

In the last set of experiments, g-gender variation in HNs was shown to be more semantically regular than in HQAS. Hence the provisional conclusion of the first set of experiments was disproved: the apparent semantic irregularity of HNs was due to comparing them with a semantically discommensurate class of adjectives. On the other hand, the experiment still highlighted that all three groups constituted distinct processes.

Although all three types of gender shifts significantly differed from one another, we observed that HQAS and HNs formed a more cohesive group. We can derive two conclusions from this. First, g-gender alternation within a category (adjectives) can vary more than across categories (adjectives vs. nouns); second, correlation with s-gender in both nouns and adjectives lead to a greater commonality in gender alternations. This result corroborates, on the basis of distributional data, the mounting sociolinguistic (McConnell-Ginet, 2013, a.o.) and psycholinguistic (Gygax et al., 2012, a.o.) evidence that, when referring to humans, g-gender always has some interpretive effects. In addition, we have shown that g-gender alternation of HNs is more regular than that of some adjectives. Given that inflection is assumed to be more semantically regular than derivation (Robins, 1959; Dressler, 1989), this suggests that gender alternations in nouns should be seen as inflectional, as argued on independent grounds by (Bonami and Boyé, in press).

This work has addressed theoretical issues regarding one grammatical feature from a data-driven perspective. Future research will determine to what extent our results are specific to gender or generalize to other grammatical features such as number. Complementarily, we plan to look in more detail at the specific contribution of gender in languages where the relationship between g-gender and s-gender is different than in French. Finally, we plan to test the potential impact of social bias on the usage of gender forms of HQAS, which was suggested in the preceding section, both from the distributional and from the psycholinguistic point of view.

Acknowledgments

We thank Heather Burnett, Alessandro Lenci, Enrico Santus, and three anonymous reviewers for useful comments on previous versions of this paper. The work was supported by two public grants overseen by the French National Research Agency (ANR) as part of the "Investissements d'Avenir" program: Labex *Empirical Foundations of Linguistics* (reference: ANR-10-LABX-0083) and Idex *Lorraine Université d'Excellence* (reference: ANR-15-IDEX-0004). Support also came from the CNRS PEPS grant *ReSeRVe*.

References

Eneko Agirre, Enrique Alfonseca, Keith Hall, Jana Kravalova, Marius Paşca, and Aitor Soroa. 2009. A study on similarity and relatedness using distributional and wordnet-based approaches. In *Proceedings of Human Language Technologies: The 2009 Annual Conference of the North American Chapter of the Association for Computational Linguistics*, pages 19–27. Association for Computational Linguistics.

Mikel Artetxe, Gorka Labaka, Eneko Agirre, Kyunghyun Cho, and CIFAR Azrieli Global Scholar. 2017. Unsupervised neural machine translation. *arXiv preprint arXiv:1710.11041*.

Marco Baroni, Silvia Bernardini, Adriano Ferraresi, and Eros Zanchetta. 2009. The wacky wide web:a collection of very large linguistically processed web-crawled corpora. *Language Resources and Evaluation*.

Douglas Bates, Martin Mächler, Ben Bolker, and Steve Walker. 2015. Fitting linear mixed-effects models using lme4. *Journal of Statistical Software*, 67(1):1–48.

Tolga Bolukbasi, Kai-Wei Chang, James Y Zou, Venkatesh Saligrama, and Adam T Kalai. 2016. Man is to computer programmer as woman is to homemaker? debiasing word embeddings. In D. D. Lee, M. Sugiyama, U. V. Luxburg, I. Guyon, and R. Garnett, editors, *Advances in Neural Information Processing Systems 29*, pages 4349–4357. Curran Associates, Inc.

Olivier Bonami and Gilles Boyé. in press. Paradigm uniformity and the French gender system. In Matthew Baerman, Oliver Bond, and Andrew Hippisley, editors, *Perspectives on Morphology*. Edinburgh University Press.

Olivier Bonami and Denis Paperno. forthcoming. A characterisation of the inflection-derivation opposition in a distributional vector space. *Lingua e Langaggio*. Forthcoming.

Heather Burnett and Olivier Bonami. in press(a). A conceptual spaces model of socially motivated language change. In *Proceedings of the 2nd Meeting of the Society for Computation in Linguistics*.

Heather Burnett and Olivier Bonami. in press(b). Linguistic prescription, ideological structure and the actuation of linguistic changes: Grammatical gender in french parliamentary debates. *Language in Society*, 48.

Maximin Coavoux. 2017. *Discontinuous Constituency Parsing of Morphologically Rich Languages*. Ph.D. thesis, Univ Paris Diderot, Sorbonne Paris Cité.

Greville G. Corbett. 1991. *Gender*. Cambridge University Press., Cambridge.

Greville G. Corbett. 2010. Canonical derivational morphology. *Word Structure*, 3:141–155.

Greville G. Corbett. 2013. Sex-based and non-sex-based gender systems. In Matthew S. Dryer and Martin Haspelmath, editors, *The World Atlas of Language Structures Online*. Max Planck Institute for Evolutionary Anthropology, Leipzig.

Wolfgang U. Dressler. 1989. Prototypical differences between inflection and derivation. *Zeitschrift für Phonetik, Sprachwissenschaft und Kommunikationsforschung*, 42:3–10.

Melody Dye, Petar Milin, Richard Futrell, and Michael Ramscar. *A functional theory of gender paradigms*. Brill, Leiden.

Cécile Fabre, Franck Floricic, and Nabil Hathout. 2004. Collecte outillée pour l'analyse des emplois discordants des déverbaux en *-eur*. Communication aux journées d'étude sur *La place des méthodes quantitatives dans le travail du linguiste*. ERSS, Université de Toulouse II-Le Mirail.

Anna Gladkova, Aleksandr Drozd, and Satoshi Matsuoka. 2016. Analogy-based detection of morphological and semantic relations with word embeddings: what works and what doesn't. In *SRW@HLT-NAACL*.

Pascal Gygax, Ute Gabriel, Arik Lévy, Eva Pool, Marjorie Grivel, and Elena Pedrazzini. 2012. The masculine form and its competing interpretations in french: When linking grammatically masculine role names to female referents is difficult. *Journal of Cognitive Psychology*, 24(4):395–408.

Nabil Hathout, Franck Sajous, and Basilio Calderone. 2014. Acquisition and enrichment of morphological and morphosemantic knowledge from the French Wiktionary. In *Proceedings of the COLING Workshop on Lexical and Grammatical Resources for Language Processing*, pages 65–74, Dublin, Ireland. Association for Computational Linguistics and Dublin City University.

Charles F. Hockett. 1958. *A course in modern linguistics*. New York: Macmillan.

Shoaib Jameel, Zied Bouraoui, and Steven Schockaert. 2018. Unsupervised learning of distributional relation vectors. In *Proceedings of the 56th Annual Meeting of the Association for Computational Linguistics*.

Guillaume Lample, Ludovic Denoyer, and Marc'Aurelio Ranzato. 2017. Unsupervised machine translation using monolingual corpora only. *arXiv preprint arXiv:1711.00043*.

Alessandro Lenci. 2018. Distributional models of word meaning. *Annual review of Linguistics*, 4:151–171.

Omer Levy and Yoav Goldberg. 2014. Linguistic regularities in sparse and explicit word representations. In *Proceedings of the Eighteenth Conference on Computational Natural Language Learning*, pages 171–180. Association for Computational Linguistics.

T. Linzen. 2016. Issues in evaluating semantic spaces using word analogies. *ArXiv e-prints*.

Marco Marelli and Marco Baroni. 2015. Affixation in semantic space: Modeling morpheme meanings with compositional distributional semantics. *Psychological review*, 122 3:485–515.

P. H. Matthews. 1974. *Morphology*. Cambridge University Press, Cambridge.

Sally McConnell-Ginet. 2013. Gender and its relation to sex: The myth of natural gender. In Greville Corbett, editor, *The Expression of Gender*, pages 3–38. De Gruyter Mouton Berlin.

Tomas Mikolov, Kai Chen, Greg Corrado, and Jeffrey Dean. 2013a. Efficient estimation of word representations in vector space. *CoRR*, abs/1301.3781.

Tomas Mikolov, Wen-tau Yih, and Geoffrey Zweig. 2013b. Linguistic regularities in continuous space word representations. In *HLT-NAACL*, pages 746–751.

R. H. Robins. 1959. In defense of WP. *Transactions of the Philological Society*, 58:116–144.

Roland Schäfer. 2015. Processing and querying large web corpora with the COW14 architecture. In *Proceedings of Challenges in the Management of Large Corpora 3 (CMLC-3)*, Lancaster. UCREL, IDS.

Andrew Spencer. 2013. *Lexical relatedness: a paradigm-based model*. Oxford University Press, Oxford.

Gregory Stump. 1998. *The handbook of morphology*, chapter Inflection. Oxford: Blackwell.

Rossella Varvara. 2017. *Verbs as nouns: empirical investigations on event-denoting nominalizations*. Ph.D. thesis, Università degli Studi di Trento.

Wolfgang Ulrich Wurzel. 1989. *Inflectional Morphology and Naturalness*. Kluwer, Dordrecht.

Wiecher Zwanenburg. 1988. *Aspects de linguistique franaise.*, chapter Flexion et dérivation: le féminin en franais.

Guess Who's Coming (and Who's Going): Bringing Perspective to the Rational Speech Acts Framework[*]

Carolyn Jane Anderson and **Brian Dillon**
University of Massachusetts
N408 Integrative Learning Center
650 North Pleasant Street
Amherst, MA 01003, USA
carolynander@umass.edu

Abstract

We present a Rational Speech Acts approach to modeling how conversation participants reason about perspectival expressions. The interpretation of perspectival expressions, such as the motion verbs *come* and *go*, depends on the point-of-view from which they are evaluated. In order to interpret a perspectival expression, the listener must jointly reason about the speaker's intended message and their choice of perspective. We propose a Bayesian approach to this inference problem and describe an extension of the Rational Speech Acts model that incorporates perspective. We lay out three sets of predictions that this model makes relating to the lexical semantics of *go*, the cost of non-speaker perspectives, and marginal inference over worlds.

1 Introduction

Recent experimental and theoretical work at the semantics/pragmatics interface has highlighted the role of perspective. Perspectival expressions are items whose meaning depends on the point-of-view from which they are interpreted. A wide range of linguistic phenomena appear sensitive to perspective, including spatial and temporal deictic expressions like *on the right* and *tomorrow* (Speas, 2000); pronouns (Loveland, 1984; Wechsler, 2010); motion verbs (Fillmore, 1975; Barlew, 2017); epithets and expressives (Doron, 1991; Harris, 2012); and logophors (Huang and Liu, 2001; Park, 2017).

Perspectival items express two kinds of information: their lexical meaning, and information about the point-of-view adopted by the speaker. Consider the sentence in (1), containing the perspectival motion verb *come*. *Come* describes motion relative to the location of a perspective holder (Fillmore, 1975). Thus (1) conveys information about the perspective holder's location in addition to its literal meaning (that Thera is in motion to Northampton).

1. Thera is coming to Northampton in an hour.

In English,[1] motion verbs like *come* and *go* allow at least three kinds of perspective holders: the speaker (e.g. *You are coming to my house*), the listener (e.g. *I am coming to your house*), or the subject of an attitude verb (e.g. *Thera says I am coming to her house*). In order to understand who is located in Northampton, however, the listener must infer who the perspective holder is. How does she do this? That is the central question that this paper addresses.

We propose to model the process of inferring a perspective holder for a perspectival expression using the Rational Speech Acts model (RSA), a framework for pragmatic modeling rooted in Bayesian inference (Frank and Goodman, 2012; Goodman and Stuhlmüller, 2013). We extend the RSA to include the inference required to identify a perspective holder in context. In particular, we model the interpretation of perspectival utterances as inference over the joint probability of a world and a perspective given an utterance. We focus on one particular class of perspectival expressions, perspectival

---

Many thanks to Lyn Frasier, Richard Futrell, and Jesse Harris, and to our SCIL reviewers for their thoughtful feedback on this work.

[1]The set of licit perspective holders is a point of cross-linguistic variation: see (Gathercole, 1987) and (Nakazawa, 2007; Nakazawa, 2009) for cross-linguistic work on the topic.

Proceedings of the Society for Computation in Linguistics (SCiL) 2019, pages 185-194.
New York City, New York, January 3-6, 2019

motion verbs, and describe the model's predictions about some of the open questions related to these verbs, including the lexical semantics of *go* and the existence of a cost for non-speaker perspectives. In what follows we describe the model and articulate its key predictions. We hope that our model and its predictions can guide further exploration of the role of perspective at the semantics-pragmatics interface.

1.1 The semantics of *come* and *go*

Perspectival motion verbs are a good test case for pragmatic modeling of perspective because there is a rich literature on the topic that provides descriptive facts to draw upon and open questions to test. We adopt a view of the lexical semantics of *come* and *go* rooted in the perspectival semantics for motion verbs described in (Barlew, 2017). We use a lexical semantics for *come* consisting of two components: a motion implication, corresponding to the lexical semantics of *come*, and an anchoring implication, corresponding to the perspectival component, expressed in (2) in a simple event semantics.

2. Semantics of *come*:

    For any world w, perspective a, destination d, and entity x, $[[Come(x, d)]]^{w,a} = $ T iff

    (a) Motion implication:
    $[[\exists e.Move(x, e) \wedge Dest(d, e)]]^{w,a} = $ T

    (b) Anchoring implication:
    $\exists y.[[Loc(y, d)]]^{w,a} = T$ and y is a salient perspective-holder with perspective a.

The motion implication is the literal meaning of the sentence: that someone moves to the destination. The anchoring implication expresses that the destination is the location of a perspective-holder.

We use a non-perspectival semantics for *go*: we propose that it has only a motion implication.

3. Semantics of *go*:

    For any world w, perspective a, destination d, and entity x, $[[Go(x, d)]]^{w,a} = $ T iff

    (a) Motion implication:
    $[[\exists e.Move(x, e) \wedge Dest(d, e)]]^{w,a} = $ T.

There are a few key points about the meaning of these motion verbs that any model must capture:

First, *come* requires that a salient perspective-holder is located at the destination. This means that *come* cannot be used to describe motion by the perspective-holder. If this were not so, the speaker would always be able to describe their own motion

with *come*, regardless of the destination.

4. Context: Matilda and Hildegard are having a conversation in New York.

    Matilda: I've always wanted to visit Antarctica, but it's so expensive.

    Hildegard: I went / #came there last year. It was so cool!

Second, the lexical semantics of *come* do not directly specify the location of the speaker or the listener, but rather the location of the perspective-holder. Although the speaker of (1) (repeated as (5)) may be the perspective-holder (as illustrated by the speaker-oriented follow-up 5a, the listener also could be (as in the listener-oriented follow-up (5b)).

5. Thera is coming to Northampton in an hour.

    (a) I wish you could come hang out too!

    (b) I wish I could come hang out too!

This means that the listener must successfully infer the perspective-holder in order to determine the interpretation of any sentence using *come*.

Third, although the lexical semantics of *go* presented here do not directly encode any anchoring implication, in practice *go* seems to imply motion away from the perspective holder. If (6) is interpreted from the speaker's perspective, then the listener will infer that the speaker is not located in Northampton.

6. Thera is going to Northampton in an hour.

The source of this anti-anchoring implication is debated. With the semantics proposed here, this implication is derived via Gricean reasoning on the part of the listener: if the perspective holder was located in Northampton, then the speaker should have used *come*; that she didn't implies that the perspective holder is not there (Wilkins and Hill, 1995; Sudo, 2018). However, in other theories, *go* has a perspectival component (Fillmore, 1975; Oshima, 2006).

2 The pragmatics of conversations

2.1 Rational Speech Act

In his foundational work on pragmatics, Lewis (1979) proposed that conversation is a cooperative game between the participants, where the goal is to determine which world the participants are in. Participants work towards this goal by sharing information, which narrows the set of possible worlds that the real world might be. Information shared between the conversation participants is stored in the Common Ground, which can be viewed as the set of accepted propositions, or as the worlds compatible with those propositions.

The Rational Speech Acts model is a framework for pragmatic modeling that extends this picture by proposing that the listener uses a Bayesian inference process to determine what message the speaker is trying to convey (Frank and Goodman, 2012). In this model, the Common Ground contains not just a set of worlds, but also a probability associated with each world, the probability that it is the real world.

At each turn in the conversation, the speaker selects a world from the set of worlds, simulating a new piece of information that the speaker wishes to contribute, and chooses an utterance to express it. Upon hearing the speaker's utterance, the listener must reason about the message that the speaker is trying to convey. The listener assumes that the speaker selects the sentence that maximizes the probability of the observed world.

The listener interprets the sentence in order to update the probability distribution over possible worlds in the Common Ground, calculating the likelihood of each world given the sentence selected, according to their model of how the speaker picks sentences.

The Rational Speech Acts model is therefore recursive. The listener's model of the speaker is called the **literal speaker**: the listener assumes that the speaker estimates the utility of each sentence based on a model of the listener, called the **literal listener**, so called because it does not involve any pragmatic reasoning. The literal listener is what the listener imagines the speaker's model of the listener to be. The listener herself is called the **pragmatic listener**.

The Rational Speech Acts framework has been applied to a range of phenomena, including projective content (Qing et al., 2016); politeness (Yoon et al., 2016); scalar implicatures (Potts et al., 2016); and word learning (Smith et al., 2013). Particularly relevant to the model we propose is the RSA lexical uncertainty model, which models joint reasoning over the lexicon and the speaker's message (Bergen et al., 2012; Kao et al., 2014; Bergen et al., 2016).

2.2 The standard RSA model

Although a RSA model is potentially infinitely recursive, we discuss just three levels: the literal listener, literal speaker, and pragmatic listener.

For the literal listener, the posterior probability of a world given an utterance is simply the literal meaning of the utterance discounted by the prior probability of the world. The meaning of the utterance is its denotation evaluated with respect to the world. Thus, the interpretation function for an utterance is an indicator function returning 1 or 0 depending on whether the utterance is true of the world.

The literal speaker is the listener's mental model of the speaker. In this model, the speaker selects a sentence in proportion to its utility, which is highest for sentences that maximize the posterior probability of the observed world according to the speaker's model of the listener (the literal listener).

The pragmatic listener is the model of the actual listener. The listener reasons about the speaker's message according to their mental model of the speaker (the literal speaker). The posterior probability over a world given the speaker's utterance is proportional to the likelihood of the literal speaker selecting the utterance given the world, discounted by the listener's prior belief in the world.

7. **Standard RSA model**
   (a) Literal listener:
   $$L_0(w|m) \propto [[m]]^w p(w)$$
   (b) Literal speaker:
   $$S_0(m|w) \propto softmax(log L_0(w|m) - Cost(m))$$
   (c) Pragmatic listener:
   $$L_1(w|m) \propto S_0(m|w) p(w)$$
   where w = world, m = message

One other consideration is usually introduced into the model: the cost of the utterance. This represents the trade-off between informativity and sentence complexity: although the speaker could theoretically select an utterance that exactly isolates the observed world, as the size of the set of possible worlds increases, the complexity of this utterance also increases. In practice, people often select a simpler, less informative utterance rather than a maximally informative but more complex utterance. The RSA model encodes this as a cost that penalizes the utility for more complex utterances at the level of the literal speaker, for some definition of complexity. A common cost function is the length of the sentence, although syntactic complexity or processing complexity can also be considered.

There are three factors important in defining a

RSA model: the set of possible worlds, the set of utterances, and the priors over the worlds. Changes to each of these affect the competition between utterances and the outcome of the inference process.

In general, a uniform distribution over the possible worlds is used, simulating the empty Common Ground at the beginning of a conversation.[2]

3 The pragmatics of perspective

What about perspectival expressions? In recent work, Roberts (2015) proposes that the Common Ground tracks a set of salient perspectives along with the set of worlds. Perspectival expressions, like *come*, are interpreted not just with respect to a world, but also with respect to a perspective.

In this view, a perspective is a set of *centered worlds*: a set of pairs consisting of a world in which the perspective-holder's beliefs are true and the spatio-temporal slice of that world that the perspective-holder self-identifies with (Stalnaker, 2014). Intuitively, a perspective can be seen as a variable assignment that picks out the individual in each world who the perspective-holder believes themselves to be. A perspectival expression is like an expression with a free variable: it cannot be interpreted unless the perspective-holder is known.

If the Common Ground is used to track salient perspectives as well as worlds, then the same inference mechanisms that track the probabilities of worlds in the Common Ground can be extended to track the probabilities of the perspectives. Here we propose just such an extension.

3.1 A perspectival extension to the RSA

We introduce the Perspectival Rational Speech Acts model, which incorporates perspective into the RSA framework. Building on Roberts (2015), we propose that conversation participants track probabilities over the set of perspectives in order to reason about the interpretation of sentences. As in the standard RSA model, the listener infers the probability of the speaker's message by reasoning about the likelihood of each sentence given the message and the prior probabilities over worlds. For perspecti-

val expressions, however, the listener must also infer the probability of speaker adopting a certain perspective. Therefore, in the perspectival RSA, the listener infers a joint probability: the probability of a paired world and perspective given the utterance. This models how listeners extract information about both the speaker's perspective and their message from sentences containing perspectival items.

The Perspectival RSA model advances the hypothesis that listeners interpret utterances not with respect to a single perspective, but by considering multiple perspectives simultaneously, each weighted by its probability in context. In this, our model departs from much previous work on the perspective in discourse, which implicitly assumes that listeners interpret utterances with respect to a single perspective (Harris, 2012; Kaiser, 2015; Roberts, 2015).

3.2 The perspectival RSA model

In the Perspectival RSA model, the literal listener reasons about the probability of a world given the utterance and the perspective. That is, in the speaker's model of the listener, the listener has access to the chosen perspective. The posterior probability of the world is proportional to the utterance's truth value with respect to the world and perspective, times the prior probability of the world given the perspective.

8. **Perspectival RSA model (preliminary)**
   (a) Literal listener:
   $$L_0(w|m, a) \propto [[m]]^{w,a} p(w|a)$$
   (b) Literal speaker:
   $$S_0(m|w, a) \propto \mathit{softmax}(\log L_0(w|m, a) - Cost(m))^3$$
   (c) Pragmatic listener:
   $$L_1(w, a|m) \propto S_0(m|w, a) p(w, a)$$
   where w = world, m = message, a = perspective

The literal speaker selects an utterance that maximizes the utility of the observed world according to the speaker's model of the listener, minus the cost of the message (we return to this below). The speaker observes a world, samples a perspective from the set of perspectives, and selects an utterance accordingly.

The pragmatic listener calculates joint probabilities for worlds and perspectives based on the utterance that the speaker selects. The joint posterior they

---

[2]However, in actual conversations, the initial Common Ground may include world knowledge that the speaker and listener have not explicitly mentioned, but are likely to agree upon.

[3]Thanks to Reviewer 1 for pointing out the need for the log term.

infer is proportional to the likelihood of the utterance given the world and perspective, according to the listener's model of the speaker, times the prior joint probability of the world and perspective.

3.3 Independence assumption

Above we showed that the inference in our model relies on the joint prior over world / perspective pairs. However, we make an independence assumption in order to simplify the calculation and assume that the prior probability of a world is independent of the prior probability of the perspective.

9. **Perspectival RSA model (intermediate)**
   (a) Literal listener:
       $$L_0(w|m, a) \propto [[m]]^{w,a} p(w)$$
   (b) Literal speaker:
       $$S_0(m|w, a) \propto softmax(log L_0(w|m, a) - Cost(m))$$
   (c) Pragmatic listener:
       $$L_1(w, a|m) \propto S_0(m|w, a) p(w) p(a)$$
   where w = world, m = message, a = perspective

3.4 The cost of a perspective

In addition to the utterance cost included in the standard RSA, we introduce a perspective cost. The perspective cost function penalizes non-speaker perspectives.[4] We use it to explore the idea that the default perspective is that of the speaker. This idea has been widely discussed in the previous literature on perspective. In theoretical work, Roberts (2015) posits that in the absence of explicit cues to the contrary, the listener always assumes that the speaker is adopting their own perspective. In experimental work, Harris (2012) and Kaiser (2015) find a strong preference for interpreting expressives, epithets, and other perspectival content from the speaker's perspective, in the absence of explicit cues otherwise.[5]

10. **Perspectival RSA model (final)**

---

[4]We use this parameter instead of manipulating the priors on perspectives because we intend to model effects of discourse salience through the perspective priors in future work. The idea is that as perspective holders are mentioned more frequently, the probability of adopting their perspectives increases. By contrast, the cost of adopting non-speaker perspectives should remain fixed over a discourse, since it reflects the cognitive difficulty in accomodating a non-speaker perspective.

[5]Note, however, that these experiments used written statements where the listener was not explicit, unlike our contexts.

(a) Literal listener:
    $$L_0(w|m, a) \propto [[m]]^{w,a} p(w)$$
(b) Literal speaker:
    $$S_0(m|w, a) \propto softmax(log L_0(w|m, a) - Cost(m) - Cost(a))$$
(c) Pragmatic listener:
    $$L_1(w, a|m) \propto S_0(m|w, a) p(w) p(a)$$
where w = world, m = message, a = perspective

In Section 5.2, we discuss the impact that this parameter has on the model's predictions.

3.5 Probabilities over perspectives

One important part of our model is the set of perspective holders that listeners track. In the Roberts (2015) view of perspective, the speaker and listener perspectives are automatically entered into the Common Ground and attitude holder perspectives are entered whenever an attitude verb is used.

Another possibility would be to introduce a new perspective whenever a new entity possessing a mental state is added to the Common Ground. We plan to test the effect of different methods for introducing perspective holders in future work.

We adopt a uniform prior over perspective holders for the moment. However, exploring different priors on perspectives might shed light on the topic of perspective maintenance. There is experimental evidence that listeners prefer to posit a coherent perspective over multiple utterances by the same speaker (Harris, 2012). This Maintain Perspective principle might be modeled well by a Dirichlet prior on perspectives, which would lead to a gradual increase in the probability of perspectives based on how frequently they are adopted by the speaker.

4 An example

To explore the predictions of the perspectival RSA model, we define toy sets of utterances and worlds.

4.1 Perspective holders

We consider a set of worlds with just three entities: Sarah, the speaker; Lydia, the listener, and Thera, a third party who is not involved in the conversation.

Although our model extends to attitude-holder perspectives, we simplify our example by considering only the speaker and listener perspectives. We adopt a uniform prior over the perspective set.

Figure 1: Worlds and utterances (destination indicated by yellow box).

4.2 Worlds

We demonstrate our model with a small set of worlds containing three individuals, Sarah, Lydia, and Thera; and two locations: Northampton (Noho) and Amherst. Since we are not considering Thera in the perspective set, we omit Thera's location. We include just the worlds in which exactly one person is moving, for a total of eight worlds (Fig.1). We use a uniform prior distribution over the worlds.

4.3 Utterances

We consider two sentence frames: *X is going to Northampton* and *X is coming to Northampton*, where X represents any of the individuals, for a total of 6 utterances (Fig. 1). One of the uses of our model is as a framework for testing the effects of different lexical semantics for *come* and *go*: we choose the relatively simple denotations in Section 1.1 for the sake of illustrating the model, but other semantics for *come* and *go* could be substituted.

5 Model predictions

We implemented our model in the WebPPL programming language (Goodman and Stuhlmüller, 2014). Using the worlds and utterances described above, we ran simulations to generate predictions about the probabilities of world/perspective pairs inferred by the listener. For each result reported, we ran 100,000 iterations of Markov Chain Monte Carlo sampling; we explored settings of {0,0.25,0.5,0.75,1.0} for perspective cost.

Our key results are: (1) perspectival interpretations of *go* can arise through pragmatic competition even if the lexical semantics of *go* are not perspectival; (2) the likelihood of non-speaker perspectives increases proportionally as the perspective cost is decreased; and (3) listeners should favor worlds that are consistent with multiple perspectives.

5.1 Competition between *come* and *go*

Our model shows how perspectival usage of *go* can arise through pragmatic competition with *come* even if the lexical semantics of *go* are not perspectival. Wilkins and Hill (1995) posit that at least in some languages, the interpretation of *go* as 'motion away from the perspective holder' is not lexically encoded, but arises through pragmatic reasoning, and Sudo (2018) proposes that Gricean reasoning is responsible for the interpretation of English *go*.

Our model verifies these theoretical proposals by showing that the perspectival interpretation of *go* can indeed arise solely through pragmatic competition with *come*. As shown in Fig. 2, our pragmatic listener infers that for sentences with *go*, the perspectival holder is unlikely to be at the destination of motion— even though our lexical semantics for *go* are not perspectival.

For the *go* sentences, world / perspective pairs where *come* is a viable alternative, such as when the perspective holder is the listener and the listener is at the destination of motion, are less likely than ones where *come* is not a possible alternative.

Thus, even without a perspectival lexical semantics, *go* acquires an interpretation that the perspective holder is unlikely to be at the destination.

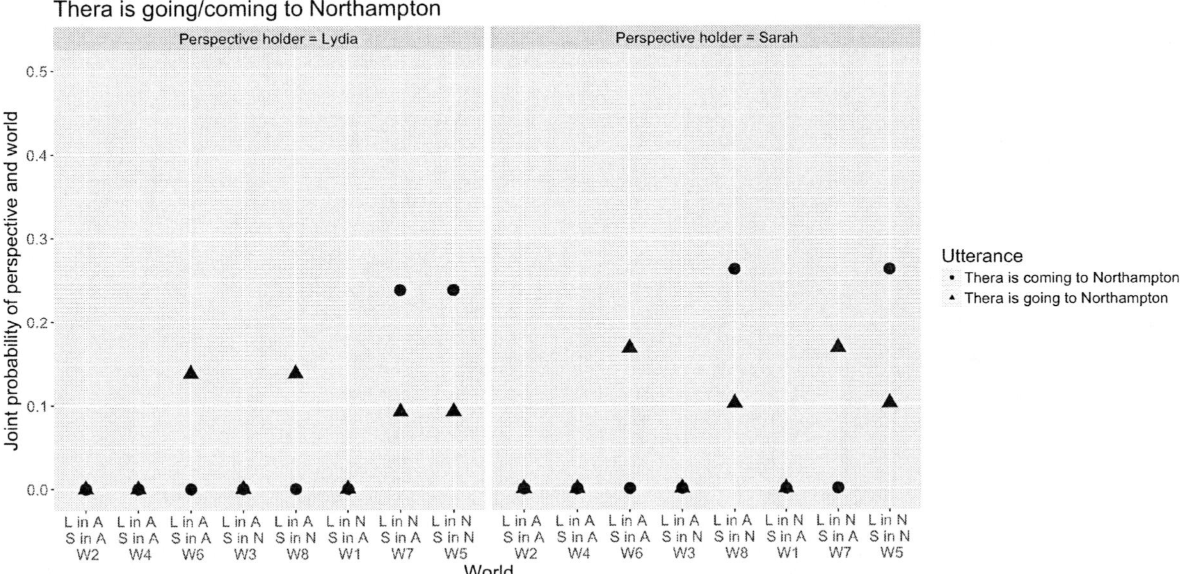

Figure 2: Model predictions for *Thera is going to Northampton* and *Thera is coming to Northampton*, speaker cost = 0.5

5.2 The cost of perspective shift

Another set of predictions relates to the perspective cost parameter. As the cost for non-speaker perspectives increases, the likelihood of a non-speaker perspective decreases. Because our cost function only assigns cost to non-speaker perspectives, with a uniform prior over perspectives, a non-speaker perspective will only be more likely than the speaker perspective when the speaker perspective is excluded by the lexical semantics of the sentence.

In our set of utterances, this occurs only with *I am coming to Northampton*, where the speaker perspective is excluded by the lexical semantics of 'come', since the speaker is moving (a person cannot be both in motion and at the destination of motion). For this sentence, the listener will infer with probability 1.0 that the perspective is the listener's (Lydia) and the world is the one in which Lydia is in Northampton.

Although decreasing in probability as perspective cost increases, the listener perspective remains possible for all sentences but *You are coming to Northampton*, where the listener perspective is eliminated because she is in motion. In this case, the speaker perspective is inferred with probability 1.0.

For a third-party mover, the listener perspective is as likely as the speaker perspective only when the perspective cost for non-speakers is set to zero. As the speaker cost increases, the listener perspective

becomes proportionally less likely (Fig. 3).

For the *go* sentences, both perspectives are always valid possibilities, since *go* does not have a perspectival component. For these sentences, the likelihood of the speaker perspective increases proportionally as the speaker cost is increased (Fig. 5).

Although the perspective cost parameter can be used to explore whether there is a processing cost for adopting non-speaker perspectives, since the cost is part of the listener's model of the speaker, it can also be used to explore the listener's beliefs about the speaker. If the listener believes that a particular speaker is more or less likely to adopt non-speaker perspectives, the listener may adjust the perspective cost parameter accordingly (for instance, if the speaker has higher rank than the listener; or limited knowledge of the listener's location).

5.3 Marginal inference

As mentioned above, one novel claim of our model is that listeners consider multiple perspectives at once when they interpret utterances. This contrasts with proposals that the default perspective holder is the speaker (Roberts, 2015), or that listeners process sentences using the most recent perspective, as Harris's Maintain Perspective proposal posits (2012).

Harris's Maintain Perspective principle is motivated by evidence that perspective shift is cogni-

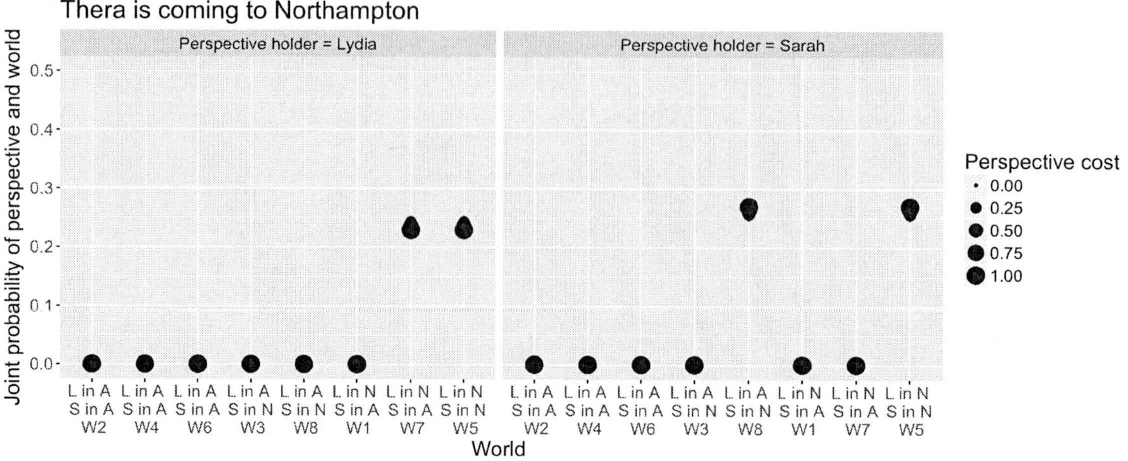

Figure 3: Model predictions for *Thera is coming to Northampton* at varying levels of speaker cost.

	Speaker	Listener	Marginal
Both in Noho:	0.26	0.24	0.5
Neither in Noho:	0	0	0
Listener in Noho:	0	0.24	0.24
Speaker in Noho:	0.26	0	0.26

Figure 4: Non-zero posterior probabilities for *Thera is coming to Northampton*, speaker cost = 0.5

tively difficult and incurs a high processing cost. He posits that listeners avoid perspective shift by processing a sentence with the last-used perspective, and only shifting perspective when motivated by sufficient contextual evidence (2012).

By contrast, our proposal posits that listeners are always weighing multiple perspectives, and that they calculate the meaning of the sentence relative to each perspective as they interpret the sentence. Considering multiple perspectives leads to a different marginal distribution over worlds than if the listener tracks just one perspective at a time.

To see this, consider the model's predictions for *Thera is coming to Northampton* when speaker cost is 0.5 (Fig. 4).The marginal distribution favors the world where both the speaker and listener are located at the destination. Although we present Fig. 4 as an example, this is true regardless of the parameter settings, so long as there is a non-zero chance that the listener is the perspective holder.

On the other hand, if the listener interprets the sentence relative to just one perspective (say, the speaker's), she would have no reason to prefer the world in which both the speaker and listener are at the destination over the world in which just the speaker is there (assuming other contextual factors, like the plausibility of conversations taking place between two people in the same location, are held steady). All worlds in which the speaker is located at the destination would be equally likely.

In this way, the 'multiple perspectives' hypothesis predicts that listeners will prefer to interpret *Thera is coming to Northampton* as conveying a message that is true for all salient perspectives; models that pick a single perspective to interpret the sentence do not. We plan to test this in an experiment where speakers are presented with perspectival sentences like *Thera is coming to Northampton* and non-perspectival equivalents like *Thera is driving to Northampton*[6], and are asked to choose the most likely scenario for each sentence from a set of pictures. If listeners perform the kind of pragmatic inference that we propose, they should prefer the world in which both possible perspective holders are at the destination in the perspectival condition.

6 Conclusion

We have outlined an extension to the Rational Speech Acts model in which the listener jointly reasons about the likelihood of the speaker's utterance and the adopted perspective. This model provides a framework for exploring the effects of various cost functions, priors, and lexical semantics for perspec-

---

[6]In order to control for the possibility that situations where the speaker and the listener are together may be more likely.

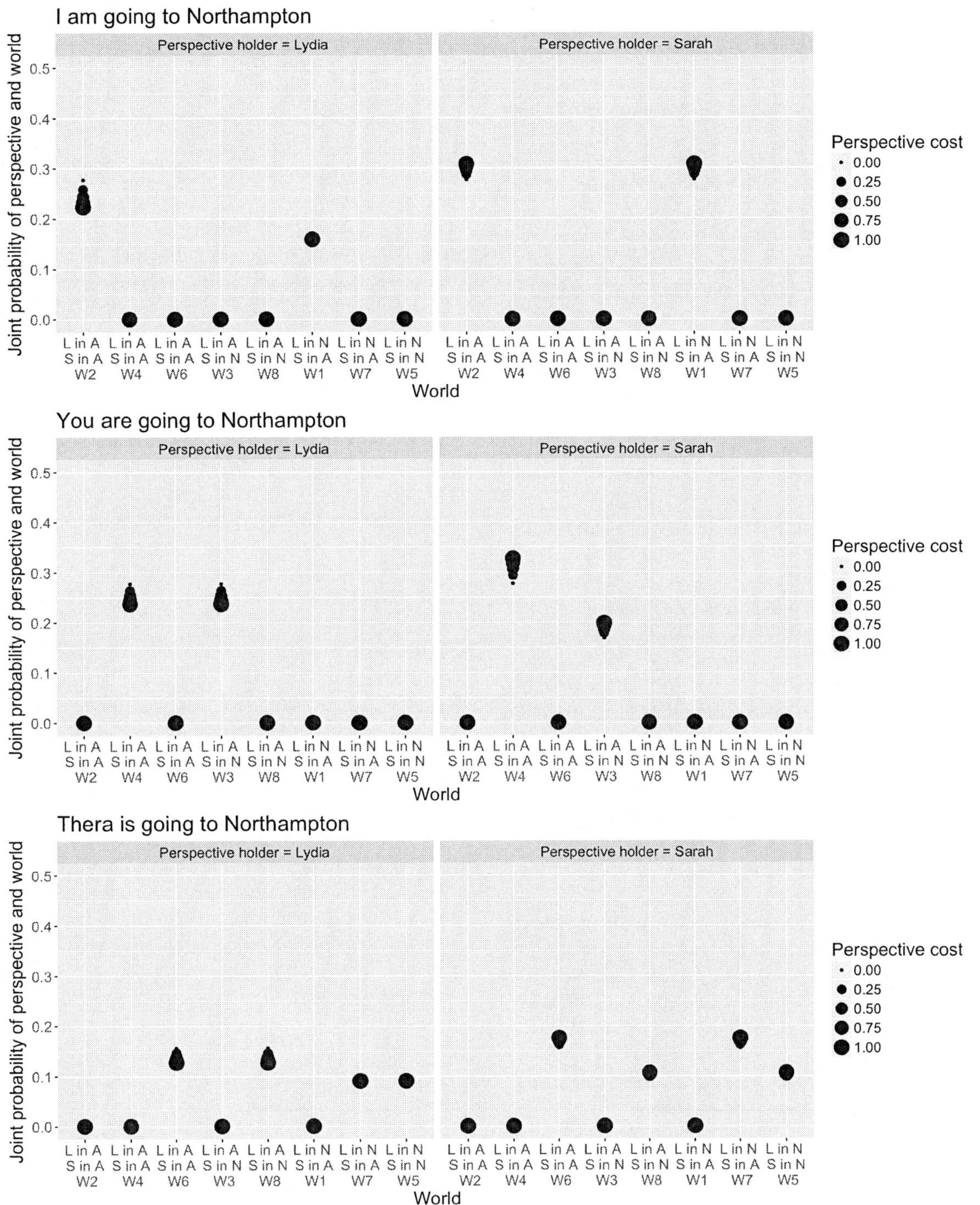

Figure 5: Model predictions for *go* sentences at varying levels of speaker cost.

tival items. We have described some of the predictions that our model makes for one kind of perspectival expression, perspectival motion verbs; we hope the model that we have outlined can serve as a useful framework for generating testable predictions about other kinds of perspectival expressions as well.

References

Jefferson Barlew. 2017. *The semantics and pragmatics of perspectival expressions in English and Bulu: The case of deictic motion verbs*. Dissertation, Ohio State University.

Leon Bergen, Noah D. Goodman, and Roger Levy. 2012. That's what she (could have) said: how alternative utterances affect language use. *Proceedings of the Annual Conference of the Cognitive Science Society*, 34.

Leon Bergen, Roger Levy, and Noah D. Goodman. 2016. Pragmatic reasoning through semantic inference. *Semantics and Pragmatics*, 9.

Edit Doron. 1991. Point of view as a factor of content. *Proceedings of tSemantics and Linguistic Theory Conference (SALT)*.

Charles J. Fillmore. 1975. *Deixis*.

Michael C. Frank and Noah D. Goodman. 2012. Predicting pragmatic reasoning in language games. *Science*, 336:998–998.

Virgina Gathercole. 1987. Towards a universal for deictic verbs of motion. *Kansas Working Papers in Linguistics*, 3.

Noah D. Goodman and Andreas Stuhlmüller. 2013. Knowledge and implicature: Modeling language understanding as social cognition. *Topics in Cognitive Science*, 5:173–184.

Noah D. Goodman and Andreas Stuhlmüller. 2014. *The Design and Implementation of Probabilistic Programming Languages*. http://dippl.org.

Jesse Harris. 2012. *Processing Perspectives*. Dissertation, University of Massachusetts, Amherst.

C. T. James Huang and C. S. Luther Liu. 2001. Logophoricity, attitudes, and *ziji* at the interface. *Long-distance reflexives*, 33:141–195.

Elsi Kaiser. 2015. Perspective-shifting and free indirect discourse: Experimental investigations.

Justine T. Kao, Jean Y. Wu, Leon Bergen, and Noah D. Goodman. 2014. Nonliteral understanding of number words. *Proceedings of the National Academy of Sciences*, 111.

David Lewis. 1979. Score-keeping in a language game. *Semantics from a Different Point of View*.

Katherine A. Loveland. 1984. Learning about points of view: spatial perspective and the acquisition of 'i/you'. *Journal of Child Language*, 11:535–556.

Tsuneko Nakazawa. 2007. A typology of the ground of deictic motion verbs as path-conflating verbs: the speaker, addressee, and beyond. *Poznan Studies in Contemporary Linguistics*, 43.

Tsuneko Nakazawa. 2009. A typology of the ground of deictic motion verbs as path-conflating verbs: the entailment of arrival and the deictic center. *Poznan Studies in Contemporary Linguistics*, 45.

David Y. Oshima. 2006. Motion deixis, indexicality, and presupposition. *Proceedings of Semantics and Linguistic Theory (SALT)*, 16.

Yangsook Park. 2017. *Attitudes de se and logophoricity*. Dissertation, University of Massachusetts, Amherst.

Christopher Potts, Daniel Lassiter, Roger Levy, and Michael C. Frank. 2016. Embedded implicatures as pragmatic inferences under compositional lexical uncertainty. *Journal of Semantics*, 33.

Ciyang Qing, Noah Goodman, and Daniel Lassiter. 2016. A rational speech-act model of projective content. *Proceedings of the Cognitive Science Society*, 38.

Craige Roberts. 2015. Indexicality: *de se* semantics and pragmatics.

Nathaniel J. Smith, Noah D. Goodman, and Michael C. Frank. 2013. Learning and using language via recursive pragmatic reasoning about other agents. *Advances in Neural Information Processing Systems (NIPS)*.

Margaret Speas. 2000. Person and point of view in navajo: direct discourse complements. *Proceedings of West Coast Conference on Formal Linguistics*.

Robert C. Stalnaker. 2014. *Context*. Oxford University Press.

Yasutada Sudo. 2018. Come vs. go and perspectival shift. Ms.

Stephen Wechsler. 2010. What 'you' and 'i' mean to each other: person indexicals, self-ascription, and theory of mind. *Language*, 86:332–365.

David P. Wilkins and Deborah Hill. 1995. When 'go' means 'come': Questioning the basicness of basic motion verbs. *Cognitive Linguistics*, 6:209–259.

Erica J. Yoon, Michael Henry Tessler, Noah D. Goodman, and Michael C. Frank. 2016. Talking with tact: Polite language as a balance between kindness and informativity. *Proceedings of the Cognitive Science Society*.

The organization of sound inventories: A study on obstruent gaps

Sheng-Fu Wang
Dept. of Linguistics
New York University
10 Washington Place
New York, NY 10003
`shengfu.wang@nyu.edu`

Abstract

This study explores the organizing principles of sound inventories by examining attested one-segment gaps in obstruent inventories. Models based on different theories of inventory organization are built and compared in a computational task where models make a binary decision to identify gaps and attested sounds. Results show that segment markedness, defined either in terms of grounded phonetic properties or typological frequencies, is a good predictor of whether a segment is likely to be gapped in an inventory. On the other hand, whether an attested segment, compared to a gapped segment, makes the feature representation more symmetric or economical, is not a good predictor of whether a segment is gapped. Finally, artificial neural networks that take inventories and segments as bags of feature values outperform all aforementioned models, demonstrating the extent to which the task of gap identification is learnable from distributional properties in the data.

1 Introduction

Sound inventories of human languages are not made up of random bags of possible speech sounds. Proposals on inventory shapes such as feature economy and symmetry (Clements, 2003a) predict that a stop inventory like /p, t, b, d/ is more likely than /p, t, b/ or /p, t, b, g/. Proposals on markedness and implicational universals (Greenberg, 1970; Gamkrelidze, 1975) also make predictions on inventory shapes. For example, when a language lacks a voiced stop, it is more likely to be /g/ than /d/. When it comes to inventory shapes, such proposals predict that /p, t, b, d/ is more likely than /p, t, b, g/.

This study compares different models on the organizing principles of inventory structure by examining the distribution of gaps in the inventories of obstruents across languages. A gap is referred to as the absence of an [α voice] stop/fricative in a certain place of articulation when a [$-\alpha$ voice] counterpart exists in the inventory. The computational task is a binary choice task, adapoted from the cloze task in Cotterell and Eisner (2017): between two sounds, the models have to decide which is the 'gap', and which is the 'foil', an attested stop/fricative that shares the [α voice] feature with the gap, with a different place of articulation. A model is more successful if it more frequently identifies the gap correctly. Examples of gaps and corresponding foils in Wogeo (Exter, 2003) is shown in (1)

(1) Inventory of obstruents in Wogeo
    b   d   ɡ
    —   t   k
    v   —
    f   s

    gap: /p/   foil: /t, k/
    gap: /z/   foil: /s/

This task can be seen as an approximation of the task of identifying phoneme categories by a human learner: The process of acquiring a phonemic inventory can be modeled as decisions to construct abstract categories based on input that has certain distributional property in an available articulatory, acoustic, and/or perceptual space (e.g., Dillon et al., 2013; McMurray et al., 2009; Vallabha et al., 2007). Take word-initial stops for example, it has been found that sounds that differ only in place of articulation differ on a continuum of time-varying spectral properties 20-40 ms after the stop release (Kewley-Port et al., 1983; Kewley-Port, 1983). A human learner has to form categories along the such dimensions, based on a mixture of bottom-up and top-down information. In forming categories, the learner makes latent decisions on whether some given types of sounds be-

Proceedings of the Society for Computation in Linguistics (SCiL) 2019, pages 195-204.
New York City, New York, January 3-6, 2019

long to a certain emergent or emerging category, and whether sounds of certain types make up a distinctive category on their own.

Two major types of models are tested: The MARKEDNESS and the FEATURE-SYSTEMIC models. The MARKEDNESS models predict that the gap is always more marked than the foils. There are two variants of the MARKEDNESS model in this study: The *grounded markedness* model ranks the markedness of obstruents based on their constriction site (Gamkrelidze, 1975): A voiced obstruent is more marked when the constriction site is further back in the vocal tract. Conversely, a voiceless obstruent is more marked if it is fronter. The *typological markedness* model uses the frequency of segments and places of articulation across inventories for ranking markedness: the less frequent sounds are more marked.

For FEATURE-SYSTEMIC models, the gap is the sound whose presence in an inventory would decrease the overall goodness of the inventory based on some feature-based metrics. Three metrics are used in this study: *feature entropy* (Mukherjee et al., 2007), *local feature symmetry*, and *global feature symmetry* (Dunbar and Dupoux, 2016). *Feature entropy* is taken as a measure of feature economy: the feature representation of a system is more economical if it can be expressed by fewer bits. *Local feature symmetry* measures the number of pairs of sounds in an inventory that differ only in one feature, and an inventory is more locally symmetric if it has more such pairs. *Global feature symmetry* measures the difference in the size of the plus and the minus feature values in a feature system: an inventory is more globally symmetric if the difference is smaller.

To further investigate to what extent the place of articulation of gaps can be learned from the distribution of segments across inventories, artificial neural networks are trained to do the gap-prediction task. The input contains inventories represented as bags of segments, which in turn are represented as bags of feature values. The training objective to either choose a gap from two sounds given the knowledge of the inventory at issue (*Inventory* model), the gap and the foil (*Segment* model), or both (*Inventory+Segment* model).

Results show that MARKEDNESS models can accounts for 65%-59% of the gapping patterns. In other words, the gap is often more marked than the foils (the attested sounds) either in terms of their places on markedness scales defined with reference to speech production, or in terms of typological segment frequencies. On the other hand, the FEATURE-SYSTEMIC models have worse performance on average, showing that the decision between a foil and a gap is not actively governed by principles on the optimality of feature representation. To locate a potential domain where these FEATURE-SYSTEMATIC models may be active, a supplement experiment is done and the results show that some of these Feature-Systematic models are able to differentiate inventories with and without gaps. Finally, artificial neural networks are able to be trained to perform better than other types of models in this task, and the architecture that utilizes information both on the inventory as a whole and on gaps and foils performs the best.

The rest of the paper is organized as follows: Section 2 reviews theories on inventory structure in a greater detail. Section 3 describes the data, task, and models in this study. Section 4 reports results and analyses. Section 5 discusses the findings and concludes the paper.

2 Theories on Inventory Structure

2.1 Segment Markedness

Gamkrelidze (1975) explicitly discusses how the markedness of sounds affects the organization of sound inventories. He proposes scales of markedness at the segmental level, shown in (2), and discusses how the scales account for attested and unattested types of stop and fricative inventories. The presentation of gaps in the inventory serves as an important way to demonstrate his main points. He proposes that voiced stops and voiceless stops have the opposite markedness scales: whereas labial stops are marked when they are voiceless, they are unmarked when they are voiced, as shown in (2). He also states that the markedness scales with respect to voicing are the same for fricatives and stops. Within voiceless stops, aspirated and unaspirated ones share the same scale.

(2)   The markedness scales in (Gamkrelidze, 1975)

marked	$\leftrightarrow$	unmarked
p	t	k
g	d	b
f	s	x
ɣ	z	v

These markedness scales are used to predict attested and unattested inventory types. The assumption is that the presence of a marked element predicts the presence of all less marked elements. On the other hand, inventories where the certain sounds exist while the less marked sounds are absent are predicted to be unattested. Examples are shown shown in (3).

(3) Inventory shapes that are predicted to be attested and unattested in Gamkrelidze (1975)

    a. Attested inventory shapes

b	d	g		b	d	—
—	t	k		p	t	k

    b. Unattested inventory shapes

b	d	g		—	d	g
p	t	—		p	t	k

The markedness scales are described to be derived from frequency counts of segments both within and across inventories. However, these scales can also be interpreted as being motivated from the aerodynamics of voicing and voicelessness in different places of articulation, especially concerning stops (Greenberg, 1970; Smith, 1975; Ohala, 1983). For voiced stops, a constriction site that is further back in the vocal tract makes the stop less optimal, since it is difficult to maintain voicing due to smaller space for air-pressure buildup behind the constriction site. This motivates why velar stops are more marked than bilabial stops. For voiceless stops, When the constriction site is further back in the oral tract, the smaller volume of cavity behind the constriction site makes it easier to build up air pressure, resulting in a stronger amplitude for the burst of the release, making the voiceless stop more perceptually salient. This motivates why bilabial voiceless stops are more optimal than velar voiceless stops.

It should be noted that even though the tendency to miss /p/ and /g/ both have aerodynamic motivations, the extent to which these motivations play a role in shaping inventory patterns has been questioned. Maddieson (2013) shows that inventories that miss /p/ have geographically concentrated distribution around the Sahara desert, where the major language families are Niger-Congo, Nilo-Saharan, and Afro-Asiatic. He argues that such clustering of these languages suggests that the aero-dynamic motivation for inventories to miss /p/ may not be valid, and areal factors may play a better role in explaining the occurrence of such inventories. Even though the present study does not seek to address the issue of areal factors in inventory shapes, the question that Maddieson raises is still relevant, as it suggests that the explanatory power of grounded markedness, thus defined, may be weaker for voiceless stops.

2.2 Feature system and inventory structure

The notion of feature economy, according to Clements (2003b), can be dated back to de Groot (1941) and Martinet (1955). It is proposed as a basic principle of sound system organization. It refers to a tendency to maximize the number of segments that can be represented per feature dimension, as shown in (4), where E refers to the economy index, S refers to the number of segments in an inventory, and F refers to the number of feature dimension necessary for representing all segments in an inventory.

(4) $E = S/F$

There have been studies that examine feature economy in attested inventories. Mackie and Mielke (2011) finds that attested inventories in P-base (Mielke, 2008) are more economical than randomly generated ones, based on four different kinds of economy metrics. Dunbar and Dupoux (2016) also have similar findings with similar simulation-based methodology.

Feature symmetry is another feature-based principle of inventory structure. It states a preference for sounds in an inventory to have symmetric distribution along feature dimensions. Thus it prefers an inventory /p, t, b, d/ over an inventory such as /p, t, b/. In other words, it can also be restated as a dispreferrence for having gaps. Clements (2003b) states that feature symmetry may be conceptualized as a tendency for languages to avoid having gaps in their inventory. This notion of symmetry is further developed and tested by Dunbar and Dupoux (2016), where they propose two non-equivalent but related symmetry metrics: local symmetry and global symmetry.

Local symmetry in an inventory refers to the notion that the number of 'oppositions' in the inventory is relatively low or high. An opposition refers to a pair of sounds that differ only in one feature. An inventory is more locally symmetric if the number of oppositions is high. Global symmetry, on the other hand, refers to whether an inventory is well-balanced among feature dimensions.

It measures whether the inventory has an imbalanced number of [+] and [−] values along all feature dimensions. It can be calculated by taking each non-redundant feature, calculating the difference between number of sounds with [+] and with [−], and summing the values across different features, divided by number of features. A lower value indicates greater global feature symmetry.

2.3 Segment Co-occurrence

Mukherjee et al. (2007) and a series of studies (Choudhury et al., 2006; Mukherjee et al., 2009) approach the issue of principles in inventory shapes by modeling the co-occurrences of segments in network models. In these models, each node represents a segment, and the weight of a node is the number of languages with that segment. The weight of the edge between two nodes is the number of languages with both segments. With actual consonant inventories from UPSID (Maddieson and Disner, 1984), the model is able to group consonants into communities that contain homogeneous sounds such as dental, retroflex, and laryngealized sounds. In addition, they also measure 'feature entropy' within each community, which calculates how many bits are needed to transfer the feature representations segments in group of sounds. They compare the feature entropy of communities formed from attested and randomly generated inventories, and find that network drawn and weighted from attested inventories have communities with lower feature entropy. The finding shows that there are some regularities in the co-occurrence pattern of sounds across inventories.

3 Method

3.1 Data

This study uses the PHOIBLE database of phoneme inventories (Moran et al., 2014), which contains 2155 inventories, where the segments are described by a phonetically detailed feature set. Only [−soronant] sounds are used in this study, which limits the scope of the study to a natural class of sounds that are more homogeneous.

After filtering out repetitive inventories, 1874 obstruent inventories remain. From these obstruent inventories, 'gaps' are identified by examining if an inventory lacks [α voice] stops and fricatives in certain places of articulation when the [−α voice] counterpart exists. The corresponding

'foils' are identified, which refer to attested sounds in an inventory that share the same [α voice] feature with the gap but with different places of articulation.

Example data points from Wogeo are shown in (5), along with the obstruent inventory. Three data points are generated from this inventory.

(5) Inventory of obstruents and data points in Wogeo

    b   d   g
    −   t   k
    v   −
    f   s

gap: /p/   foil: /t, k/
gap: /z/   foil: /s/

data point I: gap-/p/, foil-/t/
data point II: gap-/p/, foil-/k/
data point III: gap-/z/, foil-/v/

The computational task is an adaptation of the cloze task in Cotterell and Eisner (2017): a model sees each pair of sounds and labels one of the sounds as a gap and the other as a foil based on different strategies that each model employs. The success of the models is measured by how often the labels given by the model fit the actual data.

Models that require training, including the *typological markedness* model and the neural network models, are trained on data points from 70% of the inventories (training set) and tested on data points from 20% of the inventories (test set). The neural network models' hyperparameters are tunes with data points from 10% of the inventories (development set).

3.2 Models

3.2.1 Markedness Models

Two Markedness models are included in this study. The first one is *grounded markedness*, which compares segments based bases on their positions on predefined markedness scales. In the current study, the scales are expanded from the ones described in Gamkrelidze (1975), where stops and fricatives share the same scales, and voiced and voiceless sounds have inverse scales. The scale for voiced stops and fricatives are shown in (6).

(6) Markedness scale for places of articulation in voiced obstruents, presented in constraint ranking.

*pharyngeal $\gg$ *uvular $\gg$ *velar $\gg$ *labial-velar $\gg$ *palatal $\gg$ *retroflex $\gg$ *post-alveolar $\gg$ *alveolo-palatal $\gg$ *alveolar $\gg$ *dental $\gg$ *labiodental $\gg$ *bilabial

In the computational task, the model decides that the more marked segment on the corresponding scale is the gap for a data point. For example, for data point III, /z/-/v/, from Wogeo, shown in (5), the *grounded markedness* labels /z/, a voiced alveolar sound, as a gap, since the avoidance of an alveolar voiced sound (*alveolar) ranks higher than the avoidance of a labiodental sound (*labiodental).

The other markedness model, the *typological markedness* model, only takes into account the frequencies of segments or places of articulation across inventories in the task. In the computational task, the model labels the typologically less frequent sound as the gap. This model has two further variants: the frequency can either be calculated based on the typological frequency of segments or of places of articulation.

3.2.2 Feature-Systemic Models

Three models fall into this category: *global feature symmetry*, *local feature symmetry*, and *feature entropy*. All these models rely on finding a minimal feature set that is required to represent an inventory, thus the algorithm to arrive at the minimal feature set is crucial. In this study, this is done by first ranking the entropy of each feature in the training/development set. In the process of shrinking the feature set, features with lower entropy are removed first, until the point where the removal of any feature would prevent all segments in an inventory to be unique represented. As a result, the resulting minimal feature sets are more likely to contain features with high entropy, which are features with a more balanced use of [+] and [−] values in the data set.

For each of the FEATURE-SYSTEMIC models, at each data point, the algorithm to find a minimal feature set is applied twice: once to the attested inventory, and once to the 'alternative' inventory, where the foil is replaced by the gap in the attested inventory. For example, for the data point /t-p/ from the inventory of Wogeo, the algorithm will find the minimal feature set for /b, d, ɡ, **t**, k, v, f, x/ (the attested inventory) and for /b, d, ɡ, **p**, k, v, f, x/.

The three FEATURE-SYSTEMIC models can then be seen as three different metrics to score the attested and alternative inventories at a data point. When the score for a metric favors the attested inventory, the model 'scores' at this data point.

The metric for *local feature symmetry* is the number of pairs of sounds that differ only in one feature in a system. As mentioned earlier, such a pair is referred to as an 'opposition' The metric for *global feature symmetry*, on the other hand, is the averaged absolute difference between the number of sounds with the plus and the minus values in all feature dimensions.

Feature entropy uses the metric proposed in Mukherjee et al. (2007), which measures the homogeneity of segment 'communities' in a network model. It can be seen as an information-theoretic measure of the minimal bits required to convey the feature representation of a set of sounds. The metric is calculated as follows: for an inventory with N segment types that are represented with the feature set F, which contains multiple features f, where the number of segments with feature value p is referred to as p_f and the number of segments with feature value q is referred to as q_f, feature entropy is $\sum_{f \in F} \left(-\frac{p_f}{N} \log_2 \frac{p_f}{N} - \frac{q_f}{N} \log_2 \frac{q_f}{N} \right)$. The interpretation of this metric is that an inventory is more economical if it has a more skewed distribution of [+] and [−] values or/and it has fewer required features in the feature system.

3.3 Artificial Neural Network

Artificial neural network models are built and tested to see whether the shape of obstruent inventories is governed by some underlying co-occurrence principle between features and segments.

The training objective approximates the task for non-neural models: each item in the input to the model is a pair of inventories. One of them is an attested inventory, and the other is the attested inventory with a foil being replaced by a gap. The task is for the model to decide which of these inventories is the attested one. It is implemented as a binary decision task. Each data point appears twice in two different orders.

Segments are represented as bags of feature values. Each feature value (e.g., [+voice], [−voice], [+labial], etc) is represented by a 10-dimensional vector that is randomly initialized before training and updated through back propagation during training. The representation for a segment, also a 10-dimensional vector, is derived in the following way: The vector representations for its feature values are first averaged. Then, the averaged vector passes through a perceptron layer with a rectified linear unit (ReLU) to obtain the vector representation for the segment. This gives the model to capture more complicated association between feature representations and segment representation. The output representation for each segment is then summed element-wise to obtain the representation for the inventory, which is also a 10-dimensional vector.

To investigate the role of inventory-level and segment-level information in performing this task, the are three variant architectures. In the *Inventory* architecture, the representations for all segments in the attested and the alternative inventories are summed before being concatenated and passed through two layers before a softmax layer for the classification task, as shown in Figure 1. In the *Segment* architecture, the 10D representations for the gap and the foil are concatenated, while in the *Inventory+Segment* architecture, the inventory representation is still the sum of segment representations, but the 10D representation of the gap and the foil, in stead of being part of the sum of the representation for the alternative and the attested inventory, are concatenated to the inventory representation (thus yielding a 40D representation before being passed into the hidden layers). This ensures that the model has explicit access to the property of the segments that are crucial for the task.

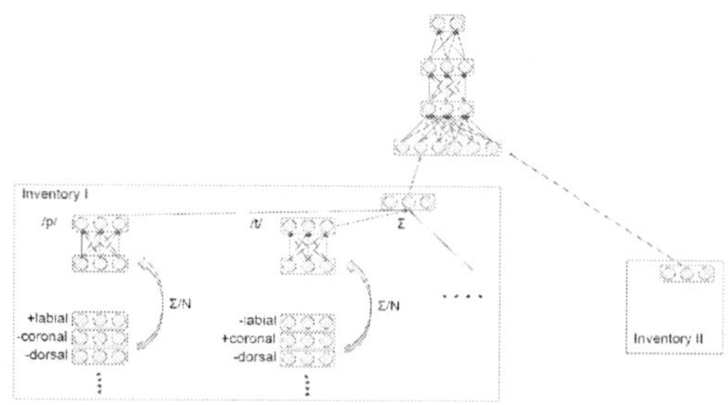

Figure 1: The *Inventory* architecture of the neural network model

For all three model architectures, hyperparameter tuning was done by a random search through 100 combinations of size of embedding dimension (between 10 and 50), learning rate (between 0.001 and 0.005) and L2 regularization weight decay (between 1×10^{-5} and 9×10^{-4}). During training, training and development set accuracies are evaluated every 100 steps. Training stops when the development accuracy does not improve after 500 steps. The best model in terms of development set performance for each architecture is used to report the result on the test set.

All the aforementioned training and testing procedures are repeated ten times over ten different random divisions of the data into training, development, and test sets. For comparison across different models, the performance of the MARKEDNESS and the FEATURE-SYSTEMIC models are also broken down into three different sets, with the test set being used for comparison.

4 Results

The overall results are shown in Table 1. Among the non-neural network models, MARKEDNESS models generally outperform the FEATURE-SYSTEMIC models. Among the former, the *typological markedness* model is the best performing one. In other words, the results shows that two third of the time the gap is less frequent than the foil. *Grounded markedness* ranks the second, showing that 62.13% of the time, the gap is more marked on the markedness scales than the foil. Another variant of the *typological markedness* model, based on the frequencies of places of articulation, ranks the third just behind grounded markedness.

The best performing FEATURE-SYSTEMIC model is the *global symmetry* model, achieving a mean accuracy of 55.91% in the test set. The *local symmetry* model is almost at chance level, while the *feature entropy* model is below chance, having a mean accuracy of 46.36%.

The neural network models are the best performing ones. The *Inventory+Segment* model, which concatenates the inventory-level summed embeddings with the embeddings of the gaps/foils for the classification task, performs the best, achieving a mean accuracy of 82.75% in the test set. The *Segment* model that only uses the embeddings of gaps and foils perform worse, with a mean accuracy of 74.89%, but is better than the performance of the *Inventory* model, which only takes the inventory-level summed embeddings. The fact that the *inventory* model can perform relatively well shows that this task can be solvable to a certain extent by information pro-

Table 1: Overall Results in average accuracy across ten different data splits. Numbers in the parentheses show standard deviations. Cells with gray numbers show that the corresponding models do not have a training component and the numbers merely indicate results of calculation in train/dev sets

Model	train	dev	test
grounded markedness	62.32 (0.57)	62.29 (2.61)	62.13 (2.65)
typological markedness – segment	66.13 (2.99)	66.91 (2.35)	65.47 (1.62)
typological markedness – place of articulation	59.49 (0.62)	60.94 (2.58)	59.36 (1.76)
feature entropy	48.18 (2.99)	46.21 (2.83)	46.36 (1.62)
local symmetry	50.29 (0.39)	48.61 (4.07)	50.38 (0.92)
global symmetry	54.95 (0.53)	54.42 (1.88)	55.91 (2.08)
NN: inv	72.21 (3.38)	73.75 (1.77)	72.16 (2.19)
NN: inv+seg	83.75 (2.35)	83.64 (2.38)	82.75 (2.51)
NN: seg	75.73 (0.60)	78.43 (2.14)	74.89 (1.09)

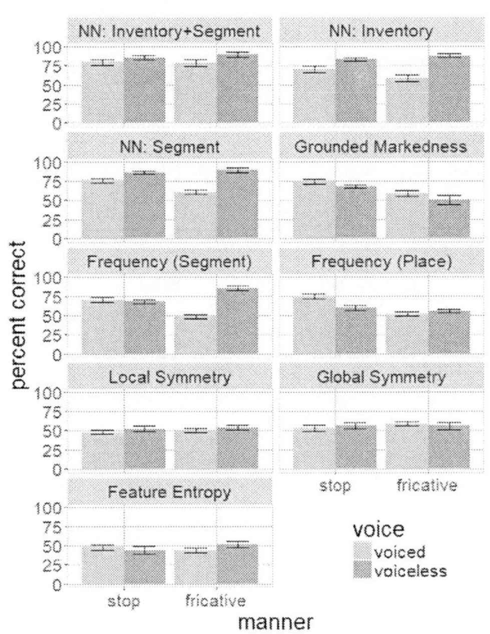

Figure 2: Model performance as a function of sound types. Note that 'Frequency (Segment)' and 'Frequency (Place)' refers to the *typological markedness* model's variants based on segments and places of articulation.

vided by the inventory as a whole. The low performance of the FEATURE-SYSTEMIC models do not really show that inventory-level information is not important for the task. It only shows that the right kind of information is not extracted via the feature-systemic measures.

Figure 2 shows the test-set results for all models, broken down in terms of segment types. Three major trends are worth noting. First, the *grounded markedness* model performs better in stops, especially for voiced stops. This is not surprising given that the grounded markedness scales are better motivated in terms of aerodynamic for stops than fricatives, and the pressure to maintain voicing in stops is considered to have stronger correlation with constriction site in the vocal tract.

Second, the *typological markedness* models have comparable performances as the *grounded markedness* models in stops, but the *typological markedness* model vastly outperforms the *grounded markedness* model in the subset with voiceless fricatives. There is a noticeable difference between the segment-based and the place-based *typological markedness* models in voiceless stops. The major reason is that since labioden-

tal sounds are overall less frequent when compared with bilabial, alveolar, and velar sounds, the place-based *typological markedness* model does not account for the fact that /f/ is a frequent fricative. Being a frequent sound among fricatives, /f/ frequently serves as a foil, and these data points can scored by simply taking into account segment-level typological frequencies. On the other hand, these *typological markedness* models struggle with voiced stops, presumably because of cases that involve /z/: /z/ is a frequent segment, and alveolar is a frequent place of articulation. However, since /s/ is a lot more frequent than /z/, it is very frequent for an inventory to have /s/ but not /z/; when that happens and when the inventory has a voicing distinction elsewhere in its fricatives, /z/ would be a gap, and the *typological markedness* models would struggle in such cases because the high-frequency /z/ should actually be a gap.

Finally, the result of neural network models are similar to frequency-based models, especially in the discrepancy of performance between voiceless and voiceless fricatives. The *Inventory+Segment* model is able to narrow down the discrepancy,

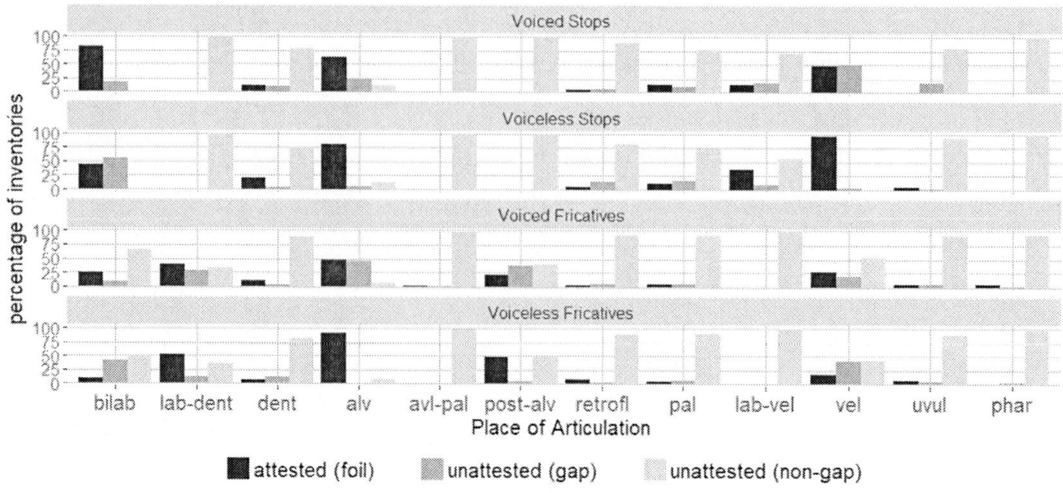

Figure 3: Distribution of attested sounds and gaps across places of articulation in the inventories in the data set

showing that it is possible to solve this problem by taking sophisticated statistical patterning at the level of both the inventory and thekey segments (the gap and the foil).

Figure 3 shows in each segment category, how often an inventory with a particular kind of gap has a gap and a foil in a particular place of articulation. For example, the dark purple bar in the 'bilab' column in the 'Voiced Stops' panel shows the following information: within inventories that have at least a gap in voiced stops, how often they have an attested bilabial voiced stop. The light purple bar shows how often do these inventories lack a bilabial voiced stop, which is defined as a gap in this study. Finally, the palest white bar, which is almost nonexistent for the 'bilab' column, shows the percentage of inventories that do not have a bilabial stop but the absence does not constitute a gap (i.e., the inventory also does not have a bilabial voiceless stop).

For voiced stops, foils are well-attested in the fronter regions of the vocal tract. Constriction in these regions supposedly makes maintenance of voicing easier. On the other hand, a more frequent distribution of gaps in the back region of the vocal tract would be advantageous for the *grounded markedness* model, which is true to a certain extent.

As for voiceless stops, the *grounded markedness* model prefers a distribution where gaps are in the front region of the vocal tract. This is again true to a certain extent, as seen in the second panel in Figure 3. For fricatives, the dis-

tributional patterns are not advantageous for the *grounded markedness* model: The gaps in voiced fricatives occur in the fronter region in the vocal tract, contradictory to how the markedness scales expect gaps to occur in the backer region. As for voiceless fricatives, the high frequency of velar gaps also goes against a preference for having gaps in the fronter region. On the other hand, as mentioned earlier, the concentration of attestedness in certain places of articulation for voiceless fricatives show why the *typological markedness* model has an advantage in this subset of data.

Due to the sub-par performance of feature-systematic models, a supplement experiment is conducted to test the following hypothesis: The feature-systematic measures do not account for where an inventory may have a gap. They simply measure a preference for inventories to not have a gap. To examine this, I compare the feature-systematic measures of obstruent inventories with and without the gaps that are investigated in this study: gaps in stops and fricatives.

The results are shown in Figure 4. To put all three measures in the same graph, the feature-systemic scores are z-transformed. Statistical tests show that the global symmetry metric is significantly lower in gapless inventories in the data set [$t(1871.9) = 5.91, p < .0001$], suggesting a better global symmetry for gapless inventories. Feature entropy is also shown to be significantly lower in gapless inventories [$t(1860.6) = 7.46, p < .0001$], suggesting a better feature economy for gapless inventories. These results may seem contradictory,

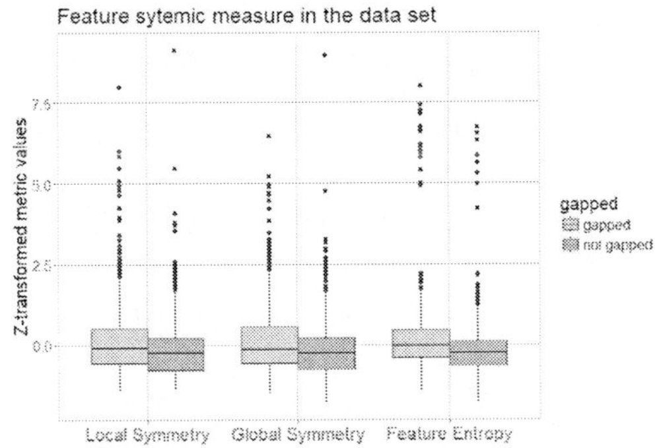

Figure 4: Comparison of gapped and non-gapped inventories in feature-systematic measures. The upper regions in the graphs indicate better symmetry and economy.

as feature entropy prefers the distribution of feature values to be skewed, while global symmetry prefers otherwise. Further inspection shows that gapless inventories requires a larger feature set [$t(1857) = 3.15, p < .01$], and this potentially explains why feature entropy and global symmetry show the same direction: it is possible that feature entropy for gapless inventories is brought down by requiring fewer features in the system. Local symmetry, on the other hand, shows an effect that is opposed as expected: gapped inventories have a significantly better local symmetry value than gapless ones [$t(1871) = 5.42, p < .0001$].

5 Discussion & Conclusion

This study shows whether a segment is more marked, either in terms of aerodynamics or typological frequencies, plays a role in deciding whether a segment is attested or gapped in an inventory. Crucially, the effectiveness of markedness in this task correlates with whether a particular markedness scale has a strong motivation in phonetic grounding.

Even though the problem of identifying gaps is more directly related to the larger question of inventory shapes, models that implement theories that directly address the nature or tendency of human sound inventories, such as feature economy or feature symmetry, do not perform well in this task. This may suggest that the drive towards a more efficient use of feature system, regardless of how it is construed, is not active in identifying what sounds should be phonemes in an inventory. However, it is possible that these theories account for inventory preference at a larger level, such as a preference for attested inventories over randomly generated sound inventories (Dunbar and Dupoux, 2016; Mukherjee et al., 2007). It remains to be seen whether the effectiveness of these metrics can be found at a level that is more accessible and related to phonological learning. As a starting point, the supplement experiment in this study has shown that these measures can differentiate inventories with and without gaps.

The performance of neural networks with different architectures complement the findings for MARKEDNESS and FEATURE-SYSTEMIC models. The good performance of the model that only looks at the key segments (i.e., the gap and the foil) shows that this task can be performed well to a certain extent by doing exactly what the MARKEDNESS models are doing, and with a more powerful statistical learner the result can be better. The performance of the Inventory model, which looks at inventories as a whole, also has good performance, showing that considering the inventory as a whole, without paying specific attention to the key segments, is also a viable way to perform this task. Finally, the *inventory+segment* model shows that the performance can be further improved when key segments are highlighted while also taking the whole inventories into account. It points to the fact that there are indeed usable information in the inventories at issue for deciding whether a segment is likely to be gapped in those particular inventories. The information is just not utilized by the FEATURE-SYSTEMIC models.

To conclude, this study shows that segmental properties and statistical patterns both play a role in shaping inventories in specific ways. In terms of methodology, this study makes two contributions: First, it demonstrates how a large database of phonemic inventories can be informative in answering phonological questions that may have ramifications for phonological learning. Seconds, it shows that models that are theoretically informed and models that only use statistical information can join force to show corroborating results. Finally, if the computational task in this study can be considered analogous to the task of phoneme identification for a human learner, this study suggests the potentially active role of segment markedness for stops, especially voiced ones, as well as the distributional patterns of feature values and segments, in learning phonemic inventories.

References

Monojit Choudhury, Animesh Mukherjee, Anupam Basu, and Niloy Ganguly. 2006. Analysis and synthesis of the distribution of consonants over languages: A complex network approach. In *Proceedings of the COLING/ACL on Main conference poster sessions*, pages 128–135. Association for Computational Linguistics.

George N Clements. 2003a. Feature economy in sound systems. *Phonology*, 20(3):287–333.

Georges N Clements. 2003b. Feature economy as a phonological universal. In *15th International Congress of Phonetic Sciences, Barcelona, Spain*.

Ryan Cotterell and Jason Eisner. 2017. Probabilistic typology: Deep generative models of vowel inventories. In *Proceedings of the 2018 Conference of the North American Chapter of the Association for Computational Linguistics: Human Language Technologies*, pages 37–46.

Brian Dillon, Ewan Dunbar, and William Idsardi. 2013. A single-stage approach to learning phonological categories: Insights from inuktitut. *Cognitive science*, 37(2):344–377.

Ewan Dunbar and Emmanuel Dupoux. 2016. Geometric constraints on human speech sound inventories. *Frontiers in psychology*, 7.

Mats Exter. 2003. Phonetik und phonologie des wogeo. Master's thesis, Institut fr Sprachwissenschaft Universitt zu Kln.

Thomas V Gamkrelidze. 1975. On the correlation of stops and fricatives in a phonological system. *Lingua*, 35(3-4):231–261.

Joseph H Greenberg. 1970. Some generalizations concerning glottalic consonants, especially implosives. *International Journal of American Linguistics*, 36(2):123–145.

Albert Willem de Groot. 1941. *Structural linguistics and phonetic law*. Noord-Hollandsche Uitgeversmaatschappij.

Diane Kewley-Port. 1983. Time-varying features as correlates of place of articulation in stop consonants. *The Journal of the Acoustical Society of America*, 73(1):322–335.

Diane Kewley-Port, David B Pisoni, and Michael Studdert-Kennedy. 1983. Perception of static and dynamic acoustic cues to place of articulation in initial stop consonants. *The Journal of the Acoustical Society of America*, 73(5):1779–1793.

Scott Mackie and Jeff Mielke. 2011. Feature economy in natural, random, and synthetic inventories. *Where do phonological features come from*, pages 43–63.

Ian Maddieson. 2013. Voicing and gaps in plosive systems. In Matthew S. Dryer and Martin Haspelmath, editors, *The World Atlas of Language Structures Online*. Max Planck Institute for Evolutionary Anthropology, Leipzig.

Ian Maddieson and Sandra Ferrari Disner. 1984. *Patterns of sounds*. Cambridge university press.

André Martinet. 1955. Economie des changements phonétiques. *Berne: Francke*.

Bob McMurray, Richard N Aslin, and Joseph C Toscano. 2009. Statistical learning of phonetic categories: insights from a computational approach. *Developmental science*, 12(3):369–378.

Jeff Mielke. 2008. *The emergence of distinctive features*. Oxford University Press.

Steven Moran, Daniel McCloy, and Richard Wright. 2014. Phoible online. *Leipzig: Max Planck Institute for Evolutionary Anthropology*.

Animesh Mukherjee, Monojit Choudhury, Anupam Basu, and Niloy Ganguly. 2007. Modeling the co-occurrence principles of the consonant inventories: A complex network approach. *International Journal of Modern Physics C*, 18(02):281–295.

Animesh Mukherjee, Monojit Choudhury, Anupam Basu, and Niloy Ganguly. 2009. Self-organization of the sound inventories: Analysis and synthesis of the occurrence and co-occurrence networks of consonants. *Journal of Quantitative Linguistics*, 16(2):157–184.

John J Ohala. 1983. The origin of sound patterns in vocal tract constraints. In *The production of speech*, pages 189–216. Springer.

BL Smith. 1975. Effects of vocalic context, place of articulation, and speaker's sex on voiced stop consonant production. *The Journal of the Acoustical Society of America*, 58(S1):S61–S61.

Gautam K Vallabha, James L McClelland, Ferran Pons, Janet F Werker, and Shigeaki Amano. 2007. Unsupervised learning of vowel categories from infant-directed speech. *Proceedings of the National Academy of Sciences*, 104(33):13273–13278.

C-command dependencies as TSL string constraints

Thomas Graf
Stony Brook University
`mail@thomasgraf.net`

Nazila Shafiei
Stony Brook University
`nazila.shafiei@stonybrook.edu`

Abstract

We provide a general formal framework for analyzing c-command based dependencies in syntax, e.g. binding and NPI licensing, from a subregular perspective. C-command relations are represented as strings computed from Minimalist derivation trees, and syntactic dependencies are shown to be input-output tier-based strictly local over such strings. The complexity of many syntactic phenomena thus is comparable to dependencies in phonology and morphology.

1 Introduction

The last decade has seen tremendous progress in the subregular analysis of phonology and morphology (see Chandlee 2017, Heinz 2018 and references therein). The subregular program is concerned with identifying proper subclasses of the regular languages that are sufficiently powerful for natural language, and to convert these tighter complexity bounds into typological predictions and new learning algorithms.

Extending the subregular approach to syntax has proven more challenging because syntactic dependencies are not regular over strings, let alone subregular (Chomsky, 1957; Huybregts, 1984; Shieber, 1985; Michaelis and Kracht, 1997; Kobele, 2006). But syntactic dependencies seem to be subregular over tree structures (Graf, 2012). More recently, a series of arguments (Graf, 2018a,b; Graf et al., 2018) has been presented that dependencies in phonology, morphology, and syntax are all of comparable subregular complexity once one picks a suitable data structure (string-like vs. trees). More precisely, all dependencies are conjectured to belong to natural extensions of the class *tier-based strictly local* (TSL; Heinz et al., 2011; Graf and Mayer, 2018).

While this claim is well-supported for phonology and morphology, it is on shakier ground for syntax. It seems to hold for subcategorization and displacement (Merge and Move in Chomskyan terms) and some kinds of NPI-licensing (Vu, 2018). But it may fail for constraints based on c-command, which are numerous in syntax. This paper argues that these dependencies are also TSL given the right kind of representation.

We define a general procedure for converting c-command dependencies to string languages. Intuitively, our procedure amounts to little more than making c-command a basic relation in syntactic representations (cf. Frank and Vijay-Shanker, 1999). Formally, we represent Minimalist grammar derivations (Stabler, 1997) as dependency trees (cf. Brody, 2000; Kobele, 2002) and then associate each node with a string of nodes that c-command it. Principle A of binding theory, for example, then requires that a string that ends in a reflexive must contain a potential binder somewhere between the reflexive and the head of its binding domain. Based on a preliminary analysis of c-command dependencies in the literature, we contend that they all fit into extensions of TSL that have been proposed for phonology and morphology.

The paper proceeds as follows. We first discuss some general preliminaries (§2), including MGs, dependency trees, and subregular syntax. After that, c-strings are introduced as a string-based representation of c-command relations (§3.1), and various syntactic phenomena are characterized in these terms (§3.2). We then show that the dependencies of these phenomena are input-output tier-based strictly local (Graf and Mayer, 2018) over c-strings (§4), and we explain why this likely holds for all c-command dependencies in syntax. Some final complications introduced by movement are discussed in §5.

Proceedings of the Society for Computation in Linguistics (SCiL) 2019, pages 205-215.
New York City, New York, January 3-6, 2019

2 Preliminaries

While the ideas presented in this paper are fairly intuitive, a sufficiently rigorous description requires a broad formal background. We first introduce some basic notation (§2.1) and then discuss Minimalist grammars as a formal model of syntax (§2.2). We also explain how their derivation can be encoded as dependency trees, which will be used in §3 to easily compute the c-commanders for any given node. After that, §2.3 surveys some recent developments on subregular syntax and why this paper pursues a different route.

2.1 Formal language theory

We follow the standard notation for strings: Σ by default denotes a fixed alphabet, ε is the empty string, S^* is the Kleene closure of set S, S^+ is $S^* - \{\varepsilon\}$, $\overline{S}$ is $\Sigma - S$, and instead of $\{a\}$ we may simply write a.

2.2 Minimalist grammars

In order to assess the complexity of syntactic dependencies, we need a formal model of syntax. We choose Minimalist grammars (MGs; Stabler, 1997, 2011). MGs are inspired by Chomsky (1995) but can incorporate a wide range of ideas from the syntactic literature (see Graf 2013 and references therein). This makes them an ideal testing ground for c-command dependencies.

Every MG is a finite set of lexical items that are annotated with strings of features to drive the structure-building operations Merge and Move.

Example 1 (Merge). The noun *car* only carries the *category feature* N^-. The determiner *the* carries a matching *selector feature* N^+. The full feature string for *the* is N^+D^-. This indicates that *the* first selects a noun and then acts as DP that can be selected by anything with the matching selector feature D^+. The possessive marker *'s*, on the other hand, must select both a noun as its complement and a DP as its specifier. Hence its feature string is $N^+D^+D^-$.

Example 2 (Move). The determiner *which* is similar to *the*, except that it also undergoes wh-movement after it has been selected. Therefore its feature string must include a *licensee feature* wh^- at the very end: $N^+D^-wh^-$. At least in some cases the landing site of the wh-mover is an empty CP-specifier. In order to allow for this, the grammar must contain a lexical item whose phonetic exponent is ε and whose feature string is $T^+wh^+C^-$. Here wh^+ is a *licensor feature* that marks the empty C-head as a landing site for wh-movement.

As every MG builds a phrase structure tree via a sequence of Merge and Move steps, every syntactic tree can be fully specified by its derivation. The derivation, in turn, can be represented as a tree, which may take the form of a dependency tree as shown in Fig. 1 (cf. Brody, 2000; Kobele, 2002). In an MG dependency tree, a node d is the daughter of node n iff n selects d. For MGs, this means that X^- on d and a matching X^+ of n were checked as part of the same Merge operation. We assume that the linear order of siblings is the reverse of the order of selection, so that the first argument of a head is its rightmost daughter. Movement is not indicated in dependency trees as it can be inferred from the distribution of licensor and licensee features.

2.3 MGs as subregular tree languages

It has been known for a long time that every MG's set of well-formed derivation trees forms a regular tree language (Michaelis, 2001; Kobele et al., 2007). While these results build on a different derivation tree format, they also hold for the dependency tree format in this paper because the latter can be obtained from the former by a regularity-preserving tree transduction.

It has also become clear, though, that MG derivation tree languages are not just regular, but subregular (Graf, 2012). Most recently, Graf (2018b) showed that they belong to the formal class TSL. This class was first defined for strings to handle some phenomena in phonology (Heinz et al., 2011). Graf lifts TSL from strings to trees. Intuitively, TSL masks out parts of the tree that are irrelevant for a given dependency and then puts locally bounded constraints on the remainder. Graf limits his attention to Merge and Move, but follow-up work has since argued that NPI-licensing and morphological case also fit into this class (Vu, 2018; Vu et al., 2019). If correct, this would not only suggest a new kind of computational parallelism between language modules, but might also prove useful for parsing and learning algorithms.

Although we believe this work to be very promising, it is still based on detailed case studies and has not yielded any general properties that guarantee that TSL is a safe upper complexity

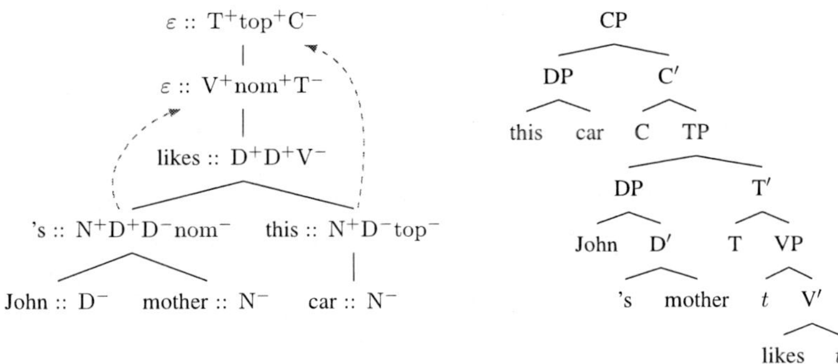

Figure 1: A dependency tree representation of an MG derivation, with its corresponding phrase structure tree to the right. Movement is indicated by arrows for the reader's convenience, it is not part of the tree. Crucially, moving phrases remain in their base position in the dependency tree.

bound for all attested syntactic dependencies. In addition, the step from strings to trees complicates the comparison to phonology and morphology. Several subregular classes besides TSL have been argued to play a central role in these domains, e.g. SP (Rogers et al., 2010) and IBSP (Graf, 2017, 2018a). The latter is difficult to lift from strings to trees, whereas the former seems ill-suited for syntactic dependencies based on preliminary work of ours. For these reasons, a string-based view of syntactic dependencies is a welcome alternative that makes it easier to compare phonology and syntax. As we argue in this paper (§4.2), it also provides some general insights that make it very likely that all c-command dependencies fall within a subregular region that is also occupied by dependencies in phonology and morphology.

3   C-command relations as strings

We are finally in a position to demonstrate how c-command dependencies reduce to constraints on strings. We first present the general idea in §3.1 and then apply it to several examples in §3.2. We only describe the relevant string languages and wait until §4 to show that they fit into (extensions of) TSL.

3.1   Idea and definition

The dependency graphs make it very easy to enforce c-command requirements for any given node — at least if one puts aside movement, as we will do until §5. Until then, "c-command" only means "c-command between base positions before movement".

If u is a left sibling of v in an MG dependency tree t, then (the phrase headed by) u c-commands

(the phrase headed by) v. This is illustrated by *John* and *mother* in Fig. 1. In addition, v is c-commanded by almost every node that dominates it. Looking again at Fig. 1, we see that the T-head and the C-head dominate *John* in the dependency tree and c-command *John* in the phrase structure tree (at the position marked by the trace in Spec,VP).

One minor wrinkle is the relation between heads and their specifiers. The former do not c-command the latter, but they do so according to our definition. Hence our notion of command is actually a hybrid of c-command and m-command (Aoun and Sportiche, 1983). One may call it *d[erivational]-command* to emphasize this difference: a node d-commands all its right siblings, all its daughters, and everything that is d-commanded by its siblings or daughters. As far as we can tell, the minor differences between c-command and d-command are immaterial for all syntactic dependencies that have been argued to involve c-command, and we will continue to use c-command as the general term instead of d-command whenever this does not cause any confusion.

Note that d-command is a highly natural relation over derivation trees as it encodes prominence with respect to feature checking. Based on the definition above, x d-commands y iff x had one of its Merge features checked more recently than y. A specifier s of head h d-commands a complement c of h because s has been selected more recently than c. And h d-commands s because h is selected by some other head after s has been selected. C-command as a basic relation of syntax is difficult to motivate (but see Epstein et al. 1998 and Chametzky 2000, 2011). D-command, on the other hand, falls out naturally from the MG feature calculus and thus is a plausible primitive for syntactic dependencies.[1]

One can automatically calculate for every node a string representation of the relevant command relations. Let T be a tree such that node m has the daughters $d_1, \ldots, d_i, d, d_{i+1}, \ldots, d_n$, with $n \geq 0$. The *immediate c[ommand]-string* $ics(d)$ of d is the string $d\, d_i \cdots d_1$. For every node n of T, its *c[ommand]-string* $cs(n)$ is recursively defined as shown below, where $\cdot$ indicates string concatenation:[2]

$$cs(n) := \begin{cases} ics(n) & \text{if } n \text{ is the root of } T \\ ics(n) \cdot cs(m) & \text{if } m \text{ is } n\text{'s mother} \end{cases}$$

Note that c-strings sort d-commanders in a bottom-up fashion, which usually yields the reverse of their linear order in the string. For improved readability, we omit all features and replace empty heads by their category.

Example 3. Consider once more the dependency graph in Fig. 1. While the immediate command string of *car* is just *car*, its c-string is *car this 's likes T C*.

The next subsection illustrates how a number of syntactic phenomena can be reinterpreted as constraints on c-strings. Even more strikingly, these constraints are fairly intuitive, and as we will see in §4, their subregular complexity is largely in line with what has been found in phonology and morphology.

3.2 Examples of syntactic constraints

It is beyond the purview of this paper to exhaustively analyze every syntactic dependency that has been claimed to involve c-command. Consequently, we limit ourselves to a representative sample of NPI-licensing (§3.2.1) and binding effects (§3.2.2–§3.2.4). Due to space restrictions, we are also limited to high-level discussions that illustrate the general ideas but do not account for all details and potential complications (cf. §3.2.5).

---

[1] If one wants to include c-command relations created by movement, it suffices to broaden the definition such that any kind of feature checking induces d-command relations, not just those affecting category and selector features.

[2] C-strings over dependency trees are closely related to the concept of spine languages (cf. Martens et al., 2008; Graf, 2012). In spine languages, $ics(n)$ and $cs(m)$ would be separated by a distinguished symbol, e.g. ♣. We omit this here for simplicity, but point out that preliminary work of ours suggests that ♣ is needed in some cases to correctly define locality domains.

3.2.1 NPI licensing

NPIs can occur in a variety of contexts, but the central syntactic licensing condition is c-command by a downward-entailing operator. We can capture this in terms of conditions on string languages. If a c-string ends in an NPI, then it must also contain a licensor such as *no* or *nobody*. So the required string language is *NPI* $\cdots$ {*no, nobody*} $\cdots$. This ensures that no NPI can ever occur without a c-commanding licensor.

Example 4. Consider the ill-formed **Every student said that the train ever arrives on time*. Assuming that *ever* is a functional head between V and T, its c-string is *ever T that every said T C*. Since this string is not a member of the NPI-licensing language, *ever* is not licensed and the sentence is illicit.

As is witnessed by *Have you ever been to Russia*, NPIs are also licensed in questions. We can readily accommodate this by adding interrogative C-heads to the set of licensors. Overall, then, the c-string pattern for NPI-licensing is *NPI* $\cdots$ *Lic* $\cdots$, where *Lic* is a downward entailing quantifier or an interrogative C-head.

3.2.2 Locally bound reflexives

Principle A requires that reflexives must be bound within their binding domain, usually a TP containing an abstract subject. When construed as a distributional constraint, this reduces to the presence of a DP in the binding domain that c-commands the reflexive and matches its ϕ-features (person, number, and gender).

In MGs, every TP with an abstract subject is headed by a lexical item with category feature T^- and licensor feature nom^+. Let T be the shorthand for any such LI, $R[\phi]$ a reflexive, and $D[\phi]$ a matching determiner. Since MGs have finite lexicons, one can list for each reflexive which determiners match its ϕ-features. Then Principle A corresponds to the string language $R[\phi]\, \overline{T}^*\, D[\phi] \cdots$, where $\overline{T}^*$ is a (possibly empty) string that contains no instances of T.

Example 5. Contrast the well-formed *John said that Mary likes herself* with the ill-formed **John said that Mary likes himself*. The former has the c-string *herself Mary likes T that John said T C*. Since *Mary* is ϕ-feature compatible with *herself* and occurs between the reflexive and the T-head, Principle A is satisfied. In the ill-formed sentence, *herself* is replaced by *himself*. The closest compatible D-head is *John*, but since a finite T-head occurs between *John* and the reflexive, Principle A is violated.

3.2.3 Non-locally bound reflexives

The reflexive *sig* in Swedish only partially obeys Principle A. It still requires a syntactic binder, but said binder must not be part of the same binding domain (Kiparsky, 2002). The corresponding c-string language is $R[\phi] \cdots T \cdots D[\phi] \cdots$.

Example 6. Suppose for the sake of argument that English *himself* behaves like Swedish *sig*, and consider again *John said that Mary likes himself/ herself*. Then the sentence with *herself* would be ill-formed, but not the one with *himself*. And as the reader may verify for themselves, only the c-string of *himself* fits the pattern above.

3.2.4 Principle B

Principle B regulates the distribution of syntactically bound pronouns. Pronouns in English can always be discourse-bound, so their distribution is unproblematic. Marathi, on the other hand, has pronouns that must be syntactically bound (Kiparsky, 2002). Like standard pronouns, they I) must be non-locally bound, and II) cannot have the same referent as a local c-commander. Condition II) makes the distribution of Marathi pronouns much harder than that of Swedish *sig*-reflexives.

From a distributional perspective, Principle B enforces a counting condition: if a pronoun is c-commanded by n pronouns in the same binding domain, then at least n potential antecedents must c-command the binding domain in order to furnish at least one grammatical reading. Temporarily putting aside ϕ-features, this yields the string template $\alpha T \beta$ such that $\alpha, \beta \in \Sigma^*$, α starts with a pronoun, and the total number of R-expressions (i.e. D-heads) in β exceeds the number of pronouns in α; pronouns are counted as R-expressions in β because they can bind pronouns in α. Without further assumptions, this pattern is context-free and thus much more complicated than any of the previous c-string languages.

But Graf and Abner (2012) show that even though a binding domain may contain an unbounded number of pronouns, most of them can share the same referent. Pronouns within distinct adjuncts can pick out the same referent, and other constructions such as coordination are very limited in how they interact with bound pronouns. As a result, there is an upper bound n on the number of distinct antecedents that are needed to license all pronouns in a binding domain. This guarantees regularity and, as we will see in §4.3, subregularity by virtue of being definable in IO-TSL.

Example 7. Suppose for the sake of argument that English pronouns always require syntactic antecedents. Then the sentence *John thinks that he likes him* is ungrammatical, whereas *John told Bill that he likes him* is well-formed. This immediately follows from the c-string of the second pronoun in each sentence. One is *him he likes T that John thinks T C* and thus does not furnish enough antecedents for *him* and *he*. The other c-string provides the required minimum of two antecedents, namely *John* and *Bill*: *him he likes T that Bill John told T C*.

3.2.5 Caveats

Each one of the phenomena above has several complications. What counts as an NPI licensor depends on the position of the NPI. For example, *every* can license an NPI if it occurs in a relative clause modifying the argument of *every*. Similarly, many reflexives are exempt from Principle A when they occur inside certain adjuncts, and some languages like Icelandic allow for long-distance binding only under specific circumstances. These are serious complications. A careful analysis of any one of these phenomena arguably requires a full-length journal paper. Nonetheless we believe that these complications would render the string patterns more complicated, but not more complex. The reason for this is explained at the end of the next section, which analyzes the subregular complexity of syntactic dependencies over c-strings.

4 Subregular complexity

We have successfully reduced c-command dependencies to regular string languages. But regularity is a loose upper bound. As we explain next, the c-string languages from the previous section all fit into IO-TSL, the class of *input-output tier-based strictly local* string languages. This class has recently been proposed as an upper bound on phonotactic complexity (Graf and Mayer, 2018). We first present the defintion IO-TSL (§4.1) and provide a general IO-TSL strategy for capturing dependencies over c-strings (§4.2). This strategy is then exemplified with IO-TSL grammars for each one of the templates from the previous section (§4.3). In §4.4, we explain why IO-TSL is a meaningful upper bound that makes testable predictions about the shape of syntactic dependencies.

4.1 Defining IO-TSL

IO-TSL is an extension of the *strictly local* (SL) languages. A language is SL iff it can be described by a list of finitely many forbidden substrings. IO-TSL enhances this with a local tier projection mechanism: whether a symbol is projected on a tier depends on the symbol itself, its local context in the string (i.e. up to m symbols before and/or after it), and up to n previous symbols on the tier.

Example 8. Unbounded tone plateauing forbids any instances of the low tone L to occur between two high tones H. So HLLL and LLLH are well-formed, but HLLLH is not. One can capture this by projecting L iff it occurs immediately to the right of H, and projecting H iff the previous symbol on the tier is L. The strings above would get the tiers L, empty, and LH, respectively. If one forbids the substring LH on tiers, HLLLH is ruled out as desired while HLLL and LLLH are still generated.

The rest of this subsection formalizes this intuitive idea. Let Σ be some fixed alphabet and $s \in \Sigma^*$. The set $f_k(s)$ of k-*factors* of s consists of all the length-k substrings of $\rtimes^{k-1} s \ltimes^{k-1}$, where $\rtimes, \ltimes \notin \Sigma$ and $k \geq 1$.

Definition 1. A stringset $L \subseteq \Sigma^*$ is *strictly k-local* (SL-k) iff there is some $G \subseteq (\Sigma \cup \{\rtimes, \ltimes\})^k$ such that $L = \{s \in \Sigma^* \mid f_k(s) \cap G = \emptyset\}$.

Intuitively, G defines a *grammar* of forbidden substrings that no well-formed string may contain. The class SL of strictly local stringsets is $\bigcup_{k \geq 0}$ SL-k.

Example 9. The string language $(ab)^+$ is generated by the grammar $G := \{\rtimes\ltimes, \rtimes b, aa, bb, a\ltimes\}$ and thus is SL-2. For instance, aba is illicit because $f_2(aba) \cap G = \{a\ltimes\} \neq \emptyset$, whereas $f_2(abab) \cap G = \emptyset$.

Example 10. The finite language of all strings of length 3 is SL-4. It is generated by the grammar $\{abcd \mid a, b, c, d \in \Sigma\} \cup \{abcd \mid a = \rtimes, d = \ltimes, b, c \in \Sigma \cup \{\rtimes, \ltimes\}\}$.

The tier projection mechanism of IO-TSL is defined in terms of contexts that specify when a given symbol should be added to the tier. An (i, j)-*context* c is a 4-tuple $\langle \sigma, b, a, t \rangle$ with $\sigma \in \Sigma$,

t a string over $\Sigma \cup \{\rtimes\}$ of length $j - 1$, and a and b strings over $\Sigma \cup \{\rtimes, \ltimes\}$ of combined length $i - 1$. The basic idea is that c specifies that σ should be projected whenever both of the following hold: it occurs between the substrings b (look-*back*) and a (look-*ahead*), and the tier constructed so far ends in t. Given a set of contexts $c_1, c_2, \ldots, c_n$, we call it an (i, j)-*context set* iff for every c_m ($1 \leq m \leq n$) there are $i_m \leq i$ and $j_m \leq j$ such that c_m is an (i_m, j_m)-context.

Definition 2. Let C be an (i, j)-context set. Then the *input-output strictly (i, j)-local* (IOSL-(i, j)) tier projection π_C maps every $s \in \Sigma^*$ to $\pi'_C(\rtimes^i, s\ltimes^i, \ltimes^j)$, where for $\sigma \in \Sigma$ and $a, b, t, u, v, w \in (\Sigma \cup \{\rtimes, \ltimes\})^*$, it holds that $\pi'_C(ub, \sigma a v, wt)$ is

$$
\begin{cases}
\varepsilon & \text{if } \sigma a v = \varepsilon, \\
\sigma \pi'_C(ub\sigma, av, wt\sigma) & \text{if } \langle \sigma, b, a, t \rangle \in C, \\
\pi'_C(ub\sigma, av, wt) & \text{otherwise.}
\end{cases}
$$

Example 11. Let $\Sigma := \{a, b, c\}$ and consider the tier projection that always projects the first and last symbol of the string, always projects a, never projects c, and projects b only if the previous symbol on the tier is a. This projection is IOSL-(2,2). The context set contains all the contexts below, and only those:

- $\langle \sigma, \rtimes, \varepsilon, \varepsilon \rangle$ for all $\sigma \in \Sigma$,

- $\langle \sigma, \varepsilon, \ltimes, \varepsilon \rangle$ for all $\sigma \in \Sigma$,

- $\langle a, \varepsilon, \varepsilon, \varepsilon \rangle$,

- $\langle b, \varepsilon, \varepsilon, a \rangle$.

Definition 3. A stringset $L \subseteq \Sigma^*$ is *input-output tier-based strictly (i, j, k)-local* (IO-TSL-(i, j, k)) iff there exists an IOSL-(i, j) tier projection π_C and an SL-k language K such that $L := \{s \in \Sigma^* \mid \pi_C(s) \in K\}$. It is IO-TSL iff it is IO-TSL-(i, j, k) for some i, j, and k.

The class TSL-k defined in Heinz et al. (2011) is identical to IO-TSL-$(1, 1, k)$. This shows that IO-TSL is indeed a generalization of TSL. In fact, I-TSL and O-TSL have been independently proposed in computational phonology (Baek, 2017; De Santo and Graf, 2017; Mayer and Major, 2018; Yang, 2018), and Graf and Mayer (2018) show that the combination of the two into IO-TSL furnishes the additional power that is required for Sanskrit n-retroflexion. Under the assumption that dependencies in phonology and syntax are of comparable complexity, IO-TSL is a natural candidate for a tighter upper bound on the complexity of constraints on c-strings.

4.2 General IO-TSL strategy

The dependencies in §3.2 — and syntactic dependencies in general — all share the common property that even though there is no upper bound on the length of c-strings, only a finitely bounded number of elements actually matter. Which elements matter depends only on the local context and which symbols are already on the tier. This allows for a very general IO-TSL strategy: construct tiers such that they only contain the relevant elements. Then there are only finitely many distinct tier configurations, and hence the set of well-formed tiers is finite. As every finite string language is SL-k for some k (cf. Ex. 10), separating the well-formed tiers from the ill-formed ones becomes trivial. So the central challenge for an IO-TSL treatment of c-command dependencies lies in the construction of tiers, not the constraints on those tiers.

The tier construction process also follows a general template. We project tiers from left to right, and the very first element is always projected — this is an input-sensitive projection step. We then use an output-sensitive projection strategy to only project relevant elements.

Example 12. Suppose the first symbol to be projected is an NPI. Then only an NPI-licensor can be projected next. After the first NPI-licensor has been projected, no more symbols are put on the tier. Since a single NPI-licensor is enough, we never project more than one. So the tier either has the form *NPI NPI-licensor* or just *NPI*. The former is well-formed, the latter is not.

Example 13. If the first element is a reflexive that is subject to Principle A, only T-heads and matching D-heads need to be projected. Again nothing is projected after this second projection step as Principle A is already satisfied or violated depending on whether the second symbol is T or $D[\phi]$. The tier then has one of the following three forms: *reflexive D*, *reflexive T*, or just *reflexive*. The first one is well-formed, the other two ill-formed.

If the first symbol on the tier is not subject to any constraints, then nothing else is projected. Proceeding in this fashion, we can define a single IO-TSL grammar that generates every well-formed c-string while forbidding those that violate one of our string patterns from §3. This shows that the whole system of syntactic dependencies is IO-TSL, not just each individual dependency.

4.3 Example grammars for dependencies

Let us now apply this idea to the c-string templates from §3, repeated here for the readers convenience:

$NPI \cdots Lic \cdots$
$R[\phi] \, \overline{T}^* D[\phi] \cdots$
$R[\phi] \cdots T \cdots D[\phi] \cdots$
$\alpha T \beta$ (α starts with pronoun,
$\quad \beta$ has more R-expressions than α has pronouns)

Now consider the corresponding projection contexts for any arbitrary MG G. We first include $\langle \sigma, \varepsilon, \ltimes, \varepsilon \rangle$ for all $\sigma \in G$ so that the first symbol is always projected. Next we add $\langle l, \varepsilon, \varepsilon, t \rangle$ for all $l \in G$ and $t \in G^*$ such that:

NPI t is an NPI and l an NPI licensor, or

Reflexive t is a reflexive, and l is either a T-head carrying nom$^+$ or a D-head with matching ϕ-features, or

sig either t is a *sig*-reflexive and l is a T-head carrying nom$^+$, or $t = uv$ with u a *sig*-reflexive and v a T-head carrying nom$^+$ and l is a D-head with matching ϕ-features.

The definition for **sig** is convoluted because it accounts for both projection of T after *sig* and projection of $D[\phi]$ after T and *sig*.

Next we forbid all bigrams of the form lp such that either l is an NPI and p is not an NPI-licensor, or l is a reflexive and p is not a matching D-head. Note that this includes cases where p is no LI at all, but rather the start/end of a tier. We also forbid all trigrams that start with a *sig*-reflexive but do not continue with a suitable T-head and a matching D-head.

Example 14. Consider once more the illicit NPI in example 4. Given the c-string *ever T that every said T C*, the constructed tier is just *ever*, which is forbidden. If *every* is replaced with *no*, the tier becomes *ever no* and thus is well-formed. If *ever* were *always* instead, the tier would just be *always*, which is never illicit because no special licensing is needed. Note that the tier never grows past *ever no*, even for sentences like *No student told no professor that no train ever arrives on time.*

Example 15. Suppose as in example 6 that English reflexives behaved like Swedish *sig* and thus require a non-local binder. The c-string *herself Mary likes T that John said T C* results in the illicit tier *herself T*. But if *herself* is replaced by *himself*, one obtains the well-formed tier *himself T John* instead. This is also the tier for much longer sentences such as *Bill thinks Peter doubts that John said that Mary likes him.*

For Principle B, the projection strategy is very similar.

- Project the first element, which is a pronoun that must be syntactically bound.

- Also project such pronouns if the tier so far contains i such pronouns and nothing else, where i is less than some fixed bound n.

- Project a T-head carrying nom$^+$ if the tier only contains pronouns so far.

- Project an R-expression if the tier already contains a T-head and at most $n - 1$ R-expressions.

With this projection strategy, the longest possible tier is of the form $pro^n\ T\ R^n$, and all illicit tiers can be filtered out by $(2n + 1)$-grams.

As pointed out earlier, this analysis ignores complicating factors such as additional licensing configurations for NPIs, or ϕ-feature matching in Principle B. But this does not affect the core property that guarantees the IO-TSL nature of c-command dependencies: Each dependency requires only a finite number of elements on the tier, and by considering the entire tier built so far one can ensure that no extraneous material is projected. In addition, each LI can only be subject to finitely many licensing conditions. These two facts jointly entail that the length of tiers can always be finitely bounded, which makes it trivial to provide an SL grammar that rules out all illicit tiers. It is because of this fixed bound on the number of elements that matter for any given c-command dependency that IO-TSL is a safe upper bound on the complexity of syntactic dependencies over c-strings. This is also the reason why we contend that IO-TSL could accommodate empirically more adequate characterizations of the phenomena in §3 — the number of relevant lexical items would still be finitely bounded within any given c-string.

Admittedly, this strategy comes at the potential cost of large contexts. Fairly small contexts seem to suffice for realistic examples, though, and a smarter, less brute-force strategy may be able to reduce their size even further. We would not be surprised if most c-command dependencies turn out to belong to IO-TSL-$(3, 3, 3)$ or perhaps even IO-TSL-$(2, 2, 2)$.

4.4 Limits of IO-TSL dependencies

IO-TSL makes some strong predictions about what shape linguistic dependencies can take and how multiple c-command conditions may be interwoven.

Example 16. Consider an unattested variant of the long-distance Principle A that applies to Swedish *sig*. In this variant, the reflexive and the antecedent not only have to be separated by a T-head, but each intervening T-head must be c-commanded by some functional head F that is lower than the next higher T-head. So the c-string language is not just $\cdots D[\phi] \cdots T \cdots R[\phi]$, but rather $\alpha R[\phi]$ such that I) α contains at least one $D[\phi]$ and, II) F occurs between every two instances of T.

This string language is not IO-TSL because we can no longer omit projecting all T-heads to the tier. To see this, contrast the well-formed pattern $D[\phi](F\ T)^*\ F\ T\ (F\ T)^*R[\phi]$ against the ill-formed $D[\phi](F\ T)^*\ T\ (F\ T)^*R[\phi]$. The only difference is the unlicensed T-head in the middle, so this T-head must end up on the tier in order to distinguish well-formed from ill-formed strings. But there is no context that can uniquely identify just this T-head without projecting other T-heads or F-heads. The set of well-formed tiers then would be an infinite subset of $\{T, F\}^*\ D[\phi]\ \{T, F\}^*\ R[\phi]$, which is not SL unless the distance between $D[\phi]$ and $R[\phi]$ is finitely bounded. Since there are no additional factors that guarantee such a bound on the distance between reflexive and licensor, our unattested variant of *sig*-licensing is not IO-TSL.

This example highlights a crucial limitation of IO-TSL: a long-distance dependency cannot apply across an unbounded number of long-distance dependencies that interact with it. The F-licensing of T-heads would be unproblematic if it were an independent constraint that must always be satisfied, rather than just being an extra condition on *sig*-licensing. For then it would be a condition on all c-strings that start with T-heads and could be omitted in c-strings that start with reflexives. Alternatively, F-licensing of T-heads could be captured if the distance between F and T were locally bounded. In this case, one could project F and T only once and skip all other locally licensed T-heads. Similarly, it would suffice to project at most one unlicensed T-head. The result would be tiers of the form $D[\phi]\alpha R[\phi]$ where α is $T\ F\ T$ or $F\ T\ T$. Then the tier language would once again be finite. So a long-distance dependency can interact with other dependencies, but either the number of those dependencies or their locus of application must be finitely bounded.

It is worth mentioning that this unattested example pattern is easily defined in first-order logic, which so far has been the only safe upper bound on syntactic dependencies (Graf, 2012). The IO-TSL perspective of c-command dependencies thus improves on previous work by ruling out some linguistically undesirable patterns.

5   Adding movement

The discussion so far has largely ignored the effects of movement on c-command relations. Under the standard raising analysis, *no* does not c-command *ever* from its base position in *[No train]$_i$ has ever seemed to me t_i to t_i arrive on time*. The c-command relation is derived by movement. Our current notion of c-strings fails to capture this.

For most dependencies discussed in this paper, it only matters that a dependent element has at least one licensor in its c-string. In this case, movement effects can be accommodated by modifying the construction of c-strings such that a mover is also copied into its landing sites. The c-string for *ever* in the previous example would be *ever no has C* after the mover *no* is copied into the position corresponding to its landing site.

But this covers only movement of a licensor. Sometimes, a dependent element is licensed only because it has moved out of a locality domain into a higher position where it is accessible to its licensor. In such cases, the c-string would be truncated by deleting all material between the licensor and the relevant occurrence, effectively pushing the licensee into a higher position.

This strategy shifts a lot of the burden to the correct construction of c-strings, which may be particularly complicated when both the licensor and the licensee move. The construction of the appropriate c-string from a dependency tree is still de-

finable in first-order logic and hence subregular, but this is a very generous upper bound. An in-depth exploration of movement from a subregular perspective has to be left for future work.

Conclusion

We have defined a string-based representation format over dependency trees that allows for c-command dependencies to be easily evaluated for any given node. The dependencies over these strings all fall within the class IO-TSL, which was first defined for phonology (Graf and Mayer, 2018). This paper marks but a first step towards a subregular theory of syntactic dependencies, and a lot remains to be done.

The current approach only measures the complexity of a syntactic dependency with respect to a specific node. To check the whole dependency tree, one has to evaluate the c-string of each node. We do not know whether the TSL-approach of Graf (2018b) provides a method for doing so. As long as all dependencies are IO-TSL, though, the well-formedness of the whole dependency tree can be verified by a deterministic top-down tree automaton with a look-ahead of 1. This implies subregular complexity and may even allow for highly efficient parsing algorithms.

Dependencies that go beyond c-command cannot be handled with our approach. This includes binding via sub-command, parasitic gaps, and across-the-board movement as an exception to the coordinate structure constraint. It remains to be seen whether they can be accommodated with tree tiers as proposed in Graf (2018b), or whether a completely new perspective is needed for these phenomena.

References

Joseph Aoun and Dominique Sportiche. 1983. On the formal theory of government. *Linguistic Review*, 2:211–236.

Hyunah Baek. 2017. Computational representation of unbounded stress: Tiers with structural features. Ms., Stony Brook University; to appear in *Proceedings of CLS 53*.

Michael Brody. 2000. Mirror theory: Syntactic representation in perfect syntax. *Linguistic Inquiry*, 31:29–56.

Robert A. Chametzky. 2000. *Phrase Structure: From GB to Minimalism*. Blackwell, Oxford.

Robert A. Chametzky. 2011. No derivation without representation. In Cedric Boeckx, editor, *The Oxford Handbook of Linguistic Minimalism*, pages 311–326. Oxford University Press, Oxford.

Jane Chandlee. 2017. Computational locality in morphological maps. *Morphology*, 27:599–641.

Noam Chomsky. 1957. *Syntactic Structures*. Mouton, The Hague.

Noam Chomsky. 1995. *The Minimalist Program*. MIT Press, Cambridge, MA.

Aniello De Santo and Thomas Graf. 2017. Structure sensitive tier projection: Applications and formal properties. Ms., Stony Brook University.

Samuel D. Epstein, Erich M. Groat, Ruriko Kawashima, and Hisatsugu Kitahara. 1998. *A Derivational Approach to Syntactic Relations*. Oxford University Press, Oxford.

Robert Frank and K. Vijay-Shanker. 1999. Primitive c-command. Ms., John Hopkins University and University of Delaware.

Thomas Graf. 2012. Locality and the complexity of Minimalist derivation tree languages. In *Formal Grammar 2010/2011*, volume 7395 of *Lecture Notes in Computer Science*, pages 208–227, Heidelberg. Springer.

Thomas Graf. 2013. *Local and Transderivational Constraints in Syntax and Semantics*. Ph.D. thesis, UCLA.

Thomas Graf. 2017. The power of locality domains in phonology. *Phonology*, 34:385–405.

Thomas Graf. 2018a. Locality domains and phonological c-command over strings. To appear in *Proceedings of NELS 2017*.

Thomas Graf. 2018b. Why movement comes for free once you have adjunction. To appear in *Proceedings of CLS 53*.

Thomas Graf and Natasha Abner. 2012. Is syntactic binding rational? In *Proceedings of the 11th International Workshop on Tree Adjoining Grammars and Related Formalisms (TAG+11)*, pages 189–197.

Thomas Graf, Alëna Aksënova, Hyunah Baek, Aniello De Santo, Hossep Dolatian, Sedigheh Moradi, Jon Rawski, Suji Yang, and Jeffrey Heinz. 2018. Tiers and relativized locality across language modules. Slides of a talk given at the 1-day workshop Parallels Between Phonology and Syntax, July 9, Meertens Instituut, Amsterdam, Netherlands.

Thomas Graf and Connor Mayer. 2018. Sanskrit n-retroflexion is input-output tier-based strictly local. To appear in *Proceedings of SIGMORPHON 2018*.

Jeffrey Heinz. 2018. The computational nature of phonological generalizations. In Larry Hyman and Frank Plank, editors, *Phonological Typology*, Phonetics and Phonology, chapter 5, pages 126–195. Mouton De Gruyter.

Jeffrey Heinz, Chetan Rawal, and Herbert G. Tanner. 2011. Tier-based strictly local constraints in phonology. In *Proceedings of the 49th Annual Meeting of the Association for Computational Linguistics*, pages 58–64.

M. A. C. Huybregts. 1984. The weak adequacy of context-free phrase structure grammar. In Ger J. de Haan, Mieke Trommelen, and Wim Zonneveld, editors, *Van Periferie naar Kern*, pages 81–99. Foris, Dordrecht.

Paul Kiparsky. 2002. Disjoint reference and the typology of pronouns. In Ingrid Kaufmann and Barbara Stiebels, editors, *More than Words*, volume 53 of *Studia Grammatica*, pages 179–226. Akademie Verlag, Berlin.

Gregory M. Kobele. 2002. Formalizing mirror theory. *Grammars*, 5:177–221.

Gregory M. Kobele. 2006. *Generating Copies: An Investigation into Structural Identity in Language and Grammar*. Ph.D. thesis, UCLA.

Gregory M. Kobele, Christian Retoré, and Sylvain Salvati. 2007. An automata-theoretic approach to Minimalism. In *Model Theoretic Syntax at 10*, pages 71–80.

Wim Martens, Frank Neven, and Thomas Schwentick. 2008. Deterministic top-down tree automata: Past, present, and future. In *Proceedings of Logic and Automata 2008*, pages 505–530.

Connor Mayer and Travis Major. 2018. A challenge for tier-based strict locality from Uyghur backness harmony. In *Proceedings of Formal Grammar 2018*. To appear.

Jens Michaelis. 2001. Transforming linear context-free rewriting systems into Minimalist grammars. *Lecture Notes in Artificial Intelligence*, 2099:228–244.

Jens Michaelis and Marcus Kracht. 1997. Semilinearity as a syntactic invariant. In *Logical Aspects of Computational Linguistics*, volume 1328 of *Lecture Notes in Artifical Intelligence*, pages 329–345. Springer.

James Rogers, Jeffrey Heinz, Gil Bailey, Matt Edlefsen, Molly Vischer, David Wellcome, and Sean Wibel. 2010. On languages piecewise testable in the strict sense. In Christan Ebert, Gerhard Jäger, and Jens Michaelis, editors, *The Mathematics of Language*, volume 6149 of *Lecture Notes in Artificial Intelligence*, pages 255–265. Springer, Heidelberg.

Stuart M. Shieber. 1985. Evidence against the context-freeness of natural language. *Linguistics and Philosophy*, 8(3):333–345.

Edward P. Stabler. 1997. Derivational Minimalism. In Christian Retoré, editor, *Logical Aspects of Computational Linguistics*, volume 1328 of *Lecture Notes in Computer Science*, pages 68–95. Springer, Berlin.

Edward P. Stabler. 2011. Computational perspectives on Minimalism. In Cedric Boeckx, editor, *Oxford Handbook of Linguistic Minimalism*, pages 617–643. Oxford University Press, Oxford.

Mai Ha Vu. 2018. Towards a formal description of NPI-licensing patterns. In *Proceedings of the Society for Computation in Linguistics*, volume 1, pages 154–163.

Mai Ha Vu, Nazila Shafiei, and Thomas Graf. 2019. Case assignment in TSL syntax: A case study. To appear in *Proceedings of SCiL 2019*.

Su Ji Yang. 2018. Subregular complexity in Korean phonotactics. Undergraduate honors thesis, Stony Brook University.

Modeling the Acquisition of Words with Multiple Meanings

Libby Barak, Sammy Floyd, and Adele Goldberg
Psychology Department
Princeton Univesrity
{lbarak,sfloyd,adele}@princeton.edu

Abstract

Learning vocabulary is essential to successful communication. Complicating this task is the underappreciated fact that most common words are associated with multiple senses (are **polysemous**) (e.g., baseball *cap* vs. *cap* of a bottle), while other words are **homonymous**, evoking meanings that are unrelated to one another (e.g., baseball *bat* vs. flying *bat*). Models of human word learning have thus far failed to represent this level of naturalistic complexity. We extend a feature-based computational model to allow for multiple meanings, while capturing the gradient distinction between polysemy and homonymy by using structured sets of features. Results confirm that the present model correlates better with human data on novel word learning tasks than the existing feature-based model.

1   Introduction

Children acquire language at a remarkable rate despite many layers of complexity in their learning environment. Previous computational models of human vocabulary learning have been primarily aimed at the mapping problem or the problem of "referential indeterminacy" (Quine, 1969), namely, determining which word maps onto which object within a noisy context (Siskind, 1996; Trueswell et al., 2013; Stevens et al., 2017; Smith et al., 2014; Fazly et al., 2010; Frank et al., 2009). These models explicitly make the simplifying but counter-factual assumption that each word can map to only one meaning in order to address how it is that learners determine which meaning a word refers to from among multiple potential referents in a scene. The models further assume that each possible meaning competes with every other possible meaning. For example, in a scene depicting "A cat drinking milk", the meaning of the word *cat* competes with the meaning of *milk*, *bowl* and every other potential meaning evoked in the scene. This perspective emphasizes the richness of visual scenes, but it overlooks the complexity associated with word meanings which very commonly refer to multiple distinct senses or meanings (Piantadosi et al., 2012). For example, a *bowl* can refer to a "dish used for feeding" in the cat scene, but to a "toilet bowl" within a different context. That is, the meaning of a word cannot be a winner-takes-all affair in which meanings compete with one another across contexts, because people learn to assign multiple meanings to many words in their vocabularies.

Multiple meanings of one word can typically not be subsumed under a general definition or rule. This is clearly true in the case of **homonyms**, which have multiple, unrelated meanings (e.g., baseball *bat* vs. flying *bat*). It is also true of many **polysemes**, which evoke conventional senses that are related to one another yet distinct. Natural language polysemy often involves extensions along multiple dimensions that are not completely predictable on the basis of a general definition or rule. For example, while baseball *caps* and bottle *caps* both cover something tightly, English speakers must learn that corks and lids, which also cover things tightly, are not called *caps*, while mushroom caps are, even though the latter do not cover anything tightly (for discussion of rule-based polysemy see e.g., (Srinivasan and Rabagliati, 2015; Srinivasan et al., 2017)). Notably, polysemes are much more frequent than homonyms, insofar as 40% of frequent English words are polysemous (Durkin and Manning, 1989), while closer to 4% of words are homonyms (Dautriche, 2015).

Even though homonyms are relatively rare, children as young as 3 years old have been found to know a number of them (Backscheider and Gelman, 1995). At least for these words, preschoolers have managed to overcome their reluctance to as-

Proceedings of the Society for Computation in Linguistics (SCiL) 2019, pages 216-225.
New York City, New York, January 3-6, 2019

sign a second meaning to a familiar word (Casenhiser, 2005). We also know that children readily generalize the meaning of a word to include new referents that share a single dimension, such as shape (Smith et al., 2002) or function (Gentner, 1978), and Srinivasan et al. (2017) has found that 4-5 year-old children can be taught that a word extends to other referents that share the same material (Srinivasan et al., 2017).

While previous psycholinguistic work has primarily focused on learning words with a single meaning or words that can be generalized along a single dimension (rule-based polysemy), a recent study that we simulate below has investigated words with multiple distinct, conventional meanings (non-rule-based). This work has demonstrated that it is easier to learn conventional polysemy when compared with homonymy, even when the polysemy follows complex, multidimensional extension patterns as in natural language. [1]

We propose a computational model that allows words to be assigned multiple meanings that cannot be generated by a one-dimensional rule, but must instead be learned through exposure (Brocher et al., 2017). We use the results from the behavioral experiment in order to inform and test the proposed model. As reported, the model not only captures the finding that people find it easier to learn polysemous words than ambiguous words, but it also closely approximates human errors. This represents a first step toward addressing the complexity involved in learning more than a single meaning of a given word.

2 Related Work

Only two recent models of human vocabulary learning allow words to evoke multiple senses. The model of Kachergis et al. (2017) implements a bias to prefer a single referent, but allows a second (unrelated) candidate meaning to be represented. Another model, Pursuit, maps each word onto a single candidate meaning per trial, and selects a new candidate meaning (at random) only when the primary meaning is disconfirmed (Stevens et al., 2017). This model retains a stipulation that only a single meaning wins. Importantly, neither of these models is evaluated on their ability to accurately represent multiple meanings. In fact, these and most other models make the simplifying assumption that each sense is represented

---

[1] Experimental results are under submission.

atomically, without any internal structure or features. This precludes them from even attempting to distinguish polysemy from homonymy, since each meaning is equally (un)related to every other meaning.

It is necessary to allow word meanings to have internal structure if we are to capture relationships among meanings of a single word. The one model of human vocabulary learning that assigns such internal structure is the feature-based associative model of (Fazly et al., 2010), which has been extended in multiple studies to account for patterns of learning complex naturalistic meaning (Nematzadeh et al., 2012, 2014). This model represents a cross-situational learner, acquiring the meaning of each word incrementally by aligning each feature in the context with a probabilistic association to each word. The model learns by ultimately representing each word's meaning as an associated "bag-of-features". We choose this model as a basis for our approach, given its successful application in many word learning tasks and its ability to represent fine-grained properties (features) of meanings.

But critically, we extend the NFS12 model in order to represent the learning of words with multiple distinct meanings that may share overlapping features to varying degrees. The key innovation we add to the bag-of-features model of NFS12 is the following: we assign each distinguishable object a distinct, albeit overlapping, **set of features**. In our version, the model learns words as associations to distinct structured collections of feature-sets rather than learning independent associations of each word to each feature. We replicate the input and tasks of recent experimental multi-meaning word learning work, and compare the performance of the extended model with NFS12 and with the performance of human learners. In the following sections, we describe the original model and our modification of it.

3 Computational Models

3.1 Cross-situational Word Learning Model

We use the implementation of the cross-situational word learner as implemented by Nematzadeh et al. (2012) (**NFS12**) as the best fitting basis for our model. While later versions of the model are also available, these versions encode assumptions regarding hierarchical-categorical learning that are irrelevant to this research and require hand-coded data of the categories in the input. NFS12 learns from <utterance, scene> input pairs that simulate what a language learner hears in the linguistic input: i.e., the utterance, and the features corresponding to the non-linguistic context (the scene). For example, the learner might first encounter the word *cap* accompanied by features that represent the scene of a parent asking a child to put a cap on a summer day, e.g.,

> Utterance = *"put your cap on"*
> Features = {sun, light, clothing, fabric,
> cover, animate,...}

The features for each utterance correspond to all relevant aspects of the understood message and the witnessed scene. This is represented as a bag-of-features in the sense that there are no boundaries to indicate which features represent each object in the visual world. The model learns the probabilistic association between each feature, f, and each word, w, through a bootstrapping process. The model initializes all $P_{t-1}(f|w)$ to a uniform distribution over all words and features. At time t, the model learns the current association of w and f as proportional to their prior learned probability:

$$assoc_t(w, f) = \frac{P_{t-1}(f|w)}{\sum_{w' \in U} P_{t-1}(f|w')} \quad (1)$$

where $P_{t-1}(f|w)$ is the probability of f being part of the meaning of w at the previous learning step. If the association of f with some other word in the utterance is particularly high, the association of f with w will be correspondingly lower. The new evidence is then used to update the probability of all observed features in a smoothed version of:

$$P_t(f|w) = \frac{assoc_t(w, f)}{\sum_{f' \in F} assoc_t(w, f')} \quad (2)$$

where F is the set of all features observed thus far. The associations are thus summed over their occurrences in the input in proportion to the time passed since last occurrence.

$$assoc_t(f, w) = \ln(\sum_{t'=1}^{t} \frac{a_{t'}(w|f)}{(t - t')^d}) \quad (3)$$

The associations are updated with every learning step to account for past experience. The denominator represents the decay of the association over time as memories of the input are assumed to

fade in memory. d is proportional to the strength of association such that stronger associations will fade less, even when significant time has passed since a previous encounter of w, i.e., $t - t'$. The learning iterations result in an association score between each feature and each word based on the observed input. The acquisition of word meaning is defined as success on a prediction task over the learned associations as described in Section 4.

3.2 Exemplar-based Learning as Sets of Features

The NFS12 model creates a bank of associations of varying strengths between features and words. It is based on the idea that over many observations of a word, the features that are actually relevant to that word will gain in probability over features that only coincidently co-occurred with the word in some subset of contexts. To date, no version of NFS12 has been evaluated on words with multiple senses. Note that if applied to multiple meanings in its current formulation, all of the features from all of the word's meanings will become associated with the word, without regard to whether certain features tend to occur with one meaning while other features tend to occur with a different meaning. That is, a word with multiple meanings will come to be associated with a merged bag-of-features. For instance, separate occurrences of the word *cap* would be associated with either $\{plastic, cover, bottle\}$ or $\{fabric, head\}$ but the model would predict that a combination of features such as $\{cover, fabric, bottle\}$ would be a reasonable interpretation of *cap*.

We predict that this vague representation will not be sufficient to approach human-like performance in recognizing distinct senses. Based on evidence that people are able to remember particular instances of objects they observe (Allen and Brooks, 1991; Brooks, 1987; Thibaut and Gelaes, 2006; Nosofsky et al., 2018), we modify the input representations to include sets of features for each word in the utterance as follows.

We propose a Structured Multi-Feature **(SMF)** model that extends NSF12, by associating each word with **sets** of features that have been learned on the basis of witnessing potential **referents** (as opposed to features) across scenes.[2] For example, if a scene involved two potential referents (the

---

[2]Like other models of human word learning, we focus our evaluation on for now the learning of words that correspond to referents in scenes.

sun and a baseball cap), the following feature
sets would be candidates for association with the
words in the utterance:

Utterance = *"put your cap on"*
Feature sets = {sun, light},
              {clothing, fabric, cover}

We modify the learning process to estimate the
association of a word, w, and a **set** of features, s,
following the formulation of the original model.

$$assoc(w, s) = \frac{P_t(s|w)}{\sum_{w' \in U} P_t(s|w')} \quad (4)$$

Thus a set of features, s, essentially represents
an hypothesized sense of a referential word. The
probability $P_t(s|w)$ is estimated from the previous
occurrences of the word, where the probability of
each set is proportional to the degree of overlap in
features rather than a direct observation of the specific set. The degree of overlap between two sets,
s_f and s_j is calculated using the Jaccard similarity coefficient, which is the proportion of shared
features across the two sets over all features in the
two sets.

$$jacc - sim(s_f, s_j) = \frac{|s_f \cap s_j|}{|s_f \cup s_j|} \quad (5)$$

The modification – making use of coherent sets
of features rather than independent features – captures a key claim about how people learn referential words. Rather than learning the degree of association between words and individual features,
e.g., learning *cap* and fabric, independently of the
association between *cap* and clothing, the model
assumes that people learn from coherent exemplars. The learner eventually learns a collection
of sets of features with various degrees of association strength among the feature sets. The association between fabric and *cap* can only be determined once other features are taken into account
as well. In this case, fabric will be more strongly
associated with *cap* in the presence of the feature,
clothing, and less associated with *cap* if the feature, bottle, is included and clothing is missing. [3]

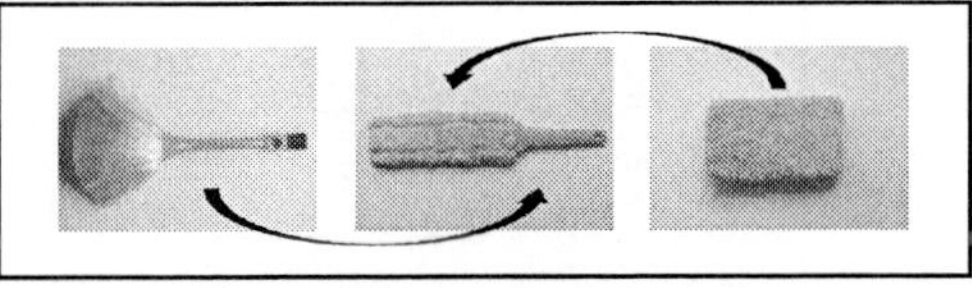

(a) Polysemy

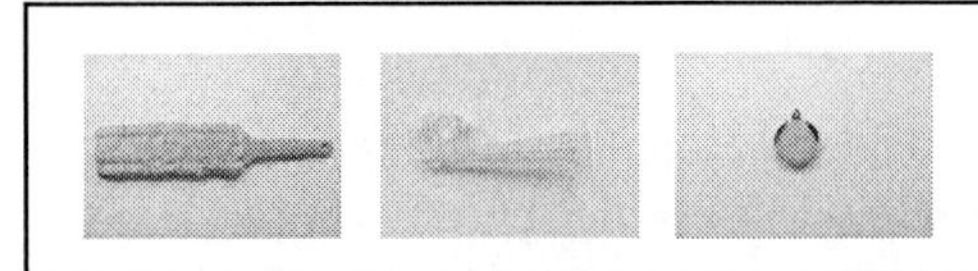

(b) Homonymy

Figure 1: A sample of the objects used in the
novel-word learning experiment. Polysemy (upper panel) - pairs share properties as marked by
arrows, with no single core feature shared by all
three exemplars. Homonymy (lower panel) - a
scrambled selection of three objects with fewer relationships among exemplars.

4 Learning Polysemy vs. Homonymy

We evaluate the NFS12 model and the present
SMF model by simulating a novel word learning task in which human participants learned several polysemous or homonymous words as described below. The experiment compared how
three populations learn words with multiple meanings: adults, typically developed children, and
children with autism spectrum disorder. Since no
previous computational models have attempted to
capture how humans learn multi-meaning words,
we focus on the adult group as a first step since
it allows us to minimize assumptions regarding
learners' development of cognitive abilities. We
follow the experimental design to investigate, for
the first time, how words with distinct but related
senses (conventional polysemy) are learned, particularly when the range of senses do not follow
from any language-wide rule.

4.1 Novel Word Learning Experiment

The experimental work explicitly compared the
distinction between homonymy and conventional
polysemy. In particular, participants learned 4
novel words, and each novel word was associated
with 3 clearly distinct novel objects. Randomly
interspersed among the 12 labeled objects were 20

<hr>

[3] A very recent publication by the authors of NFS12 experiments with the use of sets but remains limited to single-sense
word representations and still learns association of word over
features rather than sets (Nematzadeh et al., 2017).

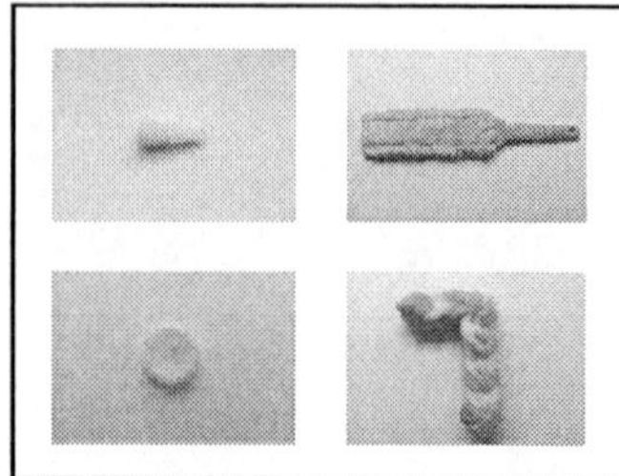

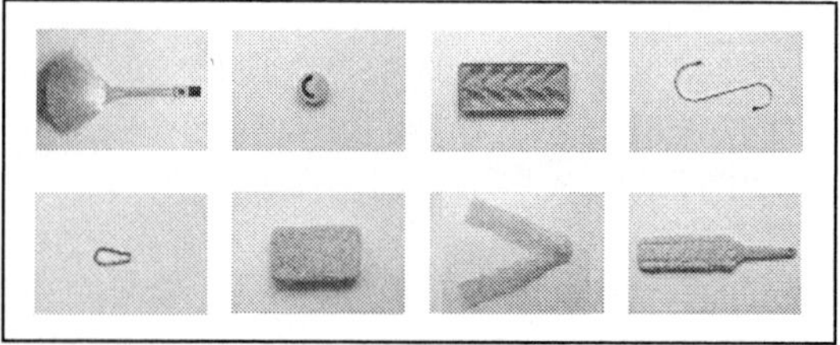

Figure 2: An example of the stimuli presented to participants in the label ID task. The target object was presented along with 3 distractors, which were targets for other novel words.

Figure 3: An example of the stimuli presented to participants in the Sense Selection task. All 3 target objects associated with one of the novel words were presented along with 5 filler objects, which had also been witnessed during the exposure but had not been labeled.

unlabeled filler (non-target) objects accompanied by tones. Novel objects were used to avoid interference from familiar words. Half of the participants were randomly assigned to a Polysemy condition in which the objects were related to one another with the 3 objects sharing distinct features with one another. The other half was assigned to a Homonymy condition, in which the 3 objects assigned to each word did now share any distinguishing features that could distinguish them from the filler objects in terms of a stronger feature-relation. (See Figure 1 for an example). The "polysemous" meanings of words were confirmed to be more similar than the "homonymous" meanings, as intended, using a separate norming study with a new group of participants.

After brief exposure, participants completed the following two tasks designed to determine whether polysemous words were easier to learn than homonymous words.

1. Label ID task - Participants were asked to select, from 4 available options, the one object that corresponded to a given label. The 3 foil objects had been labeled by each of the 3 other labels (see Figure 2). Results showed significantly higher accuracy for the polysemy condition over the homonymy condition.

2. Sense Selection task - Participants were presented with the label of one of the 4 words, and shown 8 objects (see Figure 3). Three of the objects corresponded to the 3 senses of the word and the 5 additional objects were fillers that had been witnessed during exposure. Accuracy was lower on this task, showing only slight polysemy advantage due to task difficulty.

The Label ID task allows a comparison of the two conditions, polysemy and homonymy, but participants may have used the memory of one or two words to perform well by a process of elimination by recognizing an object as related to a different label. The Sense Selection task allows for a more thorough error analysis; importantly, the particular objects selected by humans was made available to the computational analysis. We perform an error analysis on the selection rate of each filler object. The results of this task provide a crucial test of the bag-of-features meanings learned by the NFS12 model.

4.2 Experimental Simulation

We trained the model on input that reflected the exposure in the novel word study. In particular, two annotators hand-coded each object with 4 to 5 features to compose a joint a list of 40 features that jointly described all 12 labeled and 20 unlabeled (filler) objects. The features included properties related to shape, size, color, texture, material, symmetry, etc. We trained the NSF12 and SMF models independently: the features were used as a bag-of-features for the NFS12 model, and as structured sets of features for SMF. Recall that although each input item consisted of a single word associated with observable features, the models differ in the way they learn. NFS12 learns the association of a word with each feature, while SMF learns the association of a word to a subset of features.

At the end of training, we tested the models by simulating each of the two tasks described above. We first estimate the association of each word to each of the items, using the cosine distance between the learned associations and the feature rep-

	Polysemy	Homonymy
NFS12	0.88	0.37
SMF	**0.92**	**0.51**

Table 1: Pearson correlation between results from participants on the task with NSF12 and proposed SMF models.

resentation of the word. For the NFS12 model, we calculated the cosine similarity between all the associated features. For the SMF model, we calculated the maximum cosine similarity score over all the sets of features associated with the word and the feature representation of the item (i.e., we considered the sense of the word most similar to the object in question).

The likelihood of choosing an object as a target is measured by the proportional similarity of each object compared with the other objects presented in the task. For each stimuli set of 4 items used in the Label ID task (see Figure 2) and 8 items used for the Sense Selection task (see Figure 3) , we calculate

$$P(object|w) = \frac{cos(o, w)}{\sum_{o' \in O} cos(o', w)} \quad (6)$$

where, w is the word presented as visual stimuli at test. o ranges over all the objects presented at test (4 or 8 items), and O is the full set of objects for this test set.

5   Results

The experimental settings kept the alignment of sets of objects constant across participants while randomizing the word labels and the order of object presentation. For example, the same set of 4 objects in Figure 2 was used to test all 4 words. We replicated the combinations of objects to test each label in order to compare the computational models to people's choices. We used the default parameter settings included in the configuration files for NFS12.

5.1   Label ID Task

We first evaluate each model on its ability to replicate the polysemy advantage observed in human data. We obtain the item selection probability using Equation 6 for the target items only. Following the results from human experiments, we average the item probability over all targets to get the results from each model (see Figure 4).

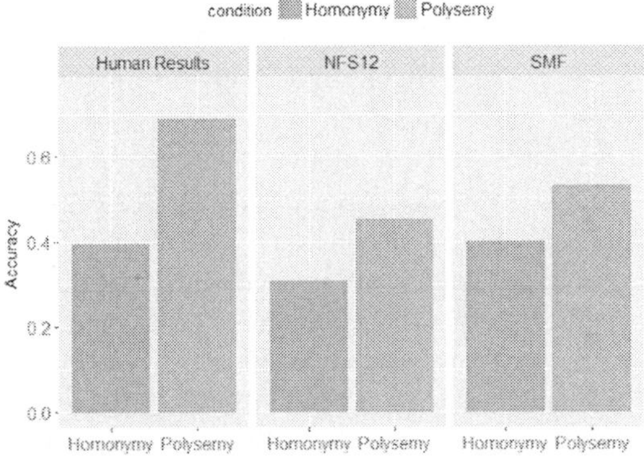

Figure 4: The likelihood of choosing an object corresponding to a target sense for Homonymy vs. Polysemy conditions in the Label ID task for (1) the human results, (2) the model of NFS12, (3) our extension of that model, SMF.

As can be seen in the middle panel of Figure 4, NFS12 replicates the human polysemy advantage in identifying the target meanings in the polysemy condition more accurately than targets in the homonymy condition. However, the accuracy of NFS12 in choosing the target object for the given label is considerably lower compared with the human results in the left most panel. The low accuracy of NFS12 compared with human performance suggests that NFS12 is prone to selecting non-target objects which do not resemble a specific sense of the learned word. Recall that because NSF12 does not maintain each exemplar's associated set of features, the model creates a superset of weighted features without respecting the co-variance among features that are associated with a particular sense. Thus, NSF12 assigns high probability to objects which share features from distinct target meanings, whereas humans are much less likely to do this.

To illustrate, Figure 1 provides example stimuli representing three senses of a polysemous vs. homonymous word. The middle object in the upper panel of Figure 1 shares some features with the left-most object (e.g., handle and overall shape), and other features with the right-most object (e.g., color, texture, and rectangular shape). However, the homonymous senses of the word share fewer features with one another (lower panel of Figure 1). Since almost no features overlap between pairs of homonymous objects, the number of features included in the superset for this word is higher than for the polysemous word.

As a result, NFS12 under-performs in accuracy for all targets presented in the upper panel of Figure 1 in both the homonymy and polysemy conditions. In homonymy (lower panel of Figure 1), the bag-of-features consists of more features compared with the polysemous condition. Probabilistically, this bag-of-features will generate a higher number of subsets that happen to coincide with the features associated with fillers, which results in lower the accuracy of NFS12 for homonymy. For instance, NFS12 accuracy is significantly lower for the translucent yellow item in the middle of the panel because it simply aggregates the highly frequent features, learning a strong association between the word label and the feature *orange*. On the other hand, SMF preserves the co-occurrence statistics of features, preventing the orange feature from being incremented in isolation from the other features of that object.

The SMF model also captures the polysemy over homonymy advantage with higher accuracy than NFS12. Overall then, accuracy more closely matches human performance more closely when compared with NFS12 (see right panel on Figure 4). To quantify the correlation of each model with the particular selections made by human participants, we calculate the Pearson correlation over all objects (targets and fillers), using the results from Equation 6. (We use the Pearson correlation as the results from both human and models have normal distributions with kurtosis values close to 3).

The correlations with human errors for both models are given in Table 1. SMF offers significant improvement over NFS12 in the homonymy condition, and mirrors human errors in the polysemy condition slightly better as well. The weaker absolute correlation in the homonymy condition of the SMF model when compared with polysemy (.51 vs. 92) stems from the model over-performing on some items while under-performing on others, when compared with humans. We hypothesize that people differ from the model in the weights they give particular features, e.g., color vs. size. For example, SMF has higher accuracy than humans in selecting the leftmost item in the homonymy condition in Figure 1, possibly by forming a bias towards large-size items, while people may not attend to size to the same degree.

The models increase probability with every

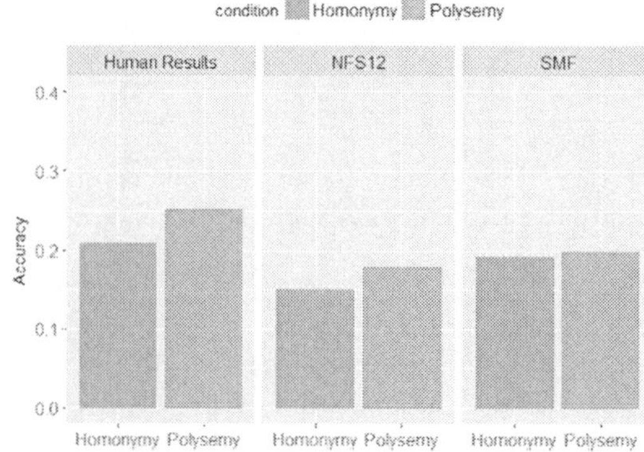

Figure 5: Sense Selection Task: The likelihood of choosing an object corresponding to a target sense for Homonymy vs. Polysemy conditions in (1) the human results, (2) the model of NFS12, (3) our extension of the model, SMF.

	Polysemy	Homonymy
NFS12	0.82	0.67
SMF	**0.91**	**0.90**

Table 2: Pearson correlation between errors produced by human participants with NSF12 and SMF models on the Sense Identification task.

overlapping feature regardless of what the feature denotes (shape, color, size, etc.). It is well known that children learn to attend to shape in learning referential novel nouns by two years of age (Smith et al., 2002). Moreover, people learn to attend to certain dimensions of meaning more closely given certain categories, e.g., using color to distinguish fruits and vegetables but not dogs and cats (Sloutsky et al., 2016). The SMF model overcomes this difficulty to some degree by having distinct memories of individual items. In order to capture these sorts of biases toward certain features for certain types of words, future models need to learn such biases over time, as we discuss further in Section 6.

5.2 The Sense Selection task

Following the results in subsection 5.1, we aim to further our analysis of the learning pattern of each model using a second task which challenges participants to recognize all senses of a word simultaneously, and includes more distractors (filler objects). The accuracy of choosing all three target items is presented in Figure 5.

Human's polysemy advantage was less pronounced in the Sense Selection task compared with the Label ID task. As shown in Figure 5, both models also show less difference between polysemy and homonymy than they did on the Label ID task. While the polysemy advantage is higher in NFS12, SMF actually shows closer performance to the human data, due to more comparable levels of accuracy.

We again evaluate the probability of choosing each of the objects over both targets and fillers. That is, we compare the probability of each model selecting each object with human performance. In particular, we calculate the Pearson correlation between each of the two models and human results; see Table 2. The correlations of SMF with human results are much better than NFS12 in both the Polysemy and Homonymy conditions. These results align with our findings in the previous simulation, especially in mirroring NFS12's difficulty in learning unrelated senses (homonymy). The SMF model, on the other hand, approaches a 0.9 correlation in both conditions. Thus, although the SMF model has a lower overall probability of choosing targets compared to people, it closely mirrors human error patterns. These results support the role of distinct memories of exemplars, while taking into account the overlap among sets of features during selection. Note that the high correlations can be attributed to similarity in the relative ranking across items for the human results and SMF. At the same time, SMF still underestimate the overall probability of predicting certain items, which results in a lower accuracy compared with the human results.

6 Discussion and Future Directions

We have presented a computational analysis of the acquisition of word meaning for words with multiple senses. Despite the growing interest in computational models for analyzing human word learning, this aspect has remained under-studied due to the complexity of the problem. Our analysis is the first, to our knowledge, to directly model differences in the acquisition of multi-sense words with varying degree of overlap across senses. The computational design enables a closer analysis of the strengths and weaknesses involved in the human learning of multi-sense words, though the analyses of human errors.

The model of Nematzadeh et al. (2012) learned the association between independent features and words. It was chosen as the benchmark for our analysis because it represents the rare model which goes beyond atomic meanings by offering feature-based representations. Results demonstrate, however, that its bag-of-features representation is not sufficient to account for human-like learning of multi-meaning words, particularly in the case of homonymy, where combining the features of unrelated senses results in a particularly noisy representation. Our modified version which is a Structured Multi-Feature model, changes both the input representation and how the model learns to associate words with meanings. In particular, SMF preserves the co-occurrence statistics of the features associated with particular objects (exemplars), as motivated by evidence in human memory research (Allen and Brooks, 1991; Brooks, 1987; Thibaut and Gelaes, 2006; Nosofsky et al., 2018).

This study offers only the first step toward a computational model that fully captures the way that human learn realistic words, which commonly evoke a range of senses that importantly include function and metaphorical extensions that are not part of the interpretation of our novel stimuli. We recognize that our hand-coding of features makes both NFS12 and SMF impractical, but insofar as words meaningfully differ on a number of distinct dimensions, the reliance on features–however they are to be determined–is reasonable. Given the quite short exposure phase in the experimental work, the current analysis has not explored the role of memory or attention mechanisms included in the original model of NFS12 (Nematzadeh et al., 2014).

We believe that correlations with human performance could potentially be improved with suprisal or novelty affecting the weights of features. We also know that people pay more attention to some features over others in a way that depends on linguistic cues, the domain involved, and their prior knowledge. For example, people attend to colors to distinguish fruits, while color is less important when identifying dogs vs. cats.

The addition of structured sets of features offers an improvement over a general bag-of-features approach and has demonstrated strong correlations with human performance. Learning words with multi-meanings is a common occurrence in natural languages so it behooves models that aim to capture this basic fact.

Future extensions of SMF should incorporate a mechanism to simulate attention, including primacy and recency effects, in order to investigate how people weight different features or dimensions of meaning in various contexts. Although, NFS12 included a mechanism in the model to encode higher attention to novel words, this only captures item-based novelty, i.e., how frequently an item is observed, which does not play a significant role within the context of our experiment.[4] The multi-meaning words, however, introduce the challenge of attending to new meanings of familiar words over a short span of time. To more fully understand the relevant mechanisms and their roles in word learning, we plan to simulate the tasks discussed here using real-world polysemes with much richer sets of features. The conclusions of this study will be further used to guide extensions of the experimental designs in order to consider the role of attention in human word learning as well.

References

Scott W Allen and Lee R Brooks. 1991. Specializing the operation of an explicit rule. *Journal of experimental psychology: General*, 120(1):3.

Andrea G Backscheider and Susan A Gelman. 1995. Children's understanding of homonyms. *Journal of Child language*, 22(1):107–127.

Andreas Brocher, Jean-Pierre Koenig, Gail Mauner, and Stephani Foraker. 2017. About sharing and commitment: the retrieval of biased and balanced irregular polysemes. *Language, Cognition and Neuroscience*, pages 1–24.

Lee R Brooks. 1987. Decentralized control of categorization: The role of prior processing episodes.

Devin M Casenhiser. 2005. Children's resistance to homonymy: An experimental study of pseudo-homonyms. *Journal of Child Language*, 32(2):319–343.

Isabelle Dautriche. 2015. *Weaving an ambiguous lexicon*. Ph.D. thesis, Sorbonne Paris Cité.

Kevin Durkin and Jocelyn Manning. 1989. Polysemy and the subjective lexicon: Semantic relatedness and the salience of intraword senses. *Journal of Psycholinguistic Research*, 18(6):577–612.

Afsaneh Fazly, Afra Alishahi, and Suzanne Stevenson. 2010. A probabilistic computational model of cross-situational word learning. *Cognitive Science*, 34(6):1017–1063.

Michael C Frank, Noah D Goodman, and Joshua B Tenenbaum. 2009. Using speakers' referential intentions to model early cross-situational word learning. *Psychological science*, 20(5):578–585.

Dedre Gentner. 1978. A study of early word meaning using artificial objects: What looks like a jiggy but acts like a zimbo? *Reading in developmental psychology*.

George Kachergis, Chen Yu, and Richard M Shiffrin. 2017. A bootstrapping model of frequency and context effects in word learning. *Cognitive science*, 41(3):590–622.

Aida Nematzadeh, Barend Beekhuizen, Shanshan Huang, and Suzanne Stevenson. 2017. Calculating probabilities simplifies word learning. *Proceedings of the 39th Annual Conference of the Cognitive Science Society*.

Aida Nematzadeh, Afsaneh Fazly, and Suzanne Stevenson. 2012. A computational model of memory, attention, and word learning. In *Proceedings of the 3rd Workshop on Cognitive Modeling and Computational Linguistics*, pages 80–89. Association for Computational Linguistics.

Aida Nematzadeh, Afsaneh Fazly, and Suzanne Stevenson. 2014. A cognitive model of semantic network learning. In *Proceedings of the 2014 Conference on Empirical Methods in Natural Language Processing (EMNLP)*.

Robert M Nosofsky, Craig A Sanders, and Mark A McDaniel. 2018. Tests of an exemplar-memory model of classification learning in a high-dimensional natural-science category domain. *Journal of Experimental Psychology: General*, 147(3):328.

Steven T Piantadosi, Harry Tily, and Edward Gibson. 2012. The communicative function of ambiguity in language. *Cognition*, 122(3):280–291.

Willard V Quine. 1969. Word and object. *Cambridge, Mass*.

Jeffrey Mark Siskind. 1996. A computational study of cross-situational techniques for learning word-to-meaning mappings. *Cognition*, 61(1-2):39–91.

Vladimir M Sloutsky et al. 2016. Selective attention, diffused attention, and the development of categorization. *Cognitive psychology*, 91:24–62.

Linda B Smith, Susan S Jones, Barbara Landau, Lisa Gershkoff-Stowe, and Larissa Samuelson. 2002. Object name learning provides on-the-job training for attention. *Psychological Science*, 13(1):13–19.

Linda B Smith, Sumarga H Suanda, and Chen Yu. 2014. The unrealized promise of infant statistical word–referent learning. *Trends in cognitive sciences*, 18(5):251–258.

[4]We use the original settings and keep this constant with future studies.

Mahesh Srinivasan, Catherine Berner, and Hugh
Rabagliati. 2017. Childrens use of lexical flexibility to structure new noun categories. In *Proceedings
of the 39th Annual Conference of the Cognitive Science Society*.

Mahesh Srinivasan and Hugh Rabagliati. 2015. How
concepts and conventions structure the lexicon:
Cross-linguistic evidence from polysemy. *Lingua*,
157:124–152.

Jon Scott Stevens, Lila R Gleitman, John C Trueswell,
and Charles Yang. 2017. The pursuit of word meanings. *Cognitive science*, 41(S4):638–676.

Jean-Pierre Thibaut and Sabine Gelaes. 2006. Exemplar effects in the context of a categorization rule:
Featural and holistic influences. *Journal of Experimental Psychology: Learning, Memory, and Cognition*, 32(6):1403.

John C Trueswell, Tamara Nicol Medina, Alon Hafri,
and Lila R Gleitman. 2013. Propose but verify:
Fast mapping meets cross-situational word learning.
Cognitive psychology, 66(1):126–156.

Evaluation Order Effects in Dynamic Continuized CCG: From Negative Polarity Items to Balanced Punctuation

Michael White
Department of Linguistics
The Ohio State University
Columbus, OH 43210 USA
`mwhite@ling.osu.edu`

Abstract

Combinatory Categorial Grammar's (CCG; Steedman, 2000) flexible treatment of word order and constituency enable it to employ a compact lexicon, an important factor in its successful application to a range of NLP problems. However, its word order flexibility can be problematic for linguistic phenomena where linear order plays a key role. In this paper, we show that the enhanced control over evaluation order afforded by Continuized CCG (Barker & Shan, 2014) makes it possible to not only implement an improved analysis of negative polarity items in Dynamic Continuized CCG (White et al., 2017) but also to develop an accurate treatment of balanced punctuation.

1 Introduction

Combinatory Categorial Grammar (CCG; Steedman, 2000) has been increasingly employed with success for a wide range of NLP problems. An important factor in its success is that its flexible treatment of word order and constituency enable it to employ a compact lexicon, making it easier to acquire lexicalized grammars automatically (Artzi and Zettlemoyer, 2013) and to train machine-learned models that generalize well (Clark and Curran, 2007; Lee et al., 2016). However, its word order flexibility can be problematic for linguistic phenomena where linear order plays a key role. In particular, linear order effects can be problematic for Steedman's (2012) treatment of negative polarity items (NPIs) as well as for implementing a treatment of balanced punctuation that attempts to track the status of the right periphery, as White & Rajkumar (2008) have previously shown.

In this paper, we show that the enhanced control over evaluation order afforded by Continuized CCG (Barker & Shan, 2014) makes it possible to successfully address both of these problems. In particular, we show that Barker & Shan's analysis of NPIs, which does not suffer from the linear order issues that we raise for Steedman's analysis, can be straightforwardly implemented in Dynamic Continuized CCG (White et al., 2017), a system that combines Barker & Shan's "tower" grammars with Charlow's (2014) monadic approach to dynamic semantics, employing Steedman's CCG on the tower bottom for predicate-argument structure. We then go on to show that the same technique used in Barker & Shan's analysis of NPIs can be used to successfully handle balanced punctuation, taking advantage of Charlow's monadic semantics to implement a novel approach to NP appositives.

Barker & Shan's continuized grammars make crucial use of continuations, a technique developed in programming language semantics to control and analyze evaluation order, and which enables the analyses presented here. Charlow's dynamic semantics implements an alternative to Steedman's (2012) approach to the exceptional scope of indefinites that fits naturally with ongoing work in dynamic semantics. Meanwhile, by combining the Barker-Shan-Charlow approach with Steedman's CCG for predicate-argument structure, the resulting system respects Steedman's Principle of Adjacency, making it attractive for computational implementations. As such, we suggest that the framework offers a promising starting point for work that tackles complex linguistic phenomena in a practical way. A prototype implementation verifying the analyses accompanies the paper.[1]

2 Negative Polarity Items in CCG

Steedman (2012) develops an approach to quantification in CCG, including a treatment of negative polarity items. Steedman's analysis follows

---

[1] `https://github.com/mwhite14850/dyc3g`

Proceedings of the Society for Computation in Linguistics (SCiL) 2019, pages 226-235.
New York City, New York, January 3-6, 2019

earlier treatments in categorial grammar (Dowty, 1994; Bernardi, 2002) in requiring negative polarity items to be licensed by an outscoping downward-entailing quantifier, negation or other licensor (e.g. verbs such as *deny*, which lexically incorporate negation). For example, Figure 1a shows how CCG can account for the difference between *No one enjoyed anything*, where the NPI *anything* is outscoped by its licensor *no one*, and **Kim enjoyed anything*, where the NPI *anything* has no licensor.[2] In Steedman's analysis, S° indicates neutral polarity, while $S^\bullet$ indicates reverse polarity. The NPI *anything* combines with the verb *enjoyed* on its left to yield $S^\bullet \backslash NP$, the category for a verb phrase with reverse polarity.[3] The downward-entailing quantifier *no one* here combines with an inverted-polarity VP on the right to yield S°, the category for a clause which again has neutral polarity. Root sentences are required to have positive polarity, which is compatible with neutral polarity. With **Kim enjoyed anything*, by contrast, the subject *Kim* does not license NPIs, and thus the derivation ends with $S^\bullet$, which is incompatible with root-level positive polarity.

As Barker & Shan observe, previous accounts in the categorial grammar literature have failed to account for the constraint that licensors must not only outscope NPIs but also precede them. Consequently, as illustrated with Steedman's account in Figure 1b, where *nothing* outscopes *anyone* but does not precede it, these accounts mistakenly predict that sentences such as **Kim gave anyone nothing* should be acceptable.[4]

3 NPIs in Continuized CCG

A continuized grammar is one where the meaning of expressions can be defined as a function on a portion of its surrounding context, or *continuation* (Barker, 2002; Shan and Barker, 2006; Barker and Shan, 2014). To make it easier to reason about continuized grammars, Barker & Shan devised the

"tower" notation illustrated in Figure 2.[5] For example, *no one* has a tower category with NP on the bottom and two Ss on top; reading counterclockwise from the bottom, this category represents a constituent that acts locally as an NP, takes scope over an S^-, and returns an S°. Here S^- represents the subtype of negative clauses, while S° is again a neutral clause.[6] The semantics is $\lambda k.\neg \exists y.ky$, a function from a continuation k of type $e \to t$ to a quantified expression of type t. A continuized meaning of this form can be abbreviated by representing the location where the continuation argument applies with $[\,]$ and putting the argument to the continuation on the bottom of the tower, as shown.

In a continuized grammar, all expressions can potentially be given continuized meanings via the Lift ($\uparrow$) operation. This is illustrated in Figure 2a where the categories for *Kim* and *gave* are lifted, taking on the semantics $\lambda k.k(\mathrm{kim})$ and $\lambda k.k(\lambda yzx.\mathrm{give}(x,y,z))$, resp. Lifting the category for *gave* allows it to combine with that of *no one* using scopal combination. The way in which scopal combination works in the tower notation is shown in Figure 3b (left): on the tower top, the syntactic categories must match in the middle (shown as matching Es here), while semantically the continuized functions $g[\,]$ and $h[\,]$ compose in surface order, yielding $g[h[\,]]$; on the tower bottom, the categories A and B with semantics a and b combine as they normally would in CCG (using the combinators in Figure 3a), yielding a category C with semantics c.[7] In the example, $[\,]$ and $\neg \exists y.[\,]$ compose to again yield $\neg \exists y.[\,]$ on the tower top, with $\lambda yzx.\mathrm{give}(x,y,z)$ applying to y and yielding $\lambda zx.\mathrm{give}(x,y,z)$ on the bottom.

As Barker & Shan observe, the explicit lifting step seen in Figure 2a can be integrated with the scopal combination step, as shown in the other recursively defined rules in Figure 3b, thereby avoiding an infinite regress when applying the lifting rule. Figure 2b shows how Lift Left ($\uparrow$L) can

---

[2] Here it's important to distinguish NPI *anything* from free-choice *anything*, where the latter is licensed instead in generic/habitual contexts, and thus can't appear in episodic sentences (as assumed in the example here).

[3] In the category for *anything*, the dollar sign matches a stack of arguments, which in this case is the single subject argument.

[4] As Barker & Shan also observe, similar linear order effects arise with binding, which Steedman handles at the level of logical form; such an approach would not seem applicable here, given that NPI licensing is generally taken to have both semantic and syntactic components.

[5] Semantic types are generally suppressed in this and subsequent figures.

[6] The subtype of positive clauses, represented by S^+, is used with positive polarity items. Note that Barker & Shan's polarity notation differs from the Dowty-style notation Steedman adopts in order to reflect its status as grammaticized rather than purely semantic information.

[7] The combinator for combining two scopal terms m and n is $\lambda mnk.m(\lambda x.n(\lambda y.k(xy)))$, assuming forward application on the tower bottom. Formulating the rules recursively allows the base combinator to be factored out while also generalizing to multi-level towers.

$$
\begin{array}{ccc}
\textit{No one} & \textit{enjoyed} & \textit{anything} \\
\hline
S^\circ/(S^\bullet\backslash NP) & (S^\circ\backslash NP)/NP & S^\bullet\$\backslash(S^\bullet\$/NP) \\
\end{array}
$$

(a)

$$
\begin{array}{cccc}
*\textit{Kim} & \textit{gave} & \textit{anyone} & \textit{nothing} \\
\hline
NP & ((S^\circ\backslash NP)/NP)/NP & S^\bullet\$\backslash(S^\bullet\$/NP) & S^\circ\$\backslash(S^\bullet\$/NP) \\
\end{array}
$$

(b)

Figure 1: Negative Polarity Item Licensing in CCG

be applied twice rather than using explicit lifting. The final representations are derived by collapsing the towers using the recursively defined Lower ($\downarrow$) operation in Figure 3c, which repeatedly applies the continuized semantics to the identity continuation $\lambda k.k$.

The polarity types in Figure 2 interact to correctly derive *Kim gave no one anything* and correctly rule out **Kim gave anyone nothing*. In Figure 2a, the licensor *no one* both precedes and outscopes the NPI *anything*, yielding a clause with neutral polarity, which is compatible with the root-level positive polarity requirement.[8] By contrast, in Figure 2b, the NPI *anyone* precedes its licensor, leading to a derivation that ends with S^-, which is incompatible with root-level positive polarity.[9] Figure 4 illustrates how the account makes the correct predictions even when Steedman's CCG, with its flexible approach to word order, is employed on the tower bottom: *Kim gave nothing to anyone* is correctly ruled in, and **Kim gave to anyone nothing* is correctly ruled out, even when the type-raised NPI PP (abbreviated as $PP^\uparrow$) swaps places places with its NP licensor using the backwards crossed composition combinatory rule ($< \mathbf{B}_\times$).

4 Flexible Word Order and Balanced Punctuation

To better serve the needs of generation, White and Rajkumar (2008) implement an approach to making the treatment of punctuation in a broad coverage grammar extracted from the CCGbank (2007) more precise by adding lexicalized punctuation categories to deal with constructions involving punctuation. In doing so, however, they observe that CCG's flexible treatment of word order is problematic when it comes to implementing a grammar-based approach to balanced punctuation, for reasons we review in this section. (Nunberg 1990 gives extensive arguments that writers have implicit knowledge of the grammar of punctuation that is comparable in intricacy to their grammatical knowledge of spoken language. Whether one agrees with Nunberg or not, there is practical value to grammars that treat punctuation with sufficient precision to satisfy the needs of parsing and generation.)

The original CCGbank corpus does not have lexical categories for punctuation; instead, punctuation marks carry categories derived from their part of speech tags and form part of a binary rule. It is assumed that there are no dependencies between words and punctuation marks and that the result of punctuation rules is the same as the non-punctuation category. Binary rules of this kind miss out on many linguistic generalizations, most glaringly the presence of manda-

---

[8] The Lower rule is compatible with subtypes of S at the tower upper right.

[9] The derivation does not go through even if *nothing* inverts to outscope *anyone*, as the *nothing*'s negation-canceling effect ends up on the wrong level. See (Barker and Shan, 2014) for discussion.

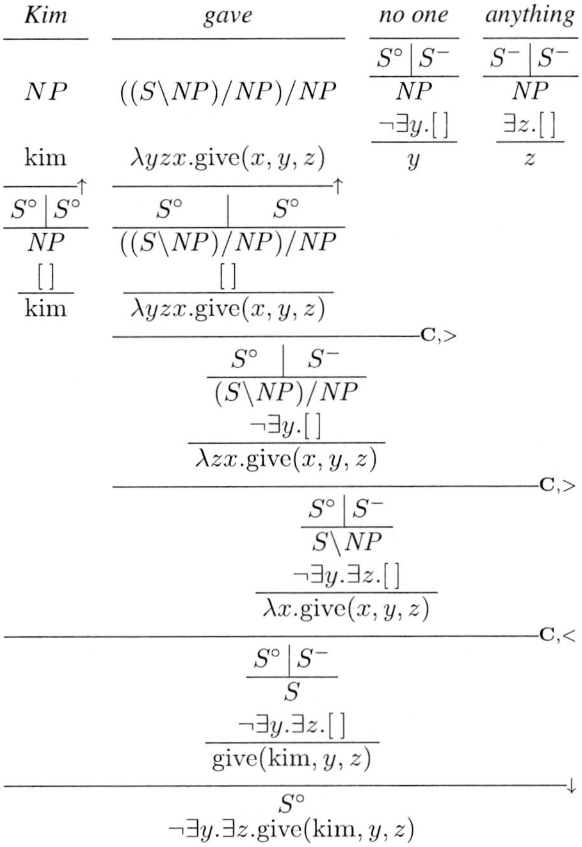

$$
\begin{array}{cccc}
Kim & gave & no\ one & anything \\
\hline
 & & \dfrac{S^\circ\,|\,S^-}{NP} & \dfrac{S^-\,|\,S^-}{NP} \\
NP & ((S\backslash NP)/NP)/NP & \neg\exists y.[\,] & \exists z.[\,] \\
kim & \lambda yzx.\mathrm{give}(x,y,z) & y & z
\end{array}
$$

$$
\dfrac{\dfrac{S^\circ\,|\,S^\circ}{NP}}{\dfrac{[\,]}{kim}}^{\uparrow}
\qquad
\dfrac{\dfrac{S^\circ\ \ |\ \ S^\circ}{((S\backslash NP)/NP)/NP}}{\dfrac{[\,]}{\lambda yzx.\mathrm{give}(x,y,z)}}^{\uparrow}
$$

$$
\cfrac{S^\circ\ \ |\ \ S^-}{\cfrac{(S\backslash NP)/NP}{\cfrac{\neg\exists y.[\,]}{\lambda zx.\mathrm{give}(x,y,z)}}}\ \mathbf{C},>
$$

$$
\cfrac{S^\circ\,|\,S^-}{\cfrac{S\backslash NP}{\cfrac{\neg\exists y.\exists z.[\,]}{\lambda x.\mathrm{give}(x,y,z)}}}\ \mathbf{C},>
$$

$$
\cfrac{S^\circ\,|\,S^-}{\cfrac{S}{\cfrac{\neg\exists y.\exists z.[\,]}{\mathrm{give}(kim,y,z)}}}\ \mathbf{C},<
$$

$$
\cfrac{S^\circ}{\neg\exists y.\exists z.\mathrm{give}(kim,y,z)}\ \downarrow
$$

(a) Negative Polarity Item Licensing, with Explicit Lifting

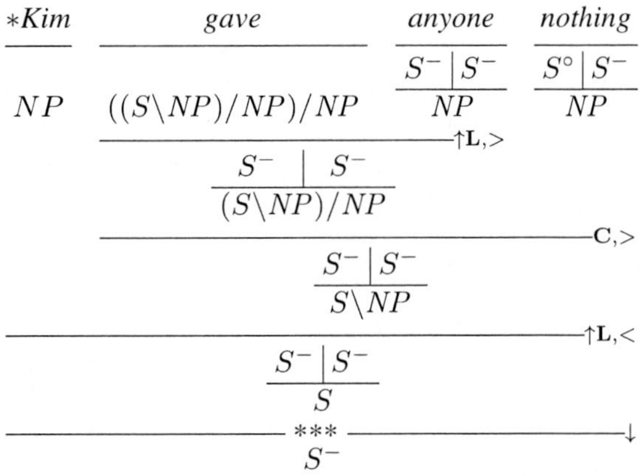

$$
\begin{array}{cccc}
{*}Kim & gave & anyone & nothing \\
\hline
NP & ((S\backslash NP)/NP)/NP & \dfrac{S^-\,|\,S^-}{NP} & \dfrac{S^\circ\,|\,S^-}{NP}
\end{array}
$$

$$
\cfrac{S^-\ \ |\ \ S^-}{(S\backslash NP)/NP}\ {\uparrow}\mathbf{L},>
$$

$$
\cfrac{S^-\,|\,S^-}{S\backslash NP}\ \mathbf{C},>
$$

$$
\cfrac{S^-\,|\,S^-}{S}\ {\uparrow}\mathbf{L},<
$$

$$
\cfrac{{*}{*}{*}}{S^-}\ \downarrow
$$

(b) Unlicensed Negative Polarity Item, with Integrated Lifting (Semantics Suppressed)

Figure 2: Continuized CCG Derivations

tory balancing marks in sentence-medial comma or dash adjuncts. For example, NP appositives can occur sentence medially or finally, and the conventions of writing mandate that sentence medial appositives should be balanced—i.e., the appositive NP should be surrounded by commas (or dashes) on both sides—while sentence final appositives should be unbalanced—i.e., they should only have one preceding comma or dash. The paradigm below illustrates:

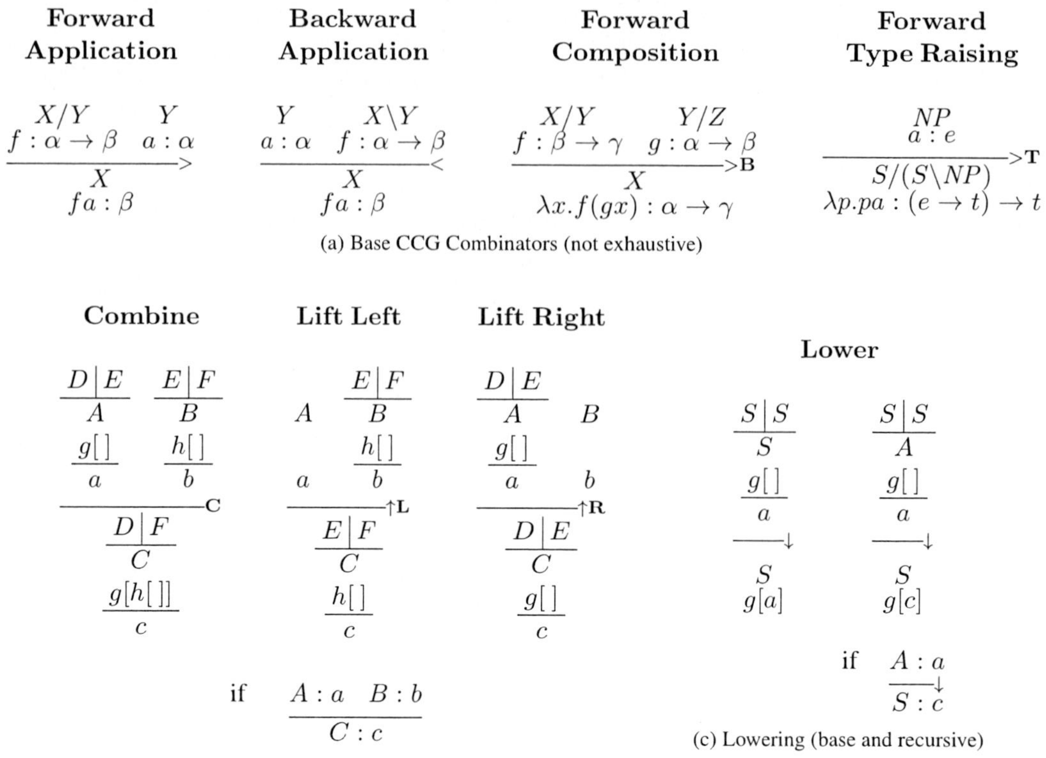

$$
\begin{array}{c}
\textbf{Forward} \\
\textbf{Application}
\end{array}
\qquad
\begin{array}{c}
\textbf{Backward} \\
\textbf{Application}
\end{array}
\qquad
\begin{array}{c}
\textbf{Forward} \\
\textbf{Composition}
\end{array}
\qquad
\begin{array}{c}
\textbf{Forward} \\
\textbf{Type Raising}
\end{array}
$$

$$
\cfrac{X/Y \quad\; Y}{\cfrac{f:\alpha\to\beta \;\; a:\alpha}{\;X\;}}\!>\;\; fa:\beta
\qquad
\cfrac{Y \quad\; X\backslash Y}{\cfrac{a:\alpha \;\; f:\alpha\to\beta}{\;X\;}}\!<\;\; fa:\beta
$$

$$
\cfrac{X/Y \quad\; Y/Z}{\cfrac{f:\beta\to\gamma \;\; g:\alpha\to\beta}{\;X\;}}\!>\!\mathbf{B}\;\; \lambda x.f(gx):\alpha\to\gamma
\qquad
\cfrac{NP}{\cfrac{a:e}{S/(S\backslash NP)}}\!>\!\mathbf{T}\;\; \lambda p.pa:(e\to t)\to t
$$

(a) Base CCG Combinators (not exhaustive)

$$
\textbf{Combine} \qquad\qquad \textbf{Lift Left} \qquad\qquad \textbf{Lift Right} \qquad\qquad\qquad \textbf{Lower}
$$

$$
\cfrac{
\begin{array}{cc}
\cfrac{D\,|\,E}{\cfrac{A}{\cfrac{g[\,]}{a}}} & \cfrac{E\,|\,F}{\cfrac{B}{\cfrac{h[\,]}{b}}}
\end{array}
}{\cfrac{D\,|\,F}{\cfrac{C}{\cfrac{g[h[\,]]}{c}}}}\mathbf{C}
\qquad
\cfrac{
\begin{array}{cc}
A & \cfrac{E\,|\,F}{\cfrac{B}{\cfrac{h[\,]}{b}}}
\end{array}
}{\cfrac{E\,|\,F}{\cfrac{C}{\cfrac{h[\,]}{c}}}}{\uparrow}\mathbf{L}
\qquad
\cfrac{
\begin{array}{cc}
\cfrac{D\,|\,E}{\cfrac{A}{\cfrac{g[\,]}{a}}} & B \;\; b
\end{array}
}{\cfrac{D\,|\,E}{\cfrac{C}{\cfrac{g[\,]}{c}}}}{\uparrow}\mathbf{R}
\qquad
\cfrac{S\,|\,S}{\cfrac{S}{\cfrac{g[\,]}{a}}}{\downarrow}\;\; \cfrac{S}{g[a]}
\qquad
\cfrac{S\,|\,S}{\cfrac{A}{\cfrac{g[\,]}{a}}}{\downarrow}\;\; \cfrac{S}{g[c]}
$$

$$
\text{if}\quad \cfrac{A:a \quad B:b}{C:c}
$$

$$
\text{if}\quad \cfrac{A:a}{S:c}{\downarrow}
$$

(b) Combination with Lifting

(c) Lowering (base and recursive)

Figure 3: Continuized CCG

(1) a.   Kim, CEO of XYZ, loves Sandy.

   b. *Kim, CEO of XYZ loves Sandy.

   c.   Kim loves Sandy, CEO of XYZ.

   d. *Kim loves Sandy, CEO of XYZ,.

   e.   Kim loves Sandy, CEO of XYZ, madly.

   f. *Kim loves Sandy, CEO of XYZ madly.

The literature discusses various means to address the issue of overgeneration: absorption rules (Nunberg, 1990), syntactic features (Doran, 1998) and (Briscoe, 1994) and semantic features (White, 2006). Nunberg (1990) argues that text adjuncts introduced by punctuation marks have an underlying representation where these adjuncts have marks on either side. They attain their surface form when a set of presentation rules are applied. This approach ensures that all sentence medial cases like (1a) and (1e) above are generated correctly, while unacceptable examples (1b) and (1f) would not be generated at all. Example (1c) would

at first be generated as (1d): to deal with such sentences, where two points happen to coincide, Nunberg posits an implicit point which is absorbed by the adjacent point. Absorption occurs according to the "strength" of the two points. Strength is determined according to the Point Absorption Hierarchy, which ranks commas lower than dashes, semi-colons, colons and periods. As White (1995) observes, from a generation-only perspective, it makes sense to generate text adjuncts which are always balanced and post-process the output to delete lower ranked points, as absorption uses relatively simple rules that operate independently of the hierarchy of the constituents. However, using this approach for parsing would involve a pre-processing step which inserts commas into possible edges of possible constituents, as described in (Forst and Kaplan, 2006). To avoid this considerable complication, Briscoe (1994) has argued for developing declarative approaches involving syntactic features in bi-directional systems, with no deletions or insertions of punctuation marks.

Following Briscoe, White and Rajkumar implement the categories shown in Figure 5 for appos-

$$
\begin{array}{c}
\textit{Kim} \quad\quad\quad \textit{gave} \quad\quad\quad \textit{nothing} \quad \textit{to anyone} \\[2pt]
\cfrac{}{NP} \quad \cfrac{}{((S\backslash NP)/PP)/NP} \quad \cfrac{S^\circ\,|\,S^-}{NP} \quad \cfrac{S^-\,|\,S^-}{PP} \\[6pt]
\cfrac{\cfrac{S^\circ\quad|\quad S^-}{(S\backslash NP)/PP}}{\;} \;\;{}^{\uparrow\mathbf{L},>} \\[6pt]
\cfrac{S^\circ\,|\,S^-}{S\backslash NP} \;\;{}^{\mathbf{C},>} \\[6pt]
\cfrac{S^\circ\,|\,S^-}{S} \;\;{}^{\uparrow\mathbf{L},<} \\[6pt]
S^\circ \;\;{}^{\downarrow}
\end{array}
\qquad\qquad
\begin{array}{c}
{*}\textit{Kim} \quad\quad\quad \textit{gave} \quad\quad\quad \textit{to anyone} \quad \textit{nothing} \\[2pt]
\cfrac{}{NP} \quad \cfrac{}{((S\backslash NP)/PP)/NP} \quad \cfrac{S^-\,|\,S^-}{PP^{\uparrow}} \quad \cfrac{S^\circ\,|\,S^-}{NP} \\[6pt]
\cfrac{S^-\quad|\quad S^-}{(S\backslash NP)/NP} \;\;{}^{\uparrow\mathbf{L},<\mathbf{B}_\times} \\[6pt]
\cfrac{S^-\,|\,S^-}{S\backslash NP} \;\;{}^{\mathbf{C},>} \\[6pt]
\cfrac{S^-\,|\,S^-}{S} \;\;{}^{\uparrow\mathbf{L},<} \\[6pt]
\overset{{*}{*}{*}}{S^-} \;\;{}^{\downarrow}
\end{array}
$$

Figure 4: Word Order Flexibility and NPI Licensing

(2) a. $, \vdash \mathsf{np}_{\langle 1\rangle\,bal=-,\,end=nil} \backslash \mathsf{np}_{\langle 1\rangle\,end=nil} /_\star \mathsf{np}_{\langle 3\rangle\,end=nil}$

   b. $, \vdash \mathsf{np}_{\langle 1\rangle\,bal=+,\,end=comma} \backslash \mathsf{np}_{\langle 1\rangle\,end=nil} /_\star \mathsf{punct}[,] /_\star \mathsf{np}_{\langle 3\rangle\,end=nil}$

Figure 5: Categories for Unbalanced and Balanced Appositive Commas in CCG (White and Rajkumar, 2008)

itive commas. Here, the unbalanced appositive comma has the category in (2a) where the comma selects as argument the appositive NP and converts it to a nominal modifier. For balanced appositives, the comma in (2b) selects the appositive NP and the balancing comma to form a nominal modifier. As these categories show, this approach involves the incorporation of syntactic features for punctuation (*bal* and *end*) into atomic categories so that certain combinations are blocked. To ensure proper appositive balancing sentence finally, the rightmost element in the sentence should transmit these features to the clause level, which the full stop can then check for the presence of right-edge punctuation; elsewhere, categories should ensure that their leftward arguments are balanced. The approach ensures that (1a)–(1f) above are all correctly generated or blocked.

The first issue with this aproach is that it does not work when crossing composition is used with adverbs in heavy-NP shift contructions, as illustrated in Figure 6.[10] Here the category for *loves* is intended to pass up the end punctuation feature from its direct object NP to the clause level (via the *PE* variable). Meanwhile, the category for *madly* is designed to combine with a balanced VP on the left to make a VP that has no end punctuation, which would be appropriate if *madly* appeared at the end of the verb phrase. However, when this category is used with backwards crossing composition as shown here, the result is category that claims to have no end punctuation when in fact it ends in a comma.

The second issue with the approach is that it is not adequate to deal with extraction involving ditransitive verbs, as shown in Figure 7. Here the comma at the end of the relative clause is not propagated to the root level. This is because the *end* feature for the relative clause should depend on the first (indirect) object of *gave*, rather than the second (direct) object as in a full ditransitive clause. Since CCG uses the same category for main and relative clauses, however, the right end punctuation is not correctly tracked.

As an interim solution to avoid overgeneration in such cases, White and Rajkumar (2008) implement an ad hoc post-filter on derivations to eliminate improperly balanced punctuation. In the next section, we'll see that continuized CCG makes it possible to successfully incorporate such constraints into the grammar itself.

---

[10]The appositive here is shortened to just *CEO* for illustration; naturally the object NP would need to be longer to count as a felicitous heavy NP.

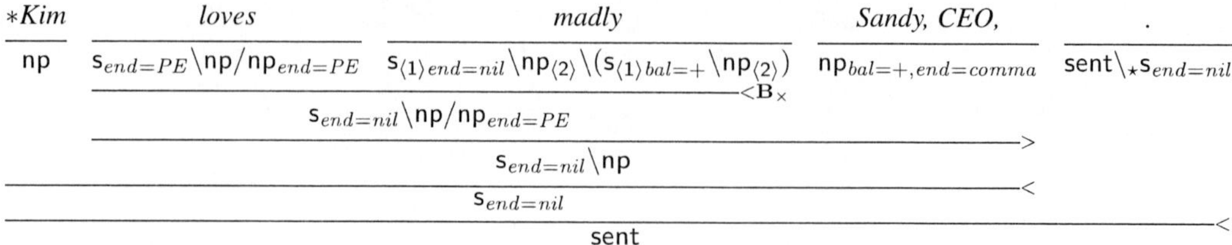

Figure 6: Crossing Composition and End Punctuation Tracking Issue in CCG

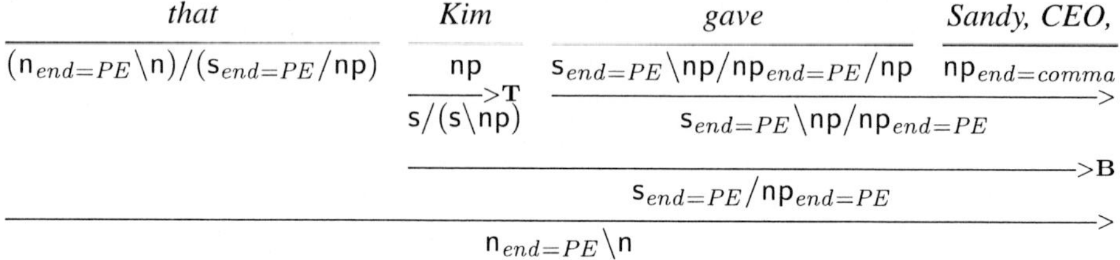

Figure 7: Object Extraction and End Punctuation Tracking Issue in CCG

5 An Evaluation Order Account of Balanced Punctuation

The approach presented in Section 3 to using the continuation layer to handle linear order constraints on NPI licensing can be generalized to also successfully track punctuation at the right periphery. As shown earlier, the category at the top left of the tower can be used to impose requirements on the preceding context, while the top right category can track information made available to the subsequent context. The idea for handling balanced punctuation is illustrated in Figure 8, where a bad comma-period sequence is correctly blocked despite the use of backwards crossed composition for heavy-NP shift. Tower categories, such as the one for *Sandy, CEO,*, ordinarily require their leftward context to have balanced punctuation, as shown with the top-left category S^{bal}; the phrase as a whole is balanced and ends with a comma, as the category S^{bal}_{comma} attests. Punctuation information on tower categories is propagated through the continuation layer via the Combination, Lift Left and Lift Right rules;[11] here, the direct object NP punctuation info is propagated up to the clausal level. At this point, combination with the full stop is blocked, since the full stop seeks a tower on the left that has no end punctuation, but the clause ends in a comma.[12] With relative clauses (not

shown), there is no problem tracking the punctuation at the right edge since this information is passed along the tower top rather than via the arguments of the CCG categories on the tower bottom, as in the problematic Figure 7.

The comma category for deriving balanced appositives is given in (3b) in Figure 9; this is the one whose result is shown in Figure 8. The corresponding unbalanced comma category—the one that would lead to a grammatical derivation—appears in (3a).

Semantically, with either comma category, the semantics of the predicative NP is added to that of the modified NP, taking advantage of the capacity of the monadic dynamic semantics to sequence constraints on entities. To show how this works, we first briefly introduce the basic idea of Charlow's monadic semantics, following White et al's (2017) presentation.

Charlow's (2014) dynamic semantics makes use of the State.Set monad (Hutton and Meijer, 1996), which combines the State monad for handling side effects with the Set monad for non-determinism. The State monad pairs ordinary semantic values with a state, which is threaded through computations. The Set monad models non-deterministic choices as sets, facilitating a non-deterministic treatment of indefinites. For example, the dynamic meaning of *a linguist swims* appears in (4): here, the proposition that x swims, where x is some linguist, is paired with a state that augments the input

---

[11]The Lift and Lift Left rules are modified to require balanced punctuation on the left.

[12]For readability, Lambek-style (result-on-top) slashes are used at the tower level, rather than Steedman-style (result-first) ones.

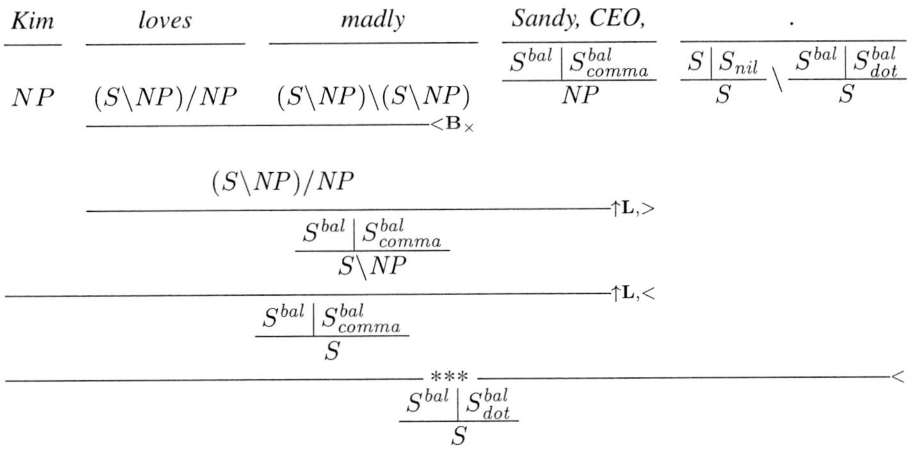

$$
\cfrac{
\cfrac{Kim}{NP} \quad
\cfrac{
\cfrac{loves}{(S\backslash NP)/NP} \quad \cfrac{madly}{(S\backslash NP)\backslash(S\backslash NP)}
}{(S\backslash NP)/NP}{}^{<\mathbf{B}_\times} \quad
\cfrac{Sandy,\ CEO,}{\cfrac{S^{bal}\,\big|\,S^{bal}_{comma}}{NP}} \quad
\cfrac{.}{\cfrac{S\,\big|\,S_{nil}}{S}\Big\backslash\cfrac{S^{bal}\,\big|\,S^{bal}_{dot}}{S}}
}{
\cfrac{
\cfrac{S^{bal}\,\big|\,S^{bal}_{comma}}{S\backslash NP}{}^{\uparrow\mathbf{L},>}
}{
\cfrac{S^{bal}\,\big|\,S^{bal}_{comma}}{S}{}^{\uparrow\mathbf{L},<}
}
}
\;{}^{***}
\cfrac{S^{bal}\,\big|\,S^{bal}_{dot}}{S}{}^{<}
$$

Figure 8: Right Edge Tracking through Crossing Composition in Dynamic Continuized CCG

$$
(3)\quad a.\ ,\ \vdash\ \cfrac{S\,\big|\,S_{nil}}{NP}\Big\backslash\cfrac{S^{bal}\,\big|\,S^{unbal}_{nil}}{NP}\Big/\cfrac{S\,\big|\,S_{nil}}{NP_{pred}}
$$

$$
b.\ ,\ \vdash\ \cfrac{S\,\big|\,S_{nil}}{NP}\Big\backslash\cfrac{S^{bal}\,\big|\,S^{bal}_{comma}}{NP}\Big/\,P_{comma}\Big/\cfrac{S\,\big|\,S_{nil}}{NP_{pred}}
$$

Figure 9: Categories for Unbalanced and Balanced Appositive Commas in Dynamic Continuized CCG

state s with the discourse referent x.

(4) $\lambda s.\{\langle \mathrm{swim}(x), \widehat{sx}\rangle \mid \mathrm{linguist}(x)\}$

More formally, the State.Set monad is defined as in (5). For each type α, the corresponding monadic type $M\alpha$ is a function from states of type s to sets pairing items of type α with such states. The η function injects values into the monad, simply yielding a singleton set consisting of the input item paired with the input state. The *bind* operation $\multimap$ sequences two monadic computations by sequencing the two computations pointwise, feeding each result of m applied to the input state s into π and unioning the results.[13] Less formally, the $\multimap$ operation can be thought of as "run m to determine v in π." Monadic sequencing with bind is what allows the meanings of *a linguist* and *swims* to compose with the indicated result.

(5) State.Set Monad

$$
\begin{aligned}
M\alpha &= s \to \alpha \times s \to t \\
a^\eta &= \lambda s.\{\langle a, s\rangle\} \\
m_v \multimap \pi &= \lambda s.\bigcup\nolimits_{\langle a, s'\rangle \in ms} \pi[a/v]s'
\end{aligned}
$$

---

[13]Note that the notation $m_v \multimap \pi$ is just syntactic sugar for $m \multimap \lambda v.\pi$, which may be more familiar.

Using these notions, the semantics of the comma-delimited appositive phrase *, CEO of XYZ,* is given in (6a) in Figure 10. As the category in (3b) takes a higher-order argument (after combining with the predicative NP and balancing comma), the semantics in (6a) takes a continuation argument k' and returns a continuized meaning (beginning with the second continuized argument k). The continuation argument k' applies the expression $\lambda x.\dots$; consequently, after combining with the continuized meaning of *Sandy*, the constant sandy substitutes for x, as shown in (6b). Via monadic sequencing, the modified noun phrase will then supply the constant sandy as the appropriate argument of the verb, in essentially the same way as it would have had *Sandy* not been modified by the appositive.

Though it's beyond the scope of the paper to go into details, the dynamic appositive semantics proposed here is consistent with Martin's (2016) treatment of supplements, where their typically projective behavior is derived by piggybacking the supplement on the scopal behavior of the modified NP. Moreover, it offers a simplification over Martin's account, as there is no need to appeal to an anaphoric mechanism in order to allow the supple-

(6) a. *, CEO of XYZ,* ⊢ $\lambda k'k.k'\lambda xs.\{\langle x, s\rangle \mid \mathrm{ceo}(x, \mathrm{xyz})\}_y \multimap ky$

    b. *Sandy, CEO of XYZ,* ⊢ $\lambda ks.\{\langle \mathrm{sandy}, s\rangle \mid \mathrm{ceo}(\mathrm{sandy}, \mathrm{xyz})\}_y \multimap ky$

Figure 10: Appositive semantics

mented NP to semantically compose with a verbal predicate.

6 Conclusion

In this paper, we have shown how Combinatory Categorial Grammar's (CCG; Steedman, 2000) flexible treatment of word order and constituency can be problematic for linguistic phenomena where linear order plays a key role. In particular, we have shown for the first time that linear order effects can be problematic for Steedman's (2012) treatment of negative polarity items, and shown that the enhanced control over evaluation order afforded by Continuized CCG (Barker & Shan, 2014) makes it possible to formulate improved analyses of NPIs that account for these effects quite naturally even in a system that combines Steedman's CCG for predicate-argument structure with Barker & Shan's for quantification. In addition, after reviewing how CCG's flexible treatment of word order and constituency are problematic for implementing constraints on balanced punctuation in the style of Briscoe (1994), we have shown how to generalize the approach to encoding evaluation order constraints to properly track punctuation information at the right boundary. As a bonus, we have also taken advantage of Charlow's monadic semantics to implement a novel approach to NP appositives that arguably improves upon Martin's (2016) treatment. Natural next steps for future work include tackling order effects found with binding and crossover as well as exploring the use of machine-learned models to guide the search for derivations.

Acknowledgements

Thanks to Simon Charlow, Dylan Bumford, Jordan Needle, Scott Martin, Mark Steedman and the anonymous reviewers for helpful comments and discussion. This work was supported in part by NSF grant IIS-1319318.

References

Yoav Artzi and Luke Zettlemoyer. 2013. Weakly supervised learning of semantic parsers for mapping instructions to actions. *Transactions of the Association for Computational Linguistics*, 1(1):49–62.

Chris Barker. 2002. Continuations and the nature of quantification. *Natural Language Semantics*, 10(3):211–242.

Chris Barker and Chung-chieh Shan. 2014. *Continuations and Natural Language*. Oxford Studies in Theoretical Linguistics.

Raffaella Bernardi. 2002. *Reasoning with polarity in categorial type logic*. Ph.D. thesis, Utrecht Institute of Linguistics (OTS), Utrecht University.

Ted Briscoe. 1994. Parsing (with) punctuation. Technical report, Xerox, Grenoble, France.

Simon Charlow. 2014. *On the semantics of exceptional scope*. Ph.D. thesis, New York University.

Stephen Clark and James R. Curran. 2007. Wide-Coverage Efficient Statistical Parsing with CCG and Log-Linear Models. *Computational Linguistics*, 33(4):493–552.

Christine Doran. 1998. *Incorporating Punctuation into the Sentence Grammar: A Lexicalized Tree Adjoining Grammar Perspective*. Ph.D. thesis, University of Pennsylvania.

David R. Dowty. 1994. The role of negative polarity and concord marking in natural language reasoning. In *Proceedings from Semantics and Linguistic Theory IV*, Ithaca. Cornell University Press.

Martin Forst and Ronald M. Kaplan. 2006. The importance of precise tokenizing for deep grammars. In *Proc. LREC-06*.

Julia Hockenmaier and Mark Steedman. 2007. CCGbank: A Corpus of CCG Derivations and Dependency Structures Extracted from the Penn Treebank. *Computational Linguistics*, 33(3):355–396.

Graham Hutton and Erik Meijer. 1996. Monadic Parser Combinators. Technical Report NOTTCS-TR-96-4, Department of Computer Science, University of Nottingham.

Kenton Lee, Mike Lewis, and Luke Zettlemoyer. 2016. Global neural CCG parsing with optimality guarantees. In *Proceedings of the 2016 Conference on*

Empirical Methods in Natural Language Processing, pages 2366–2376, Austin, Texas. Association for Computational Linguistics.

Scott Martin. 2016. Supplemental update. *Semantics and Pragmatics*, 9(5):1–61.

Geoffrey Nunberg. 1990. *The Linguistics of Punctuation*. CSLI Publications, Stanford, CA.

Chung-chieh Shan and Chris Barker. 2006. Explaining crossover and superiority as left-to-right evaluation. *Linguistics and Philosophy*, 29(1):91–134.

Mark Steedman. 2012. *Taking Scope: The Natural Semantics of Quantifiers*. MIT Press, Cambridge, MA, USA.

Michael White. 1995. Presenting punctuation. In *Proceedings of the Fifth European Workshop on Natural Language Generation*, pages 107–125.

Michael White. 2006. Efficient realization of coordinate structures in combinatory categorial grammar. *Research on Language and Computation*, 4(1):39–75.

Michael White, Simon Charlow, Jordan Needle, and Dylan Bumford. 2017. Parsing with Dynamic Continuized CCG. In *Proceedings of the 13th International Workshop on Tree Adjoining Grammars and Related Formalisms*, pages 71–83, Umeå, Sweden. Association for Computational Linguistics.

Michael White and Rajakrishnan Rajkumar. 2008. A more precise analysis of punctuation for broad-coverage surface realization with CCG. In *Coling 2008: Proceedings of the workshop on Grammar Engineering Across Frameworks*, pages 17–24, Manchester, England. Coling 2008 Organizing Committee.

Abstract Meaning Representation for Human-Robot Dialogue

Claire Bonial[1], Lucia Donatelli[2], Jessica Ervin[3], and Clare R. Voss[1]

[1]U.S Army Research Laboratory, Adelphi, MD 20783
[2]Georgetown University, Washington D.C. 20057
[3]University of Rochester, Rochester, NY 14627
claire.n.bonial.civ@mail.mil

Abstract

In this research, we begin to tackle the challenge of natural language understanding (NLU) in the context of the development of a robot dialogue system. We explore the adequacy of Abstract Meaning Representation (AMR) as a conduit for NLU. First, we consider the feasibility of using existing AMR parsers for automatically creating meaning representations for robot-directed transcribed speech data. We evaluate the quality of output of two parsers on this data against a manually annotated gold-standard data set. Second, we evaluate the semantic coverage and distinctions made in AMR overall: how well does it capture the meaning and distinctions needed in our collaborative human-robot dialogue domain? We find that AMR has gaps that align with linguistic information critical for effective human-robot collaboration in search and navigation tasks, and we present task-specific modifications to AMR to address the deficiencies.

1 Introduction

A central challenge in human-agent collaboration is that robots (or their virtual counterparts) do not have sufficient linguistic or world knowledge to communicate in a timely and effective manner with their human collaborators (Chai et al., 2017; She and Chai, 2017). We address this challenge in ongoing research directed at analyzing robot-directed communication in collaborative human-agent exploration tasks, with the ultimate goal of enabling robots to adapt to domain-specific language.

In this paper, we choose to adopt an intermediate semantic representation and select Abstract Meaning Representation (AMR) (Banarescu et al., 2013) in particular for three reasons: (i) the semantic representation framework abstracts away from surface variation, therefore the robot will only be trained to process and execute the actions corresponding to semantic elements of the representation (ii) there are a variety of fairly robust AMR parsers we can employ for this work, enabling us to forego manual annotation of substantial portions of our data and facilitating efficient automatic parsing in a future end-to-end system; and (iii) the structured representation facilitates the interpretation of novel instructions and grounding instructions with respect to the robot's current physical surroundings and set of executable actions. The latter motivation is especially important given that our human-robot dialogue is physically situated. This stands in contrast to many other dialogue systems, such as task-oriented chat bots, which do not require establishing and acting upon a shared understanding of the physical environment and often do not require any intermediate semantic representation (see §6 for further comparison to related work).

Our paper is structured as follows: First, we present background both on the corpus of human-robot dialogue we are leveraging (§2), and on AMR (§3). §4 discusses the implementation and results of two AMR parsers on the human-robot dialogue data. §5 assesses the semantic coverage of AMR for the human-robot dialogue data in particular. We then discuss related work that informs the current research in §6. Finally, §7 concludes and presents ideas for future work.

2 Background: Human-Robot Dialogue Corpus

We aim to support NLU within the broader context of ongoing research to develop a human-robot dialogue system (Marge et al., 2016a) to be used onboard a remotely located agent collaborating with humans in search and navigation tasks (e.g., disaster relief). In developing this dialogue system, we

Proceedings of the Society for Computation in Linguistics (SCiL) 2019, pages 236-246.
New York City, New York, January 3-6, 2019

are making use of portions of the corpus of human-robot dialogue data collected under this effort (Bonial et al., 2018; Traum et al., 2018).[1] This corpus was collected via a phased 'Wizard-of-Oz' (WoZ) methodology, in which human experimenters perform the dialogue and navigation capabilities of the robot during experimental trials, unbeknownst to participants interacting with the 'robot'(Marge et al., 2016b).

Specifically, a naïve participant (unaware of the wizards) is tasked with instructing a robot to navigate through a remote, unfamiliar house-like environment, and asked to find and count objects such as shoes and shovels. In reality, the participant is not speaking directly to a robot, but to an unseen Dialogue Manager (DM) Wizard who listens to the participant's spoken instructions and responds with text messages in a chat window or passes a simplified text version of the instructions to a Robot Navigator (RN) Wizard, who joysticks the robot to complete the instructions. Given that the DM acts as an intermediary passing communications between the participant and the RN, the dialogue takes place across multiple conversational floors. The flow of dialogue from participant to DM, DM to RN and subsequent feedback to the participant can be seen in table 1.

The corpus comprises 20 participants and about 20 hours of audio, with 3,573 participant utterances (continuous speech) totaling 18,336 words, as well as 13,550 words from DM-Wizard text messages. The corpus includes speech transcriptions from participants as well as the speech of the RN-Wizard. These transcriptions are time-aligned with the DM-Wizard text messages passed either to the participant or to the RN-Wizard.

The corpus also includes a dialogue annotation scheme specific to multi-floor dialogue that identifies initiator intent and signals relations between individual utterances pertaining to that intent (Traum et al., 2018).The design of the existing annotation scheme allows for the characterization of distinct information states by way of sets of participants, participant roles, turn-taking and floor-holding, and other factors (Traum and Larsson, 2003). *Transaction units (TU)* identify utterances from multiple participants and floors into units according to the realization of an initiator's intent, such that all utterances involved in an ex-change surrounding the successful execution of a command are grouped and annotated for the relations they hold to one another. *Relation types (Rel)* signal how utterances within the same TU relate to one another in the context of the ultimate goal of the TU (e.g. "ack-done" in table 1, shortened from "acknowledge-done," signals that an utterance acknowledges completion of a previous utterance; for full details on Rel types, see Traum et al. (2018)). *Antecedents (Ant)* specify which utterance is related to which. An example of a TU may be seen in table 1. It is notable that the existing annotation scheme highlights *dialogue structure* and does not provide a markup of the semantic content of participant instructions.

3 Background: Abstract Meaning Representation

The Abstract Meaning Representation (AMR) project (Banarescu et al., 2013) has created a manually annotated "semantics bank" of text drawn from a variety of genres. The AMR project annotations are completed on a sentence-by-sentence basis, where each sentence is represented by a rooted directed acyclic graph (DAG). For ease of creation and manipulation, annotators work with the PENMAN representation of the same information (Penman Natural Language Group, 1989). For example:

```
(w / want-01
   :ARG0 (d / dog)
   :ARG1 (p / pet-01
            :ARG0 (g / girl)
            :ARG1 d))
```

Figure 1: PENMAN notation of *The dog wants the girl to pet him.*

In neo-Davidsonian fashion (Davidson, 1969; Parsons, 1990), AMR introduces variables (or graph nodes) for entities, events, properties, and states. Leaves are labeled with concepts, so that (d / dog) refers to an instance (d) of the concept *dog*. Relations link entities, so that (w / walk-01 :location (p/ park)) means the walking event (w) has the relation location to the entity, park (p). When an entity plays multiple roles in a sentence (e.g., (d / dog) above), AMR employs re-entrancy in graph notation (nodes with multiple parents) or variable re-use in PENMAN notation.

AMR concepts are either English words (boy), PropBank (Palmer et al., 2005) role-

---

[1]This corpus is still being collected and a public release is in preparation.

	Left floor		Right Floor		Annotations		
#	**Participant**	**DM → Participant**	**DM → RN**	**RN**	**TU**	**Ant**	**Rel**
1	move forward 3 feet				1		
2		ok			1	1	ack-wilco
3			move forward 3 feet		1	1	trans-r
4				done	1	3	ack-done
5		I moved forward 3 feet			1	4	trans-l

Table 1: Example of a Transaction Unit (TU) in the existing corpus dialogue annotation, which contains an instruction initiated by the participant, its translation to a simplified form (DM to RN), and the execution of the instruction and acknowledgement of such by the RN. TU, Ant(ecedent), and Rel(ation type) are indicated in the right columns. (Traum et al., 2018)

sets (`want-01`), or special keywords indicating generic entity types: `date-entity`, `world-region`, `distance-quantity`, etc. In addition to the PropBank lexicon of rolesets, which associate argument numbers (ARG 0–6) with predicate-specific semantic roles (e.g., ARG0=*wanter* in ex. 1), AMR uses approximately 100 relations of its own (e.g., `:time`, `:age`, `:quantity`, `:destination`, etc.).

The representation captures *who is doing what to whom* like other semantic role labeling (SRL) schemes (e.g., PropBank (Palmer et al., 2005), FrameNet (Baker et al., 1998; Fillmore et al., 2003), VerbNet (Kipper et al., 2008)), but also represents other aspects of meaning outside of semantic role information, such as fine-grained quantity and unit information and parthood relations. Also distinguishing it from other SRL schemes, a goal of AMR is to capture core facets of meaning while abstracting away from idiosyncratic syntactic structures; thus, for example, *She adjusted the machine* and *She made an adjustment to the machine* share the same AMR. AMR has been widely used to support NLU, generation, and summarization (Liu et al., 2015; Pourdamghani et al., 2016), machine translation, question answering (Mitra and Baral, 2016), information extraction (Pan et al., 2015), and biomedical text mining (Garg et al., 2016; Rao et al., 2017; Wang et al., 2017)

4 Evaluating AMR parsers on Human-Robot Dialogue Data

To serve as a conduit for NLU in a dialogue system, the ideal semantic representation would have robust parsers, allowing the representation to be implemented efficiently on a large scale. There have been a variety of parsers developed for AMR; two parsers using very different approaches are explored in the sections to follow.

4.1 Parsers

To automatically create AMRs for the human-robot diaogue data, we used two off-the-shelf AMR parsers, JAMR[2] (Flanigan et al., 2014) and CAMR[3] (Wang et al., 2015). JAMR was one of the first AMR parsers and uses a two-part algorithm to first identify concepts and then to build the maximum spanning connected subgraph of those concepts, adding in the relations. CAMR, in contrast, starts by obtaining the dependency tree (in this case, using the Charniak parser[4] and Stanford CoreNLP toolkit (Manning et al., 2014)) and then uses their algorithm to apply a series of transformations to the dependency tree, ultimately transforming it into an AMR graph. One strength of CAMR is that the dependency parser is independent of the AMR creation, so a dependency parser that is trained on a larger data set, and therefore more accurate, can be used. Both JAMR and CAMR have algorithms that have learned probabilities from training data in order to execute their algorithms on novel sentences.

4.2 Gold Standard Data Set

In order to evaluate parser performance on our data set, we hand-annotated a subset of the participant's speech in the human-robot dialogue corpus to create a gold standard data set. We focus on only participant language because it is the natural language that the robot will ultimately need to process and act on. This selected subset comprises 10% of participant utterances from one phase of the corpus including 10 subjects. The resulting sample is 137 sentences, equally distributed across the 10 participants, who tend to have unique speech patterns. Three expert annotators familiar with both the human-robot dialogue data and AMR independently annotated this sample, ob-

---

[2]https://github.com/jflanigan/jamr
[3]https://github.com/c-amr/camr
[4]https://github.com/BLLIP/bllip-parser

taining inter-annotator agreement (IAA) scores of .82, .82, and .91 using the Smatch metric.[5]

After independent annotations, we collaboratively created the gold standard set. Notable choices made during this process include the treatment of "can you" utterances, re-entry of the subject in commands using motion verbs with independent arguments for the mover and thing-moved, and handling of disfluencies; each is described here.

In "can you" utterances, there is an ambiguity as to whether it is a genuine question of ability, or a polite request. This difference determines whether the sentence gets annotated with `possible-01` (used in AMR to convey both possibility and ability), or just as a command (figure 2). It also determines whether the robot should respond with a statement of ability, or perform the action requested. To resolve this ambiguity, we referred back to the full transcripts of the data, and inferred based on context. In our sample, only one of these utterances ("can you go that way") was deemed to be a genuine questions of ability, while the remaining 13 (e.g. "can you take a picture," "can you turn to your right") were treated as commands. Those that were commands were annotated with `:polite +`, in order to preserve what we believe to be the speaker's intention in using the modal "can."

```
(p / possible-01
    :ARG1 (p2 / picture-01
        :ARG0 (y / you))
    :polarity (a / amr-unknown))

(p / picture-01 :mode imperative
    :polite +
    :ARG0 (y / you))
```

Figure 2: Two different AMR parses for the utterance "can you take a picture," convey two distinct interpretations of the utterance: the top can be read as "Is it possible for you to take a picture?," the bottom as a command for a picturing event.

With commands like "move" or "turn," it is implied that the robot is the agent impelling motion and the thing being moved. Therefore, we used re-entry in those AMRs to infer the implied "you" as both the `:ARG0`, mover, and the `:ARG1`, thing-moved (figure 3). This is consistent with AMR's goal of capturing the meaning of an utterance, independent of syntax—all arguments that

---

[5]IAA Smatch scores on AMRs are generally between .7 and .8, depending on the complexity of the data (AMR development group communication, 2014).

can be confidently inferred should be included in the AMR, even if implicit.[6]

```
(m / move-01 :mode imperative
    :ARG0 (y / you)
    :ARG1 y
    :direction (f / forward)
    :extent (d / distance-quantity
        :quant 3
        :unit (f2 / foot)))
```

Figure 3: Gold standard AMR for "move forward 3 feet," showing the inferred argument "you" as `:ARG0` (mover) and `:ARG1` (thing-moved).

Although the LDC AMR corpus[7] does not include speech data, AMR does offer guidance for disfluencies—dropping the disfluent portion of an utterance in favor of representing only the speaker's repair utterance.[8] We followed this general AMR practice and dropped disfluent speech for the surprisingly infrequent cases of disfluency in our gold standard sample.

4.3 Results & Error Analysis

Having created a gold standard sample of our data, we ran both JAMR and CAMR on the same sample and obtained the Smatch scores when compared to the gold standard. As seen in Table 2, CAMR performs better on both precision and recall, thus obtaining the higher F-score. However, compared to their self-reported F-scores (0.58 for JAMR and 0.63 for CAMR) on other corpora, both under-perform on the human-robot dialogue data.

	Precision	Recall	F-score
JAMR	0.27	0.44	0.33
CAMR	**0.33**	**0.51**	**0.40**

Table 2: Parser performance on human-robot dialogue data.

Of the errors present in the parser output, many come from improper handling of light verb construction, imperatives, inferred arguments, and requests phrased as "can you" questions. "Take a picture" is an example of a frequent light verb construction, in which the verb ("take") is not semantically the main predicating element of the sentence. The correct parse is shown in Figure 4,

---

[6]See "implicit roles" in AMR guidelines: https://github.com/amrisi/amr-guidelines/blob/master/amr.md

[7]https://catalog.ldc.upenn.edu/LDC2017T10

[8]https://www.isi.edu/~ulf/amr/lib/amr-dict.html#disfluency

followed by the AMR that both parsers consistently create. They both incorrectly place "take" as the top node (using the grasping, caused motion sense of the verb), when in reality it should be dropped from the AMR completely according to AMR practice for light verbs. Light verb constructions occur in 60 utterances in our sample, with 59 of those being some variation on "take a picture" or "take a photo."

```
(p / picture-01 :mode imperative
    :ARG0 (y / you))

(x1 / take-01
    :ARG1 (x3 / picture))
```

Figure 4: Gold standard AMR for "take a picture" (top), followed by parser output.

Another common error shown in figure 4 is the notation `:mode imperative`, used to indicate commands, which is present in 127 sentences within our sample. Despite the prevalence of this feature in our gold standard, it is never present in parser output.

Another problematic omission on the parsers' part is a lack of inferred arguments. As discussed earlier, commands like "move forward 3 feet" have an implied "you" in both the `:ARG0` and `:ARG1` positions. However, the parsers don't include this variable, instead only including concepts that are explicitly mentioned in the sentence (figure 5).

```
(x1 / move-01
    :direction (x2 / forward)
    :ARG1 (x4 / distance-quantity
        :unit (f / foot)
        :quant 3))
```

Figure 5: CAMR output for "move forward 3 feet." The distance is mistaken for the `:ARG1` thing-moved and the implied "you"/robot is omitted. Compare with figure 3.

A fourth error made by the parsers was on "can you" requests. These were consistently handled by both parsers as questions of ability, annotated using `possible-01`, even when (as was usually the case) the utterances were intended to be polite commands (parser output is shown in the top parse of figure 2).

4.4 Discussion

The poor performance of both parsers on the human-robot dialogue data is unsurprising given the significant differences between it and the data the parsers were trained on. For both parsers,

training data came from the LDC AMR corpus, made up entirely of written text, mostly newswire.[9] In contrast, the human-robot dialogue data is transcribed from spoken utterances, taken from dialogue that is instructional and goal-oriented. Thus, running the parsers on this data set shows that the differences in domain have significant effects on the parsers, and give rise to the systematic errors described above.

Improvements to the parser output could be obtained even by just adding a few simple heuristics, due to the formulaic nature of our data. Of 137 sample sentences, 25 were "take a picture," so introducing a heuristic specific to that sentence would be a simple way to make several corrections. To obtain broader improvements, however, it's clear that it will be necessary to retrain the parsers on in-domain data. Given that retraining requires a corpus of hand-annotated data, this gives us an opportunity to examine the current features of AMR in relation to our collaborative human-robot dialogue domain, and to explore possible additions to the annotation scheme to ensure that all elements of meaning essential to our domain have coverage. The findings of this analysis are described in the sections to follow.

5 Evaluating Semantic Coverage & Distinctions of AMR

We assess the adequacy of AMR for its use in an NLU component of a human-robot dialogue system both on theoretical grounds and in light of the results and error analysis presented in §4. To our knowledge, our research is the first to employ AMR to capture the semantics of spoken language; existing corpora are otherwise text-based.[10] Here, we discuss the characteristics of our data relevant to semantic representation and highlight specific challenges and areas of interest that we hope to address with AMR (§5.1); explore how to leverage AMR for these purposes by identifying (§5.2) and remedying (§5.3) gaps in existing AMR; and conclude with discussion (§5.4).

5.1 Challenges of the Data

Our goal in introducing AMR is to bridge the gap between what is annotated currently as *dialogue*

---

[9] `https://catalog.ldc.upenn.edu/LDC2017T10`

[10] Data released at `https://amr.isi.edu/download/amr-bank-struct-v1.6.txt` (*Little Prince*) and LDC corpus (footnote 5).

structure (Traum et al., 2018), and the semantic content of utterances that comprise such dialogue (not included in the current scheme). This goal follows from the understanding that *dialogue acts* are composed of two primary components: (i) *semantic content*, identifying the entities, events, and propositions relevant to the dialogue; and (ii) *communicative function*, identifying the ways an addressee may use semantic content to update the information state (Bunt et al., 2012). The existing dialogue structure annotation scheme of Traum et al. (2018) distinguishes two primary levels of pragmatic meaning important to dialogue that our research aims to maintain. The first, *intentional structure* (Grosz and Sidner, 1986), is equivalent to a TU[11]: all utterances that explicate and address an initiator's intent. The second, *interactional structure*, captures how the information state of participants in the dialogue is updated as the TU is constructed (Traum et al., 2018). These two levels of meaning stand apart from the basic compositional meaning of their associated utterances.We seek to represent these pragmatic levels of meaning and link them to their respective semantic forms.

We also seek to represent the temporal, aspectual, and veridical/modal nature of the robot's actions. Human instructions must be interpreted for actions: the robot may respond to such instruction by asserting whether or not such an instruction is possible given the robot's capabilities and the surrounding physical environment, and the robot may also communicate whether it is in the process of completing or has completed the desired instruction. Such information is implicitly linked to the intentional and interactional structure of the dialogue. For example, the act of giving a command implies that an event (if it occurs) will happen in the future; the act of asserting that an event has occurred signals that the event is past.

The representation of space and specific parameters that contribute to the robot's understanding of how human language maps on to its physical environment is also of interest to our work here.[12] As its capabilities are presented to the participant, the 'robot' in this research is capable of performing low-level actions with specific endpoints or goals: for example, *"move five feet forward," "face the doorway on your left,"* and *"get closer to that orange object."* This robot cannot successfully perform instructions that have no clear endpoint:*"move forward"* and *"turn"* will trigger clarification requests for further specification. In our planned system, however, we would ultimately like to give the robot an instruction such as *"Robot, explore this space and tell me if anyone has been here recently."* If the robot can learn to decompose an instruction such as *explore* into smaller actions, as well as how to identify signs of previous inhabitants, such instructions may become feasible.

Finally, much of the semantic content of the data in our experiment must be situated within the dialogue context to be properly interpreted. A command of *"Do that again"* is ambiguous in terms of which action it refers back to. Similarly, a negative command such as *"No, go to the doorway on the left"* negates specific information contained in a previous command. Implicit in natural language input, as well, are subtle event-event temporal relations, such as *"Move forward and take a picture"* (sequential actions) and *"Turn around and take a picture every 45 degrees"* (simultaneous actions).

5.2 Gaps in AMR

We focus on the three elements of meaning crucial to human-robot dialogue and currently lacking in AMR: (i) speaker intended meaning (as differing from the compositional meaning of the speaker's utterances);[13] (ii) tense and aspect (and vericity, by association); and (iii) spatial parameters necessary for the robot to successfully execute instructions within its physical environment.

The goal of the AMR project is to represent *meaning*, but whether such meaning is purely semantic or also captures a speaker's intended meaning is not specified. Here, we attempt to strike a balance between capturing speaker intended meaning and overspecifying utterances. We do this to stay faithful to existing experimental dialogue annotation practices, and to enable the robot

---

[11]Transaction Unit is described in §2.

[12]Though this mapping is outside the scope of our work, we see AMR as contributing substantially richer semantic forms to the NL planning research in robotics of others, such as (Howard et al., 2014) that entails such *grounding*, the process of assigning physical meanings to NL expressions.

[13]Speaker vs. compositional meaning is arguably annotated inconsistently in the current AMR corpus; see `https://www.isi.edu/~ulf/amr/lib/amr-dict.html#pragmatics` for some specific guidelines, but note that the released annotations seem to differ from this guidance in places.

to generalize the connections between such intention and underlying semantic content.

To illustrate the need for adding tense and aspect information to existing AMRs, compare the following utterances: (i) *"move forward five feet"* (uttered by the human participant); (ii) *"moving forward five feet..."* (sent via text by the robot to signal initiation of instruction); and (iii) *"I moved forward five feet"* (sent by the robot upon completion of the action). Although distinctions between these three utterances are critical for our domain, AMR represents these three utterances the same way:[14]

```
(m / move-01
    :ARG1 (r / robot)
    :extent (d / distance-quantity
        :quant 5
        :unit (f / foot))
    :direction (f / forward))
```

Figure 6: Without tense and aspect representation, current AMR conflates commands to move forward and assertions of ongoing and/or completed motion.

Spatial parameters of actions are represented in the current AMR through the use of predicate-specific ARG numbers, as outlined in the Prop-Bank rolesets, or with the use of AMR relations, such as `:path` and `:destination`. Whether or not a relation or argument number is used, and which argument number, is specific to a predicate and therefore inconsistent across motion relations. We aim to make the representation of these parameters more consistent and enrich them with information about which are required, which are optional, and which might have assumed, default interpretations.

5.3 Proposed Refinements

We leverage the existing dialogue annotations to extract intentional and interactional meaning and, where relevant, map these annotations to proposed refinements described below.

Speech Acts. We add a higher level of pragmatic meaning to the propositional content represented in the AMR through frames that correspond to speech acts (Austin, 1975; Searle, 1969). We use the model of vocatives in existing AMR as our guide.[15] We also make use of the existing

dialogue structure annotation scheme for our corpus that identifies dialogue types similar to speech acts. Using this scheme as a starting point, we create 36 unique speech acts and corresponding AMR frames: this consists of six general dialogue types (*command, assert, request, question, evaluate, express*) with 5 to 12 subtypes each (e.g., move, send-image). An example of a speech act template for *command:move* may be seen in figure 7.[16] Notably, by adding a layer of speaker-intended meaning to the content of the proposition itself, we are able to capture participant roles within the speech act (`:ARG0` and `:ARG1` of `command-02`). Future work will be able to reference these roles and model how participant relations evolve over the course of the discourse (Allwood et al., 2000).

```
(c / command-02
    :ARG0-commander
    :ARG1-impelled agent
    :ARG2 (g / go-02 :completable +
        :ARG0-goer
        :ARG1-extent
        :ARG3-start point
        :ARG4-end point
        :path
        :direction
        :time (a / after
            :op1 (n / now))))
```

Figure 7: Speech act template for *command:move*. Arguments and relations in italics are filled in from context and the utterance.

Tense and Aspect. We also adopt the annotation scheme proposed by Donatelli et al. (2018) for augmenting AMR with tense and aspect. This scheme identifies the temporal nature of an event relative to the dialogue act in which it is expressed as past, present, or future. The aspectual nature of the event can be specified as atelic (`:ongoing -/+`), telic and hypothetical (`:ongoing -`, `:completable +`), telic and in progress (`:ongoing +`, `:complete -`), or telic and complete (`:ongoing -`, `:complete +`). A telic and hypothetical event representation can be seen in figure 7. This tense/aspect annotation scheme is specific to AMR and coarse-grained in nature, but through its use of existing AMR relations (`:time`, `before`, `after`, `now`, `:op`), it can be adapted to finer-grained temporal relations in future work.

Spatial Parameters. As seen in figure 7, all arguments of `go-02` as well as additional relations

---

[14]Utterance (i) would additionally annotate (m / move) with `:mode imperative` to signal a command. As noted in §4, parsers rarely capture this information.

[15]https://www.isi.edu/~ulf/amr/lib/amr-dict.html#vocative

[16]Annotation of tense and aspect, and the need for extra relations will be explained in continuation.

are made use of in the template. These positions correspond to parameters of the action, needed so the robot may carry out the action successfully. Having a template for each domain-relevant speech act will allow us to specify required and optional parameters for robot operationalization. In figure 7, this is either `:ARG1` or `:ARG4`, given that the robot currently needs an endpoint for each action; if both arguments are empty, this ought to trigger a request for further information by the robot. Note also that the same *command:move* AMR (including `go-02`) would be implemented for all realizations of commands for movement (e.g., *move, go, drive*), whereas these would receive distinct AMRs, headed by each individual predicate, under current practices.

5.4 Discussion

The refinements we present to the existing AMR aim to mimic a conservative learning process: we seek to provide just enough pragmatic meaning to assist robot understanding of natural language, but we do not provide specification to the point that there will be over-fitting in the form of one-to-one mappings of semantic content and pragmatic effect. As research continues and robot capabilities expand, we expect to augment the robot's linguistic knowledge based on general patterns in the current annotation scheme.

6 Related work

6.1 Semantic Representation

There is a long-standing tradition of research in semantic representation within NLP, AI, as well as theoretical linguistics and philosophy (see Schubert (2015) for an overview). In this body of research, there are a variety of options that could be used within dialogue systems for NLU. However, for many of these representations, there are no existing automatic parsers, limiting their feasibility for larger-scale implementation. A notable exception is combinatory categorical grammar (CCG) (Steedman and Baldridge, 2009); CCG parsers have already been incorporated in some current dialogue systems (Chai et al., 2014). Although promising, CCG parses closely mirror the input language, so systems making use of CCG parses still face the challenge of a great deal of linguistic variability that can be associated with a single intent. Again, in abstracting away from surface variation, AMR may offer more regular, consis-

tent parses in comparison to CCG. Universal Conceptual Cognitive Annotation (UCCA) (Abend and Rappoport, 2013), which also abstracts away from syntactic idiosyncrasies, and its corresponding parser (Hershcovich et al., 2017) merits future investigation.

6.2 NLU in Dialogue Systems

Task-oriented spoken dialogue systems have been an active area of research since the early 1990s. Broadly, the architecture of such systems includes (i) automatic speech recognition (ASR) to recognize an utterance, (ii) an NLU component to identify the user's intent, and (iii) a dialogue manager to interact with the user and achieve the intended task (Bangalore et al., 2006). The meaning representation within such systems has, in the past, been predefined frames for particular subtasks (e.g., flight inquiry), with slots to be filled (e.g., destination city) (Issar and Ward, 1993). In such approaches, the meaning representation was crafted for a specific application, making generalizability to new domains difficult if not impossible. Current approaches still model NLU as a combination of intent and dialogue act classification and slot tagging, but many have begun to incorporate recurrent neural networks (RNNs) and some multi-task learning for both NLU and dialogue state tracking (Hakkani-Tür et al., 2016; Chen et al., 2016), the latter of which allows the system to take advantage of information from the discourse context to achieve improved NLU. Substantial challenges to these systems include working in domains with intents that have a large number of possible values for each slot and accommodation of out-of-vocabulary slot values (i.e. operating in a domain with a great deal of linguistic variability).

Thus, a primary challenge today and in the past is representing the meaning of an utterance in a form that can exploit the constraints of a particular domain but also remain portable across domains and robust despite linguistic variability. We see AMR as promising because the parsers are domain-independent (and can be retrained), and the representation itself is flexible enough for the addition of some domain-specific constraints. Furthermore, since AMR abstracts away from syntactic variability to represent only core elements of meaning, some of the variability in the input language can be "tamed," to give systems more systematic input. With the proposed addition of speech acts to AMR described in §5.3, the augmented AMRs also facilitate dialogue state tracking.

Although human-robot dialogue systems often leverage a similar architecture to that of the spoken dialogue systems described above, human-robot dialogue introduces the challenge of physically situated dialogue and the necessity for symbol and action grounding, which generally incorporate computer vision. Few systems are tackling all of these challenges at this point (but see Chai et al. (2017)). A description of the preliminary human-robot dialogue system developed under the umbrella of this project, and where this research might fit into that system, is described in the next section.

7   Conclusions & Future Work

Overall, we find results to be mixed on the feasibility of AMR for NLU within a human-robot dialogue system. On one hand, AMR is attractive given that there are a variety of relatively robust parsers available for AMR, making implementation on a larger scale feasible. However, our evaluation of two parsers on the human-robot dialogue data demonstrates that retraining on domain-relevant data is necessary, and this will require a certain amount of manual annotation. Furthermore, our assessment of the distinctions made in AMR reveal gaps that must be addressed for effective use in collaborative human-robot search and navigation. Nonetheless, these AMR refinements are tractable and may also be valuable to the broader community.

Thus, we have several paths forward in ongoing and future work. First, we plan to use heuristics and manual corrections to CAMR parser output to create a larger in-domain training set following existing AMR guidelines. We plan to combine this training set with other AMRs from various human-agent dialogue data sets being annotated in parallel with this work. In addition to expanding the training set for dialogue, this will allow us to explore the extent to which our findings, with respect to AMR gaps, may also apply to other human-agent dialogue domains.

Second, we will consider how to implement AMR into the existing, preliminary dialogue system called 'Scout Bot,' which has been developed as part of our larger research project (Lukin et al.,

2018). For NLU, Scout Bot makes use of the NPCEditor (Leuski and Traum, 2011), a statistical classifier that learns a mapping from inputs to outputs. Currently, the NPCEditor currently relies on string divergence measures to associate an instruction with either a text version to be sent forward to the RN-Wizard or a clarification question to be returned to the participant. However, some of the challenging cases we analyzed in §5.1 suggest that an intermediate semantic representation will be needed within the NLU phase. Specifically, because the instructions must be grounded within physical surroundings and with respect to an executable set of robot actions, a semantic representation provides the structure needed to interpret novel instructions as well as ground instructions in novel physical contexts. Error analysis has demonstrated that the current Scout Bot system, by simply learning an association between an input string and a particular set of executed actions, cannot generalize to unseen, novel input instructions (e.g, *"Turn left 100 degrees,"* as opposed to a more typical number of degrees like 90) and fails to interpret instructions with respect to the current physical surroundings (e.g., the destination of *"Move to the door on the left"* will be interpreted differently depending where the robot is facing). The structure of the semantic representation provided by AMR will allow the system to interpret 100 degrees as a novel extent of turning, and allow destination slots like *"door on the left"* to be grounded to a location in the current physical context with the help of the robot's sensors.

Thus, in future iterations of the dialogue system incorporating AMR, we will retrain or reformulate the NPCEditor to take the automatic AMR parses as input and output the in-domain AMR templates described in §5.3. The Dialogue Manager will act upon these templates with either a response/question to the participant or pass the domain-specific AMR along to be mapped to the behavior specification of the robot for execution. Specific steps on this research trajectory will include (i) development of graph to graph transformations to map parser output to the domain-refined AMRs and (ii) an assessment of how well the domain-refined AMRs map to a specific robot planning and behavior specification, which will facilitate determining what other refinements may be necessary to effectively bridge from natural language instructions to robot execution.

References

Omri Abend and Ari Rappoport. 2013. Universal Conceptual Cognitive Annotation (UCCA). In *Proceedings of the 51st Annual Meeting of the Association for Computational Linguistics (Volume 1: Long Papers)*, volume 1, pages 228–238.

Jens Allwood, David Traum, and Kristiina Jokinen. 2000. Cooperation, dialogue and ethics. *International Journal of Human-Computer Studies*, 53(6):871–914.

John Langshaw Austin. 1975. *How to do things with words*, volume 88. Oxford University Press.

Collin F Baker, Charles J Fillmore, and John B Lowe. 1998. The Berkeley FrameNet project. In *Proc. of the 36th Annual Meeting of the Association for Computational Linguistics and 17th International Conference on Computational Linguistics-Volume 1*, pages 86–90. Association for Computational Linguistics.

Laura Banarescu, Claire Bonial, Shu Cai, Madalina Georgescu, Kira Griffitt, Ulf Hermjakob, Kevin Knight, Philipp Koehn, Martha Palmer, and Nathan Schneider. 2013. Abstract Meaning Representation for sembanking. In *Proceedings of the 7th Linguistic Annotation Workshop and Interoperability with Discourse*, pages 178–186.

Srinivas Bangalore, Dilek Hakkani-Tür, and Gokhan Tur. 2006. Introduction to the special issue on spoken language understanding in conversational systems. *Speech Communication*, 3(48):233–238.

Claire Bonial, Stephanie Lukin, Ashley Foots, Cassidy Henry, Matthew Marge, Kimberly Pollard, Ron Artstein, David Traum, and Clare R. Voss. 2018. Human-robot dialogue and collaboration in search and navigation. In *Proceedings of the Annotation, Recognition and Evaluation of Actions (AREA) Workshop at LREC, 2018*.

Harry Bunt, Jan Alexandersson, Jae-Woong Choe, Alex Chengyu Fang, Koiti Hasida, Volha Petukhova, Andrei Popescu-Belis, and David R Traum. 2012. Iso 24617-2: A semantically-based standard for dialogue annotation. In *LREC*, pages 430–437. Citeseer.

Joyce Y. Chai, Rui Fang, Changsong Liu, and Lanbo She. 2017. Collaborative Language Grounding Toward Situated Human-Robot Dialogue. *AI Magazine*, 37(4):32.

Joyce Y Chai, Lanbo She, Rui Fang, Spencer Ottarson, Cody Littley, Changsong Liu, and Kenneth Hanson. 2014. Collaborative effort towards common ground in situated human-robot dialogue. In *Proceedings of the 2014 ACM/IEEE international conference on Human-robot interaction*, pages 33–40. ACM.

Yun-Nung Chen, Dilek Hakkani-Tür, Gökhan Tür, Jianfeng Gao, and Li Deng. 2016. End-to-end memory networks with knowledge carryover for multi-turn spoken language understanding. In *INTERSPEECH*, pages 3245–3249.

Donald Davidson. 1969. The individuation of events. In *Essays in honor of Carl G. Hempel*, pages 216–234. Springer.

Lucia Donatelli, Michael Regan, William Croft, and Nathan Schneider. 2018. Annotation of tense and aspect semantics for sentential AMR. In *Proceedings of the Joint Workshop on Linguistic Annotation, Multiword Expressions and Constructions*, Santa Fe, New Mexico, USA. Association for Computational Linguistics.

Charles J Fillmore, Christopher R Johnson, and Miriam RL Petruck. 2003. Background to FrameNet. *International journal of lexicography*, 16(3):235–250.

Jeffrey Flanigan, Sam Thomson, Jaime Carbonell, Chris Dyer, and Noah A Smith. 2014. A discriminative graph-based parser for the Abstract Meaning Representation. In *Proceedings of the 52nd Annual Meeting of the Association for Computational Linguistics (Volume 1: Long Papers)*, volume 1, pages 1426–1436.

Sahil Garg, Aram Galstyan, Ulf Hermjakob, and Daniel Marcu. 2016. Extracting biomolecular interactions using semantic parsing of biomedical text. In *Proc. of AAAI*, Phoenix, Arizona, USA.

Barbara J Grosz and Candace L Sidner. 1986. Attention, intentions, and the structure of discourse. *Computational linguistics*, 12(3):175–204.

Dilek Hakkani-Tür, Gökhan Tür, Asli Celikyilmaz, Yun-Nung Chen, Jianfeng Gao, Li Deng, and Ye-Yi Wang. 2016. Multi-domain joint semantic frame parsing using bi-directional rnn-lstm. In *Interspeech*, pages 715–719.

Daniel Hershcovich, Omri Abend, and Ari Rappoport. 2017. A transition-based directed acyclic graph parser for UCCA. *arXiv preprint arXiv:1704.00552*.

Thomas Howard, Stephanie Tellex, and Nicholas Roy. 2014. A natural language planner interface for mobile manipulators. In *Proceedings of the IEEE International Conference on Robotics and Automation (ICRA 2014)*.

Sunil Issar and Wayne Ward. 1993. Cmlps robust spoken language understanding system. In *Third European Conference on Speech Communication and Technology*.

Karin Kipper, Anna Korhonen, Neville Ryant, and Martha Palmer. 2008. A large-scale classification of English verbs. *Language Resources and Evaluation*, 42(1):21–40.

Anton Leuski and David Traum. 2011. Npceditor: Creating virtual human dialogue using information retrieval techniques. *Ai Magazine*, 32(2):42–56.

Fei Liu, Jeffrey Flanigan, Sam Thomson, Norman Sadeh, and Noah A Smith. 2015. Toward abstractive summarization using semantic representations. In *Proc. of NAACL*.

Stephanie M Lukin, Felix Gervits, Cory J Hayes, Anton Leuski, Pooja Moolchandani, John G Rogers III, Carlos Sanchez Amaro, Matthew Marge, Clare R Voss, and David Traum. 2018. Scoutbot: A dialogue system for collaborative navigation. *arXiv preprint arXiv:1807.08074*.

Christopher Manning, Mihai Surdeanu, John Bauer, Jenny Finkel, Steven Bethard, and David McClosky. 2014. The Stanford CoreNLP natural language processing toolkit. In *Proceedings of 52nd annual meeting of the association for computational linguistics: system demonstrations*, pages 55–60.

Matthew Marge, Claire Bonial, Brendan Byrne, Taylor Cassidy, A. William Evans, Susan G. Hill, and Clare Voss. 2016a. Applying the Wizard-of-Oz Technique to Multimodal Human-Robot Dialogue. In *Proc. of RO-MAN*.

Matthew Marge, Claire Bonial, Kimberly A Pollard, Ron Artstein, Brendan Byrne, Susan G Hill, Clare Voss, and David Traum. 2016b. Assessing Agreement in Human-Robot Dialogue Strategies: A Tale of Two Wizards. In *International Conference on Intelligent Virtual Agents*, pages 484–488. Springer.

Arindam Mitra and Chitta Baral. 2016. Addressing a question answering challenge by combining statistical methods with inductive rule learning and reasoning. In *Proc. of AAAI*, pages 2779–2785.

Martha Palmer, Daniel Gildea, and Paul Kingsbury. 2005. The proposition bank: An annotated corpus of semantic roles. *Computational Linguistics*, 31(1):71–106.

Xiaoman Pan, Taylor Cassidy, Ulf Hermjakob, Heng Ji, and Kevin Knight. 2015. Unsupervised entity linking with Abstract Meaning Representation. In *Proc. of HLT-NAACL*, pages 1130–1139.

Terence Parsons. 1990. *Events in the Semantics of English*, volume 5. MIT Press, Cambridge, MA.

Penman Natural Language Group. 1989. The Penman user guide. *Technical report, Information Sciences Institute*.

Nima Pourdamghani, Kevin Knight, and Ulf Hermjakob. 2016. Generating English from Abstract Meaning Representations. In *Proc. of INLG*, pages 21–25.

Sudha Rao, Daniel Marcu, Kevin Knight, and Hal Daumé III. 2017. Biomedical event extraction using Abstract Meaning Representation. In *Proc. of BioNLP*, pages 126–135, Vancouver, Canada.

Lenhart K Schubert. 2015. Semantic representation. In *AAAI*, pages 4132–4139.

John Rogers Searle. 1969. *Speech acts: An essay in the philosophy of language*, volume 626. Cambridge University Press.

Lanbo She and Joyce Chai. 2017. Interactive Learning of Grounded Verb Semantics towards Human-Robot Communication. In *Proceedings of the 55th Annual Meeting of the Association for Computational Linguistics (Volume 1: Long Papers)*, pages 1634–1644, Vancouver, Canada. Association for Computational Linguistics.

Mark Steedman and Jason Baldridge. 2009. Combinatory categorial grammar. nontransformational syntax: A guide to current models. *Blackwell, Oxford*, 9:13–67.

David Traum, Cassidy Henry, Stephanie Lukin, Ron Artstein, Felix Gervits, Kimberly Pollard, Claire Bonial, Su Lei, Clare Voss, Matthew Marge, Cory Hayes, and Susan Hill. 2018. Dialogue Structure Annotation for Multi-Floor Interaction. In *Proceedings of the Eleventh International Conference on Language Resources and Evaluation (LREC 2018)*, Miyazaki, Japan. European Language Resources Association (ELRA).

David R Traum and Staffan Larsson. 2003. The information state approach to dialogue management. In *Current and new directions in discourse and dialogue*, pages 325–353. Springer.

Chuan Wang, Nianwen Xue, and Sameer Pradhan. 2015. A transition-based algorithm for AMR parsing. In *Proceedings of the 2015 Conference of the North American Chapter of the Association for Computational Linguistics: Human Language Technologies*, pages 366–375.

Yanshan Wang, Sijia Liu, Majid Rastegar-Mojarad, Liwei Wang, Feichen Shen, Fei Liu, and Hongfang Liu. 2017. Dependency and AMR embeddings for drug-drug interaction extraction from biomedical literature. In *Proc. of ACM-BCB*, pages 36–43, New York, NY, USA.

A logical and computational methodology for exploring systems of phonotactic constraints

Dakotah Lambert
Earlham College
Richmond, Indiana, USA
djlambe11@earlham.edu

James Rogers
Earlham College
Richmond, Indiana, USA
jrogers@cs.earlham.edu

Abstract

We introduce a methodology built around a logical analysis component based on a hierarchy of classes of Subregular constraints characterized by the kinds of features of a string a mechanism must be sensitive to in order to determine whether it satisfies the constraint, and a computational component built around a publicly-available interactive workbench that implements, based on the equivalence between logical formulae and finite-state automata, a theorem prover for these logics (even algorithmically extracting certain classes of constraints), wherein the alternation between these logical and computational analyses can provide useful insight more easily than using either in isolation.

We demonstrate this methodology by exploring a series of examples drawn from the StressTyp2 database (Goedemans et al., 2015) of patterns of lexical (suprasegmental) stress. Along the way we provide justification for the underlying model-theoretic approach to formalizing phonotactic patterns and demonstrate the ways in which this dual methodology can be applied to a range of phonological issues.

1 Introduction

In this paper, we introduce a set of logical (model-theoretic) and computational (automata-theoretic) tools along with a methodology for exploring systems of constraints on strings that combines them. We have incorporated these into a computational workbench, which we use to demonstrate the application of this methodology to the study of lexical (suprasegmental) stress patterns obtained from StressTyp2 (Goedemans et al., 2015).

Although the formal tools we employ here are tailored to phonotactics, the methodology we are using — alternating between the logical and computational tools in exploring the data — is applicable, with suitably modified tools, to other aspects of phonology, syntax and semantics, as well as many non-linguistic applications.

In our specific application, the phenomena we must account for are phonotactic stress patterns of human languages. Our facts are descriptions of these patterns drawn from the literature, and our methods are intended to support identification and generalization of regularities and variations both within and across languages. When we say "constraints," we are referring to these observed facts.[1] Often there will be constraints that are true of some words in a language but not others. This variation will be listed among the observed facts. There may also be constraints true of all or most languages. The expected universality of these constraints will also be among the observed facts.

With this notion of constraints, we identify the following desiderata for systems of phonotactic constraints:

1. The constraints should distinguish possible unmarked words from those that are not possible. They must be complete, licensing all and only the unmarked words, and consistent in the logical sense.

2. The constraints should provide a useful foundation for generalizing across languages. A system should provide a means to compare phonotactic constraints across languages and, in particular, a means to identify potential universals. At the same time the system must provide a means of identifying unnecessary constraints. Consequently, a system must provide a means of determining if a set of

---

[1]Our use of the term "constraint" here should not be confused with the formalized notion of constraint in Optimality Theoretic accounts of phonology, in which the violability of constraints is fundamental to the formal framework. In the sense we mean here, the constraints are the regularities of the surface structure of language that an OT account is intended to account for.

Proceedings of the Society for Computation in Linguistics (SCiL) 2019, pages 247-256.
New York City, New York, January 3-6, 2019

constraints implicitly satisfies constraints that are not explicitly stated. Finally, the system should, in principle, be capable of fully describing the entire range of attested human languages in a uniform way.

3. The phenomena the constraints describe are a consequence of actual human behavior. Thus, there actually exists some physical mechanism that can, in principle, determine whether a given set of constraints are satisfied by a given word. Further, these mechanisms do this quickly. Hence the constraints must be feasible in the sense that they lie at a relatively low level of complexity with respect to some computational model (but not necessarily all such models). Finally, the constraints are learnable. There are physical mechanisms that in principle, given some (possibly empty) set of universal constraints and sufficiently many (possibly positive or negative) examples, can generalize to an equivalent set of constraints.

In the next section we sketch the model-theoretic foundations of our methodology. We then proceed, in Sections 3 and 4 to introduce the analytic component of the methodology by applying it to examples drawn from StressTyp2.

In Section 5 we begin to explore the computational component by looking at the computational and cognitive complexity of simple propositional systems of constraints based on adjacency. We follow that, in Section 6, with a similar exploration of simple constraints based solely on precedence ("long distance" constraints).

In Section 7 we describe the algorithmic mechanisms underlying the computational component of the methodology. We then turn, in Section 8, to sketch the space of classes of stringsets definable with more powerful logical mechanisms beyond the propositional logic characterizing these simple classes.

In Sections 9 and 10 we lay out the full methodology and sketch the results of its application to Yidin. Finally, we conclude by revisiting the desiderata we list in the introduction. We then summarize some of the results that have been obtained using this methodology and close by noting some of the ways the model-theoretic approach has been generalized beyond phonotactics, all of which are candidates for potential extensions of our computational tools.

2   Logical Foundations

We interpret the descriptions of phonotactic stress patterns collected in the StressTyp2 database as sets of strings over an alphabet, Σ, of symbols, each of which denotes a particular syllable type. In this paper, we take Σ to represent syllable weight: light (L) or heavy (H);[2] along with diacritics denoting stress level: none (no mark), secondary stress (`), or primary stress (´). For our logical formulae we include symbols denoting arbitrary weight (σ) and stress marks denoting arbitrary stress (*), some stress (i.e., not unstressed) (+) and non-primary stress (i.e., either secondary or unstressed) (−). So $\sigma\overset{+}{\text{H}}\overset{-}{\text{L}}\grave{\sigma}$ would denote a word consisting of an arbitrary unstressed syllable, followed by a heavy syllable with either primary or secondary stress, followed by a light syllable with either secondary or no stress and followed by any syllable with secondary stress.

The semantics of our logic is built on two relations between strings. The first, based on adjacency, is the substring relation. A string, v, is a substring of another, w, if and only if (iff) the symbols of v occur in order as a contiguous block in w. Formally

$$v \preccurlyeq w \quad \overset{\text{def}}{\Longleftrightarrow} \quad w = w_1 v w_2,\ w_1, w_2 \in \Sigma^*$$

The second relation is based on precedence. A string, v, is a subsequence of another, w, iff the symbols of v occur in w in order but not necessarily contiguously. Formally

$$v \sqsubseteq w \quad \overset{\text{def}}{\Longleftrightarrow} \quad v = v_1 v_2 \cdots v_n,\ \text{and}$$
$$w = w_1 v_1 w_2 v_2 \cdots v_n w_{n+1},$$
$$v_i, w_i \in \Sigma^*$$

2.1   Logical formulae

Our focus, in this paper, is on a propositional logic in which the atoms are either substrings or subsequences of a string. The set of substrings occurring in a string is traditionally referred to as its set of factors. We extend this to subsequences, specifying substring factor or subsequence factor only when necessary to avoid confusion.

Substring factors are denoted with just the sequence of symbols that comprise the factor. Subsequence factors are distinguished by placing the connective '. .' between the symbols of the factor.

---

[2]The full database includes five levels of weight but we need only these two here.

φ	$\mathcal{W} \models \varphi$
$\sigma_1\sigma_2\cdots\sigma_n \in \{\rtimes\} \cdot \Sigma^* \cdot \{\ltimes\}$	$\sigma_1\sigma_2\cdots\sigma_n \preccurlyeq \{\rtimes\} \cdot \mathcal{W} \cdot \{\ltimes\}$
$\sigma_1..\sigma_2..\cdots..\sigma_n, \quad \sigma_1\sigma_2\cdots\sigma_n \in \Sigma^*$	$\sigma_1\sigma_2\cdots\sigma_n \sqsubseteq \mathcal{W}$
$\neg\varphi$	$\mathcal{W} \not\models \varphi$
$\varphi_1 \wedge \varphi_2$	$\mathcal{W} \models \varphi_1$ and $\mathcal{W} \models \varphi_2$

Figure 1: The semantics of our logical formulae

Note that we do not license atoms that mix substring and subsequence, although complex formulae may well include atoms of both types. In addition, substring factors may include either a left-end marker ('$\rtimes$') or a right-end marker ('$\ltimes$') or both, in which case we say that they are anchored. In addition to these atoms the language includes the full set of Boolean connectives with their semantics derived from the semantics of negation ('$\neg$') and conjunction ('$\wedge$').

The model-theoretic semantics of this logic are given formally in Figure 1. An atom is true of a string iff it is a factor of the appropriate kind of that string. By augmenting the models with endmarkers in defining the semantics of substring models, anchored substring factors are required to occur at the either the left end or right end of the string or to span the entire string, as appropriate. The semantics of subsequence factors is insensitive to string boundaries. The Boolean operators are defined canonically. We use the notation '$\mathcal{W} \models \varphi$' to denote the satisfaction relation between strings and formulae; a string $\mathcal{W}$ satisfies a formula φ iff φ evaluates to TRUE with respect to the string $\mathcal{W}$.

Note that, while our models (i.e., strings) have internal structure which come into play when we add quantifiers to the logic, that structure is only significant here in assigning truth values to the atoms. Each string is simply a Boolean valuation of the set of all atoms occurring in a formula; this is truly a propositional logic.

3 An example: Cambodian

Let us take for example the Cambodian language, as described in StressTyp2:

(1)   a. In words of all sizes, primary stress falls on the final syllable.

   b. In words of all sizes, secondary stress falls on all heavy syllables.

   c. Light syllables occur only immediately following heavy syllables.

   d. Light monosyllables do not occur.

We begin by examining Constraint 1a. Using our logical notation, we write this constraint as a positive literal:

(1a) $\acute{\sigma}\ltimes$ (Preliminary)

Let us now continue to Constraint 1b. Here, we may be tempted to say something like this:

(1b) $\overset{*}{\mathrm{H}} \to \grave{\mathrm{H}}$ (Wrong)

However, this would mean "If a heavy syllable happens, then a heavy syllable with secondary stress also happens." What Constraint 1b really says is "No heavy syllable without secondary stress occurs," which in turn implies "No unstressed heavy syllable occurs, and no heavy syllable with primary stress occurs." So we write instead a conjunction of two negative literals:

(1b) $\neg\mathrm{H} \wedge \neg\acute{\mathrm{H}}$ (Preliminary)

However, this is still not quite the correct constraint, as it would prevent primary stress on a heavy syllable, which Cambodian requires if it is final. As is not unusual, many of the descriptions of stress patterns rely on common phonological assumptions and are inconsistent or ambiguous in their absence. Indeed, the constraint we actually want is "No unstressed heavy syllables occur."

(1b) $\neg\mathrm{H}$ (Final)

This is a single negative literal. In fact, we can rewrite Constraint 1a as a negative literal as well:

(1a) $\neg\bar{\sigma}\ltimes$ (Preliminary)

Note that, since the semantics '$\bar{\sigma}$' is disjunctive, this expands into a conjunction of four negative literals:

(1a) $\neg\mathrm{L}\ltimes \wedge \neg\grave{\mathrm{L}}\ltimes \wedge \neg\mathrm{H}\ltimes \wedge \neg\grave{\mathrm{H}}\ltimes$ (Preliminary)

Next, we look at Constraint 1c. Its implication is that a light syllable cannot immediately follow another light syllable. Further, any light syllable must be preceded by some (heavy) syllable, so they do not begin a word:

$$\text{(1c)} \quad \neg \overset{*}{L}\overset{*}{L} \wedge \neg \rtimes \overset{*}{L} \qquad \text{(Final)}$$

Finally, we have Constraint 1d, that light monosyllables do not occur:

$$\text{(1d)} \quad \neg \rtimes \overset{*}{L} \ltimes \qquad \text{(Final)}$$

It is clear at this point that any word satisfying Constraint 1c also satisfies Constraint 1d, so including the latter is logically unnecessary. Therefore the following conjunction suffices to describe these constraints:

$$\text{(1)} \quad \neg \overset{-}{\sigma} \ltimes \wedge \neg H \wedge \neg \overset{*}{L}\overset{*}{L} \wedge \neg \rtimes \overset{*}{L} \quad \text{(Preliminary)}$$

This will be refined again at the end of the next section.

As we will see shortly, this form, a conjunction of negative literals, is significant from a cognitive and complexity-theoretic perspective.

4 Phonotactic regularities

Constraint 1d is logically unnecessary in the description of Cambodian, but it is still interesting phonologically. For example, the stress pattern of Alawa, a language with only one syllable weight and two levels of stress, is given in StressTyp2 as

(2) In words of all sizes, primary stress falls on the penultimate syllable.

This constraint, of course, cannot apply to monosyllables, which have no penultimate syllable. Again, the description relies on common phonological assumptions; in this case the meaning is ambiguous. There are four distinct possibilities for what might happen to monosyllables in Alawa:

1. Monosyllables do not occur (similar to Constraint 1d).

2. Monosyllables occur, and are always stressed.

3. Monosyllables occur, and are never stressed.

4. Monosyllables occur, and may or may not be stressed.

In the case of Alawa, monosyllables do occur and are always stressed, so Constraint 1d is not satisfied by Alawa, even though the original description suggests it would be.

This leads us naturally to consider what kinds of constraints do, in fact, occur universally across languages. One such putative universal is that all words contain exactly one syllable with primary stress (which we will call 1-Stress). Hyman (2009) argues, in the context of unifying the analysis of stress and tone, that 1-Stress is better analyzed as the conjunction of two constraints, one of which is that every word contains *some* syllable with primary stress (which, following Hyman, we will refer to as obligatoriness). The other is that no word contains *more than one* syllable with primary stress (culminativity).

Between the description of Alawa and our observation regarding monosyllables, we see that Alawa satisfies this constraint. We also see that, in Cambodian, Constraint 1a logically implies obligatoriness for words of at least one syllable. If we wanted to be truly accurate, we might rule out words of less than one syllable:

(0) When a human says something, they actually say something.

Formally:

$$\text{(0)} \quad \neg \rtimes \ltimes \qquad \text{(Final)}$$

This may be overly pedantic, but it explicitly states that every word contains at least one syllable. Such things matter when using logical machinery to test hypotheses.

Looking at Cambodian's English description, culminativity is a (pragmatic) implicature of Constraint 1a, but it is neither explicitly stated nor logically implied. If this constraint says that primary stress falls on the final syllable and we assume culminativity, then primary stress may not occur on any non-final syllable. We obtain a complete description by augmenting this constraint to account for obligatoriness and culminativity.

$$\text{(1a)} \quad \neg \overset{-}{\sigma} \ltimes \wedge \neg \rtimes \ltimes \wedge \neg \overset{'}{\sigma}\overset{*}{\sigma} \qquad \text{(Final)}$$

$$\text{(1)} \quad \neg \overset{-}{\sigma} \ltimes \wedge \neg \rtimes \ltimes \wedge \neg \overset{'}{\sigma}\overset{*}{\sigma} \wedge \neg H \wedge \neg \overset{*}{L}\overset{*}{L} \wedge \neg \rtimes \overset{*}{L}$$
$$\text{(Final)}$$

5 Local constraints

Conjunctions of negative literals, such as the final formula for Cambodian, characterize the lowest level of a strict hierarchy of logics explored by Rogers and Pullum (2011) and Rogers et al. (2012) (also see Section 8 of this paper), which characterize a range of sub-Regular classes of stringsets. These classes of stringsets are also characterized by classes of finite-state automata, grammars, and, more importantly, abstract properties of the sets in the class. The constrast between classes corresponds to a ranking of cognitive complexity based on the nature of the information in a string: each class is characterized by the kinds of features of strings that a mechanism must be sensitive to in order to determine whether a string is in a given set.

Because the pattern of phonological stress in Cambodian is completely described by a conjunction of finitely many negative atomic formulae, a mechanism that is able to make judgments as to whether a word satisfies each constraint only needs to be sensitive to whether certain substrings of some fixed length occur in the word.

Specifically, '¬H' requires sensitivity only to single syllables in isolation while the other constraints in Cambodian require a mechanism to be sensitive to pairs of consecutive syllables. Such a pattern is called "Strictly 2-Local," or "SL_2", The '2' in "SL_2" is a parameter giving the length of factors that a mechanism must necessarily be sensitive to in order to be able to make judgments about well-formedness.

From a procedural perspective, these judgments can be made by a *scanner*, a mechanism that simply scans a window of a fixed size across the input, one symbol at a time, looking at each factor in sequence. Since SL_k stringsets are defined by conjunctions of negative constraints, it suffices to look for unlicensed factors, rejecting the string if any are found.

This generalizes to any pattern completely described by a conjunction of finitely many negative literals: such a pattern is SL_k, where k is the length of the longest factor. For example, Alawa is SL_3:

$$(2) \quad \neg\bar{\sigma}\bar{\sigma}\ltimes \,\wedge\, \neg\acute{\sigma}\overset{*}{\bar{\sigma}}\overset{*}{\bar{\sigma}} \,\wedge\, \neg\overset{*}{\bar{\sigma}}\acute{\sigma}\ltimes \,\wedge\, \neg\rtimes\bar{\sigma}\ltimes \,\wedge\, \neg\rtimes\ltimes$$
$$\text{(Final)}$$

Since each k-factor can be extended to an equivalent $(k+1)$-factor by extending it with all possible next syllables, a pattern that is SL_k must also be SL_{k+1}.

If we say 'SL' with no explicit factor length, what we really mean is "SL_k for some k." A constraint can be shown to be SL simply by giving a formula that witnesses this. Of course, this merely gives an upper bound.

Generally, lower bounds can be found by appealing to the abstract properties of classes of stringsets. In this case we can show that Alawa is not SL_2 using the fact that SL_k stringsets are characterized by a *suffix substitution closure* property: if some $(k-1)$ factor occurs in two strings

that satisfy the constraint then the results of swapping suffixes of the two strings that start with that factor will also satisfy the constraint. (Intuitively, recognizing the penult requires noting that it is followed by a single syllable and no more: $\rtimes\sigma\sigma\acute{\sigma}\sigma\ltimes$ and $\rtimes\sigma\acute{\sigma}\sigma\sigma\ltimes$ share the same 2-factors, so a mechanism needs a window of size at least three.)

In SL stringsets, each constraint must be satisfied at every position in the word. Since a single violation suffices to rule out a word, a mechanism only needs to be sensitive to factors in isolation. Logical complements of SL constraints (coSL), which are defined by disjunctions of positive literals, also only require sensitivity to factors in isolation (accepting if any required factor occurs) but combinations of positive and negative literal constraints are not so simple: in order to verify that certain factors occur somewhere in the word while others do not a mechanism must be sensitive to the entire set of factors in the word. Constraints requiring sensitivity to this entire set are "Locally Testable," or "LT". Much as factor-width may be specified in SL stringsets, we may say a pattern or constraint is LT_k, where the salient factors have a length of at most k. Again like SL patterns, every LT_k pattern is LT_{k+1}.

Since a mechanism capable of making judgments based on the set of factors in a word must necessarily be able to check these factors individually, any constraint that is SL_k or $coSL_k$ must also be LT_k. Further, since the entire set of factors is available, any Boolean combination of factors may be used as an LT constraint. Giving a constraint in this form is sufficient to show that it is LT, and again we can use abstract properties of the LT stringsets to show that a constraint is not in the class.

Obligatoriness by itself is $coSL_1$, hence LT_1, as witnessed by its expression as a single positive atomic constraint: '$\acute{\sigma}$'. It is not, in itself, SL_k for any k. Obligatoriness can only be satisfied by a system of SL constraints if they require primary stress to fall within some fixed distance from either end of the word.

Similarly, culminativity is not SL. It can only be satisfied by a system of SL constraints if they require *all* syllables with primary stress to occur within a fixed distance of either end of the word. Since satisfaction of an LT constraint depends only on the set of factors of a string, LT constraints cannot distinguish between strings that have the same factorization, thus we can see by example that culminativity is also not LT$_3$, as 'LLĹLL' and 'LLĹLLĹLL' contain the same set of substring 3-factors: $\{\rtimes LL, LL\acute{H}, L\acute{H}L, \acute{H}LL, LL\ltimes\}$. This counter-example generalizes to any factor-width, so culminativity is not LT (*a fortiori* also not coSL).

6 Piecewise constraints

All local constraints are given in terms of adjacency. If we instead use precedence, then culminativity is quite a simple constraint:

$$(3) \quad \neg\acute{\sigma}..\acute{\sigma} \qquad \text{(Final)}$$

A constraint described by a negative atomic formula of length k is "Strictly k-Piecewise", or "SP$_k$". A mechanism must be sensitive to subsequences of length k in isolation in order to determine whether a string is in an SP$_k$ stringset.

Culminativity in particular is SP$_2$. Another SP constraint comes from Nubian, this one SP$_3$. It is also LT$_2$, but not SL:

(4)   a. If a word contains a non-final heavy syllable, then no light syllable with primary stress occurs in that word.

$$(4a) \quad \neg(\overset{*}{H}\overset{*}{\sigma} \wedge \acute{L}) \text{ [or: } \overset{*}{H}\overset{*}{\sigma} \rightarrow \neg\acute{L}\text{]} \quad \text{(Adjacency)}$$

$$(4a) \quad \neg\acute{L}..\overset{*}{H}..\overset{*}{\sigma} \wedge \neg\acute{H}..\acute{L} \qquad \text{(Precedence)}$$

Although Constraint 4a is both LT and SP, It is not the case that every LT constraint is SP. If a string satisfies an SP constraint, then every string formed by deleting finitely many symbols from that string also satisfies that same constraint (Rogers et al., 2010). Knowing that, it is impossible for obligatoriness to be satisfied by a system of only SP constraints.

In order to capture obligatoriness using precedence, a mechanism must be sensitive to the set of all subsequences in a string. These constraints are "Piecewise Testable", or "PT". Just as Boolean combinations of SL constraints are LT, Boolean combinations of SP constraints are PT. As with the local classes, stringsets that are the complement of SP stringsets (i.e., that are coSP), while properly PT are effectively no harder to recognize than SP stringsets. Obligatoriness is coSP as witnessed by '$\acute{\sigma}$', the same formula that witnesses that it is coSL; SL$_k$ and SP$_k$ converge for $k = 1$.

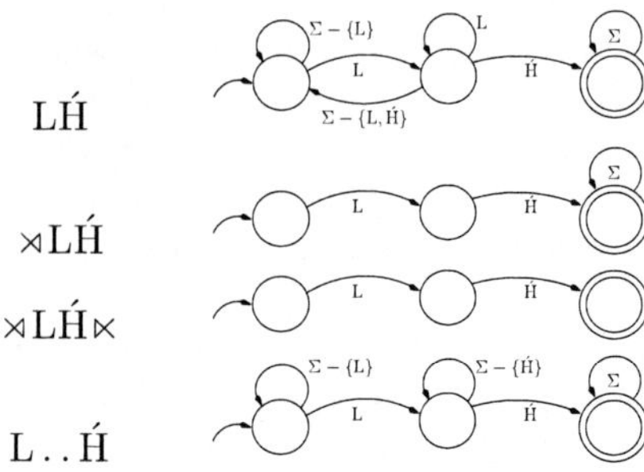

LĤ

$\rtimes$LĤ

$\rtimes$LĤ$\ltimes$

L..Ĥ

Figure 2: Automata for substring and subsequence factors.

7 Computational Foundations

Our computational workbench is a theorem prover (written in Haskell) based on the equivalence between logical formulae for finite sequences (successor models) and finite state automata established originally by Medvedev (1964); Büchi (1960) and Elgot (1961). The underlying idea is quite simple. One constructs automata for each of the atomic formulae of the logic which accept exactly those strings which satisfy that atom. Since our logic (so far) is quantifier free and our models are simply strings, the automata work directly on the models.

Examples of automata for anchored and unanchored substring formulae and for a subsequence formula are given in Figure 2. The Boolean connectives are implemented via the corresponding automaton constructions: conjunction corresponds to intersection, negation to complement.

Using this procedure on a formula for a stress pattern yields an automaton that recognizes the set of all strings that satisfy that pattern. The StressTyp2 database includes minimal deterministic finite state automata for nearly all of the lects[3] it includes and these can be read directly into the workbench. Hence we can establish the correctness of a formula relative to the automata-theoretic interpretation given in the database by testing the equivalence of that automaton and the one constructed from our formula. One way of doing this (although not the most efficient way) is to construct the automaton between the sets recognized that recognizes the set of strings that the formula incorrectly excludes (undergenerates), and another that recognizes the set that the formula incorrectly

---

[3]StressTyp2 adopts the convention of using the bare combining form 'lect' to denote a distinct pattern and, by extension, the class of languages that exhibit it.

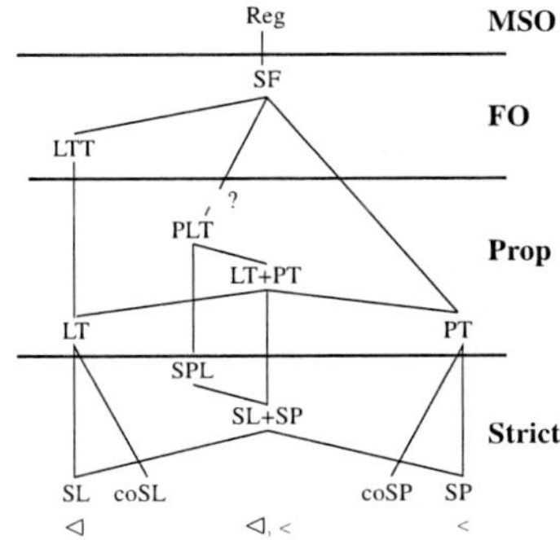

Figure 3: A cognitive complexity hierarchy.

includes (overgenerates); the formula is correct if both sets are empty.

The automata from the database are useful in analysis as well. The workbench includes algorithms that, given a finite state automaton, can determine whether the stringset it recognizes is Strictly Local (Caron, 2000) or if it is Strictly Piecewise (Rogers et al., 2010) and, if it is, determines the factor width parameter k. In addition, it includes the algorithms given by Rogers and Lambert (2017) and Rogers and Lambert (to appear) which can, given an automaton, extract the set of forbidden substring or subsequence factors which suffice to characterize the stringset recognized by that automaton if it is SL or SP (or a conjunction of $SL + SP + coSL + coSP$ constraints) and can produce an automaton that recognizes an $SL + SP + coSL + coSP$ approximation of that stringset if it is not.

In each case the approximation, if it is not exact, overgenerates and, so, by taking the difference between the approximation and the original automaton one gets a stringset that provides guidance in formulating the non-strict constraints necessary to completely characterize the original pattern.

8 Higher level constraints

Culminativity is neither SL nor LT. It is possible to enforce culminativity using only adjacency but in order to do so a mechanism must distinguish occurrences of primary stress by their position in the string. The logic we are working with here is the propositional fragment of the hierarchy of logics explored by Rogers et al. (2012). The higher levels (i.e. regular stringsets that are not $LT + PT$) represent strings as the same first-order models, with binary predicates for adjacency and prece-

dence, but also allow for quantification over positions (first-order) or sets of positions (monadic second-order). Recognizing whether a string satisfies a quantified formula requires inferring information that is not explicit in the string which changes the nature of the cognitive task, not just its magnitude.

First-order formulae that employ only adjacency characterize the Locally Threshold Testable ($LTT_{k,t}$) class. A mechanism recognizing such a stringset can count occurrences of k-factors, but only up to a threshold: the second parameter, t. It cannot distinguish t or more distinct occurrences.

If, on the other hand, these first-order formulae make use of precedence ('$<$'), then the result is something strictly stronger, the Star Free (SF) stringsets. Such stringsets are defined much like Regular stringsets, except they are closed under complement rather than the Kleene star.

Finally, if we allow monadic second-order quantification we can define all and only the Regular stringsets. This completes the sub-Regular hierarchy shown in Figure 3; the classes in the middle of the diagram are the stringsets definable by combinations of local and piecewise constraints (conjunctions at the restricted level, any Boolean combinations at the full propositional level and atoms that mix adjacency and precedence in the PL classes).

Some of the constraints listed in StressTyp2 are most naturally expressed in terms of the quantified logics but these turn out to never be necessary for stress patterns.

9 Methodology

We explore patterns by alternating between analysis based on linguistic and logical knowledge and computational analysis and synthesis using the tools of the workbench. In this paper, we began with an analytic phase, transforming the English description of a pattern into a logical description. During this translation process, one can use the abstract characterizations of the complexity classes as a guide to the form needed to express a given constraint. Assuming this translation is successful, these constraints provide an upper-bound on the complexity of the pattern as a whole.

Alternatively, for patterns already described by automata, one can start with a computational analytic phase, using the workbench to extract systems of SL, SP, coSL and coSP constraints from those automata (Rogers and Lambert, to appear). If the pattern is not simply $SL+SP+coSL+coSP$ the result of these computational methods is an approximation that is.

Another alternative is to work directly from a corpus of annotated examples using learning algorithms based on Chandlee et al. (2018), which are currently being incorporated into the workbench. Again, the result is a (possibly exact) approximation that is $SL + SP + coSL + coSP$.

In all three cases, the workbench implements a computational synthesis phase which represents these systems of constraints as automata. If an automaton is provided for the pattern the correctness and completeness of the constraints can be checked computationally against this automaton by constructing an automaton that recognizes the symmetric difference between the two, which can either be examined directly or used to generate examples of strings that satisfy the constraints but should be excluded or those that should not be excluded but fail to satisfy the constraints. If there is no existing automaton to work against, one can generate strings up to a given length-bound and look for inconsistencies. In any case, if there is under- or overgeneration the structures of these residues guide a return to the analytical phase, adding or modifying constraints in order to account for the differences.

Once the conjunction of logical constraints correctly describes the pattern in question, the workbench can minimize the description by removing constraints that are logically implied by others. Because these subregular classes form a proper hierarchy and are all closed under intersection, the complexity of the stringset is simply the maximum of the complexity of the constraints that describe it.

Our workbench can find all of the minimal independent subsets of a set of constraints constraints that describe the same pattern as the full set. However, if a constraint of higher complexity is implied by a set of lower-complexity constraints a smaller subset in which the higher-complexity constraint is explicit will be not be an accurate indication of the complexity of the stringset, rather a larger set of lower-complexity constraints would be preferred. So the workbench can also check sets of constraints provided by the user, such as the constraints identified earlier in the process either from analysis of other patterns or from theoretical

	$\triangleleft$	$<$
one $\acute{\sigma}$	$LTT_{1,2}$	PT_2
obligatoriness	$coSL_1$	PT_1
culminativity	$LTT_{1,2}$	SP_2
no $\bar{H}$ before $\acute{H}$	SF	SP_2
no $\overset{*}{H}$ with $\acute{L}$	LT_1	SP_2
nothing before $\acute{L}$	SL_2	SP_2
alternation	SL_2	SF
no light monosyllables	SL_3	PT_2

Table 1: Constraints in Yidin expressed locally and piecewise.

analysis of the linguistic phenomena under study, against the rest of the set and find independent subsets that are minimally complex. It should be noted that minimal descriptions from a linguistic perspective may well not be the same as the minimal descriptions from a complexity-theoretic perspective. But as long as they are logically equivalent, the complexity result is still valid.

One can use this same mechanism to determine whether a pattern satisfies a putative universal constraint by merely checking whether this constraint is implied by those that describe the pattern in question. When the corpus of patterns of Stress-Typ2 was tested for both obligatoriness and culminativity, it was discovered that while every lect satisfies culminativity, there are two that do not satisfy obligatoriness, namely Seneca and Cayuga. These are languages that Hyman identifies as not satisfying "the more accent-like properties of obligatoriness and culminativity" (Hyman, 2009).

When working with a set of lects, one will collect a library of non-strict constraints. The workbench can use this to automatically determine if a new pattern can be completely described by a conjunction of strict constraints and some subset of this library. When the StressTyp2 corpus was analyzed, only five non-strict constraints were needed to describe the entire set of patterns.

10 Yidin: An example

Yidin is described as:

(5)   a. In words of all sizes, primary stress falls on the left-most heavy syllable, else on the initial syllable.

       b. In words of all sizes, secondary stress falls iteratively on every second syllable in both directions from the main stress.

c. Light monosyllables do not occur.

Table 1 shows the constraints we derived from this description. The left column is an English gloss of the constraint, while the remaining two columns note the complexity class in which the constraint falls on both the local and piecewise branches of the hierarchy. Alternation, SF on the piecewise side, is only SL_2 on the local side. Similarly, "no $\bar{H}$ before $\bar{H}$" is SF on the local side, but only SP_2 on the piecewise side. Thus, considering either branch of the hierarchy in isolation brings the conclusion that the pattern is SF, but using a mix of constraints from both sides shows that the pattern is $SL_3 + coSL_1 + SP_2$.

11 Conclusion

We have introduced an approach to formalizing linguistic patterns that is based on a model-theoretic analysis of strings. We work primarily with propositional formulae for which satisfaction depends the substrings or subsequences that occur in a string. Definability of sets of strings in these logics characterizes the lowest classes of the local and piecewise subregular hierarchies.

This foundation fulfills all of the desiderata for systems of phonotactic constraints that we identify in the introduction. The logical constraints are unambiguous and fully explicit. As we have seen, the process of translating constraints stated in English to an equivalent logical form can illuminate inconsistencies and ambiguities that are usually resolved by pragmatic linguistic assumptions.

By comparing systems of logical constraints along with the sets of their models one can generalize across languages, identifying constraints that are common to classes of languages and testing putative universals against those classes. Again, using standard model-theoretic tools, one can identify minimal independent sets of constraints, eliminating those that are logically implied by the others.

We have demonstrated the breadth of coverage of this approach with respect to one range of phonotactic phenomena by using it to fully characterize the phonological stress patterns gathered in the StressTyp2 database. In Heinz (2018), Heinz argues that essentially all of phonotactics falls within the the classes of this subregular hierarchy. Moreover there is a growing body of work (Chandlee and Heinz, 2018; Chandlee et al.,

2015, 2014; Chandlee, 2014; Jardine, 2017, 2016a,b) that suggests that many phonological processes can be captured by functions based on these same sorts of logics.

Most importantly, all of these model-theoretic tools are effective in the sense of being computable. Moreover, the classes of the hierarchy correspond directly to the nature of the information about a string that any mechanism must be sensitive to in order to determine if it satisfies a constraint. Consequently, the hierarchy provides a measure of the relative complexity of constraints. They are also all learnable in the limit from positive data by algorithms of low computational complexity.

Our analysis of StressTyp2 demonstrates that phonological stress is extremely simple. Our focus is the methodology itself, not the phonological results that have been obtained using it. But we note that, as reported elsewhere, when this methodology was applied to a corpus of the 106 lects in StressTyp2 that have both English language and automata descriptions, it was found that all but eight (92.5%) were SL + SP + coSL, six more needed some subset of a library of LT constraints consisting of obligatoriness and three other constraints, and the remaining two were properly Regular, sharing a constraint based on hidden stress alternation. If secondary stress were to surface in these latter two then they would simply be SL. This means that, aside from the two patterns involving the properly Regular constraint, no pattern in the corpus requires a mechanism to infer additional information beyond that which is present in the surface string. Moreover, the only piecewise constraints are SP, forbidding the coöccurrence of certain syllables as in the case of culmanitivity, confirming Heinz (2014).

It has been verified that all patterns in this corpus satisfy culminativity, and the two patterns that do not satisfy obligatoriness, as expected by Hyman (2009), have been identified.

The logical and computational methods we use have applications beyond phonotactics. Similar techniques have proven useful in phonology in general. In particular, for exploring phonological functions (Chandlee and Heinz, 2018; Chandlee et al., 2014; Chandlee, 2014), morphology (Chandlee, 2017), and tone (Jardine, 2017, 2016a,b). These have also been used to analyze syntax (Graf, 2014; Rogers, 1998).

References

J. R. Büchi. 1960. Weak second-order arithmetic and finite automata. *Zeitschrift für mathematische Logik und Grundlagen der Mathematik* 6:66–92.

Pascal Caron. 2000. Families of locally testable languages. *Theoretical Computer Science* 242:361–376.

Jane Chandlee. 2014. *Strictly Local Phonological Processes*. Ph.D. thesis, The University of Delaware.

Jane Chandlee. 2017. Computational locality in morphological maps. *Morphology* 27:599–641.

Jane Chandlee, Rémi Eryraud, Jeffery Heinz, Adam Jardine, and Jonathan Rawski. 2018. Learning with partially ordered representations. Submitted to ALT 2019.

Jane Chandlee, Rémi Eyraud, and Jeffrey Heinz. 2014. Learning strictly local subsequential functions. *Transactions of the Association for Computational Linguistics* 2:491–503.

Jane Chandlee, Rémi Eyraud, and Jeffrey Heinz. 2015. Output strictly local functions. In Marco Kuhlmann, Makoto Kanazawa, and Gregory M. Kobele, editors, *Proceedings of the 14th Meeting on the Mathematics of Language (MoL 2015)*. Chicago, USA, pages 112–125.

Jane Chandlee and Jeffrey Heinz. 2018. Strictly locality and phonological maps. *Linguistic Inquiry* 49(1):23–60.

Calvin C. Elgot. 1961. Decision problems of finite automata design and related arithmetics. *Transactions of the American Mathematical Society* 98:21–51.

R. W. Goedemans, Jeffrey Heinz, and Harry van der Hulst. 2015. `http://st2.ullet.net/files/files/st2-v1-archive-0415.tar.gz`. Retrieved 24 Jun 2015.

Thomas Graf. 2014. Beyond the apparent: Cognitive parallels between syntax and phonology. In Carson T. Schütze and Linnaea Stockall, editors, *Connectedness: Papers by and for Sarah van Wagenen.* volume 18 of *UCLA Working Papers in Linguistics*, pages 161–174.

Jeffrey Heinz. 2014. Culminativity times harmony equals unbounded stress. In Harry van der Hulst, editor, *Word Stress: Theoretical and Typological Issues*, Cambridge University Press, Cambridge, UK, chapter 8.

Jeffrey Heinz. 2018. The computational nature of phonological generalizations. In Larry Hyman and Frank Plank, editors, *Phonological Typology*, Mouton De Gruyter, volume 23 of *Phonetics and Phonology*, chapter 5, pages 126–195.

Larry M. Hyman. 2009. How (not) to do phonological typology: the case of pitch-accent. *Language Sciences* 31(2–3):213–238.

Adam Jardine. 2016a. Computationally, tone is different. *Phonology* 32(2):247–283.

Adam Jardine. 2016b. *Locality and non-linear representations in tonal phonology*. Ph.D. thesis, University of Delaware.

Adam Jardine. 2017. The local nature of tone-association patterns. *Phonology* 34:385–405.

Yu. T. Medvedev. 1964. On the class of events representable in a finite automaton. In Edward F. Moore, editor, *Sequential Machines; Selected Papers*, Addison-Wesley, pages 215–227. Originally published in Russian in Avtomaty, 1956, 385–401.

James Rogers. 1998. *A Descriptive Approach to Language-Theoretic Complexity*. (Monograph.) Studies in Logic, Language, and Information. CSLI/FoLLI.

James Rogers, Jeff Heinz, Margaret Fero, Jeremy Hurst, Dakotah Lambert, and Sean Wibel. 2012. Cognitive and sub-regular complexity. In Glyn Morrill and Mark-Jan Nederhof, editors, *Formal Grammar 2012*, Springer, volume 8036 of *Lecture Notes in Computer Science*, pages 90–108.

James Rogers, Jeffrey Heinz, Gil Bailey, Matt Edlefsen, Molly Visscher, David Wellcome, and Sean Wibel. 2010. On languages piecewise testable in the strict sense. In Christian Ebert, Gerhard Jäger, and Jens Michaelis, editors, *The Mathematics of Language: 10th and 11th Biennial Conference, MOL 10, Los Angeles, CA, USA, July 28-30, 2007, and MOL 11, Bielefeld, Germany, August 20-21, 2009, Revised Selected Papers*, Springer Berlin Heidelberg, Berlin, Heidelberg, pages 255–265.

James Rogers and Dakotah Lambert. 2017. Extracting forbidden factors from regular stringsets. In *Proceedings of the 15th Meeting on the Mathematics of Language*. Association for Computational Linguistics, pages 36–46. http://aclweb.org/anthology/W17-3404.

James Rogers and Dakotah Lambert. to appear. Extracting subregular constraints from regular stringsets. Under review.

James Rogers and Geoffrey K. Pullum. 2011. Aural pattern recognition experiments and the subregular hierarchy. *Journal of Logic, Language and Information* 20(3):329–342.

Augmenting Compositional Models for Knowledge Base Completion Using Gradient Representations

Matthias Lalisse
Dept of Cognitive Science
Johns Hopkins University
Baltimore, MD USA
lalisse@jhu.edu

Paul Smolensky
Dept of Cognitive Science
Johns Hopkins University
& Microsoft Research AI
Seattle, WA USA
smolensky@jhu.edu

Abstract

Neural models of Knowledge Base data have typically employed compositional representations of graph objects: entity and relation embeddings are systematically combined to evaluate the truth of a candidate Knowedge Base entry. Using a model inspired by Harmonic Grammar, we propose to tokenize triplet embeddings by subjecting them to a process of optimization with respect to learned well-formedness conditions on Knowledge Base triplets. The resulting model, known as Gradient Graphs, leads to sizable improvements when implemented as a companion to compositional models. Also, we show that the "supracompositional" triplet token embeddings it produces have interpretable properties that prove helpful in performing inference on the resulting triplet representations.

1 Introduction

As they are conventionally analyzed, representations of semantic or linguistic data are "compositional": the meanings of complex representations are built up from the meanings of their constituent parts. This idea has motivated numerous models of graph data deployed in knowledge base completion (KBC), in which embeddings of entities and relations are combined into composite representations—pairs of entities in a particular relation with one another—that are built up systematically from the constituent parts. But what happens when the whole is *not* a simple function of the parts? A natural case arises in the interpretation of Noun-Noun compounds. The contrasting senses of *vampire cat* (*a-cat-that-is-a-vampire*) and *vampire stake* (*a-stake-used-to-kill-a-vampire*) has as much to do with the compatibility of the constituent nouns occurring in a given relation than with the meanings of the individual constituents.

Pursuing this line of thought, we propose **Gradient Graphs**, a neural network model for

KBC built on the principle that compositionally-obtained representations of semantic objects can be optimized to reflect context-specific aspects of the meanings of their constituents. The issue of context-conditioned, tokenized semantic representations has received little explicit attention in the KBC literature. However, precedents do exist. Bordes et al. (2011) model context-sensitive entity senses by embedding relations as pairs of matrices (R_{lhs}, R_{rhs}) that linearly transform entity embeddings into pairs of embeddings defined by the relation and the entities' positions within it (the left-hand-side or right-hand-side). The distances of the resulting embeddings are then compared. Socher et al. (2013) cope with the context-sensitivity of relation meanings by learning a $k \times d \times d$-dimensional tensor embeddings for each relation, letting their model represent polysemy by learning k versions of the relation represented in the k slices of its embedding tensor. The intuition underlying this approach is that, for instance, the relation has_part has a different sense when applied to a biological organism than when predicated of a company. While the former has parts like organs and limbs, the latter has parts like subsidiaries and workers, which occupy very different parts of the semantic space. Each relational slice is then responsible for learning the compatibility of arguments within particular semantic subspaces.

In contrast to these other works, our approach is more radical in the sense that our context-sensitive representations of knowledge base entries are not just computed from the entries' constituent elements (entity and relation embeddings), but are instead the result of a representation-optimization procedure that balances compositionally-derived representations with general knowledge about the characteristics of well-formed semantic structures. We show that this additional "supracompositional" processing, in addition to yielding sizable accuracy improvements over the compositional models we apply it to, leads to embeddings of entity tokens with interpretable characteristics.

Proceedings of the Society for Computation in Linguistics (SCiL) 2019, pages 257-266.
New York City, New York, January 3-6, 2019

1.1 Layout of the paper

Section 2 lays out the general framework, which is compatible with a variety of implementations. Section 3 presents two compositional embedding models proposed in the literature. We adapt these models to construct compositional embeddings, and in Section 4 report evaluations of Gradient versions of these models. Section 5 discusses the characteristics of the resulting semantic representations in greater detail, as well as their role in assisting inference. Section 6 concludes. Technical details about the model and the implementations are given in the Appendices.

2 Optimization of semantic tokens

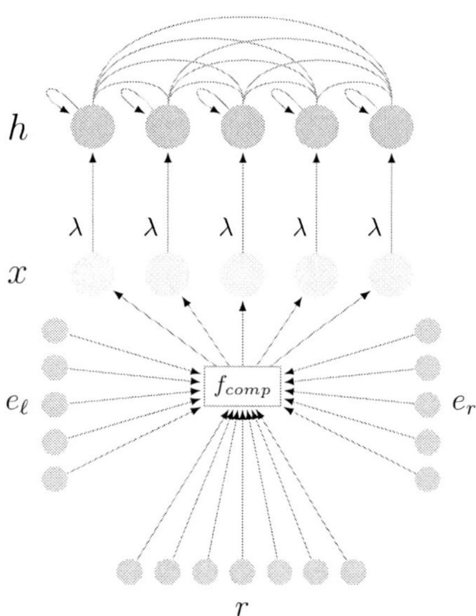

Figure 1: Gradient Graph as a recurrent neural network. In addition to bias terms (omitted in the figure) and self-connections, hidden units are densely connected to one another via a layer of connections with symmetric (undirected) weights, and receive constant input weighted by λ from a single unit in the input layer. The composition function $f_{comp}(e_\ell, r, e_r)$, which differs between implementations, computes a **compositional embedding** x, which is fed into a **hidden layer** h of the network. The continuous-time dynamics of this network compute an internal representation $\hat{h}$ of the input triplet that is optimal with respect to the Harmony (1)—a measure of the triplet's semantic well-formedness.

The hypothesis underlying the approach we propose is that noncompositional effects in knowledge base data can be modeled by subjecting candidate facts to a process of optimization with respect to a set of learned semantic coherence conditions.

These semantic coherence conditions, encoded in a symmetric matrix, map out the covariance structure of the semantic space, indicating which semantic features are likely to co-occur with one another. The embedding of a given triplet is then the vector obtained by optimizing the semantic coherence of the the triplet embedding.

We first lay out the model in abstract form, before introducing particular implementations. Let $x \in \mathbb{R}^d$ be a d-dimensional embedding of a knowledge base triplet (e_ℓ, r, e_r) obtained as some function f_{comp}—the **composition function**—of the embeddings of the left and right entities as well as the relation r. Section 3 provides several models for constructing the triplet embedding x. Also, let h be a d-dimensional vector giving the internal ("hidden") state of the network. The *Harmony* of an internal state h of the network with respect to the triplet embedding x is

$$(1) \qquad \mathcal{H}(h, x) = \tfrac{1}{2}\left[h^\top \mathbb{W}h + b^\top h - \lambda(h - x)^\top (h - x)\right]$$

where $\mathbb{W}$ is a $d \times d$ weight matrix with $\mathbb{W} = \mathbb{W}^\top$ and b is a bias vector, both learned. (1) is composed of two terms: Core Harmony, a measure of the semantic coherence of the state vector h, and Faithfulness, a penalty incurred due to the state h's deviation from the compositional triplet embedding x. λ is a hyperparameter that controls the magnitude of the penalty incurred for straying from x.

$\mathcal{H}(h, x)$ may be rewritten as (2).

$$(2) \qquad \mathcal{H}(h, x) = \tfrac{1}{2}[h^\top (\mathbb{W} - \lambda I)\, h + (b + 2\lambda x)^\top h - \lambda x^\top x)]$$

If λ is greater than the largest eigenvalue of $\mathbb{W}$, then $V = \mathbb{W} - \lambda I$ is negative-definite, and $\mathcal{H}(h, x)$ has a unique global optimum $\hat{h} = \mathrm{argmax}_h \mathcal{H}(h, x)$ for each x. In closed form, this global optimum is

$$(3) \qquad \mu(x) = \tfrac{1}{2}V^{-1}(b + 2\lambda x)$$

which depends only on the network parameters and on x. The expression $\mu(x)$ comes from observing that $\hat{h}$ is the mean of a Gaussian distribution with inverse covariance matrix V, which implies that $\hat{h}$ is the most probable state h of the network with respect to the probability distribution over the state space defined by $p(h|x) \propto \exp\{\mathcal{H}(h, x)\}$ (see Appendix A). We take the token embedding for a triplet x to be $\mu(x)$, which is the most semantically coherent triplet embedding given the compositional triplet x. In the limit as $\lambda \to \infty$, $\mu(x)$ is just x itself. Let $\lambda_\mathbb{W}$ denote the largest eigenvalue of $\mathbb{W}$; then as $\lambda \to \lambda_\mathbb{W}$, $\mu(x)$ becomes independent of the triplet embedding x.

A Gradient Graph may be viewed as a neural network with weight matrix $\mathbb{W}$ and bias vector $\frac{b}{2}$, where the synaptic weights $\mathbb{W}$ specify a feedback layer through which the values of the hidden state units affect one another. The construction is as follows. We stipulate that the hidden state of the network follows the gradient of Harmony over time:

$$(4) \qquad \frac{dh}{dt} = \frac{\partial \mathcal{H}(x,h)}{\partial h}$$

Therefore,

$$\frac{dh_i}{dt} = \frac{d}{dh_i} \frac{1}{2} \left[h^\top \mathbb{W} h + b^\top h - \lambda \left\| x - h \right\|^2 \right]$$

$$= \frac{d}{dh_i} \frac{1}{2} \left[\sum_{jk} h_j \mathbb{W}_{jk} h_k + b_i h_i - \lambda (x_i - h_i)^2 \right]$$

$$= \frac{1}{2} \left[\sum_j h_j \mathbb{W}_{ji} + \sum_k \mathbb{W}_{ik} h_k \right] + \frac{b_i}{2} + \lambda x_i - \lambda h_i$$

The above specifies the connectivity of a network whose hidden units have the linear transfer function ($f(input) = input$), bias $\frac{b}{2}$ and external input x (weighted by λ). Each h_i also receives self-inhibitory input weighted by $-\lambda$, as well as inputs $\mathbb{W}_{ij} h_j$ from each h_j. The symmetry of $\mathbb{W}$ implies that each term $\mathbb{W}_{ij} h_j = h_j \mathbb{W}_{ji}$ occurs twice, so that the factor of $\frac{1}{2}$ cancels. This connectivity structure is illustrated in Figure 1.

2.1 Relation to Harmonic Grammar

In addition to being globally optimal with respect to the Harmony function $\mathcal{H}(h, x)$ conditioned on a particular input x, $\mu(x)$ is the unique fixed point of this network's state-evolution dynamics. It is interesting to note that such networks are the connectionist foundation for Harmonic Grammar (HG) and Optimality Theory (OT) in Linguistics (Smolensky and Legendre, 2006), where the dynamics of a neural network perform optimization over internal representations of an input structure. Appropriate output representations are then selected in accordance with well-formedness constraints encoded in the network parameters. There, the output representation balances Faithfulness to the input (an Underlying Form) and the network's knowledge about the characteristics of well-formed structures in general.

Similarly, it is appealing to conceptualize the hidden layer of a Gradient Graph network as cleaning up a knowledge base triplet by subjecting it to semantic well-formedness conditions. The optimal triplet $\mu(x)$ is then the point to which the network converges in the limit of infinite computation time. However, our model differs from typical implementations of HG and OT in that the optimal structure $\mu(x)$ does not, in general, decompose into a unique combination of the input constituents (entity and relation embeddings). The resulting representations are in this sense gradient, rather than

being the product of a combination of discrete objects. Furthermore, Gradient Graphs are, to our knowledge, the first application of these ideas to the automatic learning of an appropriate semantic optimization function from a large amount of data.

2.2 Comparison with translation-based approaches

Like a large class of *Translation*-based models (Bordes et al., 2011; Yoon et al., 2016; Lin et al., 2015; Ji et al., 2016), our inference procedure consists of the application of an affine transformation to an input x (Equation (3)), which is then scored using some regular operation. In our case, this scoring function is quadratic. A particular close cousin is the bilinear SEMANTIC MATCHING ENERY (SME) method of Bordes et al. (2014), which learns a global third-order tensor $\mathbb{W}$ that, when dotted along the third mode with a relation embedding r, yields a relation-specific matrix $\mathbb{W}_r$. Along with learned left and right bias vectors b_ℓ snd b_r, this weight matrix is fed into the bilinear scoring function (5):

$$(5) \qquad \text{score}_{\text{SME}}(e_\ell, r, e_r) =$$
$$(\mathbb{W}_r e_\ell + b_\ell)^\top (\mathbb{W}_r e_r + b_r)$$

Expanding out this expression, we get (6).

$$(6) \qquad e_\ell{}^\top \mathbb{W}_r{}^\top \mathbb{W}_r e_r + b_\ell{}^\top \mathbb{W}_r e_r + b_r{}^\top \mathbb{W}_r e_l + b_\ell{}^\top b_r$$

The relation-specific bilinear form $\mathbb{W}_r{}^\top \mathbb{W}_r$ is, like our global $\mathbb{W}$ matrix, symmetric. The remaining terms, apart from the constant $b_\ell{}^\top b_r$, compute a pair of relation-specific bias vectors $b_\ell{}^\top \mathbb{W}_r$ and $b_r{}^\top \mathbb{W}_r$ applied to the pair of entity embeddings. The resulting Energy function used to score triplets has more than a passing similarity to our Harmony function (1) when $\lambda = \infty$ and, thus, no optimization takes place.

A distinctive characteristic of our approach in relation to these structurally similar models is that the transformation undergone by a Gradient Graph triplet is directly connected to the well-formedness criterion according to which triplets are evaluated in inference. As illustrated in the Discussion, our transformation of a compositional triplets using learned well-formedness criteria leads to two kinds of triplet embeddings: compositionally obtained *type* embeddings, and contextually optimized *token* embeddings. In qualitative and quantitative analyses of the learned representation, we see (1) that the space of compositionally obtained triplet embeddings has a reasonable structure, independently of the optimizing transformation, that is already sensitive to the context supplied by the relation, and (2) that semantic optimization improves these compositional representations in recognizable ways. Interestingly, improving triplets with respect to the Harmony function does *not* uniformly place them in regions that are high-Harmony in a global sense. In fact, we find that whereas positive triplets end up close to other positive triplets, plausible but negative triplets tend to be detained in clusters with other negative instances (Tables 2 and 4).

3 Compositional and Gradient Models

Optimization with respect to $\mathcal{H}$ can be implemented wherever we can construct a triplet embedding x. In our experiments, we apply Harmonic optimization of triplet representations to two compositional embedding models drawn from the knowledge base completion literature: DIST-MULT and HOLE. Both models specify a scoring function for triplet embeddings obtained via operations applied to embeddings of the three triplet components—two entity vectors and a relation vector—with no additional learned components apart from these representations of the triplet constituents. We take the terms occurring in these scoring functions to be components of the *representation* of the triplet, specifying what information about the triplet elements is important to evaluating the triplet's quality. Hence, we constructed Harmonic triplet embeddings according to the desideratum that every term occurring in the basic method's scoring function should also appear in the triplet representation x in the Harmonic model. For instance, the score of a DISTMULT triplet is a sum of three-way products of the corresponding elements of the embeddings e_ℓ, r, and e_r. Setting the products $[e_\ell]_i[r]_i[e_r]_i$ to appear in our compositional triplet embeddings (as in Eqn (8)) satisfies this desideratum.

DISTMULT (Yang et al., 2015) is a baseline model for scoring knowledge base triplets using the scoring function (7):

$$(7) \qquad score_{\text{DISTMULT}}(e_\ell, r, e_r) = e_\ell{}^\top diag(r) e_r$$

where e_ℓ, r, e_r are d-dimensional embeddings and $diag(r)$ is the $d \times d$-dimensional matrix obtained by arranging the elements of r along the diagonal. Kadlec et al. (2017) have recently shown that DISTMULT can outperform many more complicated scoring functions when hyperparameters are properly optimized, making it a strong baseline comparison for the method we propose. In addition, DISTMULT often occurs as a subcomponent in state-of-the-art KBC models—e.g. (Schlichtkrull et al., 2017; Toutanova et al., 2015). From this starting-point, we construct HARMONIC DIST-MULT (HDISTMULT) by setting the triplet embedding x to the elementwise multiplication of the relation and the pair of entity vectors:

$$(8) \qquad x_{\text{HDM}} = e_\ell \odot r \odot e_r$$

where $\odot$ denotes elementwise multiplication.

HOLOGRAPHIC EMBEDDINGS (HOLE) were introduced by Nickel et al. (2016) building on theoretical work by (Plate, 1995), as a means of constructing compressed tensor product representations of relational triplets. The method computes the score for a triplet (e_ℓ, r, e_r) from the similarity between a relation vector and the circular correlation $e_\ell \star e_r$ of the entity vectors and a relation vector:

$$(9) \qquad score_{\text{HOLE}}(e_\ell, r, e_r) = r^\top(e_\ell \star e_r)$$

where the circular correlation of e_ℓ and e_r is computed as (10).

$$(10) \qquad e_\ell \star e_r = \mathcal{F}^{-1}\left(\overline{\mathcal{F}(e_\ell)} \odot \mathcal{F}(e_r)\right)$$

$\mathcal{F}$ and $\mathcal{F}^{-1}$ denote the Fourier Transform and its inverse, and $\overline{\mathcal{F}(e_\ell)}$ is the complex conjugate of $\mathcal{F}(e_\ell)$.[1] Circular correlation is asymmetric ($e_\ell \star e_r \neq e_r \star e_\ell$)—allowing it to model asymmetric relations—and the result of the operation has the same dimensionality as the input vectors, while still carrying information about which pair of entities was bound together via correlation.

We construct HARMONIC HOLE (HHOLE) triplet embeddings via elementwise multiplication of relation vectors with the correlated pair of entity vectors:

$$(11) \qquad x_{\text{HHOLE}} = r \odot (e_\ell \star e_r)$$

In both Harmonic models, the score for a candidate triplet (e_ℓ, r, e_r) with embedding x is calculated by taking the Harmony of its optimal instantiation, $\hat{h} = \mu(x)$, i.e.

$$(12) \qquad score(x) = \mathcal{H}(\mu(x), x)$$

In the experiments, we train our networks using the log-softmax objective with negative sampling. For each positive training example (e_ℓ, r, e_r) with embedding x, we construct N negative examples $(\tilde{e}_\ell^n, \tilde{r}^n, \tilde{e}_r^n)$ obtained by deleting either the left or right entity of the true triplet and replacing it with a randomly sampled entity vector. Let $\tilde{x}^n$ denote the embedding of the nth negatively sample triplet

---

[1] The Fourier transform decomposes a function of time into its frequency components. In the context of holographic embeddings, its utility comes from the *Convolution Theorem*, which states that convolution in the time domain corresponds to elementwise multiplication in the frequency domain. This is useful in actual computations. The circular correlation—which consists of convolution with a time-reversed signal—can also be computed as a sum over off-diagonals of the tensor product of vectors, with time complexity $\mathcal{O}(d^2)$. In contrast, the Fast Fourier Transform (FFT) has time complexity $\mathcal{O}(n \log n)$ (Nickel et al., 2016).

$(\tilde{e}_\ell^n, \tilde{r}^n, \tilde{e}_r^n)$. The training objective is then to minimize (13):

(13)
$$\mathcal{L}_\mathcal{H}(e_\ell, r, e_r) = \\ -\log \frac{\exp\{\mathcal{H}(\mu(x),x)\}}{\exp\{\mathcal{H}(\mu(x),x)\}+\sum_{n=1}^{N}\exp\{\mathcal{H}(\mu(\tilde{x}^n),\tilde{x}^n)\}}$$

This has the effect of increasing the Harmony of positive examples relative to negative samples. The learning rule is thus Harmony-maximizing: the network parameters maximize the well-formedness of the positive examples relative to negative samples.

4 Experiments

We evaluated Gradient Graphs using the standard WN18 and FB15K datasets (Bordes et al., 2013)—which are subsets of the WordNet (Miller, 1995) and Freebase (Bollacker et al., 2008) databases—on the Entity Reconstruction task. In Entity Reconstruction, the network ranks completions of triplets $(\,\cdot\,, r, e_r)$ and $(e_\ell, r, \,\cdot\,)$ with deleted left and right entities. The model is successful if it ranks the true triplet above other candidate completions. We report results in the *filtered* evaluation setting (Bordes et al., 2013), in which a test triplet is only ranked against triplets that do not occur in the database. The rank of a test triplet is thus the rank of the *first* correct answer to the query. For both DISTMULT and HOLE, we report the originally reported results alongside results for our reimplementations, comparing these models with our Harmonic variants HDISTMULT and HHOLE with and without optimization of hidden layer representations. The Harmonic models with $\lambda = \infty$ have the Harmony function $\mathcal{H}(x,x)$, i.e. where the hidden representation is just the compositional embedding itself and the Faithfulness penalty in (1) is 0.

Our models used 256- to 512-dimensional embeddings and manually tuned values of the hyperparameter λ. In all models, entity and relation embeddings were normalized to $\|v\| = 1$. We do not regularize parameters, but instead set an upper bound $\lambda - \epsilon$ (ϵ a small constant) on the l_2 norm of the weight matrix $\mathbb{W}$, which helps constrain the spectral norm (maximum eigenvalue) of $\mathbb{W}$ to remain lower than λ. This is equivalent to adopting a uniform prior on weight matrices lying within the n-ball with squared radius $\lambda - \epsilon$. Importantly, this procedure keeps the matrix $V = \mathbb{W} - \lambda I$ negative-definite—a necessary condition for the existence of a unique optimum for $\mathcal{H}(h,x)$.

Results from the experiments are reported in Table 1. Overall, we found that models using our quadratic scoring function (1) to perform best across the board. This effect was particularly seen in more stringent evaluation criteria—Hits@1 and Hits@3—leading to, for instance—a 15% improvement in Hits@1 (accuracy) on Freebase between our DISTMULT reimplementation and quadratic HDISTMULT ($\lambda = \infty$). The bestDISTMULT models were those with high λ values; however, within-model comparison of HOLE shows dramatic improvements from including the optimization component—a 32% increase in FB15K accuracy between the results of (Nickel et al., 2016) and our HHOLE with a permissive λ-criterion of 1.0.

5 Discussion

In part, the appeal of our supracompositional representations stems from their ability to produce emeddings of *tokens* of semantic objects—that is, embeddings that take into account the context of a particular instance of a semantic type. Tokenized embeddings have proven useful in various settings. For instance, Dasigi et al. (2017) construct token embeddings by superposing learned vectors for WordNet senses in ratios determined by a probability distribution computed from the context. The resulting representation is a context-weighted sum of discrete senses drawn from a hand-crafted ontology. Closer to our approach, Belanger and Kakade (2015) model text as a linear dynamical system that generates texts through transitions of a continuous-state, discrete-time dynamical system across time. Estimates of the system's most probable internal state can then be extracted as an embedding of the tokens, which prove useful in language modeling and other downstream tasks.

In our framework, *types* correspond to static entity and relation embeddings that are the input to f_{comp}, and the triplet embeddings resulting from their combination. *Token* triplet embeddings are produced by optimization of the hidden layer of a GG. To understand the effect of optimizing the hidden layer of a GGRAPH both on its learned representations and on its performance in inference, we used the best-performing trained HHOLE model to produce token embeddings of database triplets in order to inspect their semantic neighborhoods. For a given compositional triplet embedding $f_{comp}(e_\ell, r, e_r) \equiv x$, we first computed the optimized triplet representation $\mu(x) \equiv \hat{h}$ using Equation (3). Treating $\hat{h}$ as the contextually optimal (token) embedding of the triplet (e_ℓ, r, e_r), we then examined the semantic neighborhood by computing the 5 closest optimized embeddings in the context of the same relation. Table 4 shows the semantic neighborhoods of compositional triplets x and optimized triplets $\hat{h}$ for different possible completions of a number of queries. Rows 1 and 2 display completions of the query $(\,\cdot\,, \texttt{office\_position\_or\_title}, \texttt{US\_President})$, and Rows 2 and 4 consider the neighborhood of the entity embedding of *Bob Dylan* in the context of

| | FB15K | | | | | | WN18 | | | | | |
| | | Rank | | Hits@ | | | | Rank | | Hits@ | | |
Model	λ	MR	MRR	1	3	10	λ	MR	MRR	1	3	10
DISTMULT	-	-	.350	-	-	.577	-	-	.830	-	-	.942
ENSEMBLE DM[†]	-	36	**.837**	**.797**	-	**.904**	-	457	.790	**.784**	-	.950
DISTMULT[*]	-	28	.710	.605	.792	.876	-	220	.825	.714	.938	.950
HDISTMULT	∞	**23**	.806	.751	**.845**	.898	∞	**164**	**.841**	.740	**.943**	**.955**
HDISTMULT	50.0	**23**	.742	.661	.799	.881	3.0	184	.831	.732	.931	.945
HOLE	-	-	.524	.402	.613	.739	-	-	.938	.930	**.945**	.949
HOLE[*]	-	39	.409	.289	.464	.647	-	205	.916	.893	.936	.946
HHOLE	∞	32	.682	.575	.763	.850	∞	293	.919	.903	.934	.942
HHOLE	1.0	**21**	**.796**	**.727**	**.848**	**.901**	2.0	**183**	**.939**	**.931**	**.945**	.951

Table 1: Results on FB15K and WN18. The results from the original DISTMULT and HOLE models are drawn from (Yang et al., 2015) and (Nickel et al., 2016). Our reimplementations[*] of DISTMULT and HOLE differ in numerous details from those in the original papers (see Appendix B for technical details). ENSEMBLE DISTMULT[†] refers to the hyperparameter-optimized Ensemble (product of experts) reimplementation of DistMult proposed by Kadlec et al. (2017). For each model, we report Mean Rank (MR) and Mean Reciprocal Rank (MRR), as well as Hits@N for $N \in \{1, 3, 10\}$. Hits@N denotes the fraction of test instances in which the true triplet completion had rank less than or equal to N. The best results within each category (DISTMULT and HOLE) are marked in **bold**, and the best results overall are additionally **underlined**.

queries about his profession ($e_\ell = \texttt{Bob\_Dylan}, r = \texttt{has\_profession}$) while varying the profession e_r. This illustrates how the representation of *Bob Dylan* varies across his different professional guises.

The table illustrates the utility of token embeddings in inference. Token embeddings of *George W. Bush* and *Barack Obama* in the context of a query about their having held the office of U.S. president are in semantic neighborhoods with a greater density of true instances of U.S. Presidents than their type embeddings. The negative examples *John McCain* and *Hilary Rodham Clinton* have type embeddings that are close to actual presidents. This is sensible since, for instance, Hilary Rodham Clinton is married to Bill Clinton—one of her nearest neighbors. But both of the negative examples' token embeddings have neighborhoods that are mostly cleared of actual presidents—despite having type embedding neighborhoods that are relatively dense with presidents.

Turning to the second half of the table, we note that *Bob Dylan*'s type embedding is already in a neighborhood dense with singer-songwriters. It is appropriate, then, that this neighborhood undergoes no change apart from minor re-ranking when the triplet (`Bob_Dylan,has_profession,singer-songwriter`) is optimized. For more difficult cases, however, where *Dylan* is not a prototypical example, the semantic neighborhoods undergo dramatic reconfiguration. For instance, optimizing the triplet (`Bob_Dylan,has_profession,disc_jockey`) correctly places *Dylan* in the neighborhood of other DJs, despite the implausibility of this association in the neighborhood of his type embedding, which contains no DJs. This places him in the token neighborhood of *Moby*, who is otherwise quite unlike *Bob Dylan* except in respect of their common career as DJs.

Combined with our finding that optimization yields the most dramatic improvements in the more stringent evaluation criteria (Hits@1 and Hits@3), this suggests that our optimization procedure is particularly helpful in arbitrating between difficult cases. This qualitative observation about the neighborhoods of compositional and supracompositional triplets can be quantified. Using the triplet classification dataset introduced by Socher et al. (2013), which contains an equal number of positive and negative triplets, we find (Table 2) that positive triplets, on average, end up in supracompositional neighborhoods that are more dense in positive examples than their compositional counterparts. On the other hands, negative triplets suffer a decrease in the number of positive triplets in the neighborhoods of their supracompositional embeddings.

To further quantify the role of semantic optimization in inference, we correlated the difference between the Harmony (score) of input triplets pre- and post-optimization with the change in its rank on the FB15K dataset. The change in Harmony is computed as $\Delta\mathcal{H} = \mathcal{H}(\mu(x), x) - \mathcal{H}(x, x)$, i.e. the difference between the Harmony of the token embedding and the Harmony of the type embedding. This comparison is model-internal—it does not compare models trained to do token inference with models trained for type inference. However, it serves as a useful index of the performance gains attributable to the optimization procedure. If optimizing a triplet representation indeed improves its relative position among all candidate triplets, we expect changes in Harmony to be negatively correlated with the change in rank of positive

	Δdensity	t statistic	p
Pos	0.241	$t = 99.7$	$p \ll 10^{-10}$
Neg	-0.059	$t = -62.4$	$p \ll 10^{-10}$

Table 2: Change in neighborhood (top-5 closest neighbors) density of true triplets (Δdensity) for positive and negative triplets drawn from the triplet classification dataset introduced by Socher et al. (2013), which is derived from the FB15K test set and consists of 59,071 positive triplets and the same number of negative triplets. This resulted in $N = 118,142$ queries for both positive and negative examples (two for each triplet, querying both the left and right entity). After computing each triplet's neighborhood, we counted the number of triplet neighbors that were in fact in the training, validation, or test sets of FB15K, yielding a measure of the concentration of true and false examples in the neighborhood of both type and token triplet embeddings.

triplets. Consistent with this, we find that optimization leads to significant improvements in raw rank in our best trained HHoLE model (Spearman's $\rho = -0.0157, p < 10^{-6}$, Figure 5). When considering the change in Mean Reciprocal Rank, a more standard evaluation metric, we find that $\Delta\mathcal{H}$ is positively associated with improvements in MRR $\left(\rho = .1370, p \ll 10^{-10}\right)$,[2] particularly when triplets whose ranks do not change at all are omitted $\left(\rho = .3746, p \ll 10^{-10}\right)$. In other words, when semantic optimization makes a difference, it does so for the better.

For HDistMult, $\Delta\mathcal{H}$ is significantly associated with increases in the rank of true triplets $\left(\rho = 0.1226, p \ll 10^{-10}\right)$, a result consistent with our finding that this class of models disprefers low settings of λ. This illustrates the importance of choices of representational format for embeddings of semantic data. Our optimization procedure can only operate over information that is contained in its compositional input. Hence, choices about how to combine the learned features of entities and relations—i.e. about the manner of composition—are central to our framework.

5.1 Desiderata of a composition function

What factors affect the success of semantic optimization in combination with a particular composition scheme? We suspect that multiplicative interactions across embedding components—which are present in HHoLE and absent in HDistMult—are essential for our optimization procedure to contribute helpfully to inference. Both

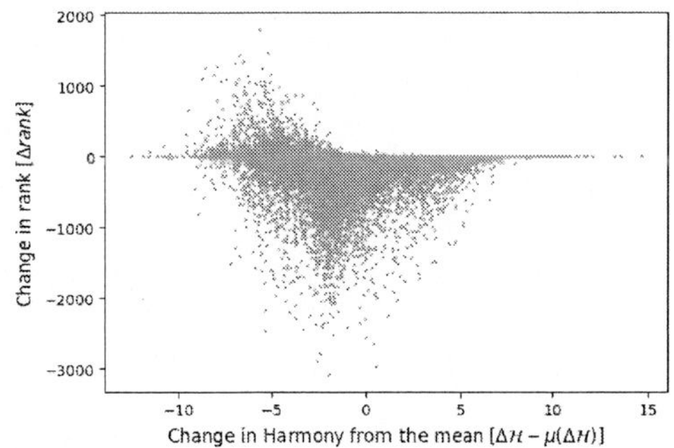

Figure 2: Effect of optimization on the rank of FB15K validation set triplets ($N = 100,000$; $50,000$ triplets with two queries per triplet) from the best-performing HHoLE model ($d = 512, \lambda = 1.0$). The horizontal axis is a triplet's change in Harmony pre- and post-optimisation ($\Delta\mathcal{H} \equiv \mathcal{H}(\mu(x), x) - \mathcal{H}(x, x)$) minus the mean change in Harmony for all triplets ($\mu(\Delta\mathcal{H})$). This is plotted against $rank_q(\mu(x)) - rank_q(x)$, the triplet's change in rank due to optimization for query q. A negative correlation indicates reductions in rank (improvements) associated with increasing optimization of triplet representations.

DistMult and HoLE are special cases of contracted Tensor Product Representations (TPRs), obtained by summing over (HoLE) or discarding (DistMult) terms from the three-way tensor product $e_\ell \otimes r \otimes e_r$.[3] In particular, DistMult retains only multiplicative interactions *within* components, omitting terms with non-matching indices. This fact appears to be crucial. In a follow-up experiment, we implemented a series of full TPR models trained on FB15K, using the composition operation (14):

$$(14) \qquad x_{\text{HTPR}} = e_\ell \otimes r \otimes e_r$$

Such models are necessarily small in size due to the rapid growth of dimensionality for TPRs as a function of the dimensionality of entity and relation embeddings. Consequently, their performance is also poor in comparison to our other implementations. However, the trend matched that which we observed within the HHoLE class: models including the optimization procedure consistently outperformed those with $\lambda = \infty$ (see Table 3). From this, we conclude that other embedding-based KBC models incorporating cross-component multiplicative interactions are likely to see improvements from the addition of a semantic optimization step prior to scoring.

---

[2]ΔMRR is computed as $\text{MRR}(\mu(x)) - \text{MRR}(x)$, i.e. the difference between the Mean Reciprocal Rank of the supracompositional and the compositional triplets.

[3]See (Nickel et al., 2016) for discussion of holographic embeddings as compressed tensor products.

λ	MR	MRR	H@1	H@3	H@10
∞	150	.278	.192	.305	.447
1.0	134	.295	.204	.326	.471

Table 3: Performance of HTPR models with and without optimization (controlled by λ). For both models, entities were 5-dimensional and relations 20-dimensional. This trend held across other hyperparameter settings.

6 Conclusion

In this paper, we proposed Gradient Graphs, a general method for augmenting compositional representations of Knowledge Graphs with a post-composition procedure that optimizes the well-formedness of triplet embeddings, highlighting the model's connection to Harmonic Grammar and Optimality Theory. The resulting model shows marked improvements over the compositional models it is implemented alongside, and also produces triplet token embeddings with properties that prove useful for inference about knowledge base entities. In future work, we intend to explore the utility of semantically-optimized token embeddings in other linguistic settings.

References

Abadi, M., Barham, P., Chen, J., Chen, Z., Davis, A., Dean, J., Devin, M., Ghemawat, S., Irving, G., Isard, M., Kudlur, M., Levenberg, J., Monga, R., Moore, S., Murray, D. G., Steiner, B., Tucker, P., Vasudevan, V., Warden, P., Wicke, M., Yu, Y., and Zheng, X. (2016). Tensorflow: A system for large-scale machine learning. In *Proceedings of the 12th USENIX Conference on Operating Systems Design and Implementation*, OSDI'16, pages 265–283, Berkeley, CA, USA. USENIX Association.

Belanger, D. and Kakade, S. (2015). A linear dynamical system model for text. In *ICML 32*, volume 37.

Bollacker, K., Evans, C., Paritosh, P., Sturge, T., and Taylor, J. (2008). Freebase: A collaboratively created graph database for structuring human knowledge. In *Proceedings of the 2008 ACM SIGMOD International Conference on Management of Data*, SIGMOD '08, pages 1247–1250, New York, NY, USA. ACM.

Bordes, A., Glorot, X., Weston, J., and Bengio, Y. (2014). A semantic matching energy function for learning with multi-relational data. *Machine Learning*, 94(2):233–259.

Bordes, A., Usunier, N., Garcia-Duran, A., Weston, J., and Yakhnenko, O. (2013). Translating embeddings for modeling multi-relational data.

In Burges, C. J. C., Bottou, L., Welling, M., Ghahramani, Z., and Weinberger, K. Q., editors, *Advances in Neural Information Processing Systems 26*, pages 2787–2795. Curran Associates, Inc.

Bordes, A., Weston, J., Collobert, R., and Bengio, Y. (2011). Learning structured embeddings of knowledge bases. In *AAAI*.

Dasigi, P., Ammar, W., Dyer, C., and Hovy, E. (2017). Ontology-aware token embeddings for prepositional phrase attachment. In *ACL55*, pages 2089–2098.

Ji, G., Liu, K., He, S., and Zhao, J. (2016). Knowledge graph completion with adaptive sparse transfer matrix. In *AAAI-16*, pages 985–991.

Kadlec, R., Bajgar, O., and Kleindienst, J. (2017). Knowledge base completion: Baselines strike back. In *2nd Workshop on Representation Learning for NLP*, pages 69–74.

Kingma, D. and Ba, J. (2015). Adam: A method for stochastic optimization. In *ICLR*.

Lin, Y., Liu, Z., Sun, M., Liu, Y., and Zhu, X. (2015). Learning entity and relation embeddings for knowledge graph completion. In *AAAI*, pages 2181–2187.

Ling, X. and Weld, D. (2012). Fine-grained entity recognition. In *AAAI 26*.

Miller, G. A. (1995). Wordnet: A lexical database for english. *Commun. ACM*, 38(11):39–41.

Nickel, M., Rosasco, L., and Poggio, T. (2016). Holographic embeddings of knowledge graphs. In *AAAI*.

Nickel, M., Tresp, V., and Kriegel, H.-P. (2011). A three-way model for collective learning on multi-relational data. In *Proceedings of the 28 th International Conference on Machine Learning*.

Plate, T. (1995). Holographic reduced representations. *IEEE Transactions on Neural Networks*, 6:623–641.

Schlichtkrull, M., Kipf, T. N., Bloem, P., Berg, R. v. d., Titov, I., and Welling, M. (2017). Modeling relational data with graph convolutional networks. *arXiv preprint arXiv:1703.06103*.

Smolensky, P. and Legendre, G. (2006). *The Harmonic Mind: From Neural Computation to Optimality-Theoretic Grammar*, volume 1: Cognitive Architecture. The MIT Press.

Socher, R., Chen, D., Manning, C. D., and Ng, A. (2013). Reasoning with neural tensor networks for knowledge base completion. In *NIPS*.

Toutanova, K., Chen, D., Pantel, P., Poon, H., Choudhury, P., and Gamon, M. (2015). Representing text for joint embedding of text and knowledge bases. In *EMNLP*. ACL – Association for Computational Linguistics.

US Presidents

	George W. Bush			Barack Obama	
n	x (compositional)	$\hat{h}$ (optimized)	n	x (compositional)	$\hat{h}$ (optimized)
1	**George H. W. Bush**	George H. W. Bush	1	Hillary Rodham Clinton	George W. Bush
2	**Bill Clinton**	Bill Clinton	2	Al Gore	Bill Clinton
3	**Jimmy Carter**	Jimmy Carter	3	George W. Bush	John F. Kennedy
4	**John F. Kennedy**	Ronald Reagan	4	Bill Clinton	Ronald Reagan
5	**Ronald Reagan**	Barack Obama	5	John F. Kennedy	George H. W. Bush

	John McCain			Al Gore	
n	x (compositional)	$\hat{h}$ (optimized)	n	x (compositional)	$\hat{h}$ (optimized)
1	John Kerry	John Kerry	1	**Barack Obama**	Condoleezza Rice
2	Hillary Rodham Clinton	Colin Powell	2	**George W. Bush**	John C. Calhoun
3	Colin Powell	Nancy Pelosi	3	Colin Powell	Colin Powell
4	**Richard Nixon**	Joe Biden	4	Condoleezza Rice	Hillary Rodham Clinton
5	**Herbert Hoover**	Dick Cheney	5	**John F. Kennedy**	John Kerry

Guises of Bob Dylan

	Singer-Songwriter			Screenwriter	
n	x (compositional)	$\hat{h}$ (optimized)	n	x (compositional)	$\hat{h}$ (optimized)
1	**Eric Clapton**	Bonnie Raitt	1	**John Lennon**	John Lennon
2	**Bonnie Raitt**	Eric Clapton	2	Jimi Hendrix	Barbara Streisand
3	**Van Morrison**	Van Morrison	3	**Barbara Streisand**	Eric Idle
4	**B.B. King**	B.B. King	4	Eric Clapton	Nick Cave
5	**Bob Seger**	Bob Seger	5	Eddie Vedder	Alan Bergman

	Disc Jockey			Writer	
n	x (compositional)	$\hat{h}$ (optimized)	n	x (compositional)	$\hat{h}$ (optimized)
1	Tom Petty	**Steven Van Zandt**	1	**John Lennon**	Alanis Morissette
2	Warren Zevon	**Erykah Badu**	2	**Alanis Morissette**	John Lennon
3	Willie Nelson	**Alice Cooper**	3	Paul McCartney	Leonard Cohen
4	John Mayer	John Mayer	4	Tina Turner	**Leonard Bernstein**
5	Steve Earle	**Moby**	5	Dolly Parton	**Prince**

Table 4: Semantic neighborhoods of type (pre-) and token (post-optimization) triplets output by the best-performing HHoLE model ($d = 512, \lambda = 1.0$). *US Presidents*: Effect of optimization on the semantic neighborhoods of entity embeddings in the context of the query (· , office_title, US_President). *Guises of Bob Dylan*: Effect of optimization on the semantic neighborhood of Bob_Dylan in the context of four queries about his profession: Bob Dylan as singer-songwriter, screenwriter, disc_jockey, and writer. Bob_Dylan is a positive instance of each of these professions in FB15K. For each entity, we retrieved the 5 closest (Euclidian Distance) compositional triplet embeddings, as well as the five closest triplets, among all candidate triplets, when all these candidates are optimized. Triplet completions that in fact occur in FB15K are marked in **bold**. Human-readable entity names were retrieved from a mapping between Freebase machine IDs and names of Wikipedia articles built by Ling and Weld (2012). See main text for discussion of the results.

265

Yang, B., Yih, W., He, X., Gao, J., and Deng, L. (2015). Embedding entities and relations for learning and infer- ence in knowledge bases. In *ICLR*.

Yoon, H., Song, H., Park, S., and Park, S. (2016). A translation-based knowledge graph embedding preserving logical property of relations. In *Proceedings of NAACL-HLT*, pages 907–916.

7   Appendix A: Model details

(15)   **Claim:** $\mu(x) = \frac{1}{2}(\mathbb{W} - \lambda I)^{-1}(b + 2\lambda x)$ is the unique global optimum for $\mathcal{H}(h, x)$ for any fixed x.

We define the Harmony of hidden state h with respect to triplet embedding x as in (1):

$$\mathcal{H}(h, x) \equiv \frac{1}{2}\left[h^\top \mathbb{W} h + b^\top h - \lambda(h - x)^\top(h - x)\right]$$

$$= \frac{1}{2}\left[h^\top(\mathbb{W} - \lambda I) h + (b + 2\lambda x)^\top h - \lambda x^\top x\right]$$

$$\equiv \frac{1}{2}\left[h^\top V h + m(x)^\top h - \lambda x^\top x\right]$$

Completing the square yields:

$$\mathcal{H}(h, x) = \frac{1}{2}\left[\left(h - \frac{1}{2}V^{-1}m(x)\right)^\top V\left(h - \frac{1}{2}V^{-1}m(x)\right)\right]$$

$$+ \frac{1}{2}\left[-\lambda x^\top x - \frac{1}{4}m(x)^\top V^{-1}m(x)\right]$$

$$\equiv \frac{1}{2}\left[(h - \mu(x))^\top V(h - \mu(x))\right] + \ell(x)$$

This is valid because $V = \mathbb{W} - \lambda I$ is symmetric. $\ell(x)$ does not depend on h, so it is sufficient to optimize $\frac{1}{2}\left[(h - \mu(x))^\top V(h - \mu(x))\right]$. Setting $\frac{\partial \mathcal{H}(h,x)}{\partial h} = 0$ yields $2V(h - \mu(x)) = 0$; $\therefore h = \mu(x)$. Since V is negative-definite, this point is a *maximum*.

The truth of the claim may also be perceived from observing that $\mathcal{H}(h, x)$ defines a Gaussian distribution over the hidden state variable h with mean $\mu(x)$ and inverse covariance matrix $\Sigma^{-1} \equiv V$. The optimality of $\mu(x)$ then follows from the unimodality of Gaussians.

The training objective (13) may be justified by the following considerations. We take the compositional triplet data to be generated by hidden states of the gradient graph network, and maximize the log probability of the training data using the maximum a posteriori point estimate of the hidden state h. The "complete data" are then $\mathcal{D} = \{\langle \hat{h}, x\rangle\} = \{\langle \mu(x), x\rangle\}$. For fixed x, $\mathcal{H}(h, x)$ models the conditional distribution $p(h|x)$, with

(16) $p(h|x) = \frac{\exp\{\mathcal{H}(h,x)\}}{Z(x)}$

where $Z(x) = \int_{h'} \exp\{\mathcal{H}(h', x)\}\, dh' = |2\pi V^{-1}|^{\frac{1}{2}}\exp\{\ell(x)\}$ is   the   partition   function

conditioned on x. Let $\chi_q = \{x'\}$ be the set of candidate triplet embeddings consistent with a given query q. Choosing the discrete distribution $p(x) = \frac{\exp\{\ell(x)\}}{\sum_{x' \in \chi_q}\exp\{\ell(x')\}}$ over triplet embeddings as the prior probability of the embedding x, we have that:

$$p(\mu(x), x|q) \propto \frac{\exp\{\mathcal{H}(\mu(x), x)\}}{|2\pi V^{-1}|^{\frac{1}{2}}\sum_{x' \in \chi_q}\exp\{\ell(x')\}}$$

For given parameters, the denominator is constant. So, renormalizing over the discrete triplets χ_q gives:

$$p(\mu(x), x|q) = \frac{\exp\{\mathcal{H}(\mu(x), x)\}}{\sum_{x' \in \chi_q}\exp\{\mathcal{H}(\mu(x), x)\}}$$

Approximating the discrete distribution over all of χ_q with a negative sample yields the objective (13).

8   Appendix B: Implementation details

In initial experiments, we searched through a number of candidate models. These included two Harmonic variants of the RESCAL model (Nickel et al., 2011), as well as models that constructed x as a simple concatenation of entity and relation vectors, as well as three-way tensor products of these vectors. These initial experiments led us to focus on DISTMULT and HOLE as the best-performing candidates. Our Harmonic models and reimplementations of the DISTMULT and HOLE baselines were written in TensorFlow (Abadi et al., 2016) and estimated using the Adam optimizer (Kingma and Ba, 2015). With the exception of the HOLE reimplementation, we uniformly used the log-softmax loss (13), which performed best in initial experiments. In contrast, Yang et al. (2015) use a margin-based ranking loss that is linear in the margin between the scores of positive and negative examples up to a threshold, and Nickel et al. (2016) use the pairwise linear margin loss applied to the scores squashed by the logistic function. For HOLE, we used the *linear* margin loss, which provided by far the best performance in the experiments. For each model, we trained until performance on the validation set decrease, then chose the best-performing embedding size from among $d \in \{256, 512\}$. Batch size (512), negative sampling rate (500), and learning rate (0.001) were kept constant across models. We note in passing that regions of the hyperparameter space for DISTMULT explored by Kadlec et al. (2017) were inaccessible to us for technical reasons. For the Harmonic models, we manually tuned the λ hyperparameter.

Case assignment in TSL syntax: a case study

Mai Ha Vu
University of Delaware
maiha@udel.edu

Nazila Shafiei
Stony Brook University
nazila.shafiei@stonybrook.edu

Thomas Graf
Stony Brook University
mail@thomasgraf.net

Abstract

Recent work suggests that the subregular complexity of syntax might be comparable to that of phonology and morphology. More specifically, whereas phonological and morphological dependencies are tier-based strictly local over strings, syntactic dependencies are tier-based strictly local over derivation trees. However, a broader range of empirical phenomena must be considered in order to solidify this claim. This paper investigates various phenomena related to morphological case, and we argue that they, too, are tier-based strictly local. Not only do our findings provide empirical support for a kind of computational parallelism across language modules, they also offer a new, computationally unified perspective of structural and lexical case. We hope that this paper will enable other researchers to fruitfully study syntactic phenomena from a subregular perspective.

1 Introduction

After significant success in phonology and morphology (Heinz, 2018 and references therein), the subregular approach has recently been extended to syntax. Graf (2018) shows that the basic Minimalist operations Merge and Move — which form the core of syntax — belong to the formal class *tier-based strictly local* (TSL; Heinz et al., 2011). More precisely, Graf shows that Minimalist grammars have TSL derivation tree languages even though their string languages are mildly context-sensitive (Joshi, 1985; Harkema, 2001; Michaelis, 2001). It has been known for a long time that many mildly context-sensitive formalisms have regular derivation tree languages (see Morawietz 2003, Kobele et al. 2007, and references therein). Graf's result is noteworthy because it identifies the very limited subclass TSL as sufficient for Minimalist grammars. Since TSL also plays a central role

in phonology (McMullin and Hansson, 2015; McMullin, 2016) and morphology (Aksënova et al., 2016), this suggests a kind of cognitive parallelism: linguistic dependencies have comparable subregular complexity across language modules.

While the findings in Graf (2018) are promising, they are far from conclusive as even the most dedicated Minimalist will readily admit that syntax consists of a lot more than just Merge and Move. Many phenomena remain to be explored, including those at the interface to morphology or semantics. Vu (2018) has already started this enterprise with an investigation of NPI licensing. This paper continues along these lines with a TSL-based analysis of morphosyntactic case.

Case is a fruitful area to explore for several reasons. First, the data is very robust compared to, say, binding or quantifier scope. Second, case exhibits few interactions with movement; such interactions still pose major challenges for TSL-accounts. At the same time, case dependencies are still sufficiently intricate that it is not immediately obvious how they could be handled by TSL mechanisms. Existing treatments of case in Minimalist grammars (Laszakovits, 2018) or agreement in general (Ermolaeva, 2018) imply that case dependencies are definable in first-order logic, but TSL is much more restricted than that. Case also lacks a unified linguistic theory. Our TSL approach combines ideas from standard case theory (Chomsky, 1981) and Dependent Case Theory (DCT; Marantz, 1991; Baker and Vinokurova, 2010) into a computationally uniform solution for both structural case (nominative and accusative) and lexical case.

The paper proceeds as follows. All necessary preliminaries are put in place in §2. This includes Minimalist grammars as a formal model of syntax, Minimalist derivation trees as the central data structure, and finally TSL itself. TSL uses a sim-

Proceedings of the Society for Computation in Linguistics (SCiL) 2019, pages 267-276.
New York City, New York, January 3-6, 2019

ple projection mechanism to construct tree tiers over which distributional constraints can be enforced in a local fashion. We then apply this idea to morphological case in §3. The central idea is that there is a single *case tier* that contains every case-carrying head. In addition, each head requires a licensor on the tier, and the licensor must be the sister of the licensee's mother. This holds for both structural and lexical case. Conceptual and methodological aspects of this subregular analysis are discussed in §4.

We deliberately keep all notation and formal machinery to a minimum in order to accommodate readers without much exposure to computational linguistics. More formally inclined readers should be able to reconstruct the formal machinery from Graf (2018) and Tab. 1.

2 TSL syntax

2.1 Minimalist grammars

Subregular syntax operates over tree structures rather than strings. Hence it requires both a linguistic theory of what those tree structures are, and a formally rigorous model for implementing these ideas. The latter is provided by Minimalist grammars (MGs; Stabler, 1997, 2011), which implement ideas of Chomsky's Minimalist syntax (Chomsky, 1995).

The technical details of MGs are largely irrelevant for the purposes of this paper. It suffices to know that phrase structure trees are assembled from feature-annotated lexical items via the structure building operations Merge and Move. The sequence of Merge and Move steps can be represented as a derivation tree, the central data structure for MGs. Derivation trees differ only minimally from phrase structure trees: I) interior nodes are labeled Merge (•) or Move, and II) moving phrases remain in their base position, and the specifier that would be occupied by the mover remains empty. To improve readability, all derivation trees in this paper are shown with the usual X′-labels for interior nodes (see e.g. Fig. 2).

Due to our reliance on MGs, the derivations we posit are closely modeled after standard accounts in Minimalist syntax: I) subjects start in a low position (Spec,VP or alternatively Spec,vP), from which they move to Spec,TP, and II) finite clauses are CPs, whereas infinitival clauses may be TPs or CPs. Most importantly, we make the less standard assumption that the head of a DP enters the

Figure 1: Long-distance sibilant harmony is tier-based strictly local over strings as it can be expressed as a local ban against [sʃ] and [ʃs] on a tier of sibilants.

derivation with a preassigned case. Consequently, the problem of case assignment amounts to regulating the distribution of case-carrying D-heads in MG derivation trees.

2.2 TSL over strings

Graf (2018) analyzes MGs from a subregular perspective by adapting the phonologically motivated class of TSL string sets for syntax. The idea behind string-based TSL is simple: if a dependency is non-local, it can be made local by masking out irrelevant material. This masking out can be understood in linguistic terms as the construction of a tier. Constraints on this tier take the form of forbidding a finite number of substrings, the length of which must be finitely bounded. For example, long-distance sibilant harmony with respect to feature f can be modeled as a TSL-dependency by first projecting all sibilants and then requiring adjacent sibilants on the tier to always agree on their value for f. If the only sibilants are [s] and [ʃ], for instance, then long-distance anteriority harmony amounts to banning the substrings [sʃ] and [ʃs] on the tier (see Fig. 1). Even though there is no limit on the length of the tier, the constraint never has to consider more than two adjacent segments at a time and thus satisfies the bounded-size requirement.

2.3 Projection of tree tiers

TSL over trees as defined by Graf (2018) is more general than string-based TSL. First, and perhaps most importantly, the tier projection function is allowed to consider the local context of a node n in the derivation tree in order to determine whether n projects. So rather than constructing a tier that contains, say, all nodes that are verbs, one may opt for more complex tiers such as "every verb that selects a DP headed by *the*". Formally, a local context for projection to tier T is specified by a subtree in which exactly one node is superscripted by T to indicate that it should be put on tier T. If a node n in the derivation tree occurs as part of a subtree that matches at least one specified context for tier

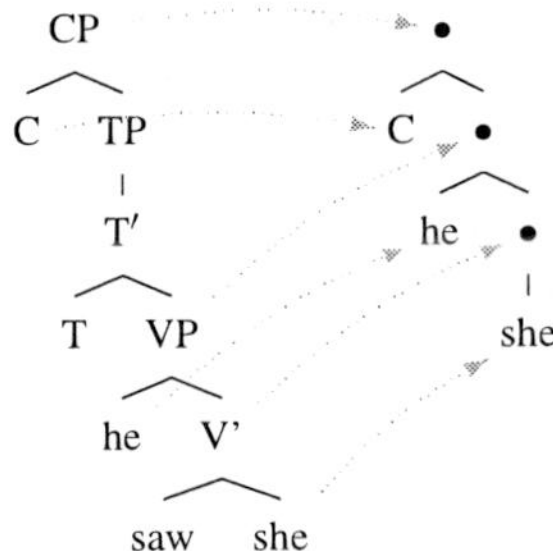

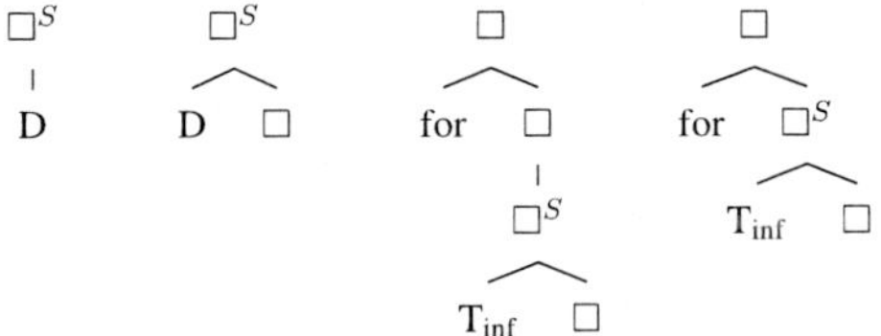

Figure 2: Nodes of the derivation tree (with X′-labels for clarity) are projected onto a tree tier based on their label and their local context. The dominance relations in the tier are inherited from the original tree.

Figure 3: Four contexts for projection to a structural case tier S; the first one projects a node whose only daughter is a D-head, whereas the second one projects a node with a D-head as the left daughter and some other node to the right ($\square$ is used as a placeholder that matches a node irrespective of its label). The third and fourth handle projection of the mother of an infinitival T-head selected by *for* in cases with and without subject movement, respectively.

T, n is projected to T. Note that the depth of the subtrees in all context specifications (i.e. the maximum distance between the root and any leaves) must be less than some fixed finite bound k, otherwise the context specifications would not be locally bounded. This is the case for our example here as it suffices for every node to look at its label and the labels of its daughters, if they exist.

Figure 2 shows the construction of a tier that contains all C-heads and their mothers as well as all D-heads with nominative case and their mothers. Crucially, the size of the context that is considered by the tier projection is finitely bounded for each node — for C-heads and D-heads only the label needs to be considered, and for all other nodes it suffices to check whether their daughter is a C-head or D-head.

Figure 3 displays two contexts. The first two ensure that every mother of a D-head is projected. The remaining two handle projection of the mother of an infinitival T-head that is selected by the C-head *for*. This is one of the most complex instances of projection used in this paper (§3.6, §3.7).

2.4 Constraints on tree tiers

Constraints on tree tiers are also allowed to be more general than in the string case. Each node on the tier is mapped to a string language that its string of daughters must belong to. Graf (2018) only discusses the simple case where this mapping considers just the label of the node. But it is easy to amend the definition so that local context information is taken into account here, too.

Continuing the example in Fig. 2, we may put in place a simple constraint to capture the fact that two distinct arguments in the same clause cannot both be nominative: if a node on the tier is labeled • and has a sister carrying nominative case, then it must not have a daughter carrying nominative case. Formally, a node n that is labeled • and appears in the context $[\square\ [\textsc{Nom}, n]]$ is mapped to the string language $(\Sigma - \{\textsc{Nom}\})^*$ (where $\square$ is a placeholder matching every node label and Σ is a fixed set of node labels). This constraint is violated in Fig. 2 as one node is labeled • and has both a Nom-carrying sister *he* and a Nom-carrying daughter *she*. If *she* were replaced by *her*, then neither *she* nor its mother would be projected on the tier, and consequently the constraint would no longer be violated.

In this paper, only Merge nodes put restrictions on their daughter strings. For each Merge node, its set of daughter strings forms a finite language of strings of length 1. Such string languages are maximally simple. The precise shape of the daughter string language for any given Merge node depends only on the siblings of the Merge node. This, too, is a very simple context specification.

The complexity of a TSL-dependency over trees is an aggregate of three different parameters: the complexity of the tier projection, the complexity of the function that associates each node on the tier with a set S of permissible daughter strings, and the complexity of S. For our treatment of morphological case, all these components will turn out to be exceedingly simple.

3 Analysis

While the preliminaries section has been kept fairly informal, it nonetheless provides all the necessary background to develop a TSL analysis of morphological case. In this section, we present our TSL account for the distribution of nominative (NOM) and accusative (ACC) in various constructions of English. We cover transitive, intransitive, and unaccusative verbs (§3.1), infinitival clauses (§3.2), ditransitives (§3.3), raising to subject (§3.4), control (§3.5), raising to object (§3.6), *for*-clauses (§3.7), and the effects of clausal subjects on case assignment (§3.8). None of the data is new, but our TSL approach represents a novel synthesis of traditional case theory and DCT that relies on a single, unified mechanism of sister-daughter dependencies on a tier.

3.1 Transitive, intransitive, and unaccusative

The core generalization of structural case assignment is that NOM is assigned to the structurally highest DP x in a case domain (modulo movement), and ACC to the DPs c-commanded by x (Marantz, 1991; Baker and Vinokurova, 2010). What constitutes a case domain is a contentious issue, but largely irrelevant for our purposes. For the sake of simplicity, we will assume that each CP is a case domain, and nothing else is.

Examples (1a-1c) show simple sentences with transitive, intransitive, and unaccusative verbs. No matter the type of verb, we observe that the subject is always NOM, and the object DP, c-commanded by the subject, carries ACC.

(1)   a. He saw her.

     b. He slept.

     c. He arrived.

Under many generative analyses, both the subject and the object enter the derivation as arguments of the verb or one of its functional projections (usually vP). They are thus part of a structural configuration of bounded size. For example, if the subject starts out in Spec,VP and the object as the complement of VP, then they are part of a subtree of size 3. Strictly speaking, then, case assignment in these configurations does not require tiers at all. Instead, one can simply list all possible subtrees of size 3 — there are only finitely many, after all — and mark a subtree as illicit if the subject does not carry NOM or the object does not carry ACC. This would be the subregular counterpart to a fully lexicalized analysis of case assignment.

But this simple account is inadequate. Merely listing all forbidden subtrees allows for arbitrary case variations. We may require two nominatives with *like*, two accusatives with *see*, and any random combination with *want*. A list cannot capture any relevant generalizations, just like listing all attested words of English is not a description of its phonology. The lack of generalizations also entails a lack of succinctness — the list of forbidden subtrees would quickly reach hundreds of thousands for even a fairly small lexicon. Most importantly, apparent cases of long-distance case assignment, e.g. ECM, cannot be handled this way. We contend that a TSL analysis that takes inspiration from DCT is empirically more adequate, more insightful, and more succinct.

Let us return to the generalization that NOM is assigned to the highest DP in a case domain, and ACC to the argument c-commanded by this DP. We have to ban the following configurations in simple sentences: two NOM DPs in a c-command relation (2a), and ACC DPs that are not c-commanded by a "licensing" NOM DP (2b).

(2)   a. * He saw she.

     b. * Him slept.

We have already seen in §2 how a TSL account can handle some of these facts. But some modifications are needed.

We still project every C-head and its mother, as well as every D-head h carrying NOM. In contrast to what was said in §2, we do not project the mother of this head, but rather the Merge node that checks its category feature. For a simple DP like *she*, this Merge node will indeed be the mother. But consider a larger DP such as *John's father*, which is commonly analyzed as [DP [DP John] [D′ 's [NP father]]]. Here the mother of 's would indicate the point where 's is merged with *father*, not the point where the whole DP is selected as an argument. Said point corresponds to when the Merge node checks the category feature of the DP's head 's. By projecting the Merge node that checks the category feature of a head h, we effectively project the mother of the whole phrase headed by h. Fortunately, it holds for every MG that there is an upper bound k such that no head is more than k steps away from the Merge node that selects its category feature (cf. Graf, 2012). Which node that is can be inferred from the feature specification of the head. This guarantees that the projection only needs to consider contexts of finitely bounded size in order to project both a case carrying D-head and the Merge node checking its category feature.

The projection function just described produces tiers that resemble the one in Fig. 2. If *he* were replaced by *John's mother* in this derivation, the tier would be almost the same except that *he* would have to be replaced by *'s*. Recall from §2 that we assume that D-heads are annotated with the morphological case of the DP, so in both instances the tier clearly indicates the presence of NOM. The constraint from §2 does not allow Merge nodes to have both a NOM sister and a NOM daughter. This rules out *he saw she* (Fig. 2), whereas *he thinks that she has arrived* is allowed thanks to the intervening C-head starting a new case domain (Fig. 4).

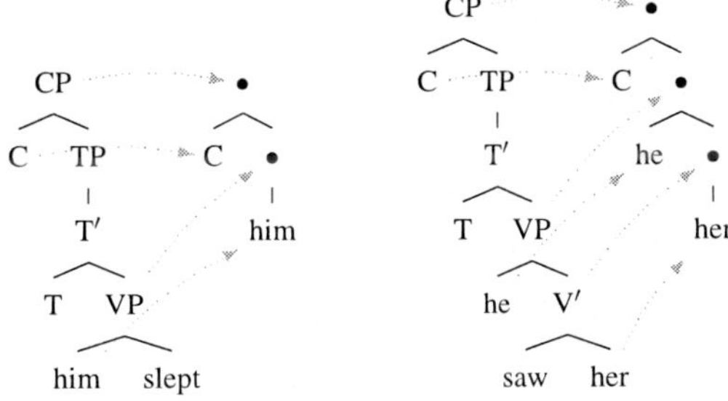

Figure 5: The left derivation is illicit because ACC is not licensed on the tier; the right one is well-formed as the required NOM sister is present on the tier.

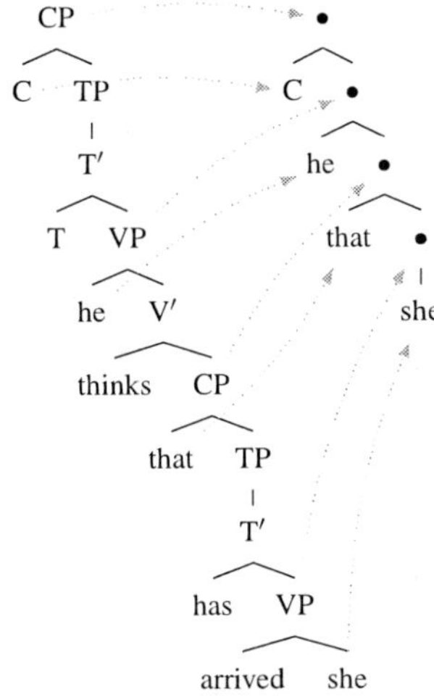

Figure 4: This case assignment pattern is permitted because no Merge node on the tier has both a NOM daughter and a NOM sister.

This takes care of double nominatives, leaving only ACC. Although ACC licensing can be enforced on a separate tier, it is easier to use a single tier for licensing of both NOM and ACC. To this end, we extend the tier projection function so that D-heads carrying ACC also end up on the tier, as do the Merge nodes checking their category features. In other words, (3b) is amended so that h is a D-head carrying NOM or ACC.

We then enforce that no Merge node without a NOM D-head as a sister may have an ACC D-head as a daughter — or equivalently, every Merge node with an ACC daughter must have a NOM sister. This correctly rules out *him slept* while allowing for *he saw her*.

(3)   **Case tier (version 1)**
      Construct a tier that contains all of the following, and only those:

      a. all C-heads and their mothers, and

      b. every D-head h carrying NOM or ACC, and

      c. the unique Merge node that checks the category feature of h.

      The following constraints hold for every Merge node m:

      i.   if a daughter of m is NOM, then no sister of m carries NOM,

      ii. if a daughter of m is ACC, the same sister of m carries NOM.

NOM and ACC thus are regulated by almost exactly the same machinery, the only difference is what daughter/sister-combinations are allowed for Merge node. In order to determine the well-formedness of a derivation with respect to case assignment, one constructs the case tier and checks each Merge node for potential constraint violations. Like DCT, the TSL approach can immediately account for the fact that subjects of passives and unaccusatives receive NOM even though they start out in object position (cf. Fig. 4), an important fact that would have to be stipulated under a purely lexicalist account.

3.2   Infinitival clauses

The current account puts no restrictions on NOM in subject position, missing the fact that subjects of infinitival clauses cannot carry NOM.

(4)   * He/Him to leave early is surprising.

While the ungrammaticality of *him* is unsurprising under our account, nothing should be wrong with *he to leave early is surprising*. One might argue that this sentence is indeed well-formed with respect to case assignment but violates some other constraint. However, we prefer to explicitly ban NOM subjects in infinitival clauses as this will simplify things later on in §3.6 and §3.7.

(5) **Case tier (version 2)**

Construct a tier that contains all of the following, and only those:

    a. all C-heads and their mothers, and

    b. all finite T-heads and their mothers, and

    c. every D-head h carrying NOM or ACC, and

    d. the unique Merge node that checks the category feature of h.

The following constraints hold for every Merge node m:

    i. if a daughter of m is NOM, then some sister of m is T_{fin},

    ii. if a daughter of m is ACC, the some sister of m carries NOM.

Note that (5i) renders the ban against multiple NOM DPs in (3i) obsolete as NOM is now much more restricted in its distribution.

3.3 Ditransitives

Ditransitive verbs in English seem to take two ACC objects.

(6) a. ?? I showed her him.

     b. I showed him to her.

According to Larson (1990), the indirect object (IO) in double object constructions starts out as the complement of the verb, and the direct object (DO) as a specifier. The subject enters the derivation as the specifier of some higher functional head. This is problematic for our treatment of ACC as this means that the tier would contain a Merge node with IO ACC as a daughter and the ACC DO as a sister. The requirement that every Merge node with an ACC daughter must have a NOM sister explicitly forbids this.

There are at least three ways to address the ditransitive challenge. Rather than picking one among them, we briefly sketch all of them because I) they illustrate the flexibility of the TSL approach to syntax, and II) each strategy may be useful in cases that do not involve ditransitives.

Chain-licensing The simplest solution is to weaken (5ii) such that an ACC daughter is also acceptable if the Merge node has an ACC sister. This effectively allows for a kind of *chain-licensing* such that each ACC is licensed by the next higher ACC. The highest ACC still needs to be licensed by NOM, though.

Dative Alternatively, one may reanalyze ACC on IO as a dative (DAT) that merely happens to be syncretic with ACC. English already displays morphological syncretism for NOM and ACC on all DPs except pronouns, so a total syncretism of ACC and DAT is conceivable. The main advantage of this solution is that it readily extends to languages that display a morphological distinction between ACC and DAT. In German, for example, IO is explicitly marked as DAT in most cases.

(7) a. Ich   zeige ihr
          1SG.NOM show 3SG.F.DAT
          den   Weg.
          the.M.ACC way

     b. * Ich   zeige sie
          1SG.NOM show 3SG.F.ACC
          den   Weg.
          the.M.ACC way

          'I show her the way.'

Dependent DAT would be handled like ACC, except that now it is ACC that functions as a licensor instead of NOM. In other words, no Merge node on the case tier may have a DAT daughter unless it also has an ACC sister. The reader is invited to verify that this blocks (7b) but not (7a), assuming that the base DO position c-commands the base IO position.

Lexical case One may also contend that (6a) is in fact ill-formed because the IO carries an unlicensed ACC, and that (6b) escapes this fate only because the preposition *to* acts as a lexical case assigner. Lexical case is handled by constructing a separate tier for lexical case. If a case-carrying D-head occurs in the local scope of a lexical case assigner, both the head and the Merge node checking its category feature are projected to the lexical case tier instead of the usual case tier. This tier also contains every lexical case assigner and its mother. On this tier, it holds for every Merge node m that its sibling assigns case c iff exactly one of the daughters of m carries case c.

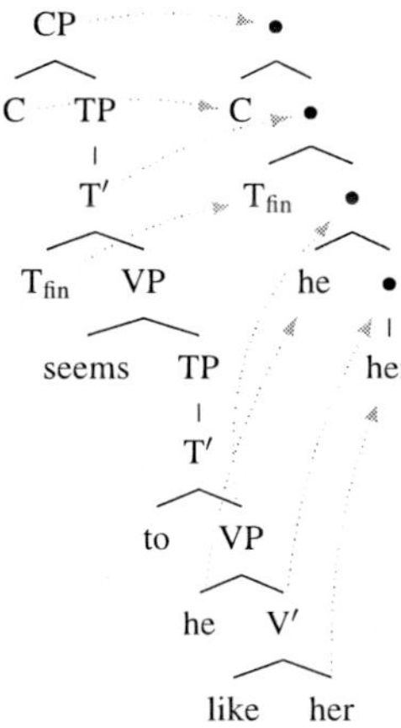

Figure 6: Case assignment in raising works exactly the same as in simple clauses.

3.4 Raising to subject

Our TSL analysis has the advantage that it readily extends to seemingly more complicated structures, e.g. subject raising. Consider the example in (8), where the subject must carry nominative case.

(8)   He/*him seems to t like her.

Assuming a transformational analysis, the embedded clause is a TP containing the surface subject, which subsequently moves into the matrix clause. This is indicated by a trace in (8).

But if the transformational analysis is indeed correct, then raising constructions do not need any special treatment in our account. As movement does not play a role in our tier-projection, the respective case tiers will mirror those for *he likes her* and *him likes her* (see Fig. 6).

3.5 Control

Control constructions as in (9) are superficially similar to subject raising, but involve a very different structure.

(9)   He persuaded her [CP PRO to leave *she/her].

The standard assumption in generative syntax is that the embedded clause in these constructions is a CP whose subject is an unpronounced PRO. In order to capture the contrast above, we expand (5) so that PRO can license ACC.

(10)   **Case tier (addendum to** (5)**)**

    a.   Also project PRO and the merge node that checks its category feature.

    b.   If a daughter of Merge node m is ACC, then some sister of m is PRO or carries NOM.

We would also like to point out an alternative analysis that might merit further exploration by syntacticians. If one allows for chain-licensing of ACC (§3.3), then one can do away with PRO and treat the embedded clause as a TP (or perhaps even just a VP). The lower ACC would then be licensed by either NOM (*He was persuaded to leave her*) or a higher ACC (*John persuaded him to leave her*). While intriguing, this view seems incompatible with the idea that other cases such as DAT in German are (at least sometimes) structurally licensed by ACC.

3.6   Exceptional Case Marking (ECM)

Another important construction is raising to object, also known as ECM.

(11)   He believes [TP *she/her to like *he/him].

Given (5i), the ungrammaticality of NOM on the embedded subject in (11) already follows from the lack of a licensing T_{fin}. This also explains why the embedded object cannot carry NOM. The only open issue, then, is the well-formedness of *he believes her to like him*.

In contrast to control, ECM does not involve an underlying PRO. Hence the PRO-less analysis of control sketched above would work exactly the same for ECM constructions: NOM on the main clause subject licenses ACC on the embedded subject, which in turn licenses ACC on the object. But this analysis depends on chain-licensing, which may run into various problems in other languages. There is, however, an alternative proposal that eschews chain-licensing, is compatible with a PRO-based analysis of control, and builds on the implementation of lexical case at the end of §3.3.

Said analysis posits that the infinitival T-head (T_{inf}) acts as a lexical licensor for both the ACC subject and the ACC object, but does so in two very different ways. First, T_{inf} and its mother are projected to the tier instead of the ACC subject, exempting the latter from any licensing requirements. The T-head then acts a licensor for the ACC object on the tier (Fig. 7). The embedded subject must carry ACC for this to work, otherwise it will project on the tier and prevent T_{inf} from licensing ACC on the object. Since the subject cannot be NOM, it cannot license the object's ACC instead

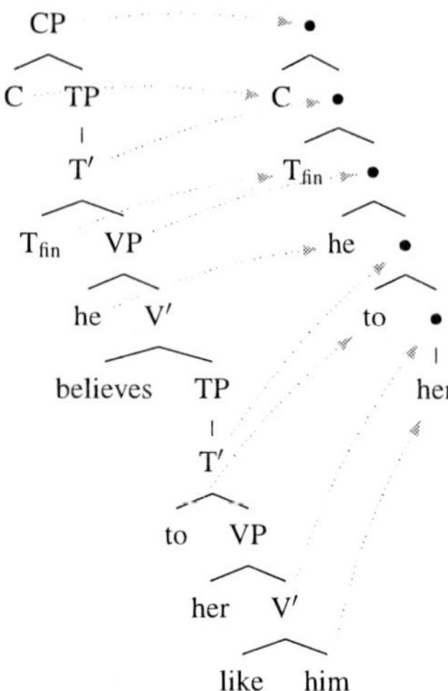

Figure 7: ECM verbs allow infinitival T to project instead of the subject to license Acc.

of the T-head, and the whole derivation is rendered illicit.

In order for this solution to work as desired, it may only apply to T-heads selected by an ECM verb, and only an Acc subject under which such a T-head may be exempt from projection. While the former is a local property, the latter is less clearcut because a clause may contain an unbounded number of VP-adjuncts. If the subject enters in a derivation below these adjuncts, then the distance to the T-head is unbounded. However, if one posits that subjects reside in the higher Spec, vP position, and that VP-adjuncts must adjoin lower than that, the projection context is still local. It is also true that the subject stands in a local configuration to the T-head by virtue of moving there, so a slightly more powerful tier projection mechanism that is at least partially aware of movement can construct the desired tier irrespective of the locus of VP-adjuncts relative to the subject.

3.7 Clauses headed by *for*

Note that the two ECM analyses presented in the previous section make slightly different predictions. With chain-linking, there has to be at least one Nom in the derivation. With lexical licensing, no Nom is needed. This predicts that there should be ECM verbs that do not take any subject, e.g. an ECM-counterpart to *seem*.

(12)   * There seems him to like her.

As far as we know, no language has such ECM-verbs. But something akin to this configuration arises with *for*-clauses.

(13)   For *he/him to leave early is surprising.

If one treats ECMs as a case of special licensing by T_{inf}, then (13) follows immediately if the special behavior of T_{inf} can also be prompted by *for* rather than an ECM verb. The chain-licensing account, on the other hand, has to project *for* as a special licensor of Acc. So the intriguing typological prediction of the chain-licensing account comes at the cost of a less unified treatment of ECM and *for*-clauses.

3.8 Clausal subjects

One final complication arises from the fact that clausal subjects are Acc licensors even though they arguably do not carry Nom.

(14)   That John left early surprised *she/her.

While this may be problematic for syntactic theories of case, it is entirely unsurprising from the TSL perspective. There is no intrinsic property of nodes that qualifies them as potential licensors. Without linguistic stipulations, case-carrying D-heads and functional heads are on equal footing regarding licensing, they are all just nodes of a tree. Suppose, then, that we not only project the mother of a C-head, but also the Merge node checking its category feature (if it exists). This would mean that C-heads are unique in that they cause two Merge nodes to project, the mother m and the selector s. Since all other elements on the tier are always projected together with their selector, clausal subjects cause a unique configuration where the Merge node s has exactly two daughters, one being the Merge node m and the other being some other Merge node dominating a case carrier or licensor. So if we expand the set of potential Acc licensors to also include •, this captures the fact that clausal subjects license Acc on their object (Fig. 8).

4   Discussion

Our treatment of case licensing is far from exhaustive. We focused almost exclusively on English, omitting many important issues such as ergative-absolutive case systems and quirky case in Icelandic. Even for English we had to put aside the complicated and little understood behavior of case assignment in coordination (Progovac, 1998).

Project …	if …		Daughter	Licensing sibling
C + mother + selecting •	always		NOM	T_{fin}
T_{fin} + mother	always		ACC	•, *for*-C, T_{inf}, PRO, NOM
T_{inf} + mother	selected by ECM-verb or *for*		DAT	ACC
PRO + selecting •	always			
NOM + selecting •	always			
ACC + selecting •	not subject under projecting T_{inf}			
DAT+ selecting •	treated as dependent case			

Table 1: Projection rules for structural case tier (left) and what sibling a Merge node must have on the tier based on its daughter(s); if case-licensing is assumed for ACC, T_{inf} need not be projected.

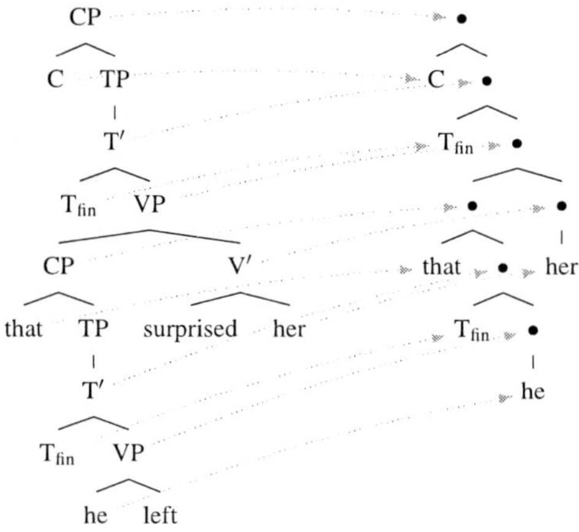

Figure 8: Licensing of an accusative object by the Merge node of a clausal subject

Some readers may also object that the case licensors we identified do not form a natural class. But this presumes a specific notion of naturalness that is based on linguistic substance. This view groups together the heads and phrases involved in case licensing according to their function or meaning. But besides uniformity of substance there is also uniformity of mechanisms, and the TSL view reveals that case is very principled from this perspective.

As can be seen in Tab. 1, the mechanisms of case licensing are highly uniform. The projection function singles out specific heads and their mother and/or selector, and all constraints on the case tier make the daughter of a Merge node m dependent on the sister of m. A single abstract pattern underlies all instances of case licensing. In addition, all parts of the formal machinery fit into TSL (with the possible exception of T_{inf} non-locally blocking projection of the subject). From a computational perspective, then, morphological case marking does not appear to be an oddity that requires special machinery, but a formally uniform phenomenon that can be handled by the compu-

tational mechanisms that are already needed for Merge and Move (Graf, 2018).

Putting substantive naturalness over formal naturalness means missing this insight. We expect that our approach will require various modifications as its empirical scope is widened, but the central role of TSL and the uniformity of mechanisms across phenomena should be preserved.

5 Conclusions

This subregular case study has shown morphological case assignment to be TSL, with ECM as the only problematic case. Even this, though, can be addressed by a tier projection function that is partially sensitive to movement. Since movement interacts with numerous syntactic dependencies, e.g. pronominal binding, a movement-aware tier projection is needed anyways and should be a high priority for future work in subregular syntax.

We also note that the TSL perspective reveals case licensing to be very uniform at a computational level. This is striking considering the lack of a unified theory of case in generative syntax. In fact, our TSL account of case exhibits many abstract parallels to the analysis of Merge and Move in Graf (2018). We are confident that the TSL perspective will prove insightful for many other syntactic phenomena, and we hope that the paper will inspire other researchers to reevaluate syntax through this lens.

References

Alëna Aksënova, Thomas Graf, and Sedigheh Moradi. 2016. Morphotactics as tier-based strictly local dependencies. In *Proceedings of the 14th SIGMOR-PHON Workshop on Computational Research in Phonetics, Phonology, and Morphology*, pages 121–130.

Mark C. Baker and Nadya Vinokurova. 2010. Two modalities of case assignment: Case in Sakha. *Natural Language and Linguistic Theory*, 28(3):593–642.

Noam Chomsky. 1981. *Lectures on Government and Binding: The Pisa Lectures*. Foris, Dordrecht.

Noam Chomsky. 1995. *The Minimalist Program*. MIT Press, Cambridge, MA.

Marina Ermolaeva. 2018. Morphological agreement in Minimalist grammars. In *Proceedings of Formal Grammar 2017*, pages 20–36, Berlin. Springer.

Thomas Graf. 2012. Locality and the complexity of Minimalist derivation tree languages. In *Formal Grammar 2010/2011*, volume 7395 of *Lecture Notes in Computer Science*, pages 208–227, Heidelberg. Springer.

Thomas Graf. 2018. Why movement comes for free once you have adjunction. To appear in *Proceedings of CLS 53*.

Henk Harkema. 2001. A characterization of Minimalist languages. In Philippe de Groote, Glyn Morrill, and Christian Retoré, editors, *Logical Aspects of Computational Linguistics (LACL'01)*, volume 2099 of *Lecture Notes in Artificial Intelligence*, pages 193–211. Springer, Berlin.

Jeffrey Heinz. 2018. The computational nature of phonological generalizations. In Larry Hyman and Frank Plank, editors, *Phonological Typology*, Phonetics and Phonology, chapter 5, pages 126–195. Mouton De Gruyter.

Jeffrey Heinz, Chetan Rawal, and Herbert G. Tanner. 2011. Tier-based strictly local constraints in phonology. In *Proceedings of the 49th Annual Meeting of the Association for Computational Linguistics*, pages 58–64.

Aravind Joshi. 1985. Tree-adjoining grammars: How much context sensitivity is required to provide reasonable structural descriptions? In David Dowty, Lauri Karttunen, and Arnold Zwicky, editors, *Natural Language Parsing*, pages 206–250. Cambridge University Press, Cambridge.

Gregory M. Kobele, Christian Retoré, and Sylvain Salvati. 2007. An automata-theoretic approach to Minimalism. In *Model Theoretic Syntax at 10*, pages 71–80.

Richard K. Larson. 1990. Double objects revisited: Reply to Jackendoff. *Linguistic Inquiry*, 21(4):589–632.

Sabine Laszakovits. 2018. Case theory in Minimalist grammars. In *Proceedings of Formal Grammar 2018*, pages 37–61, Berlin. Springer.

Alec Marantz. 1991. Case and Licensing. In *ESCOL '91: Proceedings of the Eighth Eastern states conference on linguistics*, pages 234–253.

Kevin McMullin. 2016. *Tier-Based Locality in Long-Distance Phonotactics: Learnability and Typology*. Ph.D. thesis, University of British Columbia.

Kevin McMullin and Gunnar Ólafur Hansson. 2015. Long-distance phonotactics as tier-based strictly 2-local languages. In *Proceedings of AMP 2014*.

Jens Michaelis. 2001. Transforming linear context-free rewriting systems into Minimalist grammars. *Lecture Notes in Artificial Intelligence*, 2099:228–244.

Frank Morawietz. 2003. *Two-Step Approaches to Natural Language Formalisms*. Walter de Gruyter, Berlin.

Ljiljana Progovac. 1998. Structure for coordination. *Glot International*, 3(7):3–9.

Edward P. Stabler. 1997. Derivational Minimalism. In Christian Retoré, editor, *Logical Aspects of Computational Linguistics*, volume 1328 of *Lecture Notes in Computer Science*, pages 68–95. Springer, Berlin.

Edward P. Stabler. 2011. Computational perspectives on Minimalism. In Cedric Boeckx, editor, *Oxford Handbook of Linguistic Minimalism*, pages 617–643. Oxford University Press, Oxford.

Mai Ha Vu. 2018. Towards a formal description of NPI-licensing patterns. In *Proceedings of the Society for Computation in Linguistics*, volume 1, pages 154–163.

On Evaluating the Generalization of LSTM Models in Formal Languages

Mirac Suzgun   **Yonatan Belinkov**   **Stuart M. Shieber**

John A. Paulson School of Engineering and Applied Sciences
Harvard University
Cambridge, MA 02138, USA
{msuzgun@college,belinkov@seas,shieber@seas}.harvard.edu

Abstract

Recurrent Neural Networks (RNNs) are theoretically Turing-complete and established themselves as a dominant model for language processing. Yet, there still remains an uncertainty regarding their language learning capabilities. In this paper, we empirically evaluate the inductive learning capabilities of Long Short-Term Memory networks, a popular extension of simple RNNs, to learn simple formal languages, in particular $a^n b^n$, $a^n b^n c^n$, and $a^n b^n c^n d^n$. We investigate the influence of various aspects of learning, such as training data regimes and model capacity, on the generalization to unobserved samples. We find striking differences in model performances under different training settings and highlight the need for careful analysis and assessment when making claims about the learning capabilities of neural network models.[1]

1 Introduction

Recurrent Neural Networks (RNNs) are powerful machine learning models that can capture and exploit sequential data. They have become standard in important natural language processing tasks such as machine translation (Sutskever et al., 2014; Bahdanau et al., 2014) and speech recognition (Sak et al., 2014). Despite the ubiquity of various RNN architectures in natural language processing, there still lies an unanswered fundamental question: What classes of languages can, empirically or theoretically, be learned by neural networks? This question has drawn much attention in the study of formal languages, with previous results on both the theoretical (Siegelmann and Sontag, 1992; Siegelmann, 1995) and empirical capabilities of RNNs, showing that different RNN architectures can learn certain regular (Giles et al.,

1992; Casey, 1996), context-free (Elman, 1991; Das et al., 1992), and context-sensitive languages (Gers and Schmidhuber, 2001).

In a common experimental setup for investigating whether a neural network can learn a formal language, one formulates a supervised learning problem where the network is presented one character at a time and predicts the next possible character(s). The performance of the network can then be evaluated based on its ability to recognize sequences shown in the training set and – more importantly – to generalize to unseen sequences. There are, however, various methods of evaluation in a language learning task. In order to define the *generalization* of a network, one may consider the length of the shortest sequence in a language whose output was incorrectly produced by the network, or the size of the largest accepted test set, or the accuracy on a fixed test set (Rodriguez et al., 1999; Bodén and Wiles, 2000; Gers and Schmidhuber, 2001; Rodriguez, 2001). These formulations follow narrow and bounded evaluation schemes though: They often define a length threshold in the test set and report the performance of the model on this fixed set.

We acknowledge three unsettling issues with these formulations. First, the sequences in the training set are usually assumed to be uniformly or geometrically distributed, with little regard to the nature and complexity of the language. This assumption may undermine any conclusions drawn from empirical investigations, especially given that natural language is not uniformly distributed, an aspect that is known to affect learning in modern RNN architectures (Liu et al., 2018). Second, in a test set where the sequences are enumerated by their lengths, if a network makes an error on a sequence of, say, length 7, but correctly recognizes longer sequences of length up to 1000, would we consider the model's gener-

---

[1]Our code is available at https://github.com/suzgunmirac/lstm-eval.

Proceedings of the Society for Computation in Linguistics (SCiL) 2019, pages 277-286.
New York City, New York, January 3-6, 2019

alization as good or bad? In a setting where we monitor only the shortest sequence that was incorrectly predicted by the network, this scheme clearly misses the potential success of the model after witnessing a failure, thereby misportraying the capabilities of the network. Third, the test sets are often bounded in these formulations, making it challenging to compare and contrast the performance of models if they attain full accuracy on their fixed test sets.

In the present work, we address these limitations by providing a more nuanced evaluation of the learning capabilities of RNNs. In particular, we investigate the effects of three different aspects of a network's generalization: data distribution, length-window, and network capacity. We define an informative protocol for assessing the performance of RNNs: Instead of training a single network until it has learned its training set and then evaluating it on its test set, as Gers and Schmidhuber do in their study, we monitor and test the network's performance at each epoch during the entire course of training. This approach allows us to study the stability of the solutions reached by the network. Furthermore, we do not restrict ourselves to a test set of sequences of fixed lengths during testing. Rather, we exhaustively enumerate all the sequences in a language by their lengths and then go through the sequences in the test set one by one until our network errs k times, thereby providing a more fine-grained evaluation criterion of its generalization capabilities.

Our experimental evaluation is focused on the Long Short-Term Memory (LSTM) network (Hochreiter and Schmidhuber, 1997), a particularly popular RNN variant. We consider three formal languages, namely $a^n b^n$, $a^n b^n c^n$, and $a^n b^n c^n d^n$, and investigate how LSTM networks learn these languages under different training regimes. Our investigation leads to the following insights: (1) The data distribution has a significant effect on generalization capability, with discrete uniform and U-shaped distributions often leading to the best generalization amongst all the four distributions in consideration. (2) Widening the training length-window, naturally, enables LSTM models to generalize better to longer sequences, and interestingly, the networks seem to learn to generalize to shorter sequences when trained on long sequences. (3) Higher model capacity – having more hidden units – leads to better stability, but not

necessarily better generalization levels. In other words, over-parameterized models are more stable than models with theoretically sufficient but far fewer parameters. We explain this phenomenon by conjecturing that a collaborative counting mechanism arises in over-parameterized networks.

2   Related Work

It has been shown that RNNs with a finite number of states can process regular languages by acting like a finite-state automaton using different units in their hidden layers (Giles et al., 1992; Casey, 1996). RNNs, however, are not limited to recognizing only regular languages. Siegelmann and Sontag (1992) and Siegelmann (1995) showed that first-order RNNs (with rational state weights and infinite numeric precision) can simulate a pushdown automaton with two-stacks, thereby demonstrating that RNNs are Turing-complete. In theory, RNNs with infinite numeric precision are capable of expressing recursively enumerable languages. Yet, in practice, modern machine architectures do not contain computational structures that support infinite numeric precision. Thus, the computational power of RNNs with finite precision may not necessarily be the same as that of RNNs with infinite precision.

Elman (1991) investigated the learning capabilities of simple RNNs to process and formalize a context-free grammar containing hierarchical (recursively embedded) dependencies: He observed that distinct parts of the networks were able to learn some complex representations to encode certain grammatical structures and dependencies of the context-free grammar. Later, Das et al. (1992) introduced an RNN with an external stack memory to learn simple context-free languages, such as $a^n b^m$, $a^n b^n cb^m a^m$, and $a^{n+m} b^n c^m$. Similar studies (Kwasny and Kalman, 1995; Wiles and Elman, 1995; Steijvers and Grünwald, 1996; Rodriguez et al., 1999; Bodén and Wiles, 2000) have explored the existence of stable counting mechanisms in simple RNNs, which would enable them to learn various context-free and context-sensitive languages, but none of the RNN architectures proposed in the early days were able to generalize the training set to longer (or more complex) test samples with substantially high accuracy.

Gers and Schmidhuber (2001), on the other hand, proposed a variant of Long Short-Term

Sample	a^2b^2				$a^2b^2c^2$						$a^2b^2c^2d^2$							
Input	a	a	b	b	a	a	b	b	c	c	a	a	b	b	c	c	d	d
Output	a/b	a/b	b	$\dashv$	a/b	a/b	b	c	c	$\dashv$	a/b	a/b	b	c	c	d	d	$\dashv$

Table 1: Example input-output pairs for each language under the sequence prediction formulation.

Memory (LSTM) networks[2] to learn two context-free languages, a^nb^n, $a^nb^mB^mA^n$, and one strictly context-sensitive language, $a^nb^nc^n$. Given only a small fraction of samples in a formal language, with values of n (and m) ranging from 1 to a certain training threshold N, they trained an LSTM model until its full convergence on the training set and then tested it on a more generalized set. They showed that their LSTM model outperformed the previous approaches in capturing and generalizing the aforementioned formal languages. By analyzing the cell states and the activations of the gates in their LSTM model, they further demonstrated that the network learns how to count up and down at certain places in the sample sequences to encode information about the underlying structure of each of these formal languages.

Following this approach, Bodén and Wiles (2002) and Chalup and Blair (2003) studied the stability of the LSTM networks in learning context-free and context-sensitive languages and examined the processing mechanism developed by the hidden states during the training phase. They observed that the weight initialization of the hidden states in the LSTM network had a significant effect on the inductive capabilities of the model and that the solutions were often unstable in the sense that the numbers up to which the LSTM models were able to generalize using the training dataset sporadically oscillated.

3 The Sequence Prediction Task

Following the traditional approach adopted by Elman (1991); Rodriguez (2001); Gers and Schmidhuber (2001) and many other studies, we train our neural network as follows. At each time step, we present one input character to our model and then ask it to predict the set of next possible characters, based on the current character and the prior hidden states.[3] Given a vocabulary $\mathcal{V}^{(i)}$ of size

d, we use a one-hot representation to encode the input values; therefore, all the input vectors are d-dimensional binary vectors. The output values are $(d+1)$-dimensional though, since they may further contain the termination symbol $\dashv$, in addition to the symbols in $\mathcal{V}^{(i)}$. The output values are not always one-hot encoded, because there can be multiple possibilities for the next character in the sequence, therefore we instead use a k-hot representation to encode the output values. Our objective is to minimize the mean-squared error (MSE) of the sequence predictions. During testing, we use an output threshold criterion of 0.5 for the sigmoid output layer to indicate which characters were predicted by the model. We then turn this prediction task into a classification task by *accepting* a sample if our model predicts *all* of its output values correctly and *rejecting* it otherwise.[4]

3.1 Languages

We consider the following three formal languages in our predictions tasks: a^nb^n, $a^nb^nc^n$, and $a^nb^nc^nd^n$, where $n \geq 1$. Of these three languages, the first one is a context-free language and the last two are strictly context-sensitive languages. Table 1 provides example input-output pairs for these languages under the sequence prediction task. In the rest of this section, we formulate the sequence prediction task for each language in more detail.

CFL a^nb^n: The input vocabulary $\mathcal{V}^{(i)}$ for a^nb^n consists of a and b. The output vocabulary $\mathcal{V}^{(o)}$ is the union of $\mathcal{V}^{(i)}$ and $\{\dashv\}$. Therefore, the input vectors are 2-dimensional, and the output vectors are 3-dimensional. Before the occurrence of the first b in a sequence, the model always predicts a or b (which we notate a/b) whenever it

---

[2]For a comprehensive investigation of the LSTM architecture, we invite the reader to refer to the following two papers: (Hochreiter and Schmidhuber, 1997; Greff et al., 2017).

[3]Unlike Gers and Schmidhuber (2001), we do not start each input sequence with a start symbol, since we observed

that having a start symbol in the sequence does not affect the learning capabilities of the model. However, we still use a termination symbol $\dashv$ to encode the end of the sequence in our output samples.

[4]We note that we only present positive samples from a given language to our model, but this approach is still consistent with Gold's Theorem about the inductive interference of formal languages only from positive samples (Angluin, 1980), because we give feedback to our model during training whenever it makes an error about its predictions.

sees an a. However, after it encounters the first b, the rest of the sequence becomes entirely deterministic: Assuming that the model observes n a's in a sequence, it outputs $(n-1)$ b's for the next $(n-1)$ b's and the terminal symbol $\dashv$ for the last b in the sequence. Summarizing, we define the input-target scheme for $a^n b^n$ as follows:

$$a^n b^n \Rightarrow (a/b)^n b^{n-1} \dashv \tag{1}$$

CSL $a^n b^n c^n$: The input vocabulary $\mathcal{V}^{(i)}$ for $a^n b^n c^n$ consists of three characters: a, b, and c. The output vocabulary $\mathcal{V}^{(o)}$ is $\mathcal{V}^{(i)} \cup \{\dashv\}$. The input and output vectors are 3- and 4-dimensional, respectively. The input-target scheme for $a^n b^n c^n$ is:

$$a^n b^n c^n \Rightarrow (a/b)^n b^{n-1} c^n \dashv \tag{2}$$

CSL $a^n b^n c^n d^n$: The vocabulary $\mathcal{V}^{(i)}$ for the last language $a^n b^n c^n d^n$ consists of a, b, c, and d. The input vectors are 4-dimensional, and the output vectors are 5-dimensional. As in the case of the previous two languages, a sequence becomes entirely deterministic after the observance of the first b, hence the input-target scheme for $a^n b^n c^n d^n$ is:

$$a^n b^n c^n d^n \Rightarrow (a/b)^n b^{n-1} c^n d^n \dashv \tag{3}$$

3.2 The LSTM Model

We use a single-layer LSTM model to perform the sequence prediction task, followed by a linear layer that maps to the output vocabulary size. The linear layer is followed by a sigmoid unit layer. The loss is the sum of the mean squared error between the prediction and the correct output at each character. See Figure 1 for an illustration. In our implementation, we used the standard LSTM module in PyTorch (Paszke et al., 2017) and initialized the initial hidden and cell states, h_0 and c_0, to zero.

4 Experimental Setup

4.1 Training and Testing

Training and testing are done in alternating steps: In each epoch, for training, we first present to an LSTM network 1000 samples in a given language, which are generated according to a certain discrete probability distribution supported on a closed finite interval.[5] We then freeze all the weights in our model, exhaustively enumerate all the sequences in the language by their lengths, and determine

---

[5]The strings are presented to the model in a random order.

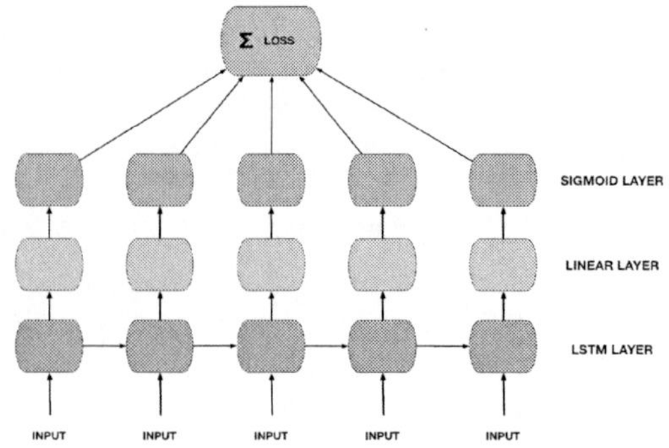

Figure 1: Our LSTM architecture

the first k shortest sequences whose outputs the model produces inaccurately.[6] We remark, for the sake of clarity, that our test design is slightly different from the traditional testing approaches used by Rodriguez et al. (1999); Gers and Schmidhuber (2001); Rodriguez (2001), since we do not consider the shortest sequence in a language whose output was incorrectly predicted by the model, or the largest accepted test set, or the accuracy of the model on a fixed test set.

Our testing approach, as we will see shortly in the following subsections, gives more information about the inductive capabilities of our LSTM networks than the previous techniques and proves itself to be useful especially in the cases where the distribution of the length of our training dataset is skewed towards one of the boundaries of the distribution's support. For instance, LSTM models sometimes fail to capture some of the short sequences in a language during the testing phase[7], but they then predict a large number of long sequences correctly.[8] If we were to report only the shortest sequence whose output our model incorrectly predicts, we would then be unable to capture the model's inductive capabilities. Furthermore, we test and report the performance of the model after each full pass of the training set. Finally, in all our investigations, we repeated each experiment ten times. In each trial, we only changed the

---

[6]In all our experiments, we decided to choose k to be 5.

[7]This phenomenon is usually observed in distributions where the training set is skewed towards having more long sequences than short sequences.

[8]We note that correctly predicting the outputs for the samples ab, abc, and $abcd$ in the languages $a^n b^n$, $a^n b^n c^n$, and $a^n b^n c^n d^n$, respectively, is a hard task, because the output sequences for these samples are $a \dashv$, $ac \dashv$, and $acd \dashv$, in this given order. While they never contain the symbol b in their outputs, the rest of the sequences in their corresponding languages do contain at least one b in their outputs.

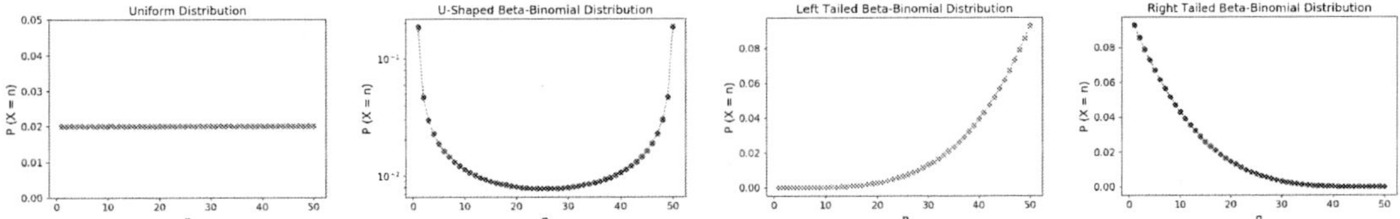

Figure 2: Distributions from Left to Right: Uniform Distribution with $N = 50$, (U-Shaped) Beta-Binomial Distribution with $\alpha = 0.25, \beta = 0.25, N = 49$, (Right-Tailed) Beta-Binomial Distribution with $\alpha = 1, \beta = 5, N = 49$, and (Left-Tailed) Beta-Binomial Distribution with $\alpha = 5, \beta = 1, N = 49$.

weights of the hidden states of the model – all the other parameters were kept the same.

4.2 Length Distributions

Previous studies have examined various length distribution models to generate appropriate training sets for each formal language: Wiles and Elman (1995); Bodén and Wiles (2000); Rodriguez (2001), for instance, used length distributions that were skewed towards having more short sequences than long sequences given a training length-window, whereas Gers and Schmidhuber (2001) used a uniform distribution scheme to generate their training sets. The latter briefly comment that the distribution of lengths of sequences in the training set does influence the generalization ability and convergence speed[9] of neural networks, and mention that training sets containing abundant numbers of both short and long sequences are learned by networks much more quickly than uniformly distributed regimes. Nevertheless, they do not systematically compare or explicitly report their findings. To study the effect of various length distributions on the learning capability and speed of LSTM models, we experimented with four discrete probability distributions supported on bounded intervals (Figure 2) to sample the lengths of sequences for the languages. We briefly recall the probability distribution functions for discrete uniform and Beta-Binomial distributions used in our data generation procedure.

Discrete Uniform Distribution: Given $N \in \mathbb{N}$, if a random variable $X \sim U(1, N)$, then the probability distribution function of X is given as follows:

$$P(x) = \begin{cases} \frac{1}{N} & \text{if } x \in \{1, \dots, N\} \\ 0 & \text{otherwise.} \end{cases}$$

To generate training data with uniformly distributed lengths, we simply draw n from $U(1, N)$ as defined above.

Beta-Binomial Distribution: Similarly, given $N \in \mathbb{Z}^{\geq 0}$ and two parameters α and $\beta \in \mathbb{R}^{>0}$, if a random variable $X \sim \text{BetaBin}(N, \alpha, \beta)$, then the probability distribution function of X is given as follows:

$$P(x) = \begin{cases} \binom{N}{x} \frac{B(x+\alpha, N-x+\beta)}{B(\alpha,\beta)} & \text{if } x \in \{0, \dots, N\} \\ 0 & \text{otherwise.} \end{cases}$$

where $B(\alpha, \beta)$ is the Beta function. We set different values of α and β as such in order to generate the following distributions:

U-shaped ($\alpha = 0.25$, $\beta = 0.25$): The probabilities of having short and long sequences are equally high, but the probability of having an average-length sequence is low.

Right-tailed ($\alpha = 1, \beta = 5$): Short sequences are more probable than long sequences.

Left-tailed ($\alpha = 5, \beta = 1$): Long sequences are more probable than short sequences.

4.3 Length Windows

Most of the previous studies trained networks on sequences of lengths $n \in [1, N]$, where typical N values were between 10 and 50 (Bodén and Wiles, 2000; Gers and Schmidhuber, 2001), and more recently 100 (Weiss et al., 2018). To determine the impact of the choice of training length-window on the stability and inductive capabilities of the LSTM networks, we experimented with three different length-windows for n: $[1, 30]$, $[1, 50]$, and $[50, 100]$. In the third window setting $[50, 100]$, we further wanted to see whether LSTM are capable of generalizing to short sequences that are contained in the window range $[1, 50]$, as well as to sequences that are longer than the sequences seen in the training set.

---

[9] We define *convergence (learning) speed* as the speed at which a sequence of numbers, the e_1 or e_5 values in our cases, converge to its stationary value.

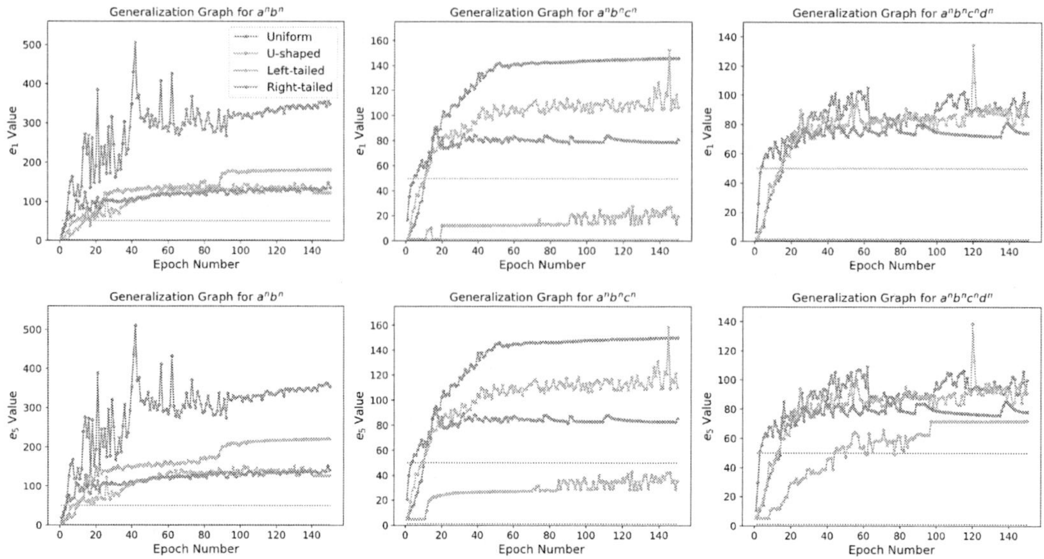

Figure 3: Generalization graphs showing the average performance of LSTMs trained under different probability distribution regimes for each language. The top plots show the e_1 values, whereas the bottom ones the e_5 values. The light blue horizontal lines indicate the training length window $[1, 50]$.

4.4 Model Capacity

It has been shown by Gers and Schmidhuber (2001) that LSTMs can learn $a^n b^n$ and $a^n b^n c^n$ with 1 and 2 hidden units, respectively. Similarly, Hölldobler et al. (1997) demonstrated that a simple RNN architecture containing a single hidden unit with carefully tuned parameters can develop a canonical linear counting mechanism to recognize the simple context-free language $a^n b^n$, for $n \leq 250$. We wanted to explore whether the stability of the networks would improve with an increase in capacity of the LSTM model. We, therefore, varied the number of hidden units in our LSTM models as follows. We experimented with 1, 2, 3, and 36 hidden units for $a^n b^n$; 2, 3, 4, and 36 hidden units for $a^n b^n c^n$; and 3, 4, 5, and 36 hidden units for $a^n b^n c^n d^n$. The 36 hidden unit case represents an over-parameterized network with more than enough theoretical capacity to recognize all these languages.

5 Results

5.1 Length Distributions

Figure 3 exhibits the generalization graphs for the three formal languages trained with LSTM models under different length distribution regimes. Each single-color sequence in a generalization graph shows the average performance of ten LSTMs trained under the same settings but with different weight initializations. In all these experiments, the training sets had the same length-window $[1, 50]$. On the other hand, we used 2, 3, and 4 hidden units in our LSTM architectures for the languages $a^n b^n$, $a^n b^n c^n$, and $a^n b^n c^n d^n$, respectively.[10] The top three plots show the average lengths of the shortest sequences (e_1) whose outputs were incorrectly predicted by the model at test time, whereas the bottom plots show the fifth such shortest lengths (e_5). We note that the models trained on uniformly distributed samples seem to perform the best amongst all the four distributions in all the three languages. Furthermore, for the languages $a^n b^n c^n$ and $a^n b^n c^n d^n$, the U-shaped Beta-Binomial distribution appears to help the LSTM models generalize better than the left- and right-tailed Beta Binomial distributions, in which the lengths of the samples are intentionally skewed towards one end of the training length-window.

When we look at the plots for the e_1 values, we observe that all the distribution regimes seem to facilitate learning at least up to the longest sequences in their respective training datasets, drawn by the light blue horizontal lines on the plots, except for the left-tailed Beta-Binomial distribution for which we see errors at lengths shorter

---

[10]The results with other configurations were qualitatively similar.

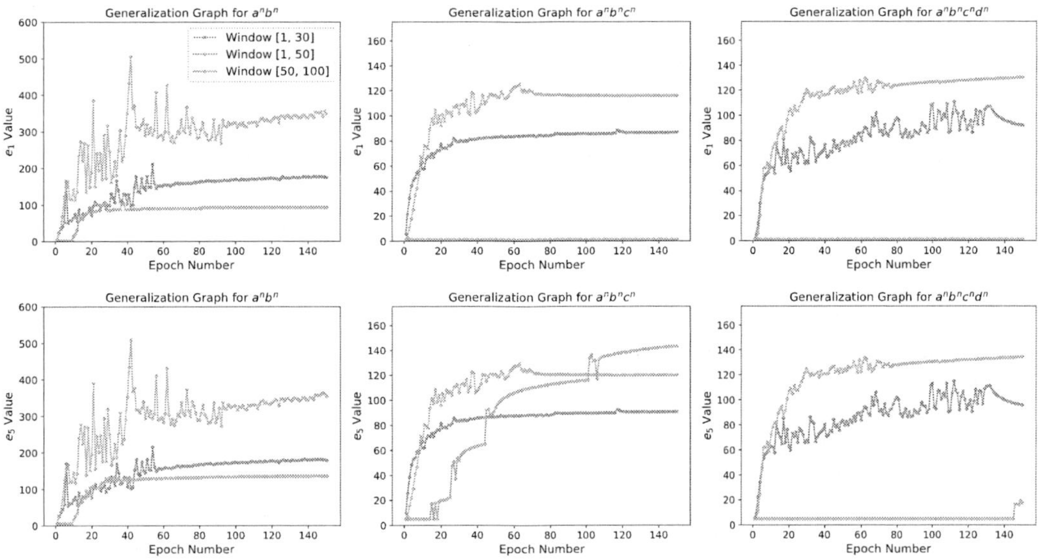

Figure 4: Generalization graphs showing the average performance of LSTMs trained under different training length-windows for each language. The top plots show the e_1 values, whereas the bottom ones the e_5 values.

than the training length threshold in the languages $a^n b^n c^n$ and $a^n b^n c^n d^n$. For instance, if we were to consider only the e_1 values in our analysis, it would be tempting to argue that the model trained under the left-tailed Beta-Binomial distribution regime did not learn to recognize the language $a^n b^n c^n d^n$. By looking at the e_5 values, in addition to the e_1 values, we however realize that the model was actually learning many of the sequences in the language, but it was just struggling to recognize and correctly predict the outputs of some of the short sequences in the language. This phenomenon can be explained by the under-representation of short sequences in left-tailed Beta-Binomial distributions. Our observation clearly emphasizes the significance of looking beyond e_1, the shortest error length at test time, in order to obtain a more complete picture of the model's generalizing capabilities.

5.2 Training Length Windows

Figure 4 shows the generalization graphs for the three formal languages trained with LSTM models under different training windows. We note that enlarging the training length-window, naturally, enables an LSTM model to generalize far beyond its training length threshold. Besides, we see that the models with the training length-window of $[50, 100]$ performed slightly better than the other two window ranges in the case of $a^n b^n c^n$ (green

line, bottom middle plot). Moreover, we acknowledge the capability of LSTMs to recognize longer sequences, as well as shorter sequences. For instance, when trained on the training length-window $[50, 100]$, our models learned to recognize not only the longer sequences but also the shorter sequences not presented in the training sets for the languages $a^n b^n$ and $a^n b^n c^n$.

Finally, we highlight the importance of the e_5 values once again: If we were to consider only the e_1 values, for instance, we would not have captured the inductive learning capabilities of the models trained with a length-window of $[50, 100]$ in the case of $a^n b^n c^n$, since the models always failed at recognizing the shortest sequence ab in the language. Yet, considering e_5 values helped us evaluate the performance of the LSTM models more accurately.

5.3 Number of Hidden Units

There seems to be a positive correlation between the number of hidden units in an LSTM network and its stability while learning a formal language. As Figure 5 demonstrates, increasing the number of hidden units in an LSTM network both increases the network's stability and also leads to faster convergence. However, it does not necessarily result in a better generalization.[11] We conjec-

---

[11]The results shown in the plot are for models that were trained on datasets with uniform length distributions with a

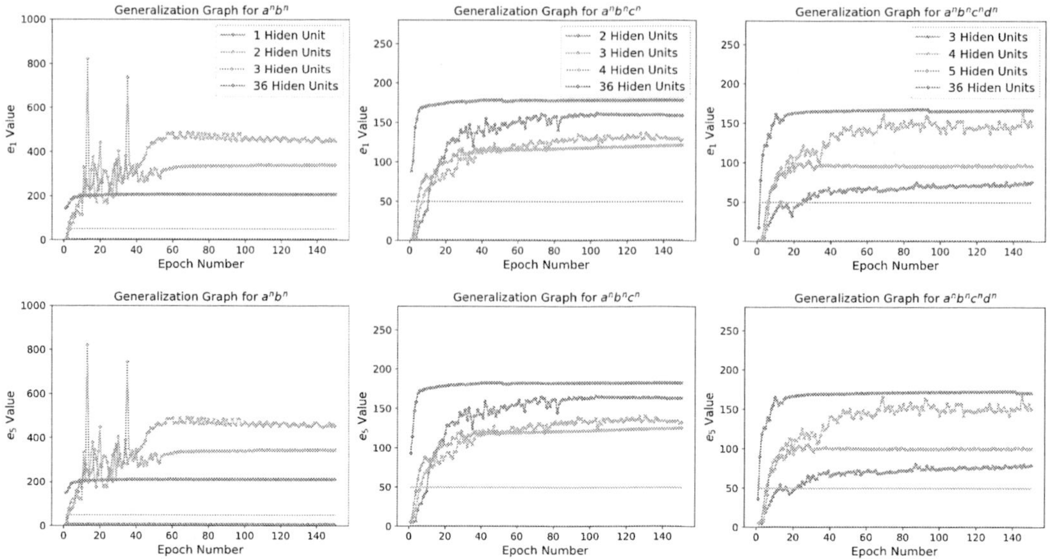

Figure 5: Generalization graphs showing the average performance of LSTM models with a different number of hidden units for each language. The top plots show the e_1 values, whereas the bottom ones the e_5 values. The light blue horizontal lines indicate the training length window $[1, 50]$.

ture that, with more hidden units, we simply offer more resources to our LSTM models to regulate their hidden states to learn these languages. The next section supports this hypothesis by visualizing the hidden state activations during sequence processing.

6 Discussion

In addition to the analysis of our empirical results in the previous section, we would like to touch upon two important characteristics of LSTM models when they learn formal languages, namely the convergence issue and counting behavior of LSTM models.

Convergence: We note that our experiments indicate that LSTM models often do not generalize to the same value in a given experiment setting. Figure 6, for instance, displays the generalization and loss graphs of LSTM models which were trained to recognize the language $a^n b^n c^n$ under a uniform distribution regime with a training window of $[1, 50]$. The figure shows the results of 10 trials with different random weight initializations. While all runs appear to converge to a similar loss value, they have different generalization values (that is, their e_1 values are all different).

____
length window of $[1, 50]$. We observed similar trends with other configurations.

This pattern is fairly common in our experiments, suggesting a disconnection between loss convergence and generalization capability. This result again highlights the importance of performing a fine-grained evaluation of generalization capability, rather than reporting a single number. Our argument is also consistent with those of Bodén and Wiles (2002) and Chalup and Blair (2003), for they also found that the weight initialization affects the inductive capabilities of an LSTM.

Counting Behavior: Here we look at the activation dynamics of the hidden states of the model when processing specific sequences. Figure 7 demonstrates that an LSTM network organizes its hidden state structure in such a way that certain hidden state units learn how to count up and down upon the subsequent encounter of some characters. In the case of $a^{100} b^{100} c^{100} d^{100}$, we observe, for instance, that certain units get activated at time steps 100, 200, and 300. In fact, some units appear to cooperate together to count.

On the other hand, when we visualized the activation dynamics of a model which was trained to learn the language $a^n b^n$ using 36 hidden units, we observed on the testing of $a^{1000} b^{1000}$ that the model still uses some of its hidden units to count up and down for all the a's and b's seen by the model, respectively, although it rejects this sam-

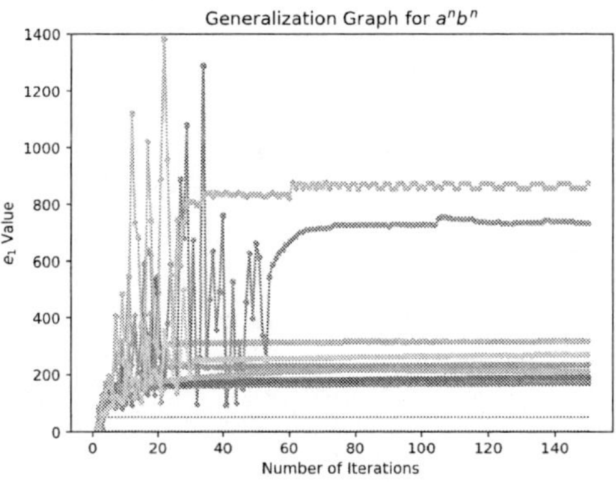
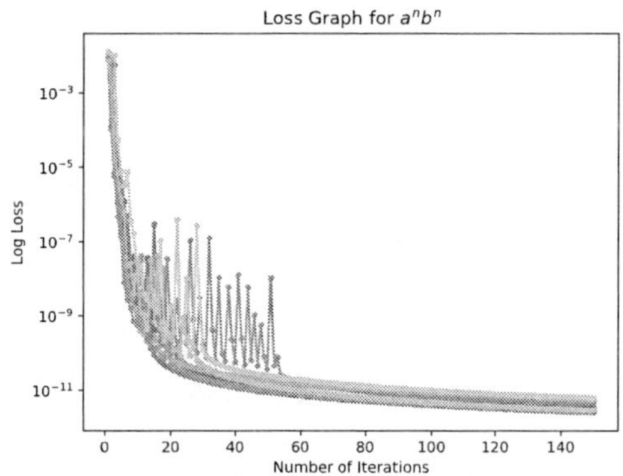

Figure 6: Generalization graph (left) and loss graph (right) with different random weight initializations.

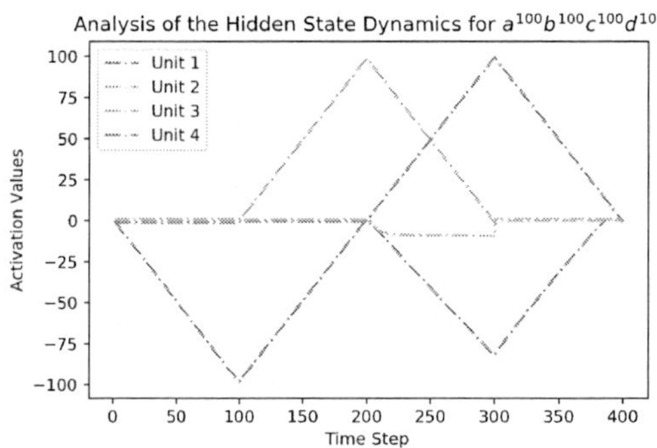

Figure 7: Hidden state dynamics in a four-unit LSTM model. We note that certain units in the LSTM model get activated at time steps 100, 200, and 300.

ple. It simply outputs $(a/b)^{1000}b^{996} \dashv^4$, instead of $(a/b)^{1000}b^{999} \dashv$. Our results corroborate and refine the findings of Gers and Schmidhuber (2001) and Weiss et al. (2018), who noted the existence of a counting mechanisms for simpler languages, while we also observe a collaborative counting behavior in over-parameterized networks.

7 Conclusion

In this paper, we have addressed the influence of various length distribution regimes and length-window sizes on the generalizing ability of LSTMs to learn simple context-free and context-sensitive languages, namely $a^n b^n$, $a^n b^n c^n$, and $a^n b^n c^n d^n$. Furthermore, we have discussed the effect of the number of hidden units in LSTM models on the stability of a representation learned by the network: We show that increasing the number of hidden units in an LSTM model improves the stability of the network, but not necessarily the inductive power. Finally, we have exhibited the importance of weight initialization to the convergence of the network: Our results indicate that different hidden weight initializations can yield different convergence values, given that all the other parameters are unchanged. Throughout our analysis, we emphasized the importance of a fine-grained evaluation, considering generalization beyond the first error and during training. We therefore concluded that there are an abundant number of parameters that can influence the inductive ability of an LSTM to learn a formal language and that the notion of *learning*, from a neural network's perspective, should be treated carefully.

8 Acknowledgment

The first author gratefully acknowledges the support of the Harvard College Research Program (HCRP) and the Harvard Center for Research on Computation and Society Research Fellowship for Undergraduate Students. The second author was supported by the Harvard Mind, Brain, and Behavior Initiative. The authors also thank Sebastian Gehrmann for his helpful comments and discussion at the beginning of the project. The computations in this paper were run on the Odyssey cluster supported by the FAS Division of Science, Research Computing Group at Harvard University.

References

Dana Angluin. 1980. Inductive inference of formal languages from positive data. *Information and control*, 45(2):117–135.

Dzmitry Bahdanau, Kyunghyun Cho, and Yoshua Bengio. 2014. Neural machine translation by jointly learning to align and translate. *arXiv preprint arXiv:1409.0473*.

Mikael Bodén and Janet Wiles. 2000. Context-free and context-sensitive dynamics in recurrent neural networks. *Connection Science*, 12(3-4):197–210.

Mikael Bodén and Janet Wiles. 2002. On learning context-free and context-sensitive languages. *IEEE Transactions on Neural Networks*, 13(2):491–493.

Mike Casey. 1996. The dynamics of discrete-time computation, with application to recurrent neural networks and finite state machine extraction. *Neural computation*, 8(6):1135–1178.

Stephan K Chalup and Alan D Blair. 2003. Incremental training of first order recurrent neural networks to predict a context-sensitive language. *Neural Networks*, 16(7):955–972.

Sreerupa Das, C Lee Giles, and Guo-Zheng Sun. 1992. Learning context-free grammars: Capabilities and limitations of a recurrent neural network with an external stack memory. In *Proceedings of The Fourteenth Annual Conference of Cognitive Science Society. Indiana University*, page 14.

Jeffrey L Elman. 1991. Distributed representations, simple recurrent networks, and grammatical structure. *Machine learning*, 7(2-3):195–225.

Felix A Gers and E Schmidhuber. 2001. LSTM recurrent networks learn simple context-free and context-sensitive languages. *IEEE Transactions on Neural Networks*, 12(6):1333–1340.

C Lee Giles, Clifford B Miller, Dong Chen, Hsing-Hen Chen, Guo-Zheng Sun, and Yee-Chun Lee. 1992. Learning and extracting finite state automata with second-order recurrent neural networks. *Neural Computation*, 4(3):393–405.

Klaus Greff, Rupesh K Srivastava, Jan Koutník, Bas R Steunebrink, and Jürgen Schmidhuber. 2017. LSTM: A search space odyssey. *IEEE transactions on neural networks and learning systems*, 28(10):2222–2232.

Sepp Hochreiter and Jürgen Schmidhuber. 1997. Long short-term memory. *Neural computation*, 9(8):1735–1780.

Steffen Hölldobler, Yvonne Kalinke, and Helko Lehmann. 1997. Designing a counter: Another case study of dynamics and activation landscapes in recurrent networks. In *Annual Conference on Artificial Intelligence*, pages 313–324. Springer.

Stan C Kwasny and Barry L Kalman. 1995. Tail-recursive distributed representations and simple recurrent networks. *Connection Science*, 7(1):61–80.

Nelson F. Liu, Omer Levy, Roy Schwartz, Chenhao Tan, and Noah A. Smith. 2018. LSTMs Exploit Linguistic Attributes of Data. In *Proceedings of the Third Workshop on Representation Learning for NLP*.

Adam Paszke, Sam Gross, Soumith Chintala, Gregory Chanan, Edward Yang, Zachary DeVito, Zeming Lin, Alban Desmaison, Luca Antiga, and Adam Lerer. 2017. Automatic differentiation in PyTorch. In *NIPS-W*.

Paul Rodriguez. 2001. Simple recurrent networks learn context-free and context-sensitive languages by counting. *Neural computation*, 13(9):2093–2118.

Paul Rodriguez, Janet Wiles, and Jeffrey L. Elman. 1999. A Recurrent Neural Network that learns to count. *Connection Science*, 11(1):5–40.

Hasim Sak, Andrew W. Senior, and Françoise Beaufays. 2014. Long short-term memory recurrent neural network architectures for large scale acoustic modeling. In *15th Annual Conference of the International Speech Communication Association (Interspeech)*, pages 338–342.

Hava T Siegelmann. 1995. Computation beyond the Turing limit. *Science*, 268(5210):545–548.

Hava T Siegelmann and Eduardo D Sontag. 1992. On the computational power of neural nets. In *Proceedings of the fifth annual workshop on Computational learning theory*, pages 440–449. ACM.

Mark Steijvers and Peter Grünwald. 1996. A recurrent network that performs a context-sensitive prediction task. In *Proceedings of the 18th annual conference of the cognitive science society*, pages 335–339.

Ilya Sutskever, Oriol Vinyals, and Quoc V. Le. 2014. Sequence to Sequence Learning with Neural Networks. In *Advances in neural information processing systems*, pages 3104–3112.

Gail Weiss, Yoav Goldberg, and Eran Yahav. 2018. On the practical computational power of finite precision rnns for language recognition. In *Proceedings of the 56th Annual Meeting of the Association for Computational Linguistics (Volume 2: Short Papers)*, pages 740–745. Association for Computational Linguistics.

Janet Wiles and Jeff Elman. 1995. Learning to count without a counter: A case study of dynamics and activation landscapes in recurrent networks. In *Proceedings of the seventeenth annual conference of the cognitive science society*, s 482, page 487. Erlbaum Hillsdale, NJ.

Verb Argument Structure Alternations in
Word and Sentence Embeddings

Katharina Kann*, Alex Warstadt*, Adina Williams* and Samuel R. Bowman
New York University, USA
{kann, warstadt, adinawilliams, bowman}@nyu.edu

Abstract

Verbs occur in different syntactic environments, or frames. We investigate whether artificial neural networks encode grammatical distinctions necessary for inferring the idiosyncratic frame-selectional properties of verbs. We introduce five datasets, collectively called FAVA, containing in aggregate nearly 10k sentences labeled for grammatical acceptability, illustrating different verbal argument structure alternations. We then test whether models can distinguish acceptable English verb–frame combinations from unacceptable ones using a sentence embedding alone. For converging evidence, we further construct LaVA, a corresponding word-level dataset, and investigate whether the same syntactic features can be extracted from word embeddings. Our models perform reliable classifications for some verbal alternations but not others, suggesting that while these representations do encode fine-grained lexical information, it is incomplete or can be hard to extract. Further, differences between the word- and sentence-level models show that some information present in word embeddings is not passed on to the downstream sentence embeddings.

1 Introduction

Artificial neural networks (ANNs) are powerful computational models that are able to implicitly learn syntactic and semantic features necessary for a variety of natural language tasks. These empirical results raise a deeper scientific question: to what extent do the features learned by ANNs resemble the linguistic competence of humans?

Studying the linguistic competence of ANNs, in addition to its intrinsic value for model evaluation, can help resolve outstanding scientific questions in linguistics about the role of prior grammatical bias

in human language acquisition. Chomsky (1965) suggests that the acquisition of rich grammatical distinctions is facilitated by an innate universal grammar (UG), which imparts specific grammatical knowledge to the learner. This proposal crucially depends on the *poverty of the stimulus* argument, which holds that the acquisition of certain linguistic features by purely domain-general data-driven learning should not be possible (Clark and Lappin, 2011). Studying the ability of low-bias learners like ANNs to acquire specific grammatical knowledge can provide evidence relevant to this argument.

In this work, we evaluate ANNs' treatment of verbs; verbs contribute to the overall meaning of sentences by encoding information about how entities are related to, and participate in, events. Concretely, we investigate if ANNs acquire the specific grammatical distinctions necessary for inferring the frame-selectional properties of verbs. Cross-linguistically, the lexical entry of a verb is associated with a set of syntactic contexts or *syntactic frames* in which it can appear. This information is lexically idiosyncratic, i.e., even verbs that are intuitively very similar in meaning may vary as to which syntactic frames they can appear in:

(1) a. Sharon **sprayed** water on the plants.
      b. Sharon **sprayed** the plants with water.
      c. Carla **poured** lemonade into the pitcher.
      d. *Carla **poured** the pitcher with lemonade.[1]

Certain verbs, e.g., *spray*, select multiple related frames and are therefore known as *alternating verbs*. In contrast, other semantically similar verbs, e.g., *pour*, select only a single frame and are thus not alternating. Information about whether a given verb alternates (as well as which frames it

---

*The first three authors contributed equally and are listed in alphabetical order.

[1] In this paper, stars mark ungrammatical sentences.

Proceedings of the Society for Computation in Linguistics (SCiL) 2019, pages 287-297.
New York City, New York, January 3-6, 2019

Verb Frame	Example Sentences		
Caus.	Jessica **dropped** the vase.	Jessica blew the bubble.	
Inch.	The vase **dropped**.	*The bubble blew.	
Dative-Prep.	Liz **gave** a gift to the boy.	Liz administered a test to the kid.	*Liz charged $50 to Jon.
Dative-2-Obj.	Liz **gave** the boy a gift.	*Liz administered the kid a test.	Liz charged Jon $50.
Spr.-Lo.-*with*	Sue **loaded** the truck with wood.	Sue coated the deck with paint.	*Sue swept the bin with sand.
Spr.-Lo.-Loc.	Sue **loaded** wood onto the truck.	*Sue coated paint on the deck.	Sue swept sand into the bin.
no-*there*	Fear **remained** in my mind.	A girl focused on the quiz.	
there	There **remained** fear in my mind.	*There focused on the quiz a girl.	
U.-Obj.-Refl.	Ada **clapped** her hands.	Ada permed her hair.	*Ada exercised herself.
U.-Obj.-No-Refl.	Ada **clapped.**	*Ada permed.	Ada exercised.

Table 1: Examples from each verb frame in the dataset. Bolded verbs evoke both verb frames; other verbs evoke only one. Transitive verb frames include: Causative, SPRAY–LOAD *with*, SPRAY–LOAD locative, UNDERSTOOD-OBJECT reflexive. Intransitive verb frames include: Inchoative, no-*there* (with locative adjunct), *there* (with locative adjunct), and UNDERSTOOD-OBJECT no-reflexive. 2-obj. class includes a ditransitive frame and a prepositional dative frame.

can appear in) has been described and classified in several verb lexica (Grishman et al., 1994; Baker et al., 1998; Fillmore et al., 2003; Kipper-Schuler, 2005; Kipper-Schuler et al., 2006). Knowledge about verb frames and their alternations is part of a human speaker's linguistic competence, and as such, should potentially be learned by ANNs.

We present two datasets and two experiments that compare ANNs' knowledge of verb frame alternations at the word level and the sentence level, respectively. First, we ask if a verb's word embedding can be used to predict which frames that verb can licitly appear in. We construct a dataset of verbs, the **Lexical Verb–frame Alternations** dataset (LaVA), based on Levin (1993), and train a multi-class classifier to identify the licit syntactic frames associated with a verb from its word embedding alone (if successful, the classifier should be able to determine, e.g., that *sprayed* alternates and can appear in sentences with *with*-alternants like (1-b), but that *poured* cannot (1-d)).

Second, we ask whether sentence embeddings encode the frame-selectional properties of their main verb. The main verb's frame-selectional properties have consequences for grammaticality at the sentence level; to give an example, (1-d) is not grammatical, because *poured* cannot participate in this frame alternation. To exploit this, we semi-automatically generate sentences in such a way to ensure that the main verb's frame alternation information is the only information determining the (un)grammaticality of the sentence. For a portion of the sentences, the main verb can participate in a given verb frame alternation, and for another portion it cannot; if the main verb cannot

participate in the alternation, then one of the sentences in the pair will be ungrammatical. Using this dataset, the **F**rames and **A**lternations of **V**erbs **A**cceptability dataset (FAVA), we train a binary classifier to judge the acceptability of sentences containing verbs in various syntactic contexts using the sentence embeddings alone.

We find that verb frame information is extractable from both word embeddings and sentence embeddings, but that these two complementary methods differ in performance. The LaVA and FAVA datasets are available under `https://nyu-mll.github.io/CoLA` for future research and model evaluation.

2 Verb Frame Alternations

The lexical meaning of each verb includes a description of an event and how entities participate in it (Fillmore, 1966; Fillmore et al., 2003), and this information is present for the various syntactic frames associated with each verb. To determine whether our ANNs encode this information, we select five verb frame alternations from Levin (1993); the verb frames which comprise each alternation vary either in the number of arguments they can take, in the order in which the arguments appear, or in both. Examples are given in Table 1, and statistics are provided in Tables 2 and 3.

To give an example, in (1-a), there is an event of *spraying* in which *Sharon* is the main actor (often referred to as *agent*), *the plants* is the entity affected by the event (i.e., the *patient*), and *water* is the entity used in the event (i.e., the *instrument* or *theme*). In (1-a), the verb frame of *spray* has three

| Levin class | CAUS.–INCH. | | DATIVE | | SPRAY–LOAD | | *there*-INSERTION | | UNDERSTOOD-OBJECT | |
	Inch.	Caus.	Prep.	2-Obj.	*with*	Loc.	no-*there*	*there*	Refl.	No-Refl.
Positive	70	120	63	72	90	81	50	145	11	81
Negative	140	(0)	356	405	220	229	185	(0)	466	396
Total	210	120	419	477	310	310	235	145	477	477

Table 2: Overview of the lexical dataset. "Positive" refers to the number of verbs that evoke each frame (i.e., will yield a grammatical sentence) and "negative" refers to the number of verbs which do not evoke those frames (i.e., will yield an ungrammatical sentence). Causative and *there* sentence frames have no negative examples (i.e., every verb participating in the alternation can instantiate these frames).

roles, and they come in a specific order: the *agent* is the subject, the *instrument* is the object, and the *patient* or *location* is part of a prepositional phrase adjoined to the verb. Participants (e.g., *Sharon* and *water*) that are provided by the verb are called *arguments* of the verb; the other argument *the plants* is within a prepositional phrase and is therefore not provided by the verb.

Whether a verb can introduce a given number of arguments can affect its sentence-level grammaticality and is therefore of interest here. Verbs can be *intransitive*, taking only one argument (e.g., *dropped* in *the vase dropped.*), *transitive*, taking two arguments (e.g., *dropped* in *Jessica dropped the vase*), or *ditransitive*, taking three arguments (e.g., *gave*, in *Liz gave the boy a gift*).

Two different verb frames may be related by the addition or deletion of an argument (e.g., CAUSATIVE-INCHOATIVE), or by realizing the same arguments in a different syntactic configuration (e.g., SPRAY-LOAD; (1-a) and (1-b)). When several verbs with similar argument structures can productively appear in such related verb frames, this is called an *argument structure alternation*. Examples are listed in Table 2.

For some alternations, there are examples of verbs that participate in both frames (e.g., are positive examples for both dative and double object frames), only the first frame (e.g., are positive examples for the dative frame, but negative examples for the double object one), or only the second frame (e.g., are positive examples for the double object frame and negative ones for the dative frame). However, full empirical coverage is not always possible for every alternation. In our corpora, two of our alternations (CAUSATIVE-INCHOATIVE and *there*-INSERTION) are sparse; some of their frames cannot be provided with negative examples. We discuss this issue in more detail in Section 3.1).

3 Datasets

In this section, we describe in detail our word-level dataset, which we call the **Lexical Verb-frame Alternations dataset (LaVA)**; and the corresponding sentence-level dataset, which we call the **Frames and Alternations of Verbs Acceptability dataset (FAVA)**. Five argument structure alternations are chosen and verbs that evoke at least one frame of the alternation are included in our lexical corpus. These verbs are subsequently used to semi-automatically create a sentence acceptability corpus for our second experiment. We describe our selected argument structure alternations in the remainder of this section and introduce our corpora.

3.1 LaVA—The Lexical Corpus

We construct LaVA from 515 verbs manually mined from five of the largest syntactic verb frame alternations provided by Levin (1993): CAUSATIVE-INCHOATIVE, DATIVE, SPRAY-LOAD, *there*-INSERTION, and UNDERSTOOD-OBJECT. Each alternation consists of two different syntactic frames. Our dataset lists whether each verb participates in each frame (wherever available, see the subsection on sparsity below); the alternations and their verb frames are described in the following.

CAUSATIVE–INCHOATIVE Alternation The CAUSATIVE–INCHOATIVE (Sundén, 1916; Fillmore, 1966; Hale and Keyser, 1986, 2002) dataset is an expanded version of the CAUSATIVE–INCHOATIVE dataset from Warstadt et al. (2018), and it contrasts verbs which can evoke both causative and inchoative frames, like *drop* in Table 1, with verbs that can evoke only the causative frame, like *blow*. Importantly, the causative frame is *transitive*—taking two syntactic arguments—and the inchoative frame is *intransitive*—taking only one. In the causative frame, the subject (e.g., *Jessica*) causes the object (e.g., *the vase*) to undergo a change of state (e.g., to be *dropped*), but, in the inchoative frame, the argument which undergoes a change of state is the subject.

DATIVE Alternation The DATIVE (Bresnan, 1980; Marantz, 1984; Larson, 1988) dataset consists of verbs that indicate transfer of possession; both frames evoked by these verbs take three arguments, but the two frames differ in the order of arguments. In the prepositional dative frame, the *theme* is the syntactic object of the verb, and the *recipient* is within a prepositional phrase; in the dative double object frame, there is no prepositional phrase, and both the *theme* and the *recipient* appear after the verb. Table 1 provides examples from the three sets of verbs: one set of verbs evokes both the prepositional dative frame and the double object frame (e.g., *give*), another set only evokes the prepositional dative frame and not the double object frame (e.g., *administered*), and the last set of verbs only evokes the double object frame, but not the prepositional dative frame (e.g., *charged*).

SPRAY–LOAD Alternation The SPRAY–LOAD (Tenny, 1987; Levin and Hovav, 1995; Arad, 2006) dataset includes transitive verb frames that relate to putting objects in places or covering things with other objects as described in Section 2.

***There*-INSERTION Alternation** The *there*-INSERTION (Poutsma, 1904; Milsark, 1974; Szabolcsi, 1986) dataset contains intransitive verbs that can evoke a frame in which the subject of the sentence (e.g., *fear*) follows the verb (as in *There remained fear in my mind.*, despite the fact that it would usually appear before the verb in other frames; for these sentences the subject position is filled with a dummy word, *there*. The *there* frame requires a prepositional phrase adjunct— e.g., *There remained fear *(in my mind)*—but the no-*there* frame does not—e.g., *Fear remained (in my mind)*. Verbs that evoke both frames are verbs of existence, spatial configuration, meandering movement, manner of motion, appearance, and inherently directed motion.

UNDERSTOOD-OBJECT Alternation The UNDERSTOOD-OBJECT (Rice, 1988; Levin, 1993) dataset contains verb frames that vary in transitivity and describe conventionalized movements of body parts. In the transitive UNDERSTOOD-OBJECT reflexive frame, the body part is the object of the verb (e.g., *Ada clapped her hands.*). In the intransitive UNDERSTOOD-OBJECT no-reflexive frame, the affected *theme* participant (e.g., the body part, or *hands*) is recoverable from the verb (e.g., *clapped*) even though the frame does not require the *theme* (i.e., we know that Ada is clapping her hands and not something else when we interpret the object-less sentence *Ada clapped*).

Sparsity Due to the nature of verb argument structure alternations, in some cases no negative examples can be obtained. For instance, there are no English verbs that can appear in the inchoative, but not the causative (see the first two columns of Table 2). This means that, for the CAUSATIVE–INCHOATIVE alternation, verbs can either evoke both causative and inchoative frames (i.e., be positive examples for both frames) or just the causative frame (i.e., be a positive example for causative and a negative example for inchoative). Similarly, there are verbs that can appear in only no-*there*, but no verbs that can only appear in the *there* frame. This leads to sparsity of annotations. As a result, word-level classifications for these frames are trivial.

Another factor that contributes to data sparsity is that our lexical corpus relies on verbs that Levin (1993) provides as positive (i.e., *grammatical*) or negative (i.e., *ungrammatical*) examples; it does not provide grammaticality judgments for each verb in every frame. In some cases, this is for a linguistic reason: CAUSATIVE–INCHOATIVE alternation verbs can take at most two arguments, and thus do not appear in frames requiring 3 arguments like the prepositional dative or double object frames. In other cases, there is no obvious reason for a particular verb to not appear in another frame, but the annotations in Levin (1993) do not provide that verb–frame combination. In many of these cases, we augment Levin's judgments with our own, also semi-automatically, in attempts to alleviate this issue. However, despite these efforts, the resulting dataset is still sparse, i.e., it does not list whether every verb is a positive or negative example for every frame.

3.2 FAVA—Acceptability Judgments Corpus

FAVA is a set of nearly 10k sentences with acceptability judgments. It is constructed semi-

Levin Class	Sentences	% Positive
CAUSATIVE–INCHOATIVE	1168	78.9
DATIVE	644	70.2
SPRAY–LOAD	5127	58.6
there-INSERTION	718	77.0
UNDERSTOOD-OBJECT	705	54.2

Table 3: Sentence counts for our acceptability corpus. "% Positive" is the percentage of sentences that count as acceptable, i.e., as positive examples.

automatically from the verbs in the lexical corpus; Table 3 provides a brief overview.

Two of the authors, both trained as linguists, manually construct lexical sets consisting of verbs with similar frame-selectional properties that are paired with semantically plausible nouns (and prepositions, where needed). These lexical sets are used to automatically generate sentences with different syntactic frames. For example, the lexical set in (2) is used to generate 18 minimal pairs of sentences as in (3) (one pair for each combination of verb, patient, location, and preposition).

(2) verbs = {hung, draped}
patients = {the blanket, the towel, the cloth}
locations = {the bed, the armchair, the couch}
prepositions = {over}

(3) a. Betty draped the blanket over the couch.
b. *Betty draped the couch with the blanket.

A similar, semi-automatic sentence creation method focusing only on the passive alternation (and non-argument structure syntactic reorderings using negation and relative clauses) was employed by Ettinger et al. (2016) and Warstadt et al. (2018).

Using this method, we construct five sentence-level datasets highlighting different verb alternations (CAUSATIVE–INCHOATIVE,[2] DATIVE, SPRAY–LOAD, *there*-INSERTION, UNDERSTOOD-OBJECT) that are chosen so that sentences could be generated with the maximum of variability in the choice of verbs. We split our data into training, development, and test sets by binning lexical sets into training and evaluation bins randomly, in equal proportions. The evaluation set is then split 80/20 into test and development set. Splitting by lexical bin rather than by sentence prevents models from finding a trivial solution to classification by learning to recognize specific verbs and verbal arguments from the training set in the evaluation or test set.

4 Pre-Trained Representations

Embeddings, i.e., vector representations of linguistic objects like characters, words, or sentences, encode helpful information for downstream applications (Mikolov et al., 2013). In particular, they can be used to leverage knowledge from one task for another and have been shown to improve performance on a diverse set of tasks. Embeddings are usually low-dimensional; common sizes differ between 100 and 300. Our experiments make use of three types of word and sentence embeddings, which we will describe in the following.

Word Embeddings For our word-level experiments, we use two different embeddings which differ in the way of their creation. First, we use 300-dimensional GloVe embeddings trained on 6B tokens (Pennington et al., 2014).[3] GloVe embeddings are used frequently in natural language processing (NLP), so evaluating them for knowledge of verb frames will be relevant for their application to and future research on tasks requiring rich syntactic features. Second, we use embeddings trained on the smaller 100M token British National Corpus[4] (BNC), optimizing a language modeling objective. The language model (LM) is a (single-directional) LSTM trained by Warstadt et al. (2018) using PyTorch and optimized using Adam (Kingma and Ba, 2015). The BNC data is tokenized using NLTK (Bird and Loper, 2004) and words outside the 100k most frequent words in the BNC are replaced with <unk>.

Our peripheral interest in how humans learn lexical frame-selectional properties motivates us to investigate these LM-trained word embeddings. We reduce the potential differences between human learners and our models by considering embeddings that are trained on an amount of data similar to what humans are exposed to during language acquisition. For this reason, most publicly available, pre-trained word vectors are a rather unnatural fit, since these embeddings are usually trained on several orders of magnitude more data than humans see in a lifetime.[5]

---

[2] The CAUSATIVE–INCHOATIVE dataset presented here is an expanded version of an analysis dataset in Warstadt et al. (2018).

[3] http://nlp.stanford.edu/data/glove.6B.zip
[4] http://www.natcorp.ox.ac.uk
[5] If we extrapolate from data gathered by Hart and Risley

Sentence Embeddings We further produce sentence embeddings with the help of an existing sentence encoder. Namely, we employ the sentence encoder trained by Warstadt et al. (2018) which performs best in their downstream acceptability classification task. The encoder is trained on a real/fake discrimination task. This is a binary classification task in which a model learns to distinguish *naturally occurring* sentences in the BNC from *fake* sentences. Fake sentences themselves are either generated by a LM or by permuting naturally occurring sentences. The real/fake dataset consists of about 12M sentences, including about 6M sentences from the BNC, about 3M million LM-generated sentences, and 3M permuted sentences. The data is tokenized and unknown words replaced in the same way as in the LM training data. A development set is used for early stopping. 20 real/fake encoders are trained for 7 days or until the completion of 4 training epochs without improvement in Matthews correlation coefficient on the development set.

The architecture of the real/fake encoder is shown in Figure 1. A bidirectional long-short term memory network (LSTM, Hochreiter and Schmidhuber, 1997) reads the words of a sentence. A fixed-length sentence embedding is then produced by a max-pooling operation over the concatenations of the forward and backward hidden states at each time-step. This encoding serves as input to a sigmoid output layer, which outputs a binary prediction. The input to the encoder are ELMo-style (Peters et al., 2018) contextualized word embeddings from a trained LM. As in ELMo, the representation for a word w_i is a linear combination of the hidden states h_i^j for each layer j in an LSTM LM, though we depart from that paper by using only a forward LM.

As argued in Warstadt et al. (2018), this sentence encoder is a reasonable model for a human learner because it is not exposed to any knowledge of language that could not plausibly be part of the input to a human learner. Its training data consists of the same 100 million tokens used to train the word embeddings, augmented with another 100 million generated tokens in the *fake* data.

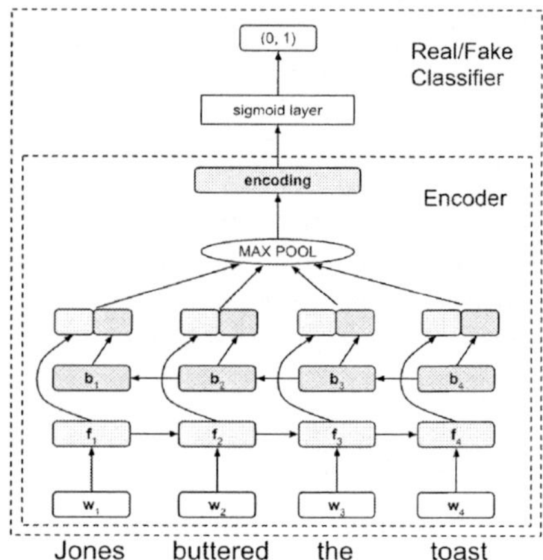

Figure 1: Real/fake model. w_i = word embeddings, f_i = forward LSTM hidden state, b_i = backward LSTM hidden state. Figure from Warstadt et al. (2018).

5 Experiment 1: From Word Embeddings to Argument Structures

In our first experiment, we aim at classifying acceptable syntactic frames, given embeddings for each of the verbs.

5.1 Model

Architecture We cast the identification of syntactic frames in which a verb can appear as a multi-label classification problem. We train one classifier per alternation, and the classes to be predicted correspond to the participating frames (cf. Table 1), i.e., each classifier predicts values for 2 different classes.

Employing a multi-layer perceptron (MLP) with a single hidden layer, the probability of a syntactic frame s being acceptable for a given verb is modeled as:

$$p(s) = \sigma(W_2(f(W_1 x))) \tag{1}$$

Here, x is the input, i.e., a word embedding representing a given verb, W_1 and W_2 are weight matrices, σ denotes the sigmoid function, and the activation function f is a rectified linear unit (ReLU).

Hyperparameters and Training Regime We employ the same hyperparameters for all word-level classifiers. In particular, we use 30-dimensional hidden states; note that the size of the embedding vectors is defined by the type of embeddings we use. During the final classification, we use a threshold of 0.7 to map the model's predictions to binary outputs.

For training, we use the Adam (Kingma and Ba, 2015) optimizer. All ANNs are trained for 15 epochs, but we apply the best performing model on the test set. Further, we use 4-fold cross-validation: the set of verbs is split into 4 equally sized parts out of which 2 are chosen to be the training set, 1 functions as the development set and 1 as the test set.

5.2 Metrics

We report both accuracy and Matthews correlation coefficient (MCC, Matthews, 1975) for this and the following experiment (cf. Section 6), but primarily rely on MCC for evaluation following Warstadt et al. (2018). MCC is a special case of Pearson's r for binary classification. It measures correlation between two binary distributions in the range from -1 to 1, with any two unrelated distributions having a score of 0, regardless of class imbalance. As such, this metric is more robust to unbalanced classification than traditional metrics like F1 or accuracy, both of which favor classifiers with a majority class bias.

5.3 Results

Table 4 shows our results. Our first observation is that, overall, accuracies for GloVe and CoLA-style embeddings are comparable for all classes. This suggests that they both contain similar information about verbs and syntactic frames, and is in line with the fact that both embeddings are based on co-occurrences of words.

Second, we find that, for GloVe embeddings, the MLP performs on par with the majority baseline for some verb frames, namely causative and *there*, as well as DATIVE prep. and DATIVE 2-Obj.; a look at the model predictions reveals that it indeed predicts the majority class for all examples. In this case, MCC will be zero, which is indicative of situations where the model predictions are no better than random. We will not further analyze these cases, since the results likely indicate that our lexical dataset does not contain enough examples for the model to learn from, and, thus, do not tell us anything meaningful about the embeddings. We would like to note that methods which explicitly account for skewed datasets might help for DATIVE prep. and DATIVE 2-Obj., but we leave an investigation of such methods for future work.

Finally, we obtain a weak (0.1–0.5) to moderate (0.5–0.7) MCC for both embedding methods and all other classes (with the MLP's accuracy also of-ten being higher than that of the majority baseline). This indicates that information about the evoked syntactic frames can indeed be extracted from verb embeddings. Relatively good performance (>0.45) is found for the inchoative frame (both embeddings), the DATIVE 2-Obj. frame (CoLA), the *with* frame (both embeddings), and *no*-there frame (both embeddings). Since our classification method (an MLP) is rather simple, our results can be considered a lower-bound on performance, thus showing that verb-frame information is rather obvious in our investigated embeddings.

6 Experiment 2: From Acceptability to Acceptable Argument Structures

Linguists are able to arrive at a classification of a verb according to its syntactic frames by interrogating whether sentences with a given verb and frame are acceptable. Analogously, we can observe whether a verb's frame-selectional properties can be extracted from a sentence embedding by training an acceptability classifier to distinguish sentences with acceptable from sentences with unacceptable verb-frame combinations. If a classifier is able to reliably classify all minimal pairs of several verbs with different frame-selectional properties from a sentence embedding alone, we can infer that the sentence embedding contains enough information to distinguish both the frame-selectional properties of the verbs and the relevant syntactic frames.

Model Our acceptability classifier is again an MLP with a single hidden layer. We model the probability that a that sentence S is acceptable as:

$$p(S) = \sigma(W_2(tanh(W_1 x))) \qquad (2)$$

Here x is the input, a sentence embedding obtained from the real/fake sentence encoder described in Section 4, W_1 and W_2 are weight matrices, σ denotes the sigmoid function, and $tanh$ is the hyperbolic tangent activation function. We use a threshold of 0.5 to map the model's predictions to binary outputs.

Training Details To select hyperparameters, we train 20 acceptability classifiers on each of the five datasets, and an additional 20 classifiers on a dataset produced by aggregating all the datasets. We repeat all experiments augmenting each dataset with the more than 10k sentences

		CAUSATIVE–INCHOATIVE		DATIVE		SPRAY–LOAD		*there*-INSERTION		UNDERSTOOD-OBJECT	
		Inch.	(Caus.)	Prep.	2-Obj.	*with*	Loc.	no-*there*	(*there*)	Refl.	Non-Refl.
CoLA: Majority BL	Acc.	66.7	(100.0)	85.0	84.9	71.0	73.9	78.7	(100.0)	97.7	83.0
CoLA: MLP	MCC	**0.555**	0.0	0.32	**0.482**	**0.645**	0.253	**0.459**	0.0	0.0	0.219
	Acc.	81.0	(100.0)	86.6	88.3	85.8	72.9	84.3	(100.0)	97.7	79.0
GloVe: Majority BL	Acc.	66.8	(100.0)	85.0	85.3	71.0	74.6	79.1	(100.0)	97.6	81.5
GloVe: MLP	MCC	**0.672**	0.0	0.0	0.0	**0.585**	0.145	**0.536**	0.0	0.0	0.3
	Acc.	85.5	(100.0)	85.0	85.3	83.9	73.4	85.8	(100.0)	97.6	73.2

Table 4: Results from Experiment 1 for CoLA-style embeddings (top) and GloVe embeddings (bottom); "Majority BL" denotes the majority baseline. Bolded MCC values represent reasonably strong correlations (above 0.45). Results for the majority baselines differ due to different words not having a vector representation within the respective embeddings. The corpus does not contain negative examples for caus. and *there* frames (parenthetical); these results cannot be interpreted and are only included for completeness.

from the corpus of linguistic acceptability (CoLA) built by Warstadt et al. (2018). Hyperparameters are chosen by random search within the following ranges: hidden size $\in [20, 100]$, learning rate $\in [10^2, 10^5]$, and dropout rate $\in \{0.2, 0.5\}$. All models are trained using early stopping with a patience of 20 epochs.

6.1 Results

Table 5 shows results for acceptability classification on the verb–frame datasets. These results lead us to conclude that the sentence encoder we test does reliably encode some fine-grained lexical information, but fails to do so in all cases. Our models are able to perform reliable acceptability classifications on several of the alternations featured in FAVA, achieving a moderate correlation (0.5–0.7) in 5 out of 12 experiments, and a strong correlation ($>$0.7) in one experiment. Most classifiers achieve a correlation above 0.3.

Across all verb classes, augmenting the training data with CoLA examples lowers MCC. However, when evaluating on the aggregate dataset augmenting the training data with CoLA improves MCC. One explanation for this might be that the distribution from which the test set is drawn does not resemble the training distribution: for instance, in the CAUSATIVE–INCHOATIVE with CoLA set, training examples illustrating the relevant alternation are outnumbered about 20:1 by CoLA examples that illustrate mostly unrelated syntactically or semantically complicated phenomena.

On the other hand, augmenting the combined dataset with sentences from CoLA helps. Performing well on the combined dataset requires an acceptability classifier with knowledge of several unrelated phenomena, so it is not surprising that augmenting the verb-alternation sentences with domain-general CoLA data improves performance.

The easiest phenomenon by a wide margin for acceptability classifiers was the UNDERSTOOD-OBJECT alternation. One explanation for this fact might be that the semantic relatedness of verbs like *blink* and objects like *her eyes* makes it easier to recognize from the sentence embedding whether their co-occurrence is expected or anomalous; for example, *eye* is the most common collocate for *blink*, *hand* is the most common one for *clap*, and *tooth* is in the top five most common collocates for *chip* (Davies, 2008, 2009).[6]

The next easiest alternations for our models to learn are CAUSATIVE–INCHOATIVE and *there*-INSERTION, both of which have at least one intransitive verb frame (both frames are intransitive in the case of *there*-INSERTION, but in one frame there is a locative adjunct). One common denominator among these three easiest alternations for the acceptability model is that they all involve verbs appearing in an intransitive frame (in the case of *there*-INSERTION a locative adjunct is present as well). By contrast, the DATIVE and SPRAY–LOAD alternations both involve verbs that take multiple arguments, appearing with up to three arguments (or possibly two arguments and a locative adjunct) in all frames. Intransitive verb frames are the simplest syntactic frames possible, and it might be expected that they are easiest to recognize.

Qualitatively, we do not find that the amount of training examples in the dataset was correlated with performance. By way of illustration, the SPRAY–LOAD alternation accounts for over half

---

[6] https://corpus.byu.edu/coca/

		Comb.	Causative–Inchoative	Dative	Spray–Load	*there*-Insertion	Understood-Object
w/o CoLA	MCC	0.290	**0.603**	0.413	0.323	**0.528**	**0.753**
	Acc.	64.6	85.4	76.0	66.2	72.9	87.4
w/ CoLA	MCC	0.361	**0.464**	0.329	0.261	**0.523**	**0.638**
	Acc.	68.7	81.2	59.0	63.4	72.5	81.8
Majority BL	MCC	0.0	0.0	0.0	0.0	0.0	0.0
	Acc.	66.6	77.6	82.1	60.3	77.5	53.7

Table 5: Results from Experiment 2. "w/o CoLA" are models trained on datasets not augmented with CoLA; "w/ CoLA" are models trained on augmented datasets; "Comb." refers to an aggregate dataset. Bolded MCC values represent moderate correlations (above 0.45).

of all the generated data, yet it was by far the hardest individual alternation for our models to learn.

7 Related Work

This investigation is part of a growing body of work which seeks to investigate the linguistic competence of ANNs. For instance, a study by Linzen et al. (2016) tested the ability of ANNs to identify mismatches in subject–verb agreement, even in the presence of intervening "distractor" nouns. Similarly, Ettinger et al. (2016) investigated whether sentence embeddings contain grammatical information, e.g., about the syntactic scope of negation.

Further previous studies on which types of information are contained in embeddings include Bjerva and Augenstein (2018), which asked whether certain phonological, morphological and syntactic information can be extracted from language embeddings. Malaviya et al. (2017) predicted features from language embeddings which were trained as part of an ANN for machine translation. Finally, Östling and Tiedemann (2017) learned language embeddings via multilingual language modeling and used them to reconstruct genealogical trees. However, we are interested in *word* or *sentence* embeddings. Extracting information from word embeddings is a common task in natural language processing. While most NLP research is application-oriented and directly or indirectly focuses on obtaining embeddings which contain as much knowledge about the task at hand as possible (e.g., by varying the training corpus or embedding method), we are interested in the question how much information is trivially contained in selected popular embeddings.

Also worth mentioning here is a lexical resource named VerbNet (Kipper-Schuler, 2005; Kipper-Schuler et al., 2006). This database contains verbs which were classified according to their semantic and syntactic properties, including their Levin classes.[7] VerbNet has been used in various NLP applications, e.g., semantic role labeling (Giuglea and Moschitti, 2006), word sense disambiguation (Brown et al., 2011), information extraction (Mausam et al., 2012), or investigation of human language acquisition (Korhonen, 2010). While this resource is very extensive, it only provides a few example sentences (generally only one or two per frame) for each verb. Since we want to investigate if argument structure information is present in sentence embeddings, we create a larger corpus.

8 Conclusions

We present complementary word-level and sentence-level datasets, LaVA and FAVA, covering five verb-alternations. We train classifiers on verb embeddings to distinguish which syntactic frames a verb can evoke and which it cannot. We further train acceptability classifiers with sentence embeddings as input for sentences which do or do not contain acceptable verb–frame combinations. We conclude that information about verb-argument structure alternations is present in both word-level and sentence-level embeddings. However, some frames seem to be easier to judge than others, and for only few frames a strong correlation can be obtained between model predictions and our gold annotations. There is considerable opportunity for future work which generalizes these experiments to other sentence encoders, verb alternations, and lexical properties.

Acknowledgments

This project has benefited from financial support to SB and KK from Samsung Research, and to SB from Google.

---

[7]To be exact, the set of classes was extended to a superset of the original Levin classes.

References

Maya Arad. 2006. *The Spray-Load Alternation*. Wiley Online Library.

Collin F Baker, Charles J Fillmore, and John B Lowe. 1998. The Berkeley FrameNet project. In *Proceedings of the 36th Annual Meeting of the Association for Computational Linguistics and 17th International Conference on Computational Linguistics*.

Steven Bird and Edward Loper. 2004. Nltk: the natural language toolkit. In *Proceedings of the ACL 2004 on Interactive poster and demonstration sessions*, page 31. Association for Computational Linguistics.

Johannes Bjerva and Isabelle Augenstein. 2018. From phonology to syntax: Unsupervised linguistic typology at different levels with language embeddings. In *Proceedings of the 2018 Conference of the North American Chapter of the Association for Computational Linguistics: Human Language Technologies*.

Joan Bresnan. 1980. Polyadicity: Part i of a theory of lexical rules and representations. *Lexical Grammar*, pages 97–121.

Susan Windisch Brown, Dmitriy Dligach, and Martha Palmer. 2011. VerbNet class assignment as a WSD task. In *Proceedings of the 9th International Conference on Computational Semantics*.

Noam Chomsky. 1965. *Aspects of the Theory of Syntax*. MIT Press.

Alexander Clark and Shalom Lappin. 2011. *Linguistic Nativism and the Poverty of the Stimulus*. John Wiley & Sons.

Mark Davies. 2008. *The corpus of contemporary American English*. BYE, Brigham Young University.

Mark Davies. 2009. The 385+ million word corpus of contemporary american english (1990–2008+): Design, architecture, and linguistic insights. *International Journal of Corpus Linguistics*, 14(2):159–190.

Allyson Ettinger, Ahmed Elgohary, and Philip Resnik. 2016. Probing for semantic evidence of composition by means of simple classification tasks. In *Proceedings of the 1st Workshop on Evaluating Vector-Space Representations for NLP*.

Charles J Fillmore. 1966. A proposal concerning english prepositions. *Monograph Series on Languages and Linguistics*, 19:19–34.

Charles J Fillmore, Christopher R Johnson, and Miriam RL Petruck. 2003. Background to framenet. *International Journal of Lexicography*, 16(3):235–250.

Ana-Maria Giuglea and Alessandro Moschitti. 2006. Semantic role labeling via framenet, verbnet and propbank. In *Proceedings of the 21st International Conference on Computational Linguistics and 44th Annual Meeting of the Association for Computational Linguistics*.

Ralph Grishman, Catherine Macleod, and Adam Meyers. 1994. COMLEX syntax: Building a computational lexicon. In *Proceedings of the 15th conference on Computational Linguistics*.

Ken Hale and Jay Keyser. 1986. Some transitivity alternations in English. *Anuario del Seminario de Filología Vasca "Julio de Urquijo"*, 20(3):605–638.

Kenneth Locke Hale and Samuel Jay Keyser. 2002. *Prolegomenon to a theory of argument structure*, volume 39. MIT press.

Betty Hart and Todd R Risley. 1992. American parenting of language-learning children: Persisting differences in family-child interactions observed in natural home environments. *Developmental Psychology*, 28(6):1096.

Sepp Hochreiter and Jürgen Schmidhuber. 1997. Long short-term memory. *Neural computation*, 9(8):1735–1780.

Diederik P Kingma and Jimmy Ba. 2015. Adam: A method for stochastic optimization. In *Proceedings of the 2015 International Conference on Learning Representations*.

Karin Kipper-Schuler. 2005. *VerbNet: A broad-coverage, comprehensive verb lexicon*. Ph.D. thesis, The University of Pennsylvania.

Karin Kipper-Schuler, Anna Korhonen, Neville Ryant, and Martha Palmer. 2006. Extending VerbNet with novel verb classes. In *Proceedings of the International Conference on Language Resources and Evaluation*.

Anna Korhonen. 2010. Automatic lexical classification: Bridging research and practice. *Philosophical Transactions of the Royal Society of London A: Mathematical, Physical and Engineering Sciences*, 368(1924):3621–3632.

Richard K Larson. 1988. On the double object construction. *Linguistic Inquiry*, 19(3):335–391.

Beth Levin. 1993. *English verb classes and alternations: A preliminary investigation*. University of Chicago press.

Beth Levin and Malka Rappaport Hovav. 1995. *Unaccusativity: At the syntax-lexical semantics interface*, volume 26. MIT press.

Tal Linzen, Emmanuel Dupoux, and Yoav Goldberg. 2016. Assessing the ability of LSTMs to learn syntax-sensitive dependencies. *Transactions of the Association for Computational Linguistics*, 4:521–535.

Chaitanya Malaviya, Graham Neubig, and Patrick Littell. 2017. Learning language representations for typology prediction. In *Proceedings of the 2017 Conference on Empirical Methods in Natural Language Processing*.

Alec Marantz. 1984. On the nature of grammatical relations. *Linguistic Inquiry Monographs*, 10.

Brian W Matthews. 1975. Comparison of the predicted and observed secondary structure of t4 phage lysozyme. *Biochimica et Biophysica Acta (BBA)-Protein Structure*, 405(2):442–451.

Mausam, Michael Schmitz, Stephen Soderland, Robert Bart, and Oren Etzioni. 2012. Open language learning for information extraction. In *Proceedings of the 2012 Joint Conference on Empirical Methods in Natural Language Processing and Computational Natural Language Learning*.

Tomas Mikolov, Wen-tau Yih, and Geoffrey Zweig. 2013. Linguistic regularities in continuous space word representations. In *Proceedings of the 2013 Conference of the North American Chapter of the Association for Computational Linguistics: Human Language Technologies*.

Gary L Milsark. 1974. *Existential sentences in English*. Ph.D. thesis, Massachusetts Institute of Technology.

Robert Östling and Jörg Tiedemann. 2017. Continuous multilinguality with language vectors. In *Proceedings of the 15th Conference of the European Chapter of the Association for Computational Linguistics*.

Jeffrey Pennington, Richard Socher, and Christopher Manning. 2014. GloVe: Global vectors for word representation. In *Proceedings of the 2014 Conference on Empirical Methods in Natural Language Processing*.

Matthew Peters, Mark Neumann, Mohit Iyyer, Matt Gardner, Christopher Clark, Kenton Lee, and Luke Zettlemoyer. 2018. Deep contextualized word representations. In *Proceedings of the 2018 Conference of the North American Chapter of the Association for Computational Linguistics: Human Language Technologies*.

Hendrik Poutsma. 1904. *A Grammar of Late Modern English: the elements of the sentence*, volume 1. P. Noordhoff.

Sally Rice. 1988. Unlikely lexical entries. In *Proceedings of the 14th Annual Meeting of the Berkeley Linguistics Society*.

Karl Fritiof Sundén. 1916. *Essay I. The Predicational Categories in English: Essay II. A Category of Predicational Change in English*, volume 1. At the University Press, E. Berling.

Anna Szabolcsi. 1986. Indefinites in complex predicates. *Theoretical Linguistic Research*, 2:47–83.

Carol Lee Tenny. 1987. *Grammaticalizing aspect and affectedness*. Ph.D. thesis, Massachusetts Institute of Technology.

Alex Warstadt, Amanpreet Singh, and Samuel R Bowman. 2018. Neural network acceptability judgments. *arXiv preprint arXiv:1805.12471*.

AUTHOR INDEX

Association for Computational Linguistics
209 N. Eighth Street
Stroudsburg, Pennsylvania 18360

ISBN 978-1-5108-7753-5